THIS IS
MY BEST

THIS IS MY BEST

ACCLAIMED QPB AUTHORS SHARE THEIR FAVORITE WORK

Edited by
Retha Powers and Kathy Kiernan

Quality Paperback Book Club
New York

Many thanks to Brigitte Weeks, Patricia Gift, Brandon Geist, Grey Thornberry, Christos Peterson, and especially Lisa Thornbloom; the QPB team; our friends and colleagues at Bookspan; and Sarah B. Williams, Jay Schaefer, and Steve Mockus of Chronicle Books, all of whom made *This Is My Best* possible.

Book design by Christos Peterson

Published by Quality Paperback Book Club, 1271 Avenue of the Americas, New York, NY 10020.

ISBN: 1-58288-157-X

Printed in the United States of America

We are tremendously grateful to the authors who shared their best.

I also thank my grandmother, Jeanette Phipps, and my parents, James Powers and the late Beverly Phipps Powers, for expecting nothing less from me.

—R.P.

Many thanks to Howard Frisch for his limitless ideas and the literary knowledge he has generously shared.

—K.K.

CONTENTS

INTRODUCTION

In 1942, more than one hundred and fifty authors declared their best to Whit Burnett, editor of *Story* magazine and the creator of the original *This Is My Best*. Over half a century later, Kathy Kiernan finds a first edition of *This Is My Best* in a friend's used bookstore. Fast forward to 2003. Retha Powers discovers a copy of the book has been sitting on a shelf in her grandparents' home for more than fifty years. Coincidence? Maybe, but we took it as a sign that we needed to revisit the idea.

Making a list of QPB's favorite authors was no easy task. Some writers were more obvious and quickly came to mind but we couldn't trust such an important task to memory. We took a field trip to the New York City booklovers' paradise Coliseum Books and went through their shelves alphabetically row by row; we also raided the QPB library, and our own private collections. The resulting list of nearly two hundred novelists, short story writers, humorists, science writers, essayists, cartoonists, playwrights, historians, and poets was our invitation list to a fabulous literary party to take place on the pages of a book.

Every day we'd rush to the mail like kids at summer camp hoping for a care package. What we received was even better than chocolate chip cookies from home. Each envelope or e-mail was loaded down with surprises and insights that only an author can know about his or her work. As Burnett wrote in his foreword to the 1942 edition, "An author is an author: he is familiar with his own work; why didn't someone think of asking him before? . . . to say, without influence or qualification: 'This is myself in my very best manner.'" Sometimes we were made to laugh for days, as with David Sedaris's introduction to "Repeat After Me." We expected to explode at Scott Adams's words and, while he did make us chuckle, we were more moved by his thoughtfulness. Authors like Laurie Garrett reminded us why their work is so important and engendered even greater respect. We found ourselves unexpectedly delighted by writers who, like Rita Dove and Arthur Miller, threw curve balls by choosing works that were less obvious.

We wanted to make sure the eclecticism that is QPB was reflected in the final product and we also insisted on bringing a freshness to Burnett's original beyond just new contributors. Our version of *This Is My Best* is much more diverse in terms of gender, age, race, and genre. Science writers such as Michael Pollan, Helen Fisher, and Natalie Angier share the stage with poets Robert Pinsky, Kathleen Norris, and Philip Levine. We even expand the definition of storytelling to include two cartoonists, Garry Trudeau and the aforementioned Scott Adams.

The writers we invited were generally excited about the project, but interesting questions arose. Some asked, Can an author really define his best? One wrote that he was flattered to be chosen but didn't feel qualified: "I haven't the least idea what my best work is, and if I knew I'm not sure it's for me to say." One submitted four choices and told us to take our pick, while another award–winning author known for the brutality of the landscape and actions of characters in her fiction wrote, "I can't do it." One writer proposed that we just select something of his and let him know what we picked, which is exactly what William Faulkner suggested to Whit Burnett back in 1942. Unlike Burnett, who used Faulkner's 1931 story "That Evening Sun Go Down," we didn't include the writer who asked us to decide. For these writers, the act of choosing her or his best seemed an elaborate form of a jinx.

But most writers saw this as welcome opportunity to pause and reflect back. QPB New Visions winner Richard Rodriguez wrote he was happy to spend time "brooding like Lear, among my several children to determine which I love best." And then there were those who seemed to be waiting for us because we were pleased and shocked to find responses within days of sending out our request. These writers lived with their best every day: greeted it in the morning, poured it a cup of tea, took it on errands, and tucked it into bed at night. Finally, for some the best seemed like a stackable Chinese lunch box of which we were served just one course. It was their best story of a given length, a point in time, or their frame of mind at that moment.

What is most exciting about *This Is My Best* is not just the impressive names we've been able to attract, but the riches the authors' introductions have yielded. For example Joyce Carol Oates reveals that her story was born of a horrific act from her family history, Jonathan Lethem shares how an unplanned character and his subconscious took over in *The Fortress of Solitude*, and Barbara Kingsolver ponders the "peculiar alchemy of the writer's words and a thousand other images, entirely personal, belonging to the reader." Ultimately, each contributor's definition of "best" is as individual as the artist.

While not all two hundred of the contributors we approached appear here, we'd like to think this finished book contains the best of them. We hope that you will enjoy the very best QPB's writers have to offer as much as we have. Each page you turn represents the exciting journey we had the privilege of sharing with these fine authors. It's our anniversary gift to you.

Retha Powers
Kathy Kiernan

THIS IS
MY BEST

SCOTT ADAMS

DILBERT, OCTOBER 8, 2001

THE HARDEST PART ABOUT picking a *best* Dilbert comic is that my tastes change over time in a predictable cycle of loving-loathing-loving-loathing. When I first get an idea for a comic, I love it. As I draw it, I begin to despise the idea because, for me, all the surprise and joy is drained out during the process. I leave each comic on a shelf for a few weeks so I can look at it later with fresh eyes, whereupon I generally start liking it. I like it more every day for a few years until it starts looking like my "older stuff" and then I am overcome with waves of self-loathing. The comic I selected as my best is one of the few that I believe will resist that pattern. It made me laugh out loud when I drew it; it made me laugh every time revisited it; and it made me laugh again when I picked it for this book.

I love to combine concepts that the brain has trouble considering together. In this case, the concepts of sandwich bags and underpants have been unnaturally paired in a way that is frankly disturbing. The comic is pathetic, unexpected, and clever; it makes a point, and it creates a visual image that is hard to get out of your head. It's everything I strive for in a comic.

My writing process is different from most cartoonists. I start with a general concept and then begin drawing without knowing what the dialog will be or how it will end. I simply populate the first panel with appropriate characters and start imagining what they might say. Sometimes, as with this comic, I finish my joke by the second panel. The newspapers wouldn't pay me if I left the third panel blank, so I had to squeeze in the extra joke about the sandwich bags. I can't explain where that idea came from. The best ones just arrive on their own. I looked at my drawing of Asok, the abused intern, and asked myself what he might say. Then I wrote down the words as they formed in my head. It's a mystery to me where that sort of idea comes from, but I blame my brother for hitting me in the head with a rock when I was a toddler.

—Scott Adams

AI

JIMMY HOFFA'S ODYSSEY

I DON'T THINK I have an all-time favorite piece of writing. I tend to have a favorite poem in each book. One that I always enjoy reading at public speaking events is "Jimmy Hoffa's Odyssey," which is also my favorite from my book *Fate*. I was inspired to write it one night while I was watching the Johnny Carson show— well, I had actually exiled myself to an antique oak horsehair-filled settee. I had not been writing much, so to make myself as uncomfortable as possible, punish and at the same time reward myself by merely "listening" to Johnny Carson, I sat impatiently waiting for the muse to tap me on the shoulder, and heard Carson tell a joke. He asked, "Who did they find under Tammy Faye Baker's makeup?" The answer was Jimmy Hoffa. The moment I heard that name, I thought to myself, I'd like to write a poem about Jimmy Hoffa. I did start writing that night, but since I research my poems based on actual people and events, I went and checked some books out of the library. After many, many drafts I found myself stuck. I simply could not seem to get a handle on the Hoffa character I had created until I read that the real Hoffa often referred to himself in the third person, as in "Hoffa don't have no machine." For some reason that opened my path into a deeper understanding of my character. Yet, I had still not really set upon what my poem's path would be until I decided that my character had not disappeared in any expected way, but had actually been kidnapped by extraterrestrials. Well, one, "a blue broccoli-looking creature." Then the poem really took off. Although it is about distressing events, I was able to make it a rather funny poem (at least to me). It is also notable to me because, until then, I had not really shown much sense of humor in my work. But because of a strange chain of events, I was able to get in touch with my inner comic, whose humor, admittedly, is rather dark. Of course, I find it downright hilarious. (Just kidding.)

—Ai

> I remember summers
> when the ice man used to come,
> a hunk of winter
> caught between his iron tongs,
> and in the kitchen, my ma with a rag,

3

wiping the floor when he'd gone;
sweet song of the vegetable man
like the music
a million silver dollars make,
as they jingle, jangle
in that big pocket of your dreams.
Dreams. Yes, and lies.
When I was a boy, I hauled ashes
in a wagon,
pulled by a bony horse
not even good enough for soap,
so later, when they called me
stocky little dockworker
with my slicked-back black hair,
my two-tone shoes, cheap suits,
and fat, smelly cigars,
I didn't care.
I had my compensation.
Bobby Kennedy didn't want to understand,
but to the teamsters back in '58 . . .
I had 'em all in my pocket then,
statesmen, lawyers, movie stars,
Joe Louis, for God's sake.
For a time I won spin after spin
on the tin wheel of fate,
but in the end, like those glory boys
Jack and Bobby,
I was only icing on the sucker cake.

I know the alibis, the lies,
stacked up like bodies
on a gurney going nowhere,
but Hoffa went, he went
walking in a parking lot one day,
while he waited for a so-called
friend, a peacemaker, ha.
See him there, bored and sweating.
See the car roll toward him
as he does a little dance, a polka step or two,
when the doors open

and the glare of sunlight off a windshield
becomes so bright
that he is blinded by it.
Later, I come to,
while a blue broccoli-looking creature
is taking tubes from my arms and legs.
Then he walks me round and round
till I can stand on my own.
He talks to me through some machine,
tells me I'm on a spaceship,
tells me he's lonely,
then he sits me down at the controls,
he talks to me about his life in some galaxy
whose name I can't pronounce.
I become a confidant of sorts, a friend,
until one day outside Roswell, New Mexico,
his skin begins to rot,
so I start collecting specimens for him:
rocks, bugs, plants,
my walks taking me farther and farther
till I find this abandoned gas station,
and when he dies,
I put up signs along the highway,
the ones that say, "10 miles, 5, 1 mile
to see THE THING!"
And fifty cents for kids, a dollar for adults,
buys a glimpse of a spaceman
in an airtight case
and Hoffa on the other side of the glass,
Hoffa who chooses to let everybody think
he was pulverized in some New Jersey nightmare.
I drink an Orange Crush, prop my feet up,
and watch the sun go down,
the moon come up. A year goes by like this,
two, when suddenly it's not enough.
In a rage, I smash the case
and burn down the shack
with the spaceman inside.
I hitch a ride to town and take a job
at McDonald's,

and when I raise enough cash,
take a Greyhound to Detroit,
but in the station,
as if commanded by a force outside myself,
buy a ticket back.
In the desert once again, I board the spaceship
and take off,
and one night,
kidnap two hunters in Maine,
later, a family in Texas,
a telephone lineman in upstate New York.
I want to tell them who I am,
but all I do is mumble, stare, and touch them,
as if I'd never been a man among men,
when the dollar sign was a benediction.
Instead of words what comes are images
of Hoffa smacked in the head
so hard he hurls himself forward,
then slams back in the seat,
and later, shot through each eye, each ear,
his mouth,
his body heaved in a trash compactor
and to its whir, whine, and moan,
crushed beyond anger.
Again and again, I play memory games
in the casino of the past.
Yes, half a chance,
I'd do it all the same,
so aim that pistol, wise guy,
and fire and keep on firing.
Let me go, let me go,
but give the bosses of the world,
the brass-assed monkeys
who haven't paid the price in blood,
this warning:
sometime when they are least expecting,
I am coming back
to take my place on the picket line,
because, like any other union man,
I earned it.

JULIA ALVAREZ

From *BEFORE WE WERE FREE*

TO BE HONEST, EVERY book I write is my best at the time I am writing it. Otherwise, I wouldn't put it out there for my readers to waste their time reading it. Would I serve a lackluster dish to guests at a dinner party?

That said, every book I have written needs improvement after I'm done with it. What I mean is that months after I've sent in the page proofs and the book finally comes out and I'm sent on a tour and I stand up in front of audiences to read from my new novel, I think, oh no, I'd change this, I'd change that. I could do a better job now if I had another chance to revise it!

I used to think that this was just me. That other writers were perfectly pleased with the job they'd done. But at the Bread Loaf Writers' Conference this past summer, I heard a writer talk about how he hates reading his own published books because he wants to go at them with a red pen. He went on to add that this is actually a good sign, a sign that he has grown as a writer, has gotten more expert in his craft, and so now, he can do a better job on the book that, by writing it, made him a better writer.

Phew, I thought. So, it's not just me.

There's the imagined novel—perfectly rendered, the writing pristine, the characters complex, the shape organic, the ending deeply satisfying—and then there's the novel you managed to get down on paper. It's with hindsight that you see that they are not one and the same. So, you keep writing, trying to close that gap.

But with my novel, *Before We Were Free*, I'd find myself giving readings and feeling *mostly* satisfied with the way I'd written it. I started saying, not that it was my best work, but that it was the book that was closest to the imagined book that I had in my head when I was writing it. I prefer explaining my selection this way rather than saying "this is my best." I hope not. I hope that in the *x* years since this novel was finished I've gotten to be a better writer.

Before We Were Free was published as "a young adult novel." Friends who know my "adult novels" ask if I think the book is "my best" because it's easier to write a book "for kids." First off, I think of all the books I write as books for readers of all ages—after all, I'm fifty-four and I'm reading them over and over and over again as I write them! Also, I do my best on whatever book I am writing. I don't dumb down my writing if my narrator is a young girl, as she is in this novel, or if my publisher is a children's book publisher. So, no, I don't think that the book turned out the way it did because I decided to be a big frog writer in the smaller pond of lit. for kids.

Another surprise on my book tour with *Before We Were Free* was that twice I gave a reading of the chapter, "Freedom Cry," and twice I had to stop near the end because I got choked up. Swallow a drink of water. Feel a little self-conscious and embarrassed because here I was, in front of a group of people, crying over something I'd made up. First time it happened, I thought, well, this is your first reading of this chapter, you'll get to be a pro, and Anita's sadness won't get to you. So, the second time, at an even bigger reading, in front of an auditorium full of college students, I read the chapter, and I got tearful again. From then on, I avoided reading from that chapter.

When I discovered that this chapter affected me this way, I couldn't help but think that it was the one chapter in the book that almost didn't get written. Briefly, *Before We Were Free* is a kind of Anne Frank story of a young girl coming of age in the Trujillo dictatorship of the Dominican Republic. Slowly, Anita (named after her namesake) experiences the brutal closing down of her world as the police state tightens around her family. When her father is taken captive, Anita and her mother go into hiding in the walk-in closet of an Italian couple who have amnesty because of their diplomatic status. In this section of the book, Anita keeps a diary, recording her day-to-day life, her dreams and fears in hiding. Finally, she and her mother are airlifted out of the country along with other families at risk. In the original version of the novel, the diary ended, and then the last chapter showed Anita, months later, watching her first snowfall with her cousins who had already emigrated to the United States.

When the manuscript came back from my editor, Andrea Cascardi, she thought the book needed a transition chapter from the end of the diary to that last chapter. The reader wanted to be with Anita as she makes her initial entry into the United States. It was too abrupt a shift.

I disagreed. I argued that I wanted the shift to be abrupt. That I loved going from the tropics to a snowfall. That I wanted Anita to be sad and resigned. That I was totally one hundred percent sure that I wanted to keep the basic structure of the book as it was.

I, I, I, I . . . As I heard myself fight for what I wanted in my book, I heard too many I's and not enough about the book. I could feel myself caving in to her suggestion.

One of the things that happens with a good editor whom you've grown to trust is that her voice becomes part of your own critical process. I trusted Andrea, and so I thought, well, let me just see what that transition chapter might be and if it makes the book a better one. That chapter was "Freedom Cry," and I think it's the best chapter in the novel.

Another lesson there for me as a writer: what I want for my book might sometimes not be what is best for the book. I might love a passage of writing which really is not right for the tone of that part of the book. I might want to save a character who has to die or disappear a difficult character. It's a big step to take, a King Solomon step; you have to love your book more than your entitled role as its writer!

Bottom line: I love writing a good book more than I love being right.

So, again and again, thanks, Andrea Cascardi!

A few months ago, I got to read "Freedom Cry" for the third time ever. I was doing the audio version of the novel, and I was closed up in a little soundproof booth with earphones on and a glass window that looked out into a bank of technicians also wearing earphones, working a dozen dials, and stopping me every other page to have me reread this or that passage, putting more oomph here and less oomph there. When we got to the "Freedom Cry" chapter, I explained that I'd had a hard time reading this chapter out loud in the past. So I just wanted to warn everybody that I might start to cry.

"Don't worry about it," Jacob Bronstein, the audio producer, said. "We'll just re-tape if we have to."

Of course, I was betting on the tell-someone-you're-going-to-mess-up approach that works the opposite results. So, I set off, confident that I'd read through, dry-eyed from having anticipated tears that, like someone saying *bless you* before you sneeze, cuts off the ach-choo at the pass.

But as we rounded toward the end of the chapter, I felt that now-familiar, tight feeling in my throat. My voice clouded up. We had to tape over, once, twice, and then I sort of got through it.

As I was getting ready to exit the taping room and face Jacob and crew, I thought, well, a good cry is appropriate for a chapter called "Freedom Cry."

Someday, soon, I might try a fourth reading of "Freedom Cry," and you know what, I'm hoping I'll still tear up a bit. It would mean that maybe this time what I got down on paper is pretty close to that perfect story in my head that almost got away if it hadn't been for my good editor, Andrea, making me go after this little piece of it.

—Julia Alvarez

FREEDOM CRY

A nita, *por favor*," Mami calls from the other room. "Turn that thing off."

I'm sitting in front of the television at the Hotel Beverly, where my grandparents have been renting an apartment on the top floor. We've been in New York City already over a month and a half. I mark off every day on the calendar. Today, I made such a heavy **X** that I tore through the paper. September 18, 1961, isn't even over, but it's already gone!

The days are getting cooler. Down on the street, ten flights below, the little toy trees are beginning to turn reddish, like someone is lighting a match to them.

Every time I get a chance, I watch TV. I tell Mami that I want to learn more about this country. But really, I just want to keep my mind off everything I could be worrying about right now.

Like the phone call Mami is about to make from the other room. Twice a week, she calls Mr. Washburn in Washington to find out if there's any news about Papi and my uncle. We all sit around—my grandparents, Mamita and Papito, Lucinda and Mundín and me— watching the reactions on her face.

"With Mr. Washburn, *por favor*," I hear Mami saying. I go up to the television to turn it off, and just then, she comes on, the only Spanish lady I've ever seen on TV. There's also a Cuban guy called Ricky Ricardo, who has a wacky American wife who reminds me of Mrs. Washburn. This lady carries a big basket of bananas on her head like the *marchantas* in the market calling out their wares.

I turn down the volume and sing along under my breath.

The first time I saw her, I couldn't believe what she was saying: "*I'm Anita Banana and I'm here to stay.*"

"*NO!*" I screamed at the TV and clapped my hands over my ears. "I am not staying, I am not staying!"

Lucinda ran into the room. "*¿Qué pasa?* What on earth are you screaming about, Anita?" Thank goodness Mami and Mamita and Papito were out with Mundín, getting him a winter jacket, otherwise my screaming would have shot their fragile nerves. "You want us to get thrown out of here?"

10

I nodded and then shook my head. Of course I didn't want to get thrown out and sent back to live in a closet. But I wanted the dictatorship to be over so we could go home to live as a family again. "The lady," I said, pointing to the silent screen.

"What about her?" Lucinda asked, turning the volume back up. She watched the rest of the commercial. "You're crying about her?"

"No, not about her, about what she said." I explained the lady's prediction as if the television were a crystal ball.

Lucinda let out one of her long-suffering sighs. "Ay, Anita, that's not what she's saying." Lucinda swirled her hips, imitating the lady, and sang a little bit of the song:

> I'm Chiquita Banana
> And I've come to say
> Bananas have to ripen
> In a certain way.

I guess my nerves were pretty shot, too.

I'm still seeing ghosts and signs everywhere. And Chucha isn't around to help me interpret them.

"I am so sorry to be molesting you, Mr. Washburn," Mami is saying as I come in the room. Lucinda has explained to her that *molestar* does not mean *bother* in English as it does in Spanish. But Mami says how is she supposed to remember all the crazy ways the American have changed Spanish around. Sometimes, sad as I am, even I have to smile at Mami.

"Yes, yes, I understand, yes, Mr. Washburn," Mami is saying. With each *yes*, I can hear her voice getting weaker. Her knuckles are bone-white from holding the receiver so tight. "No news *is* good news. You are right. We are so much in gratitude to you," she says at the end.

"Nothing," Mami says quietly after she hangs up. "They're trying to put pressure on Trujillo Junior to leave the country. Then the prisoners will be released. We just have to keep hoping and praying," she adds more cheerfully. She doesn't sound very convinced.

"*¡Exactamente!*" my grandfather agrees, trying to inject confidence into all of us. But my grandmother begins weeping. "*Mis pobres hijos, mi pobre país.*" Her poor sons, her poor country!

Lucinda joins in, and before long, Mami and I are also crying.

Mundín hurries off to the bathroom, where I'm sure he cries, too.

My grandfather puts on his overcoat and heads for the drugstore to get my grandmother some more of her blood-pressure medicine.

I want to go with him, but I can't because it's sort of illegal that we're staying in their rooms with them, as they would have to pay more. Papito has told the doorman who's Puerto Rican that ours is "a temporary situation," and the doorman says he understands, just to be *discretos*. So we try to be discreet and go out one by one, so it doesn't look like we know each other but are just separate people staying in the hotel rooms on the lower floors.

I go stand by the window and watch for Papito to come out downstairs, an old man in a Panama hat—one of the few familiar faces in this country where the only people we know are the ones who came with us.

The day we were surprised in our hiding place, I had no idea that it would be my good-bye to my country. I actually thought the SIM had discovered us and it was good-bye to my life.

That's why, scared as I was, I kept writing in my diary. I wanted someone to know what had happened to us.

But when the crawl-space doors were thrown open, it was Wimpy and his paratroopers coming to the rescue! The Mancinis, who were away at the beach, didn't even know that the airlift would be that day. A number of things had to fall in place for our evacuation, and that Sunday, July 30, they came together at the last minute.

I had been about to stash away my diary under a loose board. But Wimpy grabbed me and picked me up, and the diary came away with me in my hand. An unmarked helicopter was waiting on the embassy grounds to airlift us out, and there wasn't a minute to spare. Outside on the streets, an angry rally was going on, and the SIM were too busy with crowd control to notice a dragonfly helicopter flying by with a terrified mother and daughter inside.

North of the city, we landed on an abandoned airstrip, where a cargo plane was waiting. A van drove up with some other people, some of whom I recognized. Wimpy helped everyone climb on board, a grim look on his face, his eagle tattoo pumping away. As our plane took off, I glanced out the window at the cracked tarmac and the swaying palms waving good-bye, and I thought I saw a flash of purple getting back into the van with Wimpy.

We flew higher and higher, over green valleys and dark, ridged mountains, and then over the coast, waves breaking on the white sands. Miles below, Oscar was in one of those tiny beach houses . . . maybe looking up! How long before he returned home? Would he realize right away that I was no longer hidden in his parents' closet, using his queen of hearts to mark my place in *The Swiss Family Robinson*?

So many people and places I might not ever get to see again! Looking down, I saw a quilt of faces and memories spreading out over the sea—Monsito carrying our sack of *plátanos* in his wheelbarrow, Tío Pepe with his white socks, Porfirio watering the ginger plants while singing his sad songs—and the purple thread stitching piece to piece was Chucha, my dear Chucha, who had helped me survive this year of my life falling apart!

I stared out the window, too shocked even to cry, until we climbed into the clouds and there was nothing else to see. A little while later, I leaned against Mami and fell asleep.

When she shook me awake, it was dark outside the plane. We had landed. Somehow, I stumbled in my half-sleep across a runway, Mami holding on to me, to a bigger airplane taking us to New York City.

The next I knew, I was looking down at the view I had seen on the postcards Lucinda used to send us that left even Chucha speechless, buildings so tall that I couldn't quite believe they were real, and patches of green like scatter rugs, and tiny antlike people whom I could blot out just by putting my hand on the small square of the window. How could I live in this world full of strangers and gray light instead of a country of cousins and family and family friends and year-round sunshine?

We landed and entered a terminal where officials took us into a room to issue us special papers. Then one of them shook our hands and said, "Welcome to the United States of America," and pointed us out of Immigration. And there was my answer to how I would survive in this strange, new world: My family was waiting for us— Mundín and Lucinda, my grandparents, Carla, her sisters, and Tía Laura and Tío Carlos and Tía Mimí—all of them calling out, "Anita! Carmen!" Carla says my face was worth a thousand bucks as the family rushed forward and locked us in their arms.

By the end of September, we still have no news of Papi and Tío Toni. The Garcías have invited us to move out to their house in Queens, but Mami won't hear of it. Any day now, we will be returning home. The *campo* suburbs are for those who have decided to settle down in the United States, like the Garcías. New York City is where you stay on your way back to where you came from.

While we are waiting around, Mami decides that we should learn perfect English. Lucinda already is a pro from being here since February, but Mundín and I could use practice. "Papi will be so pleased!" she says excitedly. There is an uneasy silence when she says these things. But I so want to believe her that I'll do anything, *anything*, that might help make this happen.

Mami goes to a nearby Catholic school and asks the principal if we can sit in on any class till we go back home. The principal is a nun with a bonnet like a baby doll, except it's black. She is a Sister of Charity, and maybe that is why she is so kind and says yes, she will put us wherever there is a spot.

The next day, I don't think she is so kind. I am sitting at a small desk in the second grade, the only elementary classroom that had extra space. The teacher, Sister Mary Joseph, has a sweet face with pale whiskers and watery blue eyes as if she is always in tears. Her breath is musty, like an old suitcase that hasn't been opened in years.

"Annie is a very special student," she tells the class, "a refugee from a dictatorship." When she says this, I stare down at the wooden floor and try not to cry.

"She came here with her family in order to be free," Sister Mary Joseph is explaining. But my family is not all here, I feel like saying. And how can I be free when my mind is all worried about Papi and my whole self is so sad, I can barely get up some mornings?

"Would you like to tell the class a little something about the Dominican Republic?" the old nun prompts me.

Where do I begin telling strangers about a place whose smell is on my skin and whose memory is always in my head? To them, it's just a geography lesson; to me, it's home. Besides, talking about my country would make me too sad right now. I stand in front of this roomful of staring little kids, not saying a single word. At the very least I should show them that I can speak their language, so they don't think I'm a complete moron who is almost thirteen and still in the second grade.

"Thank you," I murmur, "for letting me into your country."

Sister Mary Joseph gives me an assignment to do on my own. I am to write a composition about what I remember from my native country.

"Maybe it'll be easier to write down memories rather than just think on your feet," she suggests. She shows me how I'm supposed to make a little cross at the top of each page, and then print the initials *J.M.J.*, dedicating my work to Jesus, Mary, and Joseph. Below, on the first line, I am to put my own name, which she writes out as *Annie Torres*, and the date, October 4, 1961.

I bend to my work, make my little cross on top of a clean page, dedicating my composition to *J.M.J.* But then, I add, *M.T.* & *A.T.*, Mundo and Antonio de la Torre.

"What's that?" Sister Mary Joseph says, peering over my shoulder.

"My father and my uncle." I point to each set of initials.

She is about to protest, but then her watery blue eyes get even more watery. "I am so sorry," she whispers—as if Papi and Tío Toni are dead!

"I will be seeing them soon," I explain.

"Of course you will, dear," Sister Mary Joseph says, nodding. Today, her breath smells like the sachets my grandmother sticks in her underwear drawer.

As the class goes over cursive letters, I work on my assignment. At first I can't think of what to say, but then I pretend I'm writing in my diary again. Soon I'm filling page after page, making lists of people and foods and places I miss, describing them using metaphors like Mrs. Brown taught us. I also write down my favorites of Chucha's sayings:

> With patience and calm, even a burro can climb a palm.
> Dress the monkey in silk, he's still a monkey.
> You can't dry yesterday's laundry with tomorrow's sun.

As I write, I can almost hear Chucha at my side whispering, "*Fly! Fly free!*" Those were the last words she ever spoke to me. But how can I be really free without Papi in my life? If something happens to him, then the part that is the wings in me would die.

When I hand in my composition, Sister Mary Joseph reads it over, marking pencil in hand. I stand by her big desk, watching her pencil dip down, correcting my mistakes. She chuckles when she gets to the page with Chucha's sayings.

"Very good," she remarks, although the pages are full of little red marks.

By the end of October, Papi is still in prison and Trujillo Junior is still in power. He is getting crazier with revenge and refuses to cooperate with the Americans, so even Mr. Washburn doesn't have a whole lot of details. I decide to write to Oscar, who always seemed to know about everything, and ask him what he knows.

I've tried writing him before. But every time I sit down, I feel a wave of homesickness, and I have to put the letter away.

But this time, I have a mission, though I've got to be extra careful on account of the censors. I start out telling him all about Nueva York; how cold it's gotten and how uncomfortable it is to wear so many heavy clothes; how the people don't smile a whole lot, so you can't really tell if they like you or not; how I am in school learning lots of English (I leave out the part about second grade); how my teacher, Sister Mary Joseph, is making me write down stories like the girl in *The Arabian Nights*; how she did a whole geography segment on the island, and Mami fried *pastelitos* for me to take in, which everyone liked a lot. I mix in the good and the bad and sometimes, I admit, when there's not much good to report, I make some things up.

Then, very casually, I slip in, *"How are things in the sultan's court?"* I underline *sultan's*, but then I erase my underlining, in case it is too obvious a clue.

I give the letter to my grandfather to mail because I don't really want Mami to know I'm writing to a boy, even if he is my cousin. But Papito looks at the address on the envelope and explains that no mail is getting through. The country is all closed up, just like this place called Berlin, where an iron curtain has come down that keeps people from going in or getting out.

I take the letter back and tear it up in lots of little pieces. Then I open the window and watch them fall, a sprinkle of white to the ground below. Some of the people on the street look up. Maybe they think it's snowing. The García girls out in Queens have told me all about winter in this country. By Christmas, they've promised, I'll get to see the snow.

"I won't be here by then," I keep telling them.

But as each day goes by, and the leaves all fall off like the trees have some disease, and October turns into November, I wonder if I'm going to be here for a lot longer than just the first snowfall of this year.

Often, on the way home from school, I'll stop at the grocery store for a visit. No matter how sad I am, every time I step in front of the door and it opens by itself, I feel a rush of excitement like I'm back at Wimpy's. I love to walk down the aisles, half expecting I'll find Chucha with the big feather duster the stock boy uses to clean the shelves. I can't believe all the boxes and brands. Soups and sauces, cans of this and cans of that, a dozen different cereals, tons of candies. Even the animals in this country get lots of choices. Six kinds of cat food! What would Monsito say about that?!

Today, I don't know what gets into me, but instead of just looking, I decide to take a cart. I go up and down each aisle, filling the basket with things I really like, pretending I have the money to buy them. When I'm done with all the aisles, the basket is piled so high, I can barely see over it. I head back the way I came, carefully putting everything back in its place.

Suddenly, a big, chesty man is barreling down the aisle toward me. He wears a white apron like a butcher and his face looks like a raw piece of meat, pinkish and maybe angry. I can't tell for sure with American faces what they are feeling, but I would say this man looks angry.

I try to act like I'm old enough to be grocery-shopping by myself. In a month, I'll be turning thirteen. Last week, a lady in the elevator at the hotel guessed I was fourteen! My baby face is sinking down to the past and a new face is coming to the surface, with my grandmother's slightly turned-up nose and my father's deep-set eyes and my mother's coffee-with-milk-color skin. I guess the only thing that is all mine is the scar above my left eye, where Mundín once hit me with a pellet from a BB gun he had aimed at the sky.

The man stops directly in front of my cart like a roadblock. "Do you have the money to buy all this, young lady?" His tone of voice suggests that he knows I don't.

I make the mistake of looking into his glaring eyes. In their harsh light, I am sure it shows that I am not one hundred percent certain I should be doing what I am doing. I stammer out a barely audible, "*Sí, señor,*" too scared at the moment to be able to speak in a second language.

"Don't you understand English?" he says, taking hold of my arm.

I'm about to tell him I do, but already he is yanking me to the front of the store and out the opening door to the sidewalk. Some people walking by turn their heads to look.

"I don't want you coming back without an adult, you hear me?" He is patting me all up and down checking to see if I've taken something.

At first, I just stand there, ashamed, submitting to his search as if I've done something wrong. But when he slaps his big hand on my chest, I cry out, "I wasn't doing anything! This is a free country!" Actually, I'm not really sure this is true. Maybe, this is a free country only for Americans? Maybe if a policeman happens by, my whole family will be deported home, where we'll all be killed by the dictator's son?

This thought is so terrifying that it's as if I have Superman strength. I wrench myself free from the man's grasp and take off running down the block, turning left, then right, trying to lose anyone who might be following me to the Beverly. When I get to the hotel, I rush past the American doorman, who is not as friendly as the Puerto Rican, and around the revolving door into the lobby, where, rather than wait for the elevator, I race up the stairs two at a time to the tenth floor, my heart pounding so hard, I'm sure it's going to explode.

I stop before our door, trying to catch my breath and calm the wild panic that I'm sure shows on my face. Inside, I hear my grandmother crying. Mami has probably just finished one of her twice-a-week calls to Mr. Washburn in Washington.

Part of me wants to avoid going in and facing even more sad news. But the terror of deportation is bigger than a disappointment I'm becoming used to. So, I knock very lightly, and call out in a little voice, "*Soy yo.*" It's just me.

Mundín opens the door, his face so drained and pale that I'm sure the police have somehow tracked me down and my family is in deep trouble.

I start crying. "I wasn't doing anything wrong."

Mundín takes my hand. "Mr. Washburn is here," he says in a flat voice, like a bulldozer has just run over it.

As I follow my brother into the main room, I'm puzzling over how Mr. Washburn could have gotten here all the way from Washington to deport us when the grocery store incident just happened. Maybe he was already in New York. Maybe the grocery-store man had planned an ambush beforehand with the State Department. But even as I entertain these farfetched possibilities, I know that I'm just trying *not* to think of the obvious reason Mr. Washburn would be here, a reason more horrible than any angry store manager or policeman coming to report me for getting into trouble.

On the couch where Mundín sleeps at night sit Mami and Lucinda holding on to each other. My grandfather is leaning forward on the recliner, listening to something Mr. Washburn is saying. Another man in a military uniform with his back to me is standing behind Mr. Washburn's chair. In the other room, I hear my grandmother crying. "She had to go lie down," Mundín explains. "She had to take a tranquilizer pill."

"Why?" I ask. My heart is tottering on the edge of a very high place, and I am waiting, breathlessly, for it to either fall down into a thousand pieces or be rescued by good news at the last minute.

Mr. Washburn stands up and folds his arms around me. When he lets go, I follow Mundín to a place on the couch beside Papito's recliner, my hand on my chest as if I could reach in and steady my heart inside my ribs. As I go by Mami, she looks up and starts crying.

My grandfather reaches over and takes my two hands in his. "We are all going to have to be very brave," he says quietly. His eyes are also red. Then he says the words I will never forget. "Your father and uncle are dead."

"We got a report yesterday," Mr. Washburn begins explaining. "The dictator's family had agreed to leave." His voice is official-sounding, but every once in a while, little clouds of sadness travel across it.

"Just before dawn, the son took off for his beach estate. Meanwhile, his SIM buddies drove over to the prison and seized the six remaining conspirators and took them to the beach—" Mr. Washburn stops abruptly.

After a moment, he adds, *"Lo siento,"* which means much more than that he is sorry, but that he feels what we are feeling.

"Tell us!" Mami orders. "I want to know how they died. I want my children to hear this. I want my country to hear this. I want the United States to hear this."

She sounds so absolutely sure, Mr. Washburn clears his throat and goes on. "Trujillo, Junior, and his cronies were quite drunk. We're not sure, but they might also have been drugged up. At any rate, they tied the prisoners to palm trees and shot them, one by one, until they were all dead. Then the bodies were taken out to sea and dumped over the side of the boat."

Before Mr. Washburn is even finished, Mami is sobbing, great big sobs, as if she is trying to scoop out all the sadness inside herself so there will be room for other feelings. Lucinda sobs, too, but in a distracted way, watching Mami, afraid of such huge grief none of us has ever seen before. Papito and Mundín dab at their eyes, my grandfather with his monogrammed handkerchief that reminds me of Papi's, Mundín with the back of his hand.

But I don't cry. Not right away. I listen carefully until the very end. I want to be with Papi and Tío Toni every step of the way.

When Mr. Washburn is done, Mami and Mundín and Lucinda and I stand up and put our arms around each other. Papito joins us, all of us crying into the empty space at the center of our family.

NATALIE ANGIER

CONFESSIONS of a LONELY ATHEIST

MAYBE IT WAS SENATOR Joe Lieberman's sermonette during the presidential campaign in 2000, when he warned against using the First Amendment's protection of religious freedom as a kind of doctor's note to get out of religious observance altogether, and added that we mustn't deceive ourselves into believing that "morality can be maintained without religion." Or maybe it was when Al Gore, Lieberman's partner in apple-polishing piety, not only boasted about how often he asked himself, "What would Jesus do?" but also began to hedge on his prior insistence that Darwin's theory of evolution by natural selection should be a mandatory part of high school science education. And these were the *Democrats*. They were supposed to be the good guys, the tolerant, enlightened Jeffersonian guys, the guys who knew enough about biology and reality to accept that, as the great geneticist Theodosius Dobzhansky put it so sonorously, "Nothing in biology makes sense, except in the light of evolution."

Rather than shoring up the ramparts against the thundering fundamentalist huns who everywhere threatened to overrun our country, however, Lieberman et al. were suddenly spinning around and pointing their spears at . . . me. Suddenly the big problem in public life was not the quickening clout of the biblical literalists, but the persistent doubts of the secular humanists. America, we were told and told and told once more, is a god-loving, god-fearing, god-cheering nation. God is in our pledge and on the money and who do you think helped us crush the communists anyway? Oh ye of little faith, ye are so little of number. Nearly every survey shows that nearly every American believes in a supreme being—and expects others to do likewise. According to the pollsters, Americans would sooner vote for a whole range of fringe characters—a woman, an African American, a Jew, a Muslim, a gay person—than choose an atheist as their president.

The statistics on that score haven't budged for years, and I'm hardly surprised to see politicians flash their religious credentials at every opportunity, no matter how ridiculous they look singing gospel. Yet when, in the midst of one of the most sanctimonious presidential campaigns in modern history, the Democrats began preaching about the moral depravity of the deity-free, and denying the overwhelming weight of evidence that supports the evolutionary narrative of how life came to be all that we see, my ordinary sense of alienation and hostility turned brimstone. And when a born-again, scrubbed-up lush opened his personal pulpit on Pennsylvania Avenue, and asked us all to put our hands together and pray with him, I had no choice but to heed my inner heathen. Enough with the genuflections, the heaven and kvelling, the baseless faith in the unbounded virtues of faith. Who says that believers are better people than nonbelievers, or that religion is the sole bedrock on which we can remain upstanding? Sure, I agree with half of the ten commandments—the ones about not killing, stealing, committing adultery or bearing false witness against thy neighbor, even if thy neighbor insists on cleaning out his Hummer with a leaf blower while Led Zeppelin blares from thy neighbor's Hummer's sound system; and especially, I tell my daughter, Commandment the Fifth, about honoring thy father and thy mother if thou knowest what is good for thee and thy college fund.

Yet I see little goodliness in the commandments that badmouth other gods, and the polytheistic and pantheistic traditions that preceded the Judeo-Christian juggernaut. Nor can any religious tract claim credit for many of the great advances in our legal and ethical systems: the abolition of slavery, universal suffrage, public education, surprisingly drinkable coffee in airports and movie theaters. If anything, religion often proves a drag on cultural evolution and the ongoing struggle to expand human rights to embrace all members of the human race. Those who oppose gay marriage, for example, are hard-pressed to defend their position on anything other than religious grounds, just as the bigoted critics of "miscegenation" did before them. Besides, do we really need ten commandments, when one golden rule will do? In my experience, nothing has worked better in inspiring my child to be as decent a human being as possible than to say, How would you feel if so-and-so did that to you?

Beyond questioning religion's claim to the civics high ground, I also question religion's claims about everything else. I can't help it. I see no evidence of a divine creator, apart from the universe itself, which is here, yes it is, and it's a gorgeous thing. I love our universe nearly all the time, except when I get angry at the stars and galaxies being so far apart from each other that we may never get a chance to meet any non-Earthlings, even if they're out there in abundance. At other times I get angry at the flip brutality of life, and the fact that most life forms are incapable of eating the sun, as plants do, and so must eat other life forms. But reality, welcome to yourself, I'm glad and grateful to meet you, and I'll be awfully sorry when I have to leave.

I wrote this story to make a case for atheism, its durability, affability, and, in my case, inevitability. I wrote it because I was dismayed by the Xtreme religiosity that had stampeded into America, right on schedule with the millennium, taken the place over, and then invited all its crazy relatives to join it. I wrote the story as confession, as catharsis, as an attempt at self-sedation. I didn't write it to make hypothetical friends or to entertain, as I've done with many of my science stories—when I wrote about dung beetles, for example, or laziness in the animal kingdom, or the history of teeth (including my dreadful ones). I didn't think I'd get a lot of sympathy with the story. Atheism? Well, aren't you a smug elitist, looking down your nose at the silly people who believe in their version of Santa Claus. My mother reminds me, whenever I go into a churl about religion, that my long-dead father spent his life on a spiritual quest, and did I really think I had a more profound insight into human nature than he did? No, I don't, I say. He was looking for meaning. He was looking for something to calm his anger and give him joy. He tried to find it in religion, but he never did. And not long before he died suddenly at the age of fifty-one, of a fast-growing melanoma tumor that had spread to his brain, I realized that he saw life for what it was: a dazzling fistful of chemistry that you can only hold so long. We were at a friend's house, and apropos of nothing except the fact that I was nineteen years old, I asked him, What do you think happens when you die? He smiled slyly and said, What happens to a candle when you blow it out? Oh, I squeaked, and then I asked if he was afraid of dying, of having his flame snuffed out. "Nope," he replied. From the pure, clipped pop of that "nope," I knew, right down to my base pairs, that he was telling the truth.

That's what I want, I tell my mother. To see things clearly, and to not feel afraid.

So I wrote about my atheism, and my anger at being marginalized for it. I combed through the surveys of who believes and who doesn't and who can be believed and who might be saying what they think the pollster wants to hear. I examined the handful of studies that asked whether there was a link between religiousness and moral behavior, and couldn't help cackling over the results. Reporting and writing the article was my version of a pilgrimage, and, the title be damned, by the end of the sojourn I felt a little less lonely.

What took me completely by surprise was how spectacularly unalone I was. In all my years of writing, I have never gotten as much response as I did to this story. Hundreds and hundreds of letters, e-mails, phone calls, limericks, home-burned CDs, and nearly all were variations on a theme. "I'm sure this will be the *only* positive feedback you get," the reader would begin, "but I wanted to thank you for expressing what I've been feeling. I thought I was the *only* one." Single-spaced letter tumbled after Georgia O'Keeffe notecard: the gratitude, the relief, the worry that religious fanatics would bomb my house, the testimonials about how the reader had shed the faith of forebears and ended up an atheist, or agnostic, or family crank. The hate mail never came, save two or three quibbles from theologians and one prayer for my errant soul.

You could argue I was preaching to the choir, but still, it gave me hope. I had no idea how many voices were out there, desperate to just say . . . nope.

—Natalie Angier

In the beginning—or rather, at the end of a very lo-o-ng beginning—George W. Bush made an earnest acceptance speech and urged our nation to "rise above a house divided." He knows, he said, that "America wants reconciliation and unity," and that we all "share hopes and goals and values." After his speech he reached out, up and down and across aisles, to embrace Republicans, Democrats, Naderites, Palm Beach Buchananites, the disaffected, the disinclined.

The only problem was what President-elect Bush wanted from me and "every American." "I ask you to pray for this great nation," he said. "I ask your prayers for leaders from both parties," and for their families too, while we're at it. Whatever else I might have been inclined to think of Bush's call for comity, with his simple little request, his assumption that prayer is some sort of miracle Vicks VapoRub for the national charley horse, it was clear that his hands were reaching for any hands but mine.

In an age when flamboyantly gay characters are sitcom staples, a Jew was but a few flutters of a butterfly wing away from being in line for the presidency and women account for a record-smiting 13 percent of the Senate, nothing seems as despised, illicit and un-American as atheism. Again and again the polls proclaim the United States to be a profoundly and persistently religious nation, one in which faith remains a powerful force despite the temptations of secularism and the decline of religion's influence in most other countries of the developed world. Every year, surveyors like Gallup and the National Opinion Research Center ask Americans whether they believe in

God, and every year the same overwhelming majority, anywhere from 92 to 97 percent, say yes.

Devils and angels alike, it seems, are in the details. In one survey, 80 percent profess belief in life after death. True to the spirit of American optimism, an even greater percentage—86 percent—say they believe in heaven, while a slightly lower number, 76 percent, subscribe to a belief in hell. When asked how often they attend church, at least 60 percent of respondents say once a month or more, and have said as much for the past 40 years. Three-quarters of all Americans proclaim a belief in religious miracles, and the same number concur with the statement that God "concerns himself with every human being personally."

These statistics contrast starkly with those from many other nations. According to the International Social Survey Program, a comparative study of beliefs and practices in 31 nations, while a mere 3.2 percent of Americans will agree flatly that they "don't believe in God," 17.2 percent of the Dutch concur with that statement, as do 19.1 of those in France, 16.8 percent of Swedes, 20.3 percent of people in the Czech Republic, 19.7 percent of Russians, 10.6 percent of Japanese and 9.2 percent of Canadians.

Other countries are also noticeably more skeptical about miracles, or their personal prospects postmortem. Anywhere from 40 to 70 percent of people in France, Sweden, Denmark, Austria, Great Britain, the Netherlands, Japan and the Czech Republic say, sorry, there probably is no life after death, there is no heaven, there is no hell, there are no Lazaruses.

Only in those countries where the Catholic Church still reigns supreme, like the Philippines or Chile, does the extent of devoutness match or even surpass America's. So, too, does the devoutness of non-Christian nations like India, Indonesia and Iran.

So who in her right mind would want to be an atheist in America today, a place where presidential candidates compete for the honor of divining "what Jesus would do," and where Senator Joseph Lieberman can declare that we shouldn't deceive ourselves into thinking that our constitutional "freedom of religion" means "freedom from religion," or "indulge the supposition that morality can be maintained without religion," and for his atheism-baiting receive the lightest possible slap on the wrist from his more secularized Jewish counterparts?

Who would want to be the low man on the voter poll? When asked in 1999 whether they would consider voting for a woman for president, 92 percent of Americans said yes, up from 76 percent in 1978; 95 percent of respondents would vote for a black, a gain of 22 points since 1978; Jews were up to 92 percent from 82 in the votability index; even homosexuals have soared in popularity, acceptable presidential fodder to 59 percent of Americans today, compared with 26 percent in 1978. But atheists, well, there's no saving them. Of all the categories in this particular Gallup poll, they scraped bottom, considered worthy candidates by only 49 percent of Americans, a gain of a mere 9 percent since 1978. "Throughout American history, there's been this belief that our country has a covenant with God and that a deity watches over America," says Michael Cromartie, vice president of the Ethics and Public Policy Center in Washington. Atheism, in other words, is practically unpatriotic.

It's enough to make one tell a nosy pollster, oh, yes, I believe in God. It's enough to make one not want to discuss belief in the first place, or to reach for palatable terms like "secular humanist," or "freethinker," or "agnostic," which sound so much less dogmatic than "atheist," so much less cocksure.

So, I'll out myself. I'm an Atheist. I don't believe in God, Gods, Godlets or any sort of higher power beyond the universe itself, which seems quite high and powerful enough to me. I don't believe in life after death, channeled chat rooms with the dead, reincarnation, telekinesis or any miracles but the miracle of life and consciousness, which again strike me as miracles in nearly obscene abundance. I believe that the universe abides by the laws of physics, some of which are known, others of which will surely be discovered, but even if they aren't, that will simply be a result, as my colleague George Johnson put it, of our brains having evolved for life on this one little planet and thus being inevitably limited. I'm convinced that the world as we see it was shaped by the again genuinely miraculous, let's even say transcendent, hand of evolution through natural selection.

I don't need pollsters like Daniel Yankelovich to tell me that I'm in the minority. I'm in the minority even among friends and family. Not long ago I was startled to learn that my older brother believes in God. ("You got a problem with that?" he practically snarled.) My older sister is rearing her two kids as semi-observant Jews, and my niece recently won raves for her bat mitzvah performance. When I sent out a casual and nonscientific poll of my own to a wide cast of acquaintances, friends and colleagues, I was surprised, but not really, to learn that maybe 60 percent claimed a belief in a God of some sort, including people I would have bet were unregenerate skeptics. Others just shrugged. They don't think about this stuff. It doesn't matter to them. They can't know, they won't beat themselves up trying to know and for that matter they don't care if their kids believe or not.

"My children's religious beliefs are their own," says Florence Haseltine, a scientist and advocate for women's health. "And as long as those beliefs do not require you to kill your parents, they're OK with me."

Rare were the respondents who considered atheism to be a significant part of their self-identities. Most called themselves "passive" atheists and said they had stopped doing battle with the big questions of life and death, meaning and eternity, pretty much when they stopped using Clearasil.

"I don't spend much time thinking about whether God exists," said Wendy Kaminer, author of *Sleeping With Extraterrestrials: The Rise of Irrationalism and Perils of Piety* and an affiliated scholar with the Radcliffe Institute for Advanced Studies. "I don't consider that a relevant question. It's unanswerable and irrelevant to my life, so I put it in the category of things I can't worry about."

To be an active atheist seems almost silly and beside the point. After all, the most famous group devoted to atheism, the American Atheists, was founded by Madalyn Murray O'Hair, an eccentric megalomaniac whose greatest claim to fame, at this point, is that she and her son were kidnapped several years ago and are presumed dead. Other atheistic groups, like the Freedom From Religion Foundation or the Council for Secular Humanism, are more concerned with maintaining an unshakable separation between church and state than they are with spreading any gospel of godlessness. Katha Pollitt, an unabashedly liberal columnist for *The Nation* who says she is listed in the "Who's Who in Hell," admits she used to feel more strongly about arguing against religion than she does today.

"I'm anticlerical, not antireligion," she says. "If somebody believes there is God, I'm not interested in trying to persuade that person there is no intelligent design to the universe. Where I become interested and wake up is about the temporal power of religion, things like prayer in schools, or Catholic-secular hospital mergers."

Or, as Tom Eisner, a neurobiologist at Cornell, put it, "I don't ring doorbells saying I'm a Seventh-Day Atheist."

And yet. There is something to be said for a revival of pagan peevishness and outspokenness. It's not that I would presume to do something as foolish and insulting as try to convert a believer. Arguments over the question of whether God exists are ancient, recurring, sometimes stimulating but more often tedious. Arrogance and righteousness are nondenominational vices that entice the churched and unchurched alike.

Still, the current climate of religiosity can be stifling to nonbelievers, and it helps now and then to cry foul. For one thing, some of the numbers surrounding the deep religiousness of America, and the rarity of nonbelief, should be held to the fire of skepticism, as should sweeping statistics of any sort. Yes, Americans are comparatively more religious than Europeans, but while the vast majority of them may say generically that they believe in God, when asked what their religion is, a sizable fraction, 11 percent, report "no religion," a figure that has more than doubled since the early 1970s and that amounts to about 26 million people.

As Pollitt points out, when one starts looking beneath the surface of things and adding together the out-front atheists with the indifferent nonbelievers, you end up with a much larger group of people than Jews, Muslims, Buddhists and Unitarians put together.

"Survey data point to an overwhelming belief in God, but when you go down a couple of layers, it can be pretty vacuous," says Cromartie. "It's striking how many people say they're Christian but don't know who gave the Sermon on the Mount."

Moreover, it seems that even good Christians sometimes lie when a pollster comes calling. Stanley Presser, a survey methodologist and sociologist at the University of Maryland in College Park, and his colleague Linda Stinson of the Bureau of Labor Statistics were impressed by the apparent stability of the number of Americans, 40 percent, who, year in and year out, told pollsters like the Gallup organization that they attended church every week. To check on the accuracy of such self-reported conscientiousness, the researchers turned to time diaries they had compiled for the Environmental Protection Agency—accounts of the daily activities of 10,000 respondents nationwide to help the agency gauge public exposure to pollutants.

"We asked people, tell us everything you did in the last 24 hours so we can know what chemicals you might have been exposed to," Presser says. "If somebody went to church, they ought to tell us, but if they didn't go, they shouldn't manufacture it. We didn't do what most polls of religious belief do, and ask, Did you go to church in the last seven days? Which some might interpret as being asked whether they were good people and good Christians."

According to their time-diary analysis, only 26 percent of Americans in 1994 went to church weekly, although the Gallup poll for the same period reported the figure at 42 percent.

What's more, in some quarters, atheism, far from being rare, is the norm—among scientists, for example, particularly high-level scientists who populate academia. Recently, Edward J. Larson, a science historian at the University of Georgia, and Larry Witham, a writer, polled scientists listed in American Men and Women of Science on their religious beliefs. Among this general group, a reasonably high proportion, 40 percent, claimed to believe in a "personal God" who would listen to their prayers. But when the researchers next targeted members of the National Academy of Sciences, an elite coterie if ever there was one, belief in a personal God was 7 percent, the flip of the American public at large. This is not to say that intelligence and atheism are in any way linked, but to suggest that immersion in the scientific method, and success in the profession, tend to influence its practitioners.

"It's a consequence of the experience of science," says Steven Weinberg, a Nobel laureate and professor of physics at the University of Texas. "As you learn more and more about the universe, you find you can understand more and more without any reference to supernatural intervention, so you lose interest in that possibility. Most scientists I know don't care enough about religion even to call themselves atheists. And that, I think, is one of the great things about science—that it has made it possible for people not to be religious."

So long, that is, as the nonbelievers remain humble. Among the more irritating consequences of our flagrantly religious society is the special dispensation that mainstream religions receive. We all may talk about religion as a powerful social force, but unlike other similarly powerful institutions, religion is not to be questioned, criticized or mocked. When the singer-songwriter Sinead O'Connor ripped apart a photograph of John Paul II to protest what she saw as his over-weening power, even the most secular humanists were outraged by her idolatry, and her career has never really recovered.

"Society bends over backward to be accommodating to religious sensibilities but not to other kinds of sensibilities," says Richard Dawkins, an evolutionary biologist and outspoken atheist. "If I say something offensive to religious people, I'll be universally censured, including by many atheists. But if I say something insulting about Democrats or Republicans or the Green Party, one is allowed to get away with that. Hiding behind the smoke screen of untouchability is something religions have been allowed to get away with for too long."

Early in December, I visited the kind of person who should be as rare as an atheist in a foxhole: a freethinker in a fire station. Bruce Monson, an affable, boyish-faced thirty-three-year-old firefighter and para-medic who works in the conservative city of Colorado Springs, where evangelical religious organizations are among the biggest boom busi-nesses, had challenged some of the religious literature, quoting New Testament Scripture, that members of the Fellowship of Christian Firefighters posted on the taxpayer-financed station's bulletin board. Fighting fire with fire, Monson posted literature of his own, this time quoting some of the less savory sections of the Old Testament, like when Lot sleeps with his daughters and impregnates them.

The Christian firefighters were outraged and demanded that Monson's posts be removed. "I was told by my superiors to take my stuff down and leave the Christian material alone," Monson said. Monson pursued his fight up the chain of command and finally won the right to his postings on the department's web page, but not with-out being described by any number of colorful terms and being told where he should, and would, go.

"I'm not antireligion," he said. "I'm anti-shoving-it-down-your-throat. Is it too much to ask for tolerance?"

Oh, yes, tolerance. How sweet a policy of respectfulness and hands-off might be, were it mutually adhered to. But when *The Atlantic Monthly* asks, in the headline of a feature article by Glenn Tinder, "Can We Be Good Without God?" the answer is, of course, "Hell, no!" And when conspicuous true believers like Lieberman make the claim that religion and ethical behavior are inextricably linked, the corollary premise is that atheists are, if not immoral, then amoral, or nihilistic misanthropes, or, worst of all, moral relativists.

"There remains a sense among a lot of Americans that someone who actively doesn't believe in God might not be morally reliable, or might not be fully trustworthy," says James Turner, a professor of history and philosophy of science at Notre Dame. Yet the canard that godliness and goodliness are linked in any way but typographically must be taken on faith, for no evidence supports it. In one classic study, sociologists at the University of Washington compared students who were part of the "Jesus people" movement with a comparable group of professed atheists and found that atheists were no more likely to cheat on tests than were Christians and no less likely to volunteer at a hospital for the mentally disabled. Recent data compiled on the religious views among federal prisoners show that nonbelievers account for less than 1 percent of the total, significantly lower than for America as a whole. Admittedly, some of those true-believing inmates may have converted post-incarceration, but the data that exist in no way support the notion that atheism promotes criminal behavior.

In fact, the foundations of ethical behavior not only predate the world's major religions; they also predate the rise of Homo sapiens. Frans de Waal, a primatologist at Emory University, has written extensively about the existence of seemingly moral behavior in non-human species. "I've argued that many of what philosophers call moral sentiments can be seen in other species," he said. "In chimpanzees and other animals, you see examples of sympathy, empathy, reciprocity, a willingness to follow social rules. Dogs are a good example of a species that have and obey social rules; that's why we like them so much, even though they're large carnivores."

As humans have sought to move beyond simple reciprocity to consider abstract issues of fairness, or to grope toward something like a universal declaration of human rights, established religions have played a surprisingly small part.

"Over the centuries, we've moved on from Scripture to accumulate precepts of ethical, legal and moral philosophy," Dawkins says. "We've evolved a liberal consensus of what we regard as underpinnings of decent society, such as the idea that we don't approve of slavery or discrimination on the grounds of race or sex, that we respect free speech and the rights of the individual. All of these things that have become second nature to our morals today owe very little to religion, and mostly have been won in opposition to the teeth of religion."

That's not to say religion has no potential to do good, or to inspire brilliant thought, art, music, indeed many of the jewels of civilization: the Song of Solomon, Handel's "Messiah," the Hagia Sophia. Perhaps Mary McCarthy was right in her lovely claim that "religion is good for good people." What remains open to question is whether religion makes anybody good or great who would otherwise be malicious or mediocre.

The capacity for religious sentiment subserves so many human interests as to suggest it may be innate. "Religions have a strong binding function and a cohesive element," de Waal says. "They emphasize the primacy of the community as opposed to the individual, and they also help set one community apart from another that doesn't share their beliefs." Certainly those in authority have long recognized the power of religion as a quick-and-dirty way of getting everybody on the same meta-bandwidth, at once focused and aroused and prepared to do battle for a putative "greater good." President-elect Bush has sought to tap into this unifying, exultant spirit in his call for a replacement of all those sterile and secular government welfare programs with a host of new "faith-based" charities. In their coming book, *Why God Won't Go Away*, the neuroscientists Andrew Newberg and Eugene d'Aquili (who died after the book was completed) argue that the "promises of religion" protected early humans from the "self-defeating fatalism" and "soul-sapping" despair of the Ingmar Bergman variety. "By providing us with helpful gods, and showing how to appeal to those gods, religions armed our ancestors—and continue to arm us—with a feeling of control," they write. "As long as we have the methods to propitiate the gods, or solicit their interest, or appeal to their sense of fairness and justice, or to connect with the presence of an eternal unity, we feel that an underlying order and purpose exist in a seemingly chaotic universe."

In his book *Consilience*, Edward O. Wilson of Harvard states that "the human mind evolved to believe in the gods. It did not evolve to believe in biology."

I'm not so sure. Religion may be innate, but so, too, is skepticism. Consider that we are the most socially sophisticated of all creatures, reliant on reciprocal altruism for so much of our success. We are profoundly dependent on the good will and good behavior of others, and we are perpetually seeking evidence that those around us are trust-worthy, are true to their word, are not about to desert us, rob us blind, murder us as we sleep. It is not enough for a newcomer to tell us: "Open your door. Trust me. I'm a swell citizen—really." We want proof. The human race resides in one great Show Me state. If we are built to have faith, we are threaded through, as well, with a desire for proof that our faith is well placed—as Bruce Monson doggedly puts it when he asks his Christian colleagues why Jesus can't step down from on high just once to bring back to life one of many children he has seen die in the line of duty.

Believers and doubters alike will always be with us—and it's just possible that we need each other more than we know. As Kevin McCullough, a member of the Fellowship of Christian Firefighters, told me of his debate with the doubting Monson: "If he's seeking the truth, I don't think he's there yet. But he makes me think, and he brings up good points, and that's good for me. It helps strengthen my own beliefs."

From my godless perspective, the devout remind me that it is human nature to thirst after meaning and to desire an expansion of purpose beyond the cramped Manhattan studio of self and its imme-diate relations. In her brief and beautiful book, *The Sacred Depths of Nature*, Ursula Goodenough, a cell biologist, articulates a sensibility that she calls "religious naturalism," a profound appreciation of the genuine workings of nature, conjoined with a commitment to pre-serving that natural world in all its staggering, interdependent splen-dor. Or call it transcendent atheism: I may not believe in life after death, but what a gift it is to be alive now.

PAUL AUSTER

From TIMBUKTU

∽

I HAVE NOTHING TO say about my choice. Writers know nothing about their own work, and the less they talk about it, the better. The work speaks for itself. Or else it doesn't. Let the reader draw his own conclusions. As for me, I sit in the dark and listen to the words inside me. I don't know where they come from. I never have, and by now I'm convinced I never will. Mr. Bones and Willy G. Christmas. Out of so many thousands of pages, why these ten? No reason that I can think of. Forgive me. I apologize for my ignorance.

—Paul Auster

Mr. Bones lifted his head. A moment later, as if the two actions were secretly connected, a shaft of light came slanting through the clouds. It struck the sidewalk an inch or two from the dog's left paw, and then, almost immediately, another beam landed just to his right. A crisscross of light and shadow began to form on the pavement in front of him, and it was a beautiful thing to behold, he felt, a small, unexpected gift on the heels of so much sadness and pain. He looked back at Willy then, and just as he was turning his head, a great bucketful of light poured down on the poet's face, and so intense was the light as it crashed against the sleeping man's eyelids that his eyes involuntarily opened—and there was Willy, all but defunct a moment ago, back in the land of the living, dusting off the cobwebs and trying to wake up.

He coughed once, then again, and then a third time before lapsing into a prolonged seizure. Mr. Bones stood by helplessly as globules of phlegm came flying from his master's mouth. Some landed on Willy's shirt, others on the pavement. Still others, the looser and more slithery ones, dribbled weakly down his chin. There they remained, dangling from his beard like noodles, and as the fit wore on, punctuated by violent jolts, lurches, and doublings over, they bobbed back and forth in a crazy, syncopated dance. Mr. Bones was stunned by the ferocity of the attack. Surely this was the end, he said to himself, surely this was the

34

limit of what a man could take. But Willy still had some fight left in him, and once he wiped his face with the sleeve of his jacket and managed to recover his breath, he surprised Mr. Bones by breaking into a broad, almost beatific smile. With much difficulty, he maneuvered himself into a more comfortable position, leaning his back against the wall of the house and stretching out his legs before him. Once his master was still again, Mr. Bones lowered his head onto his right thigh. When Willy reached out and started stroking the top of that head, a measure of calm returned to the dog's broken heart. It was only temporary, of course, and only an illusion, but that didn't mean it wasn't good medicine.

"Lend an ear, Citizen Mutt," Willy said. "It's starting. Things are falling away now. One by one they're falling away, and only strange things are left, tiny long-ago things, not at all the things I was expecting. I can't say I'm scared, though. A little sorry, maybe, a little miffed at having to make this early exit, but not crapping my drawers the way I thought I might be. Pack up your bags, amigo. We're on the road to Splitsville, and there's no turning back. You follow, Mr. Bones? Are you with me so far?"

Mr. Bones followed, and Mr. Bones was with him.

"I wish I could boil it down to a few choice words for you," the dying man continued, "but I can't. Punchy epigrams, succinct pearls of wisdom, Polonius delivering his parting shots. I don't have it in me to do that. Neither a borrower nor a lender be; a stitch in time saves nine. There's too much mayhem in the attic, Bonesy, and you'll just have to bear with me as I ramble and digress. It seems to be in the nature of things for me to be confused. Even now, as I enter the valley of the shadow of death, my thoughts bog down in the gunk of yore. There's the rub, signore. All this clutter in my head, this dust and bric-a-brac, these useless knickknacks spilling off the shelves. Indeed, sir, the sad truth is that I am a bear of but little brain.

"By way of proof, I offer you the return of O'Dell's Hair Trainer. The stuff disappeared from my life forty years ago, and now, on the last day of my life, it suddenly comes back. I yearn for profundities, and what I get is this no-account factoid, this microblip on the screen of memory. My mother used to rub it into my hair when I was just a wee thing, a mere mite of a lad. They sold it in the local barbershops, and it came in a clear glass bottle about yea big. The spout was black, I believe, and on the label there was a picture of some grinning idiot boy. A wholesome, idealized numbskull with perfectly groomed hair. No cowlicks for that lunkhead, no wobbles in the part for that pretty fellow. I was five, six years old, and every morning my mother would give me the treatment, hoping to make me look like his twin brother. I can still hear the gloppity-gluggity sound as the goo came out of the bottle. It was a whitish, translucent liquid, sticky to the touch. A kind of watered-down sperm, I suppose, but who knew about such things then? They probably manufactured it by hiring teenage boys to jerk off into vats. Thus are fortunes made in our great land. A penny to produce, a dollar to buy, and you figure out the rest. So my Polish mother would rub the O'Dell's Hair Trainer into my scalp, comb my disobedient locks, and then send me off to school looking like that ass-wipe kid on the bottle. I was going to be an American, by gum, and this hair meant that I belonged, that my parents knew what was fucking what.

"Before you break down and weep, my friend, let me add that O'Dell's was a sham concoction, a fraud. It didn't train hair so much as glue it into submission. For the first hour, it would seem to do its job, but then, as the morning wore on, the glue would harden, and little by little my hair would be turned into a mass of rigid, epoxified wires—as if a springy metallic bonnet had been clamped over my head. It felt so strange to the touch, I couldn't leave it alone. Even as my right hand gripped the pencil, making with the two plus threes and six minus fives, my left hand would be wandering around up north, poking and picking at the alien surfaces of my head. By midafternoon, the O'Dell's would be so dried out, so thoroughly drained of moisture, that each strand of coated hair would be turned into a brittle thread. That was the moment I was waiting for, the signal that the last act of the farce was about to begin. One by one, I'd reach down to the base of each strand of hair rooted in my scalp, pinch it between my thumb and middle finger, and pull. Slowly. Very slowly, sliding my nails along the entire length of the hair. Ah. The satisfactions were immense, incalculable. All the powder flying off of me! The storms, the blizzards, the whirlwinds of whiteness! It was no easy job, let me tell you, but little by little every trace of the O'Dell's would disappear. The do would be undone, and by the time the last bell rang and the teacher sent us home, my scalp would be tingling with happiness. It was as good as sex, mon vieux, as good as all the drugs and drink I ever poured into my system. Five years old, and every day another orgy of self-repair. No wonder I didn't pay attention at school. I was too busy feeling myself up, too busy doing the O'Dell's diddle.

"But enough. Enough of this tedium. Enough of this Te Deum. Hair trainer is just the tip of the iceberg, and once I start in with this childhood dreck, we'll be here for the next sixteen hours. We don't have time for that, do we? Not for castor oil, not for pot cheese, not for lumpy porridge, not for the Blackjack gum. We all grew up with that junk, but now it's gone, isn't it, and who the hell cares anyway? Wallpaper, that's what it was. Background music. Zeitgeist dust on the furniture of the mind. I can bring back fifty-one thousand details, but so what? It won't do you or me an ounce of good. Understanding. That's what I'm after, chum. The key to the puzzle, the secret formula after four-plus decades of groping in the dark. And still, all this stuff keeps getting in my way. Even as I breathe my last, I'm choking on it. Useless bits of knowledge, unwanted memories, dandelion fluff. It's all flit and fume, my boy, a bellyful of wind. The life and times of R. Mutt. Eleanor Rigby. Rumpelstiltskin. Who the fuck wants to know them? The Pep Boys, the Ritz Brothers, Rory Calhoun. Captain Video and the Four Tops. The Andrews Sisters, *Life* and *Look*, the Bobbsey Twins. There's no end to it, is there? Henry James and Jesse James, Frank James and William James. James Joyce. Joyce Cary. Cary Grant. Grant me swizzle sticks and dental floss, Dentyne gum and honey-dip doughnuts. Delete Dana Andrews and Dixie Dugan, then throw in Damon Runyon and demon rum for good measure. Forget Pall Malls and shopping malls, Milton Berle and Burl Ives, Ivory soap and Aunt Jemima pancake mix. I don't need them, do I? Not where I'm going I don't, and yet there they are, marching through my brain like long-lost brethren. That's American know-how for you. It keeps coming at you, and every minute there's new junk to push out the old junk. You'd think we would have caught on by now, wised up to the tricks they pull on us, but people can't get enough of it. They cheer, they wave flags, they hire marching bands. Yes, yes, wondrous things, miraculous things, machines to stagger the imagination, but let us not forget, no, let us not forget that we are not alone in this world. Know-how knows no borders, and when you think of the bounty that pours in from across the seas, it knocks you down a peg or two and puts you in your place. I don't just mean obvious things like turkeys from Turkey or chili from Chile. I also mean pants from France. I mean pain from Spain and pity from Italy and checks from Czechoslovakia and fleece from Greece. Patriotism has its role, but in the long run it's a sentiment best kept under wraps. Yes, we Yanks have given the world the zipper and the Zippo, not to speak of zip-a-dee doo-dah and Zeppo Marx, but we're also responsible for the H-bomb and the hula hoop. It all balances out in the end, doesn't it? Just when you think you're top gun, you wind up as bottom dog. And I don't mean you, Mr. Bones. Dog as metaphor, if you catch my drift, dog as emblem of the downtrodden, and you're no trope, my boy, you're as real as they come.

"But don't get me wrong. There's too much out there not to feel tempted. The lure of particulars, I mean, the seductions of the thing-in-itself. You'd have to be blind not to give in once in a while. I don't care what it is. Just pick a thing, and chances are a case can be made for it. The splendor of bicycle wheels, for example. Their lightness, their spidery elegance, their shining rims and gossamer spokes. Or the sound of a manhole cover rattling under a truck at three in the morning. To say nothing of Spandex, which has probably done more to spruce up the landscape than any invention since the underground telephone wire. I refer to the sight of Spandex pants plastered across the behind of a young chick as she strides by you on the street. Need I say more? You'd have to be dead not to warm to that. It darts and dives at you, keeps churning away in your head until it all melts down into a big, buttery ooze. Vasco da Gama in his puffy pantaloons. FDR's cigarette holder. Voltaire's powdery wig. Cunegonde! Cunegonde! Think of what happens when you say it. See what you say when you think of it. Cartography. Pornography. Stenography. Stentorian stammerings, Episcopalian floozies, Fudgsicles and Frosted Flakes. I admit that I've succumbed to the charms of these things as readily as the next man, am in no wise superior to the riffraff I've rubbed shoulders with for lo these many years. I'm human, aren't I? If that makes me a hypocrite, then so be it.

"Sometimes, you just have to bow down in awe. A person comes up with an idea that no one has ever thought of, an idea so simple and perfect that you wonder how the world ever managed to survive without it. The suitcase with wheels, for example. How could it have taken us so long? For thirty thousand years, we've been lugging our burdens around with us, sweating and straining as we moved from one place to another, and the only thing that's ever come of it is sore muscles, bad backs, exhaustion. I mean, it's not as though we didn't have the wheel, is it? That's what gets me. Why did we have to wait until the end of the twentieth century for this gizmo to see the light of day? If nothing else, you'd think roller skates would have inspired someone to make the connection, to put two and two together. But no. Fifty years go by, seventy-five years go by, and people are still schlepping their bags through airports and train stations every time they leave home to visit Aunt Rita in Poughkeepsie. I'm telling you, friend, things aren't as simple as they look. The human spirit is a dull instrument, and often we're no better at figuring out how to take care of ourselves than the lowest worm in the ground.

"Whatever else I've been, I've never let myself be that worm. I've jumped, I've galloped, I've soared, and no matter how many times I've crashed back to earth, I've always picked myself up and tried again. Even now, as the darkness closes in on me, my mind holds fast and won't throw in the towel. The transparent toaster, comrade. It came to me in a vision two or three nights ago, and my head's been full of the idea ever since. Why not expose the works, I said to myself, be able to watch the bread turn from white to golden brown, to see the metamorphosis with your own eyes? What good does it do to lock up the bread and hide it behind that ugly stainless steel? I'm talking about clear glass, with the orange coils glowing within. It would be a thing of beauty, a work of art in every kitchen, a luminous sculpture to contemplate even as we go about the humble task of preparing breakfast and fortifying ourselves for the day ahead. Clear, heat-resistant glass. We could tint it blue, tint it green, tint it any color we like, and then, with the orange radiating from within, imagine the combinations, just think of the visual wonders that would be possible. Making toast would be turned into a religious act, an emanation of otherworldliness, a form of prayer. Jesus god. How I wish I had the strength to work on it now, to sit down and draw up some plans, to perfect the thing and see where we got with it. That's all I've ever dreamed of, Mr. Bones. To make the world a better place. To bring some beauty to the drab, humdrum corners of the soul. You can do it with a toaster, you can do it with a poem, you can do it by reaching out your hand to a stranger. It doesn't matter what form it takes. To leave the world a little better than you found it. That's the best a man can ever do.

"Okay, snicker if you like. If I gush, I gush, and that's all there is to it. It feels good to let the purple stuff come pouring out sometimes. Does that make me a fool? Perhaps it does. But better that than bitterness, I say, better to follow the lessons of Santa Claus than to spend your life in the claws of deceit. Sure, I know what you're thinking. You don't have to say it. I can hear the words in your head, mein herr, and you won't get an argument from me. Wherefore this floundering?, you ask yourself. Wherefore this flopping to and fro, this rolling in the dust, this lifelong grovel toward annihilation? You do well to ask these questions. I've asked them many times myself, and the only answer I've ever come up with is the one that answers nothing. Because I wanted it this way. Because I had no choice. Because there are no answers to questions like these.

"No apologies, then. I've always been a flawed creature, Mr. Bones, a man riddled with contradictions and inconsistencies, the tugs of too many impulses. On the one hand, purity of heart, goodness, Santa's loyal helper. On the other hand, a loudmouthed crank, a nihilist, a besotted clown. And the poet? He fell somewhere in between, I suppose, in the interval between the best and the worst of me. Not the saint, and not the wisecracking drunk. The man with the voices in his head, the one who sometimes managed to listen in on the conversation of stones and trees, who every now and then could turn the music of the clouds into words. Pity I couldn't have been him more. But I've never been to Italy, alas, the place where pity is produced, and if you can't afford the fare, then you just have to stay at home.

"Still, you've never seen me at my best, Sir Osso, and I regret that. I regret that you've known me only as a man in decline. It was a different story back in the old days, before my spunk petered out and I ran into this . . . this engine trouble. I never wanted to be a bum. That wasn't what I had in mind for myself, that wasn't how I dreamed of my future. Scrounging for empty bottles in recycling bins wasn't part of the plan. Squirting water on windshields wasn't part of the plan. Falling down on my knees in front of churches and closing my eyes to look like an early Christian martyr so that some passerby would feel sorry for me and drop a dime or quarter in my palm—no, Signor Puccini, no, no, no, that wasn't what I was put on this earth to do. But man does not live by words alone. He needs bread, and not just one loaf, but two. One for the pocket and one for the mouth. Bread to buy bread, if you see what I mean, and if you don't have the first kind, you sure as hell aren't going to have the other.

"It was a tough blow when *Mom-san* left us. I'm not going to deny that, pupster, and I'm not going to deny that I made things worse by giving away all that money. I said no apologies, but now I want to take that back and apologize to you. I did a rash and stupid thing, and we've both paid the price. Ten thousand dollars ain't Shredded Wheat, after all. I let it slip through my fingers, watched the whole wad scatter to the winds, and the funny thing about it was that I didn't care. It made me happy to act like a big shot, to flaunt my haul like some cockamamie high-roller. Mr. Altruism. Mr. Al Truism, that's me, the one and only Alberto Verissimo, the man who took his mother's life insurance policy and unloaded every nickel of it. A hundred dollars to Benny Shapiro. Eight hundred dollars to Daisy Brackett. Four thousand dollars to the Fresh Air Fund. Two thousand dollars to the Henry Street Settlement House. Fifteen hundred dollars to the Poets-in-the-Schools Program. It went fast, didn't it? A week, ten days, and by the time I looked up again, I had divested myself of my entire inheritance. Oh well. Easy come easy go, as the old saw says, and who am I to think I could have done otherwise? It's in my blood to be bold, to do the thing that no one else would do. Buck the buck, that's what I did. It was my one chance to put up or shut up, to prove to myself that I meant what I'd been saying for all those years, and so when the dough came in I didn't hesitate. I bucked the buck. I might have fucked myself in the process, but that doesn't mean I acted in vain. Pride counts for something, after all, and when push came to shove, I'm glad I didn't back down. I walked the plank. I went the whole distance. I jumped. Never mind the sea monsters below. I know who I am, as the good sailor Popeye never said, and for once in my life I knew exactly what I was doing.

"Too bad you had to suffer, of course. Too bad we had to hit bottom. Too bad we lost our winter hideout and had to fend for ourselves in ways we weren't accustomed to. It took its toll, didn't it? The bad grub, the lack of shelter, the hard knocks. It turned me into a sick man, and it's about to turn you into an orphan. Sorry, Mr. Bones, I've done my best, but sometimes a man's best isn't good enough. If I could just get back on my feet for a few more minutes, I might be able to figure something out. Settle you in somewhere, take care of business. But my oomph is on the wane. I can feel it dribbling out of me, and one by one things are falling away. Bear with me, dog. I'll rebound yet. Once the discombobulation passes, I'll give it the old college try again. If it passes. And if it doesn't, then I'm the one who will pass, n'est-ce pas? I just need a little more time. A few more minutes to catch my breath. Then we'll see. Or not see. And if we don't, then there'll be nothing but darkness. Darkness everywhere, as far as the eye can't see. Even down to the sea, to the briny depths of nothingness, where no things are nor will ever be. Except me. Except not me. Except eternity."

T. CORAGHESSAN BOYLE

FILTHY with THINGS

I AM MARRIED TO a collector. She is so dedicated to the pursuit of accumulation, in fact, that I no longer refer to her as my wife but rather as my chief purchaser. Yes, she has given me a life of elegance and refinement, in an antique house crammed to the rafters with antique furniture, and yes, she has a fine eye for detecting potential value in the most unpromising dross (her first major acquisition was me), but still, I do tend to yearn for a more Essene environment. So what if we possess twelve examples of every article ever manufactured by man? I want space, I want order—at the very least, I want to be able to see out the windows.

Thus, I have chosen my 1992 short story, "Filthy with Things," for representation here. This story, over the years, has stricken more terror in the hearts of readers than anything our legions of horror-meisters have been able to come up with (mere ghosts, hobgoblins, and vampires will never have the same effect on you again, I guarantee). I cannot begin to count how many people—men and women alike—have come to me in penitential fervor after having read the piece, the curse of their addiction as evident on their faces as the back issues of *The New Yorker* stacked up on the porch or the silver salvers and Beanie Babies piled chest-deep on the sideboard. Aside from that, I do think that this story encapsulates some of the features of my work that have most appealed to readers—that is, it is clearly the product of a sick mind which delights in combining humor with real horror, poignance, and a love of language. The result, I hope, should be both amusing and edifying. Is this a cautionary tale? I don't think so. Not really. It's far too late for that.

—T. Coraghessan Boyle

He dreams, amidst the clutter, of sparseness, purity, the wheeling dark star-haunted reaches beyond the grasp of this constrained little world, where distances are measured in light-years and even the galaxies fall away to nothing. But dreams get you nowhere, and Marsha's latest purchase, the figured-mahogany highboy with carved likenesses of Jefferson, Washington and Adams in place of pulls, will not fit in the garage. The garage, designed to accommodate three big chromium-hung hunks of metal in the two-ton range, will not hold anything at all, not even a Japanese fan folded like a stiletto and sunk to the hilt in a horizontal crevice. There are no horizontal crevices—nor vertical, either. The mass of interlocked things, the great squared-up block of objects, of totems, of purchases made and accreted, of the precious and unattainable, is packed as tightly as the stones at Machu Picchu.

For a long moment Julian stands there in the blistering heat of the driveway, contemplating the abstract sculpture of the garage while the boy from the Antique Warehouse rolls and unrolls the sleeves of his T-shirt and watches a pair of fourteen-year-old girls saunter up the sidewalk. The sun and heat are not salutary for the colonial hardwood of which the highboy is composed, and the problem of where to put it has begun to reach critical proportions. Julian thinks of the storage shed behind the pool, where the newspapers are stacked a hundred deep and Marsha keeps her collection of Brazilian scythes and harrows, but immediately rejects it—the last time he was back there he couldn't even get the door open. Over the course of the next ten seconds or so he develops a fantasy of draining the pool and enclosing it as a sort of step-down warehouse, and it's a rich fantasy, richly rewarding, but he ultimately dismisses it, too. If they were to drain the pool, where would Marsha keep her museum-quality collection of Early American whaling implements, buoys and ship's furniture, not to mention the two hundred twelve antique oarlocks currently mounted on the pool fence?

The boy's eyes are vapid. He's begun to whistle tunelessly and edge back toward the van. "So where'd you decide you want it?" he asks listlessly.

On the moon, Julian wants to say. Saturn. On the bleak blasted ice plains of Pluto. He shrugs. "On the porch, I guess."

The porch. Yes. The only problem is, the screened-in porch is already stacked to the eaves with sideboards, armoires, butter churns and bentwood rockers. The best they can do, after a fifteen-minute struggle, is to wedge the thing two-thirds of the way in the door. "Well," says Julian, and he can feel his heart fluttering round his rib cage like some fist-sized insect, "I guess that'll have to do." The laugh he appends is curt with embarrassment. "Won't have to worry about rain till November, anyway."

The boy isn't even breathing hard. He's long-lipped and thin, strung together with wire, and he's got one of those haircuts that make his head look as if it's been put on backwards. For a long moment he leans over the hand truck, long fingers dangling, giving Julian a look that makes him feel like he's from another planet. "Yeah, that's right," the boy finally murmurs, and he looks at his feet, then jerks himself up as if to drift back to the van, the freeway, the warehouse, before stopping cold again. He looks at Julian as if he's forgotten something, and Julian digs into his pocket and gives the boy three dollars for his efforts.

The sun is there, a living presence, as the boy backs the van out of the driveway, and Julian knows he's going to have to do something about the mahogany highboy—drape a sheet over it or maybe a plastic drop cloth—but somehow he can't really seem to muster the energy. It's getting too much for him—all these things, the addition that was filled before it was finished, the prefab storage sheds on the back lawn, the crammed closets, the unlivable living room—and the butt end of the highboy hanging from the porch door seems a tangible expression of all his deepest fears. Seeing it there, the harsh light glancing off its polished flanks, its clawed feet dangling in the air, he wants to cry out against the injustice of it all, his miserable lot, wants to dig out his binoculars and the thin peeling ground cloth he's had since he was a boy in Iowa and go up to the mountains and let the meteor showers wash him clean, but he can't. That ancient handcrafted butt end represents guilt, Marsha's displeasure, a good and valuable thing left to deteriorate. He's begun to move toward it in a halfhearted shuffle, knowing from experience that he can squeeze it in there somehow, when a horn sounds breathlessly behind him. He turns, condemned like Sisyphus, and watches as Marsha wheels into the drive, the Range Rover packed to the windows and a great dark slab of furniture lashed to the roof like some primitive landing craft. "Julian! Wait till you see what I found!"

⌒

"I've seen worse," the woman says, and Julian can feel the short hairs on the back of his neck begin to stiffen—she's seen worse, but she's seen better, too. They're standing in the living room—or rather on the narrow footpath between the canyons of furniture that obscure the walls, the fireplace, even the ceiling of what was once the living room—and Julian, afraid to look her in the eye, leans back against a curio cabinet crammed with painted porcelain dolls in native costume, nervously turning her card over in his hand. The card is certainly minimalistic—*Susan Certaine*, it reads in a thin black embossed script, *Professional Organizer*, and it gives a telephone number, nothing else— and the woman herself is impressive, brisk, imposing, even; but he's just not sure. Something needs to be done, something radical—and, of course, Marsha, who left to cruise the flea markets an hour ago, will have to agree to it, at least in substance—but for all his misery and sense of oppression, for all the times he's joked about burning the place down or holding the world's biggest yard sale, Julian needs to be reassured, needs to be convinced.

"You've seen worse?" he prompts.

"Sure I have. Of course I have. What do you take me for, an amateur?"

Julian shrugs, turns up his palms, already on the defensive.

"Listen, in my business, Mr. Laxner, you tend to run across the hard cases, the ones anyone else would give up on—the Liberaces, the Warhols, the Nancy Reagans. You remember Imelda Marcos? That was me. I'm the one they called in to straighten out that mess. Twenty-seven hundred pairs of shoes alone, Mr. Laxner. Think about that."

She pauses to let her eyes flicker over the room, the smallest coldest flame burning behind the twin slivers of her contact lenses. She's a tall, pale, hovering presence, a woman stripped to the essentials, the hair torn back from her scalp and strangled in a bun, no cheeks, no lips, no makeup or jewelry, the dress black, the shoes black, the briefcase black as a dead black coal dug out of the bottom of the bag. "There's trouble here," she says finally, holding his eyes. "You're dirty with things, Mr. Laxner, filthy, up to your ears in the muck."

He is, he admits it, but he can't help wincing at the harshness of the indictment.

She leans closer, the briefcase clamped like a breastplate across her chest, her breath hot in his face, soap, Sen-Sen, Listerine. "And do you know who I am, Mr. Laxner?" she asks, a hard combative friction in the back of her throat, a rasp, a growl.

Julian tries to sound casual, tries to work the hint of a smile into the corners of his mouth and ignore the fact that his personal space has suddenly shrunk to nothing. "Susan Certaine?"

"I am the purifying stream, Mr. Laxner, that's who I am. The cleansing torrent, the baptismal font. I'll make a new man of you."

This is what she's here for, he knows it, this is what he needs, discipline, compulsion, the iron promise, but still he can't help edging away, a little dance of the feet, the condensing of a shoulder. "Well, yes, but"—giving her a sidelong glance, and still she's there, right there, breathing out her Sen-Sen like a dental hygienist—"it's a big job, it's—"

"We inventory everything—*everything*—right down to the paper clips in your drawers and the lint in your pockets. My people are the best, real professionals. There's no one like us in the business, believe me—and believe me when I tell you I'll have this situation under control inside of a week, seven short days. I'll guarantee it, in fact. All I need is your go-ahead."

His go-ahead. A sudden vista opens up before him, unbroken beaches, limitless plains, lunar seas and Venusian deserts, the yawning black interstellar wastes. Would it be too much to ask to see the walls of his own house? Just once? Just for an hour? Yes, okay, sure, he wants to say, but the immensity of it stifles him. "I'll have to ask my wife," he hears himself saying. "I mean, consult with her, think it over."

"Pah! That's what they all say." Her look is incendiary, bitter, the eyes curdling behind the film of the lenses, the lipless mouth clenched round something rotten. "Tell me something, Mr. Laxner, if you don't mind my asking—you're a stargazer, aren't you?"

"Beg pardon?"

"The upstairs room, the one over the kitchen?" Her eyes are jumping, some mad electric impulse shooting through her like a power surge scorching the lines. "Come on now, come clean. All those charts and telescopes, the books—there must be a thousand of them."

Now it's Julian's turn, the ball in his court, the ground solid under his feet. "I'm an astronomer, if you want to know."

She says nothing, just watches him out of those burning messianic eyes, waiting.

"Well, actually, it's more of a hobby really—but I do teach a course Wednesday nights at the community college."

The eyes leap at him. "I knew it. You intellectuals, you're the worst, the very worst."

"But, but"—stammering again despite himself—"it's not me, it's Marsha."

"Yes," she returns, composing herself like some lean effortless snake coiling to strike, "I've heard that one before. It takes two to tango, Mr. Laxner, the pathological aggregator and the enabler. Either way, you're guilty. Don't *ask* your wife, tell her. Take command." Turning her back on him as if the matter's been settled, she props her briefcase up against the near bank of stacked ottomans, produces a note pad and begins jotting down figures in a firm microscopic hand. Without looking up, she swings suddenly round on him. "Family money?" she asks.

And he answers before he can think: "Yes. My late mother."

"All right," she says, "all right, that's fine. But before we go any further, perhaps you'd be interested in hearing a little story one of my clients told me, a journalist, a name you'd recognize in a minute. . . ." The eyes twitch again, the eyeballs themselves, pulsing with that electric charge. "Well, a few years ago he was in Ethiopia—in the Eritrean province—during the civil war there? He was looking for some refugees to interview and a contact put him onto a young couple with three children, they'd been grain merchants before the war broke out, upper-middle-class, they even had a car. Well, they agreed to be interviewed, because he was giving them a little something and they hadn't eaten in a week, but when the time came they hung back. And do you know why?"

He doesn't know. But the room, the room he passes through twenty times a day like a tourist trapped in a museum, seems to close in on him.

"They were embarrassed, that's why—they didn't have any clothes. And I don't mean as in 'Oh dear, I don't have a thing to wear to the Junior League Ball,' but literally no clothes. Nothing at all, not even a rag. They finally showed up like Adam and Eve, one hand clamped over their privates." She held his eyes till he had to look away. "And what do you think of that, Mr. Laxner, I'd be interested to know?"

What can he say? He didn't start the war, he didn't take the food from their mouths and strip the clothes from their backs, but he feels guilty all the same, bloated with guilt, fat with it, his pores oozing the golden rancid sheen of excess and waste. "That's terrible," he murmurs, and still he can't quite look her in the eye.

"Terrible?" she cries, her voice homing in, "you're damned right it's terrible. Awful. The saddest thing in the world. And do you know what? Do you?" She's even closer now, so close he could be breathing for her. "That's why I'm charging you a thousand dollars a day."

The figure seizes him, wrings him dry, paralyzes his vocal apparatus. He can feel something jerking savagely at the cords of his throat. "A thousand—*dollars*—a day?" he echoes in disbelief. "I knew it wasn't going to be cheap—"

But she cuts him off, a single insistent finger pressed to his lips. "You're dirty," she whispers, and her voice is different now, thrilling, soft as a lover's, "you're filthy. And I'm the only one to make you clean again."

The following evening, with Julian's collusion, Susan Certaine and her associate, Dr. Doris Hauskopf, appear at the back gate just after supper. It's a clear searing evening, not a trace of moisture in the sky—the kind of evening that would later lure Julian out under the stars if it weren't for the light pollution. He and Marsha are enjoying a cup of decaf after a meal of pita, tabbouleh and dolma from the Armenian deli, sitting out on the patio amidst the impenetrable maze of lawn furniture, when Susan Certaine's crisp penetrating tones break through the muted roar of freeway traffic and sporadic birdsong: "Mr. Laxner? Are you there?"

Marsha, enthroned in wicker and browsing through a collectibles catalogue, gives him a quizzical look, expecting perhaps a delivery boy or a package from the UPS—Marsha, his Marsha, in her pastel shorts and oversized top, the quintessential innocent, so easily pleased. He loves her in that moment, loves her so fiercely he almost wants to call the whole thing off, but Susan Certaine is there, undeniable, and her voice rings out a second time, drilling him with its adamancy: "Mr. Laxner?"

He rises then, ducking ceramic swans and wrought-iron planters, feeling like Judas.

The martial tap of heels on the flagstone walk, the slap of twin briefcases against rigorously conditioned thighs, and there they are, the professional organizer and her colleague the psychologist, hovering over a bewildered Marsha like customs inspectors. There's a moment of silence, Marsha looking from Julian to the intruders and back again, before he realizes that it's up to him to make the introductions. "Marsha," he begins, and he seems to be having trouble finding his voice, "Marsha, this is Ms. Certaine. And her colleague, Dr. Doris Hauskopf—she's a specialist in aggregation disorders. They run a service for people like us . . . you remember a few weeks ago, when we—" but Marsha's look wraps fingers around his throat and he can't go on.

Blanching, pale to the roots of her hair, Marsha leaps up from the chair and throws a wild hunted look round her. "No," she gasps, "no," and for a moment Julian thinks she's going to bolt, but the psychologist, a compact woman with a hairdo even more severe than Susan Certaine's, steps forward to take charge of the situation. "Poor Marsha," she clucks, spreading her arms to embrace her, "poor, poor Marsha."

The trees bend under the weight of the carved birdhouses from Heidelberg and Zurich, a breeze comes up to play among the Taiwanese wind chimes that fringe the eaves in an unbroken line, and the house—the jam-packed house in which they haven't been able to prepare a meal or even find a frying pan in over two years—seems to rise up off its foundation and settle back again. Suddenly Marsha is sobbing, clutching Dr. Hauskopf's squared-up shoulders and sobbing like a child. "I know I've been wrong," she wails, "I know it, but I just can't, I can't—"

"Hush now, Marsha, hush," the doctor croons, and Susan Certaine gives Julian a fierce, tight-lipped look of triumph, "that's what we're here for. Don't you worry about a thing."

The next morning, at the stroke of seven, Julian is awakened from uneasy dreams by the deep-throated rumble of heavy machinery. In the first startled moment of waking, he thinks it's the noise of the garbage truck and feels a sudden stab of regret for having failed to put out the cans and reduce his load by its weekly fraction, but gradually he becomes aware that the sound is localized, static, stalled at the curb out front of the house. Throwing off the drift of counterpanes, quilts and granny-square afghans beneath which he and his wife lie entombed each night, he struggles through the precious litter of the floor to the bedroom window. Outside, drawn up to the curb in a sleek dark glittering line, their engines snarling, are three eighteen-wheel moving vans painted in metal-flake black and emblazoned with the Certaine logo. And somewhere, deep in the bowels of the house, the doorbell has begun to ring. Insistently.

Marsha isn't there to answer it. Marsha isn't struggling up bewildered from the morass of bedclothes to wonder who could be ringing at this hour. She isn't in the bathroom trying to locate her toothbrush among the mustache cups and fin-de-siècle Viennese soap dishes or in the kitchen wondering which of the coffee drippers/steamers/percolators to use. She isn't in the house at all, and the magnitude of that fact hits him now, hard, like fear or hunger.

No, Marsha is twenty-seven miles away, in the Susan Certaine Residential Treatment Center in Simi Valley, separated from him for the first time in their sixteen years of marriage. It was Dr. Hauskopf's idea. She felt it would be better this way, less traumatic for everyone concerned. After the initial twilit embrace of the preceding evening, the doctor and Susan Certaine had led Marsha out front, away from the house and Julian—her "twin crutches," as the doctor put it—and conducted an impromptu three-hour therapy session on the lawn. Julian preoccupied himself with his lunar maps and some calculations he'd been wanting to make relating to the total area of the Mare Fecunditatis in the Southeast quadrant, but he couldn't help glancing out the window now and again. The three women were camped on the grass, sitting in a circle with their legs folded under them, yoga style, while Marsha's tiki torches blazed over their heads like a forest afire.

Weirdly lit, they dipped their torsos toward one another and their hands flashed white against the shadows while Marsha's menagerie of lawn ornaments clustered round them in silent witness. There was something vaguely disquieting about the scene, and it made Julian feel like an interloper, already bereft in some deep essential way, and he had to turn away from it. He put down his pencil and made himself a drink. He flicked on the TV. Paced. Finally, at quarter to ten, he heard them coming in the front door. Marsha was subdued, her eyes downcast, and it was clear that she'd been crying. They allowed her one suitcase. No cosmetics, two changes of clothing, underwear, a nightgown. Nothing else. Not a thing. Julian embraced his wife on the front steps while Susan Certaine and Dr. Hauskopf looked on impatiently, and then they were gone.

But now the doorbell is ringing and Julian is shrugging into his pants and looking for his shoes even as Susan Certaine's whiplash cry reverberates in the stairwell and stings him to action. "Mr. Laxner! Open up! Open up!"

It takes him sixty seconds. He would have liked to comb his hair, brush his teeth, reacquaint himself with the parameters of human life on the planet, but there it is, sixty seconds, and he's still buttoning his shirt as he throws back the door to admit her. "I thought . . . I thought you said eight," he gasps.

Susan Certaine stands rigid on the doorstep, flanked by two men in black jumpsuits with the Certaine logo stitched in gold over their left breast pockets. The men are big-headed, bulky, with great slabs of muscle ladled over their shoulders and upper arms. Behind them, massed like a football team coming to the aid of a fallen comrade, are the uncountable others, all in Certaine black. "I did," she breathes, stepping past him without a glance. "We like to keep our clients on their toes. Mike!" she cries, "Fernando!" and the two men spring past Julian and into the ranked gloom of the house. "Clear paths here"—pointing toward the back room—"and here"—and then to the kitchen.

The door stands open. Beyond it, the front lawn is a turmoil of purposefully moving bodies, of ramps, ladders, forklifts, flattened boxes in bundles six feet high. Already, half a dozen workers— they're women, Julian sees now, women cut in the Certaine mold, with their hair shorn or pinned rigidly back—have begun constructing the cardboard containers that will take the measure of his and Marsha's life together. And now others, five, six, seven of them, speaking in low tones and in a language he doesn't recognize, file past him with rolls of bar-code tape, while out on the front walk, just beyond the clutter of the porch, three men in mirror sunglasses set up a gauntlet of tables equipped with computers and electric-eye guns. Barefooted, unshaven, unshowered, his teeth unbrushed and his hair uncombed, Julian can only stand and gape—it's like an invasion. It *is* an invasion.

When he emerges from the shower ten minutes later, wrapped only in a towel, he finds a small hunched Asian woman squatting on her heels in front of the cabinets under the twin sinks, methodically affixing bar-code stickers to jars of petroleum jelly, rolls of toilet paper and cans of cleanser before stacking them neatly in a box at her side. "What do you think you're doing?" Julian demands. This is too much, outrageous, in his own bathroom no less, but the woman just grins out of a toothless mouth, gives him the thumbs-up sign and says, "A-OK, Number One Charlie!"

His heart is going, he can feel it, and he tries to stay calm, tries to remind himself that these people are only doing their job, doing what he could never do, liberating him, cleansing him, but before he can get his pants back on two more women materialize in the bedroom, poking through the drawers with their ubiquitous stickers. "Get out!" he roars, "out!" and he makes a rush at them, but it's as if he doesn't exist, as if he's already becoming an irrelevance in the face of the terrible weight of his possessions. Unconcerned, they silently hold their ground, heads bowed, hands flicking all the while over his handkerchiefs, underwear, socks, over Marsha's things, her jewelry, brassieres, her ashtray and lacquered-box collections and the glass case that houses her Thimbles of the World set.

"All right," Julian says, "all right. We'll just see about this, we'll just see," and he dresses right there in front of them, boldly, angrily, hands trembling on button and zipper, before slamming out into the hallway in search of Susan Certaine.

The only problem is, he can't find her. The house, almost impossible to navigate in the best of times, is like the hold of a sinking ship. All is chaos. A dark mutter of voices rises up to engulf him, shouts, curses, dust hanging in the air, the floorboards crying out, and things, objects of all shapes and sizes, sailing past him in bizarre array. Susan Certaine is not in the kitchen, not on the lawn, not in the garage or the pool area or the guest wing. Finally, in frustration, he stops a worker with a Chinese vase slung over one shoulder and asks if he's seen her. The man has a hard face, smoldering eyes, a mustache so thick it eliminates his mouth. "And who might you be?" he growls.

"The owner." Julian feels lightheaded. He could swear he's never seen the vase before.

"Owner of what?"

"What do you mean, owner of what? All this"—gesturing at the chaotic tumble of carpets, lamps, furniture and bric-a-brac—"the house. The, the—"

"You want *Ms.* Certaine," the man says, cutting him off, "I'd advise you best look upstairs, in the den," and then he's gone, shouldering his load out the door.

The den. But that's Julian's sanctuary, the only room in the house where you can draw a breath, find a book on the shelves, a chair to sit in—his desk is there, his telescopes, his charts. There's no need for any organizing in his den. What is she thinking? He takes the stairs two at a time, dodging Certaine workers laded with artifacts, and bursts through the door to find Susan Certaine seated at his desk and the room already half-stripped.

"But, but what are you doing?" he cries, snatching at his Velbon tripod as one of the big men in black fends him off with an unconscious elbow. "This room doesn't need anything, this room is off-limits, this is mine—"

"*Mine*," Susan Certaine mimics, leaping suddenly to her feet. "Did you hear that, Fernando? Mike?" The two men pause, grinning wickedly, and the wizened Asian woman, at work now in here, gives a short sharp laugh of derision. Susan Certaine crosses the room in two strides, thrusting her jaw at Julian, forcing him back a step. "Listen to yourself—'mine, mine, mine.' Don't you see what you're saying? Marsha's only half the problem, as in any co-dependent relationship. What did you think, that you could solve all your problems by depriving her of *her* things, making *her* suffer, while all your precious little star charts and musty books and whatnot remain untouched? Is that it?"

He can feel the eyes of the big men on him. Across the room, at the bookcase, the Asian woman applies stickers to his first edition of Percival Lowell's *Mars and Its Canals*, the astrolabe that once belonged to Captain Joshua Slocum, the Starview scope his mother gave him when he turned twelve. "No, but, but—"

"Would that be fair, Mr. Laxner? Would that be equitable? Would it?" She doesn't wait for an answer, turning instead to pose the question to her henchmen. "You think it's fair, Mike? Fernando?"

"No gain without pain," Mike says.

"Amen," Fernando chimes in.

"Listen," Julian blurts, and he's upset now, as upset as he's ever been, "I don't care what you say, I'm the boss here and I say the stuff stays, just as it is. You—now put down that tripod."

No one moves. Mike looks to Fernando, Fernando looks to Susan Certaine. After a moment, she lays a hand on Julian's arm. "You're not the boss here, Julian," she says, the voice sunk low in her throat, "not anymore. If you have any doubts, just read the contract." She attempts a smile, though smiles are clearly not her forte. "The question is, do you want to get organized or not? You're paying me a thousand dollars a day, which breaks down to roughly two dollars a minute. You want to stand here and shoot the breeze at two dollars a minute, or do you want action?"

Julian hangs his head. She's right, he knows it. "I'm sorry," he says finally. "It's just that I can't . . . I mean I want to do something, anything—"

"You want to do something? You really want to help?"

Mike and Fernando are gone, already heading down the stairs

with their burdens, and the Asian woman, her hands in constant motion, has turned to his science-fiction collection. He shrugs. "Yes, sure. What can I do?"

She glances at her watch, squares her shoulders, fixes him with her dark unreadable gaze. "You can take me to breakfast."

Susan Certaine orders wheat toast, dry, and coffee, black. Though he's starving, though he feels cored out from the back of his throat to the last constricted loop of his intestines, he follows suit. He's always liked a big breakfast, eggs over easy, three strips of bacon, toast, waffles, coffee, orange juice, yogurt with fruit, and never more so than when he's under stress or feels something coming on, but with Susan Certaine sitting stiffly across from him, her lips pursed in distaste, disapproval, ascetic renunciation of all and everything he stands for, he just doesn't have the heart to order. Besides which, he's on unfamiliar ground here. The corner coffee shop, where he and Marsha have breakfasted nearly every day for the past three years, wasn't good enough for her. She had to drive halfway across the Valley to a place *she* knew, though for the life of him he can't see a whole lot of difference between the two places—same menu, same coffee, even the waitresses look the same. But they're not. And the fact of it throws him off balance.

"You know, I've been thinking, Mr. Laxner," Susan Certaine says, speaking into the void left by the disappearance of the waitress, "you really should come over to us. For the rest of the week, I mean."

Come over? Julian watches her, wondering what in god's name she's talking about, his stomach sinking over the thought of his Heinleins and Asimovs in the hands of strangers, let alone his texts and first editions and all his equipment—if they so much as scratch a lens, he'll, he'll . . . but his thoughts stop right there. Susan Certaine, locked in the grip of her black rigidity, is giving him a look he hasn't seen before. The liminal smile, the coy arch of the eyebrows. She's a young woman, younger than Marsha, far younger, and the apprehension hits him with a jolt. Here he is, sharing the most intimate meal of the day with a woman he barely knows, a young woman. He feels a wave of surrender wash over him.

"How can I persuade you?"

"I'm sorry," he murmurs, fumbling with his cup, "but I don't think I'm following you. Persuade me of what?"

"The Co-Dependent Hostel. For the spouses. The spoilers. For men like you, Mr. Laxner, who give their wives material things instead of babies, instead of love."

"But I resent that. Marsha's physically incapable of bearing children—and I *do* love her, very much so."

"Whatever." She waves her hand in dismissal. "But don't get the impression that it's a men's club or anything—you'd be surprised how many women are the enablers in these relationships. You're going to need a place to stay until Sunday anyway."

"You mean you want me to, to move out? Of my own house?"

She lays a hand on his. "Don't you think it would be fairer to Marsha? She moved out, didn't she? And by the way, Dr. Hauskopf tells me she passed a very restful night. Very restful." A sigh. A glance out the window. "Well, what do you say?"

Julian pictures a big gray featureless building lost in a vacancy of smog, men in robes and pajamas staring dully at newspapers, the intercom crackling. "But my things—"

"Things are what we're disburdening you of, Mr. Laxner. Things are crushing you, stealing your space, polluting your soul. That's what you hired me for, remember?" She pushes her cup aside and leans forward, and the old look is back, truculent, disdainful. He finds himself gazing into the shimmering nullity of her eyes. "We'll take care of all that," she says, her voice pitched low again, subtle and entrancing, "right on down to your toothbrush, hemorrhoid cream and carpet slippers." As if by legerdemain, a contract has appeared between the creamer and the twin plates of dry unadulterated toast. "Just sign here, Mr. Laxner, right at the bottom."

Julian hesitates, patting down his pockets for his reading glasses. The original contract, the one that spelled out the responsibilities of Certaine Enterprises with respect to his things—and his and Marsha's obligations to Certaine Enterprises—had run to 327 pages, a document he barely had time to skim before signing, and now this. Without his reading glasses he can barely make out the letterhead. "But how much is it, per day, I mean? Marsha's, uh, treatment was four hundred a day, correct? This wouldn't be anywhere in that ballpark, would it?"

"Think of it as a vacation, Mr. Laxner. You're going away on a little trip, that's all. And on Sunday, when you get home, you'll have your space back. Permanently." She looks into his eyes. "Can you put a price on that?"

The Susan Certaine Co-Dependent Hostel is located off a shady street in Sherman Oaks, on the grounds of a defunct private boys' school, and it costs about twice as much as a good hotel in midtown Manhattan. Julian had protested—it was Marsha, Marsha was the problem, she was the one who needed treatment, not him—but Susan Certaine, over two slices of dry wheat toast, had worn him down. He'd given her control over his life, and she was exercising it. That's what he'd paid for, that's what he'd wanted. He asked only to go home and pack a small suitcase, an overnight bag, anything, but she refused him even that—and refused him the use of his own car on top of it. "Withdrawal has got to be total," she says, easing up to the curb out front of the sprawling complex of earth-toned buildings even as a black-clad attendant hustles up to the car to pull open the door, "for *both* partners. I'm sure you'll be very happy here, Mr. Laxner."

"You're not coming in?" he says, a flutter of panic seizing him as he shoots a look from her to the doorman and back again.

The black Mercedes hums beneath them. A bird folds its wings and dips across the lawn. "Oh, no, no, not at all. You're on your own here, Mr. Laxner, I'm afraid—but in the best of hands, I assure you. No, my job is to go back to that black hole of a house and make it livable, to catalogue your things, organize. *Organize*, Mr. Laxner, that's my middle name."

Ten minutes later Julian finds himself sitting on the rock-hard upper bunk in the room he is to share with a lugubrious man named Fred, contemplating the appointments. The place is certainly Essene, but then, he supposes that's the idea. Aside from the bunk bed, the room contains two built-in chests of drawers, two mirrors, two desks and two identical posters revealing an eye-level view of the Bonneville Salt Flats. The communal bathroom/shower is down the checked linoleum hallway to the right. Fred, a big pouchy sack of a man who owns a BMW dealership in Encino, stares gloomily out the window and says only, "Kind of reminds you of college, doesn't it?"

In the evening, there's a meal in the cafeteria—instant mashed potatoes with gravy, some sort of overlooked unidentifiable meatlike substance, Jell-O—and Julian is surprised at the number of his fellow sufferers, slump-shouldered men and women, some of them quite young, who shuffle in and out of the big room like souls in purgatory. After dinner, there's a private get-acquainted chat with Dr. Heiko Hauskopf, Dr. Doris's husband, and then an informational film about acquisitive disorders, followed by a showing of *The Snake Pit* in the auditorium. Fred, as it turns out, is a belcher, tooth grinder and nocturnal mutterer of the first degree, and Julian spends the night awake, staring into the dark corner above him and imagining tiny solar systems there, hanging in the abyss, other worlds radiant with being.

Next morning, after a breakfast of desiccated eggs and corrosive coffee, he goes AWOL. Strides out the door without a glance, calls a taxi from the phone booth on the corner and checks into the nearest motel. From there he attempts to call Marsha, though both Susan Certaine and Dr. Doris had felt it would be better not to "establish contact" during therapy. He can't get through. She's unavailable, indisposed, undergoing counseling, having her nails done, and who is this calling, please?

For two days Julian holes up in his motel room like an escaped convict, feeling dangerous, feeling like a lowlife, a malingerer, a bum, letting the stubble sprout on his face, reveling in the funk of his unwashed clothes. He could walk up the street and buy himself a change of underwear and socks at least—he's still got his credit cards, after all—but something in him resists. Lying there in the sedative glow of the TV, surrounded by the detritus of the local fast-food outlets, belching softly to himself and pulling meditatively at the pint of bourbon balanced on his chest, he begins to see the point of the exercise. He misses Marsha desperately, misses his home, his bed, his things. But this is the Certaine way—to know deprivation, to know the hollowness of the manufactured image and the slow death of the unquenchable Tube, to purify oneself through renunciation. These are his thirty days and thirty nights, this is his trial, his penance. He lies there, prostrate, and when the hour of his class at the community college rolls round he gives no account of himself, not even a phone call.

On the third night, the telephone rings. Absorbed in a dramedy about a group of young musician/actor/models struggling to make ends meet in a rented beach house in Malibu, and well into his second pint of bourbon, he stupidly answers it. "Mr. Laxner?" Susan Certaine's hard flat voice drives at him through the wires.

"But, how—?" he gasps, before she cuts him off.

"Don't ask questions, just listen. You understand, of course, that as per the terms of your agreement, you owe Certaine Enterprises for six days' room and board at the Co-Dependent Hostel whether you make use of the facilities or not—"

He understands.

"Good," she snaps. "Fine. Now that that little matter has been resolved, let me tell you that your wife is responding beautifully to treatment and that she, unlike you, Mr. Laxner, is making the most of her stay in a nonacquisitive environment—and by the way, I should caution you against trying to contact her again; it could be terribly detrimental, traumatic, a real setback—"

Whipped, humbled, pried out of his cranny with a sure sharp stick, Julian can only murmur an apology.

There's a pause on the other end of the line—Julian can hear the hiss of gathering breath, the harsh whistle of the air rushing past Susan Certaine's fleshless lips, down her ascetic throat and into the repository of her disciplined lungs. "The good news," she says finally, drawing it out, "is that you're clean. Clean, Mr. Laxner. As pure as a babe sprung from the womb."

Julian is having difficulty putting it all together. His own breathing is quick and shallow. He rubs at his stubble, sits up and sets the pint of bourbon aside. "You mean—?"

"I mean twelve o'clock noon, Mr. Laxner, Sunday the twenty-seventh. Your place. You be there."

On Sunday morning, Julian is up at six. Eschewing the religious programming in favor of the newspapers, he pores methodically over each of the twenty-two sections—including the obituaries, the personals and the recondite details of the weather in Rio, Yakutsk and Rangoon—and manages to kill an hour and a half. His things have been washed—twice now, in the bathroom sink, with a bar of Ivory soap standing in for detergent—and before he slips into them he shaves with a disposable razor that gouges his face in half a dozen places and makes him yearn for the reliable purr and gentle embrace of his Braun Flex Control. He breakfasts on a stale cruller and coffee that tastes of bile while flicking through the channels. Then he shaves a second time and combs his hair. It is 9:05. The room stinks of stir-fry, pepperoni, garlic, the sad reek of his take-out life. He can wait no longer.

Unfortunately, the cab is forty-five minutes late, and it's nearly ten-thirty by the time they reach the freeway. On top of that, there's a delay—roadwork, they always wait till Sunday for roadwork—and the cab sits inert in an endless field of gleaming metal until finally the cabbie jerks savagely at the wheel and bolts forward, muttering to himself as he rockets along the shoulder and down the nearest off-ramp. Julian hangs on, feeling curiously detached as they weave in and out of traffic and the streets become increasingly familiar. And then the cab swings into his block and he's there. Home. His heart begins to pound in his chest.

He doesn't know what he's been expecting—banners, brass bands, Marsha embracing him joyously on the front steps of an immaculate house—but as he climbs out of the cab to survey his domain, he can't help feeling a tug of disappointment: the place looks pretty much the same, gray flanks, white trim, a thin sorry plume of bougainvillea clutching at the trellis over the door. But then it hits him: the lawn ornaments are gone. The tiki torches, the plaster pickaninnies and flag holders and all the rest of the outdoor claptrap have vanished as if into the maw of some brooding tropical storm, and for that he's thankful. Deeply thankful. He stands there a moment, amazed at the expanse of the lawn, plain simple grass, each blade a revelation—he never dreamed he had this much grass. The place looks the way it did when they bought it, wondering naively if it would be too big for just the two of them.

He saunters up the walk like a prospective buyer, admiring the house, truly admiring it, for the first time in years. How crisp it looks, how spare and uncluttered! She's a genius, he's thinking, she really is, as he mounts the front steps fingering his keys and humming, actually humming. But then, standing there in the quickening sun, he glances through the window and sees that the porch is empty—swept clean, not a thing left behind—and the tune goes sour in his throat. That's a surprise. A real surprise. He would have thought she'd leave something—the wicker set, the planters, a lamp or two—but even the curtains are gone. In fact, he realizes with a shock, none of the windows seems to have curtains—or blinds, either. What is she thinking? Is she crazy?

Cursing under his breath, he jabs the key in the lock and twists, but nothing happens. He jerks it back out, angry now, impatient, and examines the flat shining indented surface: no, it's the right key, the same key he's been using for sixteen years. Once again. Nothing. It won't even turn. The truth, ugly, frightening, has begun to dawn on him, even as he swings round on his heels and finds himself staring into the black unblinking gaze of Susan Certaine.

"You, you changed the locks," he accuses, and his hands are trembling.

Susan Certaine merely stands there, the briefcase at her feet, two mammoth softbound books clutched under her arms, books the size of unabridged dictionaries. She's in black, as usual, a no-nonsense business suit growing out of sensible heels, her cheeks brushed ever so faintly with blusher. "A little early, aren't we?" she says.

"You changed the locks."

She waits a beat, unhurried, in control. "What did you expect? We really can't have people interfering with our cataloguing, can we? You'd be surprised how desperate some people get, Mr. Laxner. And when you ran out on your therapy . . . well, we just couldn't take the chance." A thin pinched smile. "Not to worry: I've got your new keys right here—two sets, one for you and one for Marsha."

Her heels click on the pavement, three businesslike strides, and she's standing right beside him on the steps, crowding him. "Here, will you take these, please?" she says, dumping the books in his arms and digging into her briefcase for the keys.

The books are like dumbbells, scrap iron, so heavy he can feel the pull in his shoulders. "God, they're heavy," Julian mutters. "What are they?"

She fits the key in the lock and pauses, her face inches from his. "Your life, Mr. Laxner. The biography of your things. Did you know that you owned five hundred and fifty-two wire hangers, sixty-seven wooden ones and one hundred and sixty-nine plastic? Over two hundred flowerpots? Six hundred doilies? Potholders, Mr. Laxner. You logged in over one hundred twenty—can you imagine that? Can you imagine anyone needing a hundred and twenty potholders? Excess, Mr. Laxner," and he watches her lip curl. "Filthy excess."

The key takes, the tumblers turn, the door swings open. "Here you are, Mr. Laxner, *organization*," she cries, throwing her arms out. "Welcome to your new life."

Staggering under the burden of his catalogues, Julian moves across the barren porch and into the house, and here he has a second shock: the place is empty. Denuded. There's nothing left, not even a chair to sit in. Bewildered, he turns to her, but she's already moving past him, whirling round the room, her arms spread wide. He's begun to sweat. The scent of Sen-Sen hangs heavy in the air. "But, but there's nothing here," he stammers, bending down to set the catalogues on the stripped floorboards. "I thought . . . well, I thought you'd pare it down, organize things so we could live here more comfortably, adjust, I mean—"

"Halfway measures, Mr. Laxner?" she says, skating up to him on the newly waxed floors. "Are halfway measures going to save a man—and woman—who own three hundred and nine bookends, forty-seven rocking chairs, over two thousand plates, cups and saucers? This is tabula rasa, Mr. Laxner, square one. Did you know you owned a hundred and thirty-seven dead penlight batteries? Do you really need a hundred and thirty-seven dead penlight batteries, Mr. Laxner? Do you?"

"No, but"—backing off now, distraught, his den, his den—"but we need the basics, at least. Furniture. A TV. My, my textbooks. My scopes."

The light through the unshaded windows is harsh, unforgiving. Every corner is left naked to scrutiny, every board, every nail. "All taken care of, Mr. Laxner, no problem." Susan Certaine stands there in the glare of the window, hands on her hips. "Each couple is allowed to reclaim one item per day from the warehouse—anything you like—for a period of sixty days. Depending on how you exercise your options, that could be as many as sixty items. Most couples request a bed first, and to accommodate them, we consider a bed one item—mattress, box spring, headboard and all."

Julian is stunned. "Sixty items? You're joking."

"I never joke, Mr. Laxner. Never."

"And what about the rest—the furniture, the stereo, our clothes?"

"Read your contract, Mr. Laxner."

He can feel himself slipping. "I don't want to read the contract, damn it. I asked you a question."

"Page two hundred and seventy-eight, paragraph two. I quote: 'After expiration of the sixty-day grace period, all items to be sold at auction, the proceeds going to Certaine Enterprises, Inc., for charitable distribution, charities to be chosen at the sole discretion of the above-named corporation.'" Her eyes are on him, severe, hateful, bright with triumph. This is what it's all about, this—cutting people down to size, squashing them. "You'd be surprised how many couples never recall a thing, not a single item."

"No," Julian says, stalking across the room, "no, I won't stand for it. I won't. I'll sue."

She shrugs. "I won't even bother to remind you to listen to your-self. You're like the brat on the playground—you don't like the way the game goes, you take your bat and ball and go home, right? Go ahead, sue. You'll find it won't be so easy. You signed the contract, Mr. Laxner. Both of you."

There's a movement in the open doorway. Shadow and light. Marsha. Marsha and Dr. Hauskopf, frozen there on the doorstep, watching. "Julian," Marsha cries, and then she's in his arms, clinging to him as if he were the last thing in the world, the only thing left her.

Dr. Doris and Susan Certaine exchange a look. "Be happy," Susan Certaine says after a moment. "Think of that couple in Ethiopia." And then they're gone.

Julian doesn't know how long he stands there, in the middle of that barren room in the silence of that big empty house, holding Marsha, holding his wife, but when he shuts his eyes he sees only the sterile deeps of space, the remotest regions beyond even the reach of light. And he knows this: it is cold out there, inhospitable, alien. There's nothing there, nothing contained in nothing. Nothing at all.

BEBE MOORE CAMPBELL

From *SWEET SUMMER*

THE FIRST LINE OF my memoir, *Sweet Summer: Growing Up With and Without My Dad*, is probably the strongest and most heartfelt line I've written: "When my father died, old men went out of my life." It's an expansive line that keeps turning on itself, taking readers on a journey inside their own hearts. I like the rhythm and the poetry of that line. The truth of those words shimmers.

With this story of my relationship with my father, I manage to evoke the universal longing that all daughters have for the daddies who aren't always there. The story moves back and forth seamlessly between rural North Carolina and Philadelphia of the 1950s and 1960s. The diversity of place, and the language of characters who are educated and uneducated, black, white, male, and female give the book a richness and a fine texture. *Sweet Summer* is an important book because it is one of very few memoirs written by an African American woman that celebrates black fatherhood and depicts the tenderness of black men. This book is a stereotype slayer, and I'm as proud of it as I am of my own father.

—Bebe Moore Campbell

When my father died, old men went out of my life.

From the vantage point of my girlhood, he and his peers had always been old to me, even when they were not. In his last years, the reality of his graying head began to hit home. I no longer boogied the weekends away in smoke-clogged rooms that gyrated all night with Motown sounds, where I'd take a breather from the dancing by leaning up against the wall, sipping a sloe gin fizz and spewing out fire-laced rhetoric of "death to the pigs." I was a mature young wife, a mother even, three rungs from thirty, a home owner, a meal planner, who marched for an end to apartheid in front of the South African embassy only often enough to feel guilty. I made vague plans to care for him in his dotage. Care for him on a teacher's salary, in the middle of a marriage that was scratching against the blackboard with its fingernails, in a two-bedroom brick fixer-upper my husband, daughter and I had outgrown the moment we moved in. That was the plan.

When he died in 1977, I suppose, a theoretical weight was lifted, since Daddy was a paraplegic because of a car accident he'd had when I was ten months old. No doubt his senior-citizen years would have been expensive and exhausting for me. And then too, I had other potential dependents. I mused about the future, fantasized about my role as a nurturer of old people, feeling vaguely smug and settled, maybe a little bourgeois.

The afternoon was muggy as only a D.C. summer afternoon can be. The humidity and my afro were duking it out on the tiny sun porch of our home, the ring being the area immediately above the base of my neck, the hair coffee-colored grandmamas laughingly call the "kitchen." It is the hair I hated most as a child. The rest of my head was covered with a wavy-frizzy mixture that proclaimed my black ancestry had been intruded upon. My "kitchen" had always been hard-core naps, straight from the shores of Dahomey. Benin, they call it now. From time to time I'd tug my fingers haphazardly through the tight web of kinks, trying to make my recalcitrant hair obey me and separate into manageable clumps of curls. The hair was simply too dense back there. I would need my big black comb with the wide-spaced prongs, something heavy like that to pry my rebellious locks apart. All I was doing was hurting my fingers. I raised the window higher for more air. The faint smell of roses wafted in on a thin, damp breeze.

"I am not your responsibility, darling," Mommy had said in a brisk, businesslike tone of voice that still managed to sound loving when, on one of my frequent visits to Philly, I broached the subject of my caring for her when she got old. Each word my mother uttered stood at attention, like a soldier doing battle in the war for improved communication. But what should I have expected from a woman who was absolutely savage about enunciation, pronunciation, speaking co-rrectly, so that *they* would approve. My mother viewed speaking impeccably proper English as a strategy in the overall battle for civil rights. "Bebe, we've got to be prepared," she'd say briskly.

When as a child I said, "He be going," my mother's eyes would widen as big as silver dollars and the corners of her mouth would get dry and chalky-looking. She'd clench her throat with wide, splaying fingers and spring into action, like a fireman sniffing a cigarette in a forest and dousing it before flames erupt. "Don't say that." Her voice would be firm and patiently instructive. "That's a Negro colloquialism. Totally incorrect. They'll think you're dumb if you talk like that." They, always they.

She was sitting at her small mahogany desk in the dining room, her glasses propped on her nose, sorting papers into neat little stacks, bundling them together with rubber bands. Glancing down I saw that the papers were related to her church work. Alpha Kappa Alpha sorority, her volunteer work with a senior citizens' group and her membership on the grievance board of Holmesburg Prison, all overwhelmingly dignified pursuits. Although she was no longer a social worker for the city, my dear mother's retirement consisted of running feverishly from one volunteer gig to the next one, all for the uplifting of the race. My mother has always been and will always be a very lift-every-voice-and-sing type of sister, a woman who takes her Christian duty very seriously. Under the desk she crossed her short, brown legs and tapped her foot a little. "Clara and I will probably take a fabulous apartment together, one of those new complexes with everything inside, a laundry, a grocery store, cleaners, everything. Or by that time, my goodness, the church's senior-citizen complex will be ready and I'll just move in there. Or I'll stay here." She smiled serenely at me for a brief moment, her smooth brown face full of sunshine, then excused herself to continue working on the church bulletins.

"Senior citizens' complex!" I let my words explode in the air. "You *want* to live in an old folks' home? Mommy, that's not our culture," I finished, totally disgusted.

Mommy looked at me, her eyes squinched up in laughter, a grin spreading across her face. She loves for me to mess with her, gets a big kick out of my tongue-in-cheek assaults on her dignity. As if anything could ever put a dent in her dignity.

"Here I am, offering you a secure place in your old age, nutritious hot meals, no abuse, make sure you get your high-blood-pressure medicine. All you have to do is sign over the ole pension, SS check, bonds, CDs, deed to your property, and you get the run of the place. Do whatever you want to do. Want to have the AKAs over? The sorors can come. You get to have a boyfriend. All the sex you want! I'm talking about the best the black extended family has to offer. And you want to go..."

"I don't have high blood pressure," my mother said, chuckling and dabbing at her eyes.

"Yet, yet . . ."

My mother whooped.

"What about your arthritis?" I asked in an aha! kind of tone, truly alarmed at the notion of my aged mother hobbling to a dingy base-ment laundromat, sorting faded bras and well-worn girdles while her ancient sidekick, Clara, threw her yellowed undies into the motley heap.

Doris looked at me as if the word "lunatic" had suddenly become emblazoned on my forehead. Her shoulders and her full upper lip went stiff; the nostrils in her wide nose flared slightly. "What are you talking about, girl? I don't have any arthritis. If you're referring to the occasional stiffness in my knees, I've had that since I was a young girl and it's not going to get any worse. Darling," she said, her tone soften-ing a little, her hands still busily sorting, stacking, writing, "you have your family to look after. A baby. Don't worry about me. I'll go right on, the same as always."

So that was that; my mother was immortal. However, if by some fluke lightning struck or the rapture came and my divine mother was sent soaring away from this earth on diaphanous wings, merrily pumping her way to heaven with stiff knees, then, then I'd be duty-bound to take in Nana.

My feisty grandmother could talk the naps out of any black child's kitchen. Mouth all mighty. Mouth's mammy. I was Nan's sole choice for a caretaker, since her only other children, my Aunt Ruth and my namesake, Aunt Bebe, were dead and her only other grandchild, my cousin Michael, was engaged in a perennial search—finding himself—that made his life-style suspect. Nana wasn't into living with anyone whose phone was on one day and off the next. "Hell, I might as well have stayed in Virginia and picked cotton if I didn't want to do any better," she told me with a snort, referring to her and her parents' migration from the grips of the sharecropping South, aeons ago when she was a baby. For the record, Nana had never picked cotton a day in her life, but all the same, she was fervent about black economic progress and she found Michael's gypsy ways appalling. What was worse, what was intolerable was that her only grandson didn't have a job, at least not a steady one.

"The boy is mad," she said one day as we were snapping string beans in her kitchen. Her large almond-shaped eyes flashed. Nana's eyes were bright, the white part startlingly clear. She was small and plump, the color of a lemon wafer. "Gorgeous in my day, honey," she'd tell you in a minute. "I had all the men frothing at the mouth." Gold hoop earrings dangled at her ears. She gave off subtle whiffs of Estée Lauder, and when she spoke I could smell Doublemint chewing gum. "Smart boy like that. Nice-looking," she said disgustedly. "They need to put him in some government work camp or something." Nana's "they" was different from my mother's. More all-encompassing. Whoever made the rules, set the tone, that was Nana's "they."

"The depression is over, sweetheart. There are no work camps anymore."

"Well, then they should put his ass in the Army!" she snapped.

"Who is 'they'?" I asked, just for fun. Nana laughed. "Anyway, you can't force someone to be in the Army. And besides, he's too old"

Nana put down her beans. Her fingers were motionless in front of her. "You think he's ever gonna get himself together?" Nana's eyes were brimming with concern.

"What do you think?"

Nana sighed and began rubbing at her temples, where her hair was mostly gray, with the base of her thumbs so as to keep her fingers clean. Her eyes stared right into mine as she pulled her hands away from her hair and reached across the table and grabbed my wrist, squeezing it tightly with her thick fingers. "If anything happens to your mother you'll have to take me, Bebe," she whispered.

I simply nodded, too surprised at the sudden serious turn her outburst about Michael had taken. If I had been thinking, I would have said flippantly, "Nuh unh, honey. Sending your butt straight to the old folks' home with your daughter. Come see you every Tuesday." I could have lightened the moment a little, but I chose not to, probably because deep inside I didn't think Nana would outlive Mom. She didn't want to. Nana was seventy-five when we had this little talk and was beginning to show unmistakable signs of a disenchantment with life. Her old folks' blues would become increasingly more sorrowful as she approached her eighties. The older she got, the clearer it was that she was ready to "pass."

At seventy-nine, she called me one late afternoon and wailed into the telephone. "I don't like it anymore. I can't even go out in the winter; I'm so scared I'll fall on the ice and break my ass. And I don't even have a boyfriend," she cried, her voice high and piercing, plaintive. "What kind of life is that?"

A life with no rustling taffeta dresses, no fire-engine-red toes and fingers, no mambo nights, no baritones calling on the phone. For my jazzy grandmother (I still thought of her that way), no life. No life at all.

Whatever frailties owned her, she still possessed the strength to will herself right on out of this world. Seven years after my father's death, I believe she did just that. Only days after her eightieth birthday and a few weeks before the first Philadelphia snowstorm of 1984 could trap her for yet another season, Nana slipped off her red velvet bedroom slippers, lay down on the sofa in the living room of the house I grew up in, and fell into a dreamless, endless sleep.

When I thought about my father I realized that he had a strong will too, and maybe more reasons not to want to live to be older than Nana. You could see that will in the way he jutted out his chin, the quick way he moved and drove. He liked speed because it was powerful, as strong as he always wanted to be. I knew George Moore's mental powers would never be used to precipitate his leaving this earth any sooner than absolutely necessary. Right after the accident the doctors told him he wouldn't live out the year because of the damage that had been done to his kidneys. He made the decision right then. Put away the razor blade he'd been clutching and pressing to his throat when he saw his toes would never move again. Made a decision right then and there. Starting drinking gallons of water a day. Doing his exercises. Praying. How he forced the sadness from his eyes I do not know. Only one time did I witness him mourning the life he might have had. It was a terrible moment, but a healing one. That split second taught me that the best part of my father, the jewel stuck deep inside his core, was determination. George Moore was about living life until it was gone, wrested from him, snatched out of his clenched fist. He would play out the hand that had been dealt. My potbellied daddy wouldn't roll off resolutely to some senior citizen's palace to sip tea and play canasta, and he sure as hell didn't know any old guy he'd want for a roommate. Unmarried men living together, unless they were in the Army or Navy or something, seemed weird to him. No, he'd see his old age, his infirmities as something quite naturally to be shared with his only child. He wouldn't want to be a burden; he'd pay his way, share his little Social Security check so he would have a legitimate gripe when there weren't any pork chops in the house. And he'd be very useful; all the Moore men, my father and my seven uncles, have always had a tendency toward workaholism. They get up early and get busy; that's in their blood. Daddy would fix all the broken radios, clocks and televisions in the house. He'd do the plumbing and put in new electrical outlets. And of course, Daddy would tend the garden, since he could make anything grow. And much as he loved children, I'd have had a super built-in babysitter. If there was no work, no ball game on television and he couldn't get a decent conversation going, he'd just leave, go for a ride or something. He had a car with hand controls for the accelerator and brakes. Icy streets wouldn't keep Daddy inside a house where there was nothing to do, nobody to chew the fat and trade stories with. And we wouldn't be rushing off to attend some important, purposeful meeting called by the NAACP, the Neighborhood Association, the Coalition of 100 Black Men, or even Omega Psi Phi fraternity, of which he was a very nonactive member. He'd left behind those kinds of gatherings in his other life, the one I knew nothing about, the one he titled "Before I got hurt." No, Daddy would go riding just to hang out. And not alone, either. At least that's what I thought on that day in Washington as the fragrant, moist air mixed in my hair, rendering my kitchen absolutely impassable to my wandering fingers.

I remembered the sweet North Carolina summers of my childhood, my father's snappy "C'mon, kiddo. Let's go for a ride," when life was boring sitting in Grandma Mary's house or the yard. There was a ritual my father had to endure before he and I could zoom away down the one-car-wide dirt lane that led to the larger tar road. He'd roll his wheelchair right up between his open car door and the driver's seat and hoist himself from his chair to the car seat with one powerful thrust of his body. Then he'd clutch his leg, which would invariably start twitching with involuntary muscle spasms. When the shaking stopped, he'd lean out of his car seat, snatch his chair closed, press his body into the steering wheel, pulling the back of his seat up so that he could lift his chair into the backseat of the car. This done, he'd take out a white handkerchief, wipe his drenched forehead and look over at me and grin. Then I'd hop into the seat next to his and we'd take off. In those days I was his partner, his roadie, his little minimama homegirl. In the summer he hardly went anywhere without me. And I believed, as I engaged in my humid, sun-porch reverie, my probing fingers struggling inside the tangle of my kitchen, that I would be all those things again, that when my father got old he would need me.

The thought of our living together for the first time since I was a child delighted me, since it was in such stark contrast to the female-centered home I'd grown up in after my parents separated and my mother and I moved from North Carolina to Nana's house in Philadelphia. Realistically, though, living with my father would present special challenges. There were, of course, the implications of his paralysis, and his lack of mobility was complicated by his size. There were over two hundred pounds of him sitting in that chair. He was the black man's Chief Ironside. Well, maybe Raymond Burr had a couple of pounds on him. He tried to play it off when I teased him about his gut. Daddy would pat his belly, grin and say, "The chippies' playground, baby girl." Still, Daddy would be no fun to heave up and down stairs or in and out of a bathtub, although periodically, when he set his mind on losing weight, my father dieted quite successfully and could knock off thirty or forty pounds. When he was on a diet, I don't care how many pork chops you floated under George Moore's nose, the boy wasn't eating. That kind of doggedness enabled him in his later years finally to cut loose the Winstons he had inhaled with passion when he was younger. When he set his mind on something, that was it. Nobody had more determination than Daddy. So maybe the weight wouldn't have been a problem. What would have irritated me, though, was his innate ability to run the helpless bit into the ground at times, at least with me. Maybe only with me.

The summer before he died I drove from D.C. to the outskirts of Richmond for a visit and stayed with him at the home where he boarded with an elderly widow named Mrs. Murphy. He had only recently begun working for the federal government in personnel. He was, in affirmative-action terms, a twofer: black and disabled. Finally he was beginning to make decent money. He was sick the day I came to see him, something that rarely happened to him. Aside from his useless legs, he was robust. He rarely even got so much as a cold, although, of course, from time to time he had to go into the McGuire VA Hospital for a stay to have his damaged kidneys checked out. The day I went to visit him he had the flu and was coughing like crazy, drinking water like a fiend, snorting, trying to let out his Big Daddy Jumbo Pasquotank County farts on the sly and rattling on and on about the stock market, his latest in a long line of plans to become wealthy. To his dying day he never saw his becoming rich as something out of the realm of ordinary possibilities. His was the American dream: to work hard and have it pay off big. "Yeah, baby. Your ole daddy's gonna make us some money." He tossed off the titles of stocks and prices per share, totally losing me amid the names and numbers. Sensing my disinterest, he said disgustedly, "You ought to listen to this, girl. I'm telling you, we can make us some money." When my only response was to shrug my shoulders, Daddy shook his head. His mood turned bossy. "Bebe, go get Daddy some more cough syrup." "Bebe, go get Daddy a big ole glass of ice water." "Bebe, go empty this urine duct for your ole sick Daddy." Which was pushing it, because I hated rinsing out his urine ducts. And he knew it. But I did it that day, holding way out ahead of me the rubber duct that contained the acrid-smelling waste he could no longer control. I turned my head in the small, cramped bathroom that held his toothbrush at one end of the sink and Mrs. Murphy's teeth in a cup at the other, as I empted the urine into the toilet, and again as I rinsed the containers out in the special buckets Mrs. Murphy kept right next to the small commode.

When I returned to his bedroom, Daddy was laid up in the bed like some imperial royal highness, flashing me a slightly wan but still very dazzling smile as I handed him his duct; I turned my head as he fiddled under the covers, attaching the thing to himself. The room needed ten shots of Air-Fresh. He cleared his throat when he finished. Then he grinned at me.

My daddy had a killer of a smile and I think he knew it. I know he knew it. His teeth were so white, so perfectly straight they were startling. Big, white, even teeth. Chiclets. And his grin was just a little crooked, and that's what made him such a charming smiler. On that particular day, I wasn't falling for his charm. "Don't ask me to do one more thing, old man," I said, as sourly as I could.

"BebebebebebeMoore," Daddy sang out, throwing his big, heavy arm around my shoulder when I stopped fussing. I was sitting on the side of his bed, one leg under me, the other leg swinging, my big toe just brushing the floor as I looked at a magazine, my hips against his very still legs. The air had returned to normal and I thought to myself, George Linwood Peter Moore, please do not funk up this room with another one of those jumbo farts. I looked up and he was smiling that killer smile. "Don't bother me, old man," I said.

What can I say? Daddy would have run my ass raggedy, but he was so charming I wouldn't have minded. To have my father at the dinner table every night, to watch television with him in the early evening, to discuss books and politics, what Ted Koppel said, to go shopping with him and take rides in his car, I would have emptied his urine ducts to have all that.

But this is what I really wanted to see: Daddy and Maia being crazy about each other. He saw his granddaughter only once before he died. She was an infant at the time and I remember he took her out of my arms because I wasn't burping her right. He showed me how to do it, which didn't surprise me because whenever my father took me to visit people there were usually little kids or babies around. The children would jump up in his lap or climb on the back of his chair. He was used to burping babies. "Where'd you get this little red thing from anyway?" he teased, propping Maia up on his lap and smiling at her, lifting her up and down and shaking her gently. "Hey there, baby girl. Hey, little bit. What her got to say to ole Granddad, huh?"

They would have loved each other. I can see Maia sitting in Granddad's lap for hours, falling asleep in his arms, waking up and giggling as he rolled his wheelchair back and forth to amuse her. I can see her standing on the bracers on the back of his chair, placing her tiny arms around his neck. And when she was older, what a pair they would have made: a little brown-skinned girl and the heavyset man in the chair, she pushing him into the park near the water when they went for rides there. Daddy would go to her school plays and to open house and watch Maia as she pirouetted across the stage or recited a Paul Laurence Dunbar poem in church, his applause the loudest in the audience, his smile the brightest.

And my uncles, my father's seven brothers, would come to visit when Daddy came to live with us. John. Elijah. Eddie. Cleat. Joe. Sammy. Norman. On Sundays my husband and I would have to put the two leaves in the dining room table to accommodate two or three of my uncles and maybe their families. And my father's men friends would visit also. It wasn't such a long ride from North Carolina or Richmond to D.C. I imagine Tank Jackson, who was also paralyzed, but from World War II, driving his block-long Lincoln to our door and the two men rolling their chairs into the backyard to have beer and pretzels and me baking something whenever my uncles or Tank came to visit, a potato pie or a coconut cake, and making lemonade too, even in the winter. It would be easy enough to tear out one of the rose bushes and have a ramp put in that would lead right to the door. When Daddy pulled himself up the ramp, as he got older, I'd stand behind him and say, "Can you make it all right, old man?"

The day before my father died I was a bridesmaid in my best friend's wedding and was staying with friends in Pittsburgh. My hostess awakened me around three or four o'clock Sunday morning and told me my uncle was on the phone. Uncle Norman's signature has always been brevity, an innate ability to get to the point with a minimum of fanfare or bullshit. When I picked up the phone he said, "Bebe, this is Norman. Your father died in a car accident this morning." Just like that. Then, "Did you hear me? Honey, did you hear Uncle Norman?"

A car accident, I thought, the phone still in my hand, Uncle Norman still talking, another car accident. That wasn't supposed to happen, is what ran through my mind. How did that happen twice in one life? Twice in two lives? Somehow, with the room spinning and my head aching, I listened to the rest of his instructions. I was to return home the next day and Uncle Cleat would take me to Richmond to identify the car and sign papers at the police station. We'd get Daddy's things at Mrs. Murphy's. Uncle Johnny, the eldest of Grandma Mary's eleven children, was having my father's body transported to North Carolina, where he would be buried in the family plot behind Grandma Mary's house. "He was coming to see you, Bebe," Uncle Norman said. "He didn't know you were out of town. You know your daddy, he just hopped in the car and got on the road. He was bringing a camera to take pictures of the baby."

When Uncle Norman said that, I remembered the pictures I'd promised to send Daddy weeks before and felt the first flicker of pain course through my body. Something swept through me, hot as lightning. All at once I was shaking and crying. God. He shouldn't have died like that, all alone out on a highway, slumped over the wheel like some fragile thing who couldn't take a good hard knock. God.

It was cool and dim in the funeral parlor, and filled with a strange odor I'd never smelled before. There were three rooms full of caskets—bronze, dark wood, light wood, pastels. A dizzying array. The funeral director was a friend of the family. Mr. Walson had an uncanny affinity for professional solemnity. He referred to Daddy as "the body." Did I wish to see the body? Was I satisfied with the appearance of the body? Did I care for knotty pine or cherry wood? He said this, his dark face devoid of all emotion, his expansive belly heaving threateningly against the dangerously thin belt around his waist. The same odd smell that filled the room clung to Mr. Walson. What was that smell? I leaned against Uncle Johnny and felt his hand on my shoulder. Upon learning that my grief was buttressed by a healthy insurance policy, Mr. Walson urged me to choose the cherry wood. I looked at Uncle Johnny questioningly; he has always known how to take charge. Maybe it comes from being the oldest. If he tells you to do something, you do it. "We'll take the cherry," he told the funeral director, who assured me he would take care of everything. But he could not, of course, take care of me. My grief was private and not covered.

As we left the funeral parlor, Uncle Johnny took my hand. "Do you know what your big-head daddy wanted to do?"

I shook my head.

"After I retired and moved down here next to Mama, he tried to talk me into doing some hog farming with him. Said we could make a lot of money. I told that joker, 'Man, I came down here to rest.'" Uncle Johnny looked at me. He was smiling. "Your daddy loved making money, didn't he, girl?"

"Loved it."

The cars rolled slowly up the unpaved lane that led to Grandma Mary's house, a fleet of Cadillacs, shiny, long and black, moving quietly, and stirring up dust that flew everywhere, clinging to everyone, coating shoes and suits and dresses, blowing in hair and on faces, where particles finally lodged in eyes that blinked, blinked, blinked then looked away.

It is still cool in North Carolina in April, a perfect time for a family reunion. Crowded in Grandma's yard were all the faces that looked like her face, the resemblance lying somewhere between the chin and the character lines that ran straight across high foreheads. There were others standing next to the ones who looked like her, so many people that their feet would have crushed Grandma's zinnias had they been in bloom.

The people looked up when the Cadillacs drove into the yard. They broke away from the joyous hugs of reunion, of North once again meeting South, put their cameras back into their bags and stood silently, at attention. The gray-haired old ladies fanned themselves with miscellaneous bits of paper, the backs of magazines, newspapers, napkins, even though it wasn't warm. All of a sudden there was a circle, shoulders touching, everyone's breath mingling into a giant sigh. Somebody, my daddy's first cousin, the preacher from New York, was praying, offering to the Lord brief, familiar words that the occasion called for: higher ground, no more suffering, home. The words fell around the crowd like soft pieces of flower petals. An old woman began to sing. The lyrics came back to the people who'd taken that long-ago bus ride from Pasquotank County to Philly, Jersey, New York, in heady rushes. All wiped the dust from their eyes and joined in. The last note had scarcely disappeared before Mr. Walson's assistants began calling the names of immediate family members and leading them to the limousines: ". . . Mr. and Mrs. John Moore, Mr. and Mrs. Elijah Moore." Grandma Mary gripped my fingers as I helped her into the car where my husband and daughter were waiting. I was about to sit down when I felt a hand on my back. I turned around. "How ya making out, kiddo?" It was Sammy, my Marine uncle, the hero of my childhood. Whenever I saw him I thought of starched uniforms, even though he hadn't been in the service for years.

"Okay, so far," I said. I took his hand.

He squeezed my fingers and helped me into the car. "I'm here if you need me," he said.

Later, when I was looking into the layers of expensive satin, blinking frantically as the top of the smooth cherry-wood coffin closed, it occurred to me that more than my father had passed away. Not only had I lost a treasured friend, but gone was the ease with which I could connect to his brothers, his male friends.

After he was buried, Grandma Mary's old friend Miss Lilly or Miss Lizzy, Miss Somebody, whose face had floated in and out of my childhood summers, a wiry woman with lines like railroad tracks on skin the color of a paper bag, put her hand in mine and whispered, "Baby, you sho' put him away nice. Yes you did, chile," then, even more quietly, "God knows best, baby." She gave my arm three hard pats. Be . . . all . . . right. Don't . . . you . . . cry. Hush . . . baby . . . hush. I nodded to her, but later when I was alone I had a singular contemplation: his death wasn't for the best. That clear knowing hit me square upside my head after the last of the heavy North Carolina loam had covered the cherry-wood coffin, after Aunt Edith, my father's youngest sister, had heaved a final mournful wail that pierced through the surrounding fields of soybeans and corn that bordered my grandmother's house, then slowly faded. And what I felt wasn't even pain or grief. Just regret, gripping me like a steel claw.

In a way, it was like the end of an ordinary family reunion. I stood at the edge of the lane with Grandma Mary and watched the last of the out-of-town license plates careen down that narrow dirt road, leaving behind a cloud of dust. Pennsylvania, New Jersey, New York. Tomorrow would be another work day, regular and hard.

In the kitchen my father's mother looked tired, every one of her eighty-six years filling her eyes. She held onto the small table as she walked.

"Grandma, why don't you go to bed," I said.

"I reckon I will," she replied. I kissed her on the cheek. She stumbled and grabbed my shoulder to get her balance. "Is you gone get your daddy's car fixed?"

Her question jolted me. I hadn't given my father's Cadillac any thought since Uncle Cleat and I had left it at the mechanic's in Richmond. Soon I would be whipping around doing a "Detroit lean" out the window of George Moore's hog. Wouldn't he love to see that, I thought. "It's being fixed now, Grandma," I said.

"He sure did like that car," she mused almost to herself. "That boy loved pretty cars." She looked straight at me. "Don't bring it up the lane when you come. Hear?" I had to smile to myself. Grandma was loyal to the end. She stubbornly reasoned it was the machine at fault, and not her beloved son. I understood.

So I cleaned the kitchen, mourning my loss with each sweep of Grandma Mary's broom, each swipe of the battered dish cloth, and thought about this father whose entire possessions had fit neatly into the trunk of his yellow Cadillac, which now was mine.

I took my father's wheelchair back to D.C., even though Aunt Edith asked me if I wanted to give it to one of the old ladies in the neighborhood who was having a hard time getting around. I remember I said, "No, I want it," so fast and maybe so fiercely that Edith blinked and stepped away from me. Though why I wanted it, who knows. I put Daddy's chair in my basement and let it collect dust. Sometimes when I was washing clothes I'd look at it. The most I ever did was touch it occasionally.

In the months that followed, the fat insurance checks my father left me transformed my life-style, but at that moment I could feel his death reshaping my life, or at least the life I thought I was entitled to. There are gifts that only a father can give a daughter: his daily presence, his daily molding, his thick arm across thin girlish shoulder, his solemn declaration that she is beautiful and worthy. That her skin is radiant, the flare of her nostrils pretty. *Yeah, and Daddy's baby sure does have some big, flat feet, but that's all right. That's all right now. Come here, girl, and let Daddy see those tight, pretty curls, them kitchen curls.* I was all prepared to receive a daily ration of such gifts, albeit belatedly, but it was not to be. I would never serve beer and pretzels in the yard to Daddy and Tank. I would never have his company as I cleaned the dishes. He wouldn't see Maia's plays or her recitals. That was the way the cards had been dealt. I would go to my uncles, they wouldn't come to me. And the time for even those visits would later be eroded by obligations and miles. After April 1977 the old men in my life just plain thinned out.

For one thing, I got divorced and later remarried and moved far away to Los Angeles. After Grandma died, Uncle Johnny and Aunt Rena moved to Georgia near Aunt Rena's people. "You come see us," he told me before he left. "Don't forget; I'm your pop now." My Uncle Eddie finally sold his grocery store and moved from Philly to North Carolina, so I couldn't conveniently drop in at his market and chew the fat with him when I came to town to see Mom and Nana. Uncle Elijah died and I couldn't even go to his funeral, because my money was real funny that month. I sent flowers and called his wife, but what could I say? I should have been there.

My Marine uncle became a preacher. Uncle Sammy doesn't whoop and holler; his message is just plain good-sense gospel. He can even get scientific on you. When I hear his message I am thinking the whole time.

Uncle Norman and I still talk, but mostly on the telephone. My youngest uncle would call me up in hell, just to find out how I was getting treated. He is busy with his family and business. We don't see each other often.

The last time I saw Tank was a few weeks after the funeral, when he picked me up at the Greyhound bus station in Richmond and took me to get my father's car. Tank's skin is like a country night—no moon, no stars. You don't know what black is until you look in his face. Daddy always told me he wasn't much of a talker, and he's not, but he was just so nice and polite, sitting up in that big Lincoln, being my chauffeur. "Just tell me where you want to go," he said when I got into the car. We drove all over Richmond. Tank took me to where my father worked, to Mrs. Murphy's, everywhere.

Around two o'clock we pulled into McDonald's and he bought hamburger, french fries and sodas for our lunch; the car was filled with the aroma of greasy food. We were both famished and we ate without talking at first. All you could hear was our lips smacking against our Big Macs. Al Green was singing, "Love will make a waaay . . ." on the radio. Tank looked at me and said, "Ole Be Be," as though astonished that little girls grow up and become women. He said my name the way older southerners are wont to, two distinct syllables. I love the sound. But it was weird, because as soon as he said my name like that, I caught sight of his wheelchair in the rearview mirror and at the same time thought about Maia, whom I'd left in D.C. with a girlfriend. I was still nursing her and I immediately felt pins and needles in my breasts, and when I looked at my blouse there were two huge wet milk rings. Tank looked, he looked away, then he looked again. Then he said, as if thinking aloud, "That's right. Moore's a granddaddy."

Tank's chair was very shiny in the mirror. His words hung between us real softly for a minute before I started up, which I'd sworn I wasn't going to do. I put my head on his shoulder and I just cried and cried and cried. Tears wouldn't stop. "George was right crazy about you, Be Be. Talked about you all the time. All the time," Tank said shyly. He offered up these words as the gift they were. I just nodded.

There have never been enough idle moments really to straighten out those tight, tight curls at the nape of my neck. Untangling a kitchen calls for a protracted, concentrated effort. You have to be serious. It is not a job for weak fingers on a summer's afternoon. Still, daydreaming fingers, even those caught up in tangles, reveal much.

It has proved to be true, what I felt looking into my father's satin-lined casket: my loss was more than his death, much more. Those men who used to entice me with their storytelling, yank my plaits, throw me quarters and tell me what a pretty girl I was are mostly beyond my reach now. But that's all right. When they were with me they were very much with me. My father took to his grave the short-sleeved, beer-swilling men of summer, big bellies, raucous laughter, pipe smoke and the aroma of cigars. My daddy is really gone and his vacant place is my cold, hard border. As always, my life is framed by his absence.

HAYDEN CARRUTH

WHAT TO DO

MOST PEOPLE WOULD SAY that the quality of lyricism in literature is frivolous, now more than ever in these unfrivolous times. But I have always been fascinated by the music of language. I have written many deliberately lyrical poems. This is a short one that I like especially.

—Hayden Carruth

Tell your mind and its
    agony
to the white bloom
    of the blue plum tree,

a responding beauty,
    irreducible,
of the one earth and ground,
    and real.

Once a year
    in April
in this region
    you may tell
        for a little while.

SANDRA CISNEROS

From CARAMELO

I DON'T KNOW IF this is my best work, but I do know it is my favorite work to date. Maybe because this chapter was my life raft during the days when I was drowning.

Lots of things happened to me during the writing of *Caramelo*, the whipped cream pies of life that take one by surprise and do one in. And this chapter helped steady me, helped me to cry, and even made me laugh on days I didn't feel like laughing. At the end of a long day, my page and a quarter of production helped me to sleep and uncrease the origami in the brain, and therefore, kept me sane.

When I'm tired, when I don't feel like performing and I am asked to perform, this is the chapter I like to read. I know it in my bones, and reading the words aloud is like chanting a magic spell. It gives me power; once when I was ill, and now and always.

Maxine Hong Kingston has written in her most recent novel, "In a time of destruction, create something. A poem. A parade. A community. A vow. A moral principle. One peaceful moment."

For me, writing this chapter was my peaceful moment during the destructive season.

—Sandra Cisneros, February 8, 2004,
anniversary of my father's death

ECHANDO PALABRAS

I'm looking for Candelaria's face in the dirty windows of dirty buses lined up and roaring hot air. Father has picked me up and put me on his shoulders, but the Grandmother has marched Cande off in a hurry, and I don't know which bus is hers. Finally, I see the Grandmother making her way back to us rolling and pushing her way through the sea of people. The Grandmother swats at anyone who gets in her way, a handkerchief held to her mouth as if she isn't feeling well.

—*¡Ay, ay, qué horror!* she keeps muttering when she finally returns to Father and me. —Get me out of this inferno of Indians, it smells worse than a pigsty.

—But aren't we going to wait for Candelaria's bus to leave? I ask.

—I said let's get out of here before we catch fleas!

There is nothing else to be said. We are moving away from that heat of bus belches and song of vendors balancing trays of ham *tortas* on their heads, away from the people traveling with bulging shopping bags and cardboard boxes tied in hairy string.

We've left everyone waiting in the car, and now they're camped about in whatever patch of shade they could find, eating ice cream cones, their faces shiny, their voices whiny and impatient. —What took you so long?

Every door of our car is yawning open. Antonieta Araceli, looking miserable, is lying down in the back with a wet handkerchief on her head, because, as Aunty explains it, —*Pobrecita.* La Gorda practically fainted from the heat.

It's already the hottest part of the afternoon. To save the day from being ruined, the Grandmother suggests we drive to the port and catch a boat ride.

—I remember there are some nice inexpensive excursions. So refreshing. That way we can at least enjoy the sea breezes. You'll all thank me in the end.

But at the port, the price of the tickets is not as inexpensive as the Grandmother remembers.

—All the soft drinks you can drink! Absolutely free! the ticket seller says.

We climb on board while Father and the Grandmother haggle over a group rate with the ticket seller. —I have *siete hijos*, Father begins, bragging about his seven "sons."

At the boat's rail, we watch a bunch of noisy neighborhood boys dive for coins. Rafa is whispering orders, pinching and pulling at us. —And Lala, don't you start whining about wanting anything extra. Papa doesn't have any money.

—I wasn't going to . . .

—*Seño, seño*, the divers shout, not saying *señora* nor *señorita* but something halfway, their bodies shiny and dark as sea lions. They leap and disappear in the oily waters, followed by a trail of bubbles, and come back with the coins in their mouths. Didn't their mothers tell them never put money in your mouth? They swim as if it isn't any trouble at all, laughing and calling out to us. I'm afraid of water. The boys of Acapulco are not afraid.

Horns blast, the wooden plank is pulled up, the motor starts roaring, and we start to move away from the shore, flags fluttering in the wind, water churning about us. The Acapulco boys bobbing in the water wave to us. I take off my sun hat and wave back.

As if it has moth wings, the rose Candelaria made for me flutters away from my hat. I watch helplessly as it swirls in the air, lifts for a moment, then drops into the water, bobbing and laughing before it's swallowed by foam.

But everyone's gone. My cousin and brothers have all disappeared. Only the grown-ups are within sight, climbing the stairs to the top deck, the wind whipping their hair like flames. It's too late. By the time I catch up with them, the shore is getting smaller and smaller.

—Now what? Mother asks, because she seems I'm crying.

—My flower, it fell in the water.

—Big deal.

—Don't cry, Lalita, Father says. —I'll buy you another one.

—¿*Qué, qué, qué?* the Grandmother asks. —What are we going to waste money on?

—She's crying over some flower she says she lost.

—Crying over a flower! Why, I lost both my parents when I was your age, but do you see me crying?

—But it was the flower Cande made for me! Do you think those boys could dive and find it maybe, Father? When we get back, I mean?

—Of course, my heaven. And if they don't, I'll jump in and find it myself. Don't you cry, *corazón.*

—Yeah, Mother adds. —Now run along and leave us alone.

I walk up and down the length of the boat, twice to the bathroom, drink three Cokes on the top deck, two on the bottom, wedge myself under stairways, lie down on benches, pick the cork out of sixteen bottle caps, but I can't forget. Maybe the ocean will wash my flower up on the beach maybe. Just as I'm making another trip to the bar for another Coke, a thick hairy arm grabs me by the shoulders and holds a plastic sword to my throat. It's a pirate with a mustache and eyebrows like Groucho Marx!

—Say whiskey.

A flashbulb flashes.

—*Un recuerdo*, the photographer says. —A lovely souvenir ready for you before we return to dock, very inexpensive. Go tell your parents, kid.

But I've already remembered what Rafa told me about how there isn't any money for any extras. It's too bad no one has told the Groucho Marx pirate and the photographer. Too late; they're already busy taking pictures of my brothers.

Father and Aunty Light-Skin have had it with the wind on the top deck and are busy telling stories to Rafa and Antonieta Araceli at the bar. Only the Grandmother and Mother are still up there when I get back. I can see the Grandmother's mouth opening and closing but can't hear what she's saying over the roar of wind and motor. Mother is sitting looking straight ahead saying nothing. Behind them, the town of Acapulco with its fancy hotels where the rich people stay— Reforma, Casablanca, Las Américas, El Mirador, La Bahía, Los Flamingos, Papagayo, La Riviera, Las Anclas, Las Palmas, Mozimba.

Before the sun even sets, the sea turns wild on us. We're all sick from the free Cokes, and can't wait to get back to land. It seems like forever before we pull into port and pile into the station wagon, the big boys climbing in the back, Antonieta Araceli in front between Father and the Grandmother, the little kids in the middle row on laps. Mother takes her place behind Father.

The Grandmother in a good mood insists on telling funny stories about her sons when they were little. Everyone's jabbering like monkeys, glad to be on shore, anxious to get back to Catita's and have a nice supper after having our stomachs cleaned out with Cokes.

I must look messy because Aunty sits me on her lap, takes my hair out from its rubber band, and combs it with her fingers. Then I remember:

—My flower! Stop the car. We forgot to go look for it!

—What flower, my heaven?

—The one I lost in the water, the one Candelaria made for me!

Mother starts laughing. Hysterically. Wildly. Like a witch who has swallowed a baby. At first we laugh too. But when she won't stop, it scares us. Like when Antonieta Araceli gets one of her seizures, or Toto suffers his famous nosebleeds. We don't know if we should hold her arms up, raise her feet, force her to lie down, press down on her tongue with a spoon, or what. Then, just as suddenly as she started, she stops, aims her eyes ahead toward the rearview mirror, locks eyes with Father's, and says one word:

—How?

Father's eyebrows crumple.

—How . . . could . . . you . . . think? What do you take me for? A fool? An imbecile? A complete *alcahueta*? Do you enjoy making me look stupid in front of your family?

—*Estás histérica*, Father says. —*Domínate*. Control yourself. You don't know what you're talking about.

—That's right. I don't. That's the big joke around here, isn't it? Everyone knows but the wife.

—Zoila! For the love of God! *No seas escandalosa*.

—Your mother had the kindness to finally tell me. Now . . . you who like stories so much, tell me this story, or should I tell it for you?

Aunty tries to hug me and cover my ears, but I've never seen Mother like this, and I squirm free. The whole car is quiet, as if the world has dissolved and no one else exists except Father and Mother.

Father is silent.

Mother says, —It *is* . . . It *is* true, isn't it? Everything your mother told me. She didn't make it up this time. She didn't have to, did she? Did she? Inocencio, I'm talking to you! Answer me.

Father looks straight ahead and keeps driving as if we aren't here.

—*¡Canalla!* You lie more by what you *don't* say, than what you do. You're nothing but a goddamn, shitty, liar! Liar! Liar!! Liar!!! And then she starts hammering Father's neck and shoulders with her fists.

Father swerves the car, almost hitting a man on a bicycle with a basket of sweet bread on his head, and screeches to a stop. The Grandmother opens her macaw wings and tries to shield Father from Mother's *trancazos*, crushing a yelping Antonieta Araceli. Aunt tries to straightjacket Mother with her arms, only this makes Mother even more furious.

—Let go of me, you floozy!

—Drive, drive! the Grandmother orders, because by now a small crowd has gathered at the curb, enjoying our grief. Father floors the station wagon, but it's hopeless.

—Let me out. Let me out of this car, or I'll jump, I swear! Mother starts to shriek. She opens the door as the car is moving, and forces Father to lurch to a halt again. Before anyone can stop her, Mother springs out like a *loca*, darting across busy traffic and disappearing into a scruffy neighborhood plaza. But where can Mother go? She doesn't have any money. All she's got is her husband and kids, and now she doesn't even want us.

Father jerks the car to a stop, and we all pile out.

—Zoila! Father shouts, but Mother runs as if the Devil is chasing her.

It's the hour everyone in Mexico parades out into the streets, just as dark comes down and the night air is damp and sticky with the smell of supper frying. Men, women, children, the plaza is bubbling over with people, roiling with the scents of roasted corn, raw sewage, flowers, rotten fruit, popcorn, gasoline, the fish soup of the Pacific, sweet talc, roasted meat, and horse shit. Across the square, a scratchy big-band version of "María bonita" blasts from plaza speakers. Streetlights stutter on just as Mother bumps into a vendor sprinkling lime juice and chile powder over a huge pork rind as large as a sun hat, almost knocking it out of his hands. —¡Ey, cuidado!

Mother stumbles over shoeshine boys and shoves her way through a knot of young men as lean and dark as beef jerky, standing idly about the newspaper kiosks.

—Chulita, am I the one you're looking for?

She scurries beyond the sad horse carriages with sad horses and sad drivers.

—Where can I take you, ma'am, where?

Mother runs on hysterically.

Children with seashell necklaces draped over both arms lap at her elbows. —Seño, seño. Mother doesn't see them.

She zigzags past idling buses, freezes in the middle of the street, then darts back toward the nearest park bench, where we find her settled calm as could be next to an innocent; a little girl with a dark, square face and braids looped on her head like a tiara.

Rafa and Ito are the first to catch up with Mother, but they stop short of getting too near her. Mother ignores everyone and everything and only comes back to life when Father appears.

—Zoila! Father says, out of breath. —For the love of God! Get back in the car!

—I'm never going anywhere with you again, you big fat liar! Never! What do you take me for?

—Zoila, please don't make a scene. No seas escandalosa. Be dignified . . .

—Lárgate. Scram! I'm warning you, don't come near me!

Father clamps on to Mother's arm and tries to force her to her feet, just to show he's still the boss, but Mother jerks herself free. The little girl sitting next to Mother scowls at Father fiercely.

—*¡No me toques!* Mother says. —*Suéltame. ¡Animal bruto!* she screams at the top of her lungs.

In two languages Mother hurls words like weapons, and they thump and thud their target with amazing accuracy. Guests peer out half-naked from the windows of third-class hotels, customers at fruit-drink stands twist around on barstools, taxi drivers abandon their cars, waiters forget their tips. The corn-on-the-cob vendor ignores his customers and moves in for a better view, as if we're the last episode of a favorite *telenovela*. Vendors, townspeople, tourists, everyone gathers around us to see who it is Mother is calling a big *caca*, a goat, an ox, a fat butt, a shameless, a deceiver, a savage, a barbarian, *un gran puto*.

At the sound of bad words, the Grandmother orders Aunty to take the girls to the car. Aunty scoops me up in her arms and tries to herd us back, but by now the crowd is pressing up against us, and she's forced to put me down again.

—Zoila, just get back in the car. Look at the scandal you're creating. This is no place to discuss family matters. Let's go back to our rooms and talk calmly like decent people.

—Ha! You must be nuts! I'm not going back anywhere with you. Forget it!

—What are you saying?

—You heard me. Forget it! As of now, we're through. Finished. *Finito. Se acabó.* Understand? Then she sticks her tongue out and gives him a loud raspberry.

Father stands there humiliated, dumbfounded. My brothers look scared. By now the crowd about us shifts nervously, like an audience watching an actor painfully trying to remember his lines. Father has to say something, but what?

—All right. All right! If that's what you want, Zoila, that's what you'll have. You want to break up our family, go right ahead. Lalita, who do you want to go with, your mother or me?

I open my mouth. But instead of words, big gulpy sobs hiccup out of me laced with cobwebs of spit. Rafa suddenly remembers he's the oldest and shoves his way over to my side, picking me up and hugging me.

—*Ya ves. Ya ves,* Father says. —See? I hope you're happy.

—*Mijo,* the Grandmother intervenes. —Let her be. You're better off without her kind. Wives come and go, but mothers, you only have one!

—Who are *you* to get involved in our affairs, *metiche*! Zoila snaps.

At this, some people cheer, some jeer. Some side with Mother. Some with Father. Some with the Grandmother. Some just stand there with their mouths open as if we're the greatest show on earth.

—*¡Atrevida!* You climbed up in life marrying my son, a Reyes, and don't think I don't know it. Now you have the nerve to talk to me like that. My son could've done a lot better than marrying a woman who can't even speak a proper Spanish. You sound like you escaped from the ranch. And to make matters even more sad, you're as dark as a slave.

The Grandmother says all this without remembering Uncle Fat-Face, who is as dark as Mother. Is that why the Grandmother loves him less than Father?

—*¡Vieja cabrona!* Mother hisses.

The crowd gasps in *susto*, and in disbelief. —What a blow! —And to an elder!

Listen, you raise-heller, Mother continues. —You've wanted nothing better than to break up this marriage since day one! Well, guess what? I don't give a good goddamn what stories you've got to tell me, I'm not going to give you the satisfaction, and you know why? 'Cause that's exactly what you want, ain't it? Comes what comes, like it or not, late or early, you're going to have to get used to it. I'm Inocencio's wife and the mother of his kids, you hear. I'm his legal wife. I'm a Reyes! And there's not a damn thing you can do about it.

—*¡Aprovechada!* the Grandmother counters. —Trash! Indian! I won't stand here and be publicly insulted. Inocencio, I insist you take us home. To Mexico City! Now!

—Inocencio, if you let that cow turd in our car, you can forget about ever seeing me or your kids again. Put her on a bus with her address pinned on her slip for all I care.

—What stupidities you talk. My son would never dare to put his own mother on a bus, you little *cualquiera.* That's how much you know!

—Well, I'm not getting in that car with you even if they tie you on the luggage rack. You're a witch, I hate you!

—Quiet! Stop already. Both of you! Father orders.

—Do whatever the hell you want, I don't care anymore, Mother says. —But I'm telling you, and I'm telling you only once. I'm not going *any*where again with *that vieja!*

—Nor I with . . . *ésa.* Never, never, never! Not even if God commanded it, the Grandmother says. —*Mijo*, you'll have to choose . . . Her . . .

The Grandmother's fat finger points toward Mother, who is trembling with rage.

—Or me.

Father looks at his mother. And then at our mother. The mob around us circles tighter. Father raises his head skyward as if looking for a sign from heaven. The stars rattling like a drumroll.

Then Father does something he's never done in his life. Not before, nor since.

CHITRA BANERJEE DIVAKARUNI

MRS. DUTTA WRITES a LETTER

WHY THIS IS MY BEST

Because it grew out of painful visits
to houses of children where mothers no longer belonged

Because I struggled with it for years, (mis)placing it
in malls and amusement parks and, once,
a public restroom
before it came to rest in a backyard,
beside a white sari draped over a fence

Even my best friend said,
why don't you write something else

But the story had taken hold of me
with its bulldog teeth

It would not let go until I learned that
sometimes in tragedies
there are no villains
only people like ourselves

— Chitra Banerjee Divakaruni

When the alarm goes off at 5:00 A.M., buzzing like a trapped wasp, Mrs. Dutta has been lying awake for quite a while. Though it has now been two months, she still has difficulty sleeping on the Perma Rest mattress Sagar and Shyamoli, her son and daughter-in-law, have bought specially for her. It is too American-soft, unlike the reassuring-ly solid copra ticking she is used to at home. *Except this is home now*, she reminds herself. She reaches hurriedly to turn off the alarm, but in the dark her fingers get confused among the knobs, and the electric clock falls with a thud to the floor. Its insistent metallic call vibrates out through the walls of her room until she is sure it will wake everyone. She yanks frantically at the wire until she feels it give, and in the abrupt silence that follows she hears herself breathing, a sound harsh and uneven and full of guilt.

Mrs. Dutta knows, of course, that this turmoil is her own fault. She should just not set the alarm. There is no need for her to get up early here in Sunnyvale, in her son's house. But the habit, taught to her by her mother-in-law when she was a bride of seventeen, *a good wife wakes before the rest of the household*, is one she finds impossible to break. How hard it was then to pull her unwilling body away from her husband's sleep-warm clasp, Sagar's father whom she had just learned to love. To stumble to the kitchen that smelled of stale garam masala and light the coal unoon so she could make morning tea for them all— her parents-in-law, her husband, his two younger brothers, the widow aunt who lived with them.

After dinner, when the family sits in front of the TV, she attempts to tell her grandchildren about those days. "I was never good at start-ing that unoon—the smoke stung my eyes, making me cough and cough. Breakfast was never ready on time, and my mother-in-law— oh, how she scolded me until I was in tears. Every night I would pray to Goddess Durga, please let me sleep late, just one morning!"

"Mmmm," Pradeep says, bent over a model plane.

"Oooh, how awful," says Mrinalini, wrinkling her nose politely before she turns back to a show filled with jokes that Mrs. Dutta does not understand.

"That's why you should sleep in now, Mother," says Shyamoli, smiling from the recliner where she sits looking through the *Wall Street Journal*. With her legs crossed so elegantly under the shimmery blue skirt she has changed into after work, and her unusually fair skin, she could pass for an American, thinks Mrs. Dutta, whose own skin is brown as roasted cumin. The thought fills her with an uneasy pride.

From the floor where he leans against Shyamoli's knee, Sagar adds, "We want you to be comfortable, Ma. To rest. What's why we brought you to America."

In spite of his thinning hair and the gold-rimmed glasses which he has recently taken to wearing, Sagar's face seems to Mrs. Dutta still that of the boy she used to send off to primary school with his metal tiffin box. She remembers how he crawled into her bed on stormy monsoon nights, how when he was ill no one else could make him drink his barley water. Her heart balloons in sudden gladness because she is really here, with him and his children in America. "Oh, Sagar"—she smiles—"now you're talking like this! But did you give me a moment's rest while you were growing up?" And she launches into a description of childhood pranks that has him shaking his head indulgently while disembodied TV laughter echoes through the room.

But later he comes into her bedroom and says, a little shamefaced, "Mother, please, don't get up so early in the morning. All that noise in the bathroom, it wakes us up, and Molli has such a long day at work . . ."

And she, turning a little so he shouldn't see her foolish eyes filling with tears as though she were a teenage bride again and not a woman well over sixty, nods her head, *yes, yes.*

Waiting for the sounds of the stirring household to release her from the embrace of her Perma Rest mattress, Mrs. Dutta repeats the 108 holy names of God. *Om Keshavaya Namah, Om Narayanaya Namah, Om Madhavaya Namah.* But underneath she is thinking of the bleached-blue aerogram from Mrs. Basu that has been waiting unanswered on her bedside table all week, filled with news from home. There was a robbery at Sandhya Jewelry Store, the bandits had guns but luckily no one was hurt. Mr. Joshi's daughter, that sweet-faced child, has run away with her singing teacher, who would've thought it. Mrs. Barucha's daughter-in-law had one more baby girl, yes, their fourth, you'd think they'd know better than to keep trying for a boy. Last Tuesday was Bangla Bandh, another labor strike, everything closed down, even the buses not running, but you can't really blame them, can you, after all factory workers have to eat, too. Mrs. Basu's tenants, whom she'd been trying to evict forever, had finally moved out, good riddance, but you should see the state of the flat.

And at the very bottom Mrs. Basu wrote, *Are you happy in America?*

Mrs. Dutta knows that Mrs. Basu, who has been her closest friend since they both came to Ghoshpara Lane as young brides, cannot be fobbed off with descriptions of Fisherman's Wharf and the Golden Gate Bridge, or even anecdotes involving grandchildren. And so she has been putting off her reply while in her heart family loyalty battles with insidious feelings of—but she turns from them quickly and will not name them even to herself.

Now Sagar is knocking on the children's doors—a curious custom, this, children being allowed to close their doors against their parents—and with relief Mrs. Dutta gathers up her bathroom things. She has plenty of time. It will take a second rapping from their mother before Pradeep and Mrinalini open their doors and stumble out. Still, she is not one to waste the precious morning. She splashes cold water on her face and neck (she does not believe in pampering herself), scrapes the night's gumminess from her tongue with her metal tongue cleaner, and brushes vigorously, though the minty toothpaste does not leave her mouth feeling as clean as did the bittersweet neem stick she'd been using all her life. She combs the knots out of her hair. Even at her age, it is thicker and silkier than her daughter-in-law's permed curls. *Such vanity*, she scolds her reflection, *and you a grandmother and a widow besides*. Still, as she deftly fashions her hair into a neat coil, she remembers how her husband would always compare it to night rain.

She hears a commotion outside.

"Pat! Minnie! What d'you mean you still haven't washed up? I'm late every morning to work nowadays because of you kids."

"But, Mom, *she's* in there. She's been there forever . . ." says Mrinalini.

Pause. Then, "So go to the downstairs bathroom."

"But all our stuff is here," says Pradeep, and Mrinalini adds, "It's not fair. Why can't *she* go downstairs?"

A longer pause. Inside the bathroom Mrs. Dutta hopes Shyamoli will not be too harsh on the girl. But a child who refers to elders in that disrespectful way ought to be punished. How many times had she slapped Sagar for something far less, though he was her only one, the jewel of her eye, come to her after she had been married for seven years and everyone had given up hope already? Whenever she lifted her hand to him it was as though her heart was being put through a masala grinder. Such is a mother's duty.

But Shyamoli only says, in a tired voice, "That's enough! Go put on your clothes, hurry."

The grumblings recede. Footsteps clatter down the stairs. Inside the bathroom Mrs. Dutta bends over the sink, gripping the folds of her sari. Hard to think through the pounding in her head to what it is she feels most—anger at the children for their rudeness, or at Shyamoli for letting them go unrebuked. Or is it shame that clogs her throat, stinging, sulfuric, indigestible?

It is 9:00 A.M. and the house, after the flurry of departures, of frantic "I can't find my socks," and "Mom, he took my lunch money," and "I swear I'll leave you kids behind if you're not in the car in exactly one minute," has settled into its placid daytime rhythms.

Busy in the kitchen, Mrs. Dutta has recovered her spirits. It is too exhausting to hold on to grudges, and, besides, the kitchen—sunlight sliding across its countertops while the refrigerator hums reassuringly—is her favorite place.

Mrs. Dutta hums too as she fries potatoes for alu dum. Her voice is rusty and slightly off-key. In India she would never have ventured to sing, but with everyone gone, the house is too quiet, all that silence pressing down on her like the heel of a giant hand, and the TV voices, with their unreal accents, are no help at all. As the potatoes turn golden-brown, she permits herself a moment of nostalgia for her Calcutta kitchen—the new gas stove bought with the birthday money Sagar sent, the scoured brass pots stacked by the meat safe, the window with the lotus-pattern grille through which she could look down on children playing cricket after school. The mouth-watering smell of ginger and chili paste, ground fresh by Reba the maid, and, in the evening, strong black Assam cha brewing in the kettle when Mrs. Basu came by to visit. In her mind she writes to Mrs. Basu, *Oh, Roma, I miss it all so much, sometimes I feel that someone has reached in and torn out a handful of my chest.*

But only fools indulge in nostalgia, so Mrs. Dutta shakes her head clear of images and straightens up the kitchen. She pours the half-drunk glasses of milk down the sink, though Shyamoli has told her to save them in the refrigerator. But surely Shyamoli, a girl from a good Hindu family, doesn't expect her to put contaminated jutha things in with the rest of the food? She washes the breakfast dishes by hand instead of letting them wait inside the dishwater till night, breeding germs. With practiced fingers she throws an assortment of spices into the blender: coriander, cumin, cloves, black pepper, a few red chilies for vigor. No stale bottled curry powder for *her! At least the family's eating well since I arrived*, she writes in her mind, *proper Indian food, rutis that puff up the way they should, fish curry in mustard sauce, and real pulao with raisins and cashews and ghee—the way you taught me, Roma—instead of Rice-a-roni.* She would like to add, *They love it,* but thinking of Shyamoli she hesitates.

At first Shyamoli had been happy enough to have someone take over the cooking. It's wonderful to come home to a hot dinner, she'd say, or, Mother, what crispy papads, and your fish gravy is out of this world. But recently she's taken to picking at her food, and once or twice from the kitchen Mrs. Dutta has caught wisps of words, intensely whispered: *cholesterol, all putting on weight, she's spoiling you.* And though Shyamoli always refuses when the children ask if they can have burritos from the freezer instead, Mrs. Dutta suspects that she would really like to say yes.

The children. A heaviness pulls at Mrs. Dutta's entire body when she thinks of them. Like so much in this country they have turned out to be—yes, she might as well admit it—a disappointment.

For this she blames, in part, the Olan Mills portrait. Perhaps it had been impractical of her to set so much store on a photograph, especially one taken years ago. But it was such a charming scene—Mrinalini in a ruffled white dress with her arm around her brother, Pradeep chubby and dimpled in a suit and bow tie, a glorious autumn forest blazing red and yellow behind them. (Later Mrs. Dutta would learn, with a sense of having been betrayed, that the forest was merely a backdrop in a studio in California, where real trees did not turn such colors.)

The picture had arrived, silver-framed and wrapped in a plastic sheet filled with bubbles, with a note from Shyamoli explaining that it was a Mother's Day gift. (A strange concept, a day set aside to honor mothers. Did the sahebs not honor their mothers the rest of the year, then?) For a week Mrs. Dutta could not decide where it should be hung. If she put it in the drawing room, visitors would be able to admire her grandchildren, but if she put it on the bedroom wall, she would be able to see the photo, last thing, before she fell asleep. She had finally opted for the bedroom, and later, when she was too ill with pneumonia to leave her bed for a month, she'd been glad of it.

Mrs. Dutta was not unused to living on her own. She had done it for the last three years, since Sagar's father died, politely but stubbornly declining the offers of various relatives, well-meaning and otherwise, to come and stay with her. In this she had surprised herself as well as others, who thought of her as a shy, sheltered woman, one who would surely fall apart without her husband to handle things for her. But she managed quite well. She missed Sagar's father, of course, especially in the evenings, when it had been his habit to read to her the more amusing parts of the newspaper while she rolled out rutis. But once the grief receded, she found it rather pleasant to be mistress of her own life, as she confided to Mrs. Basu. She liked being able, for the first time ever, to lie in bed all evening and read a new novel of Shankar's straight through if she wanted, or to send out for hot brinjal pakoras on a rainy day without feeling guilty that she wasn't serving up a balanced meal.

When the pneumonia hit, everything changed.

Mrs. Dutta had been ill before, but those illnesses had been different. Even in bed she'd been at the center of the household, with Reba coming to find out what should be cooked, Sagar's father bringing her shirts with missing buttons, her mother-in-law, now old and tamed, complaining that the cook didn't brew her tea strong enough, and Sagar running in crying because he'd had a fight with the neighbor boy. But now there was no one to ask her, querulously, *Just how long do you plan to remain sick*, no one waiting in impatient exasperation for her to take on her duties again, no one whose life was inconvenienced the least bit by her illness.

There was, therefore, no reason for her to get well.

When this thought occurred to Mrs. Dutta, she was so frightened that her body grew numb. The walls of the room spun into blackness, the bed on which she lay, a vast four-poster she had shared with Sagar's father since her marriage, rocked like a mastless dinghy caught in a storm, and a great, muted roar reverberated in the cavities of her skull. For a moment, unable to move or see, she thought, *I'm dead*. Then her vision, desperate and blurry, caught on the portrait. *My grandchildren*. She focused, with some difficulty, on the bright, oblivious sheen of their child faces, the eyes so like Sagar's that for a moment she could feel heartsickness cramping her joints like arthritis. She drew in a shuddering breath; the roaring seemed to recede. When the afternoon post brought another letter from Sagar, *Mother, you really should come and live with us, we worry about you all alone in India, especially when you're sick like this*, she wrote back the same day, with fingers that still shook a little, *You're right, my place is with you, with my grandchildren*.

But now that she is here on the other side of the world, she is wrenched by doubt. She knows the grandchildren love her—how can it be otherwise among family? And she loves them, she reminds herself, though they have put away, somewhere in the back of a closet, the vellum-bound *Ramayana for Young Readers* that she carried all the way from India in her hand luggage. Though their bodies twitch with impatience when she tries to tell them stories of her girlhood. Though they offer the most transparent excuses when she asks them to sit with her while she chants the evening arati. *They're flesh of my flesh, blood of my blood*, she reminds herself. But sometimes when she listens, from the other room, to them speaking on the phone, their American voices rising in excitement as they discuss a glittering alien world of Power Rangers, Spice Girls, and Spirit Week at school, she almost cannot believe it.

Stepping into the backyard with a bucket of newly washed clothes, Mrs. Dutta views the sky with some anxiety. The butter-gold sunlight is gone, black-bellied clouds have taken over the horizon, and the air feels still and heavy on her face, as before a Bengal storm. What if her clothes don't dry by the time the others return home?

Washing clothes has been a problem for Mrs. Dutta ever since she arrived in California.

"We can't, Mother," Shyamoli had said with a sigh when Mrs. Dutta asked Sagar to put up a clothesline for her in the backyard. (Shyamoli sighed often nowadays. Perhaps it was an American habit? Mrs. Dutta did not remember the Indian Shyamoli, the docile bride she'd mothered for a month before putting her on a Pan Am flight to join her husband, pursing her lips in quite this way to let out a breath at once patient and vexed.) "It's just not *done*, not in a nice neighborhood like this one. And being the only Indian family on the street, we have to be extra careful. People here, sometimes—." She'd broken off with a shake of her head. "Why don't you just keep your dirty clothes in the hamper I've put in your room, and I'll wash them on Sunday along with everyone else's."

Afraid of causing another sigh, Mrs. Dutta had agreed reluctantly. But she knew she should not store unclean clothes in the same room where she kept the pictures of her gods. That brought bad luck. And the odor. Lying in bed at night she could smell it distinctly, even though Shyamoli claimed the hamper was airtight. The sour, starchy old-woman smell embarrassed her.

What embarrassed her more was when, Sunday afternoons, Shyamoli brought the laundry into the family room to fold. Mrs. Dutta would bend intensely over her knitting, face tingling with shame, as her daughter-in-law nonchalantly shook out the wisps of lace, magenta and sea-green and black, that were her panties, laying them next to a stack of Sagar's briefs. And when, right in front of everyone, Shyamoli pulled out Mrs. Dutta's own crumpled, baggy bras from the clothes heap, she wished the ground would open up and swallow her, like the Sita of mythology.

Then one day Shyamoli set the clothes basket down in front of Sagar.

"Can you do them today, Sagar?" (Mrs. Dutta, who had never, through the forty-two years of her marriage, addressed Sagar's father by name, tried not to wince.) "I've got to get that sales report into the computer by tonight."

Before Sagar could respond, Mrs. Dutta was out of her chair, knitting needles dropping to the floor.

"No no no, clothes and all is no work for the man of the house. I'll do it." The thought of her son's hands searching through the basket and lifting up his wife's—and her own—underclothes filled her with horror.

"Mother!" Shyamoli said. "This is why Indian men are so useless around the house. Here in America we don't believe in men's work and women's work. Don't I work outside all day, just like Sagar? How'll I manage if he doesn't help me at home?"

"I'll help you instead," Mrs. Dutta ventured.

"You don't understand, do you, Mother?" Shyamoli said with a shaky smile. Then she went into the study.

Mrs. Dutta sat down in her chair and tried to understand. But after a while she gave up and whispered to Sagar that she wanted him to teach her how to run the washer and dryer.

"Why, Mother? Molli's quite happy to . . ."

"I've got to learn it. . . ." Her voice warped with distress as she rummaged through the tangled heap for her clothes.

Her son began to object, then shrugged. "Oh very well. If that's what you really want."

But later, when she faced them alone, the machines with their cryptic symbols and rows of gleaming knobs terrified her. What if she pressed the wrong button and flooded the entire floor with soapsuds? What if she couldn't turn the machines off and they kept going, whirring maniacally, until they exploded? (This had happened to a woman on a TV show just the other day, and she had jumped up and down, screaming. Everyone else found it hilarious, but Mrs. Dutta sat stiff-spined, gripping the armrest of her chair.) So she took to washing her clothes in the bathtub when she was alone. She had never done such a chore before, but she remembered how the village washer-women of her childhood would beat their saris clean against river rocks. And a curious satisfaction filled her as her clothes hit the porce-lain with the same solid wet *thunk*.

My small victory, my secret.

This is why everything must be dried and put safely away before Shyamoli returns. Ignorance, as Mrs. Dutta knows well from years of managing a household, is a great promoter of harmony. So she keeps an eye on the menacing advance of the clouds as she hangs up her blouse and underwear. As she drapes her sari along the redwood fence that separates her son's property from the neighbor's, first wiping it clean with a dish towel she has secretly taken from the bottom drawer of the kitchen. But she isn't too worried. Hasn't she managed every time, even after that freak hailstorm last month when she had to use the iron from the laundry closet to press everything dry? The memory pleases her. In her mind she writes to Mrs. Basu, *I'm fitting in so well here, you'd never guess I came only two months back. I've found new ways of doing things, of solving problems creatively. You would be most proud if you saw me.*

When Mrs. Dutta decided to give up her home of forty-five years, her relatives showed far less surprise than she had expected.

"Oh, we all knew you'd end up in America sooner or later," they said. "It was a foolishness to stay on alone so long after Sagar's father, may he find eternal peace, passed away. Good thing that boy of yours came to his senses and called you to join him. Everyone knows a wife's place is with her husband, and a widow's with her son."

Mrs. Dutta had nodded meek agreement, ashamed to let anyone know that the night before she had awakened weeping.

"Well, now that you're going, what'll happen to all your things?"

Mrs. Dutta, still troubled over those treacherous tears, had offered up her household effects in propitiation. "Here, Didi, you take this cut-work bedspread. Mashima, for a long time I meant for you to have these Corning Ware dishes, I know how much you admire them. And, Boudi, this tape recorder that Sagar sent a year back is for you. Yes yes, I'm quite sure. I can always tell Sagar to buy me another one when I get there."

Mrs. Basu, coming in just as a cousin made off triumphantly with a bone china tea set, had protested. "Prameela, have you gone crazy? That tea set used to belong to your mother-in-law."

"But what'll I do with it in America? Shyamoli has her own set—"

A look that Mrs. Dutta couldn't read flitted across Mrs. Basu's face. "But do you want to drink from it for the rest of your life?"

"What do you mean?"

Mrs. Basu hesitated. Then she said, "What if you don't like it there?"

"How can I not like it, Roma?" Mrs. Dutta's voice was strident, even to her own ears. With an effort she controlled it and continued, "I'll miss my friends, I know—and you most of all. The things we do together—evening tea, our walk around Rabindra Sarobar Lake, Thursday night Bhagavat Geeta class. But Sagar—they're my only family. And blood is blood after all."

"I wonder," Mrs. Basu said dryly, and Mrs. Dutta recalled that though both of Mrs. Basu's children lived just a day's journey away, they came to see her only on occasions when common decency demanded their presence. Perhaps they were tightfisted in money matters too. Perhaps that was why Mrs. Basu had started renting out her downstairs a few years ago, even though, as anyone in Calcutta knew, tenants were more trouble than they were worth. Such filial neglect must be hard to take, though Mrs. Basu, loyal to her children as indeed a mother should be, never complained. In a way Mrs. Dutta had been better off, with Sagar too far away for her to put his love to the test.

"At least don't give up the house," Mrs. Basu was saying. "It'll be impossible to find another place in case—"

"In case what?" Mrs. Dutta asked, her words like stone chips. She was surprised to find that she was angrier with Mrs. Basu than she'd ever been. Or was it fear? *My son isn't like yours*, she'd been on the verge of spitting out. She took a deep breath and made herself smile, made herself remember that she might never see her friend again.

"Ah, Roma," she said, putting her arm around Mrs. Basu, "you think I'm such an old witch that my Sagar and my Shyamoli will be unable to live with me?"

Mrs. Dutta hums a popular Rabindra Sangeet as she pulls her sari from the fence. It's been a good day, as good as it can be in a country where you might stare out the window for hours and not see one living soul. No vegetable vendors with wicker baskets balanced on their heads, no knife-sharpeners calling *scissors-knives-choppers, scissors-knives-choppers* to bring the children running. No dehati women with tattoos on their arms to sell you cookware in exchange for your old silk saris. Why, even the animals that frequented Ghoshpara Lane had personality. Stray dogs that knew to line up outside the kitchen door just when leftovers were likely to be thrown out, the goat who maneuvered its head through the garden grille hoping to get at her dahlias, cows who planted themselves majestically in the center of the road, ignoring honking drivers. And right across the street was Mrs. Basu's two-story house, which Mrs. Dutta knew as well as her own. How many times had she walked up the stairs to that airy room painted sea-green and filled with plants where her friend would be waiting for her.

What took you so long today, Prameela? Your tea is cold already.

Wait till you hear what happened, Roma. Then you won't scold me for being late. . . .

Stop it, you silly woman, Mrs. Dutta tells herself severely. Every single one of your relatives would give an arm and a leg to be in your place, you know that. After lunch you're going to write a nice, long letter to Roma, telling her exactly how delighted you are to be here.

From where Mrs. Dutta stands, gathering up petticoats and blouses, she can look into the next yard. Not that there's much to see, just tidy grass and a few pale-blue flowers whose name she doesn't know. There are two wooden chairs under a tree, but Mrs. Dutta has never seen anyone using them. What's the point of having such a big yard if you're not even going to sit in it? she thinks. Calcutta pushes itself into her mind again, Calcutta with its narrow, blackened flats where families of six and eight and ten squeeze themselves into two tiny rooms, and her heart fills with a sense of loss she knows to be illogical.

When she first arrived in Sagar's home, Mrs. Dutta wanted to go over and meet her next-door neighbors, maybe take them some of her special rose-water rasogollahs, as she'd often done with Mrs. Basu. But Shyamoli said she shouldn't. Such things were not the custom in California, she explained earnestly. You didn't just drop in on people without calling ahead. Here everyone was busy, they didn't sit around chatting, drinking endless cups of sugar tea. Why, they might even say something unpleasant to her.

"For what?" Mrs. Dutta had asked disbelievingly, and Shyamoli had said, "Because Americans don't like neighbors to"—here she used an English phrase—"invade their privacy." Mrs. Dutta, who didn't fully understand the word *privacy* because there was no such term in Bengali, had gazed at her daughter-in-law in some bewilderment. But she understood enough not to ask again. In the following months, though, she often looked over the fence, hoping to make contact. People were people, whether in India or America, and everyone appreciated a friendly face. When Shyamoli was as old as Mrs. Dutta, she would know that, too.

Today, just as she is about to turn away, out of the corner of her eye Mrs. Dutta notices a movement. At one of the windows a woman is standing, her hair a sleek gold like that of the TV heroines whose exploits baffle Mrs. Dutta when sometimes she tunes in to an afternoon serial. She is smoking a cigarette, and a curl of gray rises lazily, elegantly from her fingers. Mrs. Dutta is so happy to see another human being in the middle of her solitary day that she forgets how much she disapproves of smoking, especially in women. She lifts her hand in the gesture she has seen her grandchildren use to wave an eager hello.

The woman stares back at Mrs. Dutta. Her lips are a perfect-painted red, and when she raises her cigarette to her mouth, its tip glows like an animal's eye. She does not wave back or smile. Perhaps she is not well? Mrs. Dutta feels sorry for her, alone in her illness in a silent house with only cigarettes for solace, and she wishes the etiquette of America had not prevented her from walking over with a word of cheer and a bowl of her fresh-cooked alu dum.

Mrs. Dutta rarely gets a chance to be alone with her son. In the morning he is in too much of a hurry even to drink the fragrant cardamom tea which she (remembering how as a child he would always beg for a sip from her cup) offers to make him. He doesn't return until dinnertime, and afterward he must help the children with their homework, read the paper, hear the details of Shyamoli's day, watch his favorite TV crime show in order to unwind, and take out the garbage. In between, for he is a solicitous son, he converses with Mrs. Dutta. In response to his questions she assures him that her arthritis is much better now; no, no, she's not growing bored being at home all the time; she has everything she needs—Shyamoli has been so kind—but perhaps he could pick up a few aerograms on his way back tomorrow? She recites obediently for him an edited list of her day's activities and smiles when he praises her cooking. But when he says, "Oh, well, time to turn in, another working day tomorrow," she is racked by a vague pain, like hunger, in the region of her heart.

So it is with the delighted air of a child who has been offered an unexpected gift that she leaves her half-written letter to greet Sagar at the door today, a good hour before Shyamoli is due back. The children are busy in the family room doing homework and watching cartoons (mostly the latter, Mrs. Dutta suspects). But for once she doesn't mind because they race in to give their father hurried hugs and then race back again. And she has him, her son, all to herself in a kitchen filled with the familiar, pungent odors of tamarind sauce and chopped coriander leaves.

"Khoka," she says, calling him by the childhood name she hasn't used in years, "I could fry you two-three hot-hot luchis, if you like." As she waits for his reply she can feel, in the hollow of her throat, the rapid beat of her blood. And when he says yes, that would be very nice, she shuts her eyes and takes a deep breath, and it is as though merciful time has give her back her youth, that sweet, aching urgency of being needed again.

Mrs. Dutta is telling Sagar a story.

"When you were a child, how scared you were of injections! One time, when the government doctor came to give us compulsory typhoid shots, you locked yourself in the bathroom and refused to come out. Do you remember what your father finally did? He went into the garden and caught a lizard and threw it in the bathroom window, because you were even more scared of lizards than of shots. And in exactly one second you ran out screaming—right into the waiting doctor's arms."

Sagar laughs so hard that he almost upsets his tea (made with real sugar, because Mrs. Dutta knows it is better for her son than that chemical powder Shyamoli likes to use). There are tears in his eyes, and Mrs. Dutta, who had not dared to hope he would find her story so amusing, feels gratified. When he takes off his glasses to wipe them, his face is oddly young, not like a father's at all, or even a husband's, and she has to suppress an impulse to put out her hand and rub away the indentations the glasses have left on his nose.

"I'd totally forgotten," says Sagar. "How can you keep track of those old, old things?"

Because it is the lot of mothers to remember what no one else cares to, Mrs. Dutta thinks. To tell them over and over until they are lodged, perforce, in family lore. We are the keepers of the heart's dusty corners.

But as she starts to say this, the front door creaks open, and she hears the faint click of Shyamoli's high heels. Mrs. Dutta rises, collecting the dirty dishes.

"Call me fifteen minutes before you're ready to eat so I can fry fresh luchis for everyone," she tells Sagar.

"You don't have to leave, Mother," he says.

Mrs. Dutta smiles her pleasure but doesn't stop. She knows Shyamoli likes to be alone with her husband at this time, and today in her happiness she does not grudge her this.

"You think I've nothing to do, only sit and gossip with you?" she mock-scolds. "I want you to know I have a very important letter to finish."

Somewhere behind her she hears a thud, a briefcase falling over. This surprises her. Shyamoli is always so careful with her case because it was a gift from Sagar when she was finally made a manager in her company.

"Hi!" Sagar calls, and when there's no answer," Hey, Molli, you okay?"

Shyamoli comes into the room slowly, her hair disheveled as though she'd been running her fingers through it. A hectic color blotches her cheeks.

"What's the matter, Molli?" Sagar walks over to give her a kiss. "Bad day at work?" Mrs. Dutta, embarrassed as always by this display of marital affection, turns toward the window, but not before she sees Shyamoli move her face away.

"Leave me alone." Her voice is wobbly. "Just leave me alone."

"But what is it?" Sagar says in concern.

"I don't want to talk about it right now." Shyamoli lowers herself into a kitchen chair and puts her face in her hands. Sagar stands in the middle of the room, looking helpless. He raises his hand and lets it fall, as though he wants to comfort his wife but is afraid of what she might do.

A protective anger for her son surges inside Mrs. Dutta, but she leaves the room silently. In her mind-letter she writes, *Women need to be strong, not react to every little thing like this. You and I, Roma, we had far worse to cry about, but we shed our tears invisibly. We were good wives and daughters-in-law, good mothers. Dutiful, uncomplaining. Never putting ourselves first.*

A sudden memory comes to her, one she hasn't thought of in years, a day when she scorched a special kheer dessert. Her mother-in-law had shouted at her, "Didn't your mother teach you anything, you useless girl?" As punishment she refused to let Mrs. Dutta go with Mrs. Basu to the cinema, even though *Sahib, Bibi aur Ghulam*, which all Calcutta was crazy about, was playing, and their tickets were bought already. Mrs. Dutta had wept the entire afternoon, but before Sagar's father came home she washed her face carefully with cold water and applied kajal to her eyes so he wouldn't know.

But everything is getting mixed up, and her own young, trying-not-to-cry face blurs into another—why, it's Shyamoli's—and a thought hits her so sharply in the chest she has to hold on to the bedroom wall. *And what good did it do? The more we bent, the more people pushed us, until one day we'd forgotten that we could stand up straight. Maybe Shyamoli's doing the right thing, after all. . . .*

Mrs. Dutta lowers herself heavily on to her bed, trying to erase such an insidious idea from her mind. Oh, this new country where all the rules are upside down, it's confusing her. Her mind feels muddy, like a pond in which too many water buffaloes have been wading. Maybe things will settle down if she can focus on the letter to Roma.

Then she remembers that she has left the half-written aerogram on the kitchen table. She knows she should wait until after dinner, after her son and his wife have sorted things out. But a restlessness—or is it defiance?—has taken hold of her. She's sorry Shyamoli's upset, but why should she have to waste her evening because of that? She'll go get her letter—it's no crime, is it? She'll march right in and pick it up, and even if Shyamoli stops in midsentence with another one of those sighs, she'll refuse to feel apologetic. Besides, by now they're probably in the family room, watching TV.

Really, Roma, she writes in her head as she feels her way along the unlighted corridor, *the amount of TV they watch here is quite scandalous. The children too, sitting for hours in front of that box like they've been turned into painted Kesto Nagar dolls, and then talking back when I tell them to turn it off.* Of course, she will never put such blasphemy into a real letter. Still, it makes her feel better to say it, if only to herself.

In the family room the TV is on, but for once no one is paying it any attention. Shyamoli and Sagar sit on the sofa, conversing. From where she stands in the corridor, Mrs. Dutta cannot see them, but their shadows—enormous against the wall where the table lamp has cast them—seem to flicker and leap at her.

She is about to slip unseen into the kitchen when Shyamoli's rising voice arrests her. In its raw, shaking unhappiness it is so unlike her daughter-in-law's assured tones that Mrs. Dutta is no more able to move away from it than if she had heard the call of the nishi, the lost souls of the dead on whose tales she grew up.

"It's easy for you to say 'Calm down.' I'd like to see how calm *you'd* be if she came up to you and said, 'Kindly tell the old lady not to hang her clothes over the fence into my yard.' She said it twice, like I didn't understand English, like I was an idiot. All these years I've been so careful not to give these Americans a chance to say something like this, and now—"

"Shhhh, Shyamoli, I *said* I'd talk to Mother about it."

"You always say that, but you never *do* anything. You're too busy being the perfect son, tiptoeing around her feelings. But how about mine?"

"Hush, Molli, the children . . ."

"Let them hear. I don't care anymore. They're not stupid. They already know what a hard time I've been having with her. You're the only one who refuses to see it."

In the passage Mrs. Dutta shrinks against the wall. She wants to move away, to not hear anything else, but her feet are formed of cement, impossible to lift, and Shyamoli's words pour into her ears like smoking oil.

"I've explained over and over, and she still keeps on doing what I've asked her not to—throwing away perfectly good food, leaving dishes to drip all over the countertops. Ordering my children to stop doing things I've given them permission for. She's taken over the entire kitchen, cooking whatever she likes. You come in the door and the smell of grease is everywhere, in all our clothes. I feel like this isn't my house anymore."

"Be patient, Molli, she's an old woman, after all."

"I know. That's why I tried so hard. I know having her here is important to you. But I can't do it any longer. I just can't. Some days I feel like taking the kids and leaving." Shyamoli's voice disappears into a sob.

A shadow stumbles across the wall to her, and then another. Behind the weatherman's nasal tones announcing a week of sunny days, Mrs. Dutta can hear a high, frightened weeping. The children, she thinks. It's probably the first time they've seen their mother cry.

"Don't talk like that, sweetheart." Sagar leans forward, his voice, too, miserable. All the shadows on the wall shiver and merge into a single dark silhouette.

Mrs. Dutta stares at that silhouette, the solidarity of it. Sagar and Shyamoli's murmurs are lost beneath a noise—is it in her veins, this dry humming, the way the taps in Calcutta used to hum when the municipality turned the water off? After a while she discovers that she has reached her room. In darkness she lowers herself on to her bed very gently, as though her body is made of the thinnest glass. Or perhaps ice, she is so cold. She sits for a long time with her eyes closed, while inside her head thoughts whirl faster and faster until they disappear in a gray dust storm.

When Pradeep finally comes to call her for dinner, Mrs. Dutta follows him to the kitchen where she fries luchis for everyone, the perfect circles of dough puffing up crisp and golden as always. Sagar and Shyamoli have reached a truce of some kind: she gives him a small smile, and he puts out a casual hand to massage the back of her neck. Mrs. Dutta demonstrates no embarrassment at this. She eats her dinner. She answers questions put to her. She smiles when someone makes a joke. If her face is still, as though she has been given a shot of Novocain, no one notices. When the table is cleared, she excuses herself, saying she has to finish her letter.

Now Mrs. Dutta sits on her bed, reading over what she wrote in the innocent afternoon.

Dear Roma,

Although I miss you, I know you will be pleased to hear how happy I am in America. There is much here that needs getting used to, but we are no strangers to adjusting, we old women. After all, haven't we been doing it all our lives?

Today I'm cooking one of Sagar's favorite dishes, alu dum. . . . It gives me such pleasure to see my family gathered around the table, eating my food. The children are still a little shy of me, but I am hopeful that we'll soon be friends. And Shyamoli, so confident and successful—you should see her when she's all dressed for work. I can't believe she's the same timid bride I sent off to America just a few years ago. But Sagar, most of all, is the joy of my old age.

With the edge of her sari Mrs. Dutta carefully wipes a tear that has fallen on the aerogram. She blows on the damp spot until it is completely dry, so the pen will not leave an incriminating smudge. Even though Roma would not tell a soul, she cannot risk it. She can already hear them, the avid relatives in India who have been waiting for something just like this to happen. *That Dutta-ginni, so set in her ways, we knew she'd never get along with her daughter-in-law.* Or worse, *Did you hear about poor Prameela, how her family treated her, yes, even her son, can you imagine?*

This much surely she owes to Sagar.

And what does she owe herself, Mrs. Dutta, falling through black night with all the certainties she trusted in collapsed upon themselves like imploded stars, and only an image inside her eyelids for company? A silhouette—man, wife, children—joined on a wall, showing her how alone she is in this land of young people. And how unnecessary.

She is not sure how long she sits under the glare of the overhead light, how long her hands clench themselves in her lap. When she opens them, nail marks line the soft flesh of her palms, red hieroglyphs—her body's language, telling her what to do.

Dear Roma, Mrs. Dutta writes,

I cannot answer your question about whether I am happy, for I am no longer sure I know what happiness is. All I know is that it isn't what I thought it to be. It isn't about being needed. It isn't about being with family either. It has something to do with love, I still think that, but in a different way than I believed earlier, a way I don't have the words to explain. Perhaps we can figure it out together, two old women drinking cha in your downstairs flat (for I do hope you will rent it to me on my return), while around us gossip falls—but lightly, like summer rain, for that is all we will allow it to be. If I'm lucky—and perhaps, in spite of all that has happened, I am—the happiness will be in the figuring out.

Pausing to read over what she has written, Mrs. Dutta is surprised to discover this: Now that she no longer cares whether tears blotch her letter, she feels no need to weep.

EMMA DONOGHUE

A SHORT STORY

THERE ARE STARS, AND then there are actors; think Garbo vs. Daniel Day-Lewis. The stars (who are always the same) win more fans, but I've always admired the actors (who immerse themselves in each role) far more. As a writer, I've never tried to cultivate a voice, an unmistakable style branding all my works. I figure my job is to serve the story—to choose from all the tools in my box to tell each tale (contemporary or historical, realistic or fanciful, funny or grim) the way it demands to be told.

"A Short Story," inspired by a brush with a skeleton in a museum, is an example of one of my obsessions: the digging-up of forgotten lives, generally "nasty, brutish and short." But its tone is more cold and biting than anything else I've written. I drafted it fast, trying to solve two puzzles: how do you find meaning in the life of a child who really had no independent life at all, and how do you avoid the pitfall of sentimentality? The result is half sardonic reportage, half poetic meditation. What do I like about it? The fact that it's short and as true as I could make it, and the words have sharp corners. When I read it aloud audiences tend to flinch, which I take as a compliment.

—Emma Donoghue

Formed in her mother's belly, dark filigree: the watermark of the bones.

The birth was easy. She glided out easy as a minnow into the slip-stream of life. The midwife crossed herself. The mother wept with grat-itude for this Thumbelina, this daughter of her mind's eye, embodied on the bloody sheet. The father wept with dread to see what he had spawned. Seven inches long, one pound in weight.

Hold it. Linger on the picture. Here, before poverty and ambi-tion began to pose their questions, before strangers started knocking on the door, before the beginning of the uneasy vigil that would last four years. Here for one moment, silence in the small hot room in Cork: a private wonder.

Mr. and Mrs. Crackham named their daughter Kitty.

She could not be said to have had a childhood. Her whole life was lived in proportion to her body—that is, in miniature; infancy, youth, and adulthood passed as rapidly as clouds across the sun. She was never exactly strong, in her body or her head; she was never exactly well. But Kitty Crackham did have pleasures to match her pains; she liked bright colours, and fine clothes, and if she heard music she would tap the floor with her infinitesimal foot.

At three years old she was one foot seven inches tall, and seemed to have given up growing. She never spoke, and the cough shook her like a dog. Doctor Gilligan assured the Crackhams that the air of England was much more healthful to children than that of Ireland, especially in tubercular cases such as little Kitty's. He offered to take her over the sea himself. He mentioned, only in passing, the possibility of introducing the child to certain men of science and ladies of quality. A select audience; the highest motives: to further the cause of physiological knowledge. It might help somewhat to defray the costs of her keep, he added.

Such kindness from a virtual stranger!

The Crackhams packed their daughter's tiny bag and sent her off with Doctor Gilligan, but not before he'd given them three months' rent.

Later they wished they'd said no. Later still, they wished they'd asked for twice as much. They had four other children, all full-size, all hungry.

The child was silent on the coach to Dublin, and on the ship too, even when the waves stood up like walls. The Doctor couldn't tell if she was weak-witted, or struck dumb by loss. Certainly, she was no ordinary girl. Their fellow travellers gasped and pointed as the Doctor carried Kitty Crackham along the deck in the crook of his arm. He pulled up her hood; it irked him that all these gawkers were getting a good look for free.

After dinner, when he'd thrown up the last of his lamb chops, his mind cleared. It struck him that the girl's tininess would seem even more extraordinary if she were, say, nine years old instead of three. To explain her speechlessness, he could present her as an exotic foreigner. By the time they docked, he'd taught her to stagger towards him whenever he called *Caroline*.

It was Caroline Crachami, the Dwarf from Palermo, who landed at Liverpool in the year 1823: "the smallest of all persons mentioned in the records of littleness," the Doctor's pamphlet boasted. In a fanciful touch he was rather proud of, the pamphlet suggested that her growth had been blighted in the womb by a monkey that had bitten Signora Crachami's finger.

The first exhibition, at Liverpool, drew barely a trickle of punters, but Doctor Gilligan forced himself to be patient. On to Birmingham, where the crowd began to swell, then Oxford. Town after town, room after room, month after month. Each of the child's days was crammed with strangers so big they could have crushed her with an accidental step. Such excitement in the eyes of these Brobdingnagians, now their Gulliver had come at last. Some called her *she*; others, *it*. Doctor Gilligan took to wearing a Sicilian moustache and calling her *my darling daughter.*

She made her audiences doubt their senses and cry out in delight. How strong she made them feel—but also, how clumsy. They could hardly bear to think of a child being so small and brittle, so they called her the Sicilian Fairy. As if a newborn baby had risen magically from her cradle and dressed herself to parade before them; as if her powers were in inverse proportion to her size, and she could fly out of any danger! She was the doll they had always wished would come to life.

In London Doctor Gilligan tested the weight of his moneybags and hired an exhibition room in Bond Street. He provided his *darling daughter* with a tiny ring, thimble-cup, and bed. She sat on a tea caddy that served her for a throne. He taught her to take a bit of biscuit from his hand, then rub her stomach and say "Good, good." He was delighted when after a week or two she began to talk a little more, as it increased the entertainment. "Papa," she called him, without much prompting. She had a faint high voice, not of this world, and visitors had to stoop to hear her; the Doctor repeated everything she said, adding a few touches of his own.

For a foreign child, people said, she was a quick learner of English. She put her hand over her mouth when she felt a cough coming, and she tottered across the deep carpets as if always about to drop. She was seen to express emotions of various kinds, such as gratitude, irritation, mirth, and panic.

The Doctor was less pleased when his measurements showed that she had grown a quarter of an inch.

⌒

Caroline Crachami was now one foot eight inches tall—still, by a good thirteen inches, the smallest female on record. The papers called her the Nation's Darling, the Wonder of Wonders. The King took her hand between his finger and thumb, and declared himself immensely pleased to make her acquaintance. He sat her on his footstool and had her thimble filled with a drop of his best port. She coughed and whooped and all the ladies laughed.

After that the crowds swelled and multiplied. Three hundred of the nobility visited her, three thousand of the quality, and as many of the lower sort as could beg, borrow, or steal the price of admission. Gentlemen adored Miss Crachami. Ladies grew jealous, began to call her powdery and withered.

For an extra shilling Miss Crachami could be handled. When sceptical Grub Street men came in, Doctor Gilligan invited them to handle her for free. One gentleman with a stubbled chin picked her up in one hand—she weighed only five pounds—and kissed her. She was seen to wriggle away and wipe her face. He got a highly amusing article out of the episode. Readers were assured that there was every probability of this Progeny of Nature living to an advanced age.

But nothing about Caroline Crachami took long, and her death was particularly quick. That Thursday in June she received more than two hundred visitors. A little langour was noted, and was only to be expected; a little rattle when she coughed. In the couch on the way back to their Duke Street lodgings, while Doctor Gilligan was looking out the window, she dropped soundlessly to the floor and died.

He assumed she was only in a faint. He couldn't believe it was all over.

Given the Doctor's commitment to the furthering of physiological knowledge, what came next was no surprise. He carried the body round to all the anatomists and finally sold it to the Royal College of Surgeons.

Doctor Clift was not the kind of doctor who offered cures. He was an articulator; a butcher in the service of science, or even art. His job was to draw grace and knowledge out of putridity. He needed a delicate touch in this case, as the carcass was so small.

First he cut it open, and learned what he could from the spotted lungs and shrunken organs. Then he chopped the body into convenient and logical sections, just like jointing a hen or a rabbit, and boiled it down. For several days he stirred this human soup and let it stew; finally he poured it away, leaving only the greasy bones. He'd got inured to the smell thirty years ago.

Odd, he thought, that the same people who would retch at the stench of such a soup would line up to drink in the sight of the same bones, once he had strung them together. Such was his artistry. It was the hardest of jigsaw puzzles. All his years of drawing and copying and assembling more ordinary skeletons had prepared him for this. He needed to recall every one of the two hundred and six bones in the body, and recognise their patterns, even on this miniature scale. His eyes throbbed; his fingers ached. He was going to raise a little girl from the dead, so the living might understand. With only bone and wire and glue he planned to make something that united—in the words of a recently dead poet of a medical persuasion—Beauty and Truth.

Her parents read of her death in the *Cork Inquirer*. Mr. Crackham took the night ferry. In London he banged on doors of parish authorities and magistrates' courts, and toured the hospitals and morgues, but all the bodies he was shown were too big: "This is not my daughter," he repeated.

He never caught up with Doctor Gilligan—who'd absconded from his lodgings owing £25—but he did find his way in the end to Surgeon's Hall in Lincoln's Inn Fields. He got to the laboratory a week late. Doctor Clift was putting the final touches to his masterpiece with a miniature screwdriver.

When the Irishman understood what he was looking at, he let out a roar that was not fully human. He tried to throw his arms around his Kitty, but something halted him.

This tinkling puppet was not his anymore, if she had ever been. Her clean, translucent bones were strung as taut as pearls, and her spine was a metal rod. She stood on her tiny pedestal with her frilled knees together like a nervous dancer, about to curtsey to the world. Her ankles were delicately fettered; her thumbs were wired to the looped ribbons of her hips. Her palms tilted up as if to show she had nothing to hide.

Her head was a white egg, with eye holes like smudges made by a thumb. Nine teeth on the top row, nine on the bottom, crooked as orange pips. She grinned at the man who had been her father like a child at a party, with fear or excitement, he couldn't tell which.

How lovely she was.

It occurred to Doctor Clift then, watching as the porters hauled the child's father off howling and kicking, that Kitty's bones would last longer than his own. She was a fossil, now; she had her niche in history. Shortly she would be placed on show in the Museum Hall between tanks that held a cock with a leg grafted onto its comb and a foetus with veins cast in red wax. She looked like a human house of cards, but nothing could knock her down. She would stand grinning at her baffled visitors until all those who'd ever known her were dust.

NOTE

The girl known as Caroline Crachami died on 3 June 1824, probably from a combination of tuberculosis and exhaustion. But basic facts about this child's nationality, age, medical history, and life before her arrival in England in 1823 are still disputed.

My inspiration and main source for "A Short Story" was a long and highly original article by Gaby Wood, "The Smallest of All Persons Mentioned in the Records of Littleness," published in the London Review of Books, *11 December 1997, and afterwards in volume form by Profile Books. I also drew on Richard Altick's* The Shows of London. *Crachami's skeleton, death mask, limb casts, and accessories are displayed in the Hunterian Museum at the Royal College of Surgeons in Lincoln's Inn Fields, London, next to the remains of the Giant, O'Brien.*

RITA DOVE

HER ISLAND

ORIGINALLY I INTENDED TO select one of my most popular poems, "Parsley," for my personal best, but I find myself drawn to another, quite different piece. It's a sequence of poems with a glorious formal name: a crown of sonnets. During my formative years as a poet, I never thought I'd be able to write a respectable sonnet, much less a group of sonnets with such an exacting template, much less have fun doing it. But "never say never," as Fievel the mouse sings in the movie *An American Tail,* so here's the story: I had been writing poems based on the myth of Demeter and Persephone, sonnets(!) about a daughter lost to the Underworld and returned to her mother. True to my rather superstitious research methods, I shied away from visiting the actual scene of the crime—the lake in Sicily where Persephone purportedly was kidnapped by Hades—until I had finished writing nearly all the poems I had in me on the subject. That summer when my husband and I took off for southern Italy, I told myself I was just checking facts, tanking ambiance for the final rewrites. We drove the entire circumference of Sicily, saving the lake for last . . . only to find that a racetrack had been built around it! It was a perfect oval, I reasoned, ideal for myth building and car racing. And yet my disappointment was huge—so huge that I sat down and wrote "Her Island" in a marathon stint of three nights. To my surprise, I enjoyed the rigors of the sonnet crown—where the last line of the initial sonnet becomes the first line of the succeeding one, and so on until the final sonnet ends with the very first line of the first sonnet—so much that I wrote more than the requisite seven poems. Go figure.

—Rita Dove

the heat, the stench of things,
the unutterable boredom of it all . . .
—H.D., *Notes on Thought and Vision*

Around us blazed stones, closed ground.
Waiters lounge, stricken with *sirocco*,
ice cream disintegrates to a sticky residue
fit for flies and ants. Summer, the dead season.
All the temples of Agrigento
line up like a widow's extracted wisdom teeth,
ocher-stained, proud remnants
of the last sturdy thing about her.

We wander among orange peels and wax
wrappings flecked with grease,
tilt our guidebook, pages blank from sun, and peer
up into the bottomless air. Between columns
blue slashes of a torched heaven. No.
Let it go: Nothing will come of this.

Let it go: Nothing will come of this
textbook rampaging, though we have found, by
stint and intuition, the chthonic grotto,
closed for the season behind a chicken wire gate.
We're too well trained to trespass. Clearly
we can imagine what's beyond it. Clearly
we've sought succor in the wrong corner.
Nothing melts faster than resolve in this climate;
we turn to a funny man in our path, old
as everything is here is either old
or scathingly young with whippet thighs
clamped over a souped-up Vespa. *You wish
to visit historic site?* We nod, politely;
he shuffles off to find the key.

He shuffles off to find the key,
dust blooming between us to obscure
what we had missed on the way in:
at the head of the path a shack
the size of an outhouse from which he emerges
hobbling, Quasimodo in a sunnier vein.

An eternity at the lock, then down. It's noon:
we must be madder than the English
with their dogs. Look at his shoes,
he's made them into slippers!
His touch trembles at my arm;
has he ever seen an American black
before? We find a common language: German.

Before we find a common language—German,
laced with tenth grade Spanish and
residual Latin—we descend
in silence through the parched orchard.
The way he stops to smile at me
and pat my arm, I'm surely his first
Queen of Sheba.
                        The grotto is
a disappointment, as every site has been
so far. Isn't there a way to tip him early
and get the hell back to the car?
Insulting an old man just isn't done.
Nothing to do but help him conjugate
his verbs and smile until our cheeks ache,
our hands admiring every grimy stone.

Our hands admiring every grimy stone,
we let our minds drift far afield:
there's a miracle, a lone bird
singing. What's that
he's saying? *Krieg?*
His German gathered word by word
half a century ago. I'd shudder
but it wouldn't be polite.

Now he motions my husband close, man to man:
would he like to see a true wonder?
No, not dirty. Another temple
lost to busy people—he mimics Fiats
zipping by—a man's shrine, the god
of fire. Ah, Vulcan? Emphatic nod.
He's had the key for many years, they've all forgotten.

               ∽

He's had the key for many years; they've all forgotten
the ugly god, god of everything modern.
We toil cross-town, down ever-dwindling streets
until we're certain we're about to turn into
the latest victims of a tourist scam. A sharp curve
under the *autostrada* confirms the destiny
we should at least meet head on: climb
straight through the city dump,
through rotten fruit and Tampax tubes
so our treacherous guide can deliver us into
what couldn't be: a patch of weeds sprouting six—no, seven—
columns, their Doric reserve softened by weather
to a tawny indifference. Roosters cluck among the ruins;
traffic whizzes by in heaven.

               ∽

Traffic whizzes by in heaven
for the Sicilians, of that we were certain;
why else are they practicing on earth, hell-bent
to overtake creampuff foreigners in their rented
Chrysler? Ha! Can't they guess a German
plies the wheel? We dash along beside
them, counterclockwise around the island,
not looking for the ironies we see in spades—
Palermo's golden virgin carried down to sea
as a car bomb blows a judge to smoke,
five brides whose lacquered faces echo those
ones staring, self-mocking, from lurid frescoes
at the Villa Casale: *an eye for an eye.* And
everywhere temples, or pieces of them.

Everywhere temples, or pieces of them,
lay scattered across the countryside.
These monstrous broken sticks, flung
aside in a celestial bout of I Ching, have become
Sicily's most exalted litter. (The lesser kind
flies out the windows of honking automobiles.)

We circle the island, trailing the sun
on his daily rounds, turning time back
to one infernal story: a girl
pulled into a lake, a perfect oval
hemmed all around by reeds
at the center of the physical world.
We turn inland as if turning a page in a novel:
dry splash of the cicada, no breath from the sea.

Dry splash of the cicada, no breath from the sea.
Our maps have not failed us: this is it,
the only body of water for twenty miles,
water black and still as the breath
it harbored . . . and around this perfect ellipse
they've built—a racetrack.

Bleachers. Pit stops. A ten-foot fence
plastered with ads—Castrol, Campari—
and looped barbed wire; no way to get near.
We drive the circumference
with binoculars: no cave, no reeds.
We drive it twice, first one way, then back,
to cancel our rage at the human need
to make a sport of death.

To make a sport of death
it must be endless: round and round
till you feel everything you've trained for—
precision, speed, endurance—reduced to this
god awful roar, this vale of sound.

Your head's a furnace: you don't feel it.
Your eyes two slits in a computer unit.
A vital rule: if two vehicles ahead of you
crash, drive straight toward the fire
and they will have veered away before you get
there. Bell lap, don't look to see who's
gaining. Aim for the tape, aim *through* it.
Then rip the helmet off and poke your head
through sunlight, into flowers.

Through sunlight into flowers
she walked, and was pulled down.
A simple story, a mother's deepest
dread—that her child could drown
in sweetness.

        Where the chariot went under
no one can fathom. Water keeps its horrors
while sky proclaims his, hangs them
in stars. Only the earth, wild
mother we can never leave (even now
we've leaned against her, heads bowed
against the heat) knows
no story's ever finished; it just goes
on unnoticed in the dark that's all
around us: blazed stones, the ground closed.

CAROLYN FERRELL

From *TIGER-FRAME GLASSES*

TRAVELING SHOES

I BEGAN THIS STORY when I was nine years old, writing in a small composition book I had been given by my mother and in which I had, until then, been composing calming, sunny poems. The real Bellerina changed things for me as a writer—poetry was not enough. Bellerina is the star antagonist in "Tiger-Frame Glasses" but she also existed as a real person, someone who, through sheer rage and vulnerability, gave me her life on a platter. At first I'd tried to write a poem about her. It soon became clear to me that the "true facts" of her life deserved a tougher and (in my eyes) more honest literary vehicle: how could a poem convey the fact that Bellerina was a fat, hideous, unlovable girl who made my life miserable? A harsh assessment, yes, but I was learning even then that "true facts" often bring out the harshest in us. Bellerina tortured me as I walked to and from the school bus stop each day, making fun of my lukewarm good looks and threatening to kick my butt. She thought I was too big for my britches. She couldn't understand why I took a sardine sandwich to school each day. Black people (for this was what I understood the subtext to be) didn't take sardine sandwiches to school—they ate hot lunch! We were nine years old, waiting for a bus to take us to an elementary school in the white part of the village. Bellerina got a group of school-bus girls to join her in calling me names, delivering threats, making prophecies, and so on. I remember someone (who had, in the hallways, become a new friend) suddenly shouting at me as the bus rounded the corner: "Your ass is grass!"

Escape was the only thing on my mind, that and imagining painful deaths for all the girls involved. But their deaths were never a sure bet. Mine seemed most likely to occur before I hit the sixth grade. I took to writing; my composition book became among the few consolations I had. (I could not take my mother's soft lullabies to school with me.)

My composition book made me feel better about the world; I was confident that the story I was writing would change things, would make the world nicer if I just got down all the horror that was Bellerina Brown and all the good and angelic that was myself. It felt good to get the details in place, the shouts, the cries, the hopes and dreams. The children pure of heart, and those who could not possibly be loved by anyone on earth.

Bellerina turned out, to my dismay, to play a rather small part in the story I began in my composition book when I was nine years old. All along I had craved the feeling of vindication I would get by having Bellerina destroyed in a fire or suffering a severe lack of food in an orphanage. But in my story, she took a backseat to the good characters, whose ideal lives sparkled underneath my pencil. The "chapters" of my story seethed with good deeds and Girl Scout medals and shapely girls whose names rang like bells: Vanessa Goodwin, Gorgea Gorgeous. There was a fire, but luckily there was also a fire escape and a ladder and a lifesaver's award from a fire-fighter by the name of Mr. Handy.

In spite of all this, revenge was never far from my mind. Every time I went past Bellerina Brown's house (*ran* past it), I was filled with the desire to expose their secrets. I got out my sharpened pencil. But then other things emerged on the page: the story of Vanessa saving her family from a fire (luckily she had memorized the fire drill) and her best friend, Gorgea, who was just too pretty to hate; all this growing before my eyes, under my own hand holding the sharpened pencil. I wanted to be a good writer, even as I ran like a madwoman to and from the bus stop, or dodged the garbage being flung at me from Bellerina's upstairs window, or wept as my father rolled his eyes and ordered me to grow a backbone.

⌒

This is the real Bellerina, the one who didn't make it into "Tiger-Frame Glasses": her torment of me would actually go on for years, practically until she dropped out of high school. By that time, we all had love on the brain. But it was a known fact that Bellerina disgusted all the boys, even those who would sleep with any girl. Her hair was undone (read: nappy, ungreased), her body smelled of deodorant and funk, and when you looked closely, you saw that she wore the same uniform of clothes each day, simply arranged in another raggedy order.

Years later, when I was home on a break from college, I heard that she'd been arrested trying to steal from the local five-and-dime. She hadn't taken anything glamorous; perhaps it was a can of juice, the large kind, the one that she'd have to take home and pierce with a can opener. Her mother, a shadowy presence who remained indoors at all times, left Bellerina and her mob of sisters to fend for themselves—maybe the juice was for their dinner? Maybe it was a gift for the father, but had there ever been a father? Who on the planet could rescue these girls from their bad breath, their poor eyes, their terrible yearning for love? Bellerina and her many sisters lived in the only Victorian house in our neighborhood (that is, if you didn't count the abandoned mansion that had once been a hippie commune around the corner) and they continued to live in that house for years after their mother died. Some time after the theft incident, Bellerina disappeared as well. The Victorian house was torn down in order to make room for a church basketball camp.

⌒

Somewhere I learned that revenge is actually a poor motivator for fiction. There was always the story I wanted to tell—fueled by anger, resentment, a sense of injustice—but precisely because of those feelings, the story wouldn't come. When I first began to write, I heard voices all around me saying, "Now you can get back at all those folks that did you wrong. At the very least, they make for funny characters." Once it was my mother's voice, encouraging me to get back at the wealthy East Hampton family that had hired me to "help the cook occasionally" but who treated me like a professional slave. Once it was a good friend, suggesting that a no-good boyfriend of mine would get his comeuppance *only* if he saw his disgusting name on the page.

As an undergraduate writing student, I read John Cheever's interview in *The Paris Review* in which he warned against revenge writing; slowly I realized that revenge might possibly overtake the art and leave me stranded. Writing was never therapy for me, as much as I wanted it to be. When I grew up, I realized that I was not writing to help myself. I was writing for others, writing the story I myself wanted to read. Writing became a way for me to ask better questions of the world.

At thirty-five, I returned to the story I'd tried to write about Bellerina. I didn't have the composition book any longer, but I remembered my feelings too well. I wanted to get the story down the right way, whatever that was, though even at thirty-five, I wondered if it was truly the right time to tackle this material again. I was no longer nine, but the pain would not let go, and I wondered why I would want to return to those miserable days, to that group of girls who picked my pocket on the school bus, to the parents who'd gotten up a petition against my family in order to drive us from the neighborhood, to that spelling bee I forfeited out of fear of being perceived too "smart" (as in, "She *think* she so smart"), or even to Bellerina, a desk away in the fifth-grade classroom, whispering the names of boys she'd get to get me—how could I return and create a piece of fiction, a work of art, that rose above my old feelings?

I felt more pity for the Bellerina who lived in my memory than anything else, but I knew that pity was also not a good reason to write.

The solution was simple. What I needed to do was take a journey to Mirror City.

⌒

As a visitor to Ibiza, the New Zealand writer Janet Frame once looked out onto the water from her room and saw a city mirrored there. She called it, appropriately, "Mirror City," or the city of the imagination, the place where "memories are resurrected, re-clothed with reflection and change, and their essence [left] untouched." This is a place where people and places and events cease being mere slices of life—in Mirror City, they are transformed by the creative process into art.

Trying to understand a place like Mirror City allowed me to grasp some of the challenges of this transformation. I learned how to "resurrect" and "re-clothe" the facts of my own life, and that knowledge in turn gave me greater insight into my own stories. "Putting it all down as it happens is not fiction," says Frame in her autobiography. "There must be the journey by oneself, the changing of the light focused upon the material, the willingness of the author herself to live within that light, that city of reflections governed by different laws, materials, currency."

"Tiger-Frame Glasses" is perhaps the most autobiographical piece I have ever written, and yet, there is very little of the actual me in the story. Everything is a composite, a remodeling, a challenge to the past, to the way things were. By the time I revisited Bellerina's material, my questions were larger than they'd been when I was nine: I wondered if literature could really change the world? Why write if I couldn't evoke some sort of change? What stories did I have to tell that would be of interest and/or use to anyone else on the planet?

In a fiction workshop I once attended, the wonderful Edna O'Brien said that yearning was the greatest ingredient of literature. I still love that line, and hold onto it as tightly as I hold onto my memories of Bellerina Brown at the bus stop. She has a small bit of room to move about in my mind. But on the page? There she roams freely, she becomes someone else entirely, someone I don't know I know. She points me in different directions, reminds me of what

I used to know and hands out sturdy pairs of traveling shoes. She has been renamed many times, and yet I am careful never to call out her name. There she is, Bellerina Brown, in the only Victorian on the block, remembering a lullaby her father used to sing, taking a last sip of juice before the sun sets over the neighborhood trees. How can I know this? Well, I simply have to. As a writer, I am less interested in the truthfulness of a story than I am in its honesty. And as a character in my fiction, Bellerina at least deserves to be dealt with as honestly as possible.

Though Vanessa Goodwin and Gorgea Gorgeous might disagree.

—Carolyn Ferrell

In school Mr. di Salvo asks me if I can spell the word appreciate. If I can spell it correctly, I will get to be one of the Women in the Pioneer play. I will get to sing "This Land Is Your Land" with the other Women. I will get to have Mrs. Shea from third grade sew me a bonnet and a long apron to wear over my clothes when I walk along the stage with the others. All this for appreciate on our weekly spelling bee.

Bellerina sees that I am having trouble. She and I are at the middle desk. She has not had her hair braided in days. There are all these little nubs down the back of her neck. The Ultra-Sheen grease that her mother told her to put in missed her hair and smacks down her neck and shows my reflection in it. I can almost see my corduroy pants on her neck through my tiger-frame glasses that everyone makes fun of and calls me F.E.F. cause they know I won't do nothing. I only have one pair of pants. My parents say that we are poor, but not to go out broadcasting that information. How can I help it? My knees are run down. Every Body knows. And I can't do nothing. But the school bus on page 2 of the spelling book honks to me: appreciate, appreciate. The Boloney Butcher for B whispers, I *appreciate* a truly smart girl like you. I am going stark raving for a girl in the fifth grade who is going to get it later on from the girls at the bus stop. A whole bunch of dreams. I want to do something. Will my parents finally go away with us on vacation to the mountains or the seaside like they promised? Will they send me and Bethi to private school—where we *really* belong? A truly smart girl. My brain remembers the melody lane from the day before in the backyard: Daddy mowing the dried up lawn and whistling "California Dreamer" and Mom singing the commercial for Eight O'Clock Coffee and Bethi trying to get all the words to "Shakeit Shakeit Shakeit" in one line, like there are no other words to the whole song. Me sitting in the bushes with my notebook which is the dream weavill and trying to get it all down the way I would truly like it to happen and looking up in the sunlight and wishing I had a real mother and a real father and a real sister that wanted the utmost best for me, who realized all the dynamite I have in me, like a princess or a very smart and beautiful princess/girl/student. I listen. I want to shout to Bethi, "We're going to the country, We're going to the fair" as those are the other words, but she is really too slow to get anything. I hate her.

Bellerina whispers in my ear A-P-P-R-E-S-H-E-A-T-E. I repeat her words. I want to stand in the girls circle. When I *used* to be there, Bellerina used to play the funniest jokes on me, and I wouldn't get mad. She had told Bibi in secret exactly *where* it would hurt the most on my Body to hit me, and she was right. She stold my notebook to see the stories I wrote in it so she could give the others more ammunition. She informed me that she would get her older brother Beanie from prison to take me to the Back and feel my nubs under my dress. She did all this and still. I want to stand in the girls circle. I will spin Bethi out, cause she really don't know what it means, the circle. She don't know that I should have what she has, only she don't recognize that for her genuine slowness.

Mr. di Salvo announces that I will be one of the people pulling the wagon across the prairie. They had those too, you know, when the horses died, and cattle broke down. I don't have to wear a dress if I don't want to. The girls wearing aprons and bonnets will have to wear a dress under. But I can wear whatever I want to, even my gym suit, as a puller.

The songs I will have to sing with the chorus are "Fifty Miles on the Erie Canal." "Sweet Betsy from Pike." "Carry My Back to Ole Virginny." I will have to walk slow like they did in the old days. They did not run across the prairie. I will have to learn my songs good. Bellerina holds her big teeth under her big hand. She will get to be a Pioneer Woman. She will get a bonnet and an apron. She will get to sit in the wagon while the boys and some unlucky girls pull it. Even though she weighs as much as a ninth-grader one ton and is butt-ugly.

The teacher is not expecting nothing. I was born on Easter, an Aires baby, so that makes me the kind that is innocent yet secretly commanding. I raise my hand and I get up slowly out my desk. My palms are sweaty. My long braids that I hate for my mother to make on me are messed up already because I've been putting my head down on my boring speller too much. I get up. The gray venetian blinds on the big window hold back the sun with their straight arms and tell me that I am in the right lane. Go on Girlie, they cheer! They reach down and pat my head like I'm the faithful dog. The door frame gets ready to move. The tiles on the floor are shivery with delight. Shakeit Shakeit Shakeit. Shakeit all you can. I open my mouth. "Bellerina Brown is a Fucking Ass. Hole." The class goes wild. Shakeit all you can. Shakeit like a milkshake and do the best you can. The venetian blinds nod yes you can and the clouds outside fall into the classroom and swirl my brains up in a pudding. Bellerina swings for my stomach, but I land on Mr. di Salvo's desk, where I hide with the other butterflies under the stack of math tests from last Wednesday. A staunch stunning wind from the spelling lists stampedes the stalactites on my hands. Bellerina punches but I am too fast. I'm always out her way.

With both eyes open under my tiger-frame glasses I see the pretty *one hundred* girls who are in shock and who don't want to consider me anymore for them. The rough *zero* girls have questions for me later: *we ain't know you was like us, Glory!* The snaggle tooth boys cheer Hip Hip, and Boo-Boo claps me on the back. Mr. di Salvo takes me and Bellerina out the play. We will have to sit in Mrs. Shea's class with the third-graders while the assembly is on. We will have to write out the words to "The Star Spangled Banner" ten times and maybe get locked in the closet, which is Mrs. Shea's specialty.

Bellerina looks me up and down. —Later, Today, After-school. Your Ass is Grass.

I sit back in my seat. The pencil groove on my desk smiles and asks me, Now that wasn't so hard, was it?

(The story goes on.)

Shenay is a Scorpio. She do not bother with boys at all. She is sexy, strategic and silent. She figures things out. Shenay has one mission on her mind: Find those who need help, and send in the Helper Squad. That would be her, Donna and Debbie. They all live on the same street and at night, they are all dedicated to saving.

Shenay can open her bedroom window and get the feel of the ocean waves crashing against the rock. She teaches Donna and Debbie. She tells them to look behind what you see. Look for the genuine-ality of a thing. Donna and Debbie say I don't get it. Shenay says, "Let me give you an example."

When she is lying in her bed at night, she sees gypsy moths fistfighting in the wall and hears pumpernickel swans discussing yesterday's math problems together. Did you get this one? Sure. That one was a cinch. The swans kiss her on the forehead. Honey, you ain't never told us you were such a smartie.

Shenay says, "Look."

On my way to the principal's office to get my punishment okayed I pass Bethi's classroom and wave to the teacher, Mr. Flegenheimer. Can she come out right now? I just got an important message from our mother and I just want to tell her it in the hall, Mr. Fleg. Private. It's important from our mother.

Mr. Flegenheimer brings Bethi out because he is getting too many complaints from the parents of special ed that he is not treating their kids like regular human beings. That he is holding back their bathroom and making them pee in their chairs and sit in it for a long time before calling the nurse and the janitor. That he is closing the venetian blinds and making them sit there, just like that, so he can put his head down on the desk. Mr. Flegenheimer is trying to look different now, but we all know.

—You can talk for three minutes, and I mean three minutes, Glory. I have a good mind to talk to your mother on the phone to confirm this, Mr. Flegenheimer says. Then he is gone back to the class that is howling over something. His eyes are closed.

Bethi is afraid to look at me. She just got allowed into the back of their circle this morning. She is afraid of what I will do to her. Don't worry about that till later, I assure her. I will get you back later. Right now I want you to do me a favor. I want you to go to Mr. di Salvo's classroom and tell him to send Bellerina to your classroom, Mr. Flegenheimer's orders. Can you do that? Okay Bethi? Can you do that? I whisper all this to her, but it takes a real long time before she gets the directions straight. She is not a retard. She is just slow. Her whole classroom is full of slow kids, so she don't feel so alone. They get beat up all the time, except for the large ones that are truly brainless and that can kill you just by looking your way.

Bethi goes to my classroom and gets Bellerina who calls her Stupid Ass and Brick Brain all the way back to Mr. Flegenheimer's door. I'm waiting there. Martha Madison suddenly appears out of nowhere humming her group of Women's song for Assembly "I'se Gwine Back to Dixie." She says in my direction, You Gonna Wish You Was Dead Meat. Martha is cross-eyed so she sometimes scares me and she sometimes doesn't. Now I am only thinking of my plan. Bellerina slaps her five and then Martha books. Bellerina turns and looks me dead in the eye. There, I am there. Shakeit Shakeit.

The door opened to show the first victim in need: old Mrs. Goodwin, a faithful souls who had a heart of gold. She was a white lady who trusted everyone. She lived all by herself in the black neighborhood of Tar Hill where people live in apartments instead of normal houses. She can make you believe in mankind all over again. Hallelujah for Mrs. Goodwin!

She had fell down her apartment steps and all the food stamp cans of food in her grocery bag rolled into the alleyway where Joe the town bum was laying. "Help me Joe!" she cried, but he only cried back, "Mrs. Goodwin, indeed I wish I could! I myself am too weak to do much of anything." So they both agonized in tribulations until around the corner came—the Helper Squad!

Debbie helped the old bitty to her feet, but when she found that Mrs. Goodwin couldn't walk, she carried her in her girl arms up the steps to her house and put her in the bed. Donna said, "Debbie, how come you got so strong?" Debbie didn't want to say. Modesty carnation.

Donna placed all the cans of food in their cabinets and to top it off, she cooked Mrs. Goodwin a whole dinner. Saucy Frank Supper with corn and tomatoes in it. Mrs. Goodwin closed her wrinkly eyes with tears of joy. "What would this world be without girls like you?" Donna shaked her beautiful hair and made Mrs. Goodwin feel better just by looking at her.

Meanwhile Shenay was in the alleyway helping Joe the bum to his feet. He smelled strange and warm. She was telling him, "See, if you believe in yourself, you can do it." Joe said he had never believed in himself before today. He was going downtown to get a job at the local school, doing anything. He wants to better himself. Maybe he can raise to a janitor. Shenay, you are a gold mind. Let me thank you.

"Don't thank me. Thank the Helper Squad. We want the world to be the place where you can dream and come true."

"I need to thank you Shenay."

"I said don't, old man."

Back then. The daylights whipped out of me. I said I couldn't take it no more. I felt a rippliness in my head from the punches and slides. I told them that I would never tell on them and besides my family has a pool table in our basement. Come over and use it any time. We just don't have some things that go with it. I'll never tell on you. Come over any time. But my head was getting pulverized, and in reality I was already on a cloud floating up to the sky. The voices around said, You ain't got no pool table. Your family is poor as dirt. Don't you go on putting on airs. My lips realized, How did you know that word: *airs?* Then my head got completely mashed up. Meanwhile Beanie, Bellerina's brother, waved to me from his car and laughed because it was truly funny seeing the smartass skinny one with the spy notebook of no-good gossip bout everyone on this block get the daylights whipped out of her and maybe he even saw what I wrote about a guy like him in my notebook about how strong and handsome but feeling up ladies now what a shame and why do they have to do that when all they have to do is ask and surely someone will say, Yes Please.

Bibi and Martha had my head in a lock, and then Crater had the stupendous idea of putting me between the cinder blocks to see if they could make a girl sandwich. Bellerina said, It hurts the most when something hard is lying on top of your moist spot. The other girls looked at her funny. *Where the heck is that?* Bellerina turned her head away. She said into the wind, Why am I the only one who ever knows anything.

It did not get that far. They slabbed me on a cinder block and I felt the blood bath behind my braided head go into my braided eyes and the true way Beanie's snout nose looked came clear in my mind. Spread out like a father's but he was only a guy. Even with that snout nose I saw through to Beanie's handsomeness. Didn't I say so in my notebook? Next to the made up stories about Debbie Donna and Shenay there was this gorgeous guy named B. who went to prison but who was really too handsome to really do anything prisonable. He was in secret a millionaire and he was going to fix a deserving girl up in private school where they learn. Only in real life now his car says Dodge. He is handsomely driving a Dodge. Away. I felt like laughing and then the blood trinkled to the line that was my mouth, all the way into my neck, later my eyelids. The blood burned deeper the spot of lonely that was already there. We have a pool table. Only problem is we don't have the balls that go with it. Where is every Body running? Why are you going? Wait. But it was too late. I was there half a sandwich for a pillow and no way in hell Beanie in his Dodge was going to give me another look now.

At the bus stop I am always shrinking of the girls. Fall Spring Morning Bedtime Schoolclothes PJs. I want to be with them but I am also shrinking. I wish I was dumber. I wish I was getting left back. I wish I weighed a hundred twenty pounds in the fifth grade. Then I would be in the bus stop circle. I could stop feeling Bethi breathe down my plaid dress in her waiting. She stands so close. I need to do something to her, even though she will never tell on me, and that fact makes it more stupider to do it in the first place.

My mother thinks that I am incomprehensible for wishing these kinds of things. To be left back and big. My father just laughs in the background, while he is watching *60 Minutes*. He laughs. Just one look at Glory's math grades and you can tell she's gonna be in the fifth grade a long time, maybe years. I would of got a horse whipping. You don't know how easy things are nowadays. It's the state of cultural illiteracy. Then he goes back to watching. Mother adds, And another thing: You better stop bringing up private school, girl. It's just incomprehensible. Do you think we made out of money? Then Father adds, And you better stop writing in that damn notebook and write something for Mr. di Salvo that will get you passed into sixth grade. Bethi smiles at me but I don't want it. Then they go on. Mother is folding clothes and telling Bethi what to put down on her spelling worksheet and my father is saying to the tv I Been Told You That Last Year Stupid Ass and I am doing nothing important, just standing there in an invisible cloud of butterflies, roaches, and wasps, all asking me to be their best friend.

Bellerina looks me up and down in the hallway. —What you doing here?

Before I can open my mouth she says: You want me to permanently damage that shit-ass face of yours?

—Bellerina, let's you and me go to the Back. No one will know.

—Now what in Shit's Heaven do I want to go to the Back with you for? You ain't no Body. Forget it. I'ma kill you.

—Aww no, Bellerina. I have something really big to tell you out there. If you know this you will be Boss of the Girls. You will have the Power.

—What in Shit's Heaven?

—Please come with me. Then you can whip my ass in front of the whole school. Let's run to the Back. Okay? Let's run. Let's run.

Debbie ran across little Tiffany Hammond. Tiffany was in tears, and her brown curls glittered in the sun. "What is the matter, dear child?" Debbie asked. Tiffany said it was all these words she couldn't get on her spelling quiz. She was going to fail third grade. She couldn't even make up a spelling story. She sat on the steps of her apartment and wept perfoundly. Debbie put her arms around Tiffany.

"Let me help you," she said. By magic, Donna came with Shenay. The two of them explained spelling tips to little Tiffany. They taught her how to practice to win. Meanwhile Debbie thought of a story that could put together the words Gather Garnish Gaze Gazebo Generous Generosity Genuine Ghost Gibberish. They read Tiffany's story out loud and they laughed in harmony. Tiffany said, "You saved me from impending doom, all you are geniuses" and they laughed when they realized that Genius was a spelling word too.

Shenay said why don't we start a spelling club at school cause she said girls need to know more spelling words than boys so that they wouldn't be sitting on no steps in the middle of the day crying their goddamn eyes out. "Girls can be strong, Tiffany. Tears ain't always the answer." Shenay said. Donna said that a spelling club would be just fine. Donna said that she had something to discuss with Debbie in private, so goodbye Shenay. Shenay thought a minute to herself. Then she said, "Yeah, Goodbye Girls."

Bellerina and I snuck out the window over the emergency door. I sent Bethi back to her class only I didn't know if she could make it without blabbing. Me and Bellerina walked half the way to the Back. We didn't say a word. We looked over by the handball court and saw the High Schoolers smoking there. They cursed all the time but it didn't sound like the way elementary cursed. It came over elementary lips like bowling balls except Bellerina who it was her natural way of life. High Schoolers could curse up a storm and when it was over, you realized that all they said was hi how you doing? Bellerina waved to her sister standing out there with Big Susie but they didn't notice her. Gimlet had her warm arm around Big Susie's shoulder, and their faces was really next to each other. I felt my secret long heart.

Charlie came out the shack that stood in the corner of the Back. We could see him from half way. Charlie wiped his mouth along the edges with his pointer finger and his thumb. He was big and small at the same time. He waved to us to come. "I'm feeling warm!" he shouted. He was leaning against the shack.

Bellerina looked a bit scared. She turned to me. —So what you want? What you got to tell me?

I swallowed. —Bellerina. I don't want to fight anymore. What is it about me you don't like? I can change! My notebook is only stories. Of how things can maybe be. I am really smarter than people think. I can change! Bellerina!

—I don't like your fucking face. Can you change that?

I also don't like your slobbering re-tard sister. Why she have to stand with us?

I also don't like it you think you are better than me. You think you a Brainiac. Well let me tell you. That's a damn lie. Write that in your damn notebook full of lies. Four Eye Fuck In Liar. You hurt a lot of people with them damn lies. That's what you are.

Bellerina walked away just like that. So my plan had failed. I just kept my head down and my eyes closed. Bellerina walked to the shack. It was a stupid plan when you got right down to it.

I sighed with the future. Your Body never gets used to it. It hurts more each time. I de-test the feeling of hands messing me up. I am a girl made out of brown peel, not iron and steel. I also de-test the eyes. They can mess you in a way that makes you afraid to sleep at night, get up in the morning. The eyes can push you off into a lonely circle, like the circle of me and my sister, like the circle of me. I de-test it all.

Bellerina called back to me—I'ma get you this afternoon. Me and the girls. You better be ready. Drag me out in the cold. You lucky Charlie is here for me.

She went with Charlie in the shack. Charlie said "Dag! Dag!" and I saw other High Schoolers fastwalking there. She had said: I'm his whole world.

Bellerina's sister Gimlet shook her head when she saw Bellerina going in the shack. Big Susie grinned. Gimlet usually doesn't care, even when she swears she will kick anyone's butt who messes with her little sister. She took a puff of cigarillo, down to her feet. She looked and shaked her head. Big Susie laughed, "She's going to get *lit up*."

They were needed again. Little Bobby Lee had fallen off his sister's banana seat bike and was bleeding. Another boy stood near him. "Help!" the big boy cried. Soon a crowd was there. No one was capable of doing nothing. Lucky for them Debbie, Donna and Shenay was speeding on their way to the place.

"What happened?" Debbie asked. The big boy told her. The crowd agreed. Bobby was so clumsy when you weren't looking. His sister was in tears.

Shenay stepped up and looked at the big boy. She waited a moment with eyes that didn't move. She said, "I'm waiting." The crowd growed silent. The sun didn't move from the sky. She said, "I'll wait." The big boy looked. A river of pee ran down his leg and he bawled. "It was not all my fault," he bawled.

Shenay stepped back. The crowd laughed and started smacking the big boy upside his head. Someone held little Bobby Lee in their arms and rocked him to sleep like a scared hummingbird. Shenay stepped back until she was just a speck on the distance.

I sat down on the steps of the handball court, and out the stretch of my eye, I could see the shack at the Back. High Schoolers went in and they stayed. The sky hung blue. Gimlet walked over to me out of nowhere. I had to catch my breathing. I was thinking about burning my notebook. It was just a bunch of stories. A fire would prove something. Or I could take cinder blocks and make a sandwich. That would be better proof.

Gimlet stopped in front of me and said she heard I was going to get my ass kicked. That's what she heard. She looked over at the shack. She shrugged her shoulders. But then she just kept on walking, like the air was not holding her down.

HELEN FISHER

DUMPED!

∽

IT'S AN ODD EXPERIENCE—digging through my back hallway jammed with photos of my twin sister and others of my natal family, my Elvis and Beethoven records, academic treatises on sex, driftwood, vases, trinkets from Sumatra and Easter Island, and my writings of the past thirty years. I found things I had forgotten. "My best?" Well, I rather like the description of my first spring tennis match, written in 1973, and the portrayal of the peeling beach furniture in the workroom where I used to read. That moment when humankind first descended from the trees of ancient Africa and began to "marry" and "divorce," described in *Anatomy of Love*, may be my most vivid narrative. Or perhaps it is my account of how Tia the elephant fell in love with Bad Bull, one of my examples of "animal attraction" in *Why We Love*. But I chose this article, "Dumped!," for a different reason. It isn't laced with the world's great poetry or vignettes of romance among the hunter/gatherers of Africa, as many of my writings are. Nor does it discuss global economic trends and my understanding of women's (and men's) place in the coming business world, for which I have been called America's last optimist. Instead, it proposes my ideas on the nature and evolution of rejection in love.

"Parting is," as Emily Dickinson wrote, ". . . all we need of hell." Being dumped is one of the most painful experiences a human being can endure. And studies show that 95 percent of us will suffer this excruciating sorrow at some point in our lives. This article presents, in a straightforward style, my newest theories on this important topic. And in some ways it reflects my name, Helen. I can honestly say I despised this name until I was recently told what it means, "light." I hope this article sheds some light on this universal facet of human nature.

—Helen Fisher

Emptiness, hopelessness, fear, fury: almost everyone endures the agony of romantic rejection at some point in their lives. Why do we suffer so? Sorrow and anger are metabolically expensive and time consuming. Why didn't humanity evolve a way to shrug off romantic loss and easily renew the quest to find a suitable reproductive partner?

I have been studying romantic love for ten years or so and have come to see it as an evolutionary adaptation. The ability to fall in love evolved because those who focused their courtship attention on a preferred partner saved time and energy and improved their chances of survival and reproduction.

Unfortunately, the same applies to love's darker side. We humans are soft-wired to suffer terribly when we are rejected by someone we adore—for good evolutionary reasons.

Back in 1996 I decided to use a technique called functional MRI to study the brains of men and women who had just fallen madly in love. I and several collaborators, including neuroscientist Lucy Brown of the Albert Einstein College of Medicine in New York and psychologist Arthur Aron of the State University of New York at Stony Brook, asked our subjects, a group of seven men and ten women, to look at a photograph of their beloved projected on a screen just outside the brain scanner. We also showed each participant an emotionally neutral picture—a photograph of an acquaintance for whom they had no positive or negative feelings. In between looking at these photos, we asked each to perform a "distraction task" to wash the mind clean of all emotion.

The resulting scans told us many things about the brain in love. Most significantly, when subjects were looking at their sweetheart, their brain showed increased activity in two regions: the right ventral tegmental area (VTA) in the midbrain, and parts of the caudate nucleus, a large c-shaped region near the center. The VTA is rich in cells that produce and distribute the powerful stimulant dopamine to many areas of the brain, including the caudate nucleus. It is part of the brain's network that controls general arousal, focused attention and motivation to acquire rewards. The regions of the caudate nucleus that became active are rich in dopamine receptors and are also associated with attention and motivation to acquire rewards.

The fact that intense, early-stage romantic passion is associated with areas rich in dopamine suggested to us that romantic love is not, in fact, an emotion, but primarily a motivational state designed to make us pursue a preferred partner. Indeed, romantic love appears to be a drive as powerful as hunger. No wonder people around the world live—and die—for love.

But we weren't interested in just the lovey-dovey side of romance. We wanted to understand every aspect. So in 2001 we began scanning the brains of people who were suffering the trauma of a recent rejection in love.

The study is still in progress, but we suspect we will find continued activity in the VTA and associated parts of the caudate nucleus, largely because lovers keep loving long after they have been spurned. I think we will find much more than that, however. Being rejected in love is among the most painful experiences a human being can endure, so many other brain regions may be involved as well.

Even before the results come in, there is a lot we can say about the biology of rejection which suggests that it is an evolved response with specific functions. Psychiatrists have long divided romantic rejection into two phases: "protest" and "resignation/despair." During the protest phrase, deserted lovers become obsessed with winning back the object of their affections. They agonize over what went wrong and how to rekindle the flame. They make dramatic, often humiliating, appearances at their lover's home or workplace, then storm out, only to return to berate or plead anew. They phone, e-mail and write letters. They revisit mutual haunts and mutual friends. And alas, as the adversity intensifies, so does the romantic passion. This phenomenon is so common in the psychological literature (and in life) that I coined a term for it—frustrated attraction. When romantic love is thwarted, the lover just loves harder.

What brain systems might underlie these odd behaviors? Psychiatrists Thomas Lewis, Fari Amini and Richard Lannon, all of the University of California, San Francisco, have argued that protest is a basic mammalian response to the rupturing of any social tie. They believe it is associated with dopamine, as well as with the closely related neurotransmitter norepinephrine. Elevated levels of both these chemicals lead to heightened alertness and stimulate the forlorn animal to call for help and search for its abandoner—generally its mother.

The rising level of dopamine may help explain the biology of frustration attraction. Since our research suggests that the dopamine system is activated during early-stage romantic love, one would think that as dopamine activity increased during protest the rejected lover would feel even greater passion. And another brain mechanism kicks in during the protest phase that could add to this frustration attraction—the stress system. In the short term, stress triggers the production of dopamine and norepinephrine and suppresses serotonin activity, that heady combination of neurotransmitters that I maintain in my book, *Why We Love*, is associated with romantic love.

But frustration attraction may be due to other brain activities as well. Neuroscientist Wolfram Schultz at the University of Fribourg in Switzerland reported in 2000 that when an expected reward, such as love, is delayed, "reward-expecting" neurons prolong their activities (*Nature Reviews: Neuroscience,* vol. 1, p. 199). These neurons do not make or distribute dopamine, but they are central components of the brain's reward system, the system associated with focused attention and motivation—the very behaviors that characterize romantic love.

What irony! As the beloved slips away, the brain networks and chemicals that most likely create the potent feelings of love increase.

The protest phase of rejection may also trigger activity in the brain's panic system. Neuroscientist Jaak Panksepp of Bowling Green State University in Ohio believes that this brain network generates the well-known "separation anxiety" response in infant mammals abandoned by their mother. When their mother leaves, infants become troubled. They express their alarm with a pounding heart, sucking gestures and distress calls.

Yet another brain system often becomes active as one protests against the departure of a lover: anger. Even when the departing lover severs the relationship with honesty and compassion, and honors social and parental obligations, many rejected lovers swing violently from heartbreak to fury. Psychologist Reid Meloy of the University of California, San Diego, calls this reaction "abandonment rage." I use a different term: "love hatred." Whatever you call it, it's a curious reaction. Hate and rage don't generally entice a lover to return. Why does love turn to hate?

At first I assumed that hate was the opposite of love. But it isn't. The opposite of love is indifference. Moreover, it occurred to me that love and anger might be linked in the brain, and indeed they are. The basic rage network is closely connected to centers in the prefrontal cortex that anticipate rewards, including the reward of winning a beloved. In fact, experiments in animals have shown how intimately these reward and rage circuits are intertwined. Stimulate a cat's reward circuits and it feels intense pleasure. Withdraw the stimulation and it bites. This common response to unfulfilled expectations is known as the "frustration-aggression hypothesis."

So romantic love and love hatred are probably well connected in the brain. And when the drive to love is thwarted, the brain turns passion into fury.

Why did our ancestors evolve brain links that enable us to hate the one we cherish? Rage is not good for your health: it elevates blood pressure, places stress on the heart and suppresses the immune system. So love hatred must have evolved to solve some crucial reproductive problems. Among these, I now believe that it developed to enable jilted lovers to extricate themselves from dead-end love affairs and start again.

Abandonment rage also motivates people to fight for the welfare of their offspring. This certainly occurs in divorce proceedings: men and women who are otherwise well adjusted turn vicious to get the best deal for their children. In his book *Why We Hate*, science writer Rush Dozier tells of a judge who regularly presides over child custody cases and trials of violent criminals, and reports that he is much more worried about his personal safety during the custody cases. He and other judges have even installed panic buttons in their chambers in case arguing spouses become violent.

Sadly, abandonment rage does not necessarily extinguish love. In a study of 124 dating couples, psychologists Bruce Ellis of the University of Canterbury in New Zealand and Neil Malamuth of the University of California, Los Angeles, found that romantic love and feelings of anger are independent, and can operate simultaneously. Hence, you can be terribly angry but still be very much in love.

Eventually, however, the jilted lover gives up. Then he or she must deal with new forms of torture: resignation and despair. Drugged by the potent liquor of sorrow, they cry, lie in bed, stare into space, drink too much or hole up and watch TV. Feelings of protest and anger or the desire for reconciliation sometimes resurface, but mostly they just feel deep melancholy. In 1991, sociologists at the University of California, Los Angeles, assessed 114 people who had been rejected by a sweetheart within the previous eight weeks. More than 40 percent of them were clinically depressed. Of these, 12 percent were suffering moderate to severe depression. Some people even kill themselves, and some die of a broken heart. Psychiatrist Norman Rosenthal of Georgetown University in Washington, D.C., has reported that broken-hearted lovers can expire from heart attacks or strokes caused by their depression.

Resignation and despair are well documented in other mammalian species. When infant mammals are abandoned by their mother, first they protest and panic. Later they slump into what psychologists call the "despair response."

Despair has been associated with several different networks in the brain. One is the reward system. As the abandoned partner realizes that the expected reward will never come, the dopamine-making cells in the midbrain scale down their activity. And diminishing levels of dopamine produce lethargy, despondency and depression. The stress system also plays a part. As the stress of abandonment wears on, it suppresses the activity of dopamine and other potent neurotransmitters, contributing to feelings of depression.

Like abandonment rage, the despair response seems counterproductive. Why waste time and energy moping? Some scientists now believe that depression evolved millions of years ago as a coping mechanism. Theories on this subject abound. One I particularly like has been proposed by anthropologist Edward Hagen of Humboldt University in Berlin, biologists Paul Watson and Paul Andrews of the University of New Mexico in Albuquerque and psychiatrist Andy Thomson of the University of Virginia in Charlottesville. They argue that the high metabolic and social cost of depression is actually its benefit: depression is an honest, believable signal to others that something is desperately wrong. It is a cry for help which compels stressed people to request support in times of intense need.

Imagine a young woman living in a Paleolithic tribe whose mate openly mated with another woman. First she protested, grew angry and tried to persuade her partner to give up his lover. She also appealed to her friends and kin for help. Unable to influence her mate or relatives with words or tantrums, however, she became depressed. Eventually her despondency motivated her family to drive out her unfaithful partner and console her until she could recover her vitality, find a new mate and start contributing food and childcare again.

Depression is evolutionarily advantageous for another reason: it gives you insight. Depressed people suffer what psychologist Jeffrey Zeig of the Milton H. Erickson Foundation in Phoenix, Arizona, calls a "failure of denial," allowing them to make honest assessments of themselves and others. Severe depression can push a person to face unpalatable truths and make difficult decisions that ultimately promote their survival and reproductive success.

Not everyone suffers to the same degree, of course. Still, we human beings are intricately wired to suffer when we have been rejected by a loved one, and for good evolutionary reasons. I believe romantic love is one of three primary mating drives. The sex drive evolved to enable our ancestors to seek intercourse with any remotely appropriate individual. Romantic love developed to enable our forebears to focus their attention on preferred partners, thereby conserving precious mating time and energy. And long-term attachment evolved to motivate mates to rear their babies as a team. So falling in love is one of the most important (and powerful) things we do; it profoundly affects our social and genetic future.

As a result, we are built to suffer terribly when love fails—first to protest the departure and try to win the beloved back, and later to give up utterly, dust ourselves off and redirect our energy to fall in love again. We are likely to find evidence of any combination of these myriad motivations and emotions as we examine the rejected brain in love.

AL FRANKEN

From RUSH LIMBAUGH
IS a BIG FAT IDIOT

THIS IS ONE OF my favorite pieces because it was my son's idea. Joe was ten at the time, and, as I was putting him to bed one night, he asked me about the book. He had a funny idea. Instead of a standard introduction, why not introduce the book with a "book report" about the book itself?

Joe had never read a book review, but that's really what he meant. From there it was a short leap to an angry review written by a sour Jeane Kirkpatrick, and then my letter of complaint chastising the *Times* for assigning the review to a former lover.

After the book came out, someone sent Bob Dornan a faxed copy of the "review," leading him to believe that Jeane Kirkpatrick had described him as "dangerously unstable" in *The New York Times Book Review*.

Dornan later told me that at the '96 Republican National Convention he was seated in the VIP seats next to Ambassador Kirkpatrick and asked her why she had written that. Outraged, she explained that not only was the "review" not real but that I had claimed that we had been lovers!

I ran into Kirkpatrick a few months later at a brunch at John McLaughlin's house. We were both at the buffet table and there was no ignoring each other. Within a minute or so, she grudgingly admitted the piece was funny and gave me one of those pretty smiles I remember from when we were seeing each other.

—Al Franken

1

Book Review

January 7, 1996

RUSH LIMBAUGH IS A BIG FAT IDIOT AND OTHER OBSERVATIONS

By Al Franken
288 pp. Delacorte Press:
$21.95

by Jeane Kirkpatrick

IT REMAINS a mystery why the *New York Times* would ask me to review this dreadfully foul little book. I am an expert on geopolitical strategic paradigms, not on the sort of cheap, mindless mockery that seems to be Mr. Franken's forte. It is almost as if this were the result of some awful mistake by the *Times*. Why, for example, would humorist P. J. O'Rourke be assigned this very same week to review Nigel Hodgeson's wonderful tome *The Falkland Islands War—Six Hundred Years in the Making*? Is it possible that because O'Rourke and I have the same agent, some simple mix-up occurred? Perhaps P.J., our agent, or I should have tried to sort this out. But I have simply been too busy trying to slog through this repugnant collection of vile, unfunny essays.

Rush Limbaugh Is a Big Fat Idiot

and Other Observations is not just unfunny. It is confused. While Mr. Franken decries "the loss of civility in public discourse," he himself is a most egregious offender, not just calling Rush Limbaugh "a big fat idiot," but Newt Gingrich "a big fat jerk," and House majority leader Richard Armey "a big dick."

Mr. Franken seems to want to have it both ways, criticizing Limbaugh for "demonizing" those who disagree with him, but all the while attacking *his* enemies with invective and scurrilous assertions that remain totally unproven. For example, nowhere in the 288-page screed does Franken actually show any real evidence that Limbaugh is indeed fat. There is not one footnoted reference concerning Limbaugh's body weight, and Mr. Franken seems to be relying on sheer guesswork. Indeed, on page 45, he refers to Limbaugh as "a three-hundred pound blimp," while on page 117, he refers to a "size-78 suit squeezing Rush's some six-hundred pound frame like so much sausage casing." Which is it? Three hundred or six hundred?

One begins to wonder if Franken isn't just inventing things

out of whole cloth. After a careful reread of *The Bell Curve,* nowhere in its 800-plus pages did I find Murray and Herrnstein refer to jazz as "the music created by morons." And similarly, Newt Gingrich's Contract with America did not "promise to make it easier to sue for divorce a spouse with cancer."

Occasionally Mr. Franken does succeed to amuse. When discussing the Senate Banking Committee's Whitewater investigation, he writes, "Having Al D'Amato lead an ethics investigation is like asking Bob Dornan to head up a mental health task force." I must admit that one made me chortle; Bob Dornan *is* dangerously unstable. Yet only thirty-seven pages later Mr. Franken, for all intents and purposes, *repeats* the joke. "Having Al D'Amato lead an ethics investigation is like asking *Ross Perot* [my emphasis] to head up a mental health task force." Again, funny. But which is it? Bob Dornan or Ross Perot?

As one labors through *Rush Limbaugh Is a Big Fat Idiot and Other Observations* one quickly concludes that Mr. Franken chose the title simply as a craven device to attract readers. Yes, the book's opening essay *is* "Rush Limbaugh Is a Big Fat Idiot." But in it Mr. Franken negates the whole premise of his book, when in referring to Limbaugh's enormous success, he writes: "All right. I guess Limbaugh is not an idiot. But you have to admit, he's big and fat."

In fact, one of the author's goals seems to be to draw Limbaugh into some kind of public feud, as if that would enhance the sales of his book. Calling Limbaugh "a fat bully" who is "too scared to engage in open debate with anyone other than pre-screened callers," Franken gratuitously taunts the talk radio host: "Limbaugh is able to attack women and keep the audience's sympathy for one reason and one reason only. He is clearly a sad, fat loser wounded by a pathetic history with the opposite sex." Again, Franken offers no proof, other than to cite that Limbaugh met his third, and current, wife on CompuServe.

Will Limbaugh rise to the bait? Franken seems to hope so, writing on page 187, "I hope he rises to the bait." Even so, Franken admits that Limbaugh would probably prevail in a one-on-one encounter. Franken, who insists that Bill Clinton is "by far" our best post-war President, admits to being a part of "the fuzzy-headed liberal-middle" and that mano-a-mano he would be no match for Limbaugh's clearheaded, "well thought out," right-wing doctrine. "Besides, I'm a comedian," is his weak defense. Franken's plan, as revealed in his chapter "I Have Smart Friends," is to lure Limbaugh into a live debate on ABC's *Nightline,* then act sick, getting Michael Kinsley to fill in for him at the last second.

As reprehensible as I found this strategem [my word], I was even more appalled by the flippant, smart-alecky tone of the non-Limbaugh chapters, including one entitled "If Abortions Are Outlawed, Only Outlaws Will Have Abortions." My goodness. If this is the kind of mindless tripe that passes for political satire these days, I fear for this nation!

Letters

He Said, She Said

To the Editor:

It was with great horror that I picked up Sunday's *Times* to see that you had assigned Jeane Kirkpatrick to review my book, "Rush Limbaugh Is a Big Fat Idiot and Other Observations" (January 7). It had been my understanding that in the interest of objectivity your paper has had a long-standing policy of not assigning an author's former lover to review his book. As anyone who was familiar with the Manhattan eighties' club scene knows, Ms. Kirkpatrick and I endured a somewhat stormy and all too public affair during her tenure as our country's U.N. Ambassador. Even then Ms. Kirkpatrick, though my lover, had no discernible sense of humor. In fact, a primary cause of our breakup was her almost obdurate unwillingness to understand irony, an unwillingness which is woefully apparent in her uncomprehending review of my very funny book. Come on! Be fair. Next time get someone who isn't my former lover to review my book!

AL FRANKEN
New York

Ambassador Kirkpatrick replies:

I don't know what this horrible, horrible man is talking about. During the time that I served as ambassador to the United Nations I was far too busy defending the people of America, including (unfortunately) Mr. Franken, against the dark forces of Soviet Communism to cheat on my husband, let alone "go clubbing" (my phrase) as Mr. Franken suggests. After careful examination of my appointment calendars from that period, I admit that I did on one occasion step foot inside Studio 54, but I can assure you that once I saw what was going on in that place, I quickly turned on my heel and left. I can assure you as well that Mr. Franken will be hearing from my attorney, as will the *New York Times*. How on ,earth the *Times* could print his letter and take part in this abhorrent calumny is beyond me.

The editors reply:

It is our policy to allow authors to respond to reviews in the manner they see fit. Since Mr. Franken's claim of an affair between Ms. Kirkpatrick and himself comes down to a matter of "he-said, she-said," we felt the Ambassador's denial was insufficient to prevent us from printing his response. We did, however, edit Mr. Franken's letter, omitting a number of gratuitously lurid descriptions which were entirely irrelevant to his complaint. And, yes, it *is* our policy not to allow a former lover to review an author's book. Our apologies to Mr. Franken.

MARTIN GARDNER

SURPRISE

MY ESSAY ON SURPRISE is Chapter 20 of my confessional, *The Whys of a Philosophical Scrivener*. The book defends what has come to be called "philosophical theism," a belief, independent of any religion, in a transcendent Creator—a belief resting not on logical proofs (there are none) or on empirical evidence (there is none). It rests solely on a mysterious somersault of the will prompted by the heart, not by the head.

The impulse behind this Quixotic "leap of faith" may even have a slight genetic basis. For many eminent philosophers who were compelled to make the leap—Kant, William James, Charles Peirce, Miguel de Unamuno—the leap springs from a profound sense of awe, not far from terror, toward the impenetrable mystery of being. "Why," Stephen Hawking recently asked, "does the universe go to all the bother of existing?" It would be so much simpler if nothing existed at all!

No writer expressed this emotion more strongly than G. K. Chesterton. He called it the central idea of his life. It is also the central idea of mine. In this essay on surprise I did my best to arouse a Chestertonian sense of wonder in the readers of my *Whys*. Consider the Big Bang. In the first few seconds the entire cosmos, including you and me, were potentially *there*, somehow locked into the future interactions of quantum fields and their particles. To an atheist, Chesterton once remarked, "The universe is the most exquisite mechanism ever constructed by nobody."

—Martin Gardner

WHY I CANNOT TAKE THE WORLD FOR GRANTED

We glibly talk of nature's laws
but do things have a natural cause?
Black earth turned into yellow crocus
is undiluted hocus-pocus.

—Piet Hein

Will science someday discover everything? The question is hopelessly blurry, so let's try to sharpen it. If living organisms are no more than complex arrangements of molecules, it is conceivable that biology and psychology will eventually be reduced to physics. And if waves and particles dissolve into mathematical equations, it is conceivable that physics may eventually become a single deductive system. If this ever occurs, will all the laws of physics, and hence all the laws of the universe, become discoverable in principle?

This notion of physics as a formal system is carried to an ultimate extreme in David Hume's *Dialogues Concerning Natural Religion*. In Part IX, Cleanthes is attacking the ontological argument. If God is necessarily existent, he says, may not the universe itself be necessarily existent? "We dare not affirm that we know all the qualities of matter; and for aught we can determine, it may contain some qualities, which, were they known, would make its non-existence appear as great a contradiction as that twice two is five."

In other words, total nothingness is impossible. I have no idea what this could mean. Indeed, if we could know something about matter that would render its nonexistence absurd, that knowledge would solve the superultimate question. I can, however, imagine that, given a small set of axioms (about space, time, matter, logic, and mathematics), all the laws of the universe will follow in the way a theorem follows from the axioms of Euclidean geometry.

Physics seems to me a long long way from this goal, though occasionally an eminent physicist will voice contrary sentiments. In an 1894 speech Albert A. Michelson made the following notorious statement: "The more important fundamental laws and facts of physical science have all been discovered, and these are now so firmly established that the possibility of their ever being supplanted in consequence of new discoveries is exceedingly remote. . . . Future discoveries must be looked for in the sixth place of decimals."[1]

Other famous physicists have made similar remarks. I find in my files a 1931 assertion by Arthur H. Compton that there are only three basic things in the physical universe: protons, electrons, and photons.[2] That was a year before the neutron was discovered. In 1959, in his *Principles of Modern Physics*, Robert B. Leighton wrote: "With the rapid advances that are being made in particle physics, perhaps it is not too much to expect that in a few more decades *all* physical phenomena will be equally well understood."[3] George Gamow once compared the growth of scientific knowledge with a circle that was rapidly expanding on the surface of a sphere. Beyond a certain point the circle begins to shrink.[4] As late as 1971, Werner Heisenberg was talking about the near approach of the day when there would be no more "surprises" in particle physics.[5]

In 1965, Richard P. Feynman expressed the opinion that ours is an age in which the fundamental laws of nature are being discovered, and that this day, like the discovery of America, "will never come again." Of course there will be other tasks, such as exploring the solar system and investigating the way fundamental laws operate on levels such as biology, but the "perpetual novelty" of finding new structural levels cannot go on "say for a thousand years." To this view he gave the following twist:

> It seems to me that what can happen in the future is either that all the laws become known—that is, if you had enough laws you could compute consequences and they would always agree with experiment, which would be the end of the line—or it may happen that the experiments get harder and harder to make, more and more expensive, so you get 99.9 percent of the phenomena, but there is always some phenomenon which has just been discovered, which is very hard to measure, and which disagrees; and as soon as you have the explanation of that one there is always another one, and it gets slower and slower and more and more uninteresting. That is another way it may end. But I think it has to end in one way or another.[6]

Most physicists, I suspect, hold contrary views. For them nature is infinitely inexhaustible, and there will always be wheels within wheels, and wheels outside wheels. Murray Gell-Mann once compared physics to the task of perpetually cleaning out a cluttered basement. No sooner is the basement's outline seen than somebody finds a cleverly hidden trapdoor leading to a vast sub-basement.[7] David Bohm and Stanislaw

Ulam are among those who believe that the universe has infinitely many levels of structure in both directions, toward the large and toward the small.

"Perhaps the pattern will be summed up," said Philip Morrison; "perhaps it will become lost in an endless regress of intricacy. I do not know. But I would bet right now that matter, like logic, is destined to remain forever in part within, and in part without, the reach of any closed form."[8]

In an admirable essay on "The Art of Teaching Science," Lewis Thomas proposes that the best way to interest young people in science is to teach not only what is known, but also what is unknown. There should be "courses dealing systematically with ignorance," with "informed bewilderment." To see science as a great adventure, young minds should be told that "every important scientific advance that has come in looking like an answer has turned, sooner or later—usually sooner—into a question. And the game is just beginning."

> On any Tuesday morning, if asked, a good working scientist will tell you with some self-satisfaction that the affairs of his field are nicely in order, that things are finally looking clear and making sense, and all is well. But come back again on another Tuesday, and the roof may have just fallen in on his life's work. All the old ideas—last week's ideas in some cases—are no longer good ideas. The hard facts have softened, melted away and vanished under the pressure of new hard facts. Something strange has happened. And it is this very strangeness of nature that makes science engrossing, that keeps bright people at it, and that ought to be at the center of science teaching.[9]

Suppose for argument's sake that someday physics will indeed reach the closed form of an axiomatic system. There will still be severe limitations on what science can tell us. For one thing, we could never be absolutely sure that the axioms are permanent. We do not know if they were the same in the far distant past, especially before the big bang, if indeed there was a "before." We do not know if they will be the same in the far future, or if they hold in parallel universes, if there are parallel universes. It may be, as John Wheeler and other physicists have suggested, that many of our basic laws are the result of pure chance events that occurred during the first few seconds of the primeval explosion; that if those events had been slightly different, as they might well have been, some of the fundamental constants of nature would have been different.

For another thing, in a formal system such as Euclidean geometry there is an infinity of theorems to discover, even though they are, in a sense, given by the system's finite axioms and rules. If physics is ever formalized, an infinity of laws could follow, many of which—perhaps an infinity of which—will be beyond the reach of the human species, even though in principle they may be discoverable on the unlikely assumption that the human race has an endless future. The decimal expansion of pi, to give a simple analog, follows inexorably from the axioms of number theory, but no one will ever calculate pi to the last decimal digit because pi *has* no last digit.

Since the discoveries of Kurt Gödel, the situation has become even more hopeless. If physics turns out to be a formal system, or at least describable by one, there will be undecidable laws that can be expressed in the system's language but established only by adopting a new system with new axioms. Physicists may find themselves burdened with an infinite hierarchy of formal systems similar to the infinite hierarchy of such systems in logic and mathematics.

It is hard for me to imagine how any mathematician could be distressed by Gödel's incompleteness theorem. In his marvelous book, *Infinity and the Mind*, Rudy Rucker speaks of how an understanding of Gödel's theorem can hit one like a religious conversion, bringing with it a great feeling of liberation from anxiety. Rucker describes Gödel's laughter as frequent, rhythmic, and hypnotic.[10] I sometimes fancy that God invaded Gödel's mind (note the "God" in his name) for the purpose of letting us mortals in on one of Heaven's transcendent jokes; that even in elementary number theory there are truths we will never know with certainty to be true.

A still deeper limitation of science is built into the nature of all formal systems. At any stage of the game one may ask: Why this particular system? Obviously there is no way to answer if the question is asked about the ultimate system. The only way science can explain a law is to subsume it under a more general law. Suppose that physicists eventually discover one monstrous equation that describes how spacetime gets itself tied into all those fantastic little knots called particles. We could then ask: Why *that* equation? Clearly physics, regardless of how close it gets to bedrock axioms, has to accept the ultimate structure of the universe as something given. It is the nature of the scientific enterprise that it cannot in principle ever answer the superultimate question of why there is something rather than nothing, or even the lesser question of why the something that is our universe has the basic structure it has. The statement that science can in principle discover everything is defensible only when reduced to the trivial tautology that science can discover everything science is capable of discovering.

Anyone who has read this far surely realizes that I believe there are truths totally beyond the reach of science and reason, even assuming an infinite time for the human mind to evolve. I do not mean anything so trivial as whether the cosmos will stop expanding, or whether there are black holes, or if gravity and electromagnetism can be unified, or if there are intelligent creatures on other planets, or whether Fermat's last theorem and Goldbach's conjecture are true. I mean questions that are in principle beyond the capacity of any mind (other than God's) to formulate; truths that lie beyond the farthest rim science is capable of reaching.

Georg Cantor was criticized by some of his unworthy opponents for implying that God did not exist, because in Cantor's transfinite set theory, one can prove there is no highest transfinite number. Cantor not only did not imply this, he did not even believe it. He was a deeply religious man who placed God in a region that transcends all finite and infinite sets. It is because I, too, believe in this "wholly other" realm, a realm in which our universe is an infinitesimal island, that I can call myself a mystic in the Platonic sense.

I am, of course, not arguing a case but only expressing an emotion. It has no agreed-upon name. There is no way you can talk someone into feeling it, any more than you can talk someone into falling in love or liking a piece of music or a type of cheese. Rudolf Otto, the German Protestant theologian, coined the word *numinous* (from the Latin *numen*, meaning divine power) to express this emotion. (The word should not be confused with Immanuel Kant's *noumena*, which refers to the unknowable realities behind the *phenomena* of our experience.) For Otto, the essence of the emotion is an awareness of what he called the *mysterium tremendum*, the tremendous mystery of the wholly other. Otto did not invent the phrase "wholly other." It is a translation of what Saint Augustine called the *aliud valde*. Two thousand years earlier, the Hindus called it the *anyad eva*, applying it to Brahman, their ultimate God.

For Otto, the sense of the numinous is compounded of feelings expressed by such words as awe, terror, dread, mystery, fascination, astonishment, wonder. If one is a theist, the emotion combines with strong feelings of humility, of the littleness of one's self, of holiness, of gratitude for the privilege of existing. I believe that the degree to which a person feels such emotions is roughly proportional to the strength of that person's faith in God. I know of no great theologians, in or out of any organized religion, who did not have a profound sense of the numinous. It is the secret of the book of Job. It is the emotion that engenders and sustains all the religious faiths of history.

Pantheists vary widely in the degree to which they are moved by the numinous. The emotion is understandably weak among those for whom all existence is no more than a dreary repetition of the fields we know. It is strong among pantheists who see the universe as a shadow of some vaster realm, as a world of illusion, the maya of the Hindus. It is strong in Taoism, for the Tao is as far beyond our comprehension as Brahman. It is strong in Spinoza, who, although he had no personal God to whom he could pray, thought of Being as having an infinite number of attributes that transcend human comprehension. The emotion was strong in Albert Einstein, who considered himself a Spinozist.

"The most beautiful experience we can have is the mysterious," Einstein wrote in a passage that is often quoted.

> It is the fundamental emotion which stands at the cradle of true art and true science. Whoever does not know it and can no longer wonder, no longer marvel, is as good as dead, and his eyes are dimmed. It was the experience of mystery—even if mixed with fear—that engendered religion. A knowledge of the existence of something we cannot penetrate, our perceptions of the profoundest reason and the most radiant beauty, which only in their most primitive forms are accessible to our minds—it is this knowledge and this emotion that constitute true religiosity; in this sense, and in this alone, I am a deeply religious man.[11]

The last sentence could almost have been lifted out of Otto's best-known work, *The Idea of the Holy.*

We all know the statement by Sir Isaac Newton, about how he thought of himself as a boy playing on the seashore and diverting himself by now and then finding "a smoother pebble or a prettier shell than ordinary, whilst the great ocean of truth lay all undiscovered before me." Using a less familiar metaphor, Einstein once said to an interviewer:

We are in the position of a little child, entering a huge library whose walls are covered to the ceiling with books in many different tongues. The child knows that someone must have written those books. It does not know who or how. It does not understand the languages in which they are written. The child notes a definite plan in the arrangement of the books, a mysterious order, which it does not comprehend, but only dimly suspects. That, it seems to me, is the attitude of the human mind, even the greatest and most cultured, toward God.[12]

"Madam," said Dr. Lao, "the role of skeptic becomes you not; there are things in the world not even the experience of a whole life spent in Abalone, Arizona, could conceive of." "Human knowledge," Jean Henri Fabre somewhere wrote, "will be erased from the world's archives before we possess the last word that a gnat has to say to us." Substitute *stone* for *gnat* and I think the statement is still true. Jorge Luis Borges recalls an old Buddhist text that says: "If there were as many Ganges Rivers as there are grains of sand in the Ganges and again as many Ganges Rivers as grains of sand in those new Ganges Rivers, the number of grains of sand would be smaller than the number of things *not known* by the Buddha."[13]

One of Hamlet's familiar remarks is that "there are more things in heaven and earth, Horatio, than are dreamt of in your philosophy." It is quoted less often these days than a similar remark by J.B.S. Haldane. "Now, my own suspicion is that the universe is not only queerer than we suppose, but queerer than we *can* suppose."[14] Change *we* to *you* and Haldane's statement is a good summary of what God shouts to Job out of the whirlwind.

Herbert Spencer, more than any other British philosopher who called himself an agnostic or atheist, stressed the mystery of the wholly other. Spencer called it the Unknowable—not the Unknown. It contains all the transcendent truths of Kant's noumena as well as the infinity of other truths totally beyond our grasp. Theodore Dreiser was so taken by the concept of the Unknowable that he closes his novel *The Genius* by reproducing a long passage in which Spencer writes about the mystery of space and the Sartrean "nausea" it arouses in him:

Beyond the reach of our intelligence as are the mysteries of the objects known by our senses, those presented in this universal matrix are, if we may say so, still further beyond the reach of our intelligence, for whereas, those of the one kind may be, and are, thought of by many as explicable on the hypothesis of creation, and by the rest on the hypothesis of evolution, those of the other kind cannot by either be regarded as thus explicable. Theist and Agnostic must agree in recognizing the properties of Space as inherent, eternal, uncreated—as anteceding all creation, if creation has taken place. Hence, could we penetrate the mysteries of existence, there would still remain more transcendent mysteries. That which can be thought of as neither made nor evolved presents us with facts the origin of which is even more remote from conceivability than is the origin of the facts presented by visible and tangible things. . . . The thought of this blank form of existence which, explored in all directions as far as eye can reach, has, beyond that, an unexplored region compared with which the part imagination has traversed is but infinitesimal—the thought of a space, compared with which our immeasurable sidereal system dwindles to a point, is a thought too overwhelming to be dwelt upon. Of late years the consciousness that without origin or cause, infinite space has ever existed and must ever exist produces in me a feeling from which I shrink.[15]

Here is atheist Bertrand Russell in one of his rare numinous moods: "I want to stand at the rim of the world and peer into the darkness beyond, and see a little more than others have seen of the strange shapes of mystery that inhabit that unknown night. . . ." That was from a letter Russell wrote when he was in prison during the First World War.[16] Later, in a philosophical book, he wrote: "But if there be a world which is not physical, or not in space-time, it may have a structure which we can never hope to express or to know." Russell hastens to add that he has now "lapsed into mystical speculation," and will say no more because by the very nature of the case there is nothing more he can *say*.[17]

George Santayana, another honest atheist, admired Spencer's concept of the Unknowable, and occasionally allowed himself to report on this region. "A really naked spirit," he wrote, "cannot assume that the world is thoroughly intelligible. There may be surds, there may be hard facts, there may be dark abysses before which intelligence must be silent for fear of going mad."[18] Do you not sense, behind that casual remark, Santayana's awareness of the *mysterium tremendum*?

H. G. Wells, another atheist (aside from his momentary flirtation with a finite God), also had occasional glimpses of the tremendous mystery. His most numinous writing is a section on "Ultimate Truth" in *The Work, Wealth and Happiness of Mankind*:

> It may be that we exist and cease to exist in alternations, like the minute dots in some forms of toned printing or the succession of pictures on a cinema film. It may be that consciousness is an illusion of movement in an eternal, static, multidimensional universe. We may be only a story written on a ground of inconceivable realities, the pattern of a carpet beneath the feet of the incomprehensible. We may be, as Sir James Jeans seems to suggest, part of a vast idea in the mediation of a divine circumambient mathematician. It is wonderful exercise for the mind to peer at such possibilities. It brings us to the realization of the entirely limited nature of our intelligence, such as it is, and of existence as we know it. It leads plainly towards the belief that with minds such as ours the ultimate truth of things is forever inconceivable and unknowable. . . .
>
> It is impossible to dismiss mystery from life. Being is altogether mysterious. Mystery is all about us and in us, the Inconceivable permeates us, it is "closer than breathing and nearer than hands and feet." For all we know, that which we are may rise at death from living, as an intent player wakes up from his absorption when a game comes to an end, or as a spectator turns his eyes from the stage as the curtain falls, to look at the auditorium he has for a time forgotten. These are pretty metaphors, that have nothing to do with the game or the drama of space and time. Ultimately the mystery may be the only thing that matters, but *within the rules and limits of the game of life*, when you are catching trains or paying bills or earning a living, the mystery does not matter at all.[19]

Commenting on these pages in his autobiography, Wells summarizes:

> I realize that Being is surrounded east, south, north and west, above and below, by wonder. Within that frame, like a little house in a strange, cold, vast and beautiful scenery, is life upon this planet, of which life I am a temporary speck and impression. There is interest beyond measure within that house; use for my utmost. Nevertheless at times one finds an urgency to go out and gaze at those enigmatical immensities. But for such a thing as I am, there is nothing con-

ceivable to be done out there. Ultimately those remote metaphysical appearances may mean everything, but so far as my present will and activities go they mean nothing.[20]

Nothing? Observe how quickly Wells, like Russell, dismisses the *mysterium tremendum* as unworthy of worship or prolonged contemplation.

Among recent philosophers John Dewey seems to me the outstanding example of an atheist for whom a sense of the numinous was minimal. I have been unable to find a single passage in all of Dewey's writings that strikes me as a memorable expression of wonder about the mystery of being. Nothing seems ever to have mystified Dewey. Never, so far as I can recall, did he see anything tragic or comic or absurd about the human condition. We are all organisms interacting with our environment, and that's that. I suggest it is this almost total absence of a sense of mystery in Dewey, and a sense of the comic, that makes his writing so incredibly dull. Who can read him anymore?

I find in my files a reference to a letter in *The New Leader* in which someone complains of Dewey's lack of a sense of wonder. I have saved only the published reply, a letter from Corliss Lamont. On the contrary, says Lamont, Dewey had a "keen awareness of the awesome and grand totality of the cosmos." To prove it, Lamont quotes the following passage from Dewey's *A Common Faith*:

> The community of causes and consequences in which we, together with those not born, are enmeshed is the widest and deepest symbol of the mysterious totality of being the imagination calls the universe. It is the embodiment for sense and thought of that encompassing scope of existence the intellect cannot grasp. It is the matrix within which our ideal aspirations are born and bred. It is the source of the values that the moral imagination projects as directive criteria and as shaping purposes.[21]

I rest my case. If this is the most numinous statement Lamont can find in Dewey's books (and I have not found a better one), it testifies to Dewey's remarkable uninterest in the wholly other. Indeed, as Lamont recognizes, the purpose of *A Common Faith* was to redefine *religion* and *faith* so that all feeling for the supernatural would be eliminated. In this respect Dewey is a type of the practical down-to-earth person who finds metaphysical speculation a waste of time. I do not mean someone who recognizes there are no rational or empirical ways to solve metaphysical puzzles, but one who seems never to be troubled by the puzzles. Greatly as I admire Rudolf Carnap for his contributions to the philosophy of science, I find him akin to Dewey in this respect. Both men recognized the mystery that envelops all scientific knowledge, yes, but emotionally they were low in metaphysical awe. In Richard Burgin's *Conversations with Jorge Luis Borges*, Borges recalls a highly intelligent woman he once knew who was incapable of getting anything out of the books by Bishop Berkeley and William James that he gave her:

> She didn't see why people should be poring over things that seemed very simple to her. So I said, "Yes, but are you sure that time is simple, are you sure that space is simple, are you sure that consciousness is simple?" "Yes," she said. "Well, but could you define them?" She said, "No, I don't think I could, but I don't feel puzzled by them."

Unlike most atheists and agnostics, Borges is perpetually astonished by the world, even though he is not sure there is a God, even though he professes no desire to live again. The majority of men and women, and especially women, he told Burgin (I do not go along with Borges in distinguishing between the sexes here), take the universe for granted:

> They never wonder at anything, no? They don't think it's strange that they should be living. I remember the first time I felt that was when my father said to me, "What a queer thing," he said, "that I should be living, as they say, behind my eyes, inside my head, I wonder if that makes sense?" And then, it was the first time I felt that, and then instantly I pounced upon that because I knew what he was saying. But many people can hardly understand that. And they say, "Well, but where else could you live?"[22]

No modern writer lived with a more pervasive sense of ontological wonder, of surprise to find himself alive, than Gilbert Chesterton. Surely it is one reason why Borges was so fond of GK's poetry and fiction. In his autobiography Chesterton accurately calls it "the chief idea of my life" and defines it as not taking the world for granted, but taking it with humility and gratitude. It is to see everything, even the most common thing, as something both unexpected and undeserved. "The only way to enjoy a weed is to feel unworthy even of a weed."[23] All the evils of the world are a small price to pay for the privilege of existing.

One could assemble a large volume of excerpts from GK's books in which he plays beautiful and amusing variations on this theme of enjoying the world the way a happy child enjoys it, as something miraculous. It would include Chesterton's preface to an edition of Job. It would include that refreshing rhapsody to order in the opening chapter of *The Man Who Was Thursday*. An anarchist poet maintains that order is dull, that disorder is the soul of poetry. Why do the riders on the London subway look so sad and tired? "It is because they know that the train is going right. . . . It is because after they have passed Sloane Square they know that the next station must be Victoria, and nothing but Victoria. Oh, their wild rapture! oh, their eyes like stars and their souls again in Eden, if the next station were unaccountably Baker Street!"

Nonsense, replies Gabriel Syme. "The rare, strange thing is to hit the mark; the gross, obvious thing is to miss it. We feel it is epical when man with one wild arrow strikes a distant bird. Is it not also epical when man with one wild engine strikes a distant station? Chaos is dull; because in chaos the train might indeed go anywhere, to Baker Street or to Bagdad. But man is a magician, and his whole magic is in this, that he does say Victoria, and lo! it is Victoria."

My anthology would include many of Chesterton's short stories, such as "The Unthinkable Theory of Professor Green" in which an astronomer, stricken suddenly by a sense of awe toward ordinary things, delivers a solemn lecture on his discovery of a new planet. As he talks on, it slowly dawns on his learned listeners that he is talking about the earth.[24]

My anthology would include at least two of GK's poems. One of them, "The Sword of Surprise," is short enough to quote in full:

> Sunder me from my bones, O sword of God,
> Till they stand stark and strange as do the trees;
> That I whose heart goes up with the soaring woods
> May marvel as much at these.
>
> Sunder me from my blood that in the dark
> I hear that red ancestral river run,
> Like branching buried floods that find the sea
> But never see the sun.

Give me miraculous eyes to see my eyes,
Those rolling mirrors made alive in me,
Terrible crystal more incredible
Than all the things they see.

Sunder me from my soul, that I may see
The sins like streaming wounds, the life's brave beat;
Till I shall save myself, as I would save
A stranger in the street.

The other poem, "A Second Childhood," is so much longer that I shall quote only the first two stanzas. If you don't know this poem, I urge you to look it up in *The Collected Poems of G. K. Chesterton.*[25] I think it is one of the greatest religious lyrics ever written:

When all my days are ending
And I have no song to sing,
I think I shall not be too old
To stare at everything;
As I stared once at a nursery door
Or a tall tree and a swing.

Wherein God's ponderous mercy hangs
On all my sins and me,
Because He does not take away
The terror from the tree
And stones still shine along the road
That are and cannot be.

My book of Chestertonian wonder would include many essays and passages in which GK praised the glory and mystery of ordinary things—*Tremendous Trifles*, as he calls them in the title of one of his best books. And there are those passages in which he combines awe with a sense of absurdity, seeing the pelican as one of God's jokes, seeing men and women as four-footed animals balancing precariously on their hind legs. I find in my GK files a clipping (dated 1945) of the comic strip "Blondie." Dagwood has made one of his giant sandwiches, and while eating it he startles Blondie by reflecting aloud: "Eating is a silly thing. In order to get food into your stomach you've got to push it through your face." The sentiment is pure Chesterton. In *The Napoleon of Notting Hill*, GK describes eating as the stuffing of alien substances through a hole in the head, and somewhere else he sees drinking as pouring liquid through an opening the way one fills a bottle. If he hadn't thought it bad taste he could have written hilarious descriptions of the sex act. A great admirer of Edward Lear and Lewis Carroll, GK often called attention to the role of nonsense in arousing an emotion of spiritual wonder toward the world.

My anthology would be incomplete without the chapter on "The Ethics of Elfland" from *Orthodoxy*.[26] In the spirit of Hume, though Hume is never mentioned, Chesterton argues that all natural laws should be looked upon as magic because there is no logical connection between any cause and its effect. Fairy tales, said GK, remind us that the laws of nature have an arbitrary quality in that they could, for all we know, be quite other than what they are. Maybe the regularities of nature, its weird repetitions, as Chesterton called them, are not logically necessary but exist because God, like a small child is:

> strong enough to exult in monotony. It is possible that God says every morning "Do it again" to the sun; and every evening, "Do it again" to the moon. It may not be automatic necessity that makes all daisies alike; it may be that God makes every daisy separately, but has never got tired of making them. It may be that He has the eternal appetite of infancy; for we have sinned and grown old, and our Father is younger than we. The repetition in Nature may not be a mere recurrence; it may be a theatrical *encore*. Heaven may *encore* the bird who laid an egg.

This way of viewing Nature as sheer magic, which of course implies a Magician, is surely part of the fascination of watching a great conjuror. The art of prestidigitation has been one of the loves of my life, and like Chesterton I find it intimately connected with a love of fantasy fiction. Science reminds us of the reason behind things. Magic and fantasy remind us of the unreason behind things.

> Reason has moons, but moons not hers
> Lie mirror'd on her sea,
> Confounding her astronomers,
> But, O! delighting me.[27]

Conjuring, wrote Max Beerbohm in his novel about a beautiful lady magician, *Zuleika Dobson*, is "an art which, more potently perhaps than any other, touched in mankind the sense of mystery and stirred the faculty of wonder; the most truly romantic of all the arts. . . ." We enjoy seeing a conjuror perform because his counterfeit miracles make us realize that natural laws could easily permit women to float in the air and elephants to disappear. A spectator with a sense of the numinous leaves the theater with heightened surprise that objects fall when dropped, that stars vanish in the daytime only to reappear mysteriously at night.

You can be sure that Chesterton, like Charles Dickens (who actually performed magic on the stage) and Lewis Carroll, enjoyed seeing magic shows. In fact, GK wrote an unusual play called *Magic*, in which a professional conjuror is the main character. I can easily imagine Wells and Einstein and Santayana sitting entranced through a magic show. It is hard to imagine Dewey or Carnap watching a magician without being bored.[28] Both men, although no doubt they would have agreed that natural laws could be other than they are, saw little value in speculating about such nonsense possibilities. They were like the man from Cadiz in an anonymous limerick:

> There was a young man of Cadiz
> Who inferred that life is what it is,
>> For he early had learnt,
>> If it were what it weren't,
> It could not be that which it is.

To the atheist and positivist the world is what it is. How could it be otherwise? Where else could we live? There is no point in speculating on why it is what it is, because there is no way reason or science can get a handle on the question. Accept the only universe we know. Find out what you can about its structure. Try to be as happy as possible before you vanish back into the Black Hat from which you popped into existence.

Just as knowing how a magic trick is done spoils all its wonder, so let us be grateful that wherever science and reason turn they plunge finally into stygian darkness. I am not in the least annoyed because I do not understand time and space, or consciousness, or free will, or evil, or why the universe is made the way it is. I am relieved beyond measure that I do not need to comprehend more than dimly the nature of God or an afterlife. I do not want to be blinded by truths beyond the capacity of my eyes and brain and heart. I am as contented as a Carnap with the absence of rational methods for penetrating ultimate mysteries.

Must we conclude, then, that all metaphysical speculation is futile? A metaphysician asks this question in one of Raymond Smullyan's wry dialogs, and a mystic answers as follows:

> Oh, not at all! It is sometimes absolutely necessary to bat one's head against a stone wall trying to use objective methods which cannot possibly work before one sees for oneself the necessity of direct introspective methods. Metaphysics is essentially one giant koan, not for an individual, but for the human race as a whole—a koan whose purpose is to force the realization of the impossibility of metaphysical methods being pushed any further. Stated otherwise, metaphysics is the necessary ripening process of the human race to prepare it for mysticism.[29]

I agree with Smullyan—for the mystic's voice is his. There *are* no metaphysical methods. There is no rational way to approach God—or, as Smullyan would prefer to say, the Tao—except inwardly. As for the heart's leap that leads to theism, I confess again that I do not know why some people are compelled to make it and others find it impossible. I do not even know if a sense of the numinous is essential for such a leap.

In the second Oz book, when Tip brings a wooden sawhorse to life with Mombi's magic powder, the creature is more surprised than Tip. "He rolled his knotty eyes from side to side, taking a first wondering view of the world in which he had now so important an existence." Have none of the quotations in this chapter aroused in you, patient reader, a similar sense of surprise and wonder? Have you never felt amazed to find yourself not only living in an Ozzy world but, more incredibly, aware of the fact that you are alive? Are you capable of identifying with the Sawhorse when he says, in the third Oz book, "A creature like me has no business to live"?

If you are looking puzzled and shaking your head, that small cave-like region in which you are so mysteriously hiding for a time—and for so brief a time!—then my book of *Whys* is not for you. After all, where else could you hide?

NOTES

1. The lecture is reprinted in Albert A. Michelson's book *Light Waves and Their Uses* (1903). However, Michelson attributed the remark about the search for new decimal places to an "eminent physicist," and no one seems to know who he had in mind. Robert Millikan, in his *Autobiography* (1950), says he thinks it was Lord Kelvin, and adds: "Later, in conversation with me, he [Michelson] was to upbraid himself roundly for this remark." (See Stephen Brush's letter, "Romance in Six Figures," *Physics Today*, January 1969, page 9.) It was only a few decades after Michelson's speech that the paradoxes of relativity and quantum mechanics introduced depths of previously unimagined richness.

2. Arthur H. Compton's remark is quoted in *The University of Chicago Magazine*, February 1931, page 191.

3. Robert B. Leighton, *Principles of Modern Physics* (1959).

4. I was unable to locate the source of Gamow's statement about the expanding circle, but here is a similar remark from an article of his in *Physics Today* (January 1949) that I found quoted in William H. Whyte, Jr.'s *The Organization Man* (1956):

> It seems to me that our science definitely shows signs of convergence, although this statement can also be easily classified as wishful thinking. We see, nevertheless, from our analysis, that in the field of microphenomena there is only one big region remaining to be explored: the theory of elementary length in its relation to the problem of elementary particles.

5. My source for Werner Heisenberg's remark is an interview by Walter Sullivan in *The New York Times*, December 13, 1971. Heisenberg said he agreed with Plato that the ultimate constituents of matter are ideal mathematical forms. The notion of an infinite complexity of smaller and smaller entities, going on forever, he called an "old-fashioned" and "foolish idea." On these philosophical grounds he expressed skepticism about the reality of quarks, and questioned the advisability of building more powerful atom smashers, because, in Sullivan's phrasing, "the ultimate has probably been reached in probing the innermost sanctum of matter."

6. Richard P. Feynman, *The Character of Physical Laws* (1965).

7. Murray Gell-Mann is quoted in *Time*, January 2, 1960. "In the village of World's End," writes Lord Dunsany (in his *Book of Wonder*, 1912),

> at the furthest end of Last Street, there is a hole that you take to be a well, close by the garden wall, but if you lower yourself by your hands over the edge of the hole, and feel about with your feet till they find a ledge, that is the top step of a flight of stairs that takes you down over the edge of the World. "For all that men know, those stairs may have a purpose and even a bottom step," said the arch-idolator, "but discussion about the lower flights is idle." Then the teeth of Pompo chattered, for he feared the darkness, but he that made idols of his own explained that those stairs were always lit by the faint blue gloaming in which the World spins.

8. Philip Morrison's remark is in his article "Science May Beggar Predictions," *The New York Times Annual Educational Review*, January 12, 1970.

9. Lewis Thomas, "The Art of Teaching Science," *The New York Times Magazine*, March 14, 1982.

10. Rudy Rucker, *Infinity and the Mind* (1982).

11. From Albert Einstein's essay "What I Believe," in *Forum and Century*, Vol. 84, 1930, pages 193-194; reprinted in the thirteenth of the *Forum* series, *Living Philosophies* (1931).

12. I copied this from a deteriorating newspaper clipping that I failed to date or identify. Peter Michelmore, in his *Einstein, Profile of the Man* (1962), gives almost the same quotation. He attributes it to an interview by George Sylvester Viereck, published in Viereck's *Glimpses of the Great* (1930).

13. Dr. Lao's statement is in *The Circus of Dr. Lao* (1935), by Charles Finney. I do not know the source of the Fabre quote. The Buddhist text is given by Jorge Luis Borges in a footnote to his essay "From Someone to Nobody," in his *Other Inquisitions: 1937-1952* (1964).

14. From J.B.S. Haldane's essay "Possible Worlds," in his book of the same name (1928).

15. Eugene Witla, the artist and protagonist of Dreiser's novel, reads this passage ("the sanest interpretation of the limits of human thought I have ever read," he says to himself) from *Spencer's Facts and Comments* (1902). For Spencer's fullest discussion of the Unknowable, see the first section of his *First Principles* (1862).

16. I have copied this from a newspaper clipping, but I do not know where the letter was printed.

17. Bertrand Russell, *Some Problems of Philosophy* (1927), retitled *Philosophy* for its United States edition, Chapter 24.

18. From George Santayana's address "Ultimate Religion," published in his *Obiter Scripta* (1936).

19. H. G. Wells, *The Work, Wealth and Happiness of Mankind* (1931).

20. Wells's *Experiment in Autobiography* (1934), Chapter 5, section 2.

21. I failed to date my clipping of Corliss Lamont's letter. The passage he quotes from John Dewey (to which I added the paragraph's final sentence) can be found in the last chapter of *A Common Faith* (1934).

22. Borge's remarks are in the first chapter of Richard Burgin's *Conversations with Jorge Luis Borges* (1969).

23. *The Autobiography of G. K. Chesterton* (Sheed and Ward, New York, 1936), pages 90-91, 132, 341-350.
    In his life of Samuel Johnson (April 15, 1778 section), Boswell records an interesting conversation between Johnson and a lady about the fear of annihilation at death.

Although a person who does not exist obviously can feel no pain, reasoned Johnson, "It is in the apprehension of it that the horror of annihilation consists." "Mere existence," he said, "is so much better than nothing, that one would rather exist even in pain, than not exist." Miguel de Unamuno often recalled his childhood fears of hell, when he took the doctrine of eternal punishment seriously, and how even then he found the prospect of life in torment preferable to ceasing to exist.

24. The story about Professor Oliver Green is in Chesterton's *Tales of the Long Bow* (1925).

25. *The Collected Poems of G. K. Chesterton* (1932).

26. The chapter derives from an earlier essay, "A Fairy Tale" (1906), that was one of the weekly columns Chesterton wrote for the London *Daily News*. The column is reprinted in Chesterton's posthumous *Lunacy and Letters* (1958), edited by Dorothy Collins. Admirers of "The Ethics of Elfland" will find the column much worth reading.

27. "Reason," a one-stanza poem by the British poet Ralph Hodgson. It is surely in one of his books, but I have not tried to run it down.

28. Perhaps this is unfair to both Dewey and Carnap. Charles W. Morris, a philosopher whose views were close to, and strongly influenced by, Dewey and Carnap, not only loved conjuring but actually performed magic semiprofessionally in his youth. However, Morris's philosophy had a romantic side, a passionate interest in Maitreyan Buddhism. In temperament he was closer to Charles Peirce (who invented several unusual mathematical card tricks) than to Dewey or Carnap.

29. "When the Time is Ripe—," the last essay in Smullyan's book *The Tao Is Silent* (1977). The passage could almost have been written by either of the two German fideists and opponents of Kant: Johann Georg Hamann and Friedrich Heinrich Jacobi. Both men praised Hume's skepticism as having demonstrated the inability of reason to solve any fundamental metaphysical question, thereby preparing the way for unencumbered faith.

LAURIE GARRETT

A HIDDEN KILLER
in CAJUN COUNTRY

SHORTLY AFTER I RETURNED from Zaire, having spent a month there covering the Ebola virus outbreak of 1995, one of my *Newsday* colleagues started calling me "Germ Lady." To his possibly twisted delight, the moniker caught on and I carried the unsought label for years. I don't mind, of course: Few things in the world from my perspective can possibly be as important as the global HIV/AIDS pandemic and its twin epidemics of tuberculosis and drug resistant malaria.

Still, I would hope writers and readers see greater dimension in my work than the nickname "Germ Lady" would describe.

I started my career as a general science correspondent for National Public Radio, covering everything from quarks to quinine, particle physics to pollen particulates. And though the microbes have always held a special interest for me, there have been stories far afield from virology and microbiology that elicited my intellectual "Wow Factor" and touched my heart.

Back in 1990, when I'd only been a newspaper reporter for about a year and a half, I was on the phone with a source at Tulane University in New Orleans, yammering about primate research. As an aside she mentioned a recent, rather curious discovery that involved a rare genetic disease, Cajuns in rural western Louisiana, Jews, and Catholics. That combination caught my attention. I was on a New Orleans-bound plane a couple of days later.

I spent many emotionally charged days in Louisiana's Cajun country, falling in love with the people and their culture. It was a dangerous romance, peppered with seductive Zydeco music, fattening but irresistible cuisine, delicious linguistic patois, intriguing history, and terrible tragedy. Maintaining reportorial objectivity, especially when looking at dying babies, proved nearly impossible. My youthful talents were sorely tested, and the Cajun people generously gave of themselves, helping me to hone my craft as they shared their deepest secrets and fears.

Several days into my Cajun sojourn an athletic young man who had spent his entire life within a fifty-mile perimeter of Lafayette suddenly interrupted our interview about his family to ask, "Are you Jew? Wha's a Jew? You Jew?"

His question was so earnest and naive that I smiled, saying, "No, I'm not Jewish. But I live in New York, City, which is arguably the most Jewish place in America, and I know some Yiddish."

"Yiddish? Wha's that?"

And so I, a fifth-generation Los Angeleno of Irish/Scot/Croatian descent, found myself explaining Hebrew history, the Torah, and Lenny Bruce to a Catholic man whose Acadian ancestors were forced out of France in the seventeenth century and had, for generations, ventured few miles from their original Louisiana settling point. With apologies to all my Jewish friends, I suspect that to this day there are folks in Cajun country telling Lenny Bruce jokes with a Laurie Garrett accent.

—Laurie Garrett

Three-year-old Brentan Brown was so sick he couldn't crawl, talk or even hold up his head. It was a condition so well-known that generations of Cajuns had dubbed the victims "lazy babies" because life just seemed to drain away.

So on a hot July day in 1985, Michelle and Greg Brown placed their son on the back seat of their mini-van and drove an hour through the sparsely populated farms of rice, soybeans and crawfish to see a neurologist in the nearest big city, Lafayette.

"When we went in his office the first question he asked was, 'Are any of you Jew?'" Michelle, now twenty-nine, said. "My husband and I looked at each other.

"We're Cajuns," Michelle replied. "French-Canadians, maybe a little French-French, a little German."

The doctor explained that Brentan had Tay-Sachs, an incurable and fatal disease caused by a gene rarely seen in anyone other than Ashkenazi Jews. It runs in families so, Michelle was told, "your son is the first of many more you're going to see in the area with Tay-Sachs."

Four years later, that medical forecast has turned into tragic truth. That diagnosis was just the first of a string of events that rocked the small, self-proclaimed capital of Cajun country literally all the way back to its roots.

Since that diagnosis, Brentan and at least one other child have succumbed. Two more are fighting for their lives, including Jordan

McClelland, two and a half, who was discharged from the hospital after more than ten days battling double pneumonia. His parents believe it is their unshakable faith in God that is keeping their baby alive despite Tay-Sachs.

Genetic tests show that members of some families are six times more likely to carry the gene for Tay-Sachs than anyone else known in the world. For religious and political reasons, abortion, the only way aside from abstinence to prevent the spread of the disease, is just not an acceptable option for the region's Roman Catholics and Christian fundamentalists.

"I don't believe that it's a Jewish disease any more," said Renee Abshire, whose daughter Maigon died of Tay-Sachs in 1989. "It's a Cajun disease."

Things used to be easy in this farming town of 1,250 people who pride themselves on their French heritage, the spicy cuisine, zydeco music and the distinct patois passed from ancestors exiled from Nova Scotia by the British in the late 1700s.

"Everything revolves around family and food," said Dr. Glenn Bourne, a local pediatrician. "Whether it's barbequing or roasting a pig or boiling crawfish—that sense of closeness and family is probably the most important thing to the people of southwest Louisiana."

Children seldom leave. Despite high unemployment and few career opportunities, young adults marry and settle in because they can't imagine leaving the all-embracing Cajun lifestyle. "You don't believe what I say?" one older woman bragged. "Well, you just come by and taste my etouffee—then you tell me if you want to leave. I guarantee you, you stay."

Mayor-elect Gerard Frey agreed. Most people simply marry their high school sweethearts. "Everybody in Iota is kin."

Which, of course, is why the Tay-Sachs problem exists, said Dr. Emmanuel Shapira, of Tulane University of New Orleans, who diagnosed two of the local cases.

"In these little communities you find people stayed and intermarried for generations," leading to a higher prevalence of other rare genetic disorders, he said. Throughout southwest Louisiana unusual disorders can be found, particularly among Cajuns. Ushers Disease, Maroteaux-Lamy Syndrome and Charcot-Marie-Tooth Disease—all, like Tay-Sachs, metabolic disorders that cause painful and early death—have been diagnosed near Iota.

Shapira is the top genetic sleuth in Louisiana and found many of the diseases hidden among Cajuns. He came to the United States some two decades ago from Israel and retains his Hebrew accent.

Knowing his reputation, three Iota-area mothers with sick babies drove three and a half hours last spring to his Hayward Genetics Center to urge Shapira to begin general genetic testing.

In July, Shapira and his team arrived here. "We wanted to see: Is it a problem of three or four families, or is it a problem of a whole community? That was the question we had to answer," he said.

The scientists were surprised by the size of the crowd that filled the Knights of Columbus Hall as Mayor Robert Walker set the example by rolling up his sleeve so that blood could be drawn. After using up all of his 230 test kits, Shapira said he had to turn away a still sizable crowd.

The results were even more surprising. Shapira said that an average of 7.5 percent of the 230 are carriers of the Tay-Sachs gene. Among those related to one of the four Tay-Sachs babies, a startling 17 percent carry the gene.

Even among residents who do not believe that they share any common ancestor with a Tay-Sachs family, an astounding 3.5 percent turn out to be carriers. The highest previously known Tay-Sachs carrier rate was 3 percent, seen in isolated communities of Ashkenazi Jews around the world. Iota's rate "is without a doubt the highest in the world," Shapira said.

Children are born with Tay-Sachs if they inherit a defective gene from each parent. Inheriting one gene means the child is a healthy carrier. Inheriting both genes is a death sentence.

Tay-Sachs babies are barely functional, lacking an enzyme, beta-hexosaminidase-A, a chemical vital to the proper breakdown of fats stored in the brain and nerve cells. Because fats accumulate in their brains, the babies eventually become blind, deaf, paralyzed, demented and have frequent seizures. Symptoms usually appear in the sixth month of life when the children are listless. They rarely survive to their fourth birthdays.

When Brentan Brown was diagnosed, Michelle Brown said she thought her family was unique among Cajuns. Then, Renee Abshire called in late 1987, "You don't know me but I'm from [nearby] Lake Charles and I have a little girl with Tay-Sachs."

In December, 1988, Abshire met Gail McClelland, another local woman whose son, Jordan, had just been diagnosed with Tay-Sachs. "We started talking about it the minute I walked in her house and I stayed all night crying and talking with Gail," Abshire recalled. "The next day we went to Brentan's funeral."

Since then, another Tay-Sachs case has surfaced in Lafayette—the parents are originally from Iota, as are Renee's husband, David, and the other women. At least one member of each of the four couples had attended Iota High School, which graduates about one hundred students each year. Everyone sensed Iota was the link, no one could figure out how.

At first, it seemed logical to assume the Cajuns carried a previously seen, although even rarer, type of Tay-Sachs found in some French-Canadians. But, Dr. Miriam Blitzer, of the University of Maryland Medical School, who was working with Shapira, analyzed the deoxyribonucleic acid (DNA) of some residents and found they have the classic mutations found in Ashkenazi Jews.

Despite the scientific evidence, there were no records indicating that Jews had ever lived in the area. In fact, archives at the prestigious and authoritative New Orleans Historic Collection adamantly state, "There is no positive documentary evidence known that any Jew came to Louisiana during the early years of the colony," and, no Jew even set foot in New Orleans until at least the nineteenth century.

On the day Shapira began his tests, Dr. Philip Fabacher, an obstetrician, was in town from his distant home in Shreveport to visit his great-aunt, Lucille Fabacher Gravot. He later said he found the puzzle "positively delightful." Twenty-one years earlier, while attending Iota High School, Fabacher started tracing local family trees as a class project. "And it just became a sort of obsessive hobby," he said. "I never thought any of this would be useful."

Fabacher plowed through his records and found the missing links. "I've been able to trace most of the Iota carriers back to four brothers and sisters who married three brothers and a sister and their uncle back in 1780," Fabacher said.

The families, the Millers and the Meyers, were in-laws, and all of their children shared a common ancestor, Abraham Edelmeier, a farmer from a town called Palatinate, Germany, that, together with the villages of Worms, Spire and Mainz, were known among Jews in the eleventh century as Ashkenaz. Edelmeier's son, Johann Adam, left his war-ravaged land in 1720 on one of seven ships commissioned on behalf of the French king by Scotsman John Law, whose charge was to settle the Louisiana territory, "with 4,000 persons and 6,000 negroe slaves." Law's ship logs state the passengers included "French as well as German and Jews."

Although records list Johann Adam Edelmeier as Catholic as early as 1724, he almost certainly was an Ashkenazi Jew and most likely brought the Tay-Sachs gene with him, according to Fabacher and Shapira. Edelmeier would have had ample reason to hide his Jewish origins. In 1724, King Louis XV issued Le Code Noir, a set of edicts primarily aimed at regulating the slave trade and defining the colony's races.

But, the code's first article orders the king's officers "to chase out" of Louisiana "all Jews who have established their residence there, whom, as declared enemies of the Christian faith, We command to get out within three months upon penalty of the confiscation of their persons and property."

Edelmeier was not baptized as a Catholic until 1743, the year King Louis XV reaffirmed Le Code Noir.

Edelmeier moved to Iota, then called Pointes aux Loupes. His grandchildren settled in and married locally, eventually becoming the Miller and Meyer families. The Miller family had three boys and one girl. The Meyers had three unmarried sisters. In an area so sparsely populated that intermarriage was virtually the only option available, the two families simply merged. Fifty years later, their descendants intermarried with the Acadian, or Cajun, settlers, and today the most common Iota-area surnames are French.

"It's very difficult to find any family in Iota who wasn't traceable back to intermarriage back there," Fabacher said. "They're all at some point connected to that pedigree."

Shapira said the Iota Cajuns brought to mind the story of the ten lost tribes of Israel. "According to legend those tribes are behind something called the Sambatyon River. Well, I figure they spelled it wrong—it should have been spelled M-I-S-S-I-S-S-I-P-P-I.

"So that's what I'm doing here in New Orleans—looking for the lost tribes of Israel."

Having a Jewish ancestor is not something that most of Iota ever thought about. No one remembers there ever being a Jew around and Jewish culture is completely foreign. "No one seems to say anything about the Jewish, really," Michelle Brown said. "It's just something that has come upon us and we have to live with it. And right now, it really doesn't matter where it comes from, we can't do anything about it anyway. It's here."

Frey, who takes over as mayor in January, shrugged. "Now we're going to find out that some of these Cajuns have Jewish histories. Cajuns aren't prejudiced, they're caring, generous, open people. So I don't expect this will be a problem."

The gene, however, is a problem in their eyes because of the disease. It is only in the past thirty years that anyone has maintained reliable birth and death records. Older residents tell of generations of "lazy babies," listless children who died in their first three years of life.

"I had a child when I was sixteen with a girl I was dating in high school," said Kurt McClelland, husband of Gail. "He died before his first birthday with a strange disease nobody could put a finger on. After he died, my grandmother told me about 'lazy disease,' and said there were lots of 'lazy babies' in her day," he said.

Kurt's mother, Grace Quebodeaux McClelland, her brother and sister, mother and uncle were tested and were found to carry the Tay-Sachs gene. Grace McClelland remembers that her brother and sister also had "lazy babies" that died in the late 1930s.

Another of Iota's senior citizens, Lucille Fabacher Gravot, said, "Long ago children had that, people didn't know what it was. But I definitely heard about 'lazy babies' when I was young." Gravot's nephew, Fabacher, found an unusually high incidence of child mortality going back well into the eighteenth century, when baby deaths often went unrecorded. His search through records shows that births were recorded but that the babies often disappeared from later censuses, presumably because they had died in infancy.

Last month, Shapira mailed letters to the 230 Iota residents who were tested, informing them of their genetic status. He explained Tay-Sachs is a recessive genetic trait, and a baby will only have the disease if both parents pass on the gene. Because each parent carries two genes—one Tay-Sachs, one normal—a baby has a 50 percent chance of being a healthy carrier and a 25 percent chance of being a healthy noncarrier, even if both parents carry a copy of the gene.

"They are going to Las Vegas with 75 percent win odds, 25 percent lose odds," Shapira said. "Those are terrific—I'd love to play with those odds."

Many Iota residents don't think 3-1 odds is worth betting on.

"If we find out we both have it, we won't have children," said Dorla Frey, Gerard's wife. She missed her chance to be tested by Shapira and now is scared to the point of tears. "It will be devastating because I'm twenty-seven. I feel God hasn't decided to bless me with children yet, but I want to bear a child. It scares the hell out of me."

It also has put the rest of the town on edge.

As residents gathered at the Iota High School polling booth on Election Day, Michelle Brown entered with two-year-old daughter Megan. "Is that one healthy," one woman whispered behind Brown's back. When the rambunctious Megan jumped to the floor and scampered over to one of her cousins, the woman was visibly relieved. She then asked aloud if anyone knew someone who had tested positive for the gene.

"I hear all the LeJeunes have it," one woman said.

"No. That's not true. But there's the Legers and the Poussons—they got it," another asserted.

Marcus LeJeune, a physical education teacher at Iota High School, was relieved when his test came back negative for the Tay-Sachs gene, but is "amazed at how many relatives are positive." Around the high school a handful of teenagers were tested; all are relieved to learn they don't carry the gene.

Both seventeen-year-old Todd Fruge, the high school's star quarterback, and his girlfriend, Kay Cart, tested negative, and they said they weren't worried about Tay-Sachs. Todd's real worry was carrying the Iota Bulldogs all the way through the state championship. They entered the playoffs in mid-November after a 10-0 season.

There's no privacy in small-town Louisiana. Everybody knew who got to sit on the 50-yard line—and everybody now knows who came up positive in Shapira's test. Fingers are already being pointed, guilt cast and family tensions aggravated.

"My granddaughters just found out they both carry the gene," Gravot said. "They're scared to death. They're in their twenties and they don't have any children yet."

She said she is angry because her daughter-in-law, the granddaughters' mother, refuses to be tested. "She's a LeJeune, you know," Gravot says, raising her eyebrows.

One of Greg Brown's brothers is a carrier, but his other brother and sister have so far refused testing. "They're bozos. I think they're crazy. That's something that I consider dangerous," he said.

David Abshire's entire family refused to be tested, despite having witnessed the suffering and death of his daughter, Maigon. When asked about his family's obstinance, Abshire slowly shakes his head.

"But most people in the community of Iota are just crying out for them [Shapira's group] to come back and test everybody," Renee Abshire said. "Now people know, 'Hey, my cousin might carry the gene, what about me?' And they want to know how far it branches, and if it branches outside Iota, maybe all over Cajun country."

Shapira plans to return to Iota later this winter to lecture residents about the significance of his findings. He will teach the people about their odds of having a Tay-Sachs baby, Shapira said, by playing cards. "See? I flip up a card and say, 'What are the chances this is an ace? If you're afraid of having an ace, do you throw out the whole deck of cards?' That's how I teach human genetics."

Shapira also would like to return to do a large-scale genetic screening, and to conduct tests in nearby communities. "We have opened a Pandora's box that we did not expect. We must see this through," he said.

But Shapira needs financial support from the state to test the 5,000—perhaps 100,000—Cajuns who might wish to know if they are Tay-Sachs carriers.

"What kind of numbers do we have to have to get a federal program or state program going to screen people and educate them in Louisiana?" asked Kurt McClelland. "What do we have to do, have an outbreak of thousands of these kids?"

The state health officer, Dr. Louis Trachtman, said in New Orleans that his agency is "looking into the problem but has no immediate plans and aren't required by Louisiana law to do such testing." Furthermore, he said, it is unlikely Louisiana would support such screening because it might promote abortion.

In the Ashkenazi Jewish community, Tay-Sachs is considered a genetic success story because only a handful of Tay-Sachs babies are born each year, because of genetic testing and abortion.

Nancy Pousson, in her late twenties, had a daughter who died from an undiagnosed genetic disease that may also affect future children.

"People say, 'Look at the fetus; if it's diagnosed as having Tay-Sachs, well, just don't carry it any further,' " she said. "Well, we don't

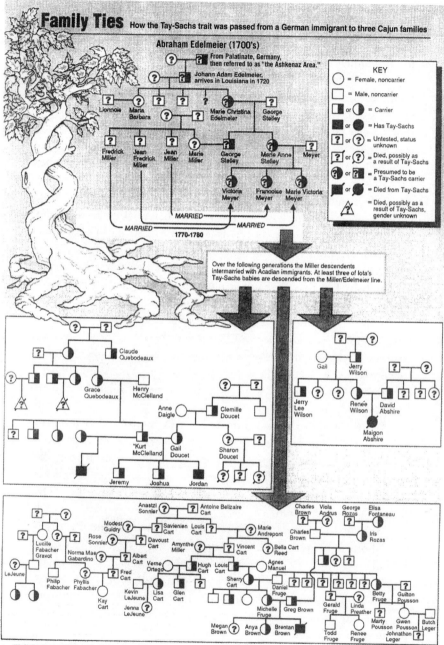

Family Ties
How the Tay-Sachs trait was passed from a German immigrant to three Cajun families

Abraham Edelmeier (1700's)
From Palatinate, Germany, then referred to as "the Ashkenaz Area."
Johann Adam Edelmeier, arrives in Louisiana in 1720

KEY

- ○ = Female, noncarrier
- ☐ = Male, noncarrier
- ◑ or ◐ = Carrier
- ■ or ● = Has Tay-Sachs
- ? or ⦵? = Untested, status unknown
- ?̸ or ⦵?̸ = Died, possibly as a result of Tay-Sachs
- ◐̸ or ◑̸ = Presumed to be a Tay-Sachs carrier
- ■̸ or ●̸ = Died from Tay-Sachs
- ⚠ = Died, possibly as a result of Tay-Sachs, gender unknown

Lionnois — Maria Barbara — Marie Christina Edelmeier — George Stelley

Fredrick Miller — Jean Fredrick Miller — Jean Miller — Marie Miller — George Stelley — Marie Anne Stelley — Meyer

Victoria Meyer — Francoise Meyer — Marie Victoria Meyer

MARRIED
MARRIED — MARRIED
1770-1780

Over the following generations the Miller descendents intermarried with Acadian immigrants. At least three of Iota's Tay-Sachs babies are descended from the Miller/Edelmeier line.

Claude Quebodeaux

Grace Quebodeaux — Henry McClelland

Anne Daigle — Clemille Doucet

*Kurt McClelland — Gail Doucet — Sharon Doucet

Jeremy — Joshua — Jordan

Gail — Jerry Wilson

Jerry Lee Wilson — Renée Wilson — David Abshire

Maigon Abshire

Anastzi Sonnier — Antoine Belizaire Cart — Charles Brown — Viola Andrus — George Rozas — Elisa Fontaneau

Modest Guidry — Savienien Cart — Louis Cart — Marie Andrepont — Charles Brown — Iris Rozas

Lucille Fabacher Gravot — Rose Sonnier — Davoust Cart — Amynthe Miller — Vincent Cart — Bella Cart Reed

LeJeune — Norma Mae Gabardino — Albert Cart — Verne Ortego — Hugh Cart — Louis Cart — Agnes Manuel

Philip Fabacher — Phyllis Fabacher — Fred Cart — Kevin LeJeune — Lisa Cart — Glen Cart — Sherry Cart — Daniel Fruge — Betty Fruge — Guiton Pousson

Kay Cart — Jenna LeJeune — Michelle Fruge — Greg Brown — Gerald Fruge — Linda Preather — Marty Pousson — Gwen Pousson — Butch Leger

Megan Brown — Anya Brown — Brentan Brown — Todd Fruge — Renee Fruge — Johnathon Leger

Philip Dionisio

*McClelland had a child outside of wedlock that later died.

look at that as a solution. We want to find a cure for it, we don't want to find a termination for a life."

After suffering Maigon's Tay-Sachs, the Abshires—members of the fundamentalist Assembly of God Church—decided not to have any more children, rather than face the abortion issue. They believe their decision best reflects their religious beliefs. "I know probably you're sitting there thinking why in the world are they talking so much about God, but when that is where you get your strength, and that is what you eat and you sleep—when that's your everything, you can't help but give Him the praise and the glory because He's the one. I mean, there is nothing in me—it's totally Him."

But when Michelle Brown, also a member of the Assembly of God Church, was pregnant with Megan, shortly before Brentan died, she went to New York to have her fetus tested at Mt. Sinai. "We had considered abortion, if she came up positive," Brown said. "In my case, with what I'm dealing with, I don't consider it abortion. Look at the life my baby boy lived—that was nothing. No life at all. I just don't consider that abortion."

Bourne, the Browns' pediatrician, tells couples who ask to be screened for Tay-Sachs they must consider abortion. "Anybody who has seen anybody who has gone through Tay-Sachs should make an exception. Look, Louisiana is very pro-life. And I'm definitely pro-life. But this is the time I wouldn't argue. I would consider it justified," he said.

Ted McWhortor runs a nursing services company that has provided twenty-four-hour-a-day home care for all four Tay-Sachs babies in the Iota area. He said insurance companies resist footing the bill, which generally tops $250,000, and the suffering of the families is overwhelming. Even his nurses, he said, have been deeply affected by caring for these children.

"I'd like to see the Catholic church seriously examine this situation," he said. "I don't think the church is ready to deal with this. I'm not sure it can."

McWhortor spoke in Crowley Hospital, where he was visiting two-and-a-half-year-old Jordan McClelland. Heavily sedated to prevent the numerous seizures he suffers most days, Jordan needs a respirator to breathe and an intravenous tube to eat.

Just before Election Day, Jordan was rushed to the hospital with a case of double pneumonia, a common Tay-Sachs complication. The doctor, Michael Quinn, told the McClellands to consider whether they wanted heroic measures taken to keep Jordan alive, hooked to machines.

"We called members of our church, and they joined us at Jordie's bedside," Kurt McClelland said. "We prayed all night long, and when the sun rose, the Lord had kept Jordan with us another day."

"The Lord is going to save Jordan. I have faith," McClelland insisted.

Exhausted, lying on a bed beside his ailing son, McClelland stared at the respirator pumping air into his son's diseased lungs. His wife sat down beside him, and the couple fixed their eyes on the pump as the room darkened at the end of the day.

Two weeks ago, Jordan went home.

MARITA GOLDEN

From MIGRATIONS of the HEART

I HAVE SENT THE opening pages from *Migrations of the Heart*, which I selected because it was my first book and as such holds a special place for me. I chose these pages because whenever I reread this section I feel so much satisfaction that I made my debut with writing this strong. I am conflicted about the idea of choosing my "best," as I like to think I am always journeying toward that elusive goal. I have made peace with the inevitable imperfections in my writing as I have with the imperfections in myself. These imperfections are often the starting point for strong writing and fearless living. I think this excerpt represents my best because it comes from such a deep place within my memory, imagination, soul, and spirit. So much is here—yearning, nostalgia, regret, love—rendered in specific, concrete, and poetic language that, I have been told, pulls the reader into this world—which is really all we writers want to do.

—Marita Golden

My father was the first man I ever loved. He was as assured as a panther. His ebony skin was soft as the surface of coal. The vigorous scent of El Producto cigars was a perfume that clung to him. The worn leather seat of his taxi, a stubborn aroma, had seeped into his pores, and like a baptism the smells rubbed onto me from the palms of his hands.

In school he went as far as the sixth grade, then learned the rest on his own. Part of the rest he bequeathed to me—gold nuggets of fact, myth, legend dropped in the lap of my mind, shiny new pennies meant to be saved. By his own definition he was "a black man and proud of it." Arming me with a measure of this conviction, he unfolded a richly colored tapestry, savored its silken texture and warned me never to forget its worth.

Africa: "It wasn't dark until the white man got there."

Cleopatra: "I don't care WHAT they tell you in school, she was a black woman."

Hannibal: "He crossed the Alps with an army of five hundred elephants."

The Sphinx (pointing with a tobacco-stained index finger to a page in the encyclopedia): "Look at the nose, see how broad it is? That's your nose. That's my nose too."

Bitter, frightening tales of slavery dredged by his great-grand-parents from memories that refused to be mute. Passed to him. Passed to me. And when he recounted the exploits of Toussaint L'Ouverture, pausing to remind me that L'Ouverture meant "The Opener," inside his eyes I saw fire and smoke float over the hills of Haiti, and his voice stalked the room amid the clanging of swords, the stomp of heavy boots.

Our most comfortable stage was his taxicab. On frigid winter Saturday afternoons and warm summer evenings, I rode in the front seat with him. Always, it was an adventure. As much as anything else in his life, my father cherished the look of surprise and unease that invaded the faces of white passengers as he regaled them with quotes from Jefferson, Tolstoy or Frederick Douglass. Pouncing on them unawares with the sharpness of his intellect, he brought their blanched faces from behind *The Wall Street Journal* or *The New York Times.* Their baffled respect, blooming in the form of a generous tip or an awed, "Mister, you're pretty smart," sealed his victory.

Together we visited the homes of women, who plied me with Kool-Aid and cookies and spoke to him in a language of double mean-ings and invisible but obvious desire. Women adored my father. He took them seriously enough to strip his fantasies before them. He lis-tened as intensely as he spoke, and his reactions confirmed the legiti-macy of their dreams. All of his women were like my mother, women who had turned daydream desire into tangible reality through houses, cars, money. All theirs. And, like my mother, these women, who had flexed their muscles in the face of fate and circumstance, looked at him with eyes that said, "I will give this all to you." My father never refused anything. He accepted their allegiance or a loan of money with equal ease as his due. He was a hard, nearly impossible man to love when love meant exclusive rights to his soul. Yet he relied on their steadfast-ness to enhance the improvisational nature of his life. Hearing their screen doors slam behind us as we walked to my father's cab, I trem-bled as though implicated in a crime. For, returning home, I met my mother's worried interrogation and watched her large hands tie themselves in knots after I helplessly nodded in assent when she asked if we'd visited Dorothy or Mamie that day.

My father's friends were men with names like Lucky and Sweets, men whose eyes rendered other verdicts on their lives. I watched them develop potbellies and saw gray sprout at their hairlines as they stood, year after year, before the fire-engine-red Coke machine in Sam's Sunoco gas station, waiting for the number to come out. In a shifting, eternal circle, they parried and joked, voices edgy, cloaked in gruff humor as they stood wondering if 301 or 513 would come out that day and "make them a man." Because of his luck with women and money, they called my father Goldie.

They were not his real friends—they feared him too much. Shuddered in the wake of his determination, which cast consideration aside. And they trembled, windswept and lost, in the face of his poorly hidden belief that he was and always would be better than the rest. Much like the characters who peopled the Africa he created for me, and for whom he felt an unbridled affinity, my father viewed his life as a stage. Those around him were an audience from whom he demanded total loyalty but to whom he gave mere lightning flashes of his soul. And I loved him with blind faith. Could never imagine having to forgive him anything. So when I had to, I could not.

My father grabbed life by the arm and wrestled it into squealing submission. My mother cleared the same terrain with a faith and self-possession that both fueled and ruined some of her dreams.

Greensboro, North Carolina, must have fit her like a coat too small, buttons missing, hem unraveling and torn. The town steeped and cured in humility and patience, could never have imagined her hopes. So at nineteen she fled. One summer night, while her parents and younger brothers slept, she crept out of bed. Crouching on the floor, she retrieved a cardboard suitcase wrapped in string that had been hidden beneath her bed for three days. After pinning a note to her pillow, she walked out into the full-moon night. Standing on the porch, she felt her heart hacking a path out of her chest. Placing the suitcase on the porch, she rubbed her sweating palms on the side of her dress. Crickets echoed in the night air and fireflies illuminated the web of knee-high front-yard grass. And, as on every evening of what had been her life up to then, the pure, heartfelt country silence reached out for her. Struggling out of its grasp, she picked up the suitcase. Licked her lips for courage. And, imagining her mother's face the next morning discovering the empty bed and her wizened hands reaching for the letter, she scurried down the steps. It was 1928 and she was headed north.

Washington, D.C., was as far north as she got. There she settled with a cousin who'd arrived the year before. Her first job was cleaning government office buildings. But soon she discovered more gratifying outlets for her industry. Driven by caution, she scrupulously saved her earnings yet daringly, shrewdly bet small amounts on the numbers. She hit them regularly and plowed the winnings into property. Soon she owned four boarding houses and leased two others, a material affluence which at that time equaled a virtual empire for a black woman. Indeed, my mother was blessed, for she had her own. Each month, when she wrote her parents, she slipped a money order between the pages of the folded letter. And seven years after her arrival in the city dotted with historical monuments and scarred by Jim Crow laws, my mother drove, prosperous and proud, back to Greensboro in her own 1935 Ford.

Her mother sat on the porch in a rocking chair, stringing beans that afternoon. Her feet touched the splintered boards and she set the bowl of beans on the table beside her, stood up and clutched the banister. "Be-*A*-trice, whose car that you drivin?" she called out with only modest interest.

"It's mine, mama," her daughter called back, parking the car before the house with considerable skill.

"Yours?"

"Yes, mama, mine."

My mother was now walking dramatically up the steps to the porch. She wore a dark-purple suit and a hat that resembled a box was perched on her head. Her hands held white gloves and a small brown leather clutch bag.

"You want to go for a ride?" she asked, delighted to be offering such a treat.

Her mother, who had witnessed greater miracles than this every Sunday in church, merely folded her arms and shook her head in disgruntled amazement. "Be-*A*-trice, can't you write your own folks no more? It's been three months since we last heard from you."

If she'd had her way, my mother would have been an actress. Like the best of them, her presence was irresistible. My father used words to control and keep others at bay. For my mother language was a way to reassure and reward. My father demanded loyalty. My mother inspired it in the host of friends whom she cared for and melded into her life. She was a large, buxom woman, with caramel-colored skin and a serene face that gave little indication of the passion with which she imbued every wish, every commitment. Her hands were large, long-fingered. Serious hands that rendered punishment swiftly and breathlessly, folded sheets and dusted tables in a succession of white folks' homes long after she was mistress of several of her own. Hands that offered unconditional shelter and love. In every picture of her there is freeze-framed a look of sadness rippling across her glance, as though there is still just one more thing she wants to own, to do, to know. She wore perfume, fox fur throws casually slung over her shoulders and lamb coats, as though born to wear nothing else. My father confided to me offhandedly once, "When I met your mother I thought she was the most beautiful woman I'd ever seen."

She had been married once before. That husband had loved her with a precision and concern my father could never imagine. But after ten years she divorced him, his spirit routed, mauled by years of drinking into a shape she could barely recognize.

My father was her Armageddon. The thirteen years of their marriage, a music box wound too tight, played an off-key song of separation and reunion. The arguments and fights were nearly always murderous. Sculpted like hot wax around the dry bones of their unyielding wills was a love that joined and informed them of each other in ways that were unbearable and soothing. They fought over my father's women. But mostly, with a special viciousness, over power, symbolized by my mother's property. Her will shimmered with so much eloquence and strength that my father felt duty bound to try to break it. He almost did.

Year after year he insisted the houses be put in his name. Some were, and my father lost them with obscene swiftness, bartering them to pay his own gambling debts. My mother, now more reckless than wise and entrapped and enshrined by her love for my father, lost the rest. She gambled the way she had lived her life—with everything she had. Soon the modest empire dwindled to one house. Like pearls falling to the floor, the houses scattered, rolling across my mother's hopes into unseen cracks and crevices. Finally, irretrievable.

A. M. HOMES

THE FORMER FIRST LADY and the FOOTBALL HERO

ALL TOO OFTEN THERE is a gap between what one aspires to and what one is able to accomplish—this is my best because it is that rare thing—a piece of fiction that on paper matches what I saw in my mind's eye.

I had the idea for the story for more than a year before I was able to begin—I couldn't start until I knew the pitch of the piece in the most musical sense.

The story occurs at the intersection of fact and fiction; what one thinks is made up is likely true and what feels accurate is perhaps the work of the imagination.

In this case, writing about real people, I wanted to be sure to get it right. Taking on the experience of a couple at once so public and so entirely unknowable seemed like both fair game and a violation. If I was going to attempt it, I wasn't going to just make fun of the people involved—that would be too easy; I was going to sympathize/empathize. It is black comedy and it is deadly serious—the funnier it gets the more serious the story becomes.

Not long ago a bookseller told me the story of how someone high up in President Reagan's cabinet came into his store and asked, "Do you know this young woman who's written a story about Ron and Nancy?" The bookseller nodded. "Well," the former cabinet member said, "I don't know how she knows what she knows but it's true. She got it all right." I took it as a high compliment—confirmation from the inside.

—A. M. Homes

The white van accelerates. He is in black, strapped in, seat-belted, shoulder-harnessed, sitting between two men in suits. She, too, is supposed to be in back, but she is up front, next to the driver. Wherever they go, she is always up front—-she gets carsick.

There are escort cars front and rear, small unmarked sedans—white on the West Coast, black on the East.

"Trash day," one of the agents in the back seat says, trying to make conversation. All along the curb are large black plastic trash cans and blue recycle bins. The path is narrow, the van takes the curves broadly, swinging wide, as though it owns the road.

Something happens; there is a subtle shift, a tremor in the tectonic plates below, and the trash cans begin to roll. They pick up speed, careering downhill toward the motorcade.

"Incoming on the right," the agent shouts.

The lead car acts like a tank, taking the hit head on, the trash can explodes, showering the convoy with debris: empty Tropicana containers, Stouffer's tins, used Bounty. Something red gets stuck on the van's antenna and starts flapping like a flag.

"Son of a bitch," she says.

In the lead car, an agent whips a flashing light out of the glove compartment, slaps it down on the roof, and they take off, accelerating rapidly.

The motorcade speeds in through the main gate. Agents hover in the driveway and along the perimeter, on alert, guns drawn.

"The Hummingbird has landed. The package has been returned. We are at sea level." The agents speak into their lapels.

The gates automatically pull closed.

"What the hell was that—terrorists on St. Cloud Road?" she asks.

"Earthquake," the agent says. "We're confirming it now." He presses his ear bud deeper into his ear.

"Are you all right, sir?" they ask, helping him out of the van.

"Fit as a fiddle," he says. "That was one hell of a ride, let's saddle her up and go out again."

His eye catches the shiny red fabric stuck on the antenna. He lifts it off with his index finger, twirling it through the air—bright red panties, hooked on their lacy trim. The underpants fly off his finger and land on the gravel. Whee.

"Where are we?" he asks, kicking gravel in the driveway. "You call this a quarry? Who's directing this picture? What the hell kind of a movie is this? The set is a shambles."

The problem isn't taking him out, it's bringing him back.

"Home," she says.

"Well, it's no White House, that's for sure." He pushes up his sleeve and picks at the Band-Aid covering the spot where they injected the contrast.

Earlier, at the doctor's office, two agents waited in the exam room with him, doing card tricks, while she met with Dr. Sibley.

"How are you?" Sibley asks when she sat down.

"Fine. I'm always fine, you know that."

"Are you able to get out at all?"

She nods. "Absolutely. I had lunch at Chasen's with the girls earlier this week."

There is a pause. Chasen's closed several years ago. "Nothing is what it used to be," she says, catching herself. "How's he?"

Dr. Sibley turns on the light boxes. He taps his pencil against the films. "Shrinking," he says. "The brain is getting smaller."

She nods.

"Does he seem different to you? Are there sleep disturbances? Does he wander? Has he ever gotten combative? Paranoid?"

"He's fine," she says.

Now he stands in the driveway, hands on his hips. Behind him is blue sky. There is another tremor, the ground vibrates, shivers beneath his feet.

"I love that," he says. "It reminds me of a carnival ride."

She puts her arm through his and leads him into the house.

"I don't know what you're thinking," he says, "but any which way, you've got the wrong idea."

She smiles and squeezes his arm. "We'll see." Soledad, the housekeeper, rings a bell.

"This must be lunch," he says when Soledad puts a bowl of soup in front of him. Every day they have the same thing—routine prevents confusion, and besides they like it that way; they have always liked it that way.

If you feed him something different, if you give him a nice big chef's salad, he gets confused. "Did they run out of bread? What the hell kind of commissary is this?"

"What's the story with Sibley?" he asks, lifting his bowl, sipping from the edge.

She hands him a spoon. She motions to him how to use it. He continues drinking from the bowl.

"He doesn't seem to be getting me any work. Every week I see him; squeeze this, lift that, testing me to see if I've still got the juice.

But then he does nothing for me. Maybe we should fire him and get someone new. How about the folks over at William Morris—there has to be someone good there. How about Swifty Lazar, I always thought he was a character." He puts the bowl down.

"Swifty's dead."

"Is he? Well, then, he's not much better than Sibley." He trails off. "Who am I?" he asks her.

"You're my man," she says.

"Well, they certainly did a good job when they cast you as my wife—whose idea was that?"

"Dore Schary," she says.

He nods. "And who am I really?"

"Who would you like to be?"

They sit in silence. "May I be excused?"

She nods. He gets up from the table and heads down the hall toward his office. Every afternoon he writes letters and pays bills. He uses an out-of-date checkbook and one-cent stamps, sometimes a whole sheet on a single envelope. He spits on the back of the sheet of stamps, rubs the spit around, and wraps the letter in postage.

"Would you like me to mail that?" she asks when he is done.

"This one's for you," he often says, handing her an envelope.

"I look forward to receiving it," she says, taking the envelope from him.

Once, a letter was accidentally mailed—a five-thousand dollar donation to a Palestinian Naturalists' Organization—Nude in the Desert.

Every day he writes her a letter. His handwriting is unsteady and she can't always read every word, but she tries.

Mommy—

I see you. I love you always. Love, Me.

He smiles. There are moments when she sees a glimmer, the shine that tells her he's in there, and then it is gone.

"Lucky?" he says.

"Lucky's no more," she says.

"Lucy?"

She shakes her head. "That was a long time ago," she says. "Lucky is long gone."

She gives him a pat on the head and a quick scratch behind the ears. "Errands to run," she says. "I'm leaving you with Philip."

"Philip?"

"The pool boy," she says.

"Is Philip the same as Bennett?" Bennett was his bodyguard and chauffeur from gubernatorial days.

"Yes," she says.

"Well, why don't you just say so? What's all the mystery? Why don't you call him Bennett?"

"I don't want to confuse him," she says.

Philip is the LPN. He fills the daily minder—pill container, doles out the herbal supplements, and gives the baths. The idea of a male nurse is so unmasculine that it sickens her. She thinks of male nurses as weaklings, serial killers, repressed homosexuals.

Philip was Dr. Sibley's idea. For a while they had part-time help, a girl in the afternoons. One afternoon she came home from shopping and asked how he was.

"He have good lunch," the girl said, followed by, "Your husband have very big penis."

She found him in the sunroom with an erection. "Would you look at me," he said.

"Sometimes, as memory fades, a man becomes more aggressive, more sexual," Sibley said. "The last thing we'd want is a bastard baby claiming to be the President's child. Avoid the issue," Sibley advised. "Hire this Philip fellow. He comes highly recommended. Call him the President's personal trainer."

From the beginning, there is something about Philip that she doesn't like—something hard to put her finger on, something sticky, almost gooey, he is soft in the center like caramel.

She picks up the phone, dialing the extension for the pool house.

"Should I come in now?" Philip asks.

"Why else would I call?"

"Philip is going to give you your treatment, and then maybe you'll take a little nap."

His treatment is a bath and a massage. He has become afraid of the shower—shooting water. Every day Philip gives him a treatment.

"Don't leave me here alone," he says, grabbing at the edge of her skirt, clinging, begging her not to leave.

"I can't disappoint the people, now can I?" She pries his fingers off.

"I wouldn't be myself without you," he says rummaging around, looking for something. "Where is my list? My lines? I've got calls to make. Remind me, what's her name, with the accent? Mugs?"

"Margaret Thatcher?" Philip says.

He looks at her for confirmation. She nods.

"See you later," she says.

He picks up the phone. It automatically rings in the kitchen. In order to get an outside line you have to dial a three-digit code.

"Operator," Soledad says, picking up.

"Put me through to Margaret Thatcher," he says.

"One moment, please," Soledad says. She makes the ring, ring sound. "Good afternoon, London here." Soledad mimics an English accent. "America calling," she says, switching back to her operator voice. "I have the President on the line."—"Jolly well, then, put him through," she says in her English accent. "You're on the line, sir, go ahead," she says.

"Margaret," he says, "she's left me, gone for good, now it's just the two of us. Are we on the same team? Are all our soldiers in a line? Are you packed and ready to go at a moment's notice? Is there enough oil? Are we on the same team? Did I just ask you that?"

When she goes, she's gone. She passes through her dressing room, freshens her face, sprays her hair, puts a red suit on, and practically runs out to the car.

Whenever she wants to be seen she wears a red suit—she has a dozen of them: Adolfo, Armani, Beene, Blass, Cassini, Dior, Galanos, Saint Laurent, Ungaro. When she goes out with him, when she goes incognito, she wears pastels. No one looks at an old woman in pastel pull-on pants.

"The Hummingbird is in the feeder." Her agents talk into their lapels.

"Where to?" Jim asks as the gate swings open.

"Let's go down to Rodeo and window-shop. Maybe we'll stop at Saks or Barney's."

Sometimes she has the men drive her to Malibu to clear her head, sometimes she goes walking down Beverly Boulevard, like a tourist attraction. Sometimes she needs to be recognized, reminded of who she is, reminded that she is not the one evaporating.

"Notify BHPD that we'll be in their jurisdiction. Anticipate R&W." They radio ahead. "R&W" stands for the vicinity of Rodeo and Wilshire.

They notify the Los Angeles field office and the local police department just in case. A couple of months ago an old drag queen paraded up and down Rodeo Drive doing a convincing imitation of her, until he asked to use the ladies' room in the Gap and came out with his skirt tucked into the back of his panty hose, flashing a flat ass and hairy thighs.

They pull into the public lot on Rodeo Drive.

The attendant waves the white car away. "Lot full," he says.

"It's okay," one of the special agents says, putting the OFFICIAL GOVT. BUSINESS placard in the window.

She carries a small purse with almost nothing in it: a lipstick, some old Republican Party pens and tie tacks to pass out as little gifts, and a bottle of liquid hand sanitizer. She is one of the few who, with good reason, regrets gloves having gone out of style—too many clammy hands in the world.

A couple comes up to her on the sidewalk. "We're here from Terre Haute," the husband says, snapping a picture of his wife with her.

"We're such big fans," the woman says. "How is the President feeling?"

"He's very strong," she says.

"We voted for you, twice," the husband says, holding up two fingers like a peace sign.

"We miss you," someone calls out.

"God bless," she says.

"I've been hoping you'd come in," Mr. Holmes in the shoe department of Saks confides. He is her regular salesman. "I'm holding some Ferragamos for you—they're on sale." He whispers as though protecting her privacy.

"There's nothing nicer than new shoes," she says, sliding into the pumps. She looks at her legs in the half mirror. "At least my ankles are still good," she says.

"You are very thin," Mr. Holmes says, shaking his head.

For years she was a six, and then a four, and now she's a two. After a lifetime of dieting she is just four sticks and a brain, her thin hair teased high, like spun caramel sugar, hard.

"The shoes are down to one-sixty but with my discount I can get them for you at one-thirty-five."

"You've always been good to me."

He knows enough to have them sent. He knows to put it on

account, not to bring her the bag or the paperwork. She doesn't sign bills of sale or carry bags, and the agents need to keep their hands free.

In Barney's, she stops at the makeup counter.

"Is that really you?" the salesgirl asks.

"Yes." She glances into the magnifying mirror. Blown-up, she looks scary, preserved like something dipped in formaldehyde. "I need something for my skin," she tells the girl.

"I've got just the thing for you," the girl pulls out a cotton ball. "May I?"

She nods. "You may."

"It goes on light." The girl dabs her face with the moisturizer. "But it has enough body to fill in any uneven spots. Your skin is lovely, you must have a good regimen."

"Smoke and mirrors," she says. "Hollywood magic."

The agents look away, their eyes, ever vigilant, scan the room. In Los Angeles, the agents dress down. They dress like golf pros—knitted short-sleeved shirts, sweaters, and permanent-press pants. They keep their guns in fanny packs under their sweaters. Their ear buds are clear plastic, like hearing aids.

"That's lovely," she says. "I'll take a jar."

A woman comes rushing across the store toward her, the agents pull in. "I heard you were here." The woman moves to kiss her on the cheek, they brush the sides of their faces, their hairdos against each other.

"You look fantastic," she says, unable to remember the woman's name—she thinks it might be Maude.

"Of course I do," the woman says. "I'm like a time machine. Every year, I intend to look five years younger. By the time I die I'll look like JonBenet."

"Could I trouble you for an autograph?" someone interrupts, handing her a piece of paper to sign.

A woman standing off to the side pushes her little girl in the First Lady's direction. "Go and shake her hand," she says. "She used to be married to the President of the United States."

The First Lady, practiced in the art of greeting children, reaches out. The child extends a single finger, touching her like she's not quite real, like tagging her—You're it. The little girl touches the former First Lady the way you'd touch something that had cooties, the way you'd touch something just to prove you were brave enough to do it. She touches the former First Lady and then runs.

In Niketown she buys him a pair of aqua socks—they won't fall off the way his slippers do, and he can wear them everywhere: inside, outside, in the bath, to bed. She buys the aqua socks and when she realizes that no one there knows who she is, she leaves quickly.

"That was nice," she says when they are back in the car. She has started to enjoy these impromptu excursions more than official functions. At First Lady events, at library luncheons, disease breakfasts, she is under the microscope. People look at her, checking for signs of wear and tear. She keeps up a good front, she has always kept up a good front. She is careful not to be caught off guard.

"Removed from public view"—that's how they describe him on his Web site. He was removed from public view in 1988, like a statue or a painting. She will not allow him to be embarrassed, humiliated. She will not allow even the closest of their friends to see him like this. They should remember him as he was, not as he is.

Meanwhile, the two of them are in exile, self-imposed, self-preserving.

When she gets home, he is in the backyard with Philip, playing catch with a Nerf football.

"Did you miss me?" she asks.

"Liz Taylor called," he says. "She's not well. I couldn't understand a word of what she said."

Is he making it up—getting back at her for having gone out for an hour? She turns to Philip. "Did Liz Taylor really call? Do I have to call her back?"

Philip shrugs. "I don't know."

"Don't play games with me, Philip. He's not a toy, he's a man. He's a man," she repeats. "How am I supposed to know what's real? How am I supposed to know what the truth is anymore?" She shouts and then storms off to her room.

Philip and the President resume tossing the ball.

"My grip is stronger than it ever was," he says, squeezing the ball, squishing it, not realizing that it's not a real football. "I could never have done that as a young man."

Philip, running for a pass, stumbles over a lounge chair and plunges into the pool.

The President instantly dives in, wrapping his arm around Philip's neck, pulling. Philip, afraid to fight, afraid he will accidentally drown the President, guides them toward the shallow end. Philip climbs out, pulling the President out of the water, the President's arm still wrapped around his neck, choking him.

"They call me the Gripper, because I don't let go."

"I think it was the Gipper, sir. They called you the Gipper, as in 'win one for the Gipper.'"

"Seventy-eight," he says.

"What's seventy-eight?"

"You're the seventy-eighth person I saved. I used to be a life guard," he says, and it is entirely true. "Hey, does that count as a bath?"

She is in her dressing room. It started as a walk-in closet and kept expanding. They broke through a wall into one of the children's bedrooms and then through another into the guest room, and now it is a dressing suite, a queen's waiting room. The carpet is Wedgwood blue, the walls white with gold trim, calmly patriotic, American royal. It is her hideaway, her fortress, command and control. She's got a computer, fax, private telephone lines, and a beauty parlor complete with a professional hair dryer. There's a divan that used to belong to Merv Griffin, photographs of her with everyone—the little lady with the big head standing next to Princess Di, Mikhail Baryshnikov, the Gorbachevs.

In her favorite velour sweat suit, she mounts the contraption—a recumbent bike with built-in screen—she can watch TV, go online, surf the Web, write e-mails, or pedal her way down an animated bucolic country lane.

She needs to be in motion—constant motion. That's one of the reasons they call her the Hummingbird.

She logs on, checking in with her secretary—would she be willing to host a Los Angeles event with the head of the Republican Party? "OK as per N.R.," she types. She reviews a proposed album of photographs and sends a message to the chief archivist at the Presidential Library. "Dig deeper. There is a better picture of me with Raisa, also a nice one of the President and me waltzing. That should be the closing image."

She e-mails the lawyer, the business manager, the White House Alumni Office. Nothing happens without her knowledge, without her approval. She is in communication because he can't be.

Using a series of code words, she moves in further, signing into the First Ladies' Club, a project started by Barbara Bush as a way of keeping in touch; trading helpful hints about difficult subjects such as transition times—when you're not elected, you're not wanted—and standing by your man when indictments come down. They keep each other updated on their special interests, literacy, mental health, addiction, "Just Say No." They all talk about Hillary behind her back—she's a little too ambitious for them. And Hillary doesn't update her weekly "What I Did for the Good of the Country" column, instead just sending impersonal perky messages like "You Go Girl!"

The communications man has her wired up, six accounts under a variety of names—virtually untraceable. This is her solace, her salvation. This is the one place where she can be herself, or better yet, be someone else.

Under the name Edith Iowa she logs into an Alzheimer's support group.

"What do you do when they don't recognize you anymore? 'I know you from somewhere,' he says, looking at me, worried, struggling."

"He asked for more light. He kept asking more light, more light. I turned on every light in the house. He kept saying, Why is it so dark in here? Don't we pay the electric bills? I grabbed the flashlight and shined it in his face—is this enough light for you? He froze. I could see right through him and there was nothing there. Am I horrible? Did I hurt him? Is someone going to take him away? Do I ever say how much I miss him?"

She reads the stories and cries. She cries because she knows what they're talking about, because she lives in fear of the same things happening to her, because she knows that despite everything it will all come true. After a lifetime of trying not to be like everyone else, in the end she is just like everyone else.

When the doctor told them it was Alzheimer's, she thought they'd deal with it the same way they'd dealt with so many things—cancer, the assassination attempt, more cancer. But then she realized that it was not something they'd deal with, it was something she would deal with, alone. She cries because it is the erasing of a marriage, the erasing of history, as though the experiences, the memories which define her, never happened, as though nothing is real.

"How brave you are," Larry King said to her. What choice does she have?

She orders products online, things to make life easier: plastic plugs for the electric outlets, locks for the cabinets, motion detectors that turn on lamps, flood alarms, fold-down shower seats, a nonslip rubber mat for around the toilet, diapers. They arrived at a post box downtown, addressed to Western Industries. She stores them in what used to be Skipper's room. Like preparing for the arrival of an infant, she orders things in advance, she wants to have whatever he'll need on hand, she wants there to be no surprises.

Under her most brazen moniker, Lady Hawke, she goes into chat rooms, love online. The ability to flirt, to charm, is still important to her. She lists her interests as homemaking and politics. She says she's divorced with no children and puts her age at fifty-three.

—Favorite drink?

—Whiskey sour.

—Snack food?

—Caviar.

She is in correspondence with EZRIDER69, a man whose Harley has a sidecar.

—Just back from a convention in Santa Barbara—ever been there?

—Used to go all the time.

—U ride?

—Horses.

—Would love to take you for a spin in my sidecar.

—Too fast for me.

—How about on a Ferris wheel?

She feels herself blushing, it spreads through her, a liquidy warm rush.

—Dinner by the ocean?

EZ is asking her out on a date. He is a motorcyclist, a self-described leather man with a handlebar mustache, a professional hobbyist, he likes fine wines, romance, and the music of Neil Diamond.

"Not possible," she writes back. "I am not able to leave my husband. He is older and failing."

—I thought U were divorced?

She doesn't respond.

—U still there?

—Yes.

—I don't care what you are—Divorced, Married, Widowed. You

could be married to the President of the United States and it wouldn't change anything—I'd still like to take you to dinner.

It changes everything. She looks at herself in the mirrored closet doors, a seventy-seven-year-old woman flirting while riding an exercise bike.

A hollow body, an elected body, a public body. The way to best shield yourself in a public life is simply to empty the inside, to have no secrets, to have nothing that requires attention, to be a vessel, a kind of figurehead, a figurine like a Staffordshire dog.

She goes to the entertainment channel and gets the latest on Brad and Jennifer. They are all in her town, down the road, around the corner. She could summon any of them and they would come quickly, out of curiosity, but she can't, she won't. Like a strange Siamese twin, the more removed he becomes the more removed she becomes.

She changes screen names again—STARPOWER—and checks in with her psychic friends, her astrological soul mates. You have to believe in something and she has always loved the stars—she is a classic Cancer, he is a prototypical Aquarius. Mercury is in retrograde, the planets are slipping out of alignment, hold on, Cancer, hold on. The planets are transiting, ascending—she works hard at keeping her houses in order.

She is pushing, always pushing. She rides for three hours, fifty miles a day. Her legs are skinny steel rods. When she's done, she showers, puts on a new outfit, and emerges refreshed.

Philip has taken him out for an hour. He still gets great pleasure from shaking hands, pressing the flesh. So, occasionally Philip dresses him up like a clown, brings him to random parking lots around town, and lets him work the crowd. In his costume, he looks like a cross between Ronald McDonald and Howdy Doody. It makes the agents very nervous.

"Mommy," he calls when he's back.

"Yes?"

"Come here." He is alone in the bedroom.

"Give me a minute," she says. "I'm powdering my nose."

She goes into the room. He beckons to her, whispering, "There's a strange man over there who keeps talking to me." He points at the television.

"That's not a strange man, that's Dan Rather—you know him from a long time ago."

"He's staring at me."

"He's not watching you, you're watching him. It's television." She goes to the TV and blows a raspberry at the screen. Dan Rather doesn't react. He keeps reporting the news.

"See," she says. "He can't see you."

"Did I like him? I don't think I liked him."

She changes the channel. "You always liked Tom Brokaw."

At twilight, he travels through time, lost in space. Terrified of the darkness, of the coming night, he follows her from room to room, at her heels, shadowing.

"It's cocktail time," she says. "Would you like a drink?"

He looks at her blankly. "Are you plotting something? Is there something I'm supposed to know? Something I'm supposed to be doing? I'm always thinking there's a paper that needs to be signed. What am I trying to remember?"

"You tell me," she says, making herself a gin and tonic.

He wanders off, in search. She stands in the living room sipping, enjoying the feel of the heavy crystal glass in her hand, running her finger over the facets, taking a moment to herself before going after him.

He is in her dressing room. He has opened every drawer and rummaged through, leaving the floor littered with clothing. Her neatly folded cashmere sweaters are scattered around the room. He's got a pair of panty hose tied around his neck like an ascot.

He has taken out a suitcase and started packing. "I've been called away," he says, hurriedly going to and from the closet. He pulls out everything on a hanger, filling the suitcase with her dresses.

"No," she screams, seeing her beloved gowns rolled into a ball and stuffed into the bag. She rushes towards him, swatting him, pulling a Galanos out of his hands.

"It's all right," he says, going into the closet for more. "I'll be back."

Soledad, having heard the scream, charges through the door.

The place is a mess, ransacked.

"Sundowning," Philip says, arriving after the fact. "It's a common phenomena."

"Where the heck are all my clean shirts?" he asks. At the moment he is wearing four or five, like a fashion statement, piled one atop the other, buttoned so that part of each one is clearly visible. "I'm out of time."

"It's early," she says, leading him out of the room. On one of the sites she read that distraction is good for this kind of disorientation. "It's not time for you to go," she says. "Shall we dance?"

She puts on an old Glenn Miller record and they glide around the living room. The box step is embedded in his genes, he has not forgotten. She looks up at him. His chest is still deep, his pompadour still high, though graying at the roots.

"Tomorrow, when Philip gives you your bath, we'll have him dye your hair," she says, leading him into the night.

"I don't want to upset you," he whispers in her ear. "But we're being held hostage."

"By whom?" she whispers back.

"It's important that we stay calm, that we not give them any information. It's good that I'm having a little trouble with my memory, Bill Casey told me so many things that I should never have known . . . Did I have some sort of an affair?"

She pulls away from him, unsettled. "Did you?"

"I keep remembering something about getting into a lot of trouble for an affair, everyone being very unhappy with me."

"Iran Contra?"

"Who was she? A foreign girl, exotic, a beautiful dancer on a Polynesian island? Did my wife know?" he asks. "Did she forgive me? I should have known better, I should not have put us in that position, it almost cost us everything."

She changes the record to something faster, happier, a mix tape someone made her—Gloria Gaynor, Donna Summer. She spins in circles around him.

He looks at her blankly. "Have we known each other very long?"

They have dinner in the bedroom on trays in front of the television set. This is the way they've done it for years. As early as six or seven o'clock they change into their night clothes: pajamas, bathrobe, and slippers for him; a zipped red housedress with a Nehru collar and gold braiding, like a queen's robe, for her. They dress as though they are actors playing a scene—the quiet evening at home.

She slips into the closet to change. She always undresses in the closet.

"You know my mother used to do that," he says while she's gone.

Red. She has a dozen red housedresses, cocktail pajamas, leisure suits. The Hummingbird, the elf, the red pepper, cherry tomato, royal highness, power and blood.

"Why is the soup always cold?"

"So you won't burn yourself," she says.

He coughs during dinner, half-choking.

"Chew before you swallow," she says.

After dinner she pops one of his movies into the VCR. A walk down memory lane is supposed to be good for him, it is supposed to be comforting to see things from his past.

"Do you recall my premiere in Washington?"

"Your inaugural? January 20, 1981?"

"Now that was something." He stands up. "I'd like to thank each and every one of you for giving me this award."

"Tonight it's *Kings Row*," she says.

He gets a kick out of watching himself—the only hitch is that he thinks everything is real, it's all one long home movie.

"My father-in-law-to-be was a surgeon, scared the hell out of me when he cut off my legs."

"What are you talking about?" she asks, offended. "Dr. Loyal never wanted to hurt you," she said. "He liked you very much."

"Where's the rest of me?" he screams. "Where's the rest of me?" He's been so many different people, in so many different roles, and now he doesn't know where it stops or starts—he doesn't know who he is.

"What movie are we in?"

"We're not in a movie right now, this is real," she says, moving his dinner tray out of the way, reaching out to hold his hand.

"What time does the flight get in?"

"You're home," she says. "This is your home."

He looks around. "Oh yeah, when did we buy this place?"

At eight, Soledad comes in with her knitting, trailed by Philip with a plate of cookies, four glasses of milk.

Philip flips on the game and the four of them settle in on the king-sized bed, Philip, the President, she, and Soledad, lined up in a row, postmodern Bob & Carol & Ted & Alice. When the game begins, the President puts his hand over his heart and starts to sing.

"Oh say can you see . . ."

"Did you see that?" Soledad asks him. "He had that one on the rebound."

Philip, wanting to practice his reflexology, tries it on the President. He slips off the President's bedroom slippers and socks.

"Hey, quit tickling me." The President jerks his feet away.

Philip offers his services to her.

"Oh, I don't know," she says. "My feet aren't in good shape. I haven't had a pedicure in weeks." She pauses. "What the hell," she says, kicking her slippers off. He is on the floor at the bottom of the bed. "That feels fantastic," she says after twenty minutes.

Soledad is crocheting a multicolored afghan to send to her mother for Christmas.

"What color next?" she asks the President. "Blue or orange?"

"Orange," the President says.

At night she is happy to have them there; it is a comfort not to be alone with him, and he seems to enjoy the company.

He sits on his side of the bed, picking invisible lint off himself.

"What are you going for there?" Philip asks.

"Bugs," he says. "I'm crawling with bugs."

Philip uses an imaginary spray and makes the spraying sound. Philip sprays the President and then he sprays himself. "You're all clean now," Philip says. "I sprayed you with disinfectant." The President stops picking.

At a certain point he gets up to go to the bathroom.

"He's getting worse," she says when he's gone.

They nod. The slow fade is becoming a fast forward.

He is gone a long time. After a while they all look at each other. "Are you all right?" she calls out.

"Just give me a minute," he says. He comes out of the bathroom with black shoe polish all over his face and red lipstick in a circle around his mouth. "My father used to do this one for me," he says, launching into an old Amos 'n' Andy routine.

"What did you use?" she asks, horrified.

"Kiwi," he says.

"I'm sorry," she says to Soledad, mortified that she is having to watch. Luckily, Soledad is from the islands and doesn't quite understand how horrible it is.

At eleven, Philip puts the rail on his side of the bed up, turns on the motion detector pad on the floor, tucks him in, and they call down to the gatehouse and tell them that the package is down for the night.

"Good night," she says.

"See you in the morning," Soledad says.

She stays up for a while, sitting next to him reading while he sleeps. This is her favorite part of the night. He sleeps and she can pretend that everything isn't as it is, she can pretend this is a dream, a nightmare, and in the morning it will all be fine.

She could remove herself, live in another part of the house and receive reports of his progress, but she remains in love with him, profoundly attached. She doesn't know how to be without him, and without her, he is nothing.

The motion detector goes off, turning on the light by her side of the bed. It is six-thirty in the morning.

"Is this conversation being taped?" He speaks directly into the roses, tapping his finger on the open flower as if testing the microphone. Petals fall to the floor. "Who's there? Is someone hiding over there?" He picks up the remote control and throws it into the billowing curtains.

"Hey, hey," she says, pushing up her eye mask, blinking. "No throwing."

"Go away, leave us alone," he says.

She takes his hand and holds it over the vent.

"It's the air," she says, "the air is moving the curtains."

He picks up the red toy telephone that he carries around everywhere—"just in case."

"I can't get a goddamned dial tone. How can I launch the missiles if I can't get a dial tone?"

"It's early," she says. "Come back to bed." She turns the television on to the morning cartoons, pulls her eye mask down, and crawls back into bed.

He is in the bathroom with the water running. "There's someone around here who looks familiar."

She pops her head in. "Are you talking to me?"

"Yes," he whispers. "That man, I can't remember that man's name." He points at the mirror.

"That's you," she says.

"Look, he waves and I'm waving back."

"You're the one waving."

"I just said that."

She notices an empty bottle of mouthwash on the sink.

"Did you spill your mouthwash?"

"I drank it," he belches. Hot, minty-fresh air fills the bathroom.

In the morning, she has to locate him in time and space. To figure out when and where he is, she runs through a list of possible names.

"Honey, Sweetheart, Running Bear, Chief, Captain, Mr. President."

He stands before her, empty, nonreactive. She sticks a finger first into one ear and then the other, feeling for his hearing aid, they're both in, she plucks one out, cranks up the volume until it squeals.

"I'm checking the battery," she yells. "Can you hear me?"

"Of course I can. I'm not deaf." He takes the hearing aid from her and stuffs it back into his ear, putting it into the ear that already has one.

"Wrong ear," she says, fishing it out. She starts again. "Mr. President, Sir, Rough Rider, Rick, Daddy, Dutch." There is a flicker of recognition.

"Now that sounds familiar."

"Do you know who you are?"

"Give me a clue."

She continues. "Mr. P., Junior, Jelly Bean."

"Rings a bell."

"Jelly Bean?"

"That's me."

"Oh. Jelly Bean," she says, relieved to have found him. "What's new?" She hands him his clothing one piece at a time, in order, from under to outer.

Soledad rings a bell.

"Your breakfast is ready." She urges him down the hall. "Send the gardener in when he gets here," she instructs Soledad as she steps into a morning meeting with Philip and the agents.

"Don't call him Mr. President anymore—it's too confusing. It's best not to use any particular name; he's played so many roles, it's hard to know where he is at any given moment. This morning he's responding to Jelly Bean and talking about things from 1984."

"We're not always sure what to do," the head agent says, "how far to go. Yesterday he cleaned the pool for a couple of hours, he kept taking the leaves out, and whenever he looked away we just kept dumping them back, the same leaves over and over."

She nods.

"And then there were the holly berries. He was chewing on the bushes," the agent says.

"Halle Berry? George and Barbara?" Philip asks.

"The shrubbery—like a giraffe he was going around eating—" The agent stops in mid-sentence.

Jorge, the gardener, is standing in the doorway. He has taken off his shoes and holds them in his hand. He curtsies when he enters.

"Thank you," she says. She takes out a map and lays it on the table for everyone to see. "We need a safer garden; this is a list of the plants—they're all nontoxic, edible."

In the distance there is a heavy thump. The phone rings. She pushes the speakerphone button.

"Yes?"

"The President has banged into the sliding glass door."

"Is he hurt?"

"He's all right—but he's got a bump on his head."

She sends Philip to check on him and she, Jorge, and the agents go into the yard and pace off where the wandering garden will be.

"Everything poisonous has to come out," she says. "Azaleas, birds of paradise, calla lilies, and daffodils. No more holly berries, hydrangea, tulips, poppies. No wisteria. No star-of-Bethlehem."

Jorge gets down on his knees, ready to begin.

She stops him. "Before you get dirty. I need you to put a lock on my dressing room door."

He is in the sunroom with a bag of ice on his face.

"Are you in pain?" she asks. He doesn't answer. "Did you have a nice breakfast?"

Again he belches, mint mouthwash.

"It won't happen again," Philip says, using masking tape to make a grid pattern on the sliding glass door, like a hurricane warning, like an Amish stencil in a cornfield, like the bars of a cattle crossing. "For some reason it works—they see it as a barrier and they don't cross it."

"Soledad, may I have a word?" She refrains from saying more until they are out of the room. "We need to make a few changes."

"I will miss you very much," Soledad says.

"It's time to get the house ready," she says, ignoring the comment, taking Soledad from room to room, pointing out what's not needed, what has to go in order to make life simpler, less confusing, safer.

"Put it away, send it to storage, keep that for yourself, this goes and this goes and this goes. Up with the rug, out with the chair."

They put safety plugs in every outlet, toddler latches on every cabinet. She moves quickly, as though time is limited, as though preparing for a disaster, a storm front of some sort.

"Send someone to one of the thrift shops and get a couple of Naugahyde sofas and some chairs."

"But you have such nice furniture," Soledad says.

"Exactly."

"Are we expecting a hurricane?" he asks, passing through. "I saw the boy taping up the window."

He knows and he doesn't know.

Jorge is in the bedroom, putting a huge combination lock on the dressing room door.

"Do we have any white paint?" she asks George.

"No, Señora."

"We'll need some," she says. "Until then use this." She hands Soledad a bottle of Maalox. "Paint his mirror with it. Use a sponge if there isn't a brush. Put it on thick, so he can't see himself. It may take a couple of coats."

He is alone with Philip. They are in the kitchen, making chocolate chip cookies—slice and bake. The President plays with a hunk of dough, molding it into a dog.

"There are a couple of things I wanted to ask you, if you don't mind."

The President nods. "Go ahead, Tom."

"Who were your heroes?"

"Tarzan and Babe Ruth."

"Who was the most exciting person you ever met?"

"That would have to be Knute Rockne. I used to play ball with him. One hell of a guy."

"And in that whole Iran-Contra thing, what was the bit about using the chocolate cake as a bribe?"

"Funny you mention it." He tilts his head, adopting the interview pose of careful consideration. "I was just thinking about her last night." He pauses. "You know, Bob, America is a country of families, companies, individuals who care about each other. This is another of those unavoidable tragedies, but in the end . . . It's them I worry about, the people who are out there."

"Any regrets?"

"I never walked on the moon. I was a little too old, they gave the part to another fella." He eats a clump of dough. "Listen," he says. "When I come to, everything will be fine, we'll get back on course. We're strong people, Mike, we'll get through."

She is online, catching up. The king of Toda has died and all the first ladies are going to the funeral. She can't leave him alone. "Now's not the time," she e-mails her secretary. "Tell them I have the flu, so no one gets suspicious."

She checks into the Alzheimer's chat rooms.

—Her life must be a living hell. Imagine having everything in the world, all that help, and still you're on a sinking ship.

—She's an inspiration, how gracefully they handled it, and that letter he wrote about going off into the sunset.

-Do you think she even sees him? Does he recognize her? What condition is he in? We never hear a word.

They are talking about her. She is tempted to chime in, to defend herself. She wants to say, I am N.R. and you know nothing about my life.

—Think of all the people she got to meet and all the free clothes. She got a good deal. It's more than enough for one lifetime.

—Got to go, Earl just wet himself. It's one thing when it's a twenty-two-pound infant the size of a turkey; it's another when it's a two-hundred-forty-pound man the size of a sofa.

She pedals faster. She's gone about thirty miles, when EZRIDER69 sends her an instant message.

—Where did you disappear to?, EZ wants to know. Hope I didn't scare you.

—Telephone rang. Long distance.

—Where did we leave off?

—You were taking me for a ride on a Ferris wheel, we were high above it all . . .

There is a knock at her door. She ignores it. It comes again, harder. "What the hell is it?"

The door opens. It's one of the agents. "Sorry to interrupt, but the President has disappeared."

She continues pedaling.

"We can't find him. We've searched the house, the perimeter, and Mike and Jeff are going up and down the block on foot." Mike and Jeff, he says—it sounds like Mutt and Jeff. "Should we call the police?"

She logs off, calmly gets off the bike, and punches the panic button on the wall. They all come running.

"Who last saw him, where, and when?"

"We were baking cookies about twenty minutes ago, the last batch just went into the oven, he said he had to go to the bathroom," Philip says.

"He was in the yard," one of the agents says, "relieving himself against a tree. That was maybe twenty-five minutes ago."

"He's eloped," Philip says. "It happens all the time, they have the urge to go, and then, as if summoned, they're gone."

"How many cars do we have?" she asks.

"The sedan, the van, Soledad's, and mine," Philip says.

"Divide into teams. Philip, you go on foot, I'll go with Soledad, does everyone have a cell phone?"

They quickly get their phones and exchange numbers.

"Those lines aren't secure," the agent says.

"No hysterical calls," she says. "Code name Francine."

She hurries out to the driveway and into Soledad's old red Mercury.

"We can't send you without an agent."

"Your agents can't find my husband," she says, slamming the door, missing the man's fingers by an eighth of an inch.

"We should call the police."

"The last thing we need to do is draw attention to what Keystone cops you are," she says, signaling to Soledad to start the engine.

"I think we're required to by law," one of the younger agents says. "We've never had a President disappear."

"Oh sure we have," one of the older men says. "We just don't talk about it. John Kennedy was gone for seventy-two hours once and we didn't have a clue."

She and Soledad take off. They see Mike down the street, talking to the Bristol Farms deliveryman, and Jeff following the mailman from house to house.

"Take a right," she says, and she and Soledad go up the hill, looking for signs.

Philip moves from door to door with an old glossy head shot. He rings the bell and holds the head shot in front of the electric eye. "Have you seen this man?" he asks, and then repeats the question in Spanish.

It can't end here, with him disappearing, the Amelia Earhart of politics. She is in the car with Soledad, imagining stories of mysterious sightings, dinner parties with him as the prize guest, him being held hostage in a Barcalounger in some faux paneled recreation room. She imagines him being found months later, when they get tired of taking care of him and pitch him out of a car in the Cedars-Sinai parking lot in the middle of the night, dirty and dehydrated.

They come upon a dog walker with eight dogs on eight different leashes, each dog a statement of sorts.

"Have you seen anyone walking around here? We've misplaced an older white man."

The dog walker shakes her head. "No one walks—if they want to walk, they get on the treadmill and watch TV."

They climb up St. Cloud, higher still. She remembers when she first came to Hollywood in the late 1940s as a young actress. She remembers going to parties at these houses, before they were married, when they used to spend evenings with Bill and Ardis Holden, when Jimmy Stewart lived on Roxbury Drive. She recalls the first time she visited Frank Sinatra's place on Foothill Road. She is reading it all now, like a map of the stars' homes.

The air is unmoving, smog presses down, hanging like a layer of dust waiting to fall, sealing them in. Soledad's car doesn't have air-conditioning; they drive with the windows down, it's the first time she's been in real air in years. She is sweating, there's a clammy glow to her skin.

Mike and Jeff wind downhill toward Westwood, UCLA, and Beverly Hills.

"Have you seen Ronald Reagan?"

"You might want to check on the quad—a lot of people were going over there, there's a puppet show or something."

"Ollie-ollie-oxen-free," Philip yells down the street. "Come out, come out, wherever you are. Come on down, The Price Is Right."

The Bel Air police pull him over. "Where do you belong?"

"At 668. I'm the President's personal trainer."

"You're the trainer?"

Philip pulls out his card. "Yes, the trainer. Now if you'll excuse me." He walks on, singing loudly, "hi-de-hi, hi-de-ho."

She is panicked that someone has him, she worries that they won't know who he is, they won't treat him well. She worries that they know exactly who he is and they won't give him back. She worries that he is wondering who he is.

"We had a dog who disappeared," she tells Soledad. "There was something about it that was horrible, the idea that he was out there somewhere, suffering, hurt, lost, wanting to get home and unable to."

"He can't have gotten far," Soledad says.

She has never told anyone, not even herself, but there are times lately when she just wishes it was over. As there is less and less of him, it becomes more painful, and she wishes it would end before he is no longer a man, but a thing, like a potted plant. She imagines making it happen, hastening the process, putting him out of her misery—she can't go on like this forever.

The cell phone rings. It's a conference call from the agents.

"Mike and Jeff are at the circle by the Beverly Hills Hotel. They believe they see Francine. She's out there in the middle of the circle directing traffic and apparently doing a pretty good job of it. They're waving at him—I mean her—and she's waving back. They're parking now and walking over. Yes, we have Francine. Francine has been found."

She is back at the house when the white van pulls through the gate.

He gets out, wearing an orange reflective safety vest.

"Where'd he get that?"

"We don't know."

She puts her hand in his pockets; there's money—singles and a five.

"Did someone take you away? Did someone give you a ride?"

"I got tips," he says.

The Bel Air police pull up with Philip in the back of the car. "Sorry to bother you," one of the cops says.

The agents grab the President, like a mannequin, and protectively pull him behind the van for cover.

"Do you know this man?" the cop asks.

"Has he done something wrong?" she asks.

"He was out, walking and singing, and he has a glossy photo of your husband and, well, we thought he looked a little like John Hinckley."

"He's our trainer," she says.

"That's what he said. And you're sure about that?"

"Quite."

"All right then, I'm sorry." The cop gets out, lets Philip out of the back of the car, and unlocks the handcuffs. "You can never be too careful."

"Of course you can't. Thank you."

"How did he get all the way to Beverly Hills?" Philip asks, when he finds out where they found him.

"I don't think he walked," she says.

She is livid. She wants to take him and shake him and tell him that if he ever does that again she's sending him away, putting him in a home under lock and key.

Instead she goes inside, picks up the phone, and calls Washington. "Head of the Secret Service, please, this is Nancy Reagan on the line."

"Can I have him return?" his secretary says.

"No."

"One moment, please."

The head of the service comes on the line. She reads him the riot act, starting calmly and working her way up. "I don't know what kind of agency you're running . . ." By the time she's finished she is screaming and the man on the other end is blithering. "How many men have you got there? We'll do a full investigation. I'll replace the whole crew. I don't know what to say. Maybe they weren't thinking. Maybe they're burned out."

"Burned out . . . You're supposed to be the best in the world and the man wandered away from his own home." She slams the phone down.

Philip helps him take a shower and change into clean clothing— jeans and a cowboy shirt. Philip has a cowboy hat for him, a toy guitar, and a piece of rope. They are in the backyard doing rope tricks.

"I've upset Mother," he says.

"It's all right, Chief, you gave us all quite a scare."

She is brittle, flash-frozen. And she has a backache. She takes a couple of aspirin and tries to catch her breath.

Later he is in the bedroom, sitting on the floor playing with his toy guitar.

She goes to the padlock, starts spinning the numbers, one to the right, two to the left. She takes a sharp breath, makes an odd sound, turns around, gives him a surprised look—and falls face down on the floor. The sound is like a plank of light wood; there's a distinct snap— her nose breaking, her beak bending to the side.

"The hummingbird is down, the hummingbird is down." The call goes out when Philip finds her.

He rolls her over and attempts CPR. "Someone dial 911—dial 911," he shouts.

"That man is kissing Mother," he says, strumming his guitar.

Philip's breath, his compressions are useless. The paramedics arrive and try to jump-start her. Her body bounces off the floor, ribs snap. They are about to call for backup when Soledad steps forward, living will in hand, and tells them to stop. "No heroic measures," she says. "It's enough."

Soledad calls Dr. Sibley, who arranges for someone to meet them at Saint Johns, and they slide her into a garment bag, and discreetly tuck her into the back of Jorge's gardening truck under a pile of grass clippings. The ambulance stays out front while she is taken out the back. Jorge's Ever Green Gardening Service pulls away just as the news trucks pull up, raising their satellite dishes into the sky.

And he still sits on the bedroom floor strumming the guitar and singing an old cowboy song—"Yippee-ti-yi-yay, get along little dogies, you know that Wyoming will be your new home."

ARIANNA HUFFINGTON

From FANATICS and FOOLS

⁓

THE FOLLOWING SELECTION IS an excerpt from my book, *Fanatics and Fools: The Game Plan for Winning Back America*, which was inspired and informed by the lessons I learned while running for governor in the California recall race. My temporary transformation from pundit to candidate brought me face-to-face with the fact that while criticism and outrage are perfectly legitimate responses to our current political landscape, they are not nearly enough to get us out of the mess we are in—no matter how witty, quotable, or justified. What is needed is a clear, broad, and accessible moral vision that counters the Bush Republicans' messianic vision of a new world built on tax cuts, tax cuts, and more tax cuts. A vision that answers the fundamental question: What sort of America do we want to live in?

The campaign trail taught me that more than laying out clearly articulated policies and a clear critique of your opponent, what is needed is a powerful narrative. And to take back America from the GOP fanatics who now occupy the White House, that narrative must be exceptionally bold—transcending not just what passes for the current Democratic vision but even the vision of the politically successful Clinton years. It has to go back to the founding of our country, to the spiritual absolutes the Founding Fathers grounded America in when they declared "all men are created equal"—a premise Abraham Lincoln called "the father of all moral principle."

Here then is a look at what is perhaps the greatest failing of George W. Bush's failed presidency—his refusal to call on the American people to care about anything more than our own narrow self-interest—along with an explanation of what a candidate would have to do to embody this new vision.

—Arianna Huffington

SACRIFICE IS FOR SUCKERS

And all our military families that mourn can know this: our nation will never forget the sacrifice their loved one made." That was the president speaking to assembled military families at Fort Carson last November. I wish a member of a mourning military family had asked Mr. Bush why soldiers and their families are the only ones being asked to sacrifice. What about the rest of the country?

The truth is that in speech after speech since September 11, the president has been asking very little of us. During one speech he recommended we "be a Boy Scout leader or a Girl Scout leader." At another he suggested that Americans "put their arm around somebody who hurts and say, 'I love you. What can I do to help you? How can I make a difference in your life?'" Unfortunately, he failed to mention what to do when the answer comes back: "Take your arm off me and get me some affordable health insurance!"

Now, I'm not saying that there is anything wrong with being a Boy Scout leader or telling people that you love them (even when you don't; by the way, Mr. President, I love you). Indeed, I'm all in favor of these things. But there is a world of difference between urging easy, spare-change charity and championing a cause that will transform our society. It's the difference between patronizing us with flaccid, stump-speech rhetoric and invoking patriotism to rally us as a nation to a common cause. Imagine how different our country would be if President Bush had used his political capital after 9/11 to call on the American people to commit themselves to a large, collective purpose.

So here is a new bargain that the Democratic nominee should strike with the American people: "Let's put an end to the tyranny of low expectations," he should say. "You can expect a lot more of me, and I will ask a lot more of you."

President Bush claims to believe in our country. So why doesn't he believe in us enough to ask us to make a collective commitment to confront both the horrors wrought by terrorists and the horrors wrought by random violence in our inner cities and by woefully inadequate health care, education, and housing? Why doesn't he believe in us enough to ask us to share in the sacrifices necessary to build a country of real opportunity for all, and a sturdy social safety net? I believe the country was ready to do that after September 11, and I believe it's still ready.

Far from asking us to share in the sacrifice, since September 11 all the president has asked us to do is return to our normal lives. His opponent should ask, "But why stop there? Why not commit ourselves to larger goals and a greater purpose? To living not merely normal but better lives?" George Bush urged us to "get down to

Disney World in Florida," and Arnold Schwarzenegger urged us to "Buy cars! Buy new cars! Buy used cars!" But spending a wad of cash cannot be all our leaders ask of us. The truest expression of American character has always been not our will to amuse ourselves but our choice to give of ourselves.

Remember September 12, 2001? On that day blood banks overflowed, tens of millions of dollars poured into charities, and such a throng of people showed up to help at Ground Zero that most had to be turned away. It was the worst of times, yet it was the best of times. It was in the middle of that horrible crisis that the best aspects of the American character—generosity, selflessness, courage—came to the fore and reminded us of those intangible qualities that make our nation great.

Despite the passage of time, the values and spirit that emerged that day are still very much part of who we are, and can still be harnessed, if the right leader issues the challenge. Instead of talking straight to the American people, President Bush is telling the nation that we can carry the burden of a worldwide war on terror and the Iraqi occupation while giving ourselves a multitrillion-dollar tax cut and a huge new prescription drug benefit without cost containment. We can't, of course. But he assumes that he will be safely reelected before enough Americans realize it. The Democratic nominee will have to make sure they realize it in time.

He will also have to stay connected to the movement for real reform that is larger than any one candidate—and use the momentum and passion of the movement to put forward the kind of grand, bold vision the times demand. To accomplish this, he must ask us to imagine a country where all people—not just the privileged ones—can send their children off to school in the morning confident that they will be safe and that they will learn.

He must ask us to imagine a country where everyone has comprehensive health care as a basic right. If your family doctor is the local emergency room, it's hard to enjoy life, liberty, or the pursuit of happiness.

He must ask Americans to imagine a country where the environment is an asset to be treasured, not a resource to be exploited, and where clean air and water are the norm, not the exception.

He must ask Americans to imagine a country where elected officials belong to the voters instead of being owned by special interests, and where policies are determined by what is in the public interest and not in the best interest of some corporation that eludes its tax obligations by opening a post office box in Bermuda.

And he has to paint a picture of a different kind of economy—one where productivity doesn't come at the cost of quality of life and where work is structured to allow parents to take care of their children.

This shouldn't be too much to ask for, yet in recent years our economy and society have been moving in the opposite direction: air and water quality are threatened; more families have been forced to have both parents working longer hours to make ends meet, if, that is, they can find jobs at all; our public education infrastructure is crumbling; disgracefully large numbers of people are homeless and millions are going without health insurance. This is the state of the union that Bush claimed in his 2002 address had "never been stronger." That would be true only if you measure the strength of our union by military might and the economic benefits that have accrued over the past twenty years to the wealthiest one percent of households.

Thirty-six years ago, Robert Kennedy stood in front of an audience at the University of Kansas and asked them to look at our economy in a radically different way. "Our gross national product is now over $800 billion a year," Kennedy said, "but that GNP—if we should judge America by that—counts air pollution and cigarette advertising, and ambulances to clear our highways of carnage. It counts special locks for our doors, and the jails for those who break them. It counts the destruction of our redwoods and the loss of our natural wonder in chaotic sprawl. It counts napalm and the cost of a nuclear warhead, and armored cars for police who fight riots in our streets."

The 2004 Democratic nominee will have to engage in a similar, soul-stirring questioning of many unquestioned assumptions. He will have to display a concern for the poor people of this nation and the beleaguered middle class lacking among those currently in charge of public policy.

He will have to recapture the language of morality from the fundamentalists who have hijacked it and reduced it to sexual morality, and use it to spotlight the rampant immorality of the corporate sector instead.

He will have to force his own party to make a choice Democratic leaders have desperately been trying to avoid: between their corporate donors and the urgent need to articulate a powerful, populist case against the sordid actions of corporate America.

He will have to forge the kind of alliance that includes minorities and the dispossessed together with those among the influential, the affluent, and the powerful who are sick of the country we are becoming and of the grotesque parody of democracy we are being served.

He will have to provide an outlet for idealistic young people to be active in shaping our nation's future. And he will have to appeal to what is best in us after years of politicians appealing to what is most selfish in us.

It's a tall order but nothing less will do. Great social movements are not sparked by subtle shifts in policy or new and improved versions of familiar proposals. Nor are they sparked by attacks alone, no matter how brilliant and justified. "Ronald Reagan," said Reagan speechwriter Peggy Noonan, "was a great communicator not because he said things in a big way but because he said big things. It wasn't the way he said it, it was what he said." The Democratic nominee, too, has to speak of big things, and if he does, I have faith that we can make the journey to the other side of the mountain.

P. D. JAMES

From A TASTE for DEATH

UNLESS A NOVELIST'S WORK is very uneven, it is surely impossible for her to choose which book is the best. Certainly some are easier to write than others, but the book which is most enjoyable for the author would not necessarily be judged the most successful by readers. I have never been able to choose one book as my best, but it is possible for me to name those of my novels which I would most regret permanently to lose, and high among them is one first published in 1986, *A Taste for Death*.

It is certainly one in which I feel I have managed to combine all the effects of a successful mystery novel—setting, characterisation, theme, and plot—into a coherent whole. It is set in London, a city I love and about which I enjoy writing. The story, like most of my novels, features Commander Adam Dalgliesh as its detective-hero and it is the one in which my professional woman detective, Inspector Kate Miskin, first appears:

> The new squad had been set up in C1 to investigate serious crimes that, for political or other reasons, needed particularly sensitive handling. It had been so self-evident to Dalgliesh that the squad would need a senior woman detective that he had devoted his energy to choosing the right one, rather than to speculating how well she would fit into the team. He had selected the 27-year-old Kate Miskin on her record and her performance at interview, satisfied that she had the qualities for which he was looking. They were also the ones he most admired in a detective: intelligence, courage, discretion and common sense.

Kate fulfilled Dalgliesh's aspirations so successfully that she has remained on his team ever since, and indeed featured in my latest mystery novel, *The Murder Room*.

In *A Taste for Death*, two bodies are discovered in the vestry of a London church, their throats cut with brutal precision. One is an alcoholic tramp, the other Sir Paul Berowne, a recently resigned minister of the Crown. The characters cover the whole spectrum of English social life from Sir Paul Berowne's

aristocratic mother, Lady Ursula Berowne, and his elegant house in a prestigious area of Kensington, to the humble spinster who discovers the bodies
and the home of a prostitute and her delinquent truant son.

The passage I have chosen to include in this compilation is Book One,
Section 8, which describes the arrival on the scene of crime of the forensic
pathologist Miles Kynaston. To say that *A Taste for Death* is my best book
would be to suggest that all novels since have been a deterioration of talent,
but it does still remain a favorite.

—P. D. James

Dalgliesh remembered a surgeon once telling him that Miles
Kynaston had shown promise of becoming a brilliant diagnosti-
cian, but had given up general medicine for pathology at registrar
level because he could no longer bear to watch human suffering. The
surgeon had sounded a note of amused condescension as though he
were betraying a colleague's unfortunate weakness, wryly observed,
which a more prudent man would have detected before beginning his
medical training, or at least would have come to terms with before his
second year. It could, Dalgliesh thought, have been true. Kynaston
had fulfilled his promise, but now he applied his diagnostic skills to
the unrepining dead, whose eyes couldn't implore him to offer hope,
whose mouths could no longer cry out. Certainly he had a taste for
death. Nothing about it disconcerted him: its messiness, its smell, the
most bizarre of its trappings. Unlike most doctors, he saw it not as the
final enemy, but as a fascinating enigma, each cadaver, which he
would gaze at with the same intent look as he must once have fixed
on his living patients, a new piece of evidence which might, if rightly
interpreted, bring him closer to its central mystery.

Dalgliesh respected him more than any other pathologist with
whom he had worked. He came promptly when called and was equally prompt reporting on a post-mortem. He didn't indulge in the crude
autopsy humour which some of his colleagues found necessary to bol-
ster their social self-esteem; dinner guests could know themselves safe
from distasteful anecdotes about carving knives or missing kidneys.
Above all he was good in the witness box, too good for some people.
Dalgliesh remembered the sour comment of a defending counsel after
a verdict of guilty: "Kynaston's getting dangerously infallible with
juries. We don't want another Spilsbury."

He never wasted time. Even as he greeted Dalgliesh he was taking off his jacket and was drawing his fine latex gloves over stubby-fingered hands which looked unnaturally white, almost bloodless. He was tall and solidly built, giving an impression of shambling clumsiness until one saw him working in a confined space, when he would seem physically to contract and become compact, even graceful, moving about the body with the lightness and precision of a cat. His face was fleshy, the dark hair receding from a high speckled forehead, the long upper lip as precisely curved as an arrowhead, and the full, heavily lidded eyes dark and very bright, giving his face a look of sardonic, humorous intelligence. Now he squatted, toad-like, by Berowne's body, his hands hanging loosely in front of him, palely disembodied. He gazed at the throat wounds with extraordinary concentration, but made no move to touch the body except to run his hand lightly over the back of the head, like a caress. Then he said: "Who are they?"

"Sir Paul Berowne, late MP and junior Minister, and a tramp, Harry Mack."

"On the face of it, murder followed by suicide. The cuts are textbook: two fairly superficial from left to right, then one above, swift, deep, severing the artery. And the razor neatly to hand. As I say, on the face of it obvious. A little too obvious?"

Dalgliesh said:

"I thought so."

Kynaston stepped gingerly over the carpet to Harry, prancing on tiptoe like an inexpert dancer.

"One cut. Enough. Again from left to right. Which means that Berowne, if it was Berowne, stood behind him."

"So why isn't Berowne's right shirt sleeve soaked with blood? All right, it's heavily bloodstained, his own or Harry's blood or both. But if he killed Harry, wouldn't you expect a greater amount of soaking?"

"Not if he turned up his shirt sleeve first and took him from behind."

"And turned it down again before slitting his own throat? Unlikely, surely."

Kynaston said:

"Forensic should be able to identify Harry's blood, or what could be Harry's blood, on the shirt sleeve as well as Berowne's own. There seem to be no visible stains between the bodies."

Dalgliesh said:

"Forensic have been over the carpet with the fibre-optic lamp. They may get something. And there is one discernible smudge under Harry's jacket and a trace of what looks like blood on the jacket lining immediately above it."

He lifted the corner. Both of them looked at the stain on the carpet in silence. Dalgliesh said:

"It was under the jacket when we found it. That means it was there before Harry fell. And if it proves to be Berowne's blood, then he died first, unless, of course, he staggered across to Harry after making one or more of the superficial cuts in his own throat. As a theory, it strikes me as ludicrous. If he were in the very act of cutting his own throat, how could Harry have stopped him? So why bother to kill him? But is it possible, medically possible?"

Kynaston looked at him. Both knew the importance of the question. He said:

"After the first superficial cut, I'd say that it was."

"But would he still have had the strength to kill Harry?"

"With his own throat partly cut? Again, after that first superficial cut, I don't think one can rule it out. He'd be in a state of high excitement, remember. It's amazing what strength people do find. After all, we're supposing that he was interrupted in the act of suicide. Hardly the moment when a man is at his most rational. But I can't be certain. No one can. You're asking the impossible, Adam."

"I was afraid so. But it's too neat."

"Or you want to believe it's too neat. How do you see it?"

"From the position of the body I think he could have been sitting on the edge of the bed. Assuming he was murdered, assuming that the murderer went first into the kitchen, then he could have crept back silently and attacked Berowne from behind. A blow, a cord round the throat. Or he grabs him by the hair, drags back the head, makes the first deep cut. The others, the ones designed to look tentative, could have come afterwards. So we look for any mark under the cuts, or for a bump on the back of the head."

Kynaston said:

"There is a bump but it's small. It could have been caused by the body falling. But we'll know more at the pm."

"An alternative theory is that the killer knocked him out first, then went into the kitchen to strip and came back for the final throat-cutting before Berowne had a chance to come round. But that raises obvious objections. He'd have to judge the force of the blow very carefully, and you'd expect it to leave more than a slight bump."

Kynaston said:

"But it raises fewer objections than the first theory, that he came in half-naked and armed with a razor and yet there are no obvious signs that Berowne put up any resistance."

"He could have been taken by surprise. He could expect his visitor to come back through the door to the kitchen. It's possible that he tiptoed down the passage and came in by the main door. That's the most likely theory, given the position of the body."

Kynaston said:

"You're assuming premeditation then? That the killer knew he'd find a razor to hand?"

"Oh yes. If Berowne was murdered, then the killing was premeditated. But I'm theorizing in advance of the facts, the unforgivable sin. All the same, there's something contrived about it, Miles. It's too obvious, too neat."

Kynaston said:

"I'll finish the preliminary examination and then you can take them away. I would normally do the pm first thing tomorrow, but they aren't expecting me back at the hospital until Monday and the pm room is tied up until the afternoon. Three thirty is the earliest. Is that all right for your people?"

"I don't know about the lab. The sooner the better for us."

Something in his voice alerted Kynaston. He said:

"Did you know him?"

Dalgliesh thought: This is going to come up again and again. You knew him. You're emotionally involved. You don't want to see him as mad, a suicide, a killer. He said:

"Yes, I knew him slightly, mostly across a committee table."

The words seemed to him grudging, almost a small treachery. He said again:

"Yes, I knew him."

"What was he doing here?"

"He had some kind of religious quasi-mystical experience here in this room. He may have been hoping to recapture it. He'd arranged with the parish priest to stay the night here. He gave no explanation."

"And Harry?"

"It looks as if Berowne let him in. He may have found him sleeping in the porch. Apparently Harry couldn't tolerate being with other people. There's evidence that he was proposing to sleep further along the passage in the larger vestry."

Kynaston nodded and got down to his familiar routine. Dalgliesh left him to it and went out into the passage. Watching this violation of the body's orifices, preliminaries to the scientific brutality to follow, had always made him feel uncomfortably like a voyeur. He had often wondered why he found it more offensive and ghoulish than the autopsy itself. Was it, perhaps, because the body was so recently dead, sometimes hardly cold? A superstitious man might fear that the spirit, so recently released, hovered around to be outraged at this insult to the discarded, still vulnerable, flesh. There was nothing for him to do now until Kynaston had finished. He was surprised to find himself tired. He expected to be exhausted later in an investigation when he would be working a sixteen-hour day, but this early heaviness, the feeling that he was already spent in mind and body, was new to him. He wondered whether it was the beginning of age or one more sign that this case was going to be different.

He went back into the church, sat down in a chair in front of a statute of the Virgin. The huge nave was empty now. Father Barnes had gone, escorted home by a police constable. He had been readily helpful about the mug, identifying it as one Harry had often had with him when he was found sleeping in the porch. And he had tried to be helpful about the blotter, staring at it with almost painful intensity before saying that he thought that the black markings hadn't been there when he had last seen the blotter on Monday evening. But he couldn't be sure. He had taken a sheet of writing paper from the desk and used it to make notes during the meeting. This had covered the blotter so that he had really only seen it for a short time. But, as far as his memory went, the black markings were new.

Dalgliesh was grateful for these minutes of quiet contemplation. The scent of incense seemed to have intensified, but it smelt to him overlaid with a sickly, more sinister smell, and the silence wasn't absolute. At his back he could hear the ring of footsteps, an occasional raised voice, calm, confident and unhurried, as the unseen professionals went about their work behind the grille. The sounds seemed very far off and yet distinct, and he had the sensation of a secret, sinister busyness, like the scrabbling of mice behind the wainscot. Soon, he knew, the two bodies would be neatly parcelled in plastic sheeting.

The rug would be carefully folded to preserve bloodstains, and in particular that one significant stain of dried blood. The scene-of-crime exhibits packed and tagged would be carried to the police car: the razor, the crumbs of bread and cheese from the larger room, the fibres from Harry's clothing, that single burnt match head. For the moment he would keep possession of the diary. He needed to have it with him when he went to Campden Hill Square.

At the foot of the statue of the Virgin and Child stood a wrought-iron candleholder bearing its triple row of clotted sockets, the tips of burnt wick deep in their rims of wax. On impulse he felt in his pocket for a tenpenny piece and dropped it in the box. The clatter was unnaturally loud. He half expected to hear Kate or Massingham moving up beside him to watch, unspeaking but with interested eyes, this untypical act of sentimental folly. There was a box of matches in a brass holder chained to the candlerack, similar to the one at the back of the church. He took one of the smaller candles and struck a match, holding it to the wick. It seemed to take an unduly long time before it took hold. Then the flame burnt steadily, a limpid, unflickering glow. He stuck the candle upright in a socket, then sat and gazed at the flame, letting it mesmerize him into memory.

GISH JEN

WHO'S IRISH?

I DON'T REALLY KNOW that this story is "my best"—whatever that means. However, I do like some things in it, for example the way the mood shifts when Bess Shea starts to talk. There are the Sheas and the narrator, seated at the same table but completely without sympathy for each other. Then Bess Shea speaks, and something softens. The narrator had been rightly offended by the Shea family's use of the word "brown," but by the time Bess Shea says "a little brown granddaughter, she is so precious to me," "brown" has mysteriously lost its sting. I don't know where that little sea change came from, but I still smile to think of the new water; there is something so human and hopeful in it.

I like too the humor of this piece. And I like the narrator's spunk—her no-holds-barred forthrightness. In stories I often discover characters and voices I can use in novels; stories can be a kind of lab for me. In writing this piece, for example, I felt the pull of the narrator immediately, and knew I'd be coming back to her. I don't know that I'd say she's been reborn as Mama Wong in *The Love Wife*, but she does seem a clear precursor.

—Gish Jen

In China, people say mixed children are supposed to be smart, and definitely my granddaughter Sophie is smart. But Sophie is wild, Sophie is not like my daughter Natalie, or like me. I am work hard my whole life, and fierce besides. My husband always used to say he is afraid of me, and in our restaurant, busboys and cooks all afraid of me too. Even the gang members come for protection money, they try to talk to my husband. When I am there, they stay away. If they come by mistake, they pretend they are come to eat. They hide behind the menu, they order a lot of food. They talk about their mothers. Oh, my mother have some arthritis, need to take herbal medicine, they say. Oh, my mother getting old, her hair all white now.

I say, Your mother's hair used to be white, but since she dye it, it become black again. Why don't you go home once in a while and take a look? I tell them, Confucius say a filial son knows what color his mother's hair is.

My daughter is fierce too, she is vice president in the bank now. Her new house is big enough for everybody to have their own room, including me. But Sophie take after Natalie's husband's family, their name is Shea. Irish. I always thought Irish people are like Chinese people, work so hard on the railroad, but now I know why the Chinese beat the Irish. Of course, not all Irish are like the Shea family, of course not. My daughter tell me I should not say Irish this, Irish that.

How do you like it when people say the Chinese this, the Chinese that, she say.

You know, the British call the Irish heathen, just like they call the Chinese, she say.

You think the Opium War was bad, how would you like to live right next door to the British, she say.

And that is that. My daughter have a funny habit when she win an argument, she take a sip of something and look away, so the other person is not embarrassed. So I am not embarrassed. I do not call anybody anything either. I just happen to mention about the Shea family, an interesting fact: four brothers in the family, and not one of them work. The mother, Bess, have a job before she got sick, she was executive secretary in a big company. She is handle everything for a big shot, you would be surprised how complicated her job is, not just type this, type that. Now she is a nice woman with a clean house. But her boys, every one of them is on welfare, or so-called severance pay, or so-called disability pay. Something. They say they cannot find work, this is not the economy of the fifties, but I say, Even the black people doing better these days, some of them live so fancy, you'd be surprised. Why the Shea family have so much trouble? They are white people, they speak English. When I come to this country, I have no money and do not speak English. But my husband and I own our restaurant before he die. Free and clear, no mortgage. Of course, I understand I am just lucky, come from a country where the food is popular all over the world. I understand it is not the Shea family's fault they come from a country where everything is boiled. Still, I say.

She's right, we should broaden our horizons, say one brother, Jim, at Thanksgiving. Forget about the car business. Think about egg rolls.

Pad thai, say another brother, Mike. I'm going to make my fortune in pad thai. It's going to be the new pizza.

I say, You people too picky about what you sell. Selling egg rolls not good enough for you, but at least my husband and I can say, We made it. What can you say? Tell me. What can you say?

Everybody chew their tough turkey.

I especially cannot understand my daughter's husband John, who has no job but cannot take care of Sophie either. Because he is a man, he say, and that's the end of the sentence.

Plain boiled food, plain boiled thinking. Even his name is plain boiled: John. Maybe I grew up with black bean sauce and hoisin sauce and garlic sauce, I always feel something is missing when my son-in-law talk.

But, okay: so my son-in-law can be man, I am baby-sitter. Six hours a day, same as the old sitter, crazy Amy, who quit. This is not so easy, now that I am sixty-eight, Chinese age almost seventy. Still, I try. In China, daughter take care of mother. Here it is the other way around. Mother help daughter, mother ask, Anything else I can do? Otherwise daughter complain mother is not supportive. I tell daughter, we do not have this word in Chinese, *supportive*. But my daughter too busy to listen, she has to go to meeting, she has to write memo while her husband go to the gym to be a man. My daughter say otherwise he will be depressed. Seems like all his life he has this trouble, depression.

No one wants to hire someone who is depressed, she say. It is important for him to keep his spirits up.

Beautiful wife, beautiful daughter, beautiful house, oven can clean itself automatically. No money left over, because only one income, but lucky enough, got the baby-sitter for free. If John lived in China, he would be very happy. But he is not happy. Even at the gym things go wrong. One day, he pull a muscle. Another day, weight room too crowded. Always something.

Until finally, hooray, he has a job. Then he feel pressure.

I need to concentrate, he say. I need to focus.

He is going to work for insurance company. Salesman job. A paycheck, he say, and at least he will wear clothes instead of gym shorts. My daughter buy him some special candy bars from the health-food store. They say THINK! on them, and are supposed to help John think.

John is a good-looking boy, you have to say that, especially now that he shave so you can see his face.

I am an old man in a young man's game, say John.

I will need a new suit, say John.

This time I am not going to shoot myself in the foot, say John.

Good, I say.

She means to be supportive, my daughter say. Don't start the send her back to China thing, because we can't.

Sophie is three years old American age, but already I see her nice Chinese side swallowed up by her wild Shea side. She looks like mostly Chinese. Beautiful black hair, beautiful black eyes. Nose perfect size, not so flat looks like something fell down, not so large looks like some big deal got stuck in wrong face. Everything just right, only her skin is a brown surprise to John's family. So brown, they say. Even John say it. She never goes in the sun, still she is that color, he say. Brown. They say, Nothing the matter with brown. They are just surprised. So brown. Nattie is not that brown, they say. They say, It seems like Sophie should be a color in between Nattie and John. Seems funny, a girl named Sophie Shea be brown. But she is brown, maybe her name should be Sophie Brown. She never go in the sun, still she is that color, they say. Nothing the matter with brown. They are just surprised.

The Shea family talk is like this sometimes, going around and around like a Christmas-tree train.

Maybe John is not her father, I say one day, to stop the train. And sure enough, train wreck. None of the brothers ever say the word *brown* to me again.

Instead, John's mother, Bess, say, I hope you are not offended.

She say, I did my best on those boys. But raising four boys with no father is no picnic.

You have a beautiful family, I say.

I'm getting old, she say.

You deserve a rest, I say. Too many boys make you old.

I never had a daughter, she say. You have a daughter.

I have a daughter, I say. Chinese people don't think a daughter is so great, but you're right. I have a daughter.

I was never against the marriage, you know, she say. I never thought John was marrying down. I always thought Nattie was just as good as white.

I was never against the marriage either, I say. I just wonder if they look at the whole problem.

Of course you pointed out the problem, you are a mother, she say. And now we both have a granddaughter. A little brown grand-daughter, she is so precious to me.

I laugh. A little brown granddaughter, I say. To tell you the truth, I don't know how she came out so brown.

We laugh some more. These days Bess need a walker to walk. She take so many pills, she need two glasses of water to get them all down. Her favorite TV show is about bloopers, and she love her bird feeder. All day long, she can watch that bird feeder, like a cat.

I can't wait for her to grow up, Bess say. I could use some female company.

Too many boys, I say.

Boys are fine, she say. But they do surround you after a while.

You should take a break, come live with us, I say. Lots of girls at our house.

Be careful what you offer, say Bess with a wink. Where I come from, people mean for you to move in when they say a thing like that.

Nothing the matter with Sophie's outside, that's the truth. It is inside that she is like not any Chinese girl I ever see. We go to the park, and this is what she does. She stand up in the stroller. She take off all her clothes and throw them in the fountain.

Sophie! I say. Stop!

But she just laugh like a crazy person. Before I take over as baby-sitter, Sophie has that crazy-person sitter, Amy the guitar player. My daughter thought this Amy very creative—another word we do not talk about in China. In China, we talk about whether we have difficulty or no difficulty. We talk about whether life is bitter or not bitter. In America, all day long, people talk about creative. Never mind that I cannot even look at this Amy, with her shirt so short that her belly button showing. This Amy think Sophie should love her body. So when Sophie take off her diaper, Amy laugh. When Sophie run around naked, Amy say she wouldn't want to wear a diaper either. When Sophie go *shu-shu* in her lap, Amy laugh and say there are no germs in pee. When Sophie take off her shoes, Amy say bare feet is best, even the pediatrician say so. That is why Sophie now walk around with no shoes like a beggar child. Also why Sophie love to take off her clothes.

Turn around! say the boys in the park. Let's see that ass!

Of course, Sophie does not understand. Sophie clap her hands, I am the only one to say, No! This is not a game.

It has nothing to do with John's family, my daughter say. Amy was too permissive, that's all.

But I think if Sophie was not wild inside, she would not take off her shoes and clothes to begin with.

You never take off your clothes when you were little, I say. All my Chinese friends had babies, I never saw one of them act wild like that.

Look, my daughter say. I have a big presentation tomorrow.

John and my daughter agree Sophie is a problem, but they don't know what to do.

You spank her, she'll stop, I say another day.

But they say, Oh no.

In America, parents not supposed to spank their child.

It gives them low self-esteem, my daughter say. And that leads to problems later, as I happen to know.

My daughter never have big presentation the next day when the subject of spanking come up.

I don't you want to touch Sophie, she say. No spanking, period.

Don't tell me what to do, I say.

I'm not telling you what to do, say my daughter. I'm telling you how I feel.

I am not your servant, I say. Don't you dare talk to me like that.

My daughter have another funny habit when she lose an argument. She spread out all her fingers and look at them, as if she like to make sure they are still there.

My daughter is fierce like me, but she and John think it is better to explain to Sophie that clothes are a good idea. This is not so hard in the cold weather. In the warm weather, it is very hard.

Use your words, my daughter say. That's what we tell Sophie. How about if you set a good example.

As if good example mean anything to Sophie. I am so fierce, the gang members who used to come to the restaurant all afraid of me, but Sophie is not afraid.

I say, Sophie, if you take off your clothes, no snack.

I say, Sophie, if you take off your clothes, no lunch.

I say, Sophie, if you take off your clothes, no park.

Pretty soon we are stay home all day, and by the end of six hours she still did not have one thing to eat. You never saw a child stubborn like that.

I'm hungry! she cry when my daughter come home.

What's the matter, doesn't your grandmother feed you? My daughter laugh.

No! Sophie say. She doesn't feed me anything!

My daughter laugh again. Here you go, she say.

She say to John, Sophie must be growing.

Growing like a weed, I say.

Still Sophie take off her clothes, until one day I spank her. Not too hard, but she cry and cry, and when I tell her if she doesn't put her clothes back on I'll spank her again, she put her clothes back on. Then I tell her she is good girl, and give her some food to eat. The next day we go to the park and, like a nice Chinese girl, she does not take off her clothes.

She stop taking off her clothes, I report. Finally!

How did you do it? my daughter ask.

After twenty-eight years experience with you, I guess I learn something, I say.

It must have been a phase, John say, and his voice is suddenly like an expert.

His voice is like an expert about everything these days, now that he carry a leather briefcase, and wear shiny shoes, and can go shopping for a new car. On the company, he say. The company will pay for it, but he will be able to drive it whenever he want.

A free car, he say. How do you like that.

It's good to see you in the saddle again, my daughter say. Some of your family patterns are scary.

At least I don't drink, he say. He say, And I'm not the only one with scary family patterns.

That's for sure, say my daughter.

Everyone is happy. Even I am happy, because there is more trouble with Sophie, but now I think I can help her Chinese side fight against her wild side. I teach her to eat food with fork or spoon or chopsticks, she cannot just grab into the middle of a bowl of noodles. I teach her not to play with garbage cans. Sometimes I spank her, but not too often, not too hard.

Still, there are problems. Sophie like to climb everything. If there is a railing, she is never next to it. Always she is on top of it. Also, Sophie like to hit the mommies of her friends. She learned this from her playground best friend, Sinbad, who is four. Sinbad wear army clothes every day and like to ambush his mommy. He is the one who dug a big hole under the play structure, a foxhole he call it, all by himself. Very hardworking. Now he wait in the foxhole with a shovel full of wet sand. When his mommy come, he throw it right at her.

Oh, it's all right, his mommy say. You can't get rid of war games, it's part of their imaginative play. All the boys go through it.

Also, he like to kick his mommy, and one day he tell Sophie to kick his mommy too.

I wish this story is not true.

Kick her, kick her! Sinbad say.

Sophie kick her. A little kick, as if she just so happened was swinging her little leg and didn't realize that big mommy leg was in the way. Still I spank Sophie and make Sophie say sorry, and what does the mommy say?

Really, it's all right, she say. It didn't hurt.

After that, Sophie learn she can attack mommies in the playground, and some will say, Stop, but others will say, Oh, she didn't mean it, especially if they realize Sophie will be punished.

This is how, one day, bigger trouble come. The bigger trouble start when Sophie hide in the foxhole with that shovel full of sand. She wait, and when I come look for her, she throw it at me. All over my nice clean clothes.

Did you ever see a Chinese girl act this way?

Sophie! I say. Come out of there, say you're sorry.

But she does not come out. Instead, she laugh. Naaah, naah-na, naaa-naaa, she say.

I am not exaggerate: millions of children in China, not one act like this.

Sophie! I say. Now! Come out now!

But she know she is in big trouble. She know if she come out, what will happen next. So she does not come out. I am sixty-eight, Chinese age almost seventy, how can I crawl under there to catch her? Impossible. So I yell, yell, yell, and what happen? Nothing. A Chinese mother would help, but American mothers, they look at you, they shake their head, they go home. And, of course, a Chinese child would give up, but not Sophie.

I hate you! she yell. I hate you, Meanie!

Meanie is my new name these days.

Long time goes on, long long time. The foxhole is deep, you cannot see too much, you don't know where is the bottom. You cannot hear too much either. If she does not yell, you cannot even know she is still there or not. After a while, getting cold out, getting dark out. No one left in the playground, only us.

Sophie, I say. How did you become stubborn like this? I am go home without you now.

I try to use a stick, chase her out of there, and once or twice I hit her, but still she does not come out. So finally I leave. I go outside the gate.

Bye-bye! I say. I'm go home now.

But still she does not come out and does not come out. Now it is dinnertime, the sky is black. I think I should maybe go get help, but how can I leave a little girl by herself in the playground? A bad man could come. A rat could come. I go back in to see what is happen to Sophie. What if she have a shovel and is making a tunnel to escape?

Sophie! I say.

No answer.

Sophie!

I don't know if she is alive. I don't know if she is fall asleep down there. If she is crying, I cannot hear her.

So I take the stick and poke.

Sophie! I say. I promise I no hit you. If you come out, I give you a lollipop.

No answer. By now I worried. What to do, what to do, what to do? I poke some more, even harder, so that I am poking and poking when my daughter and John suddenly appear.

What are you doing? What's going on? say my daughter.

Put down that stick! say my daughter.

You are crazy! say my daughter.

John wiggle under the structure, into the foxhole, to rescue Sophie.

She fell asleep, say John the expert. She's okay. That is one big hole.

Now Sophie is crying and crying.

Sophia, my daughter say, hugging her. Are you okay, peanut? Are you okay?

She's just scared, say John.

Are you okay? I say too. I don't know what happen, I say.

She's okay, say John. He is not like my daughter, full of questions. He is full of answers until we get home and can see by the lamplight.

Will you look at her? he yell then. What the hell happened?

Bruises all over her brown skin, and a swollen-up eye.

You are crazy! say my daughter. Look at what you did! You are crazy!

I try very hard, I say.

How could you use a stick? I told you to use your words!

She is hard to handle, I say.

She's three years old! You cannot use a stick! say my daughter.

She is not like any Chinese girl I ever saw, I say.

I brush some sand off my clothes. Sophie's clothes are dirty too, but at least she has her clothes on.

Has she done this before? ask my daughter. Has she hit you before?

She hits me all the time, Sophie say, eating ice cream.

Your family, say John.

Believe me, say my daughter.

A daughter I have, a beautiful daughter. I took care of her when she could not hold her head up. I took care of her before she could argue with me, when she was a little girl with two pigtails, one of them always crooked. I took care of her when we have to escape from China, I took care of her when suddenly we live in a country with cars everywhere, if you are not careful your little girl get run over. When my husband die, I promise him I will keep the family together, even though it was just two of us, hardly a family at all.

But now my daughter take me around to look at apartments. After all, I can cook, I can clean, there's no reason I cannot live by myself, all I need is a telephone. Of course, she is sorry. Sometimes she cry, I am the one to say everything will be okay. She say she have no choice, she doesn't want to end up divorced. I say divorce is terrible, I don't know who invented this terrible idea. Instead of live with a telephone, though, surprise, I come to live with Bess. Imagine that. Bess make an offer and sure enough, where she come from, people mean for you to move in when they say things like that. A crazy idea, go to live with someone else's family, but she like to have some female company, not like my daughter, who does not believe in company. These days when my daughter visit, she does not bring Sophie. Bess say we should give Nattie time, we will see Sophie again soon. But seems like my daughter have more presentation than ever before, every time she come she have to leave.

I have a family to support, she say, and her voice is heavy, as if soaking wet. I have a young daughter and a depressed husband and no one to turn to.

When she say no one to turn to, she mean me.

These days my beautiful daughter is so tired she can just sit there in a chair and fall asleep. John lost his job again, already, but still they rather hire a baby-sitter than ask me to help, even they can't afford it. Of course, the new baby-sitter is much younger, can run around. I don't know if Sophie these days is wild or not wild. She call me Meanie, but she like to kiss me too, sometimes. I remember that every time I see a child on TV. Sophie like to grab my hair, a fistful in each hand, and then kiss me smack on the nose. I never see any other child kiss that way.

The satellite TV has so many channels, more channels than I can count, including a Chinese channel from the Mainland and a Chinese channel from Taiwan, but most of the time I watch bloopers with Bess. Also, I watch the bird feeder—so many, many kinds of birds come. The Shea sons hang around all the time, asking when I will go home, but Bess tell them, Get lost.

She's a permanent resident, say Bess. She isn't going anywhere.

Then she wink at me, and switch the channel with the remote control.

Of course, I shouldn't say Irish this, Irish that, especially now I am become honorary Irish myself, according to Bess. Me! Who's Irish? I say, and she laugh. All the same, if I could mention one thing about some of the Irish, not all of them of course, I like to mention this: Their talk just stick. I don't know how Bess Shea learn to use her words, but sometimes I hear what she say a long time later. *Permanent resident. Not going anywhere.* Over and over I hear it, the voice of Bess.

MARY KARR

From CHERRY

THE LETTERS I GET from readers about this section of *Cherry*, where I finally get to hunker up close to the clueless boy whose name I've been scrawling on my notebooks for years, would have filled a bushel basket. Many professed joy that someone finally wrote about the great passion that accompanies the G-rated sexual encounters of youth. Joyce Carol Oates also praised the scene in some detail for *The New York Review of Books*. Those readers' votes of confidence in part prompt my selecting this particular hunk.

I do know, from teaching classes in literary memoir over the decades, that the wealth of material about boys' sexual coming-of-age—from Nabokov's *Speak, Memory* to Frank Conroy's *Stop-Time*—is matched by a dearth of material on the women's side of the fence. Women's memoirs can deal in great detail with aberrant sexual events, or unwanted advances, from Mary McCarthy's *Memories of a Catholic Girlhood* to Kathryn Harrison's *The Kiss*. In Maya Angelou's *I Know Why the Caged Bird Sings*, a rape is described in intimate detail, but her romance with a neighbor boy, resulting in an unwanted pregnancy, is skimmed over.

Girls lack the kind of goofy, innocent-sounding vernacular for libidinal events that are essentially part of childhood. Where are the female equivalents of words like *chubbie* or *woodie* to describe a sixth-grade boy's erection? In this passage I set myself the task of finding a language that evokes both passion and innocence, since a girl's ardor at age thirteen doesn't mean she wants to be boffed into guacamole, as it's been suggested that boys of that age wish to be (not being a boy, I can't testify with certainty). Girls want something else—the infinite kiss. But that difference doesn't mean less passion: The feeling differs in kind from a boy's, not in intensity. Or so it seemed to me.

—Mary Karr

I've been sitting in the crotch of this itchy damn tree with my feet dangling down so long they both feel like concrete. I shinnied up here to find John Cleary in the park's spread out fireworks crowd where folks have been gathering since dusk. They've come on foot toting stripey lawn chairs and knitting bags and metal coolers. There are quilts spread out over the stiff grass so babies can lay down without taking in cockleburrs and starting to bellow. My eyes glide over the mess and seem to latch down on everybody in town who's not John Cleary.

Eventually from the swarm of bobbing-heads, I find his crew-cut stubble, bleached white into a jagged, low-flying halo. He's astride his banana-seat bike, one foot on the ground while he waits for the mosquito truck to show up so he can pedal behind it with his buddies. There's a cowboy song about ghost riders galloping across the clouds with their faces blurred by dust. That's what I think when I see the truck and John Cleary riding off behind it, leaned over his motorcycle handlebars, his thighs pumping.

John Cleary is what Daddy would call my huckleberry (not that John's agreed to that position yet). So sometimes I get so engrossed watching him, I forget myself entirely. That's how it got dark around me. That's how I wound up with these heavy throbbing feet hung out of the tree, like the elephant feet in the *Textbook of Medical Anomalies* I like to sneak peeks at in the library section marked ADULTS ONLY when the librarian goes onto the steps to smoke.

Meanwhile, John Cleary managed to vanish into the crowd, as did Clarice, who's sleeping over tonight.

Not until the last sparks go out when folks start folding their blankets and collapsing their beach chairs do I finally make them out over by the tilted merry-go-round with Bobbie Stuart and Davie Ray Hawks. They're all squatting over a patch of dirt with their arms dangling inside their knees like something out of *National Geographic*. Maybe somebody's lit one of those caterpillars of ash you can buy at Moak's fireworks stand out on Hogaboom Road. I never purchase fireworks myself, but I often find myself repeating the phrase Hogaboom Road at night to see how fast I can say it without slipping up: *hogaboom road hogaboom road hogaboom road.*

Clarice never does anything like this, and if she's spending the night and hears me prattling like this, she'll roll over and prop up on one elbow and tell me flat out that's why everybody thinks you're weird. It's not your mother or Pete, or the nudes on your walls or the fact that your parents divorced then got back later. It's you chattering to yourself like a gerbil instead of just going to sleep. But Clarice doesn't give a big rat's ass if I saw Hogaboom Road till the kitchen kettle whistles for coffee. "You are a marvel," she likes to say, shaking her head and drawing one side of her mouth down in a half frown. But she watches me as if I warrant pondering, and she never doesn't laugh at my jokes.

John and Bobbie sword-fight with sparklers, joist and parry, while dumbass Davie Ray Hawks tries to get his sparkler going with what they call a punk—a little brown straw with a coal on the end that'll light a cherry bomb fuse but is useless on a sparkler. Finally, I get so tired of holding back unspoken opinions like this that I holler, and they come running from the edge of the field in a quick herd.

Clarice looks up at me with her hands on her hips like I'm in trouble. "That's where you've been hiding," she says.

"Ya'll get me down from here," I say. "My feet fell asleep hanging."

"Why should we?" Davie Ray Hawks says. He's the only one who keeps his bangs slung across his forehead in a surfer cut.

"Because we'll let you in our club if you do," I say.

"What kind of club?" Bobbie wants to know. His sparkler's hit a wet spot and sizzled out, so he's holding a bent silver wire in a way that seems forlorn, like a flower with all its petals stripped off.

Clarice pops out with, "A sex club." Which sends the boys into a fit of giggling and punching each other on the shoulder.

Only Davie Ray Hawks is unconvinced. "Y'all don't have any sex club."

"We didn't start it," Clarice says, "but we're in it. It's a junior high thing." To me, she seems to be holding down laughs, but the boys doubtless think she's serious as a heart attack.

John fakes being wholly engrossed in his sparkler, but if he were a dog, his ears would be pricked forward. He says, "Who all's in this club?"

Clarice names Larry Miller, the lifeguard at the pool, whose bathing suit we spend a lot of time trying to look up the leghole of. I shush her, for I spend whole hours hung on the side of his lifeguard stand and don't want these peckerheads to shoo him off talking to me by dragging his name through the mud.

"Uh-uh!" Davie Ray says, with more force than seems necessary. "He's in a fraternity in college. My cousin Janie's gone to dances with him."

"He's not having sex with y'all," Bobbie says.

"We never said he was," Clarice said. "It's all broken up by grade."

"Get me down outa here," I finally say, for Clarice is leading us down a path I no way want to miss by being stuck up a tree. John and Bobbie come to the tree's base and hold up their arms. I put the heels of my hands where my butt's been in the tree crotch and lower myself till they can each grab a leg. First, it's like a princess being helped down from a carriage by two pages. But when their hands clamp on my thighs, I get a powerful jolt from them grabbing hold. The feeling slides clear up to my middle and lodges just under my rib cage where it presses against my hard-thumping heart.

It's strange. We've known each other our whole entire lives, since we were babies splashing bare assed in the same wading pool. We have hauled each other up on tree house ropes and built human pyramids on each other's backs and red-rovered through each other's joined arms. But this touch is different. Feeling those strong hands on my legs suddenly startles me. Suddenly and deeply, these two boys are not like me.

They must feel it too, because they practically let go at the same time like they grabbed an electric wire or something. They back off and start looking in opposite directions like nothing happened.

Clarice goes into detail about the different levels of the sex club. How at our level you get to practice French kissing and slow dancing. Davie Ray Hawks claims he already knows how to tongue-kiss, a phrase I've never heard that makes the whole thing way too overt sounding. In my head flashes a drawing I had to label and fill in with map colors—the esophagus and sinuses and tonsils floating in some hollow man, whose whole existence is devoted to demonstrating body parts to kids who want to hork looking at them. That said, I lately like watching Clarice's brother French-kiss his girlfriend Peg on the couch when they think we're asleep. By TV sign-off time, it's fairly clear their mouths are open. What I can't figure is if their tongues are slipping around in there the whole time, lapping on each other, or if they just lip-lock and every now and again touch tongues.

The sex club notion causes initiation rites to pop up, and it's an idea we all glom onto. Me and Clarice put our heads together and conjure some pretty good ones too, tests that if you pass, you get to practice kissing with me and Clarice. Here's what we gin up:

1. Pour lighter fluid on your hand and set a match to it.

2. Roll a cherry bomb in peanut butter, then mash a bunch of BBs on it, then drop it lit in the mailbox on Main to see if the whole thing explodes.

3. Take a shit-bomb (paper sack filled with somebody's doo) to the home of the junior high principal, Lead-Head Briggs. Light the sack on fire, then hide in the ditch while he stomps it out.

4. Blindfold Davie Ray Hawks and tell him he's putting his finger up somebody's butt, but really it's just wet bread wadded up in a soup can.

We stand on the edge of the field swatting mosquitoes, not sure where else to go. All around in other fields and neighborhoods, you can hear the sharp pop of fireworks like gunfire from some far off war. Kids are hollering, and Huey Ladette's mama calls him in because goddamn it, it's late, and she's gonna tear him a new asshole.

Somehow we get to my garage by meandering, nothing on purpose. I find the key to Mother's padlocked studio, where we're scared to turn on the light in case my parents look out back and wonder. Something's about to start, and we stand on the brink of it, still pretending to be shadows to one another amid the paint fumes. If I close my eyes, I can almost feel the mountain pines that give off this smell. The air hangs heavy as gauze between us all. Outside, about a zillion crickets have gone into *chirrup, chirrup,* each in a different soprano voice. The toads come back in alto, and they're worse than any choir I ever sang in, if matching up notes is a measure. Still they blend somehow, a kind of curtain of sounds woven together, and the firecrackers go *pop pop pop*, and the bottle rockets whish out sparks then burst.

After my eyes get used to the dark, I make out John's crew cut. He's walked over to a canvas propped in a puddle of moonlight, an old nude Mother never framed. "Lookit this!" he says. There's a slow foot-shuffle in the dark as Bobbie and Davie Ray and Clarice congregate in front of it.

"Get a load of those knockers," Davie Ray says, and there's hissed whispers to shut the fuck up.

"Boy she got some headlights, don't she," Bobbie says.

"Lecia pose for this?" Davie Ray says, which draws stuffed giggles from all the boys. The unsaid comparison to my little ace-bandaged-looking chest pins me like a spear.

"Y'all are gross," Clarice says, and John says that's her sister, chris-sake. Then to make sure nobody thinks he's a goodie-goodie, or too much on a girl's side, he reaches a hand up and tickles one painted boob, saying, *Gootchie gootchie goo.*

Somebody comes up with rules for a kissing game, but basically Clarice and me each kiss a boy while one of them sits out. Then we switch. If I had my druthers, Davie Ray Hawks would just go home and let me kiss John while Clarice kissed Bobbie. But the whole point of a game like this is how everybody's kiss is at the same level, so each of us holds the same value, even though in matters of kissing, opin-ions always run fairly deep. But only by leveling the ground like this does the kiss get possible as activity.

The first boy I kiss is Bobbie, who holds my elbows as if we're about to spin toplike through the dark. His lips are chapped dry as parchment and sweet. Then somebody says switch, and Davie Ray Hawks is on me. His lips are blubbery and wet. He puts his hand in the small of my back and leans into me. But I don't feel danced with. Plus once he gets me arched back a good ways, I can feel what must be his dick hard as a crescent wrench poking my leg. The raw fact of it grosses me out, and this whole scene starts to feel all blunt and greasy.

Then Bobbie's voice says switch, and John Cleary draws me to him, and there's such a surge inside me I can't locate where it's bubbled up from.

I hold my breath, afraid of messing up. That corn dog I ate earlier flashes through my head, and I get a weird urge to draw back, dash out the studio and up the back steps and into the bathroom to brush my teeth, rinse, spit, and rinse again with Lecia's Listerine before blinking myself magically back to John's arms.

None of which I do, of course. I hold my breath and count to myself like during a storm: *one Mississippi, two Mississippi.*

There's a TV commercial for some thick green shampoo that they drop a pearl in to show how rich and heavy it is, the pearl falling through this heavy green goop. And that's what John smells like. Prell, it's called. All the cut grass in the world gets mashed into a bottle of this stuff. And the time we move into is that slow-falling, underwater shampoo time. John does not hold my elbows like he's scared to get too close. He makes a cage of his arms I step right in (colt in a corral, I think). He tilts his head and says with a breath like Juicy Fruit right before he kisses me, "Is this okay?" Before I can say yes, we bump teeth a little, then he's breathing the Juicy Fruit right into my mouth, my lips, and his lips come closer till the softnesses match up.

John's tongue is not hard and pointy like Davie Ray's or plumb absent like Bobbie's. It parts my lips a little as if testing the warmth of water. And after a second I get the idea that my tongue's supposed to do something other than lay there or draw back hiding. I ease it forward so as not to poke at him the way Davie Ray Hawks did me. I taste the coppery flesh of his soft tongue on my wet one. My breathing seizes up again. And I put my hands up and press them flat against his chest because half of me is afraid I'll fall entirely into him if he keeps holding me. And there over his breast pocket, a small embroidered seahorse dips its head down and coils its tail inward till it's a perfect figure for how shy I suddenly feel. Through the shirt cotton is John's own strong heart.

I try to reteach myself to breathe normal, but it comes out in halts and jags. I feel grit in the crook of my elbow and creases in my neck and a single dot of sweat bumping down my spine to the small of my back. Then I feel John's hands tremble on my back, and I try to draw him out of that trembling with my own tongue, and it's like we're drinking from each other.

Suddenly, I know so much. I understand about waves and cross tides and how jellyfish float and why rivers empty themselves in the Gulf. I understand the undulating movement of the stingray on *Sea Hunt* and the hard forward muscle of the shark. Now I know why they call it petting, for even though I'm more still in the plush warmth of his mouth than I can ever get in church, my whole body is purring. I let myself breathe into him a breath that tastes like ashes from a long fire.

Outside there's the bump of a screen door. Maybe my folks letting the cat out. I hear it latch back careful the way Daddy would do. There's the far off whine of a bottle rocket shedding sparks across some field. Then nothing.

Then the crunch of foot on gravel sets us all in a panic. Everybody rears back from kissing and starts mouthing stuff I can't make out. Clarice has her knees squinched together like she has to pee. She flaps her hands like a bird fighting its way out of a nosedive. Davie Ray Hawks sneaks over to the curtain and looks out a sliver. When he wheels around in the moonlight, his face is bug-eyed, his hands held out wide in an expression copied from Frankenstein right when he got zapped in the head with lightning. Daddy's crunching barefoot down the gravel path alongside the garage, closer and closer till the door on the other side of this studio door aches on its old hinge.

I think of explicit threats he's made about using his straight razor to slice up anybody who ever messed with Lecia and me. I think this qualifies as messing. He wouldn't actually use a razor on those boys, of course, or lay a hand on me or Clarice, but they might well catch an ass-whipping. But a whipping would be way better than this waterfall of shame I feel at the prospect of him knowing I've been standing around with boys in the dark letting them put their tongues in my mouth. This is definitely not what he expects me to be doing.

In the hot dark, John Cleary's eyes are blue as struck matches. Plus he's drawn his whole head turtle-like inside his shirt collar, and pulled that up over his nose like Pud in *Bazooka Joe* comics. I start figuring our way out of it.

Wolfman, I could say to Daddy. *We were playing wolfman.* Or better still, *We were gonna make a play about a mummy where lightning knocks out the electricity right before the mummy staggers in . . .*

Daddy's in the garage now, easing the door back flush to the frame. When I hear him talking, at first I think it's aimed at us. I take his sugary tone for a kind of sideways menace. "Poor old fella," he says. Then the black cat Daddy thinks of as his yowls like he's been picked up in the middle. That's when I know we're safe. Daddy's not heading in here at all. The other kids probably don't twig to it, but I wouldn't breathe a word that might spark Daddy's Indian ears into hearing us. Still the air starts to ease back into the room.

We stand like statues in freeze tag listening to him in the dark. "Don't nobody love old Roy like he has coming," Daddy says. Clarice tries to stuff down her giggles at that. Davie Ray's waving his arms and miming *shhh*, John draws an invisible hankie out of his breast pocket and mops his forehead.

Meanwhile, my own daddy is talking out loud to this shiny black tomcat. "Works hard all day being a cat," he says, then, "I know it. Nobody even rubs his chin. He's chasing mice all day. Keeping his whiskers slicked nice." Daddy heaves open his truck door then shuts it. The whiskey bottle clinks against the seat adjuster as he draws it out. I can picture the broken paper seal and the gold twisty lid and my daddy's whiskey throat guzzling under the dome light.

Nobody's folks drink like mine. John Cleary's daddy has had the same case of Lone Star in the garage so long spiders have nested all

over it. Knowledge of that difference in my family makes me suddenly alone in the room, though an instant before in John's arms, I'd stood
embrace in more warm than I could recall. Now Daddy's drinking has
carved me away from everybody else. He's sucking down whiskey and
talking to a cat, saying, "Just tell old Pete about it." And maybe Roy
does tell him, for the room is a gray velvet tomb we're all buried in listening hard. After a long time, Daddy says, "Dadgum 'em all to hell."

Then the door opens and his steps crunch away, and our exhalings
of relief are so loud, I miss hearing the house door.

Outside, the night has grown exponentially larger. The roads to the
horizon seem to stretch farther. We're small under the sky's dome. There's
mist at our ankles, and the moon is low. I still feel quivery as a rabbit from
where John held me. I can barely look at him because I know he possesses that soft mouth that matches up with mine so right. How can you know
such a thing about a person and not lean into it? I squat down and pretend to sift for quartz pebbles in the road gravel till I think his blue eyes
glide over my shoulder's curve, but when I sneak a look, he's staring back
toward Bobbie's house. Bobbie says, "Old Pete's tough as a boot."

John says, "I wouldn't wanna tangle with him."

Davie Ray makes the sign of the cross. "We damn near died back
there," he says. This puffs me up a little, that Daddy's so formidable in
everybody's mind. Clarice isn't saying diddly. Like me she's doubtless
thinking of all that softness these otherwise scabby-looking boys
embody. But she also knows that the whole sex-club idea has swept
past us, that interval in the garage gone to ether. We're back on our
own separate islands. Nobody could even say "sex club" or mention
what happened without being thought of as warped in the head.

Bobbie says, "Let's go back to my house and make Jiffy Pop and
watch *Thriller*." Then they're slapping away, no goodbye, no see you
later. They practically vaporize before us.

When they're far enough away, Clarice asks me if I felt myself getting hot back there in the studio. "And I don't mean temperature." I
say hell yes. We stand there a second, unable to either say more about
it or to let the feeling go.

Finally, Clarice says she wants popcorn too, but I don't want to go
back in my house now. Just seeing Mother and Daddy would somehow banish how I feel. As long as they're away from me, I can close
my eyes and taste John Cleary's Juicy Fruit, feel the unexploded
weight of him breathing on me.

Mother harps all the time on how sex and even touching your-self is normal as can be. Her only worry is that I'll get what she calls hot pants and get knocked up. She'll let me look at her erotic art book with folks entwined and rolling around like weasels whenev-er I want. But while lately I consider cracking it open most every day, I always wait till she and Daddy aren't home.

Somehow even letting Mother and Daddy whiz through my head totally wipes away the girl John Cleary just held. She's long gone, and in her place stands this skinned-up kid again. I want to stave off going home wicked bad.

I ask Clarice if she wants to go over to Bobbie's house to ask the boys to share their Jiffy Pop. She says that, as excuses go, that's really pitiful sounding. To show up there would be asking for it. Since the boys have probably got blue balls from kissing us, no telling what they'd do. Her brothers have explained to her that unchanneled sperm makes your balls swell and somehow backs it up into your brain. "They don't think straight with blue balls," Clarice says.

Because John Cleary's kisses have plugged my body into some unspecified socket still humming on high, I ask Clarice what girls get to have that even approximates blue balls.

"Diddly shit, that's what," Clarice says. Or else you get a Reputation. If you let boys suck hickies on your neck or if you do the shimmy at the skating rink so your boobs slap back and forth like Marilyn Fruget, then you get guys standing around lagging pennies off a wall behind the raceway, talking about how they finger-fucked you and your yin-yang made their hand smell like tuna fish. Clarice is going to high school year after next and has big plans for improving her social standing. She says a novena every night to grow titties, and when that crop finally comes in, the last thing she can have is A Reputation.

Nor, she warns me, do I want one when I start junior high this fall. I tell her that tonight I'm not so sure.

There's a line Mother read me from a book about poor crackers dragging their dead mama across Mississippi or Alabama or some god-awful place: "I feel like a wet seed wild in the hot blind earth," the girl says. Just hearing that told me something about being a girl I didn't know. But standing inside John Cleary's breath and body temperature with our mouths melting into each other makes me really know it. *Really, really,* as Clarice would say, *down south of your neck.*

BARBARA KINGSOLVER

From THE POISONWOOD BIBLE

THE BEAUTY OF A written passage is in the mind's eye of the beholder, assembled there by a peculiar alchemy of the writer's words and a thousand other images, entirely personal, belonging to the reader. I'm endlessly amazed that when my readers send me the nuggets of my writing that have most moved them, they're like snowflakes: no two selections are alike. So it's pointless for me to try to guess which passage of my writing is "best," in the terms by which a reader might judge. I decided instead to look for a passage I'd worked hardest to create, because that's an objective measure, and one that's known only to me. I knew where to look: one of my novels took longer to write, by a decade, than any of the others. I could have chosen any of several chapters, so the particulars of my choice were somewhat arbitrary, but picking one person out of the lineup was easy.

The character of Adah Price in *The Poisonwood Bible* brought to that novel a point of view I needed in order to fully develop my theme. But getting her onto the page took years, not just of writing and revision but also research in medical and physiology books, and a special form of word crafting in which I sometimes even enlisted the help of my family. Adah is hemiplegic: half her brain suffered devastating damage at birth, so she's extremely weak on one side of her body and has the sort of mind an intelligent adolescent could have if the right hemisphere of her brain had been forced to compensate entirely for the left. She sees the world in geometric shapes, she has an unusual ethical sense, she reads both forward and backward, and she expresses herself frequently in palindromes. As hard as she was for me to write, I've been told she was an even harder taskmaster for my translators.

—Barbara Kingsolver

Walk to learn. I and Path. Long one is Congo.
Congo is one long path and I learn to walk.

That is the name of my story, forward and backward. *Manene* is the word for path: *Manene enenam, amen.* On the Congo's one long *manene* Ada learns to walk, amen. One day she nearly does not come back. Like Daniel she enters the lions' den, but lacking Daniel's pure and unblemished soul, Ada is spiced with the flavors of vice that make for a tasty meal. Pure and unblemished souls must taste very bland, with an aftertaste of bitterness.

Tata Ndu reported the news of my demise. Tata Ndu is chief of Kilanga and everything past it in several directions. Behind his glasses and striking outfit he possesses an imposing bald forehead and the huge, triangular upper body of a comic-book bully. How would he even know about a person like me, the white little crooked girl as I was called? Yet he did. The day he visited my family I had been walking alone, making my way home on the forest path from the river. It was a surprising event for him to come to our house. He had never gone out of his way to see my father, only to avoid him, though he sometimes sent us messages through Anatole, his own sons, or other minor ambassadors. This day was different. He came because he had learned I was eaten by a lion.

Early that afternoon, Leah and I had been sent to bring back water. Sent together, the twin and the *niwt,* chained together always in life as in prelife. There was little choice, as Her Highness Rachel is above manual labor, and Ruth May beneath it so to speak, so Leah and I were considered by our mother, by default, disposed for her errands. It is always the twin and the niwt she sends out to the *marché* on market day, to walk among all those frightening women and bring back fruit or a kettle or whatever thing she needs. She even sends us sometimes to bring back meat from the butcher *marché*, a place where Rachel will not set foot on account of the intestines and neatly stacked heads. We can look out our door and know when the butcher *marché* is open for business, if the big kapok tree down there is filled with black buzzards. This is the truth. We call them the Congolese billboard.

But above all else and every day, she would send us to get water. It was hard for me to carry the heavy pail with my one good hand, and I went too slowly. *Slow lee two went I.* My habit on that path was reciting sentences forward and back, for the concentration improved my walking. It helped me forget the tedium of moving only one way through the world, the way of the slow, slow body. So Leah took all the water and went ahead. As all ways.

The forest path was a live thing underfoot that went a little farther every day. For me, anyway, it did. First, it went only from one side of our yard to the other: what our mother could see and deem safe if she stood in the middle. At first we only heard stories about what happened to it on the north, after the forest closed down on it: a stream, a waterfall, clear pools for swimming. It went to a log bridge. It went to another village. It went to Léopoldville. It went to Cairo. Some of these stories were bound to be true, and some were not; to discover the line between, I decided to walk. I became determined to know a few steps more of that path every day. If we stayed long enough I would walk to Johannesburg and Egypt. My sisters all seemed determined to fly, or in Rachel's case, to ascend to heaven directly through a superior mind-set, but my way was slowly and surely to walk. What I do not have is *kakakaka*, the Kikongo word for hurrying up. But I find I can go a long way without *kakakaka*. Already I had gone as far as the pools and the log bridge on the north. And south, to clearings where women wearing babies in slings stoop together with digging sticks and sing songs (not hymns) and grow their manioc. Everyone knows those places. But without *kakakaka* I discover sights of my own: how the women working the field will stand up one after another, unwrap the *pagne* of bright cloth tied under their breasts, stretch it out wide before retying. They resemble flocks of butterflies opening and closing their wings.

I have seen the little forest elephants that move in quiet bands, nudging the trees with their small, pinkish tusks. I have seen bands of Pygmies, too. When they smile they reveal teeth filed to sharp points, yet they are gentle, and unbelievably small. You can only believe they are men and women by their beards and breasts, and the grown-up way they move to protect their children. They always see you first, and grow still as tree trunks.

I discovered the *bidila dipapfumu*, the cemetery of witch doctors.

I discovered a bird with a black head and mahogany-colored tail as long as my arm, curved like a bow. In the *Field Guide to African Birds* left by our fowl-minded patron Brother Fowles, my bird is called the *paradise flycatcher*. In the notebook I keep in my pillowcase, in which I draw pictures of all things I know, I put a smile on the face of the paradise flycatcher and printed underneath, in my backward code for secrecy:

NEVAEH NI SEILF FO FOORP WEN .REHCTACYLF ESIDARAP

I also made a habit of following Methuselah (the parrot) as he made his way around our house in insecure spirals. He roosts right inside our latrine, which is near where his empty cage was thrown by the Reverend into the weeds. Its hulk rots there like a shipwreck. Methuselah, like me, is a cripple: the Wreck of Wild Africa. For all time since the arrival of Christ, he had lived on seventeen inches of a yardstick. Now he has a world. What can he possibly do with it? He has no muscle tone in his wings. They are atrophied, probably beyond hope of recovery. Where his pectoral muscles should be, he has a breast weighed down with the words of human beings: by words interred, free-as-a-bird absurd, unheard! Sometimes he flaps his wings as if he nearly remembers flight, as he did in the first jubilant terror of his release. But his independence was frozen in that moment. Now, after stretching his wings he retracts them again, stretches out his head, and waddles, making his tedious way up one branch and down another. Now Methuselah creeps each morning out of the little hole under the rafters of our latrine house, cocks his head, and casts one nervous eye upward as if in prayer: *Lord of the feathers, deliver me this day from the carnivores that could tear me breast from wishbone!* From there, I track his path. I set out small offerings of guava and avocado I have picked and broken open, exposing them to him as food. I do not think he would recognize these fruits wholly concealed in their own skins. After he learns to do that, it will be another whole step to make him see that fruit is not a thing he must rely on the hands of mankind for, but grows on trees. *Treason grows but for kind man.*

In following Methuselah on his slow forays through the forest, I discovered the boys and men practicing drills. This was not the Belgian Army, official conscripted protectors of white people, but a group of young men who held secret meetings in the woods behind our house. I learned that Anatole is more than a teacher of schoolboys and translator of sermons. *Ah Anatole, the lot an aha!* Anatole carried no gun in the clearing where I spied him, but he spoke to armed men who listened. Once he read aloud a letter about the Belgian setting a timetable for independence. Anatole said 1964. "*Mil neuf cent soixante quatre!*" The men threw back their heads at this and laughed ferociously. They cried out as if their skin had been torn.

I feared not, and grew accustomed to walking alone. Our mother did not think she allowed it, especially near dark. It was my secret. She never did realize that whenever she sent me anywhere with Leah, such as to the creek that day to carry water, it would mean coming back alone.

It was already late afternoon, and I passed through spotted light, then brighter clearings, with grass so tall it bent from both sides to form a tunnel overhead, then back under trees again. Leah long gone ahead of me with the water. But someone was behind, some one or some thing. I understood perfectly well that I was being followed. I cannot say I heard anything, but I knew. I wanted to think: Methuselah is playing a trick on me. Or the Pygmies. But I knew better. I paid attention to the small hairs rising on my nape. I did not feel afraid because it does no good in my case. I cannot run away on the muscular effects of adrenaline, but I could taste fear in the back of my throat and feel its despairing weight in my slack limbs. For some, I am told, this weighted-down helplessness comes in dreams. For me it is my life. In my life as Adah I must come to my own terms with the Predator.

I stopped, slowly turned, looked back. The movement behind me also stopped; a final swish in the tall grass by the path, like the swinging of a velvet curtain dropped. Each time I paused, this happened. Then I would wait in the still and growing darkness, till I could not wait anymore and had to walk on.

This is what it means to be very slow: every story you would like to tell has already ended before you can open your mouth. When I reached our house it was nighttime in another life.

Sunset at six o'clock means that life does go on after dark: reading by lamplight on the porch, our family's evening event. Leah had come home with the buckets of water, Mother had boiled it and set it out to cool while she worked on dinner, Rachel had dipped a cloth in it to drape across her forehead while she lay in the hammock examining her pores with the hand mirror. Ruth May had attempted to convince every family member in turn that she could lift a full water bucket by herself with her one remaining unbroken arm. I know all this without having been there. Somewhere in this subdued family din I was presumed to have been minding my own business for many hours. When I finally did return home it was as if, as usual, I had shown up late for my own life, and so I slipped into the hammock at the end of the porch and rested under the dark bougainvilleas.

A short while later Tata Ndu emerged out of darkness. He came up the steps to explain in his formal French that the tracks of a large lion, a solitary hunting male, had been spotted on the path from the river. Tata Ndu's eldest son had just come back from there and brought this report. He had seen the marks of the little girl who drags her right foot, and the lion tracks, very fresh, covering over her footprints. He found the signs of stalking, the sign of a pounce, and a smear of fresh blood trailing into the bush. And that is how they knew the little crooked white child, the little girl without *kakakaka*, had been eaten. *La petite blanche tordue a été mangée.* This was Tata Ndu's sad news. Yet he looked pleased. As a favor to my parents, a party of young men, including his sons, had gone in search of the body, or what might be left of it.

I found I could not breathe as I watched his face tell this story, and the faces of the others as they received the news. My sisters could not comprehend Tata Ndu's word salad of French and Kikongo, so were merely spellbound by the presence of a celebrity on the porch. I was the last thing on their minds, even Leah's. Leah who had left me to the lion's den in question. But my mother: Yes. No! She understood. She had hurried out to the porch from the cooking hut and still carried a large wooden paddle in her hand, which dripped steaming water onto the floor. Part of her hair fell in a wave across her face. The rest of her seemed unalive, like a pale wax model of my mother: the woman who could not fight fire with fire, even to save her children. Such affliction I saw on her face I briefly believed myself dead. I imagined the lion's eyes on me like the eyes of an evil man, and felt my own flesh being eaten. I became nothing.

Our Father rose and said in a commanding voice, "Let us pray to the Lord for mercy and understanding."

Tata Ndu did not bow his head but raised it, not happily but proudly. Then I understood that he had won, and my father had lost. Tata Ndu came here personally to tell us that the gods of his village did not take kindly to the minister of corruption. As a small sign of Their displeasure, They ate his daughter alive.

It was very nearly impossible to make myself stand and come forward. But I did. Our Father stopped praying, for once. Tata Ndu drew back, narrowing his eyes. Perhaps it was not so much that he wanted me eaten, but that he did not like being wrong. He said no more than *mbote*—fare thee well. Then turned on his heel in a dignified way and left us to ourselves. He would not come back to our house again until much later, after many things had changed.

The next morning we heard the search party had found what the lion killed in my place: a yearling bushbuck. I wonder about its size and tenderness, whether the lion was greatly disappointed, and whether the bushbuck loved its life. I wonder that religion can live or die on the strength of a faint, stirring breeze. The scent trail shifts, causing the predator to miss the pounce. One god draws in the breath of life and rises; another god expires.

MAXINE HONG KINGSTON

From CHINA MEN

CHINA MEN MUST BE my best writing. It's the perfect book, the one I use as a model for my creative writing students. (*The New York Times* called it a "perfect book"—or was that "a *nearly* perfect book"?) The form of *China Men* is just right—it truly fits the lives of all the characters, including the narrator and the author.

Writing *China Men*, I was able to imagine and think my way to truth. Short chapters of myths and long chapters about everyday life reverberate through one another. The seen and the unseen play now in darkness, now in light.

The excerpt below tells two versions of how my father came to be in America. I have asked readers, Which version is it that you believe to have actually happened? Most choose the scene about the father on Angel Island. It's impossible that my actual father could have really stowed away among the sea dragons. Afraid that someone from the INS might read *China Men*, and arrest and deport my father, I had to write about his immigration in this diverting way.

In fact, *China Men* tells two more stories about BaBa's arrival in the U.S. There's documentation that he was born in San Francisco, but that birth certificate was burned along with the Hall of Records during the Earthquake and Fire of 1906.

And Chinese women are magical. My grandmother in China had the power to give birth at a distance. To account for the population of Chinese in the U.S., given the Exclusion Acts and the antimiscegenation laws, each Chinese woman here must have given birth to hundreds of baby boys.

(The real story was even more fantastic. As in a fairy tale, my father was caught twice and deported. On his third try, he landed in New York on the very day Lindbergh landed in Paris. Too bad I didn't hear this story until after *China Men* was published.)

It is not because I am a writer that I can make up four stories about one event. Most people of my parents' generation have many stories in their repertoire—one for the INS, others for trusted friends, one in Chinese, another in English. Such fictional ways are true to our culture.

—Maxine Hong Kingston

I think this is the journey you don't tell me:

The father's friends nailed him inside a crate with no conspicuous air holes. Light leaked through the slats that he himself had fitted together, and the bright streaks jumped and winked as the friends hammered the lid shut above his head. Then he felt himself being lifted as in a palanquin and carried to a darker place. Nothing happened for hours so that he began to lose his bearings—whether or not he was in a deep part of the ship where horns and anchor chains could not be heard, whether or not there had already been a pulling away from land, a plunging into the ocean, and this was steady speed. The father sat against a corner and stretched each limb the diagonal of the box, which was a yard by a yard by a yard. He had padded the bottom with his bedding and clothes. He had stuffed dried food, a jar of water, and a chamber pot in a bag. The box contained everything. He felt caught.

Various futures raced through his mind: walking the plank, drowning, growing old in jail, being thrown overboard in chains, flogged to tell where others were hiding, hung by the neck, returned to China—all things that happened to caught chinamen.

Suddenly—a disturbance—a giant's heart came to life; the ship shook and throbbed. A pulse had started up, and his box vibrated with it. He thought he could hear men running and calling. He must be near the engine room or a deck, near people.

The father's thoughts reached out as if stretching in four directions—skyward, seaward, back toward land, and forward to the new country. Oh, he did yearn for the open sea. The nerves in his chest and legs jumped with impatience. In the future he had to walk on deck the entire voyage, sleep on it, eat there.

He ought to have brought a knife to cut holes in the wood, or at least to carve more lines into the grain. He wanted to look out and see if his box had dropped overboard and was floating atop water, a transparency that ought not to be able to bear weight; he could have been immersed and this wooden air bubble hanging at a middle depth, or falling through the whale waters. People said that a Dragon King ruled an underwater city in the Yellow River; what larger oceanic unknown—tortoises twenty feet across, open-mouthed fish like the marine monster that swallowed the sutras—swam alongside or beneath him. What eels, sharks, jellies, rays glided a board's-width away? He heard the gruff voices of water lizards calling for the night rain. He must not be afraid; it was sea turtles and water lizards that had formed a bridge for King Mu of Chou.

Because of fear, he did not eat nor did he feel hungry. His bowels felt loose and bladder full, but he squeezed shut ass and sphincter against using the chamber pot. He slept and woke and slept again, and time seemed long and forever. Rocking and dozing, he felt the ocean's variety—the peaked waves that must have looked like pines; the rolling waves, round like shrubs, the occasional icy mountain; and for stretches, lulling grasslands.

He heard voices, his family talking about gems, gold, cobbles, food. They were describing meat, just as they had his last evenings home. "They eat it raw." "All you can eat." The voices must have been the sounds of the ocean given sense by his memory. They were discussing a new world. "Skyscrapers tall as mountains." He would fly an aeroplane above the skyscrapers tall as mountains. "They know how to do things there; they're very good at organization and machinery. They have machines that can do anything." "They'll invent robots to do all the work, even answer the door." "All the people are fat." "They're honest. If they say they'll do something, they do it. A handshake is enough." "They arrive for appointments at the very moment they say they will." "They wrap everything—food, flowers, clothes. You can use the paper over again. Free paper bags." "And westward, there are wild horses. You can eat them or ride them." It alarmed him when the strange talk did not cease at his concentration. He was awake, not dozing, and heard mouth noises, sighs, swallows, the clicking and clucking of tongues. There were also seas when the waves clinked like gold coins, and the father's palm remembered the peculiar heaviness of gold. "Americans are careless; you can get rich picking over what they drop." "Americans are forgetful from one day to the next." "They play games, sports; grown men play ball like children." "All you have to do is stay alert; play a little less than they do, use your memory, and you'll become a millionaire." "They have swimming pools, elevators, lawns, vacuum cleaners, books with hard covers, X-rays." The villagers had to make up words for the wonders. "Something new happens every day, not the same boring farming."

The sea invented words too. He heard a new language, which might have been English, the water's many tongues speaking and speaking. Though he could not make out words, the whispers sounded personal, intimate, talking him over, sometimes disapproving, sometimes in praise of his bravery.

"It's me. It's me." A solid voice. Concrete words. "I'm opening the box." It was the smuggler, who squeaked the nails out and lifted the lid. He helped the father climb out of the box with firm and generous hands. "You're safe to come out and walk," he said. The size of the room outside the box seemed immense and the man enormous. He brought fresh food from the dining room and fresh water and he talked to the father.

Suddenly they heard a march of footsteps, the leather heels of white demons. Coming steadily toward them. The two men gave each other a look, parted, and ran between the hallways of cargo, ducked behind crates. The door clanked open, shut, and the father heard the footsteps nearing. He made out the sounds of two people pacing, as if searching for a stowaway. Crouched like a rabbit, he felt his heart thud against his own thigh. He heard talking and fervently wished to know whether they were discussing stowaways. He looked for other places to dart, but the crates, lashed with rope, towered above him in straight stacks. He was in a wedge with an opening like a cracked door. The cargo room was small after all, a mere closet, and he could not step from aisle to aisle without being seen; his footsteps would echo on the metal floor. If only there were portholes to jump through or tarpaulins to hide under.

The white demons' voices continued. He heard them speak their whispery language whose sentences went up at the end as if always questioning, sibilant questions, quiet, quiet voices. The demons had but to walk this far and see into the wedge. His friend, the smuggler, could say, "I came to check the ropes," or "The captain ordered me to take inventory." Or "I'm looking for stowaways, and I found one," and deliver him up. But there were no explanations for him, a stowaway chinaman. He would not be able to talk convincingly; he would have to fight. He hardly breathed, became aware of inadequate shallow breaths through his nose.

Then, so close to his face he could reach out and touch it, he saw a white trouser leg turn this way and that. He had never seen anything so white, the crease so sharp. A shark's tooth. A silver blade. He would not get out of this by his own actions but by luck.

Then, blessedness, the trouser leg turned once more and walked away.

He had not been caught. The demons had not looked down. After a time of quiet, the two hiders called to each other and came out hysterical with relief. Oh, they had the luck of rich men. The trousers had practically brushed his face.

"It's time to go back in your box," said the smuggler. A moment before, the father had thought it would be a joy to be back in, but as the lid shut on him again, reluctance almost overwhelmed him. He did not visit outside of the box again. He rode on, coming to claim the Gold Mountain, his own country.

The smuggler came occasionally and knocked a code on the wood, and the stowaway father signaled back. Thus he knew that he had not been forgotten, that he had been visited. This exchange of greetings kept him from falling into the trance that overtakes animals about to die.

At last the smuggler let him out; the ship had docked at a pier in New York. He motioned the father up hatches, across empty decks, around corners to an unguarded gangway. He would not have to swim past patrol boats in the dark. "Come. Come. Hurry," the smuggler guided him. He staggered along on cramped legs; the new air dizzied him. As they were saying good-bye, the smuggler said, "Look," and pointed into the harbor. The father was thrilled enough to see sky and skyscrapers. "There." A gray and green giantess stood on the gray water; her clothes, though seeming to swirl, were stiff in the wind and the moving sea. She was a statue, and she carried fire and a book. "Is she a goddess of theirs?" the father asked. "No," said the smuggler, "they don't have goddesses. She's a symbol of an idea." He was glad to hear that the Americans saw the idea of Liberty so real that they made a statue of it.

The father walked off the ship and onto the Gold Mountain. He disciplined his legs to step confidently, as if they belonged where they walked. He felt the concrete through his shoes. The noise and size of New York did not confuse him; he followed a map that his kinsmen had drawn so clearly that each landmark to Chinatown seemed to be waiting to welcome him. He went to the Extending Virtue Club, where people from his own village gave him a bed in a basement; it could have been a grocery shelf or an ironing table or the floor under a store counter. To lie stretched out on any part of the Gold Mountain was a pleasure to him.

Of course, my father could not have come that way. He came a legal way, something like this:

Arriving in San Francisco Bay, the legal father was detained for an indefinite time at the Immigration Station on Angel Island, almost within swimming distance of San Francisco. In a wooden house, a white demon physically examined him, poked him in the ass and genitals, looked in his mouth, pulled his eyelids with a hook. This was not the way a father ought to have been greeted. A cough tickled his chest and throat, but he held it down. The doctor demon pointed to a door, which he entered to find men and boys crowded together from floor to ceiling in bunkbeds and on benches; they stood against the walls and at the windows. These must be the hundred China Men who could enter America, he thought. But the quota was one hundred a year, not one hundred per day, and here were packed more than one hundred, nearer two hundred or three. A few people made room for him to set down his suitcases. "A newcomer. Another newcomer," they called out. A welcome party made its way to him. "I'm the president of the Self-Governing Association," one of them was telling him in a dialect almost like his. "The most important rule we have here is that we guard one another's chances for immigration." He also asked for dues; the father gave a few dimes toward buying newspapers and phonograph records, an invention that he had never heard before. "Now you're eligible to vote," said the president, who then said that he had won his office by having been on the island the longest, three and a half years. The legal father's heart sank, and rose again; there must be something wrong with this man, not a good man, a criminal to be jailed for so long. "Do you want to spend money on a rubber ball? Vote Yes or No." The legal father voted No. How odd it would be to say to these men, "Play ball. Go ahead. Play with it," as if they were boys and could play. Even the boys wouldn't play. Who can be that lighthearted? He wasn't really going to stay here for more than a day or two, was he? He made his way across the room. Some of the men were gambling, others exercising, cutting one another's hair, staring at their feet or folded hands or the floor. He saw two men handcuffed to each other. Readers chanted San Francisco newspapers, *Young China* and *Chinese World*. The legal father, who was skillful and lucky, joined a game and won forty silver dollars, and gave away one for the rubber ball. He learned who was being deported and who was serving a year's sentence before deportation.

A bell went off like a ship's alarm, but it was a dinner bell. The father followed the others to a dining hall. About ten women were coming out. They were the first women he had seen since China, and they already belonged to husbands. He did not know that he had come to a country with no women. The husbands and wives talked quickly as the guards pushed them past one another. The father saw the man ahead of him hold hands with a woman for a moment and—he saw it—pass her a note. She dropped it. She knelt and, fixing her shoe with one hand, snatched the piece of paper with the other. A big white matron grabbed her arm and took the paper. Though these people were all strangers, the father joined the men who surrounded the matron. They wrested the paper from her and tore it up. The legal father ate some of the shreds. That was the last time the men's and women's mealtimes overlapped. There seemed to be no other immediate consequences; perhaps denial of entry would be the punishment.

The China Men who worked in the kitchen brought food cooked and served in buckets. "Poison," the prisoners grumbled. "A couple of years ago," said the president of the Self-Governing Association, "the demons tried to starve us to death. They were taking the food money for themselves. If it weren't for us rioting, you newcomers wouldn't be eating so much today. We faced bayonets for this food." The legal father wasn't sure he would've wanted any more of the slop they were eating.

The men spent the long days rehearsing what they would say to the Immigration Demon. The forgetful men fingered their risky notes. Those who came back after being examined told what questions they had been asked. "I had to describe all the streets in my village." "They'll ask, 'Do you have any money?' and 'Do you have a job?'" "They've been asking those questions all this week," the cooks and janitors confirmed. "What's the right answer?" asked the legal fathers. "Well, last week they liked 'No job' because it proves you were an aristocrat. And they liked 'No money' because you showed a willingness to work. But this week, they like 'Yes job' and 'Yes money' because you wouldn't be taking jobs away from white workers." The men groaned, "Some help." The demons did not treat people of any other race the way they did Chinese. The few Japanese left in a day or two. It was because their emperor was strong.

Footsteps walked across the ceiling, and bedsprings squeaked above their heads. So there were more of them locked on the second floor. "The women are up there," the father was told. Diabolical, inauspicious beginning—to be trodden over by women. "Living under women's legs," said the superstitious old-fashioned men from the backward villages. "Climbed over by women." It was bad luck even to walk under women's pants on clotheslines. No doubt the demons had deliberately planned this humiliation. The legal father decided that for a start in the new country, he would rid himself of Chinese superstitions; this curse would not count.

He read the walls, which were covered with poems. Those who could write protested this jailing, this wooden house (*wood* rhyming with *house*), the unfair laws, the emperor too weak to help them. They wrote about the fog and being lonely and afraid. The poets had come to a part of the world not made for honor, where "a hero cannot use his bravery." One poet was ready to ride his horse to do mighty American deeds but instead here he sat corralled, "this wooden house my coffin." The poets must have stayed long to carve the words so well. The demons were not going to free him, a scholar, then. Some were not poems exactly but statements. "This island is not angelic." "It's not true about the gold." One man blamed "the Mexican Exclusion Laws" for his imprisonment. The writers were anonymous; no official demon could trace them and penalize them. Some signed surname and village, but they were still disguised; there were many of that name from that village, many men named Lee from Toi Sahn, many a Hong of Sun Woi, and many a Three District Man and Four District No Such Man. There were dates of long stays.

Night fell quickly; at about four o'clock the fog poured down the San Francisco hillsides, covered the bay, and clouded the windows. Soon the city was gone, held fast by black sea and sky. The fog horns mourned. San Francisco might have been a figment of Gold Mountain dreams.

The legal father heard cries and thumps from someone locked in a separate shed. Words came out of the fog, the wind whipping a voice around the Island. "Let me land. Let me out. Let me land. I want to come home."

In the middle of one night when he was the only man awake, the legal father took out his Four Valuable Things, and using spit and maybe tears to mix the ink, he wrote a poem on the wall, just a few words to observe his stay. He wrote about wanting freedom. He did not sign his name; he would find himself a new American name when he landed. If the U.S. government found out his thoughts on freedom, it might not let him land. The next morning the readers sang the new poem for the others to hear. "Who wrote this wonderful poem during the night?" they asked, but the father modestly did not say.

For one another's entertainment, the men rehearsed and staged skits, puppet shows, and heroic parts of operas. They juggled fruit, bottles, and the new rubber ball. The father, who was traveling with the adventures of Yüeh Fei, the Patriot, in six volumes, read aloud the part where Yüeh Fei's mother carved on his back four words: FIRST—PROTECT MY NATION. He held up for all to see the illustrations of warriors in battle. He also carried the poems of Li Po, the best poet, the Heavenly Poet, the Great White Light, Venus. The father sang about a sentry stopping Li Po from entering a city. Li Po was drunk as usual and riding a mule. He refused to give his name to the sentry, but wrote a daring poem that he was a man from whose mouth the emperor had wiped the drool; the emperor's favorite wife had held his inkslab. The impressed sentry granted him entrance. This poem heartened the men; they laughed and clapped at Li Po's cleverness and the sentry's recognition of him and poetry.

"What is a poem exactly?" asked an illiterate man, a Gold Mountain Sojourner who had spent twenty years in America and was on his way back to his family. "Let me give it a try," he said. "A short poem: 'On the Gold Mountain, I met black men black like coal' Is that a poem?" The literate men were delighted. "Marvelous," they said. "Of course, it's a poem." "A simile. A simile. Yes, a poem." The legal father liked it so much, he remembered it forever.

The legal father learned many people's thoughts because he wrote their letters. They told their wives and mothers how wonderful they found the Gold Mountain. "The first place I came to was The Island of Immortals," they told him to write. "The foreigners clapped at our civilized magnificence when we walked off the ship in our brocades. A fine welcome. They call us 'Celestials.'" They were eating well; soon they would be sending money. Yes, a magical country. They were happy, not at all frightened. The Beautiful Nation was glorious, exactly the way they had heard it would be. "I'll be seeing you in no time." "Today we ate duck with buns and plum sauce," which was true on days when the China Men in San Francisco sent gifts.

Every day at intervals men were called out one by one. The legal father kept himself looking presentable. He wore his Western suit and shined shoes, constantly ready.

One morning the barracks awoke to find a man had hanged himself. He had done it from a railing. At first he looked as if he had been tortured, his legs cut off. He had tied his legs bent at the knees like an actor or beggar playing a man with no legs, and hung himself by pushing over his chair. His body had elongated from hanging all night. The men looked through his papers and found X's across them. When new arrivals looked for beds, nobody told them that a dead, hung man had slept in that one.

Also, the rumor went, a woman upstairs had killed herself by sharpening a chopstick and shoving it through her ear. Her husband had sent for her, and she did not understand why he did not come to take her home.

At last came the legal father's turn to be interrogated. He combed his hair again. He said his good-byes. Inside the interrogation room were several white demons in formal wear; the legal father gauged by the width of lapels and ties that his own suit was not quite stylish. Standing beside the table was a Chinese-looking soldier in American uniform and a demon soldier in the same uniform. This Chinese American was the interpreter. The legal father sat opposite the interrogators, who asked his name, his village, where he was born, his birth date—easy questions.

"Can you read and write?" the white demon asked in English and the Chinese American asked in Cantonese.

"Yes," said the legal father.

But the secretary demon was already writing No since he obviously couldn't, needing a translator.

"When did you cut off your pigtail?" asked the translator.

"In 1911," said the legal father. It was a safe answer, the year he would have picked anyway, not too early before the Republic nor too late, not too revolutionary nor too reactionary. Most people had cut their hair in 1911. He might have cut it for fashion as much as for revolution.

"Do you have relatives who are American citizens?"

The janitor, a China Man, who just then entered the room with dustpan and broom, nodded.

"Yes."

"Who?"

"My grandfather is an American. My father is an American. So I'm an American, also my three older brothers and three uncles—all Americans."

Then came the trap questions about how many pigs did they own in 1919, whether the pig house was made out of bricks or straw, how many steps on the back stoop, how far to the outhouse, how to get to the market from the farm, what were the addresses of the places his grandfather and father and brothers and uncles had lived in America. The interrogators liked asking questions with numbers for answers.

Numbers seemed true to them. "Quick. How many windows do you have in your house?" "How many times did your grandfather return to the United States?" "Twice." "Twice?" "Yes, twice. He was here once and returned twice. He was here three times altogether. He spent half his life in America and half in China." They looked into his eyes for lies. Even the Chinese American looked into his eyes, and they repeated his answers, as if doubting them. He squelched an urge to change the answers, elaborate on them. "Do you have any money?" "Yes." "How much?" He wondered if they would charge him higher fees the more money he reported. He decided to tell the truth; lying added traps. Whether or not he spoke the truth didn't matter anyway; demons were capricious. It was up to luck now.

They matched his answers to the ones his relatives and fellow villagers gave. He watched the hands with yellow hair on their backs turn the copies of his grandfather's and father's papers.

They told him to go back to the jail, where he waited for more weeks. The next time he was called to be examined—*searched* the Chinese word—they asked again, "What American relatives do you have?"

"My grandfather and father," he said again, "and also my three brothers and three uncles."

"Your grandfather's papers are illegal," the Chinese American translated. "And your father is also an illegal alien." One by one the demons outlawed his relatives and ancestors, including a Gold Rush grandfather, who had paid a bag of gold dust to an American Citizenship Judge for papers. "There are no such things as Citizenship Judges," said the Immigration Demon and put an X across the paper that had been in the family for seventy-five years. He moved on to ask more trap questions, the directions the neighbors' houses faced and the number of water buffaloes in 1920, and sent him back to the barracks.

He waited again. He was examined again, and since he had an accurate memory, he told them the same number of pigs as the last two times, the same number of water buffaloes (one), the same year of cutting his queue, and at last they said, "You may enter the United States of America." He had passed the American examination; he had won America. He was not sure on what basis they let him in—his diploma, his American lineage (which may have turned out to be good after all), his ability to withstand jailing, his honesty, or the skill of his deceits.

This legal father then worked his way across the continent to New York, the center of America.

NEIL LaBUTE

A GAGGLE of SAINTS

IT'S A DANGEROUS GAME, rating anything—good, better, best—and especially when that "anything" is yourself. As soon as you've done it you immediately begin to doubt your choice. In my case, not so much that you've picked the wrong piece, but that you even have a piece that deserves a title in the first place. Don't get me wrong, I can do this—what you're about to read attests to that—but I stand by my earlier statement that self-aggrandizement is indeed a tricky and treacherous path. Actually, I'm mixing metaphors now, but you no doubt get my point.

The reason I've chosen "A Gaggle of Saints" is because I like it. Simple as that. It's a playlet that I've gone back to on several occasions—to read, to examine when a producer or director has forwarded a question about it to me, etc.—and it has continued to hold up both as a piece of writing and as a piece of entertainment. Throughout my career, I've tried to remain a person of the theater, and I feel that this piece represents my theatrical sensibilities quite well. I continue to believe that the monologue is the greatest weapon afforded the playwright, so what could be better than using two of them, running in tandem, to tell a story? Now, I suppose they actually call this technique a "duologue" or something like that in the dark, hallowed halls of dramaturgy, but whatever it is, I know it works. I enjoy the characters and the story of "A Gaggle of Saints," but most of all I like the talk. Lots and lots of talk. It seems that the theater is our last great bastion for talk, and I'm happy to travel there as both a patron and a practitioner. Again and again.

I hope you enjoy the read. If you don't, do not fear—it's a relatively short play, and you'll be on to the next author before you know it.

—Neil LaBute

silence, darkness.

a young attractive couple sitting apart
from one another, they are dressed in the
popular evening fashion of the day.

JOHN

so, okay, there was this big bash . . .

SUE

a party . . .

JOHN

party, bash, whatever, in the city. that's what we came down for. the thing, this get-together. 's why we did it in the first place . . .

SUE

's our old youth group. i got a flyer in the mail . . .

JOHN

couple churches together, i think, mixed, and meeting in the city, ballroom over at the plaza . . .

SUE

which really sounded nice, you know . . .

JOHN

's expensive.

SUE

i mean, elegant . . .

JOHN

but that's cool, manhattan, always have a good time there, right?

SUE

people from high school were going . . .

JOHN

'cause we're juniors up at b.c., so, like, there's still lots of guys we know . . .

SUE

seniors now, mostly . . .

JOHN

all these seniors, guys like that, who we're still in touch with. friends, you know . . .

SUE

this was just after midterms . . .

JOHN

sue's a year ahead, almost, two semesters, we're juniors, but nearly a year . . . (BEAT) both going to b.c. . . .

SUE

boston college, you know, we almost didn't get in. i mean, both of us . . .

JOHN

my g.p.a., but we'd decided, i mean, early—like back at greeley, junior year, maybe—that we'd do college together.

SUE

and boston seemed about right, you know, four hours from home . . .

JOHN

's a little over three, if you push it. i don't like to go crazy with my v.w., but it's only about three hours if you're really moving, three, three and a half . . .

SUE

it's beautiful up around there, i mean, massachusetts. new england, all that's just gorgeous this time of year. leaves turning . . .

JOHN

it just sounded really great, weekend back in new york. stop in, maybe, say "hi" to the folks . . . be good to go down for a couple days.

SUE

so i contacted the three people going to school with us . . . you know, from home, three friends going to b.c. as well . . .

JOHN

one guy's even in my house, david's his name . . . didn't really hang out with him at home or anything, he does gymnastics, but he's cool . . .

SUE

he's nice. nice guy . . .

JOHN

ended up, we talked two other couples into going back with us . . . guy from the house, this david guy.

SUE

we took his car down . . .

JOHN

. . . and a friend of mine, tim. year behind me, but studying at b.c., same time . . .

SUE

's a beautiful red truck he had.
(PAUSE)
jeep or something . . .

JOHN

'cause i've got this old v.w., i said that, right? it's great, '73, with the metal bumpers and all that . . . but needs a tune-up and i'm not gonna drive three hours with all these guys . . .

SUE

we all thought we could go down together, one car. everybody wanted to, gonna be in the city at this hotel, live band and everything . . .

JOHN

and so six of us, a girl that's going out with this david from my fraternity, karen's her name, i think . . . she was coming too. she knew the
city pretty well, grew up just off the park and they were getting along
good . . . so it's six altogether now, six for the ride and the v-dub's definitely out of the question.

SUE

david said he'd drive if we wanted.

JOHN

's got one of those isuzu troopers. 's roomy, big.

SUE

and we're all picked up at three in the afternoon, saturday.

JOHN

it was greek week, well, same weekend as the black & white ball up at
school . . . but we hadn't committed to going, you know, and then sue
gets the flyer and suddenly, i'm rushing around, fighting for tuxedos,
ten minutes to six, friday afternoon! (BEAT) i ended up buying a perry
ellis, finally. a size big, but i got one . . . looks okay, doesn't it?

SUE

it looked good on him . . . i had to put a safety pin in the vest, in the
back of it, but it was really nice when he had it on . . .

JOHN

we left 'em in the bags, the three of us guys, hanging in the trooper for
the ride. i mean, no sense getting 'em messed up for no reason, right?

SUE

i had this dress i'd been saving . . . all taffeta, i'd been saving it for
something like this . . . did i mention that? (BEAT) i needed to find
some shoes, but i thought the dress was perfect . . .

JOHN

we missed the game, b.c.'s first conference—'s away, but we could've watched it at our place with a bunch of guys, they always order in pizza and everything, but we said "no," jump in with all these people . . . road trip.

SUE

tim's girlfriend, patrice, i've known for years . . .

JOHN

with about a dozen overnight bags, tuxedos hanging from all corners of dave's isuzu . . . (BEAT) the girls decided to wear their outfits . . .

SUE

it was my black dress.

JOHN

sue's got this knockout thing, kind of a cutaway in the front, what's it called?

SUE

. . . with a scalloped neckline . . .

JOHN

"scalloped," I think . . . in the front, you know, over her chest and no back to it at all, not any sleeves, just very little on top. but chic, too, right? classic lines, see, it's a dinner dress, dress you'd wear out to dinner, dining, not something a girl would pick out, junior prom, with spaghetti straps all clotting it up . . . (BEAT) she looked great, proud to be with her . . .

SUE

i knew it'd get wrinkled, a little . . . i did. taffeta's terrible for that, but i thought it sounded wonderful, you know, getting out at some amoco, middle of connecticut, in this wave of taffeta . . . and buying, i don't know, a milky way, a can of soda. and the attendant's mouth just hanging open at the sight of us . . .

JOHN

i'm putting gas in, one time we stopped, and look up . . . i see nothing but chiffon and silk and whatnot, miles of it, going down the snack aisle, that killed me! . . .

SUE

i was carrying my shoes—i did find a pair, even had time to dye them to match—but i took 'em off in the car, and i was just holding them in the store. so, i'm standing there, in my stockings, carrying these shoes . . .

JOHN

i'll always remember that. her smiling at me, through the glass there, little bit of chocolate on her lips . . . and carrying her shoes.

SUE

this was going to be a great party . . .
(PAUSE)
. . . i could feel it.

JOHN

the church usually threw a pretty good bash, i mean, times we'd go into the city.

SUE

it was our anniversary . . .

JOHN

last minute, got her a corsage, not the wrist kind, hate those . . . but this was beautiful, white blossoms. don't know what kind, but they were white, i remember that . . .

SUE

i loved it! the softest pink, it was . . . john thought it was white, but it was really just the lightest shade of pink. the last shade of pink it could be, before turning into something else . . . (BEAT) and you know? he pricked his finger, john did. as he pinned it on me, pricked his index finger . . .

JOHN

stupid pin! . . .

SUE

and then . . . a spot of blood, just a drop, but he ended up with this touch of blood on his shirt . . .

JOHN

couldn't even see it if i buttoned the jacket . . .

SUE

but see, in a weird way, though, it excited me. the blood, is that stupid to say? . . . probably, but it did. (BEAT) i mean, it was stunning to look at, you know? all that white on him, the bright of his shirt . . . and then this splash of . . .

JOHN

red . . .

SUE

. . . blood on his chest.

JOHN

didn't get any on her dress, however, nothing. felt good about that . . . wouldn't want to ruin her anniversary dress.

SUE

four years . . .

JOHN

huh? believe that? four . . . since fall of our third year in high school, wow . . .

SUE

i saw him on the track one day. lived six blocks away all my life, in history together, but i never really saw him until he was jogging one time . . .

JOHN

i like to keep in shape . . .

SUE

he'd always kept his hair short, trimmed up . . .

JOHN

my dad cut it. believe that?! sixteen years old and my father drags me
into the kitchen, every other sunday. i could just count on the standard
"sears portrait" cut. (BEAT) i was always a little worried about my
ears. stick out a bit.

SUE

but i see him running, really running, blistering by people who are just
jogging or walking and i don't know this guy. 's cute. nice body. and i
don't know him . . . (BEAT) kind of long hair . . .

JOHN

my dad was away on sabbatical over in london or some type of thing
. . . i didn't really know or care. i could let my hair grow, that's what
i saw coming out of the whole deal. my mom didn't mind at all . . .

SUE

so i put down my pom-poms, and my purse and all that, and i start
running, too. i mean, i can't keep up with him but i go a little slower
or a little faster every so often so that he's catching me more quickly on
every lap.

JOHN

i knew who she was. she was dating a guy i knew . . .

SUE

that was over. we broke up, like, two weeks before. he was this, i don't
know, he'd kind of left the church, and there's this completely bad
scene at a party, the screaming, and he's sort 'a drunk, and so it's over.
i mean, we're still calling each other but it's definitely over . . .

JOHN

i'd heard this. i mean, you hear everything at some time in your life,
right, and this was a thing you keep up on in high school, girls you
secretly like but can't get at 'cause they're dating somebody, maybe a
friend, and so you file 'em away and hope the guy joins the army and
gets sent to laos or something . . . held back in school, even, and you
and she end up on the same floor, some dorm in florida. (BEAT) the
best would be, like, a major football moment, touchdown to take the
state championship, something majestic like that, but anything . . .
camp counselors even, would do, she was that kind of girl . . .

SUE

and we're running together now, he's pretending he's winded and needs to slow down and i'm just trying to keep up and around we go. sun going down, we're not speaking at all, and we just keep going in circles . . .

JOHN

then he shows up . . .

SUE

we really had stopped dating, but he was going to give me a ride home, just friendly, because the track and the practice fields and everything are, like, three miles from my house . . .

JOHN

he pulls his car right on the track, into the lanes. nice new scirocco, all black, that he got as a graduation gift from his dad. he was a year or so older . . .

SUE

i slowed down a little.

JOHN

and i can see what's coming because i know him and we've had some laughs together, not friends, exactly, but friends of friends, that's what we are . . .

SUE

but i don't want to leave.

JOHN

this is how we first got together, it's kind of a funny story . . .

SUE

so he chases me down on the track, because we just jog by him, right around his car for a couple laps, and keep going . . .

JOHN

why am i gonna stop? he's not my boyfriend . . .

SUE

we weren't really dating, you couldn't call it that, anymore . . .

JOHN

see, and he grabs me. turns me around, after grabbing me, he turns me and says, "hey!" and he's holding onto me, about my size, and one of his nails is digging into my nipple, holding my chest like he is. he's got these, like, long nails on one hand . . .

SUE

he plays guitar, he's very good . . .

JOHN

and this hurts and i'm standing there thinking, "this doesn't need to be happening . . ." and i turn on him. never spoke to him the whole time, just turned on him and flipped him over onto the ground and started pounding on his head. it's a surface track so he's not getting too banged up but i'm hitting him pretty good and sue's just standing there . . . waiting.

SUE

i'd never seen this happen before . . .

JOHN

finally he stops squirming around and i hit him one more time, you know high schoolers, right, you go a bit overboard in a fight, and then i walk over and grab her stuff and give it to her and we take off. scirocco's still standing there, people having to jog around it, sun dancing off the hood of the thing as we head home.

SUE

we walked all the way . . .

JOHN

noticed my reflection in it as we go by. bloody nose, him grabbing at me . . .

SUE

i had, like, two huge blisters the next day.

JOHN

and i kissed her, standing there on her porch, still didn't say anything but we've been dating four years since then and never heard back from the other guy after that. (BEAT) i shot baskets with him about a year ago, over at the elementary, and he didn't seem so mad . . .

SUE

sometimes we fight, we do, like anybody else, or break up . . . whatever, john dated someone for a week or so, freshman year, i met this guy in a biology class. didn't last . . . (BEAT) we're getting engaged this summer, we already planned it . . .

JOHN

point being, it's our anniversary, right, and we're hoping for this great time and whatnot, want it all to be special, weekend in the city, girls wanna go shopping in "the village" if there's time, whatever . . . (BEAT) we talked about taking the train on the way back, alone, sleeping car . . .
(PAUSE)
. . . i'm kidding, they don't even have those . . .

SUE

midterms last week everybody just needed to get away.

JOHN

ends up we do go to my parents' house on sunday . . . dad makes me sit down, "you look like a bushman," first thing out of his mouth—what's he mean by that?—and he tries to give me a haircut! halfway through my pre-med, he's still trying to cut my bangs!

SUE

i thought it was kind of funny . . . i could hear them arguing in the other room. his hair really does look better when it's long. it does . . .

JOHN

but that's later, anyway . . .

SUE

so we make it to the city in, like, less than four hours, weekend traffic, that's not bad.

JOHN

does it look stupid? seriously . . . no, i mean it. are my ears funny at all?

SUE

$28.50 for ten hours parking, that's a lot, i thought . . . and then we all walk over to the hotel, the guys carrying these big dry cleaning bags over their shoulders . . .

JOHN

we decided to go in on a room, all of us . . . not for anything, i mean, you know. i'm just telling you, so we could change and everything. better than wrinkling our stuff up. right?

SUE

we get in, still a few hours before the party's going to start, so we all decide to use the facilities, you know, take a jacuzzi, whatever, lots of time to get changed again . . . 's fun. (BEAT) i got back into my dress . . .

JOHN

i'm tying up my shoes, lacing 'em up . . . she comes out of the bathroom, like i said, this is four years we've been going together and i'm still staring at the best-looking girl i've ever seen. i'm just completely in love. serious . . .

SUE

makeup, try and put makeup on in some hotel bathroom and you'll understand the meaning of devotion, sinks in those places, even the plaza, are impossibly small, postage stamp of a mirror i'm using . . . but i want to look nice for him. (BEAT) i bought a new lipstick in the lobby, they had a counter there . . . 's vivid, crimson . . .

JOHN

she steps into the living room of this hotel suite, city full of models and actresses . . . the beautiful people . . . and i can't see anything else. 's like we're thrown back to the garden, the two of us, watching one another across this great green meadow, my side still hurting from the missing rib and all, but she's revealed to me, golden hair and a face like fresh snow and i'm thinking . . . hey, screw the bone, you know, here's why he rested on the seventh day. 'cause they can't get any better than this. (BEAT) i mean, i'm not so poetic or whatever, but this is exactly what i'm thinking.

SUE

the dress helps a lot, because I'm not going to kid myself, it does, but i can see he's happy, and his tux looks really handsome, it was going to be great, a really good evening, i could feel it . . .

JOHN

and we walk downstairs, arm in arm. man, feels so nice to stroll past all these people, i mean, rich guys, girl like that on my arm! made me feel strong, you know? powerful . . . the crowd almost glides apart as we approach.

SUE

we've got nowhere to go. the party's not until later . . . nothing but possibilities . . . wherever we looked, i really felt that, walking along.

JOHN

so on and on . . . couple hours pass, david's girlfriend, karen, takes the lead at some point, walking us through the park . . . over by that one bridge, the big pond? by the delacorte, moon's smiling down and all, romance hanging over a night like this out of some storybook, some tale by, maybe, scott fitzgerald or those guys . . . i really do love this girl. that's the thing that's screaming out in my head right then . . .

SUE

he was holding my hand so tight . . .

JOHN

there's a swan or two out on the water, some geese, maybe. little breeze, october, but still warm, you know how that can be . . . perfect, a perfect night, and then, just off to our left, there's this, like, patch of woods near the path. comes this rustling . . .

SUE

i thought it might be some teenagers or who knows what. we all started to walk a bit faster . . .

JOHN

i'm not scared but it's night, city all around . . what else can you do, girls with you? so we walk along. (BEAT) and two guys, middle-aged guys, l.l. bean shirts on and the whole thing . . . come out of the dark. smiling, and i don't need a map to tell me what's been going on . . .
(PAUSE)
. . . i don't.

SUE

it was just two men. walking along . . . no big deal.

JOHN

coming out of the weeds, they were, off in the park alone, and these smiles, i don't know, i just don't know what to think about it. i mean, we're going to this party, all dressed up, what should we care, right? one dude looks like my father, a little, it's dark but he had that look, right, that settled, satisfied sort of . . . anyway, off they head, arms linked together and nothing we say ever going to change what they are . . .
(PAUSE)
dance all night, sue as stunning as she's ever looked and i'm telling you, i can't get that picture, the image of it, out of my head. those smiles, i can't do it . . . (BEAT) but the party is great, it really is . . .

SUE

i haven't danced like that in a long time . . .

JOHN

it was, like, the beginning of a magical evening . . . everything was right, it was pristine, you know? soothing, and we just kept dancing, the two of us. danced for hours . . . round and round.

SUE

they'd done the whole place, the room, i mean, when we finally got inside . . . in blues, and golds, with these great moons, these golden crescents hanging above us . . .

JOHN

like smiles, like the moon smiling down . . .

SUE

i think we looked pretty nice together, looked like a couple, you know?

JOHN

it was fun, back like that, in the city . . . 's always fun. saw a lot of guys we know . . .

SUE

my little sister was there . . . there with some boy from greeley, he's in debate, he said. seemed nice enough . . . she likes him.

JOHN

we ran into sue's sister, did she mention that?

SUE

hadn't seen her since august . . .

JOHN

younger sister, maureen, with some kid . . .

SUE

he'd been drinking . . .

JOHN

ahh, he was okay. (BEAT) had a good band going. reggae . . .

SUE

i'd never been to the plaza before, i mean, past it, shopping and whatever, with my mom, but never to it. it was tremendous! so much glass,
high white walls, it was like . . . a cake, some wedding cake, left on the
corner there, downtown. 's what it reminded me of . . . (BEAT) the
whole thing, though . . . the trip, dance and all . . . made me sleepy.

JOHN

sue went upstairs to our room, room we'd rented, with karen and tim's
girlfriend . . . patrice . . .

SUE

i'd known patrice since kindergarten . . .

JOHN

said they wanted to take a quick nap, just a half hour, whatever, then
we'd go get a bite. this was, like, maybe, one-thirty . . .

SUE

's a king-size bed. a gold comforter on it . . .

JOHN

so, we hung out downstairs a bit, talked to some guys from home . . .
david, tim, and me.

SUE

we all fell asleep, together on that bed . . .

JOHN

i was a touch bored, you know, room was warm, and lots of people we
didn't recognize . . . so i suggested a walk. "let's head over to the park."
about six, seven guys all together, it was still nice out . . .

SUE

i'm not sure what time it was . . .

JOHN

we strolled around a bit, over by the paris theatre, some guy, younger guy, kicked over a garbage can . . . i mean, it happens, you get together, doing stuff, no big deal. 's just garbage . . .
(PAUSE)
fifteen, twenty minutes later we split up, lot of the high schoolers want to get back to the bash, but us three, tim, david, and me . . . no hurry, we just kind 'a wander around, hanging out. after a while, we shoot over into central park, the 59th street entrance . . . looking around, talking. 's really dark in there, only lights coming from the buildings, way off. kind of exciting.

SUE

i thought i looked up at two, or two-fifteen . . . but i'm not sure. 'cause i kept sleeping . . .

JOHN

. . . and then i saw 'em. both of them. those guys . . .

SUE

i was so tired . . .

JOHN

they were saying "goodnight . . ." well, not saying it exactly, but kissing, two men, grown men, standing in this park, public park in the middle of new york and kissing like something out of a clark gable film. tongues out, and the arms around each other, and nothing else in the world matters to these two . . . just finishing off the date, big night at the symphony, or some foreign film, who knows? but it's this "see you soon" and "thanks so much" and hands all where they shouldn't be. i mean, come on, i know the scriptures, know 'em pretty well, and this is wrong. (BEAT) we all kind 'a squeeze up against a couple trees, off in the shadows, tim crouching on the ground, watching this. out near "the ramble." oh man . . . man! you know, you read about it, or even see that film, what is it, with the "superman" guy? *deathtrap*, right, and you live with it. don't love it, don't condone it for the world, still, you go on living, live and let live, whatever, but this, i figure, is flaunting it. i mean, as much our park as theirs, and we're in town one night, that's all, one . . . and we got 'a witness this?

(PAUSE)
men old enough to be our fathers—i mean, middle-aged, and clutching
at one another like romeo and juliet! (BEAT) they whisper something,
and chuckle for a second, hand on each other's bottoms . . . i start to feel
sick, i mean it, nauseous. then a last peck on the cheek and one disappears down a trail, headed for the west side. he's gone. the other glances
around, taking in the night, i guess, big smile up at the moon . . . and
he kind of casually strolls over to this "men's room." 50 yards off. concrete building, with the steps down into it. whistling while he goes . . .
he was whistling, i don't even stop to think this through, but motion the
guys to follow me.

SUE

i thought about getting out of my dress, but i couldn't move. all of us,
we were sleeping so peacefully . . . (BEAT) did you know patrice
snores? she does . . . a little.

JOHN

as we're moving down the landing into the restroom, i glance at tim
. . . 's got that look. recognize that look anywhere, and he's starting to
smile . . .

SUE

i don't think i even dreamed that night . . .

JOHN

before going in i told the guys to hold off, wait out here for me 'til they
got my signal . . . and that's the plan. wait for me to flush him out,
make sure no one wanders by. when i get inside, 's like another world
. . . walls are exploding with graffiti, place stinks, two bulbs burnt out.
some old dude curled up, asleep in a corner, and our friend's legs, i
spot, patiently sitting in a stall, waiting, and not a care in this world, i
slip into the booth next to his, start fumbling with my belt, this, that,
and like clockwork, this guy's hand comes up under my side of the
partition, his signal, pink fingers, wiggling up at me. imploring, i
notice this thin gold band on his little finger, catching the light.
(BEAT) so, i lay my open palm in his and two minutes later we're
standing near the mirrors—big pieces of stainless steel, really—standing, and sizing each other up. small talk. name's "chet," he says, and i
don't even bat an eyelash as he moves in, his lips playing across my

cheek, let his tongue run along my teeth and a hand, free hand, tracing down my fly . . . i just smile at him, smile and even lick his chin for a second, for a single second, i see his shoulders relax. then i whistle, i let out a whistle that sends him stumbling back, blinking, and kind of waving his hands in the air as tim and dave appear in the doorway, he looks at them, looks and comes back from his fantasies long enough to touch down on earth, a flicker in his eyes, realizing no good can come from this . . . and starts babbling, this guy, "chet," probably a vp some bank on park avenue, and he's babbling and wetting himself like an infant, i don't remember exactly, but i think he even got on his knees, down on his knees and the pleading, begging. (BEAT) my first shot catches him against the cheek, just under the eye and he slams into a sink. all snot and blood running down. with so many of us hitting, tearing at him, it's hard to get off a clean punch but i know i connect a few more times, i feel his head, the back of it, softening as we go, but i just find a new spot and move on. tim kicking him long after he's blacked out . . .
(PAUSE)
finally, we start to relax a bit, looking at what we've done. exhausted, spent, i mean, this man is not moving, may never move again and we know it's time to leave, believe this, guy in the corner, sleeps through it all?! (BEAT) before we go, tim leans into it one more time, takes a little run at it, smashing his foot against the bridge of this man's nose and i see it give way. just pick up and move to the other side of his face. wow. and then it's silence, not a sound, and for the first time, we look over at dave. tim and me. i mean, really look at him. us together, tim, myself, that's one thing, it's unspoken, our bond, but we don't know david. don't really know him . . . what's he thinking? and right then, as if to answer us through revelation . . . he grabs up the nearest trash can, big wire mesh thing, raises it above his head as he whispers, "fag." i'll never forget that . . . "fag." that's all. and brings that can down right on the spine of the guy, who just sort of shudders a bit, expelling some air. boom! right on his back, as i'm leaning down, pulling that ring off his pinkie. (BEAT) i told you i noticed it . . .
(PAUSE)
then, and i still can't even believe this, then tim does the most amazing thing, this'll go down, the record books, there, with the three of us over this guy's body, he starts offering up a short eulogy, i mean, i'm getting delirious, this is, like, almost surreal . . . and halfway through,

tim's praying along, we all start giggling, like schoolboys, we're howling, tears running down, can't catch our breath we find it all so funny! and that's how we leave him . . . (BEAT) slip out, one by one, running back toward the plaza in the dark and whooping it up like indians, war cries, and running with just a trace of moonlight dancing off the pond as we go . . .

SUE

the phone woke me up . . .

JOHN

we called the room from the street, wanted to take the girls out to breakfast, say they'll be down in fifteen minutes . . .
(PAUSE)
we waited outside.

SUE

i got the other girls up . . . took a minute, but i got them up. i felt really refreshed . . .
(PAUSE)
. . . i did.

JOHN

dave's walking around on the curb, talking to himself, and tim pulls me aside, asks me, wants to know one thing. "what?" i say. wants to know why i touched the guy. let him kiss me. see, he'd seen it happen, glanced inside, and seen it. (BEAT) but i didn't know, didn't have an answer, isn't that strange?

SUE

it was so quiet in the lobby as we were leaving, i started tiptoeing out. isn't that funny?

JOHN

i couldn't answer him, and you know, he never asked me again, he didn't. (BEAT) he pointed out to me, though, that my shirt had blood on it, a misting of blood, probably off the guy as i was getting the ring. my tux was covered, so, got 'a think quick, i asked tim to hit me in the face, give me a bloody nose so i could explain it to sue. (BEAT) only hurt for a second . . .

SUE

we all met in front of the hotel, and i saw john's face. aaah! all cut up like it was . . . see, he'd fallen down, racing along the fountain out front, balancing on it, and slipped, scraped himself up and blood on everything. (BEAT) silly games . . .

JOHN

had a great meal . . . you know, you can't get those german sausages for breakfast, the big fat ones, anywhere but manhattan, you can't . . .

SUE

i was eating my french toast, just eating along and i notice this glint in my water glass, a spark of light. (BEAT) john'd slipped a ring in it! a beautiful gold thing . . . i loved him so much at that moment.

JOHN

"happy anniversary," i said . . .

SUE

it was a little big, but fit pretty well. had this wonderful leaf pattern, all the way around . . .

JOHN

looked nice on her, i liked it . . .

SUE

i kissed him there, in front of everybody, and he blushed a bit. we all laughed, i can't tell you what a wonderful weekend we had . . .

JOHN

we did end up taking the amtrak back up . . . just sue and myself, dave dropped us at grand central and, you know, lots of "thank you" and "see you monday!" (BEAT) tim even gave me a hug. first time he's even done that . . .

SUE

it was my idea . . . the train.

JOHN

and we saw our parents, stopped in sunday and even made it to church . . . that was really nice.

SUE

i like sunday school at home so much better . . .

JOHN

had dinner with the folks, then the late train up to boston.

SUE

you know, on the way back—it's funny, i shouldn't even bring this up—a fight broke out. well, not really a fight but this argument between a man and his girlfriend, a lot of yelling, she stands up, and starts pulling on her coat and this guy, i mean, middle of a crowded compartment, just backhands her. he did . . .

JOHN

knocked her up against the window, really hard . . .

SUE

everybody got quiet, i could feel john tense up, getting all tense, but the couple was, i don't know, kind of dirty-looking and they seemed like, you know, those kind of people—i don't know what i mean by that, exactly, but they were—so i asked john, whispered to him, to "let it go." (BEAT) and you know what? he didn't so much as bat an eyelash. just kept holding my hand. holding it and playing with the ring on my finger, that made me so happy . . .

JOHN

i could see he'd given her a bloody nose . . .

SUE

and they pretty much quieted down right after that. 's no big deal . . .

JOHN

anyway . . .

SUE

anyway, we are getting engaged this summer, for sure. did i tell you that?

JOHN

and finally, as we tumbled along toward massachusetts, nearly midnight . . . i could feel sue fall asleep against my shoulder, all warm. protected.

SUE

i hope it's a fall wedding, you know? I always think they're the most beautiful . . .

JOHN

but not me . . . i couldn't drift off. just couldn't do it. so i sat up, watching the lights dance by, the moon grinning down. and you know, i started whistling to myself, i did . . .

SUE

i was sleeping, asleep there on john's arm, but i'd swear i could hear music . . .

JOHN

not loud, i mean, don't even recall the tune. but i was whistling, i was. that much i remember . . .

SUE

. . . this beautiful music as i was sleeping, like the sound of angels calling us home . . .

**they sit together in silence for a moment,
finally, they rise and embrace,
waiting for their picture to
be taken, they smile broadly.**

harsh bulb of a camera's flashbulb.

silence, darkness.

DORIS LESSING

From UNDER MY SKIN

❧

I LIKE THIS PIECE because it concentrates so much into a few paragraphs. If nothing else survived of my history, the essentials are all here.

First the family situation, dominated by my father's lost leg, blown away in the First World War, his ironical view of life, my mother's competence, her bravery, her refusal to see obstacles. Then, the war; it took a long time for that war to loosen its hold on those who were part of it—if it ever did.

Outside the train, so much going on: here is my first introduction to the world's ills, above all the children without fathers and mothers, wild, desperate, and hungry—their numbers have immeasurably increased since then.

I was not yet five years old. How much is conveyed about that child's helplessness, and, too, her ways of coping with it.

How well I do remember the small girl and her teddy, the suitcase of clothes which had to be ordered just so used to keep control of such anxiety—her mother apparently disappeared, the threats from the angry mob.

These are some of my earliest memories.

The scene in the Moscow Hotel, one of the brightest: there I am in the corridor, shut out of the room, the handle of the door far above my reach.

Not least is the comedy of the British abroad in the last refulgence of the British Empire, triumphing over civil war and chaos.

—Doris Lessing

When my mother decided to travel to England via Moscow, across Russia, because she did not want to expose her little children to the heat of the Red Sea, she did not know what she was doing—as she often said herself. *"If I'd only known!"* She did know we would be the first foreign family to travel in an ordinary way since the Revolution. It was 1924. That it would be difficult, of course she knew, but difficulties are made to be overcome. The journey turned out to be horrendous, told and told again, the vividest chapter in the family chronicle. What I was told and what I remember are not the same, and the most dramatic moment of all is nowhere in my memory. At the Russian frontier, it turned out we did not have the right stamps in our passports, and my mother had to browbeat a bemused official into letting us in. Both my mother and my father loved this incident: she because she had achieved the impossible, he because of his relish for farce. "Good Lord, no one would dare to put that on the stage," he would say, recalling the calm, in-the-right, overriding British matron, and the ragged and hungry official who had probably never seen a foreign family with well-dressed and well-fed children.

The most dangerous part was at the beginning, when the family found itself on an oil tanker across the Caspian, which had been used as a troop carrier, and the cabin, "not exactly everyone's idea of a cruise cabin," was full of lice. And, probably, of typhus, then raging everywhere.

The parents sat up all night to keep the sleeping children inside the circles of lamplight, but one arm, mine, fell into the shadow and was bitten by bugs, and swelled up, red and enormous. The cabin was usually shared by members of the crew, and was small. For me it was a vast, cavernous, shadowy place, full of menace because of my parents' fear, but above all, the smell, a cold stuffy metallic stink which is the smell of lice.

From the Caspian to Moscow took several days, and the tale went like this: "There was no food on the train, and Mummy got off at the stations to buy from the peasant women, but they only had hard-boiled eggs and a little bread. The samovar in the corridor most of the time didn't have water. And we were afraid to drink unboiled water. There was typhoid and typhus, and filthy diseases everywhere. And every station was swarming with beggars and homeless children, oh it was horrible, and then Mummy was left behind at a station because the train just started without warning and we thought we would never see her again. But she caught us up two days later. She made the station master stop the next train, and she got on to it and caught us up. All this without a word of Russian, mind you."

What I remember is something different, parallel, but like a jerky stop-and-start film.

The seats in the compartment, which was like a little room, were ragged, and they smelled of sickness and sweat and of mice, in spite of the Keating's Insect Powder my mother sprinkled everywhere. Mice scurried under the seats and ran between our feet looking for crumbs. The lamps on the wall were broken, but luckily my mother had thought of candles. At night I woke to see long pale dangerous flames swaying against the black panes where cracks let in air, warm in the south, cold in the north. I held my face in it, because of the smell. It was April. My father had flu, and lay on an upper bunk, away from the two noisy children and our demands. My mother was frightened: the great Flu Epidemic was over, but the threat of it would be heard in people's voices for years yet. There were little bloody dots and spatters on the seats, and that meant lice had been here. Years later I had to sit myself down and work out why the words flu and typhus made me afraid. Flu was easy, but typhus? It was from that journey. For years the word "Russia" meant station platforms, for the train stopped all the time, at sidings as well as big towns, on the long journey from Baku to Moscow.

The train groaned and rattled and screamed and strained to a stop among crowds of people, and what frightening people, for they were nothing like the Persians. They were in rags, some seemed like bundles of rags, and with their feet tied in rags. Children with sharp hungry faces jumped up at the train windows and peered in, or held up their hands, begging. Then soldiers jumped down from the train and pushed back the people, holding their guns like sticks to hit them with, and the crowds fell back before the soldiers, but then swarmed forward again. Some people lay on the platforms, with their heads on bundles and watched the train, but not expecting anything from it. My parents talked about them, and their voices were low and anxious and there were words I did not know, so I kept saying, what does that mean, what does that mean? The Great War. The Revolution. The Civil War. Famine. The Bolsheviks. But why, Mummy, but why, Daddy? Because we had been told that the *besprizorniki*—the gangs of children without families—attacked trains when they stopped at stations, as soon as my mother got out to buy food, the compartment door was locked and the windows pushed up. The locks on the door were unsafe and suitcases were pushed against it. This meant my father had to come down from his high shelf. He wore his dark heavy dressing gown, bought for warmth in the Trenches, but under it he kept on all his gear and tackle for the wooden leg, so he could put it on quickly. Meanwhile the pale scarred stump sometimes poked out from the dressing gown, because, he joked, it had a life of its own, for it did not know it was only part of a leg, and in moments of need, as when he leaned forward to open the compartment door to let in my mother—triumphant, holding up her purchases, a couple of eggs, a bit of bread—it tried to behave like a leg, instinctively reaching out to take weight. The two little children fearfully watched our mother out there among those frightening crowds, as she held out money to the peasant women for the hard eggs, the half-loaves of the dark sour stuff that was called bread. The story said we were hungry because there was not enough food, but I don't remember feeling hungry. Only the fear and the anguish, looking at those swarms of people, so strange, so unlike us, and at the ragged children who had no parents and no one to look after them. When the train jerked forward, the soldiers jumped on to it, clutching what they had managed to buy from the women, and then turned to keep their guns pointed at the children who ran after the train.

The story says we were read to, we played with plasticine, we drew pictures with chalks, we counted telegraph wires and played "I-Spy" out of the windows, but what is in my mind is the train rattling into yet another station—surely it was the same one?—the ragged people, the ragged children. And again my mother was out there, among them all. And then, when the train was pulling out, she did not appear in the corridor outside the compartment, holding up what she had bought to show us. She had been left behind. My sick father held himself upright in the corner and kept saying it was all right, she would come soon, nothing to worry about, don't cry. But he was worried and we knew it. That was when I first understood the helplessness of my father, his dependence on her. He could not jump down out of the train with his wooden leg and push through the crowds looking for food. "You had to share an egg between you and there were some raisins we brought with us, but that was all." She would have to reappear, she would have to, and she did, but two days later. Meanwhile our train had been slowing, groaning and screeching, again and again, into stations, into sidings, into the crowds, the *besprizorniki*, the soldiers with guns. I don't remember crying and being frightened, all that has gone, but not the rough feel of the dressing gown on my cheek as I sat on my father's good knee and saw the hungry faces at the window, peering in. But I was safe in his arms.

A small girl sits on the train seat with her teddy and the tiny cardboard suitcase that has teddy's clothes in it. She takes the teddy's clothes off, folds them just so, takes another set of clothes from the case, dresses the teddy, tells it to be good and sit quietly, takes this set of clothes off the teddy, folds them, takes a third set of trousers and jacket out, puts the taken-off clothes back in the case, folded perfectly, dresses the teddy. Over and over again, ordering the world, keeping control of events. There, you're a good teddy, nice and clean.

From Moscow comes the most powerful of all my early memories. I am in a hotel corridor, outside a door whose handle is high above my head. The ceiling is very far away up there, and the great tall shiny doors go all along the corridor, and behind every door is a frightening strangeness, strange people, who appear suddenly out of a doorway or walk fast past all the shut doors, and disappear, or arrive at the turn of the corridor and then vanish into a door. I bang my fists against our door, and cry and scream. No one comes. No one comes for what seems like for ever, but that cannot have been so, the door must have soon opened, but the nightmare is of being shut out, locked out, and the implacable tall shiny door. This shut door is in a thousand tales, legends, myths, the door to which you do not have the key, the door which is the way to—but that is the point, I suppose. Probably it is in our genes, I wouldn't be surprised, this shut door, and it is in my memory for ever, while I reach up, like Alice, trying to touch the handle.

JONATHAN LETHEM

From THE FORTRESS of SOLITUDE

THE FORTRESS OF SOLITUDE is the best book I've written. These pages, from about a hundred pages in, are where I really began cooking. When the character of Arthur Lomb appeared, I knew my subconscious was going to take the book further than even my (very ambitious) conscious designs could aspire. I'm grateful to him, poor wretch. I still read these pages aloud in bookstores more than any other part of the book.

—Jonathan Lethem

It was entirely possible that one song could destroy your life. Yes, musical doom could fall on a lone human form and crush it like a bug. The song, *that song*, was sent from somewhere else to find you, to pick the scab of your whole existence. The song was your personal shitty fate, manifest as a throb of pop floating out of radios everywhere.

At the very least the song was the soundtrack to your destruction, the *theme*. Your days reduced to a montage cut to its cowbell beat, inexorable doubled bassline and raunch vocal, a sort of chanted sneer, surrounded by groans of pleasure. The stutter and blurt of what—a *tuba*? French horn? Rhythm guitar and trumpet, pitched to mockery. The singer might as well have held a gun to your head. How it could have been allowed to happen, how it could have been allowed on the *radio*? That song ought to be illegal. It wasn't racist—you'll never sort that one out, don't even start—so much as anti-*you*.

Yes they were dancing, and singing, and movin' to the groovin', and just when it hit me, somebody turned around and shouted—

Every time your sneakers met the street, the end of that summer, somebody was hurling it at your head, *that song*.

September 7, 1976, the week Dylan Ebdus began seventh grade in the main building on Court Street and Butler, Wild Cherry's "Play That Funky Music" was the top song on the rhythm and blues charts.

Fourteen days later it topped *Billboard*'s pop charts. Your misery's anthem, number-one song in the nation.

Sing it through gritted teeth: *WHITE BOY!*

Lay down the boogie and play that funky music 'til you die.

Seventh grade was where it turned out when you finally joined Mingus Rude in the main building Mingus Rude was never there. The only evidence he existed was the proliferation of DOSE tags on lamp-posts and mailboxes, Mingus's handiwork spread in a nimbus with the school building at the center. Every few days, it seemed, produced a fresh supply. Dylan would covertly push a forefinger against the metal, wondering if he could measure in the tackiness of the ink the tag's vintage. If his finger stuck slightly Dylan imagined he'd followed Mingus by minutes to the spot, barely missed catching him in the act.

For three weeks Mingus Rude was a rumor Dylan couldn't confirm. Mingus's vacancy from his own schooldays, and from Dylan's, was the secret premise of an existence which was otherwise unchanged except by being worse every possible way. Seventh grade was sixth grade desublimated, uncorked. It was the *Lord of the Rings* trilogy to sixth grade's *The Hobbit*, the real story at last, all the ominous foreshadowed stuff flushed from the margins and into view. It wasn't for children, seventh grade. You could read the stress of even entering the building in the postures of the teachers, the security guards. Nobody could relax in such a racial and hormonal disaster area.

Bodies ranged like ugly cartoons, as though someone without talent was scribbling in flesh.

Chinese kids had apparently gotten some warning well in advance, and had thoroughly disappeared.

Puerto Rican or Dominican kids seemed to be tiptoeing away from the scene of everything. They decorated themselves differently and spoke more Spanish each passing hour.

The scariest fights were between black girls.

When Dylan Ebdus first spotted Arthur Lomb the other boy was feigning pain in the far corner of the schoolyard. At some distance Dylan heard the cries and turned from the entrance of the school to look. Catching sight of Arthur Lomb was like noticing the flight and fall of a bird across a distance of leaf-blurred sky, that flicker at the corner of vision, the abrupt plummeting. It occurred at that moment after the bell had rung and the gym teachers who patrolled the yard had returned inside, ahead of the flood of students, so the yard became a lawless zone, that terrible sudden reframing of space which could happen anywhere, even inside the corridors of the school. Nevertheless it was a clumsy mistake for the boy now cringing on the ground to be caught so far from the yard's entrance, a mistake Dylan felt he couldn't forgive. He wouldn't have forgiven it in himself.

Arthur Lomb fell to his knees and clutched his chest and keened. His words were briefly audible across the depopulating yard.

"I can't breathe!"

Then, each syllable riding a sharp insuck of air, *"I!"* Pause. *"Can't!"* Pause. *"Breathe!"*

Arthur Lomb was pretending asthma or some other weakness. It was an identifiable method: preemptive suffering. Nobody could do much with a kid who was already crying. He had no spirit to crush and it was faintly disgusting, in poor taste. Anyway, this weirdly gasping kid might not know the rules and talk, tattle to some distant cloddish figure of authority what he imagined had been done to him. He might even be truly sick, fucked up, in pain, who knew? Your only option was to say *dang, white boy, what's your problem? I didn't even touch you.* And move on.

Dylan admired the strategy, feeling at once a cool quiver of recognition and a hot bolt of shame. He felt that he was seeing his double, his stand-in.

From that point on Arthur Lomb's reddish hair and hunched shoulders were easy to spot. He dressed in conspicuous striped polo shirts and wore soft brown shoes. His pants were often highwaters. Dylan once heard a couple of black girls serenading Arthur Lomb with a couplet he hadn't himself elicited since fourth grade, snapping their fingers and harmonizing high and low like a doo-wop group: *The flood is over, the land is dry, so why do you wear your pants so high?*

Arthur Lomb carried an enormous and bright blue backpack, an additional blight. All his schoolbooks must be inside, or maybe a couple of stone tablets. The bag itself would have tugged Arthur Lomb to the ground if he'd stood up straight. The bag glowed as a target, begged to be jerked downward to crumple Arthur Lomb to the corridor floor to enact his shortness-of-breath routine. Dylan had seen it done five times already before he and Arthur Lomb ever spoke. Dylan had even heard kids chanting *the song* at Arthur Lomb as they slapped at his reddened neck or the top of his head while he squirmed on the floor. Play that *fucking* music, white boy! Stretching the last two words to a groaning, derisive, Bugs-Bunnyesque *whyyyyyyyboy*!

It was the library where they finally spoke. Dylan and Arthur Lomb's two homerooms had been deposited there together for a period, the school librarian covering some unexplained absence of teachers. Below a poster advertising *A Hero Ain't Nothin' But a Sandwich*, a book the library didn't actually offer, Dylan placed himself against a wall and flipped open issue number two of the Marvel Comics adaptation of *Logan's Run*. As the period ticked away glacially, Arthur Lomb buzzed him twice, squinting to see the title of the comic, then pursing lips in false concentration as he mimed browsing the half-empty shelves nearby, before stepping close enough for Dylan to hear him speak in an angry, clenched whisper.

"That guy George Perez can't draw Farrah Fawcett to save his life."

It was a startling allusion to several bodies of knowledge simultaneously. Dylan could only glare, his curiosity mingled with the certainty that he and Arthur Lomb were more objectionable, more unpardonable, together than apart. Up close Arthur Lomb had a blinky agitated quality to his features which made Dylan himself want to knock him down. His face seemed to reach for something, his features like a grasping hand. Dylan wondered if there might be a pair of glasses tucked in the background somewhere, perhaps in a side pocket of the monumental blue backpack.

"Seen it?"

"What?"

"*Logan's Run.*"

Fuck you looking at? Dylan wanted to shriek at Arthur Lomb, before it was too late, before Dylan succumbed to his loneliness and allowed himself to meet Arthur, the other white boy.

"Not yet," Dylan said instead.

"Farrah Fawcett is a *fox*."

Dylan didn't answer.

"Don't feel bad. I bought ten copies of *Logan's Run #1*." Arthur Lomb spoke in a hurried whisper, showing some awareness of his surroundings, but compelled to spill what he had, to force Dylan know to him. "You *have* to buy number ones, it's an investment. I've got ten of *Eternals*, ten of *2001*, ten of *Omega*, ten of *Kobra*. And all those comics stink. Number one's a number one, doesn't matter. You know *Fantastic Four #1* goes for four hundred dollars? Kobra might be an all-time record for the stupidest character ever. Doesn't matter. Put it in plastic and put it on the shelf, that's what I say. You use plastic, don't you?"

"Of course," said Dylan resentfully.

He understood every word Arthur Lomb said. Worse, he felt his sensibility colonized by Arthur's, his future interests co-opted.

They were doomed to friendship.

PHILIP LEVINE

MY FATHER with CIGARETTE TWELVE YEARS BEFORE the NAZIS COULD BREAK HIS HEART

THERE ARE OTHER POEMS by me that are far better known and in fact may be better poems: I'm thinking specifically of "They Feed They Lion," which is the most anthologized of my poems, and "A Walk with Tom Jefferson," which captures better than any other poem I've written the complex of emotions I feel about my city, Detroit, and I love it because it took me so long to write and required more patience than I knew I had. "My Father," by contrast, came quickly in a sudden rush that consumed a single morning. A few days before I wrote it I'd gone, grudgingly, with my wife to the Museum of American Folk Art in its old home near Lincoln Center. Besides the museum's permanent collection, there was a visiting show of the work of Harry Lieberman, a Polish Jew, born in 1880, who'd immigrated to the U.S. in 1906, about the same time as my father. Nephew of a Hassidic rabbi, Lieberman had prepared for the rabbinate, but abandoned that life to work in New York City, first as a clothing cutter and later as a candy manufacturer. At the age of seventy-six, bored with retirement, he took up painting, and had the good luck to have Larry Rivers as a teacher. Most of his paintings reflect his early interest in the folklore and imagery of Orthodox Judaism. During the thirties he'd returned to Poland to urge the remaining members of his family to come to the U.S., for Lieberman was aware of the Nazi's designs on his people. He was unsuccessful and returned alone to New York. One of the paintings, the one that moved me the most, reflected an impression from that trip; in it his father is smoking what looked to me like an enormous cigarette, one that appears completely out of proportion to the rest of the painting, which was titled, "My Father with Cigarette." My own father had died in 1933 at the age of thirty-five. For the first time I realized that awful as that event was it did spare him the knowledge of what was ahead for all those he'd left behind.

—Philip Levine

I remember the room in which he held
a kitchen match and with his thumbnail
commanded it to flame: a brown sofa,
two easy chairs, one covered with flowers,
a black piano no one ever played half
covered by a long-fringed ornamental scarf
Ray Estrada brought back from Mexico
in 1931. How new the world is, you say.
In that room someone is speaking about money,
asking why it matters, and my father exhales
the blue smoke, and says a million dollars
even in large bills would be impossible.
He's telling me because, I see now, I'm
the one who asked, for I dream of money,
always coins and bills that run through my hands,
money I find in the corners of unknown rooms
or in metal boxes I dig up in the backyard
flower beds of houses I've never seen.
My father rises now and goes to the closet.
It's as though someone were directing a play
and my father's part called for him to stand
so that the audience, which must be you,
could see him in white shirt, dark trousers,
held up by suspenders, a sign of the times,
and conclude he is taller than his son
will ever be, and as he dips into his jacket,
you'll know his role calls for him to exit
by the front door, leaving something
unfinished, the closet light still on,
the cigarette still burning dangerously,
a Yiddish paper folded to the right place
so that a photograph of Hindenburg
in full military regalia swims up
to you out of all the details we lived.
I remember the way the match flared
blue and yellow in the deepening light
of a cool afternoon in early September,
and the sound, part iron, part animal,
part music, as the air rushed toward it

out of my mouth, and his intake of breath
through the Lucky Strike, and the smoke
hanging on after the door closed and the play
ran out of acts and actors, and the audience—
which must be you—grew tired of these lives
that finally come to nothing or no more
than the furniture and the cotton drapes
left open so the darkening sky can seem
to have the last word, with half a moon
and a showering of fake stars to say what
the stars always say about the ordinary.
Oh, you're still here, 60 years later,
you wonder what became of us, why
someone put it in a book, and left
the book open to a page no one reads.
Everything tells you he never came back,
though he did before he didn't, everything
suggests it was the year Hitler came
to power, the year my grandmother learned
to read English novels and fell in love
with *David Copperfield* and *Oliver Twist*
which she read to me seated on a stool
beside my bed until I fell asleep.
Everything tells you this is a preface
to something important, the Second World War,
the news that leaked back from Poland
that the villages were gone. The truth is—
if there is a truth—I remember the room,
I remember the flame, the blue smoke,
how bright and slippery were the secret coins,
how David Copperfield doubted his own name,
how sweet the stars seemed, peeping and blinking,
how close the moon, how utterly silent the piano.

BARRY LOPEZ

THE MAPPIST

I'M NOT AT EASE with the idea that a short story must have a point, anymore than I'm comfortable with the thought that I can cast an eye back over thirty-five years and say, "This is the best story I ever wrote."

I've never written a story to make a point—I've never known, in fact, how a story was going to end until I finished writing it. The short story, as I see it, is a pattern that strikes the reader in the end as true, a set of relationships—events, settings, characters, images—that coheres emotionally. It is not meant to be an explanation of life, but by the very way the parts of the pattern fit together the reader comes to feel well situated again in the larger tapestry of life, as if something once known but then forgotten has reemerged.

The title of this story occurred to me many years before I wrote it. It lay around in my imagination, as I picture it, gathering to itself various moments (for example, my personal experience one night in the Sanseido Book Store; my fascination with the landscapes of North Dakota, where I've set four other stories; my anxiety about the loss of authenticity in modern life; my preoccupation with maps) until I sat down at my typewriter one day and that long-lived title generated this story.

Had I written "The Mappist" earlier, it might simply have ended with an encounter between Phillip Trevino and Corlis Benefideo, though perhaps in a setting different from this one in Corlis's home. But with four children in my life by the time I actually drafted the story (as opposed to none when the title first came to me), it represents another kind of knowing than the one I had without children.

I can see in "The Mappist" themes I believe relevant to our times. I want to continue to explore these perceptions about modern life in other stories, especially the social and political dangers inherent in a free-floating culture, in, literally, an ungrounded existence.

On the day that I drafted this story, this was the best I could do with my claim to a knowledge of life. I mean it as a kind of proof against the threat of being alone in the world. I hope it fares well with you, as you bring to it an imagination different from mine.

—Barry Lopez

When I was an undergraduate at Brown I came across a book called *The City of Ascensions*, about Bogotá. I knew nothing of Bogotá, but I felt the author had captured its essence. My view was that Onesimo Peña had not written a travel book but a work about the soul of Bogotá. Even if I were to read it later in life, I thought, I would not be able to get all Peña meant in a single reading. I looked him up at the library but he had apparently written no other books, at least not any in English.

In my senior year I discovered a somewhat better known book, *The City of Trembling Leaves*, by Walter Van Tilburg Clark, about Reno, Nevada. I liked it, but it did not have the superior depth, the integration of Peña's work. Peña, you had the feeling, could walk you through the warrens of Bogotá without a map and put your hands directly on the vitality of any modern century—the baptismal registries of a particular cathedral, a cornerstone that had been taken from one building to be used in another, a London plane tree planted by Bolívar. He had such a command of the idiom of this city, and the book itself demonstrated such complex linkages, it was easy to believe Peña had no other subject, that he could have written nothing else. I believed this was so until I read *The City of Floating Sand* a year later, a book about Cape Town, and then a book about Djakarta, called *The City of Frangipani*. Though the former was by one Frans Haartman and the latter by a Jemboa Tran, each had the distinctive organic layering of the Peña book, and I felt certain they'd been written by the same man.

A national library search through the University of Michigan, where I had gone to work on a master's degree in geography, produced hundreds of books with titles similar to these. I had to know whether Peña had written any others and so read or skimmed perhaps thirty of those I got through interlibrary loan. Some, though wretched, were strange enough to be engaging; others were brilliant but not in the way of Peña. I ended up ordering copies of five I believed Peña had written, books about Perth, Lagos, Tokyo, Venice, and Boston, the last a volume by William Smith Everett called *The City of Cod*.

Who Peña actually was I could not then determine. Letters to publishers eventually led me to a literary agency in New York where I was told that the author did not wish to be known. I pressed for information about what else he might have written, inquired whether he was still alive (the book about Venice had been published more than fifty years before), but got nowhere.

As a doctoral student at Duke I made the seven Peña books the basis of a dissertation. I wanted to show in a series of city maps, based on all the detail in Peña's descriptions, what a brilliant exegesis of the social dynamics of these cities he had achieved. My maps showed, for example, how water moved through Djakarta, not just municipal water but also trucked water and, street by street, the flow of rainwater. And how road building in Cape Town reflected the policy of apartheid.

I received quite a few compliments on the work, but I knew the maps did not make apparent the hard, translucent jewel of integration that was each Peña book. I had only created some illustrations, however well done. But had I known whether he was alive or where he lived, I would still have sent him a copy out of a sense of collegiality and respect.

After I finished the dissertation I moved my wife and three young children to Brookline, a suburb of Boston, and set up a practice as a restoration geographer. Fifteen years later I embarked on my fourth or fifth trip to Tokyo as a consultant to a planning firm there, and one evening I took a train out to Chiyoda-ku to visit bookstores in an area called Jimbocho. Just down the street from a bridge over the Kanda River is the Sanseido Book Store, a regular haunt by then for me. Up on the fifth floor I bought two translations of books by Japanese writers on the Asian architectural response to topography in mountain cities. I was exiting the store on the ground floor, a level given over entirely to maps, closing my coat against the spring night, when I happened to spot the kanji for "Tokyo" on a tier of drawers. I opened one of them to browse. Toward the bottom of a second drawer, I came upon a set of maps that seemed vaguely familiar, though the entries were all in kanji. After a few minutes of leafing through, it dawned on me that they bore a resemblance to the maps I had done as a student at Duke. I was considering buying one of them as a memento when I caught a name in English in the corner—Corlis Benefideo. It appeared there on every map.

I stared at that name a long while, and I began to consider what you also may be thinking. I bought all thirteen maps. Even without language to identify information in the keys, even without titles, I could decipher what the mapmaker was up to. One designated areas prone to flooding as water from the Sumida River backed up through the city's storm drains. Another showed the location of all shops dealing in Edo Period manuscripts and artwork. Another, using small pink arrows, showed the point of view of each of Hiroshige's famous One Hundred Views. Yet another showed, in six time-sequenced panels, the rise and decline of horse barns in the city.

My office in Boston was fourteen hours behind me, so I had to leave a message for my assistant, asking him to look up Corlis Benefideo's name. I gave him some contacts at map libraries I used regularly, and asked him to call me back as soon as he had anything, no matter the hour. He called at three A.M. to say that Corlis Benefideo had worked as a mapmaker for the U.S. Coast and Geodetic Survey in Washington from 1932 until 1958, and that he was going to fax me some more information.

I dressed and went down to the hotel lobby to wait for the faxes and read them while I stood there. Benefideo was born in Fargo, North Dakota, in 1912. He went to work for the federal government straight out of Grinnell College during the Depression and by 1940 was traveling to various places—Venice, Bogotá, Lagos—in an exchange program. In 1958 he went into private practice as a cartographer in Chicago. His main source of income at that time appeared to be from the production of individualized site maps for large estate homes being built along the North Shore of Lake Michigan. The maps were bound in oversize books, twenty by thirty inches, and showed the vegetation, geology, hydrology, biology, and even archaeology of each site. They were subcontracted for under several architects.

Benefideo's Chicago practice closed in 1975. The fax said nothing more was known of his work history, and that he was not listed in any Chicago area phone books, nor with any professional organizations. I faxed back to my office, asking them to check phone books in Fargo, in Washington, D.C., and around Grinnell, Iowa—Des Moines and those towns. And asking them to try to find someone at what was now the National Geodetic Survey who might have known Benefideo or who could provide some detail.

When I came back to the hotel the following afternoon, there was another fax. No luck with the phone books, I read, but I could call a Maxwell Abert at the National Survey who'd worked with Benefideo. I waited the necessary few hours for the time change and called.

Abert said he had overlapped with Benefideo for one year, 1958, and though Benefideo had left voluntarily, it wasn't his idea.

"What you had to understand about Corlis," he said, "was that he was a patriot. Now, that word today, I don't know, means maybe nothing, but Corlis felt this very strong commitment to his country, and to a certain kind of mapmaking, and he and the Survey just ended up on a collision course. The way Corlis worked, you see, the way he approached things, slowed down the production of the maps. That wasn't any good from a bureaucratic point of view. He couldn't give up being comprehensive, you understand, and they just didn't know what to do with him."

"What happened to him?"

"Well, the man spoke five or six languages, and he had both the drafting ability and the conceptual skill of a first-rate cartographer, so the government should have done something to keep the guy—and he was also very loyal—but they didn't. Oh, his last year they created a project for him, but it was temporary. He saw they didn't want him. He moved to Chicago—but you said you knew that."

"Mmm. Do you know where he went after Chicago?"

"I do. He went to Fargo. And that's the last I know. I wrote him there until about 1985—he'd have been in his seventies—and then the last letter came back 'no forwarding address.' So that's the last I heard. I believe he must have died. He'd be, what, eighty-eight now."

"What was the special project?"

"Well Corlis, you know, he was like something out of a WPA project, like Dorothea Lange, Walker Evans and James Agee and them, people that had this sense of America as a country under siege, undergoing a trial during the Depression, a society that needed its dignity back. Corlis believed that in order to effect any political or social change, you had to know exactly what you were talking about. You had to know what the country itself—the ground, the real thing, not some political abstraction—was all about. So he proposed this series of forty-eight sets of maps—this was just before Alaska and Hawaii came in—a series for each state that would show the geology and hydrology, where the water was, you know, and the botany and biology, and the history of the place from Native American times.

"Well, a hundred people working hundred-hour weeks for a decade might get it all down, you know—it was monumental, what he was proposing. But to keep him around, to have him in the office, the

Survey created this pilot project so he could come up with an approach that might get it done in a reasonable amount of time—why, I don't know; the government works on most things forever—but that's what he did. I never saw the results, but if you ever wanted to see disillusionment in a man, you should have seen Corlis in those last months. He tried congressmen, he tried senators, he tried other people in Commerce, he tried everybody, but I think they all had the same sense of him, that he was an obstructionist. They'd eat a guy like that alive on the Hill today, the same way. He just wasn't very practical. But he was a good man."

I got the address in Fargo and thanked Mr. Abert. It turned out to be where Benefideo's parents had lived until they died. The house was sold in 1985. And that was that.

When I returned to Boston I reread *The City of Ascensions*. It's a beautiful book, so tender toward the city, and proceeding on the assumption that Bogotá was the living idea of its inhabitants. I thought Benefideo's books would make an exceptional subject for a senior project in history or geography, and wanted to suggest it to my older daughter, Stephanie. How, I might ask her, do we cultivate people like Corlis Benefideo? Do they all finally return to the rural districts from which they come, unable or unwilling to fully adapt to the goals, the tone, of a progressive society? Was Corlis familiar with the work of Lewis Mumford? Would you call him a populist?

Stephanie, about to finish her junior year at Bryn Mawr, had an interest in cities and geography, but I didn't know how to follow up on this with her. Her interests were there in spite of my promotions.

One morning, several months after I got back from Tokyo, I walked into the office and saw a note in the center of my desk, a few words from my diligent assistant. It was Benefideo's address—Box 117, Garrison, North Dakota 58540. I got out the office atlas. Garrison is halfway between Minot and Bismarck, just north of Lake Sakakawea. No phone.

I wrote him a brief letter, saying I'd recently bought a set of his maps in Tokyo, asking if he was indeed the author of the books, and telling him how much I admired them and that I had based my Ph.D. dissertation on them. I praised the integrity of the work he had done, and said I was intrigued by his last Survey project, and would also like to see one of the Chicago publications sometime.

A week later I got a note. "Dear Mr. Trevino," it read.

I appreciate your kind words about my work. I am still at it. Come
for a visit if you wish. I will be back from a trip in late September, so
the first week of October would be fine. Sincerely, Corlis Benefideo.

I located a motel in Garrison, got plane tickets to Bismarck,
arranged a rental car, and then wrote Mr. Benefideo and told him I
was coming, and that if he would send me his street address I would
be at his door at nine A.M. on October second. The address he sent,
15088 State Highway 37, was a few miles east of Garrison. A hand-
rendered map in colored pencil, which made tears well up in my eyes,
showed how to get to the house, which lay a ways off the road in a
grove of ash trees he had sketched.

The days of waiting made me anxious and aware of my vulnerability. I asked both my daughters and my son if they wanted to go. No,
school was starting, they wanted to be with their friends. My wife
debated, then said no. She thought this was something that would go
best if I went alone.

Corlis was straddling the sill of his door as I drove in to his yard. He
wore a pair of khaki trousers, a khaki shirt, and a khaki ball cap. He
was about five foot six and lean. Though spry, he showed evidence of
arthritis and the other infirmities of age in his walk and handshake.

During breakfast I noticed a set of *The City of* books on his
shelves. There were eight, which meant I'd missed one. After breakfast he asked if I'd brought any binoculars, and whether I'd be interested in visiting a wildlife refuge a few miles away off the Bismarck
highway, to watch ducks and geese coming in from Canada. He made
a picnic lunch and we drove over and had a fine time. I had no binoculars with me, and little interest in the birds to start with, but with his
guidance and animation I came to appreciate the place. We saw more
than a million birds that day, he said.

When we got back to the house I asked if I could scan his book-
shelves while he fixed dinner. He had thousands of books, a significant
number of them in Spanish and French and some in Japanese. (The
eighth book was called *The City of Geraniums*, about Lima.) On the
walls of a large room that incorporated the kitchen and dining area
was perhaps the most astonishing collection of hand-drawn maps I

had ever seen outside a library. Among them were two of McKenzie's map sketches from his exploration of northern Canada; four of FitzRoy's coastal elevations from Chile, made during the voyage with Darwin; one of Humboldt's maps of the Orinoco; and a half-dozen sketches of the Thames docks by Samuel Pepys.

Mr. Benefideo made us a dinner of canned soup, canned meat, and canned vegetables. For dessert he served fresh fruit, some store-bought cookies, and instant coffee. I studied him at the table. His forehead was high, and a prominent jaw and large nose further elongated his face. His eyes were pale blue, his skin burnished and dark, like a Palermo fisherman's. His ears flared slightly. His hair, still black on top, was close-cropped. There was little in the face but the alertness of the eyes to give you a sense of the importance of his work.

After dinner our conversation took a more satisfying turn. He had discouraged conversation while we were watching the birds, and he had seemed disinclined to talk while he was riding in the car. Our exchanges around dinner—which was quick—were broken up by its preparation and by clearing the table. A little to my surprise, he offered me Mexican tequila after the meal. I declined, noticing the bottle had no label, but sat with him on the porch while he drank.

Yes, he said, he'd used the pen names to keep the government from finding out what else he'd been up to in those cities. And yes, the experience with the Survey had made him a little bitter, but it had also opened the way to other things. His work in Chicago had satisfied him—the map sets for the estate architects and their wealthy clients, he made clear, were a minor thing; his real business in those years was in other countries, where hand-drawn and hand-colored maps still were welcome and enthused over. The estate map books, however, had allowed him to keep his hand in on the kind of work he wanted to pursue more fully one day. In 1975 he came back to Fargo to take care of his parents. When they died he sold the house and moved to Garrison. He had a government pension—when he said this he flicked his eyebrows, as though in the end he had gotten the best of the government. He had a small income from his books, he told me, mostly the foreign editions. And he had put some money away, so he'd been able to buy this place.

"What are you doing now?"

"The North Dakota series, the work I proposed in Washington in '57."

"The hydrological maps, the biological maps?"

"Yes. I subdivided the state into different sections, the actual number depending on whatever scale I needed for that subject. I've been doing them for fifteen years now, a thousand six hundred and fifty-one maps. I want to finish them, you know, so that if anyone ever wants to duplicate the work, they'll have a good idea of how to go about it."

He gazed at me in a slightly disturbing, almost accusatory way.

"Are you going to donate the maps, then, to a place where they can be studied?"

"North Dakota Museum of Art, in Grand Forks."

"Did you never marry, never have children?"

"I'm not sure, you know. No, I never married—I asked a few times, but was turned down. I didn't have the features, I think, and, early on, no money. Afterward, I developed a way of life that was really too much my own on a day-to-day basis. But, you know, I've been the beneficiary of great kindness in my life, and some of it has come from women who were, or are, very dear to me. Do you know what I mean?"

"Yes, I do."

"As for children, I think maybe there are one or two. In Bogotá. Venice. Does it shock you?"

"People are not shocked by things like this anymore, Mr. Benefideo."

"That's too bad. I am. I have made my peace with it, though. Would you like to see the maps?"

"The Dakota series?"

Mr. Benefideo took me to a second large room with more stunning maps on the walls, six or eight tiers of large map drawers, and a work-table the perimeter of which was stained with hundreds of shades of watercolors surrounding a gleaming white area about three feet square. He turned on some track lighting which made the room very bright and pointed me to a swivel stool in front of an empty table, a smooth, broad surface of some waxed and dark wood.

From an adjacent drawer he pulled out a set of large maps, which he laid in front of me.

"As you go through, swing them to the side there. I'll restack them."

The first map was of ephemeral streams in the northeast quadrant of the state.

"These streams," he pointed out, "run only during wet periods, some but once in twenty years. Some don't have any names."

The information was strikingly presented and beautifully drawn. The instruction you needed to get oriented—where the Red River was, where the county lines were—was just enough, so it barely impinged on the actual subject matter of the map. The balance was perfect.

The next map showed fence lines, along the Missouri River in a central part of the state.

"These are done at twenty-year intervals, going back to 1840. Fences are like roads, they proliferate. They're never completely removed."

The following map was a geological rendering of McIntosh County's bedrock geology. As I took in the shape and colors, the subdivided shades of purple and green and blue, Mr. Benefideo slid a large hand-colored transparency across the sheet, a soil map of the same area. You could imagine looking down through a variety of soil types to the bedrock below.

"Or," he said, and slid an opaque map with the same information across in front of me, the yellows and browns of a dozen silts, clays, and sands.

The next sheet was of eighteenth- and nineteenth-century foot trails in the western half of the state.

"But how did you compile this information?"

"Inspection and interviews. Close personal observation and talking with long-term residents. It's a hard thing, really, to erase a trail. A lot of information can be recovered if you stay at it."

When he placed the next map in front of me, the summer distribution of Swainson's hawks, and then slid in next to it a map showing the overlapping summer distribution of its main prey species, the Richardson ground squirrel, the precision and revelation were too much for me.

I turned to face him. "I've never seen anything that even approaches this, this"—my gesture across the surface of the table included everything. "It's not just the information, or the execution—I mean, the technique is flawless, the water-coloring, your choice of scale—but it's like the books, there's so much more."

"That's the idea, don't you think, Mr. Trevino?"

"Of course, but nobody has the time for this kind of fieldwork anymore."

"That's unfortunate, because this information is what we need, you know. This shows history and how people fit the places they occupy. It's about what gets erased and what comes to replace it. These maps reveal the foundations beneath the ephemera."

"What about us, though?" I blurted, resisting his pronouncement. "In the books, in *City in Aspic* in particular, there is such a palpable love of human life in the cities, and here—"

"I do not have to live up to the history of Venice, Mr. Trevino," he interrupted, "but I am obliged to shoulder the history of my own country. I could show you here the whole coming and going of the Mandan nation, wiped out in 1837 by a smallpox epidemic. I could show you how the arrival of German and Scandinavian farmers changed the composition of the topsoil, and the places where Charles Bodmer painted, and the evolution of red-light districts in Fargo—all that with pleasure. I've nothing against human passion, human longing. What I oppose is blind devotion to progress, and the venality of material wealth. If we're going to trade the priceless for the common, I want to know exactly what the terms are."

I had no response. His position was as difficult to assail as it would be to promote.

"You mean," I finally ventured, "that someone else will have to do the maps that show the spread of the Wal-Mart empire in North Dakota."

"I won't be doing those."

His tone was assertive but not testy. He wasn't even seeking my agreement.

"My daughter," I said, changing the subject, "wants to be an environmental historian. She has a good head for it, and I know she's interested—she wants to discover the kind of information you need to have to build a stable society. I'm sure it comes partly from looking at what's already there, as you suggest, like the birds this morning, how that movement, those movements, might determine the architecture of a society. I'm wondering—could I ever send her out? Maybe to help? Would you spend a few days with her?"

"I'd be glad to speak with her," he said, after considering the question. "I'd train her, if it came to that."

"Thank you."

He began squaring the maps up to place them back in the drawer.

"You know, Mr. Trevino—Phillip, if I may, and you may call me

Corlis—the question is about you, really." He shut the drawer and gestured me toward the door of the room, which he closed behind us.

"You represent a questing but lost generation of people. I think you know what I mean. You made it clear this morning, talking nostalgically about my books, that you think an elegant order has disappeared, something that shows the way." We were standing at the corner of the dining table with our hands on the chair backs. "It's wonderful, of course, that you brought your daughter into our conversation tonight, and certainly we're both going to have to depend on her, on her thinking. But the real question, now, is what will *you* do? Because you can't expect her to take up something you wish for yourself, a way of seeing the world. You send her here, if it turns out to be what she wants, but don't make the mistake of thinking you, or I or anyone, knows how the world is meant to work. The world is a miracle, unfolding in the pitch dark. We're lighting candles. Those maps— they are my candles. And I can't extinguish them for anyone."

He crossed to his shelves and took down his copy of *The City of Geraniums.* He handed it to me and we went to the door.

"If you want to come back in the morning for breakfast, please do. Or, there is a cafe, the Dogwood, next to the motel. It's good. However you wish."

We said good night and I moved out through pools of dark beneath the ash trees to where I'd parked the car. I set the book on the seat opposite and started the engine. The headlights swept the front of the house as I turned past it, catching the salute of his hand, and then he was gone.

I inverted the image of the map from his letter in my mind and began driving south to the highway. After a few moments I turned off the headlights and rolled down the window. I listened to the tires crushing gravel in the roadbed. The sound of it helped me hold the road, together with instinct and the memory of earlier having driven it. I felt the volume of space beneath the clear, star-ridden sky, and moved over the dark prairie like a barn-bound horse.

YANN MARTEL

From *THE FACTS BEHIND the HELSINKI ROCCAMATIOS*

I STARTED WRITING SERIOUSLY when I was nineteen. I wrote a play about a young man who falls in love with a door; when a friend finds out and destroys the door, our hero commits suicide. It was as bad as it sounds. But that first effort was a capital step for me because, for the first time in my life, I wrote something for its own sake; that is, the sake of art.

Before that, writing had always been homework. Writing doesn't come easily—to anyone. Children draw without being prompted. They sing and babble without being prompted. They do all kinds of things on their own. But they don't write. Precocious children may compose sonatas, like Mozart. But you never hear parents exclaim, "Look! Junior has written a three-hundred-page novel! And he's only seven years old!" It just doesn't happen. Words are boring; they just sit there on the page. They are hard to spell. There are so many of them to learn. Some you can't even pronounce. And then you must order them into something called "sentences"—so, so difficult. Worse, there's grammar, which never gives you a break. And all this struggle for what? For something boring that just sits there on the page.

Playing cops and robbers or hide and seek is more fun. Swimming is more fun. Nearly everything is more fun. The child can't imagine anyone who would enjoy writing. Except perhaps one person: its older sibling, who is miserable and inward-looking, who is racked by doubts and covered in pimples.

Adolescence is the savior of writing, just as—to some teenagers—writing is the savior of adolescence. It is at that age that the effort involved in writing begins to bear fruit. With words, one can express oneself; and since every teenager is at one point or another misunderstood, there is much to express. Suddenly the possibilities of words begin to explode in the mind. The teenager reads and writes in search of answers.

Then, normally, in the late teen years, the angst settles, the pen is dropped and life goes on. The poems and stories one wrote as a teenager are relegated to yellowed diaries stored in boxes in attics. Normally.

But some of us don't want to drop the pen. The intoxication of words and stories goes beyond merely calming us. On the contrary. Words and stories and books fire us up. After looking in with language, we start looking out. We feel the urge to continue writing. We have more stories and poems in us. Writing becomes something serious.

Thus is born the writer. Or at least this writer. I kept writing to learn, to explore, to create, to renew.

At first what I wrote was terrible, trapped in immaturity. But by dint of practice I got better. This story is the result. "The Facts Behind the Helsinki Roccamatios," and the three other stories that became my first book, are the best results of my early years as a writer. With them, the door of the imagination was flung open and I entered a room—a bejeweled world—I never wanted to leave. It was a thrill I'll never forget.

For me, the best was the first.

—Yann Martel

I hadn't known Paul for very long. We met in the fall of 1986 at Ellis University, in Roetown, just east of Toronto. I had taken time off and worked and travelled to India: I was twenty-three and in my last year. Paul had just turned nineteen and was entering first year. At the beginning of the year at Ellis, some senior students introduce the first-years to the university. There are no pranks or mischief or anything like that; the seniors are there to be helpful. They're called "amigos" and the first-years "amigees," which shows you how much Spanish they speak in Roetown. I was an amigo and most of my amigees struck me as cheerful, eager and young—very young. But right away I liked Paul's laidback, intelligent curiosity and his sceptical turn of mind. The two of us clicked and we started hanging out together. Because I was older and I had done more things, I usually spoke with the authority of a wise guru, and Paul listened like a young disciple—except when he raised an eyebrow and said something that threw my pompousness right into my face. Then we laughed and broke from these roles and it was plain what we were: really good friends.

Then, hardly into second term, Paul fell ill. Already at Christmas he had had a fever, and since then he had been carrying around a dry, hacking cough he couldn't get rid of. Initially, he—

we—thought nothing of it. The cold, the dryness of the air—it was something to do with that.

Slowly things got worse. Now I recall signs that I didn't think twice about at the time. Meals left unfinished. A complaint once of diarrhea. A lack of energy that went beyond phlegmatic temperament. One day we were climbing the stairs to the library, hardly twenty-five steps, and when we reached the top, we stopped. I remember realizing that the only reason we had stopped was because Paul was out of breath and wanted to rest. And he seemed to be losing weight. It was hard to tell, what with the heavy winter sweaters and all, but I was certain that his frame had been stockier earlier in the year. When it became clear that something was wrong, we talked about it—nearly casually, you must understand—and I played doctor and said, "Let's see . . . breathlessness, cough, weight loss, fatigue. Paul, you have pneumonia." I was joking, of course; what do I know? But that's in fact what he had. It's called *Pneumocystis carinii* pneumonia, PCP to intimates. In mid-February Paul went to Toronto to see his family doctor.

Nine months later he was dead.

AIDS. He announced it to me over the phone in a detached voice. He had been gone nearly two weeks. He had just got back from the hospital, he told me. I reeled. My first thoughts were for myself. Had he ever cut himself in my presence? If so, what had happened? Had I ever drunk from his glass? Shared his food? I tried to establish if there had ever been a bridge between his system and mine. Then I thought of him. I thought of gay sex and hard drugs. But Paul wasn't gay. He had never told me so outright, but I knew him well enough and I had never detected the least ambivalence. I likewise couldn't imagine him a heroin addict. In any case, that wasn't it. Three years ago, when he was sixteen, he had gone to Jamaica on a Christmas holiday with his parents. They had had a car accident. Paul's right leg had been broken and he'd lost some blood. He had received a blood transfusion at the local hospital. Six witnesses of the accident had come along to volunteer blood. Three were of the right blood group. Several phone calls and a little research turned up the fact that one of the three had died unexpectedly two years later while being treated for pneumonia. An autopsy had revealed that the man had severe toxoplasmic cerebral lesions. A suspicious combination.

I went to visit Paul that weekend at his home in wealthy Rosedale.

I didn't want to; I wanted to block the whole thing off mentally. I asked—this was my excuse—if he was sure his parents cared for a visitor. He insisted that I come. And I did. I came through. I drove down to Toronto. And I was right about his parents. Because what hurt most that first weekend was not Paul, but Paul's family.

After learning how he had probably caught the virus, Paul's father, Jack, didn't utter a syllable for the rest of that day. Early the next morning he fetched the tool kit in the basement, put his winter parka over his housecoat, stepped out onto the driveway, and proceeded to destroy the family car. Because he had been the driver when they had had the accident in Jamaica, even though it hadn't been his fault and it had been in another car, a rental. He took a hammer and shattered all the lights and windows. He scraped and trashed the entire body. He banged nails into the tires. He siphoned the gasoline from the tank, poured it over and inside the car, and set it on fire. That's when neighbours called the firefighters. They rushed to the scene and put the fire out. The police came, too. When he blurted out why he had done it, all of them were very understanding and the police left without charging him or anything; they only asked if he wanted to go to the hospital, which he didn't. So that was the first thing I saw when I walked up to Paul's large, corner-lot house: a burnt wreck of a Mercedes covered in dried foam.

Jack was a hard-working corporate lawyer. When Paul introduced me to him, he grinned, shook my hand hard and said, "Good to meet you!" Then he didn't seem to have anything else to say. His face was red. Paul's mother, Mary, was in their bedroom. I had met her at the beginning of the university year. As a young woman she had earned an M.A. in anthropology from McGill, she had been a highly ranked amateur tennis player, and she had travelled. Now she worked part-time for a human rights organization. Paul was proud of his mother and got along with her very well. She was a smart, energetic woman. But here she was, lying awake on the bed in a fetal position, looking like a wrinkled balloon, all the taut vitality drained out of her. Paul stood next to the bed and just said, "My mother." She barely reacted. I didn't know what to do. Paul's sister, Jennifer, a graduate student in sociology at the University of Toronto, was the most visibly distraught. Her eyes were red, her face was puffy—she looked terrible. I don't mean to be funny, but even George H., the family Labrador, was grief-stricken. He had squeezed himself under the living-room sofa, wouldn't budge, and whined all the time.

The verdict had come on Wednesday morning, and since then (it was Friday) none of them, George H. included, had eaten a morsel of food. Paul's father and mother hadn't gone to work, and Jennifer hadn't gone to school. They slept, when they slept, wherever they happened to be. One morning I found Paul's father sleeping on the living-room floor, fully dressed and wrapped in the Persian rug, a hand reaching for the dog beneath the sofa. Except for frenzied bursts of phone conversation, the house was quiet.

In the middle of it all was Paul, who wasn't reacting. At a funeral where the family members are broken with pain and grief, he was the funeral director going about with professional calm and dull sympathy. Only on the third day of my stay did he start to react. But death couldn't make itself understood. Paul knew that something awful was happening to him, but he couldn't grasp it. Death was beyond him. It was a theoretical abstraction. He spoke of his condition as if it were news from a foreign country. He said, "I'm going to die," the way he might say, "There was a ferry disaster in Bangladesh."

I had meant to stay just the weekend—there was school—but I ended up staying ten days. I did a lot of housecleaning and cooking during that time. The family didn't notice much, but that was all right. Paul helped me, and he liked that because it gave him something to do. We had the car towed away, we replaced a phone that Paul's father had destroyed, we cleaned the house spotlessly from top to bottom, we gave George H. a bath (George H. because Paul really liked the Beatles and when he was a kid he liked to say to himself when he was walking the dog, "At this very moment, unbeknown to anyone, absolutely incognito, Beatle Paul and Beatle George are walking the streets of Toronto," and he would dream about what it would be like to sing "Help!" in Shea Stadium or something like that), and we went food shopping and nudged the family into eating. I say "we" and "Paul helped"—what I mean is that I did everything while he sat in a chair nearby. Drugs called dapsone and trimethoprim were overcoming Paul's pneumonia, but he was still weak and out of breath. He moved about like an old man, slowly and conscious of every exertion.

It took the family a while to break out of its shock. During the course of Paul's illness I noticed three states they would go through. In the first, common at home, when the pain was too close, they would pull away and each do their thing: Paul's father would destroy something sturdy, like a table or an appliance, Paul's mother would lie on her bed in a daze, Jennifer would cry in her bedroom, and George H. would hide under the sofa and whine. In the second, at the hospital often, they would rally around Paul, and they would talk and sob and encourage each other and laugh and whisper. Finally, in the third, they would display what I suppose you could call normal behaviour, an ability to get through the day as if death didn't exist, a composed, somewhat numb face of courage that, because it was required every single day, became both heroic and ordinary. The family went through these states over the course of several months, or in an hour.

I don't want to talk about what AIDS does to a body. Imagine it very bad—and then make it worse (you can't imagine the degradation). Look up in the dictionary the word "flesh"—such a plump word— and then look up the word "melt."

That's not the worst of it, anyway. The worst of it is the resistance put up, the I'm-not-going-to-die virus. It's the one that affects the most people because it attacks the living, the ones who surround and love the dying. That virus infected me early on. I remember the day precisely. Paul was in the hospital. He was eating his supper, his whole supper, till the plate was clean and shiny, though he wasn't at all hungry. I watched him as he chased down every last pea with his fork and as he consciously chewed every mouthful before swallowing. *It will help my body fight. Every little bit counts*—that's what he was thinking. It was written all over his face, all over his body, all over the walls. I wanted to scream, "Forget the fucking peas, Paul. You're going to die! DIE!" Except that the words "death" and "dying," and their various derivatives and synonyms, were now tacitly forbidden from our talk. So I just sat there, my face emptied of any expression, anger roiling me up inside. My condition got much worse every time I saw Paul shave. All he had were a few downy whiskers on his chin; he just wasn't the hairy type. Still, he began to shave every day. Every day he lathered up his face with a mountain of shaving cream and scraped it off with a disposable razor. It's an image that has become engraved in my memory: a vacillatingly healthy Paul dressed in a hospital gown standing in front of a mirror, turning his head this way and that, pulling his skin here and there, meticulously doing something that was utterly, utterly useless.

I botched my academic year. I was skipping lectures and seminars constantly and I couldn't write any essays. In fact, I couldn't even read anymore; I would stare for hours at the same paragraph of Kant or Heidegger, trying to understand what it was saying, trying to focus, without any success. At the same time, I developed a loathing for my country. Canada reeked of insipidity, comfort and insularity. Canadians were up to their necks in materialism and above the neck it was all American television. Nowhere could I see idealism or rigour. There was nothing but deadening mediocrity. Canada's policy on Central America, on Native issues, on the environment, on Reagan's America, on everything, made my stomach turn. There was nothing about this country that I liked, nothing. I couldn't wait to escape.

One day in a philosophy seminar—that was my major—I was doing a presentation on Hegel's philosophy of history. The professor, an intelligent and considerate man, interrupted me and asked me to elucidate a point he hadn't understood. I fell silent. I looked about the cosy, book-filled office where we were sitting. I remember that moment of silence very clearly because it was precisely then, rising through my confusion with unstoppable force, that I boiled over with anger and cynicism. I screamed, I got up, I projected the hefty Hegel book through the closed window, and I stormed out of the office, slamming the door as hard as I could and kicking in one of its nicely sculptured panels for good measure.

I tried to withdraw from Ellis, but I missed the deadline. I appealed and appeared in front of a committee, the Committee on Undergraduate Standings and Petitions, CUSP they call it. My grounds for withdrawing were Paul, but when the chairman of CUSP prodded me and asked me in a glib little voice what exactly I meant by "emotional distress," I looked at him and I decided that Paul's agony wasn't an orange I was going to peel and quarter and present to him. This time, however, I didn't make a scene. I just said, "I've changed my mind. I would like to withdraw my petition. Thank you for your attention," and I walked out.

As a result I failed my year. I didn't care and I don't care. I hung around Roetown, a nice place to hang around.

But what I really want to tell you about, the purpose of this story, is the Roccamatio family of Helsinki. That's not Paul's family; his last name was Atsee. Nor is it my family.

You see, Paul spent months in the hospital. When his condition was stable he came home, but mostly I remember him at the hospital. The course of his illnesses, tests and treatments became the course of his life. Against my will I became familiar with words like azidothymidine, alpha interferon, domipramine, nitrazepam. (When you're with people who are really sick, you discover what an illusion science can be.) I visited Paul. I was making the trip to Toronto to see him once or twice during the week, and often on weekends too, and I was calling him every day. When I was there, if he was strong enough, we would go for a walk or see a movie or a play. Mostly, though, we just sat around. But when you're between four walls and neither of you wants to watch television anymore, and the papers have been read, and you're sick of playing cards, chess, Scrabble and Trivial Pursuit, and you can't always be talking about *it* and *its* progress, you run out of ways to whittle away the time. Which was fine. Neither Paul nor I minded just sitting there, listening to music, lost in our own thoughts.

Except that I started feeling we should do something with that time. I don't mean put on togas and ruminate philosophically about life, death, God, the universe and the meaning of it all. We had done that in first term, before we even knew he was sick. That's the staple of undergraduate life, isn't it? What else is there to talk about when you've stayed up all night till sunrise? Or when you've just read Descartes or Berkeley or T. S. Eliot for the first time? And anyway, Paul was nineteen. What are you at nineteen? You're a blank page. You're all hopes and dreams and uncertainties. You're all future and little philosophy. What I meant was that between the two of us we had to do something constructive, something that would make something out of nothing, sense out of nonsense, something that would go beyond *talking* about life, death, God, the universe and the meaning of it all and actually *be* those things.

I gave it a good thinking. I had plenty of time to think: in the spring I got a job as a gardener for the city of Roetown. I spent my days tending flowerbeds, clipping shrubbery and mowing lawns, work that kept my hands busy but left my mind free.

The idea came to me one day as I was pushing a gas mower across an expanse of municipal lawn, my ears muffled by industrial ear protectors. Two words stopped me dead in my tracks: Boccaccio's *Decameron.* I had read a beaten-up copy of the Italian classic when I was in India. Such a simple idea: an isolated villa outside of Florence;

the world dying of the Black Death; ten people gathered together hoping to survive; *telling each other stories to pass the time.*

That was it. The transformative wizardry of the imagination. Boccaccio had done it in the fourteenth century, we would do it in the twentieth: we would tell each other stories. But we would be the sick this time, not the world, and we wouldn't be fleeing it, either. On the contrary: with our stories we would be remembering the world, recreating it, embracing it. Yes, to meet as storytellers to embrace the world—there, that was how Paul and I would destroy the void.

The more I thought about it, the more I liked it. Paul and I would create a story about a family, a large family, to allow diverse yet related stories, to ensure continuity and development. The family would be Canadian and the setting would be contemporary, to make the historical and cultural references easy. I would have to be a firm guide and not let the stories slide into mere autobiography. And I would have to be well prepared so that I could carry the story all by myself when Paul was too weak or depressed. I would also have to convince him that he had no choice, that this storytelling wasn't a game or something on the same level as watching a movie or talking about politics. He would have to see that everything besides the story was useless, even his desperate existential thoughts that did nothing but frighten him. Only the imaginary must count.

VALERIE MARTIN

From PROPERTY

⌁

WHEN I FIRST STARTED writing, I wrote plays, and I've always felt that dialogue is my strength. I like to use it to do several things at once: reveal character, advance the action, suggest an ideological undercurrent, and create a narrative tension that is the result of the interplay between verifiable facts and what the reader recognizes as lies. Naturalness is not what I'm after, as ordinary dialogue is seldom packed in this way, but it is important that the conversation *seem* natural, that the characters do not mouth my ideas or give speeches to one another. I find it helps if they each have something at stake. These are the conversations that keep us awake at night going over all the things we should have said.

The scene I've chosen is from my novel *Property*. I think it is my "best" because the characters are revealed to one another as equal antagonists and the matter at stake is the fate of an innocent person whom they both, in a very concrete sense, seek to own. It's the stuff of high drama, but it takes place in a banal domestic setting.

The year is 1828 and the narrator, Manon Gaudet, a white slaveholder who lives in New Orleans, has agreed to meet with Mr. Everett Roget, a free man of color, who desires to purchase Manon's slave Sarah. Sarah has run away, probably with the assistance of Mr. Roget, taking her infant daughter with her, but leaving behind her eight-year-old son, Walter. Both of Sarah's children were fathered by Manon's husband, who was recently killed in a slave insurrection.

—Valerie Martin

After breakfast I consulted with my aunt, who agreed with me that Mr. Roget knew exactly where Sarah was and intended to make an offer pending her return. "He may seem sure of himself," she said. "He has established some means of contacting Sarah quickly and he thinks she is so well hidden no one can find her. But he must know Mr. Leggett has been commissioned to apprehend her. This is a desperate measure."

Mr. Roget did not appear in the least desperate when he arrived at my door that afternoon. As he followed Rose into the parlor his eyes darted confidently over the cornices, the mantel, the baseboards, then settled upon me with much the same quality of appraisal and assurance. He was neatly dressed, though not elegant in any part, except for his walking stick, which had a silver knob. He took the seat I directed him to, set his hat upon the side table, and held the stick between his legs. His hands, I noticed, were large, chapped from the cold and the dry plaster of his trade, the nails neatly trimmed. One was bruised black at the quick. He was light-skinned, though not so light as Sarah, and his features were pleasing, especially his eyes, which were wide, dark brown, the lashes thick for a man. He began almost at once, offering his condolences for my recent losses and apologizing for having taken the liberty to disturb me in my mourning.

"It is for just that reason that I must ask you to come directly to the point of your visit," I said.

He compressed his lips in a tight, self-satisfied smile that suggested he had not expected to be treated courteously, and was now justified in that expectation. I leaned forward over the arm of my chair, giving him my close attention.

"I have come in hopes that you will accept an offer for the purchase of your servant Sarah."

"Sarah?" I pretended surprise. "But she is not for sale. Are you in the habit of offering to buy servants who are not for sale?"

He raised his eyes to mine. "No," he said.

"Then I wonder what has driven you to such impertinence in this case."

"I made Sarah's acquaintance when she was with her former owner, and I have long been desirous of purchasing her."

"You know, of course, that she has run away."

"I do," he said. "My offer is made in the event of her return."

"What makes you think she will return?" I asked. "She has eluded capture for over a month now."

He looked down at the knob of his cane, making no reply. After a moment he rubbed at a smudge on the silver with his palm.

"How soon after I accept your offer might I expect her return?" I asked.

Still the infuriating man did not speak. His eyes wandered over the objects on the side table, stopping at the portrait of my father. How

Father would have detested him, I thought, and seen through his despicable game. He wanted a wife lighter than he was, but no free quadroon would have him. In spite of his fortune, which I didn't doubt was considerable, he was a laborer. Sarah was perfect for him. They could raise a houseful of yellow brats, one more useless than the next. But what, I wondered, would he do with the baby Sarah already had?

"You know that Sarah has a child with her," I said.

He looked up from the portrait, his expression candid and businesslike. "I do," he said.

"I assume that your offer would include that child. It is too young to be separated from its mother."

"Of course," he said.

"You have figured that into the offer, have you?" I said.

He frowned at my persistence on this point. "I have," he said.

"Did you know that Sarah has another child?" I asked, watching his face closely. His eyes widened almost imperceptibly. She didn't tell him, I thought.

"No," he said. "I didn't."

"A boy," I said. "A healthy child. She left him behind." I stood up and pulled the cord for Rose. "He is eight years old." Rose came in at the dining room door. "Send Walter to me," I said. She looked past me at Mr. Roget, then turned back hurriedly. She and Delphine were probably huddled together over the kitchen table in a fit of jabbering. I turned, smiling, to my guest, who had not moved, though his shoulders drooped. The interview was not going exactly as he had planned. "Walter is old enough to be separated from his mother," I observed, "but that is a policy I have always abhorred. It is a cruelty to sell a child away from his only protector. My father, that is his portrait"—I lifted my chin indicating the picture—"was strongly opposed to the unnecessary breakup of family connections among our people, and I have tried to follow his example."

Mr. Roget listened to these sentiments absently, his eyes focused on the dining room door. I kept my back to it, as I knew exactly what he was about to discover and I felt a great curiosity to see his face when he experienced what I imagined would be a series of hard shocks to the foundations of his scheme. We listened to the patter of bare feet as the wild creature charged across the dining room. Then with what amusement I heard the gleeful bark with which Walter is wont to greet new faces! His hand brushed against my skirt as he hurried past me to clutch the knees of the astounded Mr. Roget. I pressed my lips together to keep from laughing. "It was too bad of Sarah not to tell you about Walter," I said solemnly. "I expect she feared you might be disappointed in some way." Walter was working up to a scream as he attempted to divest Mr. Roget of his walking stick. "You can't have it," Mr. Roget said. "You might hurt yourself with it."

"He can't hear you," I pointed out helpfully. "He is deaf. He has been examined by a physician, and I'm afraid there is no hope that he will ever be normal."

Walter gave up the stick and held out his arms to be picked up. When Mr. Roget did not respond, he turned to me, stretching his arms up and mewing. He persists in this behavior, though I never touch him if I can avoid it. He was wearing only a slip made from sacking, his face was smeared with what looked like dried egg yolk, his hands and feet were filthy, and his hair was a mass of knots. I looked back to see Rose watching from the far door. "Come take him," I said, and she came in quickly. As soon as he saw her, the boy ran to her arms. He was carried back to the courtyard, simpering and patting Rose's cheek. "He is much improved since our move here," I observed to Mr. Roget as I resumed my seat. My guest raised his hand and commenced rubbing the corner of his eye with his finger, evidently thunderstruck. "But the truth is," I continued, "as you can see, he will never be worth anything to anyone."

"No," he agreed. He left off rubbing his eye and gave me a look of frank ill will mixed with grudging admiration, such as one gives a worthy opponent. This gratified me, but his lips betrayed the faintest trace of a smile, an habitual insolence, I thought, which made me want to slap him.

"Perhaps you wish to reconsider your offer," I suggested.

"No," he said. "But as you say yourself, this boy has no value. If I were to agree to take him, I would not offer more."

"Well, I am curious to hear the figure you have in mind."

"Two thousand dollars," he said coolly.

It was twice what Sarah was worth. I allowed the notion of making such a profit and getting rid of Walter in the bargain to tempt me for a moment. I've no doubt I gave Mr. Roget the same adversarial scrutiny he had just given me. "It is a generous offer," I said. "You must be very determined to have her."

"I am," he said.

What possessed the man? He had already gone to the expense of financing Sarah's escape. He was probably paying someone to hide her as we sat there. If I agreed, he would have to pay to bring her back, then take on two children not his own, one ugly and dark, the other no better than a mad yellow dog. Then he would have to go through the long, expensive process of manumission, applying bribes all round, as the laws are strict. He leaned back in his chair, bringing his stick to the side and stretching his legs out before him, nonchalantly examining his trouser leg. He found a bit of plaster stuck to the seam and flicked it away with his fingernail. It fell onto the carpet near his shoe. I focused my eyes and my mind upon this small fleck of white plaster. The fact of it enraged me, but I counseled myself to remain calm. Mr. Roget was waiting for my answer, having no idea that a bit of plaster had sealed his fate and Sarah's as well.

"I fear you are improvident," I said. "And that you will regret your offer."

"That will be my lookout," he said. "My offer is firm. I am prepared to write you a check for half the amount today."

"Let me propose a counteroffer," I said. "I think it might prove a more practical solution for us all."

He glanced at the mantel clock, reminding me that he was a busy man.

"I have no intention of selling Sarah," I said. "It's that simple. She is not for sale. However, I would have no objection to a marriage between you. I think that is your object, is it not? She would continue to live here during the week, but she could come to you on Sundays and she would be free to visit one or two evenings a week when I am dining out."

"You aren't serious," he said flatly, leaving me to imagine the extent of his outrage. A free man married to a slave! His children would be mine, to do with as I pleased.

"I'm afraid that's all I can offer you," I said. "In the event of Sarah's capture, of course, which I firmly believe can only be a matter of days."

"Then we have nothing more to discuss," he said, leaning forward upon his cane.

"There are laws against harboring a fugitive, Mr. Roget," I said, "as I'm sure you know. Assisting Sarah in any way is strictly unlawful. The fines are heavy. Once she has been returned to me, it is my intention to prosecute anyone who can be proved to have aided her in her flight. I don't think of her as having run away, you see, I think of her as having been stolen. She would never take such a risk had she not been encouraged by someone who has no respect for the law, who is so morally derelict that he fails to comprehend the difference between purchase and blackmail."

Mr. Roget stood up, frowning mightily. As I spoke, he drew his head back, as if to dodge the thrust of my argument. "It is a mystery to me," I continued, "how you could find the nerve to come here and offer to pay me for what you have stolen. You seem to think I care for nothing but money. I am going to considerable expense to recover what is mine, by right and by law, and recover her I will."

"Good day, Mrs. Gaudet," he said, making for the door. I got up from the chair to watch him go. There was the usual bite of pain in my shoulder as my arm stretched down at my side. I didn't expect him to stop, but he did, turning in the doorway to deliver an interesting bit of information. "You will never find her," he said. "She is no longer your property nor anyone else's, and you will never see her again."

ARTHUR MILLER

From SALESMAN in BEIJING

I CAN'T THINK OF another work of mine that gave me as much pleasure in the writing as this one did. I suppose it is partly because initially I was not writing for publication but simply to keep the days from melting into one another incoherently. The working hours of the Chinese theatre in those days were rather odd for an outsider. We began work at ten in the morning and went until around two when everybody disappeared and resumed again at four and went to about eight. The hiatus in the afternoon was to let everyone rush around for food since no one had a refrigerator and they had to buy fresh stuff every day. Those were the times when cabbages arrived on open trucks, which then tipped and dumped them all on the sidewalk in front of a food market.

The adventure of this production was what made it so lovely an experience. Nobody really knew if the Chinese would ever understand *Death of a Salesman* nor could I understand a word of what the actors were saying, relying completely on the interpreting of my star, Ying Ruocheng, who played Willy.

All that was left was the pure emotional context, reading people through their eyes, and the expressions on their faces. The Chinese in social matters tend to be very reticent and work to disguise what they really think if a conflict is imminent. But in the writing of what turned out to be this book I found myself sinking into their way of concealing and admitting what I felt to be true, and it was a new venture for me into a completely alien culture that in the end turned out to be simpler and more familiar than I had ever imagined.

If nothing more, these selections may at least suggest my enthusiasm and perhaps that's why at least in spirit they are some of my best work.

—Arthur Miller

MARCH 24 [1983]

In every production the moment arrives when the honeymoon is over and the marriage begins out of which, one hopes, a living rather than stillborn birth will emerge. I still do not understand a word of Chinese, of course, and to be candid with myself, I find toward the end of a rehearsal period a certain grating quality to its general sound, something Inge [Morath, Miller's late wife] stoutly denies. I suppose it is as much my frustration at trying to penetrate an incomprehensible gibberish hour after hour as any objective quality of the language itself. In any case, after running and reading Act One two or three times I realize that I have penetrated not the language but many of the actors' intentions, and some of them, I now think, are sentimental, untrue.

Linda, who at first seemed so charmingly devoted to Willy and yet so much herself, so dignified, tends to verge on warbling, especially in her two-page-long aria where she pleads with the boys to help save Willy, who she fears is trying to kill himself. I stop the scene at one point (and only then wonder if I am perhaps breaching etiquette by correcting her before others), and as diplomatically as possible, I remind her that she is talking not about a dead husband toward whom she has these retrospective feelings, but one who is alive in a crisis right now. There is no time to feel pity for oneself in such an emergency situation; she has a task to perform in the scene, which is to get Biff to find a job in New York and begin rescuing his old man from certain suicide.

Looking into her eyes I feel at home, gratified that all actors are the same. She has the spark of recognition, the wit, one might call it, of the aware performer who can turn it on or off almost at will. She is far too experienced not to know what she has been doing—drawing audience sympathy rather than playing the scene—and I begin to fear that she will easily outwit me or wear me down before the end. Nevertheless, she starts again, and this time it is much more simple, direct, almost but not quite free of the warbling. I learn that, like the actor playing Happy, she is of a tradition—in her case, that of the Mother, who in effect is always a warbler. In this play, however, such exploiting of the sentiments will sink them all in a morass of brainless "feeling" that finally is not feeling at all but an unspecific bath of self-love. I suppose it is inevitable that she reminds me of the bits of Yiddish theatre I saw years ago in New York. There, too, the Mother was a lachrymose fount; crying was what Mothers are for. But on thinking about it I see that this is no monopoly of Jews or, for that matter, of Chinese. If one recalls the early movies, most of them performed by actors of Irish background, Mother was always on the verge of tears, too. Lachrymosity must represent some stage in the evolution of society, nationality having little to do with it.

MARCH 25

Our press conference. I have finally had to resort to this mass interview or spend most of my time saying the same things to the foreign and Chinese reporters who have put in requests. In a large room in the theatre Ying and I face perhaps fifty people packed together, including four or five TV crews from the American and Canadian networks and a dozen still photographers of many nationalities.

For once the bulk of the questioning is not trivial or fatuous. Why was *Salesman* chosen? Was it as propaganda against the American way of life? Is it really possible for Chinese to relate to the very American situation and to Willy Loman's character? Do Chinese actors work differently from Americans in creating their roles? Is the humor likely to register? Are there really any parallels in Chinese society? Will the production be closed to the public, and with "certain strata" let in to see it (as apparently had been the case with some productions in the past)? How much will tickets cost? Are tickets going to be sold to anyone at the box office or distributed to organizations?

I take a positive stance, since we have only rehearsed two full days and I do not yet know all the problems. I tell them that I feel I am quickly learning how to read the actors' signals; that while it is obvious that our cultural semaphores are vastly different, perhaps they are really referring to the same basic information deep within us. I theorize a universality of human emotions; I hope that the production here of this very American play will simply assert the idea of a single humanity once again.

At this point I can only say that the actors seem to have no difficulty in putting themselves into the parts; there must surely be some exotic mysteries for them in this play, but, after all, the Chinese practically invented the family, which is the core of the play, and the social interrelationships with the family struggle have been a part of Chinese life for a very long time.

As for the humor, at least the cast is laughing when laughter is called for, so I presume we have a chance to do the same with an audience. Parallels exist in the play with Chinese society, I have reason to think, assuming that people want to rise in the world everywhere. And if there aren't as yet traveling salesman in this country, I conjecture that the idea of such a man is easily enough grasped from the text itself. In any case, the salesman motif is in some great part metaphorical; we must all sell ourselves, convince the world of a persona that perhaps we only wish we really possessed.

Ying Ruocheng now takes some questions about the theatre and the production. He is, of course, a star in China, and all the reporters know him and seem to have confidence in his candor. Tickets, he says, will cost one yuan (about fifty cents), and anyone who comes to the box office can buy them, the more the better (a remark in which I sense a little more confidence than he really has). The production will run as long as there is a strong enough demand by the public. He disapproves of the practice of distributing tickets through unions and other organizations in order to dragoon an audience. In fact, "that kind of thing only demonstrates that you've got a flop."

It begins to sound more and more like Broadway, and one of the reporters interrupts to ask me if I had an agreement as to how long they were to run the play. I had nothing of the kind, I said; I expect it to run as long as the public cares to attend, but of course at fifty cents a ticket that has to be a lot longer than my plays have sometimes run at American prices.

Which leads us to ticket prices in New York, a problem I had left behind only a few days before when I attempted to get the eighteen-to-thirty-two-dollar range lowered for the revival of *A View from the Bridge* at the Ambassador Theatre. When I tell them the New York price range—to which Ying Ruocheng adds that he paid forty-five dollars to see *Cats*—there is a gasp of incredulity from the Chinese reporters present. Forty-five dollars is more than a month's wage for most of them and double for some, intellectuals being among the lowest-paid people in China.

I think the best part of the conference is Ying's way of dealing with the propaganda question. "When it was announced that we were thinking about this project for our theatre, there was quite a bit of press comment in Taiwan," he contentedly begins. "They said, 'Cao Yü and Ying Ruocheng must be crazy to think they will be allowed to do *Death of a Salesman* in Beijing, let alone have Miller admitted to direct it.' So you see," Ying continues, "some people apparently think it a different kind of propaganda than others. But actually my own interest in it is basically aesthetic. I think it can open new territory to our own playwrights, since it does break out of the conventions that by and large have held us back. And of course I would love to play Willy, as any actor would."

Inge is then brought up to the front to account for having learned to speak and write Chinese so fluently. She has always tried to learn the language of a country in which she intends to photograph intensively, believing that the linguistic imagery can lead her deeper into the visual. She learned Russian before working in the Soviet Union for the same reason. What she does not say is that she is even more fluent in five other languages.

As a compromise I promise the TV reporters to open the theatre to them all for one afternoon's rehearsal, the alternative being to let in each crew separately, a disastrously time-consuming request. I will pick some afternoon after the middle of April. The trouble with filming a rehearsal, of course, is that I shall have to pretend I am "directing" or it will not seem to be a rehearsal. Actually my physical interference on the set will be quite rare.

MARCH 26

After yesterday evening's rehearsal Ying Ruocheng, with barely visible irritation, asked me if I would let him run lines with the cast next morning. I would not have to be present, since it would simply involve rote repetition. I was happy to hear this, because scene after scene has been collapsing due to their having to stop to retrieve lines. Ying knows almost all his words and has been the worst victim of the others' lapses. I asked him at the same time to press upon Linda the need to focus her mind on Willy rather than herself and to suppress her bad tendency to weep. I also wanted him to talk to Biff, who I think is now taking on the same sentimentality in spots. Ying Ruocheng, who is fantastically energetic and steady-minded, refusing either to illusion himself or to despair, said he would do his best with both actors. Aware that Zhu Lin's presence in the play will sell more tickets than any other factor, she being the biggest star in the cast, I am grateful that she pulls no rank and is always eager for direction—which of course she does not always use. She dresses in the same brown trousers and quilted brown tapestried short coat each day. In one sense I am glad she and I cannot converse, for she would doubtless have a lot to tell me about her reasons for acting the role as she does. This way, as two mutes, I say what I have to say and she can only nod pleasantly, often with what I take to be pleased surprise. But I am going to struggle with her to the end. She is really too good an actress and attractive a woman to waste her energy on tears.

It now appears that our Happy's speech pattern was not at all an acquired affectation, as Ying had thought, but a way of speaking common in his birthplace, a small town some fifty miles from Beijing. This information encouraged me to stop him in the middle of his first scene with Biff—where he should rather deliciously bemoan his success with women and business. Ying Ruocheng had several times pressed me to give him one simple line of direction rather than any kind of discussion about Happy's nature or his interactions with Biff. It suddenly occurred to me that what he lacked was enjoyment of his dilemma. I called up to the elevated bedroom, "You must be happy, that's all! The character is a very happy man!" His smile was one of relief. He went back to the scene, stood straight, and ticked it off as though he'd been playing it for months, his strain gone and with it a certain overlay of "tragic darkness." But he is still not right temperamentally.

Biff's sentimentality has largely disappeared. At one point he has to pick his old football helmet out of a chest beside his bed and, staring at it, say, "I've always made a point of not wasting my life, and . . . all I've done is to waste my life." The self-pity in it is difficult to watch. I told him that it is an ironical statement, a passing remark rather than something philosophically final. Now he does the speech again but with a grin of light self-mockery, then tosses the helmet back into the chest and walks away. It is really quite good, and gives his character strength. Remarkable how quickly they can shift like this. But it also implies how technical their approach is. I wonder whether our concept of an actor's inner life is at all useful to them, at least at this stage. The whole idea of theatre, it seems, is quite distant from a reflection of actual life, much closer to something formal and ritualistic. That he could change so quickly, and Happy likewise, must mean that they are playing purely by ear.

I must begin working on Act Two on Monday, so the time has come to turn some screws. I get onto the set and take the wild family fight scene, pointing out where the climaxes are and making them drill the cues for me so that we begin to get something approaching the rapid rhythms required. Since I am a head taller than any of them and my voice louder, I yell Willy's climactic line "Big shot!" and Biff's furious response, and Happy's "Wait a minute! I got a feasible idea!" throwing my arms out and belting at the top of my lungs. The shock in their faces tells me that they had never dreamed it went so loud and so far, that the threat in my tone was closer to danger than they had ever anticipated. Nevertheless they seem eager to do the scene again, and this time it goes so wild that the onlooking actors begin making noises as they watch, half-smiling, half-laughing with the excitement, and Ying blows himself out, losing *his* lines in the final tangle. But they seem to catch on to how high it must all reach, and there is some real excitement up there at last.

And so at the end of the first week I think they are capable of creating an American kind of performance, the direct, confrontational style of behavior the play requires. I am beginning to feel particularly good about Linda; on the final afternoon's run she has been far simpler, much more the woman on whom Willy relies, rather than the type to mop up after him. I suppose my hope in her springs from her intelligent, rather nobly commanding nature offstage. It will, I think, lead her to a stringent performance as best not only for the play but for her. At the end of rehearsals I decide it is time to tell her specifically that there is only one moment in Act One when she may actually weep, and that is on the single line "His life is in your hands." She opens her eyes even wider and looks surprised, but she nods deeply. I hope I understand what this means.

Ying Ruocheng's performance is already a joy. A real pro, yet a man full of intelligent feeling who is ready to try anything. He is about the size and shape of Cagney, balanced on short legs, a compact man who is able to come on cold, step onto the forestage and simply call up the feelings and joys of his great moment, decades ago, when through Biff he felt he was within inches of some fabled victory over life's ignominious leveling.

He seems to see Willy more and more accurately, as a little bantam with quick fists and the irreducible demand that life give him its meaning and significance and honor. I found myself standing up the other day and making a speech, to my own and everyone's surprise, and regretting it even as it was happening. But it suddenly seemed to me that with all their progress they were still being actors rather than humans who were privileged to express a poetic vision that lies within the play. They were not moving into the vision. I let myself say that the one red line connecting everyone in the play was a love for Willy; not admiration, necessarily, but a kind of visceral recognition that in his fumbling and often ridiculous way he is trying to lift up a belief in immense redeeming human possibilities. People can't stand him often, they flee from him, but they miss him when he isn't there. Perhaps it's that he hasn't a cynical bone in his body, he is the walking believer, the bearer of a flame whose going-out would leave us flat, with merely what the past has given us. He is forever signaling to a future that he cannot describe and will not live to see, but he is in love with it all the same.

Death of a Salesman, really, is a love story between a man and his son, and in a crazy way between both of them and America.

When I finished I feared I'd simply confused them. But two days later, in a car leaving an American Embassy reception for the whole company, Ying Ruocheng, in typical Chinese fashion, simply let drop that he was trying to get my speech written down; it apparently affected the cast, although at the time there was no visible reaction of any kind in their faces. This can drive you crazy, but it is still necessary to simply assert what has to be asserted and hope it has some effect.

There is a certain sensitive diffidence in the Chinese that, I confess, I never really considered before. It is difficult for them to put themselves forward except after some struggle. Ying Ruocheng, for one, does not volunteer to contradict another's mistaken information with what he knows to be accurate until asked his opinion. One comes upon frequent loud arguments in the neighborhood lanes, but I suspect it takes a lot to get their feelings to overleap the bounds, although of course when they do they are wildly passionate. I find that I must persist in drawing out the actors' own views in a way I would not be having to do in America, for example. I sensed yesterday that Charley was still having doubts about the reasons for his kindness to Willy—I can now read their eyes a bit better, I believe—and he admitted in a rather movingly hesitant way that this was so. I told him then what I had forgotten to in our earlier talks: that Charley has a deep feeling for Linda, whom he greatly admires. His face lit up then; he could act that. Paradoxically enough, it is also a kind of envy he feels for Willy's imagination, the condiments with which he sprinkles his life as contrasted with the blandness of Charley's more rational existence. Charley can laugh at Willy as a fool, but he is never bored by him. This seemed to help.

Ying Ruocheng feels that their diffidence, or reluctance to put themselves forward, is a legacy of Confucian self-abnegation, on top of which is laid the second grid of Communist suppression of individual personality, the leveling instinct; in both systems people really exist to serve the higher order, rather than the other way around as the American scheme has it. This may also lie at the root of what outsiders interpret merely as Chinese sexual puritanism. But Ying and others, too, deny that a puritan fear of sexuality is particularly Chinese; it is rather their sense of form that frowns on its public display. And in truth they do attempt to show a cool front in public quite apart from sexual matters. All the more baffling, then, how a monstrosity like the Cultural Revolution could have swept this country, when one of its chief features was to demand public avowals of proletarian loyalty and the most lavish public repentances for past sins against the workers' alleged interests. It actually got to where tens of thousands of people would be assembled in stadiums to witness and enjoy painful humiliations of some of their brightest intellectual and political stars. Ba Gin, one of their most praised novelists (and a major talent, I think), was forced to wear a dunce cap and kneel on broken glass before such a howling mob that packed the stadium.

MAY 7, THE OPENING

In the afternoon I go to Ying Ruocheng and Wu Sheliang's house to sit together one more time. As well to give me a chance to do something that there has not been time for—I have been wanting to take down some samples of the imagery he has used in his translation of the play that differed from the original. And while Inge and Wu Sheliang sit together on one side of the cool, book-lined living room that faces their little courtyard, Ying tries to remember some of his images.

I have never had this kind of relationship with an actor—primarily, I think, because Ying is also a scholar and approaches concepts passionately; thus he can draw feeling from ideas as well as from sheer psychological experience. I have never really seen myself as a director, probably because actors can ordinarily use only one impulse at a time rather than the clusters that life offers at any one moment. I have to warn myself against overcomplicating matters, something that can lead an actor to a hard intellectualized rendering rather than a felt performance. In this production, forced to find the central lines of motion by the sheer difficulties of translation, I have inadvertently undergone a kind of exercise that has kept me stimulated and sensitized to a play I wrote more than three decades ago. Ying Ruocheng has been my rock, a man of double consciousness, Eastern and Western, literary and show business. And he has managed to contain his actor's necessary selfishness through all our trials. I am happy to be in his house now with nothing to do but enjoy the delightful absence of necessity. We are merely going to talk about images.

In the opening scene of Act Two Willy is full of optimism and promises to talk to his boss, Howard, about giving him a New York job. "I'll put it to him straight and simple. He'll just have to take me off the road."

The translation is a four-character image: "Open door see mountain," or, in other words, a direct confrontation. Ying explains, "There is a famous line by a Tang Dynasty poet saying, 'End of the mountain, end of the river, so one feels the road should end there; however, with the shade from the willow and brightness from the flowers the road meanders and goes on.' This, of course, is the opposite image. But for Willy there can be no more meandering—he will open the door and face the mountain right in front of the door."

I ask about the play's own store of time-worn clichés, like "Business is business"—a phrase without any meaning in Chinese, it now turns out. "I made it, in effect, 'Kin is kin, money is money,'" says Ying. This resonates destructively upon Willy's repeated "I named him. I named him Howard"—his attempt to transcend the money relationship with his employer.

This reminds me of "Blood is thicker than water," which in turn reminds Ying that it is precisely the phrase used to describe Taiwan's separation from China, where indeed Chinese kin are separated from each other by a body of water.

Referring to his dead brother Ben, Willy says, "That man was a genius, that man was success incarnate!" I know that this bit of Lomanesque hyperbole has intrigued Ying Ruocheng from our first rehearsals. "In Chinese this is a very dense image, and a pun," he explains. "Genius in Chinese is conveyed by a double symbol—Heaven-Talent, *Tian-Cai. Tian* written one way can mean talent or another way it can mean money—money in a rather abstract way, not the coin or bill, more like 'wealth.' So the word *far-tian*, which we use all the time in this play, means 'get rich' but also 'success.' Hong Kong people eat a water plant that looks like hair that is called '*far-tian*'—they eat it for luck. For thousands of years somebody is said to have '*far-tian*-ed'—either become a big official or a landlord or some way struck it big (like 'lucked-out').

"Now 'incarnate' I translate as 'heaven-sent,' so it embraces the gift, like a talent that comes from off the earth, combining with money and success and the power to prevail—all of this packed together in one image. So . . . *tian-cai* is a slightly ludicrous punning on 'heaven,' 'success,' and 'making a buck.' And the audience laughed lightly at this last night—they caught it."

"In other words," I concluded, "to exaggerate slightly, it's like being blessed by heaven with the power and the talent to collect second mortgages."

Through our laughter we both acknowledge our mutual attempt to find the common ground beneath both our cultures. If Chinese has a more pictorial imagery it is nevertheless expressing like human situations far down below. (And this, as we both realize, makes the success of the production of far more importance than merely a theatrical success.)

Which leads to Ying's telling how he experienced American culture for the first time, years ago. "Superficially, everything is opposite between American and Chinese ways. Like we have soup at the end of the meal and you at the beginning; and the first time I had a haircut in the United States, I was amazed that they washed my hair before they cut it. Here we wash it afterward. But there are great similarities, and for me the main reason is the immense size of both countries; when a country is so large it tends to break down narrow-mindedness because people have experience with all kinds of other people, unlike in very small countries. America is very young, but people have been endlessly moving around in it, and China—at least for the last twenty-five hundred years—has been a unified state; but it is a mistake to think that China was created by a single tribe, it melded a large number of intermingling peoples. You've been to Datong, the great cave sculptures by the Meo Dynasty, who were entirely nomadic. There are dozens of other examples of very high cultures being worked into the Chinese culture. So that you don't get that provincial outlook, the narrow-minded thing."

"China was really a melting pot."

"Oh, very definitely, and in many ways like the American one. Last time I was in California—"

"Incidentally, California's going to have an Hispanic majority soon, you know—"

"I'm not surprised. Almost all the workers in the hotel were Hispanic, with a thin layer of Chinese above them, and the customers were all white." And he added, "And Japanese, of course."

My next image—"I won't take the rap for this"—he has translated, "I won't carry this blackened cooking pot on my back." And he calls across the room to Wu Sheliang, "What is the origin of that 'black cooking pot'?" She has no idea either, except that the soot blackens the clothes of the carrier.

I wondered if Chinese actually "saw" a man with a cooking pot when they used this common phrase, or the actual picture of any common metaphor.

"Not at all," Ying says. "Any more than you actually see a little mouse when you say 'quiet as a mouse,' or the vision of a hill when somebody is 'going downhill' in his career."

"It is only consciously poetic to foreigners."

"In any language, I should think."

As he is parting from Willy at the end of the scene in Charley's office, Bernard tries to cheer him up with "Good-bye, Willy, and don't worry about it. You know, 'If at first you don't succeed . . .'"

WILLY: Yes, I believe in that.
BERNARD: But sometimes, Willy, it's better for a man just to
walk away.
WILLY: Walk away?
BERNARD: That's right.
WILLY: But if you can't walk away?

How had he translated the last line? In our two previews the audiences had laughed, inappropriately it would seem.

Ying grinned. "Literally, 'walk away' doesn't mean anything in Chinese. So Bernard is saying, 'It's good to be able to pick things up but also to be able to put things down.' And Willy answers, 'Suppose I can't put them down?' He is implying he can only pick things up, and by that time the audience, I think, has identified themselves with Willy as a man who picks up all sorts of things without being able to put them down. And that's funny."

With our rehearsals past now and the play all but finally launched and a well-prepared cast of actors relaxing all over the town, it is time to relish some of the fruits of work—the power that the play obviously exercised over the second audience.

"That first audience was the worst you are going to get in China. First of all they don't pay, and on top of that they have no idea what theatre is, anyway—they're the people who provision our canteen."

"They think it's a place where you bring meat and vegetables."

"Right!" He laughs. "And then there's also our messengers. Most of our people, including myself, of course, have no telephones, so we need messengers. And to buy them the best Japanese motorbikes, to have an adequate supply of gasoline, to have a place to fix them up—you have to keep all those people happy. Then various clubs and universities, factories, are in a position to order five hundred, a thousand tickets at a time—these people are not really interested in art, it's their job, that's all, to get tickets. The second audience, as far as we're concerned, was perfect. But of course with our noisy seats you have the feeling that they've all left just because four or five have gotten up to go to the johns. But last night with those curtain calls I was surprised and I thought, Nobody left! Chinese are quick to leave a performance, you know, and that kind of applause at the end is very rare."

ANCHEE MIN

FROM MAO to AMERICA: A WRITER'S REMARKABLE JOURNEY

THIS IS MY FAVORITE piece because I still can't believe that I lived it. The Yangtze River runs in my blood, and the time dust of the yellow-earth culture frames my bones. I am Chinese and a female, the kind an old saying describes as "grass born to be stepped on."

—Anchee Min

My memory stirred when I saw images of Afghani children reading the Koran while I was at home near Los Angeles. I recognized my own childhood, except that what I had held in my hands was a book of Mao's quotations. Children of China were instructed in Mao's teachings beginning in the nursery. Learning Mao was the goal of my entire schooling, ten years in total. The concepts for all subjects were intended to deepen our understanding of Mao's teachings. A typical question in first-grade math would be: "During the battle to break an encirclement in the midmountain area, fifty of Mao's Red Army soldiers defeated ten times their number. How many enemy soldiers were there when the battle started?"

Pictures of Mao were on the jackets of all my textbooks. His large head was centered in the red sun, the rays of which spread out and filled the page. "I love you, Chairman Mao" was the first sentence taught to a toddler before he or she said "Mama" or "Papa." Each morning we bowed to Mao's portrait, which hung in the front of every classroom. Anyone who failed to wear a Mao pin or bring Mao's books to school or the work unit would be considered disloyal and therefore punished. My biggest fear was that my mother would unintentionally violate the rules. She was unable to learn her lessons, no matter how hard she tried. I witnessed that in the name of Mao adults held grudges against each other and teens formed violent gangs.

I strove hard to become a Mao loyalist. It was not because I truly loved Mao, although I claimed to do so. It was to escape beatings from the school bullies. Whenever I was struck with sticks, umbrellas, or abacuses, I would begin to recite Mao's teachings. The act worked, but the beatings would resume the next day. I grew to love Mao for the magical power his words held. I was fluent in reciting his important writings, essays, poems, and *The Little Red Book* in its entirety. It didn't matter that I had little understanding of the meaning. We worshipped Mao as a god, and there was no doubt in our minds that only he could lead us out of hunger. I never dreamt of anything else but food in my childhood.

When I was twelve I was honorably selected by the school to be a youth leader. I was sent to the Shanghai Garrison to be trained to use a gun and throw grenades. I was also taught combat skills. When I came back I was expected to teach others. At the garrison the military officer made us understand that the Americans were slaughtering people in Vietnam, and China was going to be next. Besides training and chanting Mao quotations we studied the lives of revolutionary martyrs. I was so moved and inspired that I couldn't wait to be sent to Vietnam—I wanted to model myself after the martyrs. Nothing was more glorious than honoring Mao and my country. We watched a movie titled *The Heroes*, and we sang its theme song, "Let Our Blood and Ashes Fertilize the Motherland," as loud as we could.

Every day I dreamed of tying grenades to my body and hurling myself into a group of American soldiers. I saw myself performing the same task the hero did in the movie. The scene that got my tears running every time was when the hero lit the explosive. He shouted his last words through his radio headphones to his commander: "In my direction, fire the cannons! For Mao, good-bye comrades!" He jumped and we saw the faces of terrified American soldiers while smoke filled the screen. I imagined my remains being brought back home wrapped in the communist red flag, and my school, family, and neighbors shedding sad but proud tears.

Today, the images of airplanes crashing into the Twin Towers continue to haunt me. I know what must have gone through the minds of the hijackers. It must have been the thrill of being given the opportunity to serve God, as I would have served Mao. Think of it: I could have died without experiencing the life I now have—a wonderful husband, an adorable daughter, a spacious house with shining white porcelain toilets, a car, plenty of food, plum trees in the backyard, and most of all, the tremendous love and happiness I feel.

My hatred of Americans dissolved after three years in a labor camp near the East China Sea and one day back in Shanghai. It was a cold and wet winter in 1979. My neighbor, Mr. Kang, was allowed to contact his relatives in Hong Kong for the first time. Right before the New Year he received a big box that contained a gift. It was my first time seeing a television set. Fearing that he might be accused of indulging himself with the TV, Mr. Kang offered to share it with everyone in the lane for a few days. It turned out to be a party that was grander than New Year's Eve. The public cafeteria was crowded. Old people came with canes and the young in their mothers' arms. Soon the room was packed, but more people wanted in. The manager tried to close the door, but people wouldn't let him. Eventually the door popped out of its frame. Shivering in the cold, we sat tightly together. My toes and fingers ached from frostbite and infections. Everyone's eyes were glued to the nine-inch black-and-white screen.

We were aware that the program had gone through government censorship, and we expected that it would show nothing but the worst of the enemy nation. Still, our jaws dropped. I couldn't believe what I saw: the laid-off American workers, to whose liberation and freedom we had devoted our lives, were not skeletons in rags. The translation said that these people were picketing in front of Chicago City Hall where they had worked. My saliva ran when the camera panned over the background, and I saw handsome buildings, fancy shops, and people eating in neon-sign-decorated restaurants.

What followed for the next few years was China's awakening. It became impossible for the Communist Party to rule through deception. To survive and keep order our government loosened its grip. Books and music started to be smuggled in from Hong Kong and Taiwan. By 1984 the theaters were permitted to show American movies. It was then that I first saw *Snow White*. I remember walking out of the theater in confusion: how was it possible that people who created this wanted to kill us? Following Snow White was Mickey Mouse, *The Sound of Music*, love songs, the Beatles, and Karen Carpenter. I grew up with slogan-shouting propaganda songs and had never heard a woman sing in a natural and unstrangled voice. I couldn't understand a word she said, but I played the tape until it broke. I remember fighting with my siblings over a borrowed tape player.

My twenty-seven years in China helped me greatly as a writer. The tough part of my writing has been English. I think in Chinese and have to translate while writing. All my outlines and detailed notes are in Chinese. When I get tired, the "translator" inside my head slows down. Sometimes it just quits working. I speak Chinese to my American husband and he calls our daughter, Lauryann, and asks her to translate. Lauryann was born in Chicago, and her Chinese is naturally poor. She doesn't mind being the translator because it makes her feel powerful.

I wrote *Red Azalea* in eight years because of my struggle with English. My ideas, concepts, and word order were in Chinese. The problem was that I didn't have enough vocabulary to describe emotions. In my English-Chinese dictionary all the definitions carried a communist tone. For example, the first definition for the word *love* reads, "Affection, admiration: we have ardent love for our great leader Chairman Mao"; "Show great *love* towards one's comrades/one's country." The definition for the word *last* reads: "Last, the only one that's left: fight the enemy to the *last* drop of one's blood."

The preface of my dictionary offers an even clearer idea: "The New English-Chinese Dictionary is a product of the Great Proletarian Cultural Revolution. We believe in Karl Marx, who said, 'A foreign language is a weapon against our enemies.' The purpose of this edition is to serve to win our war against the Imperialists [meaning the United States] and the Revisionists [the USSR] . . . We offer criticisms while translating. It is to help our readers identify the unacceptable parts that English bears as a language, such as bourgeois reactionary ideas, words used to depict corrupted lifestyles, and most of all we must warn our users of the danger in English that promotes humanism. The guidelines we as editors follow is Mao's teaching, which says, 'It is a matter of principle who you serve.'"

It was through English that I discovered my true expression. The humanistic elements in English motivated me to turn back to Chinese to look for the same. As a result I relearned Chinese and discovered with great delight and satisfaction the beauty of my mother tongue. Looking back, I would say that the act of writing was more therapeutic than anything else. Ten years later I wrote *Wild Ginger*, and it only took me two weeks. It was because my English had improved and the translator in my head was smoother. The stories, many of which I recalled with unbearable grief, came to me easily. There was a subtle difference between the parts I imagined and the parts I had lived. *Red Azalea* is an autobiography; *Katherine* and *Wild Ginger* were largely based on my own experiences and characters I knew well. There was not much to plot or invent.

The longer I live in the United States the more clearly I know what to do with my life. I didn't realize that I had written an alternative history until *Red Azalea* was published in 1994. I only knew that China's official history of the Cultural Revolution did not tell the truth. I was aware of my role when I decided to write *Becoming Madame Mao*. The most consuming part of my writing was research. I wanted to find out the "whys" and "hows"—the basic-basic, so to speak. I was denied entrance to libraries in China, and no one in the government dared to help. My only choice was to use what we call in China "the back door"—to obtain documents through bribery. For interviews I had to go through a chain of "middlemen." My being a former Communist helped a great deal: at least I knew which doors to knock on. I found exciting material, especially when it helped answer the questions that I had always had. Such as Madame Mao's motivation in silencing people who knew her background, and what made her shout, "I am Mao's dog!" during her trial.

I was not confident that I could do a good job when I began *Empress Orchid*. The only thing I knew was that she was a demon. I was taught, like every child in China, that Empress Tzu-Hsi (Orchid), who ruled for forty-seven years, was responsible for the downfall of the Ch'ing Dynasty, which ended our millennia-long imperial tradition. The good thing was that I distrusted the official version. I sailed on my own journey and was determined to discover the truth. I used nothing but common sense when I put together my findings. To construct the narrative, I chose the simplest format. With a story as fascinating as that of the empress, less is truly more.

I almost took my good life for granted and forgot how privileged I have been as an American writer until I recently learned about the ban in China. It was a historical TV series titled *Going Republic*, which reflected for the first time the empress's true role in history. The writer, a journalist and historian whom I admired, was said to be under house arrest, which would have been my fate if I lived in China. I was pleased that the empress in the banned version was a close match of mine.

JAN MORRIS

From FAREWELL the TRUMPETS

⌒

I AM EASILY MOVED, not least by my own writing, and the maudlin in me was paramount when I came to the end of a long trilogy, the Pax Britannica trilogy, about the climax and decline of the British Empire. As a Welsh patriot I was not much disturbed by the end of the empire itself, whose ideology had long been discredited, but having spent ten years thinking about its meaning and wandering its lost territories, I found myself truly saddened by its sacrifices and good intentions, so often gone to waste—by the graves of its activists scattered across the continents, by the memorials of its real grandeur, and most of all, perhaps, by the departure from the scene of its most fascinating archetype, Winston Churchill. This passage concludes the work, and is sentimentally lubricated by my tears.

—Jan Morris

TEARS AT THE END OF EMPIRE

Across the continents stood those tombs, from the triumphant mausolea of Anglo-Indian conquerors to the pathetic mementos of defeat, carved in prison workshops in the graveyards of Hong Kong and Singapore. Many expressed pride in death, many more contentment, but often the epitaphists were concerned less with the dead than with the living—

> *O! ye in the far distant place,*
> *O'er the infinite seas;*
> *When ye think of the sons of our race,*
> *Think deep upon these!*

> *When you go home, tell them of us and say*
> *For your tomorrows we gave our today.* *

---

*The first comes from a memorial at Wagon Hill, outside Ladysmith; the second is from the famous memorial to the 14th Army at Kohima, and is an English version of Leonidas' message from Thermopylae in 480 B.C.—*Go, tell the Spartans, thou who passest by, / That here obedient to their laws we lie.*

This is because they believed that there were lessons to be learnt from the example of the imperial dead, that the Empire and the world would be a better place because of the manner of their lives, and the penalty of their deaths. Nobody who wandered among the imperial gravestones, though, pondering the sadness of their separate tragedies, could fail to wonder at the waste of it all, the young lives thrown away, the useless courage, the unnecessary partings; and the fading image of Empire, its ever dimmer panoply of flags and battlements, seemed then to be hazed in a mist of tears, like a grand old march shot through with melancholy, in a bandstand by the sea.

The end of it was not surprising. Once the almost orgiastic splendour of its climax had been achieved, once the zest went out of it, it became rather a sad phenomenon. Its beauty had lain in its certainty and momentum, its arrogance perhaps. In its declining years it lost the dignity of command, and became rather an exhibition of ineffectual good intentions. Its memory was terrific; it had done much good in its time; it had behaved with courtesy as with brutality, rapaciously and generously, rightly and in error; good and bad had been allied in this, one of the most truly astonishing of human enterprises. Now its contribution was over, the world had moved on, and it died.

They performed its obsequies, with Sir Winston's, on a grey London day in January, and for the last time the world watched a British imperial spectacle. Melancholy though the occasion was, intuitively though the British felt its deeper significance, they did it, as Churchill wished, in the high old style. Big Ben was silenced for the day. Mourning guns were fired in Hyde Park. The great drum-horse of the Household Cavalry, drums swathed in black crêpe, led the funeral procession solemnly through London to St. Paul's, while band after band across the capital played the Dead March from *Saul*, and the soldiers along the way bared their heads and reversed their arms.

Five Field Marshals, four Prime Ministers, an Admiral of the Fleet and a Marshal of the Royal Air Force were among the pallbearers when the coffin, draped with the flags of the Cinque Ports and of the Spencer-Churchill family, was carried up the great steps into the cathedral. A hundred nations were represented there, and twenty of them had once been ruled from this very capital. A bugle played the *Last Post* in the Whispering Gallery, another answered with *Reveille* from the west door, and after the funeral service they took the coffin down to the River Thames. There, as the pipers played "The Flowers of the Forest," six tall guardsmen, their cold sad faces straining with the weight, carried it on board a river launch: and away up the London river it sailed towards Westminster, escorted by black police boats. "Rule Britannia" sounded from the shore, fighter aircraft flew overhead, farewell guns fired from the Tower of London, and as the little flotilla disappeared upstream, watched by the great mourning crowd below the cathedral, all the cranes on the riverside wharves were dipped in salute. Everyone knew what was happening, even the enemies of Empire. "The true old times were dead, when every morning brought a noble chance, and every chance a noble knight."

In the afternoon they put the old statesman's body reverently on a train, for he was to be buried in the family churchyard in Oxfordshire: and so as dusk fell, with white steam flying from the engine's funnel, and a hiss of its pistons through the meadows, it carried him sadly home again, to the green country heart of England.

HARUKI MURAKAMI

From THE WIND-UP BIRD CHRONICLE

∼

I WROTE THIS NOVEL while I was living in America from 1991 to 1995, first in Princeton, New Jersey, for two and a half years, and then Cambridge, Massachusetts, for two years. Writing it was hard work, probably the hardest one so far, but I was totally absorbed in it, sometimes even mesmerized.

Writing something while you are living abroad can be quite an interesting experience. You are a stranger in the country, but you think you are not a stranger in your own internal world. So you write about your own world. But then, suddenly, you find yourself a total stranger even in your own realm. Something has happened there and the outer strangeness has intruded into your place.

So you have to go deep, deeper, and find a secret path leading you to the core of yourself, where you are the real YOU. To me, *The Wind-Up Bird Chronicle* is the story of a search for something—something essential to me as an individual and as a novelist. And I like to think that, at the end of it, I found what I was looking for.

—Haruki Murakami

TUESDAY'S WIND-UP BIRD

SIX FINGERS AND FOUR BREASTS

When the phone rang I was in the kitchen, boiling a potful of spaghetti and whistling along with an FM broadcast of the overture to Rossini's *The Thieving Magpie*, which has to be the perfect music for cooking pasta.

I wanted to ignore the phone, not only because the spaghetti was nearly done, but because Claudio Abbado was bringing the London Symphony to its musical climax. Finally, though, I had to give in. It could have been somebody with news of a job opening. I lowered the flame, went to the living room, and picked up the receiver.

"Ten minutes, please," said a woman on the other end.

I'm good at recognizing people's voices, but this was not one I knew.

"Excuse me? To whom did you wish to speak?"

"To *you*, of course. Ten minutes, please. That's all we need to understand each other." Her voice was low and soft but otherwise nondescript.

"Understand each other?"

"Each other's feelings."

I leaned over and peeked through the kitchen door. The spaghetti pot was steaming nicely, and Claudio Abbado was still conducting *The Thieving Magpie*.

"Sorry, but you caught me in the middle of making spaghetti. Can I ask you to call back later?"

"Spaghetti? What are you doing cooking spaghetti at ten-thirty in the morning?"

"That's none of your business," I said. "*I* decide what I eat and when I eat it."

"True enough. I'll call back," she said, her voice now flat and expressionless. A little change in mood can do amazing things to the tone of a person's voice.

"Hold on a minute," I said before she could hang up. "If this is some new sales gimmick, you can forget it. I'm out of work. I'm not in the market for anything."

"Don't worry. I know."

"You know? You know what?"

"That you're out of work. I know about that. So go cook your precious spaghetti."

"Who the hell—"

She cut the connection.

With no outlet for my feelings, I stared at the phone in my hand until I remembered the spaghetti. Back in the kitchen, I turned off the gas and poured the contents of the pot into a colander. Thanks to the phone call, the spaghetti was a little softer than *al dente*, but it had not been dealt a mortal blow. I started eating—and thinking.

Understand each other? Understand each other's feelings in ten minutes? What was she talking about? Maybe it was just a prank call. Or some new sales pitch. In any case, it had nothing to do with me.

After lunch, I went back to my library novel on the living room sofa, glancing every now and then at the telephone. What were we supposed to understand about each other in ten minutes? What *can* two people understand about each other in ten minutes? Come to think of it, she seemed awfully sure about those ten minutes: it was the first thing out of her mouth. As if nine minutes would be too short or eleven minutes too long. Like cooking spaghetti *al dente*.

I couldn't read anymore. I decided to iron shirts instead. Which is what I always do when I'm upset. It's an old habit. I divide the job into twelve precise stages, beginning with the collar (outer surface) and ending with the left-hand cuff. The order is always the same, and I count off each stage to myself. Otherwise, it won't come out right.

I ironed three shirts, checking them over for wrinkles and putting them on hangers. Once I had switched off the iron and put it away with the ironing board in the hall closet, my mind felt a good deal clearer.

I was on my way to the kitchen for a glass of water when the phone rang again. I hesitated for a second but decided to answer it. If it was the same woman, I'd tell her I was ironing and hang up.

This time it was Kumiko. The wall clock said eleven-thirty. "How are you?" she asked.

"Fine," I said, relieved to hear my wife's voice.

"What are you doing?"

"Just finished ironing."

"What's wrong?" There was a note of tension in her voice. She knew what it meant for me to be ironing.

"Nothing. I was just ironing some shirts." I sat down and shifted the receiver from my left hand to my right. "What's up?"

"Can you write poetry?" she asked.

"Poetry!?" Poetry? Did she mean . . . poetry?

"I know the publisher of a story magazine for girls. They're looking for somebody to pick and revise poems submitted by readers. And they want the person to write a short poem every month for the frontispiece. Pay's not bad for an easy job. Of course, it's part-time. But they might add some editorial work if the person—"

"Easy work?" I broke in. "Hey, wait a minute. I'm looking for something in law, not poetry."

"I thought you did some writing in high school."

"Yeah, sure, for the school newspaper: which team won the soccer championship or how the physics teacher fell down the stairs and ended up in the hospital—that kind of stuff. Not poetry. I can't write poetry."

"Sure, but I'm not talking about great poetry, just something for high school girls. It doesn't have to find a place in literary history. You could do it with your eyes closed. Don't you see?"

"Look, I just can't write poetry—eyes open or closed. I've never done it, and I'm not going to start now."

"All right," said Kumiko, with a hint of regret. "But it's hard to find legal work."

"I know. That's why I've got so many feelers out. I should be hearing something this week. If it's no go, I'll think about doing something else."

"Well, I suppose that's that. By the way, what's today? What day of the week?"

I thought a moment and said, "Tuesday."

"Then will you go to the bank and pay the gas and telephone?"

"Sure. I was just about to go shopping for dinner anyway."

"What are you planning to make?"

"I don't know yet. I'll decide when I'm shopping."

She paused. "Come to think of it," she said, with a new seriousness, "there's no great hurry about your finding a job."

This took me off guard. "Why's that?" I asked. Had the women of the world chosen today to surprise me on the telephone? "My unemployment's going to run out sooner or later. I can't keep hanging around forever."

"True, but with my raise and occasional side jobs and our savings, we can get by OK if we're careful. There's no real emergency. Do you hate staying at home like this and doing housework? I mean, is this life so wrong for you?"

"I don't know," I answered honestly. I really didn't know.

"Well, take your time and give it some thought," she said. "Anyhow, has the cat come back?"

The cat. I hadn't thought about the cat all morning. "No," I said. "Not yet."

"Can you please have a look around the neighborhood? It's been gone over a week now."

I gave a noncommittal grunt and shifted the receiver back to my left hand. She went on:

"I'm almost certain it's hanging around the empty house at the other end of the alley. The one with the bird statue in the yard. I've seen it in there several times."

"The alley? Since when have you been going to the alley? You've never said anything—"

"Oops! Got to run. Lots of work to do. Don't forget about the cat."

She hung up. I found myself staring at the receiver again. Then I set it down in its cradle.

I wondered what had brought Kumiko to the alley. To get there from our house, you had to climb over the cinder-block wall. And once you'd made the effort, there was no point in being there.

I went to the kitchen for a glass of water, then out to the veranda to look at the cat's dish. The mound of sardines was untouched from last night. No, the cat had not come back. I stood there looking at our small garden, with the early-summer sunshine streaming into it. Not that ours was the kind of garden that gives you spiritual solace to look at. The sun managed to find its way in there for the smallest fraction of each day, so the earth was always black and moist, and all we had by way of garden plants were a few drab hydrangeas in one corner—and I don't like hydrangeas. There was a small stand of trees nearby, and from it you could hear the mechanical cry of a bird that sounded as if it were winding a spring. We called it the wind-up bird. Kumiko gave it the name. We didn't know what it was really called or what it looked like, but that didn't bother the wind-up bird. Every day it would come to the stand of trees in our neighborhood and wind the spring of our quiet little world.

So now I had to go cat hunting. I had always liked cats. And I liked this particular cat. But cats have their own way of living. They're not stupid. If a cat stopped living where you happened to be, that meant it had decided to go somewhere else. If it got tired and hungry, it would come back. Finally, though, to keep Kumiko happy, I would have to go looking for our cat. I had nothing better to do.

I had quit my job at the beginning of April—the law job I had had since graduation. Not that I had quit for any special reason. I didn't dislike the work. It wasn't thrilling, but the pay was all right and the office atmosphere was friendly.

My role at the firm was—not to put too fine a point on it—that of professional gofer. And I was good at it. I might say I have a real talent for the execution of such practical duties. I'm a quick study, efficient, I never complain, and I'm realistic. Why is why, when I said I wanted to quit, the senior partner (the father in this father-

and-son law firm) went so far as to offer me a small raise.

But I quit just the same. Not that quitting would help me realize any particular hopes or prospects. The last thing I wanted to do, for example, was shut myself up in the house and study for the bar exam. I was surer than ever that I didn't want to become a lawyer. I knew, too, that I didn't want to stay where I was and continue with the job I had. If I was going to quit, now was the time to do it. If I stayed with the firm any longer, I'd be there for the rest of my life. I was thirty years old, after all.

I had told Kumiko at the dinner table that I was thinking of quitting my job. Her only response had been, "I see." I didn't know what she meant by that, but for a while she said nothing more.

I kept silent too, until she added, "If you want to quit, you should quit. It's your life, and you should live it the way you want to." Having said this much, she then became involved in picking out fish bones with her chopsticks and moving them to the edge of her plate.

Kumiko earned pretty good pay as editor of a health food magazine, and she would occasionally take on illustration assignments from editor friends at other magazines to earn substantial additional income. (She had studied design in college and had hoped to be a free-lance illustrator.) In addition, if I quit I would have my own income for a while from unemployment insurance. Which meant that even if I stayed home and took care of the house, we would still have enough for extras such as eating out and paying the cleaning bill, and our lifestyle would hardly change.

And so I had quit my job.

⌒

I was loading groceries into the refrigerator when the phone rang. The ringing seemed to have an impatient edge to it this time. I had just ripped open a plastic pack of tofu, which I set down carefully on the kitchen table to keep the water from spilling out. I went to the living room and picked up the phone.

"You must have finished your spaghetti by now," said the woman.

"You're right. But now I have to go look for the cat."

"That can wait for ten minutes, I'm sure. It's not like cooking spaghetti."

For some reason, I couldn't just hang up on her. There was something about her voice that commanded my attention. "OK, but no more than ten minutes."

"Now we'll be able to understand each other," she said with quiet certainty. I sensed her settling comfortably into a chair and crossing her legs.

"I wonder," I said. "What can you understand in ten minutes?"

"Ten minutes may be longer than you think," she said.

"Are you sure you know me?"

"Of course I do. We've met hundreds of times."

"Where? When?"

"Somewhere, sometime," she said. "But if I went into that, ten minutes would never be enough. What's important is the time we have now. The present. Don't you agree?"

"Maybe. But I'd like some proof that you know me."

"What kind of proof?"

"My age, say?"

"Thirty," she answered instantaneously. "Thirty and two months. Good enough?"

That shut me up. She obviously did know me, but I had absolutely no memory of her voice.

"Now it's your turn," she said, her voice seductive. "Try picturing me. From my voice. Imagine what I'm like. My age. Where I am. How I'm dressed. Go ahead."

"I have no idea," I said.

"Oh, come on," she said. "Try."

I looked at my watch. Only a minute and five seconds had gone by. "I have no idea," I said again.

"Then let me help you," she said. "I'm in bed. I just got out of the shower, and I'm not wearing a thing."

Oh, great. Telephone sex.

"Or would you prefer me with something on? Something lacy. Or stockings. Would that work better for you?"

"I don't give a damn. Do what you like," I said. "Put something on if you want to. Stay naked if you want to. Sorry, but I'm not interested in telephone games like this. I've got a lot of things I have to—"

"Ten minutes," she said. "Ten minutes won't kill you. It won't put a hole in your life. Just answer my question. Do you want me naked or with something on? I've got all kinds of things I could put on. Black lace panties . . ."

"Naked is fine."

"Well, good. You want me naked."

"Yes. Naked. Good."

Four minutes.

"My pubic hair is still wet," she said. "I didn't dry myself very well. Oh, I'm so wet! Warm and moist. And soft. Wonderfully soft and black. Touch me."

"Look, I'm sorry, but—"

"And down below too. All the way down. It's so warm down there, like butter cream. So warm. Mmm. And my legs. What position do you think my legs are in? My right knee is up, and my left leg is open just enough. Say, ten-oh-five on the clock."

I could tell from her voice that she was not faking it. She really did have her legs open to ten-oh-five, her sex warm and moist.

"Touch the lips," she said. "Slooowly. Now open them. That's it. Slowly, slowly. Let your fingers caress them. Oh so slowly. Now, with your other hand, touch my left breast. Play with it. Caress it. Upward. And give the nipple a little squeeze. Do it again. And again. And again. Until I'm just about to come."

Without a word, I put the receiver down. Stretching out on the sofa, I stared at the clock and released a long, deep sigh. I had spoken with her for close to six minutes.

The phone rang again ten minutes later, but I left it on the hook. It rang fifteen times. And when it stopped, a deep, cold silence descended upon the room.

~

Just before two, I climbed over the cinder-block wall and down into the alley—or what we called the alley. It was not an "alley" in the proper sense of the word, but then, there was probably no word for what it was. It wasn't a "road" or a "path" or even a "way." Properly speaking, a "way" should be a pathway or channel with an entrance and an exit, which takes you somewhere if you follow it. But our "alley" had neither entrance nor exit. You couldn't call it a cul-de-sac, either: a cul-de-sac has at least one open end. The alley had not one dead end but two. The people of the neighborhood called it "the alley" strictly as an expedient. It was some two hundred yards in length and threaded its way between the back gardens of the houses that lined either side. Barely over three feet in width, it had several spots at which you had to edge through sideways because of fences sticking out into the path or things that people had left in the way.

About this alley, the story was—the story I heard from my uncle, who rented us our house for next to nothing—that it used to have both an entrance and an exit and actually served the purpose of providing a shortcut between two streets. But with the rapid economic growth of the mid-fifties, rows of new houses came to fill the empty lots on either side of the road, squeezing it down until it was little more than a narrow path. People didn't like strangers passing so close to their houses and yards, so before long, one end of the path was blocked off—or, rather, screened off—with an unassertive fence. Then one local citizen decided to enlarge his yard and completely sealed off his end of the alley with a cinder-block wall. As if in response, a barbed-wire barrier went up at the other end, preventing even dogs from getting through. None of the neighbors complained, because none of them used the alley as a passageway, and they were just as happy to have this extra protection against crime. As a result, the alley remained like some kind of abandoned canal, unused, serving as little more than a bugger zone between two rows of houses. Spiders spread their sticky webs in the overgrowth.

Why had Kumiko been frequenting such a place? I myself had walked down that "alley" no more than twice, and Kumiko was afraid of spiders at the best of times. Oh, what the hell—if Kumiko said I should go to the alley and look for the cat, I'd go to the alley and look for the cat. What came later I could think about later. Walking outside like this was far better than sitting in the house waiting for the phone to ring.

The sharp sunshine of early summer dappled the surface of the alley with the hard shadows of the branches that stretched overhead. Without wind to move the branches, the shadows looked like permanent stains, destined to remain imprinted on the pavement forever. No sounds of any kind seemed to penetrate this place. I could almost hear the blades of grass breathing in the sunlight. A few small clouds floated in the sky, their shapes clear and precise, like the clouds in medieval engravings. I saw everything with such terrific clarity that my own body felt vague and boundless and flowing . . . and hot!

I wore a T-shirt, thin cotton pants, and tennis shoes, but walking in the summer sun, I could feel a light film of sweat forming under my arms and in the hollow of my chest. The T-shirt and pants had been packed away in a box crammed with summer clothing until I pulled them out that morning, the sharp smell of mothballs penetrating my nostrils.

The houses that lined the alley fell into two distinct categories: older houses and those built more recently. As a group, the newer ones were smaller, with smaller yards to match. Their clothes-drying poles often protruded into the alley, making it necessary for me to thread my way through the occasional screen of towels and sheets and undershirts. Over some back walls came the clear sound of television sets and flushing toilets, and the smell of curry cooking.

The older houses, by contrast, gave hardly any sense of life. These were screened off by well-placed shrubs and hedges, between which I caught glimpses of manicured gardens.

An old, brown, withered Christmas tree stood in the corner of one garden. Another had become the dumping ground for every toy known to man, the apparent leavings of several childhoods. There were tricycles and toss rings and plastic swords and rubber balls and tortoise dolls and little baseball bats. One garden had a basketball hoop, and another had fine lawn chairs surrounding a ceramic table. The white chairs were caked in dirt, as if they had not been used for some months or even years. The tabletop was coated with lavender magnolia petals, beaten down by the rain.

I had a clear view of one living room through an aluminum storm door. It had a matching leather sofa and chairs, a large TV, a sideboard (atop which sat a tropical-fish tank and two trophies of some kind), and a decorative floor lamp. The room looked like the set of a TV drama. A huge doghouse occupied a large part of another garden, but there was no sign of the dog itself, and the house's door stood open. The screen of the doghouse door bulged outward, as if someone had been leaning against it for months at a time.

The vacant house that Kumiko had told me about lay just beyond the place with the huge doghouse. One glance was all I needed to see that it was empty—and had been for some time. It was a fairly new two-story house, yet its wooden storm shutters showed signs of severe aging, and the railings outside the second-story windows were caked with rust. The house had a cozy little garden, in which, to be sure, a stone statue of a bird stood. The statue rested on a base that came to chest height and was surrounded by a thick growth of weeds. Tall fronds of goldenrod were almost touching the bird's feet. The bird—I had no idea what kind of bird it was supposed to be—had its wings open as if it wanted to escape from this unpleasant place as soon as possible. Aside from the statue, the garden had no decorative features. A pile of aging plastic lawn chairs stood against the house, and beside them an azalea bush displayed its bright-red blossoms, their color strangely unreal. Weeds made up the rest.

I leaned against the chest-high chain-link fence for a while, contemplating the garden. It should have been a paradise for cats, but there was no sign of cats here now. Perched on the roof's TV antenna, a single pigeon lent its monotonous cries to the scene. The stone bird's shadow fell on the surrounding undergrowth, breaking apart.

I took a lemon drop from my pocket, unwrapped it, and popped it into my mouth. I had taken my resignation from the firm as an opportunity to quit smoking, but now I was never without a pack of lemon drops. Kumiko said I was addicted to them and warned me that I'd soon have a mouthful of cavities, but I had to have my lemon drops. While I stood there looking at the garden, the pigeon on the TV antenna kept up its regular cooing, like some clerk stamping numbers on a sheaf of bills. I don't know how long I stayed there, leaning against the fence, but I remember spitting my lemon drop on the ground when, half melted, it filled my mouth with its sticky sweetness. I had just shifted my gaze to the shadow of the stone bird when I sensed that someone was calling to me from behind.

I turned, to see a girl standing in the garden on the other side of the alley. She was small and had her hair in a ponytail. She wore dark sunglasses with amber frames, and a light-blue sleeveless T-shirt. The rainy season had barely ended, and yet she had already managed to give her slender arms a nice, smooth tan. She had one hand jammed into the pocket of her short pants. The other rested on a waist-high bamboo gate, which could not have been providing much support. Only three feet—maybe four—separated us.

"Hot," she said to me.

"Yeah, right," I answered.

After this brief exchange of views, she stood there looking at me. Then she took a box of Hope regulars from her pants pocket, drew out a cigarette, and put it between her lips. She had a small mouth, the upper lip turned slightly upward. She struck a match and lit her cigarette. When she inclined her head to one side, her hair swung away to reveal a beautifully shaped ear, smooth as if freshly made, its edge aglow with a downy fringe.

She flicked her match away and exhaled smoke through pursed lips.

Then she looked up at me as if she had forgotten that I was there. I couldn't see her eyes through the dark, reflective lenses of her sunglasses.

"You live around here?" she asked.

"Uh-huh," I wanted to motion toward our house, but I had turned so many odd angles to get here that I no longer knew exactly where it was. I ended up pointing at random.

"I'm looking for my cat," I explained, wiping a sweaty palm on my pants. "It's been gone for a week. Somebody saw it around here somewhere."

"What kind of cat?"

"A big tom. Brown stripes. Tip of the tail a little bent."

"Name?"

"Noboru. Noboru Wataya."

"No, not *your* name. The cat's."

"That *is* my cat's name."

"Oh! Very impressive!"

"Well, actually, it's my brother-in-law's name. The cat sort of reminds us of him. We gave the cat his name, just for fun."

"How does the cat remind you of him?"

"I don't know. Just in general. The way it walks. And it has this blank stare."

She smiled now for the first time, which made her look a lot more childlike than she had seemed at first. She couldn't have been more than fifteen or sixteen. With its slight curl, her upper lip pointed up at a strange angle. I seemed to hear a voice saying "Touch me"—the voice of the woman on the phone. I wiped the sweat from my forehead with the back of my hand.

"A brown-striped cat with a bent tail," said the girl. "Hmm. Does it have a collar or something?"

"A black flea collar."

She stood there thinking for ten or fifteen seconds, her hand still resting on the gate. Then she dropped what was left of her cigarette and crushed it under her sandal.

"Maybe I did see a cat like that," she said. "I don't know about the bent tail, but it was a brown tiger cat, big, and I think it had a collar."

"When did you see it?"

"When *did* I see it? Hmm. No more than three or four days ago. Our yard is a kind of highway for the neighborhood cats. They all cut across here from the Takitanis' to the Miyawakis'."

She pointed toward the vacant house, where the stone bird still spread its wings, the tall goldenrod still caught the early-summer sun, and the pigeon went on with its monotonous cooing atop the TV antenna.

"I've got an idea," she said. "Why don't you wait here? All the cats eventually pass through our place on their way to the Miyawakis'. And somebody's bound to call the cops if they see you hanging around like that. It wouldn't be the first time."

I hesitated.

"Don't worry," she said. "I'm the only one here. The two of us can sit in the sun and wait for the cat to show up. I'll help. I've got twenty-twenty vision."

I looked at my watch. Two twenty-six. All I had to do today before it got dark was take in the laundry and fix dinner.

I went in through the gate and followed the girl across the lawn. She dragged her right leg slightly. She took a few steps, stopped, and turned to face me.

"I got thrown from the back of a motorcycle," she said, as if it hardly mattered.

A large oak tree stood at the point where the yard's lawn gave out. Under the tree sat two canvas deck chairs, one draped with a blue beach towel. Scattered on the other were a new box of Hope regulars, an ashtray and lighter, a magazine, and an oversize boom box. The boom box was playing hard-rock music at low volume. She turned the music off and took all the stuff out of the chair for me, dropping it on the grass. From the chair, I could see into the yard of the vacant house—the stone birds, the goldenrod, the chain-link fence. The girl had probably been watching me the whole time I was there.

The yard of this house was very large. It had a broad, sloping lawn dotted with clumps of trees. To the left of the deck chairs was a rather large concrete-lined pond, its empty bottom exposed to the sun. Judging from its greenish tinge, it had been without water for some time. We sat with our backs to the house, which was visible through a screen of trees. The house was neither large nor lavish in its construction. Only the yard gave an impression of large size, and it was well manicured.

"What a big yard," I said, looking around. "It must be a pain to take care of."

"Must be."

"I used to work for a lawn-mowing company when I was a kid."

"Oh?" She was obviously not interested in lawns.

"Are you always here alone?" I asked.

"Yeah. Always. Except a maid comes mornings and evenings. During the day it's just me. Alone. Want a cold drink? We've got beer."

"No, thanks."

"Really? Don't be shy."

I shook my head. "Don't you go to school?"

"Don't you go to work?"

"No work to go to."

"Lost your job?"

"Sort of. I quit a few weeks ago."

"What kind of job?"

"I was a lawyer's gofer. I'd go to different government offices to pick up documents, put materials in order, check on legal precedents, handle court procedures—that kind of stuff."

"But you quit."

"Yeah."

"Does your wife have a job?"

"She does."

The pigeon across the way must have stopped its cooing and gone off somewhere. I suddenly realized that a deep silence lay all around me.

"Right over there is where the cats go through," she said, pointing toward the far side of the lawn. "See the incinerator in the Takitanis' yard? They come under the fence at that point, cut across the grass, and go out under the gate to the yard across the way. They always follow exactly the same route."

She perched her sunglasses on her forehead, squinted at the yard, and lowered her glasses again, exhaling a cloud of smoke. In the interval, I saw that she had a two-inch cut next to her left eye—the kind of cut that would probably leave a scar the rest of her life. The dark sunglasses were probably meant to hide the wound. The girl's face was not a particularly beautiful one, but there was something attractive about it, probably the lively eyes or the unusual shape of the lips.

"Do you know about the Miyawakis?" she asked.

"Not a thing," I said.

"They're the ones who lived in the vacant house. A very proper family. They had two daughters, both in a private girls' school. Mr. Miyawaki owned a few family restaurants."

"Why'd they leave?"

"Maybe he was in debt. It was like they ran away—just cleared out one night. About a year ago, I think. Left the place to rot and breed cats. My mother's always complaining."

"Are there so many cats in there?"

Cigarette in her lips, the girl looked up at the sky.

"All kinds of cats. Some losing their fur, some with one eye . . . and where the other eye used to be, a lump of raw flesh. Yuck!"

I nodded.

"I've got a relative with six fingers on each hand. She's just a little older than me. Next to her pinkie she's got this extra finger, like a baby's finger. She knows how to keep it folded up so most people don't notice. She's really pretty."

I nodded again.

"You think it's in the family? What do you call it . . . part of the bloodline?"

"I don't know much about heredity."

She stopped talking. I sucked on my lemon drop and looked hard at the cat path. Not one cat had shown itself so far.

"Sure you don't want something to drink?" she asked. "I'm going to have a Coke."

I said I didn't need a drink.

She left her deck chair and disappeared through the trees, dragging her bad leg slightly. I picked up her magazine from the grass and leafed through it. Much to my surprise, it turned out to be a men's magazine, one of the glossy monthlies. The woman in the foldout wore thin panties that showed her slit and pubic hair. She sat on a stool with her legs spread out at weird angles. With a sigh, I put the magazine back, folded my hands on my chest, and focused on the cat path again.

A very long time went by before the girl came back, with a Coke in her hand. The heat was getting to me. Sitting under the sun, I felt my brain fogging over. The last thing I wanted to do was think.

"Tell me," she said, picking up her earlier conversation. "If you were in love with a girl and she turned out to have six fingers, what would you do?"

"Sell her to the circus," I answered.

"Really?"

"No, of course not," I said. "I'm kidding. I don't think it would bother me."

"Even if your kids might inherit it?"

I took a moment to think about that.

"No, I really don't think it would bother me. What harm would an extra finger do?"

"What if she had four breasts?"

I thought about that too.

"I don't know."

Four breasts? This kind of thing could go on forever. I decided to change the subject.

"How old are you?" I asked.

"Sixteen," she said. "Just had my birthday. First year in high school."

"Have you been out of school long?"

"My leg hurts if I walk too much. And I've got this scar near my eye. My school's very strict. They'd probably start bugging me if they found out I hurt myself falling off a motorcycle. So I'm out 'sick.' I could take a year off. I'm not in any hurry to go up a grade."

"No, I guess not," I said.

"Anyhow, what you were saying before, that you wouldn't mind marrying a girl with six fingers but not four breasts . . ."

"I didn't say that. I said I didn't know."

"Why don't you know?"

"I don't know—it's hard to imagine such a thing."

"Can you imagine someone with six fingers?"

"Sure, I guess so."

"So why not four breasts? What's the difference?"

I took another moment to think it over, but I couldn't find an answer.

"Do I ask too many questions?"

"Do people tell you that?"

"Yeah, sometimes."

I turned toward the cat path again. What the hell was I doing here? Not one cat had showed itself the whole time. Hands still folded on my chest, I closed my eyes for maybe thirty seconds. I could feel the sweat forming on different parts of my body. The sun poured into me with a strange heaviness. Whenever the girl moved her glass, the ice clinked inside it like a cowbell.

"Go to sleep if you want," she whispered. "I'll wake you if a cat shows up."

Eyes closed, I nodded in silence.

The air was still. There were no sounds of any kind. The pigeon had long since disappeared. I kept thinking about the woman on the telephone. Did I really know her? There had been nothing remotely familiar about her voice or her manner of speaking. But she definitely knew me. I could have been looking at a De Chirico scene: the woman's long shadow cutting across an empty street and stretching toward me, but she herself in a place far removed from the bounds of my consciousness. A bell went on ringing and ringing next to my ear.

"Are you asleep?" the girl asked, in a voice so tiny I could not be sure I was hearing it.

"No, I'm not sleeping," I said.

"Can I get closer? It'll be . . . easier if I keep my voice low."

"Fine with me," I said, eyes still closed.

She moved her chair until it struck mine with a dry, wooden clack. Strange, the girl's voice sounded completely different, depending on whether my eyes were open or closed.

"Can I talk? I'll keep real quiet, and you don't have to answer. You can even fall asleep. I don't mind."

"OK," I said.

"When people die, it's so neat."

Her mouth was next to my ear now, so the words worked their way inside me along with her warm, moist breath.

"Why's that?" I asked.

She put a finger on my lips as if to seal them.

"No questions," she said. "And don't open your eyes. OK?"

My nod was as small as her voice.

She took her finger from my lips and placed it on my wrist.

"I wish I had a scalpel. I'd cut it open and look inside. Not the corpse . . . the lump of death. I'm sure there must be something like that. Something round and squishy, like a softball, with a hard little core of dead nerves. I want to take it out of a dead person and cut it open and look inside. I always wonder what it's like. Maybe it's all hard, like toothpaste dried up inside the tube. That's it, don't you think? No, don't answer. It's squishy on the outside, and the deeper you go inside, the harder it gets. I want to cut open the skin and take out the squishy stuff, use a scalpel and some kind of spatula to get through it, and the closer you get to the center, the harder the squishy stuff gets, until you reach this tiny core. It's sooo tiny, like a tiny ball bearing, and really hard. It must be like that, don't you think?"

She cleared her throat a few times.

"That's all I think about these days. Must be because I have so much time to kill every day. When you don't have anything to do, your thoughts get really, really far out—so far out you can't follow them all the way to the end."

She took the finger from my wrist and drank down the rest of her cola. I knew the glass was empty from the sound of the ice.

"Don't worry about the cat—I'm watching for it. I'll let you know if Noboru Wataya shows up. Keep your eyes closed. I'm sure Noboru Wataya is walking around here someplace. He'll be here any minute now. He's coming. I know he's coming—through the grass, under the fence, stopping to sniff the flowers along the way, little by little Noboru Wataya is coming closer. Picture him that way, get his image in mind."

I tried to picture the image of the cat, but the best I could do was a blurry, backlighted photo. The sunlight penetrating my eyelids destabilized and diffused my inner darkness, making it impossible for me to bring up a precise image of the cat. Instead, what I imagined was a failed portrait, a strange, distorted picture, certain distinguishing features bearing some resemblance to the original but the most important parts missing. I couldn't even recall how the cat looked when it walked.

The girl put her finger on my wrist again, using the tip to draw an odd diagram of uncertain shape. As if in response, a new kind of darkness—different in quality from the darkness I had been experiencing until that moment—began to burrow into my consciousness. I was probably falling asleep. I didn't want this to happen, but there was no way I could resist it. My body felt like a corpse—someone else's corpse—sinking into the canvas deck chair.

In the darkness, I saw the four legs of Noboru Wataya, four silent brown legs atop four soft paws with swelling, rubberlike pads, legs that were soundlessly treading the earth somewhere.

But where?

"Ten minutes is all it will take," said the woman on the phone. No, she had to be wrong. Sometimes ten minutes is not ten minutes. It can stretch and shrink. That was something I did know for sure.

KATHLEEN NORRIS

THE WEDDING at the COURTHOUSE

I CHOSE THIS POEM for personal reasons, as it is a slightly fictionalized account of my wedding to the poet David J. Dwyer in the Sundance, Wyoming, county courthouse. I was the third generation of women in my family to elope—my respectable Presbyterian grandmother, Charlotte Hutton, with Frank C. Totten, M.D., in 1910, and my mother, Lois Totten, with John Heyward Norris in 1938. Both of these marriages lasted sixty-five years, so I thought that eloping was a good bet. My husband and I had thirty rich and rewarding years together until his death in 2003, and whenever I read this poem, I have to smile.

—Kathleen Norris

I don't like weddings.
When you live here long enough
the spindly-legged girls
grow up like weeds
to be mowed down: matrons
at twenty-five, all edges taken off.
When the music starts
they're led down the aisle
in their white dresses
and we celebrate sentiment
and money.

There's only one wedding
I'd go to again.
I happened to be on an errand
at the county courthouse
and Lucille came running:
"Will you be a witness?
We need two,
and the girls can't leave their desks."

They'd shown up
that morning, no family or friends.
Not kids: he looked about thirty
and she just a little younger.
She may have been pregnant,
but you couldn't tell.
It might have been the denim jumper
she was wearing.

I can picture Lucille
chain-smoking, surprised
and pleased
to interrupt routine.
And the Deputy Sheriff,
a young man, blushing,
loaded gun in his holster,
arms hanging loose.
He looked at his shoes.

It's the words I remember most.
Lucille put out a cigarette
and began: "Dearly beloved,"
and we were!

LYNN NOTTAGE

From INTIMATE APPAREL

I'VE SELECTED AN EXCERPT from my play *Intimate Apparel*, which is set in New York City in 1905; it's the story of Esther, a lonely African American seamstress who longs for intimacy. Ironically, she creates beautiful lingerie for wealthy socialites and prostitutes, helping them fulfill their desires, but remains unfulfilled herself.

With the aid of a client, Esther begins a long-distance correspondence with a Caribbean laborer stationed in the Panama Canal Zone. We, however, learn that her heart secretly belongs to an Orthodox Jewish fabric salesmen, who, due to circumstance, can't return her love. Therefore, when the Panama Canal laborer proposes marriage via mail, Esther willingly accepts, afraid that it might be her last chance for love. But when the laborer arrives, Esther is forced to deal with the consequences of marrying a man she does not even know.

This excerpt comes near the end of the first act. It is the moment at which Esther is resolved to leave her old life behind for the possibility of the unknown. She fears if she remains in the boarding house where she lives, she'll be condemned to a life of inconsequence. In the scene I've selected, Mrs. Dickson, her landlady, tries to prepare innocent Esther for the life of a married woman, cautioning that a marriage without love is no better than being alone. I like the scene because it's really about two close friends recognizing that their relationship will never be the same. As such, they permit themselves to be momentarily naked.

It is one of the more surprisingly intimate moments in the play, and no matter how many times I've seen it performed, it remains one of the scenes that I most look forward to seeing again.

—Lynn Nottage

(*Lights cross fade. Esther's Boudoir. Mrs. Dickson is packing Esther's suitcase. Esther enters.*)

MRS. DICKSON:

Who is going to sit next to me at the table? There is Bertha, but she has no conversation. Oh, I could move Erma down closer, but she and Bertha don't speak. It'll be an absolute mess at the dinner table without you. That's for certain. Oh, it's gonna be a shame to let this room to anybody else. It has so many of your sweet touches. Yes.

ESTHER: You wasn't always pleased with my conversation if I recall.

MRS. DICKSON:

Who told you that? Well, they lie.

(*Mrs. Dickson holds up a dress.*)

Oh no. Not this little frumpy thing, really Esther. My grandmother wouldn't even wear a collar like so and she was a right proud Christian soldier. Yes.

ESTHER: Well, I like it. It's the most refined thing I own. I paid five whole dollars for it.

MRS. DICKSON:

You'll scare off your gentleman, and it ain't worth five dollars of misery. You needn't be a prude. Trust me, your man'll have needs, and it's your duty to keep his member firmly at home. Yes.

ESTHER: Excuse me?

MRS. DICKSON:

> I shan't repeat it. But there ain't no greater disappointment than a husband without much . . . vigor. Believe me, I know. And sometime he gotta be pleasured to ensure your own satisfaction. You understand. I ain't an expert, but I do have some experience. And I'll tell you, give and take make for the best of partnerships. Never mind what the minister tells you about decency, what go on between a man and wife be their own business. He will test you and he will try you, but don't let him beat on you, don't take no shit from him, understand.

ESTHER: Mrs. Dickson.

MRS. DICKSON:

> Excuse me, for saying, but if he raises his hand once, he'll do it again. I thought we should have this conversation before you go off. I don't mean to scare you, but I know you come as an innocent and we're friends so I feel I can speak plainly.

ESTHER: Thank you, but I do believe I'm old enough to handle things for myself.

MRS. DICKSON:

> Just the same, I thought I'd say it. Now whatcha want me to do with this dress?

ESTHER: It that bad?

MRS. DICKSON:

> Let's just say we'll give it to Deacon Wynn and let the church ladies fight over it. Yes.

(Mrs. Dickson sits on the bed.)

> You really going to do this, ain't you?

ESTHER: You didn't expect me to be here for the rest of my life?

MRS. DICKSON:

> I guess I sort of did. I'm so used to hearing your sewing machine and foot tapping up here. Yes, I reckon I'm going to miss it.

ESTHER: Another gal will move into this room, and by supper you'll be fussing about something new.

MRS. DICKSON:

> You say that with such certainty. You hurt my feelings, Miss Esther Mills.

(Mrs. Dickson dabs her eyes with a handkerchief.)

> Eighteen years is a long time. Yes. I don't reckon I've known anyone else that long. It'll be lonely.

ESTHER: You have plenty of suitors to keep you busy.

MRS. DICKSON:

> But ain't a working man amongst them.

(A moment.)

> You know you don't have to do this.

ESTHER: Yes, I do. I stay on here I'll turn to dust one day, get swept up and released into the garden without notice. I've finally found someone. Just as you found Mr. Dickson.

MRS. DICKSON:

> I married him, because I was thirty-seven years old, I had no profession and there wasn't a decent colored fella' in New York City that would have me.

ESTHER: But you come to love each other.

MRS. DICKSON:

> I suppose. He give me some laughs. But you see, my moth-
> er wanted me to marry up. She was a washerwoman, and
> my father was the very married minister of our mission.
> He couldn't even look out at her there in the church pews,
> but she'd sit there proudly every Sunday, determined to
> gain God's favor. Marry Good. She didn't ever want me to
> be embarrassed of my fingers the way she was of hers. I'd
> watch her put witch hazel and hot oil on her delicate
> hands, but they remained raw and chapped and she kept
> them hidden inside gray wool gloves. In the winter they'd
> bleed so bad sometimes, but she'd plunge her hands into
> the hot water without flinching, knead and scrub the cloth-
> ing clean. Fold and press for hours and hours, the linen, the
> bedding, the stockings and the britches, sometimes wear-
> ing the frayed gloves so as not to leave bloodstains on her
> precious laundry. She wouldn't even let me help her, she
> didn't want my hands to show the markings of labor. I was
> going to marry up. Love was an entirely impractical thing
> for a woman in her position. "Look what love done to me,"
> Mama used to say. "Look what love done to me."

(A moment.)

> So I did what was necessary to gain favor. I allowed myself
> to be flattered by gentlemen. You understand? Yes, this
> "pretty" gal done things, un-pretty things, for this marble
> mantle, gaslights in every room, a player piano and an
> indoor toilet.

ESTHER: But Mr. Dickson was a good man.

MRS. DICKSON:

> Bless his broken-down soul. He had fine suits and perfect
> diction, and was too high on opium to notice that he was
> married. But I would not be a washerwoman if it killed
> me. And I have absolutely marvelous hands to prove it.

(Mrs. Dickson laughs, displaying her hands.)

MRS. DICKSON:

> But you have Godly fingers and a means, and you deserve a gentleman. Why gamble it all away for a common laborer?

ESTHER: . . . Love.

MRS. DICKSON:

> Don't you let a man have no part of your heart without getting a piece of his.

(*Lights cross fade to George.*)

JOYCE CAROL OATES

THE GIRL with the BLACKENED EYE

THIS SHORT STORY, PLACED at the core of my collection *I Am No One You Know* (Ecco/HarperCollins, 2004), belongs to a cycle of stories of mine that dramatize the aftermath of trauma. Though less complex and less ambitious than longer stories of mine, it seems to me "my best" in its structural brevity and in the eerie, matter-of-fact cadences of its narrative voice.

I'm sure that there are personal reasons for my choice, some of them unconscious. At the heart of my mother's family history in the twentieth century there was a single act of violence that altered the course of numerous lives, including my own. No one ever explained this "motiveless malignancy" and so it remained a mystery through the decades. Like a ghost who is herself haunted, I am drawn to reenacting the circumstances of such trauma, often in ways very different from the original. Contrary to what is often said about my writing, it isn't so much about violence but about the aftermath of violence in the lives of victims, predominantly women and children. My rapt attention is upon survivors, not perpetrators. I stand in awe of the young female narrator of "The Girl with the Blackened Eye" who carries the memory of her terrifying experience so guardedly within her, it burns like a votive candle. For the killer who'd been so cruel to others allowed her to live, having seen in her something "special."

—Joyce Carol Oates

This black eye I had, once! Like a clown's eye painted on. Both my eyes were bruised and ugly but the right eye was swollen almost shut, people must've seen me and I wonder what they were thinking, I mean you have to wonder. Nobody said a word, didn't want to get involved, I guess. You have to wonder what went through their minds, though.

Sometimes now I see myself in a mirror, like in the middle of the night getting up to use the bathroom, I see a blurred face, a woman's face I don't recognize. And I see that eye.

Twenty-seven years.

In America, that's a lifetime.

This weird thing that happened to me, fifteen years old and a sopho-
more at Menlo Park High, living with my family in Menlo Park,
California, where Dad was a dental surgeon (which was lucky: I'd
need dental and gum surgery, to repair the damage to my mouth).
Weird, and wild. Ugly. I've never told anybody who knows me now.
Especially my daughters. My husband doesn't know, he couldn't have
handled it. We were in our late twenties when we met, no need to drag
up the past. I never do. I'm not one of those. I left California forever
when I went to college in Vermont. My family moved, too. They live
in Seattle now. There's a stiffness between us, we never talk about that
time. Never say that man's name. So it's like it never did happen.

Or, if it did, it happened to someone else. A high school girl in the
1970s. A silly little girl who wore tank tops and jeans so tight she had
to lie down on her bed to wriggle into them, and teased her hair into a
mane. That girl.

When they found me, my hair was wild and tangled like broom
sage. It couldn't be combed through, had to be cut from my head in
clumps. Something sticky like cobwebs was in it. I'd been wearing it
long since ninth grade and after that I kept it cut short for years. Like
a guy's hair, the back of my neck shaved and my ears showing.

I'd been forcibly abducted at the age of fifteen. It was something that
could happen to you from the outside, *forcibly abducted*, like being in a
plane crash, or struck by lightning. There wouldn't be any human
agent, almost. The human agent wouldn't have a name. I'd been walking through the mall parking lot to the bus stop, about 5:30 P.M., a
weekday, I'd come to the mall after school with some kids now I was
headed home, and somehow it happened, don't ask me how, a guy was
asking me questions, or saying something, mainly I registered he was
an adult my dad's age possibly, every adult man looked like my dad's
age except obviously old white-haired men. I hadn't any clear impression of this guy except afterward I would recall rings on his fingers
which would've caused me to glance up at his face with interest except
at that instant something slammed into the back of my head behind
my ear knocking me forward, and down, like he'd thrown a hook at
me from in front, I was on my face on the sun-heated vinyl upholstery

of a car, or a van, and another blow or blows knocked me out. Like anesthesia, it was. You're out.

This was the *forcible abduction*. How it might be described by a witness who was there, who was also the victim. But who hadn't any memory of what happened because it happened so fast, and she hadn't been personally involved.

⌒

It's like they say. You are there, and not-there. He drove to this place in the Sonoma Mountains, I would afterward learn, this cabin it would be called, and he raped me, and beat me, and shocked me with electrical cords and he stubbed cigarette butts on my stomach and breasts, and he said things to me like he knew me, he knew all my secrets, what a dirty-minded girl I was, what a nasty girl, and selfish, like everyone of my *privileged class* as he called it. I'm saying that these things were done to me but in fact they were done to my body mostly. Like the cabin was in the Sonoma Mountains north of Healdsburg but it was just anywhere for those eight days, and I was anywhere, I was holding onto being alive the way you would hold onto a straw you could breathe through, lying at the bottom of deep water. And that water opaque, you can't see through to the surface.

He was gone, and he came back. He left me tied in the bed, it was a cot with a thin mattress, very dirty. There were only two windows in the cabin and there were blinds over them drawn tight. It was hot during what I guessed was the day. It was cool, and it was very quiet, at night. The lower parts of me were raw and throbbing with pain and other parts of me were in a haze of pain so I wasn't able to think, and I wasn't awake most of the time, not what you'd call actual wakefulness, with a personality.

What you call your personality, you know?—it's not like actual bones, or teeth, something solid. It's more like a flame. A flame can be upright, and a flame can flicker in the wind, a flame can be extinguished so there's no sign of it, like it had never been.

My eyes had been hurt, he'd mashed his fists into my eyes. The eyelids were puffy, I couldn't see very well. It was like I didn't try to see, I was saving my eyesight for when I was stronger. I had not seen the man's face actually. I had felt him but I had not seen him, I could not have identified him. Any more than you could identify yourself if you had never seen yourself in a mirror or in any likeness.

In one of my dreams I was saying to my family I would not be seeing them for a while, I was going away. *I'm going away, I want to say good-bye.* Their faces were blurred. My sister, I was closer to than my parents, she's two years older than me and I adored her, my sister was crying, her face was blurred with tears. She asked where was I going and I said I didn't know, but I wanted to say good-bye, and I wanted to say *I love you.* And this was so vivid it would seem to me to have happened actually, and was more real than other things that happened to me during that time I would learn afterward was eight days.

It might've been the same day repeated, or it might've been eighty days. It was a place, not a day. Like a dimension you could slip into, or be sucked into, by an undertow. And it's there, but no one is aware of it. Until you're in it, you don't know; but when you're in it, it's all that you know. So you have no way of speaking of it except like this. Stammering, and ignorant.

Why he brought me food and water, why he decided to let me live, would never be clear. The others he'd killed after a few days. They went stale on him, you have to suppose. One of the bodies was buried in the woods a few hundred yards behind the cabin, others were dumped along Route 101 as far north as Crescent City. And possibly there were others never known, never located or identified. These facts, if they are facts, I would learn later, as I would learn that the other girls and women had been older than me, the oldest was thirty, and the youngest he'd been on record as killing was eighteen. So it was speculated he had mercy on me because he hadn't realized, abducting me in the parking lot, that I was so young, and in my battered condition in the cabin, when I started losing weight, I must've looked to him like a child. I was crying a lot, and calling *Mommy! Mom-my!*

Like my own kids, grown, would call *Mom-my!* in some nightmare they were trapped in. But I never think of such things.

The man with the rings on his fingers, saying, There's some reason I don't know yet, that you have been spared.

Later I would look back and think, there was a turn, a shifting of fortune, when he first allowed me to wash. To wash! He could see I was ashamed, I was a naturally shy, clean girl. He allowed this. He might have assisted me, a little. He picked ticks out of my skin where they were invisible and gorged with blood. He hated ticks! They disgusted him. He went away, and came back with food and Hires Diet Root Beer. We ate together sitting on the edge of the cot. And once when he allowed me out into the clearing at dusk. Like a picnic. His greasy fingers, and mine. Fried chicken, french fries, and runny coleslaw, my hands starting shaking and my mouth was on fire. And my stomach convulsing with hunger, cramps that doubled me over like he'd sunk a knife into my guts and twisted. Still, I was able to eat some things, in little bites. I did not starve. Seeing the color come back into my face, he was impressed, stirred. He said in mild reproach, Hey: a butterfly could eat more'n you.

I would remember these little pale-yellow butterflies around the cabin. A swarm of them. And jays screaming, waiting to swoop down to snatch up food.

I guess I was pretty sick. Delirious. My gums were infected. Four of my teeth were broken. Blood kept leaking to the back of my mouth making me sick, gagging. But I could walk to the car leaning against him, I was able to sit up normally in the passenger's seat, buckled in, he always made sure to buckle me in, and a wire wound tight around my ankles. Driving then out of the forest, and the foothills I could not have identified as the Sonoma hills, and the sun high and gauzy in the sky, and I lost track of time, lapsing in and out of time but noticing that highway traffic was changing to suburban, more traffic lights, we were cruising through parking lots so vast you couldn't see to the edge of them, sun-blinded spaces and rows of glittering cars like grave markers I saw them suddenly in a cemetery that went on forever.

He wanted me with him all the time now, he said. Keep an eye on you, girl. Maybe I was his trophy? The only female trophy in his abducting/raping/killing spree of an estimated seventeen months to be publicly displayed. Not beaten, strangled, raped to death, kicked to death and buried like animal carrion. (This I would learn later.) Or maybe I was meant to signal to the world, if the world glanced through the windshield of his car, his daughter. A sign of—what? *Hey, I'm normal. I'm a nice guy, see.*

Except the daughter's hair was wild and matted, her eyes were bruised and one of them swollen almost shut. Her mouth was a slack puffy wound. Bruises on her face and throat and arms and her ribs were cracked, skinny body covered in pus-leaking burns and sores. Yet he'd allowed me to wash, and he'd allowed me to wash out my clothes, I was less filthy now. He'd given me a T-shirt too big for me, already soiled but I was grateful for it. Through acres of parking lots we cruised like sharks seeking prey. I was aware of people glancing into the car, just by accident, seeing me, or maybe not seeing me, there were reflections in the windshield (weren't there?) because of the sun, so maybe they didn't see me, or didn't see me clearly. Yet others, seeing me, looked away. It did not occur to me at the time that there must be a search for me, my face in the papers, on TV. My face as it had been. At the time I'd stopped thinking of that other world. Mostly I'd stopped thinking. It was like anesthesia, you give in to it, there's peace in it, almost. As cruising the parking lots with the man whistling to himself, humming, talking in a low affable monotone, I understood that he wasn't thinking either, as a predator fish would not be thinking cruising beneath the surface of the ocean. The silent gliding of sharks, that never cease their motion. I was concerned mostly with sitting right: my head balanced on my neck, which isn't easy to do, and the wire wound tight around my ankles cutting off circulation. So my feet were numb. I knew of gangrene, I knew of toes and entire feet going black with rot. From my father I knew of tooth-rot, gum-rot. I was trying not to think of those strangers who must've seen me, sure they saw me, and turned away, uncertain what they'd seen but knowing it was trouble, not wanting to know more.

Just a girl with a blackened eye, you figure she maybe deserved it.

He said, there must be some reason you are spared.

He said, in my daddy's voice from a long time ago, Know what, girl?—you're not like the others. That's why.

They would say he was insane, these were the acts of an insane person. And I would not disagree. Though I knew it was not so.

The red-haired woman in the khaki jacket and matching pants. Eventually she would have a name but it was not a name I would wish to know, none of them were. This was a woman, not a girl. He'd put me in the backseat of his car now, so the passenger's seat was empty. He'd buckled me safely in. O.K., girl? You be good, now. We cruised the giant parking lot at dusk. When the lights first come on. (Where was this? Ukiah. Where I'd never been. Except for the red-haired woman I would have no memory of Ukiah.)

He'd removed his rings. He was wearing a white baseball cap.

There came this red-haired woman beside him smiling, talking like they were friends. I stared, I was astonished. They were coming toward the car. Never could I imagine what those two were talking about! I thought *He will trade me for her* and I was frightened. The man in the baseball cap wearing shiny dark glasses asking the red-haired woman—what? Directions? Yet he had the power to make her smile, there was a sexual ease between them. She was a mature woman with a shapely body, breasts I could envy and hips in the tight-fitting khaki pants that were stylish pants, with a drawstring waist. I felt a rush of anger for this woman, contempt, disgust, how stupid she was, unsuspecting, bending to peer at me where possibly she'd been told the man's daughter was sitting, maybe he'd said his daughter had a question for her? needed an adult female's advice? and in an instant she would find herself shoved forward onto the front seat of the car, down on her face, her chest, helpless, as fast as you might snap your fingers, too fast for her to cry out. So fast, you understand it had happened many times before. The girl in the backseat blinking and staring and unable to speak though she wasn't gagged, no more able to scream for help than the woman struggling for her life a few inches away. She shuddered in sympathy, she moaned as the man pounded the woman with his fists. Furious, grunting! His eyes bulged. Were there no witnesses? No one to see? Deftly he wrapped a blanket around the woman, who'd gone limp, wrapping it tight around her head and chest, he shoved her legs inside the car and shut the door and climbed into the driver's seat and drove away humming, happy. In the backseat the girl was crying. If she'd had tears she would have cried.

Weird how your mind works: I was thinking I was that woman, in the front seat wrapped in the blanket, so the rest of it had not yet happened.

It was that time, I think, I saw my mom. In the parking lot. There were shoppers, mostly women. And my mom was one of them. I knew it couldn't be her, so far from home, I knew I was hundreds of miles from home, so it couldn't be, but I saw her, Mom crossing in front of the car, walking briskly to the entrance of Lord & Taylor.

Yet I couldn't wave to her, my arm was heavy as lead.

Yes. In the cabin I was made to witness what he did to the red-haired woman. I saw now that this was my importance to him: I would be a witness to his fury, his indignation, his disgust. Tying the woman's wrists to the iron rails of the bed, spreading her legs and tying her ankles. Naked, the red-haired woman had no power. There was no sexual ease to her now, no confidence. You would not envy her now. You would scorn her now. You would not wish to be her now. She'd become a chicken on a spit.

I had to watch, I could not close my eyes or look away.

For it had happened already, it was completed. There was certitude in this, and peace in certitude. When there is no escape, for what is happening has already happened. Not once but many times.

When you give up struggle, there's a kind of love.

The red-haired woman did not know this, in her terror. But I was the witness, I knew.

They would ask me about him. I saw only parts of him. Like jigsaw puzzle parts. Like quick camera jumps and cuts. His back was pale and flaccid at the waist, more muscular at the shoulders. It was a broad pimply sweating back. It was a part of a man, like my dad, I would not see. Not in this way. Not straining, tensing. And the smell of a man's hair, like congealed oil. His hair was stiff, dark, threaded with silver hairs like wires, at the crown of his head you could see the scalp beneath. On his torso and legs hairs grew in dense waves and rivulets like water or grasses. He was grunting, he was making a high-pitched moaning sound. When he turned, I saw a fierce blurred face, I didn't recognize that face. And nipples. The nipples of a man's breasts, wine-colored like berries. Between his thighs the angry thing swung like a length of rubber, slick and darkened with blood.

I would recall, yes, he had tattoos. Smudged-looking like ink blots. Never did I see them clearly. Never did I see him clearly. I would not have dared as you would not look into the sun in terror of being blinded.

He kept us there together for three days. I mean, the red-haired woman was there for three days, unconscious most of the time. There was a mercy in this. You learn to take note of small mercies and be grateful for them. Nor would he kill her in the cabin. When he was finished with her, disgusted with her, he half-carried her out to the car. I was alone, and frightened. But then he returned and said, O.K., girl, goin for a ride. I was able to walk, just barely. I was very dizzy. I would ride in the backseat of the car like a big rag doll, boneless and unresisting.

He'd shoved the woman down beside him, hidden by a blanket wrapped around her head and upper body. She was not struggling now, her body was limp and unresisting for she too had weakened in the cabin, she'd lost weight. You learned to be weak to please him for you did not want to displease him in even the smallest things. Yet the woman managed to speak, this small choked begging voice. Don't kill me, please. I won't tell anybody. I won't tell anybody don't kill me. I have a little daughter, please don't kill me. Please, God. Please.

I wasn't sure if this voice was (somehow) a made-up voice. A voice of my imagination. Or like on TV. Or my own voice, if I'd been older and had a daughter. *Please don't kill me. Please, God.*

For always it's this voice when you're alone and silent you hear it.

Afterward they would speculate he'd panicked. Seeing TV spot announcements, the photographs of his "victims." When last seen and where, Menlo Park, Ukiah. There were witnesses' descriptions of *the abductor* and a police sketch of his face, coarser and uglier and older than his face which was now disguised by dark glasses. In the drawing he was clean-shaven but now his jaws were covered in several days' beard, a stubbly beard, his hair was tied in a ponytail and the baseball cap pulled low on his head. Yet you could recognize him in the drawing, that looked as if it had been executed by a blind man. So he'd panicked.

The first car he'd been driving he abandoned somewhere, he was driving another, a stolen car with switched license plates. You came to see that his life was such maneuvers. He was tireless in invention as a willful child and would seem to have had no purpose beyond this and when afterward I would learn details of his background, his family life in San Jose, his early incarcerations as a juvenile, as a youth, as an adult "offender" now on parole from Bakersfield maximum-security prison, I would block off such information as not related to me, not related to the man who'd existed exclusively for me as, for a brief while, though lacking a name, for he'd never asked me my name, I'd existed exclusively for him. I was contemptuous of "facts" for I came to know that no accumulation of facts constitutes knowledge, and no impersonal knowledge constitutes the intimacy of knowing.

Know what, girl? You're not like the others. You're special.

That's the reason.

Driving fast, farther into the foothills. The road was ever narrower and bumpier. There were few vehicles on the road, all of them mini-vans or campers. He never spoke to the red-haired woman moaning and whimpering beside him but to me in the backseat, looking at me through the rearview mirror, the way my dad used to do when I rode in the backseat, and Mom was up front with him. He said, How ya doin, girl?

O.K.

Doin O.K., huh?

Yes.

I'm gonna let you go, girl, you know that, huh? Gonna give you your freedom.

To this I could not reply. My swollen lips moved in a kind of smile as you smile out of politeness.

Less you want to trade? With her?

Again I could not reply. I wasn't certain what the question was. My smile ached in my face but it was a sincere smile.

He parked the car on an unpaved lane off the road. He waited, no vehicles were approaching. There were no aircraft overhead. It was very quiet except for birds. He said, C'mon, help me, girl. So I moved my legs that were stiff, my legs that felt strange and skinny to me, I climbed out of the car and fought off dizziness helping him with the bound woman, he'd pulled the blanket off her, her discolored swollen face, her face that wasn't attractive now, scabby mouth and panicked eyes, brown eyes they were, I would remember those eyes pleading. For they were my own, but in one who was doomed as I was not. He said then, so strangely: Stay here, girl. Watch the car. Somebody shows up, honk the horn. Two-three times. Got it?

I whispered yes. I was staring at the crumbly earth.

I could not look at the woman now. I would not watch them move away into the woods.

Maybe it was a test, he'd left the key in the ignition. It was to make me think I could drive the car away from there, I could drive to get help, or I could run out onto the road and get help. Maybe I could get help. He had a gun, and he had knives, but I could have driven away. But the sun was beating on my head, I couldn't move. My legs were heavy like lead. My eye was swollen shut and throbbing. I believe it was a test but I wasn't certain. Afterward they would ask if I'd had any chance to escape in those days he kept me captive and always I said no, no I did not have a chance to escape. Because that was so. That was how it was to me, that I could not explain.

Yet I remember the keys in the ignition, and I remember that the road was close by. He would strangle the woman, that was his way of killing and this I seemed to know. It would require some minutes. It was not an easy way of killing. I could run, I could run along the road and hope that someone would come along, or I could hide, and he wouldn't find me in all that wilderness, if he called me I would not answer. But I stood there beside the car because I could not do these things. He trusted me, and I could not betray that trust. Even if he would kill me, I could not betray him.

Yes, I heard her screams in the woods. I think I heard. It might have been jays. It might have been my own screams I heard. But I heard them.

A few days later he would be dead. He would be shot down by police in a motel parking lot in Petaluma. Why he was there, in that place, about fifty miles from the cabin, I don't know. He'd left me in the cabin chained to the bed. It was filthy, flies and ants. The chain was long enough for me to use the toilet. But the toilet was backed up. Blinds were drawn on the windows. I did not dare to take them down or break the windowpanes but I looked out, I saw just the clearing, a haze of green. Overhead there were small planes sometimes. A helicopter. I wanted to think that somebody would rescue me but I knew better, I knew nobody would find me.

But they did find me.

He told them where the cabin was, when he was dying. He did that for me. He drew a rough map and I have that map!—not the actual piece of paper but a copy. He would never see me again, and I would have trouble recalling his face for I never truly saw it.

Photographs of him were not accurate. Even his name, printed out, is misleading. For it could be anyone's name and not *his*.

In my present life I never speak of these things. I have never told anyone. There would be no point to it. Why I've told you, I don't know: you might write about me but you would respect my privacy.

Because if you wrote about me, these things that happened to me so long ago, no one would know it was me. And you would disguise it so that no one could guess, that's why I trust you.

My life afterward is what's unreal. The life then, those eight days, was very real. The two don't seem to be connected, do they? I learned you don't discover the evidence of any cause in its result. Philosophers debate over that but if you know, you know. There is no connection though people wish to think so. When I was recovered I went back to Menlo Park High and I graduated with my class and I went to college in Vermont, I met my husband in New York a few years later and married him and had my babies and none of my life would be different in any way, I believe, if I had not been "abducted" when I was fifteen.

Sure, I see him sometimes. More often lately. On the street, in a passing car. In profile, I see him. In his shiny dark glasses and white baseball cap. A man's forearm, a thick pelt of hair on it, a tattoo, I see him. The shock of it is, he's only thirty-two.

That's so young now. Your life all before you, almost.

ROBERT PINSKY

IMPOSSIBLE to TELL

I THINK—IT'S A kind of vanity, I realize—that I get bored sooner or more easily than most people.

That is why I like poetry, because it moves so quickly: one second you are talking to the Western Wind and thinking about the small rain, then suddenly it's "Christ!" and then immediately after that it's wanting to be in bed with my love again. The four-line poem has gone somewhere, but with the speed of an ice-skater, muscles flicking the momentum from one direction to another.

Poetry accelerates on the curves, powered by the speech-muscles as it covers a lot of ground quickly. If at its most thrilling poetry resembles ice-skating, too much writing (and some TV, some film, some social occasions) is more like wading: you can stare at one place, as you labor along. Wading may have its virtues (notice that anemone next to your left foot), but it lacks the thrill of the poetry I love.

In my own work, "Impossible to Tell" strives for that ideal of rapid, unpredictable movement that gets somewhere.

I choose the poem for personal reasons, too: my friend Elliot Gilbert died the same year our friend Robert Hass was completing his marvelous anthology of haiku. I had always been a bit haiku-deaf, but Robert's brilliant introduction and notes made me understand haiku in relation to the *renga*: a collaborative linking poem, in which poet-friends in the course of an evening pick up images or figures from one another, so that if the snow is popcorn in your winter stanza I might improvise the smell of popcorn into my summer stanza.

That's how it is for people who love telling jokes, as Elliot did and I do. (When I say "jokes," I don't mean witty remarks, but *A parrot, St. Peter, and Senator Orrin Hatch go into a bar*, and then there is a punchline.)

A joke session like a *renga* evening has its links, and its collaborations. An optometrist joke inspires a dentist joke, and if the dentist in my joke meets the Pope then the Pope may appear in your joke. And so goes the night's laughter and companionship. Elliot would nearly tremble with a mixture of joy that he was hearing a new one and frustration that *you* were telling it to *him*, instead of the other way around.

He was a brilliant, lovable, and well-loved man, and I still miss him. He died at sixty during a routine procedure because of blunders by doctors who lied about their blunders. My poem contains two full-scale jokes, in tribute to Elliot and in recognition of certain absurdities and inevitabilities.

—Robert Pinsky

To Robert Hass and in Memory of Elliot Gilbert

Slow dulcimer, gavotte and bow, in autumn,
Bashō and his friends go out to view the moon;
In summer, gasoline rainbow in the gutter,

The secret courtesy that courses like ichor
Through the old form of the rude, full-scale joke,
Impossible to tell in writing. *"Bashō"*

He named himself, "Banana Tree": banana
After the plant some grateful students gave him,
Maybe in appreciation of his guidance

Threading a long night through the rules and channels
Of their collaborative linking-poem
Scored in their teacher's heart: live, rigid, fluid

Like passages etched in a microscopic circuit.
Elliot had in his memory so many jokes
They seemed to breed like microbes in a culture

Inside his brain, one so much making another
It was impossible to tell them all:
In the court-culture of jokes, a top banana.

Imagine a court of one: the queen a young mother,
Unhappy, alone all day with her firstborn child
And her new baby in a squalid apartment

Of too few rooms, a different race from her neighbors.
She tells the child she's going to kill herself.
She broods, she rages. Hoping to distract her,

The child cuts capers, he sings, he does imitations
Of different people in the building, he jokes,
He feels if he keeps her alive until the father

Gets home from work, they'll be okay till morning.
It's laughter *versus* the bedroom and the pills.
What is he in his efforts but a courtier?

Impossible to tell his whole delusion.
In the first months when I had moved back East
From California and had to leave a message

On Bob's machine, I used to make a habit
Of telling the tape a joke; and part-way through,
I would pretend that I forgot the punchline,

Or make believe that I was interrupted—
As though he'd be so eager to hear the end
He'd have to call me back. The joke was Elliot's,

More often than not. The doctors made the blunder
That killed him some time later that same year.
One day when I got home I found a message

On my machine from Bob. He had a story
About two rabbis, one of them tall, one short,
One day while walking along the street together

They see the corpse of a Chinese man before them,
And Bob said, sorry, he forgot the rest.
Of course he thought that his joke was a dummy,

Impossible to tell—a dead-end challenge.
But here it is, as Elliot told it to me:
The dead man's widow came to the rabbis weeping,

Begging them, if they could, to resurrect him.
Shocked, the tall rabbi said absolutely not.
But the short rabbi told her to bring the body

Into the study house, and ordered the shutters
Closed so the room was night-dark. Then he prayed
Over the body, chanting a secret blessing

Out of Kabala. "Arise and breathe," he shouted;
But nothing happened. The body lay still. So then
The little rabbi called for hundreds of candles

And danced around the body, chanting and praying
In Hebrew, then Yiddish, then Aramaic. He prayed
In Turkish and Egyptian and Old Galician

For nearly three hours, leaping about the coffin
In the candlelight so that his tiny black shoes
Seemed not to touch the floor. With one last prayer

Sobbed in the Spanish of before the Inquisition
He stopped, exhausted, and looked in the dead man's face.
Panting, he raised both arms in a mystic gesture

And said, "Arise and breathe!" And still the body
Lay as before. Impossible to tell
In words how Elliot's eyebrows flailed and snorted

Lake shaggy mammoths as—the Chinese widow
Granting permission—the little rabbi sang
The blessing for performing a circumcision

And removed the dead man's foreskin, chanting blessings
In Finnish and Swahili, and bathed the corpse
From head to foot, and with a final prayer

In Babylonian, gasping with exhaustion,
He seized the dead man's head and kissed the lips
And dropped it again and leaping back commanded,

"Arise and breathe!" The corpse lay still as ever.
At this, as when Bashō's disciples wind
Along the curving spine that links the *renga*

Across the different voices, each one adding
A transformation according to the rules
Of stasis and repetition, all in order

And yet impossible to tell beforehand,
Elliot changes for the punchline: the wee
Rabbi, still panting, like a startled boxer,

Looks at the dead one, then up at all those watching,
A kind of Mel Brooks gesture: "Hoo boy!" he says,
"Now that's what I call *really dead*." O mortal

Powers and princes of earth, and you immortal
Lords of the underground and afterlife,
Jehovah, Raa, Bol-Morah, Hecate, Pluto,

What has a brilliant, living soul to do with
Your harps and fires and boats, your bric-a-brac
And troughs of smoking blood? Provincial stinkers,

Our languages don't touch you, you're like that mother
Whose small child entertained her to beg her life.
Possibly he grew up to be the tall rabbi,

The one who washed his hands of all those capers
Right at the outset. Or maybe he became
The author of these lines, a one-man *renga*

The one for whom it seems to be impossible
To tell a story straight. It was a routine
Procedure. When it was finished the physicians

Told Sandra and the kids it had succeeded,
But Elliot wouldn't wake up for maybe an hour,
They should go eat. The two of them loved to bicker

In a way that on his side went back to Yiddish,
On Sandra's to some Sicilian dialect.
He used to scold her endlessly for smoking.

When she got back from dinner with their children
The doctors had to tell them about the mistake.
Oh swirling petals, falling leaves! The movement

Of linking *renga* coursing from moment to moment
Is meaning, Bob says in his Haiku book.
Oh swirling petals, all living things are contingent,

Falling leaves, and transient, and they suffer.
But the Universal is the goal of jokes,
Especially certain ethnic jokes, which taper

Down through the swirling funnel of tongues and gestures
Toward their preposterous Ithaca. There's one
A journalist told me. He heard it while a hero

Of the South African freedom movement was speaking
To elderly Jews. The speaker's own right arm
Had been blown off by right-wing letter-bombers.

He told his listeners they had to cast their ballots
For the ANC—a group the old Jews feared
As "in with the Arabs." But they started weeping

As the old one-armed fighter told them their country
Needed them to vote for what was right, their vote
Could make a country their children could return to

From London and Chicago. The moved old people
Applauded wildly, and the speaker's friend
Whispered to the journalist, "It's the Belgian Army

Joke come to life." I wish that I could tell it
To Elliot. In the Belgian Army, the feud
Between the Flemings and Walloons grew vicious,

So out of hand the army could barely function.
Finally one commander assembled his men
In one great room, to deal with things directly.

They stood before him at attention. "All Flemings,"
He ordered, "to the left wall." Half the men
Clustered to the left. "Now all Walloons," he ordered,

"Move to the right." An equal number crowded
Against the right wall. Only one man remained
At attention in the middle: "What are you, soldier?"

Saluting, the man said, "Sir, I am a Belgian."
"Why, that's astonishing, Corporal—what's your name?"
Saluting again, "Rabinowitz," he answered:

A joke that seems at first to be a story
About the Jews. But as the *renga* describes
Religious meaning by moving in drifting petals

And brittle leaves that touch and die and suffer
The changing winds that riffle the gutter swirl,
So in the joke, just under the raucous music

Of Fleming, Jew, Walloon, a courtly allegiance
Moves to the dulcimer, gavotte and bow,
Over the banana tree the moon in autumn—

Allegiance to a state impossible to tell.

MICHAEL POLLAN

From THE BOTANY of DESIRE

THE WHOLE IDEA OF pointing to a single piece of one's own work and declaring it "the best" gives me the willies, frankly; I mean, how do *I* know? Isn't that for others to decide? And yet there are things you write you can bear to reread years later without wincing too sharply and, even more rare, passages you actually don't mind reading aloud to perfect strangers. This passage, from the marijuana section of *The Botany of Desire*, is one of those pieces.

As much as anything on the page, though, what I like about it is the memory it summons of its composition, a process that was as close to pleasurable as writing ever comes. Which most of the time is not very close, believe me. But I remember the months spent drafting the marijuana chapter of *Botany of Desire* as a kind of pleasant fever, when scenes and ideas and readings fell into place like puzzle pieces, and a desultory train of associations—from Nietzsche to religious meditation to Emerson to the garden to George Eliot to the munchies to Huxley to the Grateful Dead—brought me places I didn't know I could go.

The kind of writing I like best, and the kind I think I managed here with some success, layers many different ways of looking at the same thing to arrive at an understanding richer than any single lens could hope to provide. What I like particularly about this passage is its transit from one vocabulary to another: from memoir to science to philosophy to religion to speculation and back again to memoir—to a man standing in his garden. I don't think any one of those vocabularies can by itself approach the mysteries of what a plant like marijuana does to consciousness with much success. But put those disparate lens together, layer them atop the other, and you find the elusive object in view begin to come into a certain focus. That for me is one of the great satisfactions of writing, and happy proof that the old-fashioned idea of approaching the world as a free-ranging essayist rather than the monocled expert is a venture still worth the candle.

—Michael Pollan

I am not by nature one of the world's great noticers. Unless I make a conscious effort, I won't notice what color your shirt is, the song playing on the radio, or whether you put one sugar in your coffee or two. When I'm working as a reporter I have to hector myself continually to mark the details: checked shirt, two sugars, Van Morrison. Why this should be so, I have no idea, except that I am literally absent-minded, prone to be thinking about something else, something past, when I am ostensibly having a fresh experience. Almost always, my attention can't wait to beat a retreat from the here and now to the abstract, frog-jumping from the data of the senses to conclusions.

Actually, it's worse than that. Very often the conclusions or concepts come first, allowing me to dispense with the sensory data altogether or to notice in it only what fits. It's a form of impatience with lived life, and though it might appear to be a symptom of an active mind, I suspect it's really a form of laziness. My lawyer father, once complimented on his ability to see ahead three or four moves in a negotiation, explained that the reason he liked to jump to conclusions was so he could get there early and rest. I'm the same way in my negotiations with reality.

Though I suspect that what I have is only an acute case of an attention disorder that is more or less universal. Seeing, hearing, smelling, feeling, or tasting things as they "really are" is always difficult if not impossible (in part because doing so would overwhelm us, as George Eliot understood), so we perceive each multisensory moment through a protective screen of ideas, past experiences or expectations. "Nature always wears the colors of the spirit," Emerson wrote, by which he meant we never see the world plainly, only through the filter of prior concepts or metaphors. ("Colors" in classical rhetoric, are tropes.) In my case this filter is so fine (or is it thick?) that a lot of the details and textures of reality simply never get through. It's a habit of mind I sorely wish I could break, since it keeps me from enjoying the pleasures of the senses and the moment, pleasures that, at least in the abstract, I prize above all others. But right there you see the problem: *in the abstract.*

All those who write about cannabis's effect on consciousness speak of the changes in perception they experience, and specifically of an intensification of all the senses. Common foods taste better, familiar music is suddenly sublime, sexual touch revelatory. Scientists who've studied the phenomenon can find no quantifiable change in the visual, auditory, or tactile acuity of subjects high on marijuana, yet these people invariably report seeing, and hearing, and tasting things with a new keenness, as if with fresh eyes and ears and taste buds.

You know how it goes, this italicization of experience, this seemingly virginal *noticing* of the sensate world. You've heard that song a thousand times before, but now you suddenly *hear* it in all its soul-piercing beauty, the sweet bottomless poignancy of the guitar line like a revelation, and for the first time you can understand, *really* understand, just what Jerry Garcia meant by every note, his unhurried cheerful-baleful improvisation piping something very near the meaning of life directly into *your* mind.

Or that exceptionally delicious spoonful of vanilla ice cream—*ice cream!*—parting the drab curtains of the quotidian to reveal, what?—the heartrendingly sweet significance of *cream*, yes, bearing us all the way back to the breast. Not to mention the never-before-adequately-appreciated wonder of: *vanilla*. How astonishing it is that we happen to inhabit a universe in which this quality of vanilla-ness—this *bean!*—happens also to reside? How easily it could have been otherwise, and just where would we be (where would *chocolate* be?) without that singular irreplaceable note, that middle C on the Scale of Archetypal Flavors? (*Paging Dr. Plato!*) For the first time in your journey on this planet you are fully appreciating *Vanilla* in all its italicized and capitalized significance. Until, that is, the next epiphany comes along (*Chairs! People thinking in other languages! Carbonated water!*) and the one about ice cream is blown away like a leaf on the breeze of free association.

Nothing is easier to make fun of than these pot-sponsored perceptions, long the broad butt of jokes about marijuana. But I'm not prepared to concede that these epiphanies are as empty or false as they usually appear in the cold light of the next day. In fact, I'm tempted to agree with Carl Sagan, who was convinced that marijuana's morning-after problem is not a question of self-deception so much as a failure to communicate—to put "these insights in a form acceptable to the quite different self that we are when we're down the next day." We simply don't have the words to convey the force of these perceptions to our straight selves, perhaps because they are the kinds of perceptions that precede words. They may well be banal, but that doesn't mean they aren't also at the same time profound.

Marijuana dissolves this apparent contradiction, and it does so by making us temporarily forget most of the baggage we usually bring to our perception of something like ice cream, our acquired sense of its familiarity and banality. For what is a sense of the banality of something if not a defense against the overwhelming (or at least whelming) power of that thing experienced freshly? Banality depends on memory, as do irony and abstraction and boredom, three other defenses the educated mind deploys against experience so that it can get through the day without being continually, exhaustingly astonished.

It is by temporarily mislaying much of what we already know (or think we know) that cannabis restores a kind of innocence to our perceptions of the world, and innocence in adults will always flirt with embarrassment. The cannabinoids are molecules with the power to make romantics and transcendentalists of us all. By disabling our moment-by-moment memory, which is ever pulling us off the astounding frontier of the present and throwing us back onto the mapped byways of the past, the cannabinoids open a space for something nearer to direct experience. By the grace of this forgetting, we temporarily shelve our inherited ways of looking and see things as if for the first time, so that even something as ordinary as ice cream becomes *Ice cream!*

There is another word for this extremist noticing—this sense of first sight unencumbered by knowingness, by the already-been-theres and seen-thats of the adult mind—and that word, of course, is *wonder.*

⌒

Memory is the enemy of wonder, which abides nowhere else but in the present. This is why, unless you are a child, wonder depends on forgetting—on a process, that is, of subtraction. Ordinarily we think of drug experiences as additive—it's often said that drugs "distort" normal perceptions and augment the data of the senses (adding hallucinations, say), but it may be that the very opposite is true—that they work by subtracting some of the filters that consciousness normally interposes between us and the world.

This, at least, was Aldous Huxley's conclusion in *The Doors of Perception*, his 1954 account of his experiments with mescaline. In Huxley's view, the drug—which is derived from peyote, the flower of a desert cactus—disables what he called "the reducing valve" of consciousness, his name for the conscious mind's everyday editing faculty. The reducing valve keeps us from being crushed under the "pressure of reality," but it accomplishes this at a price, for the mechanism prevents us from ever seeing reality as it really is. The insight of mystics and artists flows from their special ability to switch off the mind's reducing valve. I'm not sure any of us ever perceives reality "as it really is" (how would one know?), but Huxley is persuasive in depicting wonder as what happens when we succeed in suspending our customary verbal and conceptual ways of seeing. (He writes with a wacky earnestness about the beauty of fabric folds, a garden chair, and a vase of flowers: "I was seeing what Adam had seen on the morning of his creation—the miracle, moment by moment, of naked existence.")

I think I understand Huxley's reducing valve of consciousness, though in my own experience the mechanism looks a little different. I picture ordinary consciousness more as a funnel or, even better, as the cinched waist of an hourglass. In this metaphor the mind's eye stands poised between time past and time to come, determining which of the innumerable grains of sensory experience will pass through the narrow aperture of the present and enter into memory. I know, there are some problems with this metaphor, the main one being that all the sand eventually gets to the bottom of an hourglass, whereas most of the grains of experience never make it past our regard. But the metaphor at least gets at the notion that the principal work of consciousness is eliminative and defensive, maintaining perceptual order to keep us from being overwhelmed.

So what happens under the influence of drugs or, for that matter, inspiration? In Huxley's metaphor, the reducing valve is opened wide to admit more of experience. This seems about right, though I'd qualify it by suggesting (as Huxley's own examples do) that the effect of altered consciousness is to admit a whole lot more information about a much smaller increment of experience. "The folds of my gray flannel trousers were charged with 'is-ness,'" Huxley tells us, before dilating on Botticelli draperies and the "Allness and Infinity of folded cloth." The usual process by which the grains of perception pass us by slows way down, to the point where the conscious I can behold each grain in its turn, scrupulously examining it from every conceivable angle (sometimes from more angles than it even has), until all there is is the still point at the hourglass's waist, where time itself appears to pause.

⌒

But is this wonder the real thing? At first glance, it wouldn't seem to be: a transcendence that's chemically induced must surely be fake. *Artificial Paradises* was what Charles Baudelaire called his 1860 book about his experiences with hashish, and that sounds about right. Yet what if it turns out that the neurochemistry of transcendence is no different whether you smoke marijuana, meditate, or enter a hypnotic trance by way of chanting, fasting, or prayer? What if in every one of these endeavors, the brain is simply prompted to produce large quantities of cannabinoids, thereby suspending short-term memory and allowing us to experience the present deeply? There are many technologies for changing the brain's chemistry; drugs may simply be the most direct. (This doesn't necessarily make drugs a *better* technology for changing consciousness—indeed, the toxic side effects of so many of them suggest that the opposite is true.) From a brain's point of view, the distinction between a natural and an artificial high may be meaningless.

Aldous Huxley did his best to argue us out of the view that a chemically conditioned spiritual existence is false—and he did so long before we knew anything about cannabinoid or opiod receptor networks. "In one way or another, *all* our experiences are chemically conditioned, and if we imagine that some of them are purely 'spiritual,' purely 'intellectual,' purely 'aesthetic,' it is merely because we have never troubled to investigate the internal chemical environment at the moment of their occurrence." He points out that mystics have always worked systematically to modify their brain chemistry, whether through fasting, self-flagellation, sleeplessness, hypnotic movement, or chanting.* The brain can be made to drug itself, as seems to happen with certain placebos. We don't merely imagine that the placebo antidepressant is working to lift our sadness or worry—the brain is actually producing extra serotonin in response to the mental prompt of swallowing a pill containing nothing but sugar and belief. What all this suggests is that the workings of consciousness are both more and less materialistic than we usually think: chemical reactions can induce thoughts, but thoughts can also induce chemical reactions.

Even so, the use of drugs for spiritual purposes feels cheap and false. Perhaps it is our work ethic that is offended—you know, no pain, no gain. Or maybe it is the provenance of the chemicals that troubles us, the fact that they come *from outside*. Especially in the Judeo-Christian West, we tend to define ourselves by the distance we've put between ourselves and nature, and we jealousy guard the borders

---

*Huxley suggests that the reason there aren't nearly as many mystics and visionaries walking around today, as compared to the Middle Ages, is the improvement in nutrition. Vitamin deficiencies wreak havoc on brain function and probably explain a large portion of visionary experiences in the past.

between matter and spirit as proof of our ties to the angels. The notion that spirit might turn out in some sense to *be* matter (and plant matter, no less!) is a threat to our sense of separateness and godliness. Spiritual knowledge comes from above or within, but surely not from plants. Christians have a name for someone who believes otherwise: pagan.

⌒

Two stories stand behind the taboos that people in the West have placed on cannabis at various times in its history. Each reflects our anxieties about this remarkable plant, about what its Dionysian power might do to us if it is not resisted or brought under control.

The first, brought back from the Orient by Marco Polo (among others), is the story of the Assassins—or rather, a corruption of the story of the Assassins, which may or may not be apocryphal to begin with. The time is the eleventh century, when a vicious sect called the Assassins, under the absolute control of Hassan ibn al Sabbah (aka "the Old Man of the Mountain") is terrorizing Persia, robbing and murdering with brutal abandon. Hassan's marauders will do anything he tells them to, no questions asked; they have lost their fear of death. How does Hassan secure this perfect loyalty? By treating his men to a foretaste of the eternal paradise that will be theirs should they die in his service.

Hassan would begin his initiation of new recruits by giving them so much hashish that they passed out. Hours later the men would awaken to find themselves in the midst of a most beautiful palace garden, laid with sumptuous delicacies and staffed with gorgeous maidens to gratify their every desire. Scattered through this paradise, lying on the grounds in pools of blood, are severed heads—actually actors buried to their necks. The heads speak, telling the men of the afterlife and what they will have to do if they hope ever to return to this paradise.

The story was corrupted by the time Marco Polo retold it, so that the hashish was now directly responsible for the violence of the Assassins. (The word itself is a corruption of "hashish.") By erasing the Assassins' fear of death, the story suggested, hashish freed them to commit the most daring and merciless crimes. The tale became a staple of orientalism and, later, of the campaign to criminalize marijuana in America in the 1930s. Harry J. Anslinger, the first director of the Federal Bureau of Narcotics and the man most responsible for marijuana prohibition, mentioned the Assassins at every opportunity. He skillfully used this metanarrative—publicizing every contemporary crime story he could cut to its lurid pattern—to transform a little-known drug of indolence into one of violence, a social menace. Even after Anslinger's "reefer madness" had subsided, the moral of the tale of the Assassins continued to trail cannabis—the notion that, by severing the ink between acts and their consequences, marijuana unleashes human inhibitions, thereby endangering Western civilization.

The second story is simply this: In 1484, Pope Innocent VIII issued a papal condemnation of witchcraft in which he specifically condemned the use of cannabis as an "antisacrament" in satanic worship. The black mass celebrated by medieval witches and sorcerers presented a mocking mirror image of the Catholic Eucharist, and in it cannabis traditionally took the place of wine—serving as a pagan sacrament in a counterculture that sought to undermine the establishment church.

The fact that witches and sorcerers were the first Europeans to exploit the psychoactive properties of cannabis probably sealed its fate in the West as a drug identified with feared outsiders and cultures conceived in opposition: pagans, Africans, hippies. The two stories fed each other and in turn the plant's power: people who smoked cannabis were Other, and the cannabis they smoked threatened to let their Otherness loose in the land.

⌒

Witches the Church simply burned at the stake, but something more interesting happened to the witches' magic plants. The plants were too precious to banish from human society, so in the decades after Pope Innocent's fiat against witchcraft, cannabis, opium, belladonna, and the rest were simply transferred from the realm of sorcery to medicine, thanks largely to the work of a sixteenth-century Swiss alchemist and physician named Paracelsus. Sometimes called the "Father of Medicine," Paracelsus established a legitimate pharmacology largely on the basis of the ingredients found in flying ointments. (Among his many accomplishments was the invention of laudanum, the tincture of opium that was perhaps the most important drug in the pharmacopoeia until the twelfth century.) Paracelsus often said that he had learned everything he knew about medicine from the sorceresses. Working under the rational sign of Apollo, he domesticated their forbidden Dionysian knowledge, turning the pagan portions into healing tinctures, bottling the magic plants and calling them medicines.

Paracelsus's grand project, which arguably is still going on today,** represents one of the many ways the Judeo-Christian tradition has deployed its genius to absorb, or co-opt, the power of the pagan faith it set out to uproot. In much the same way that the new monotheism folded into its rituals the people's traditional pagan holidays and spectacles, it desperately needed to do something about their ancient devotion to magic plants. Indeed, the story of the forbidden fruit in Genesis suggests that nothing was more important.

The challenge these plants posed to monotheism was profound, for they threatened to divert people's gaze from the sky, where the new God resided, down to the natural world all around them. The magic plants were, and remain, a gravitational force pulling us back to Earth, to matter, away from the there and then of Christian salvation and back to the here and now. Indeed, what these plants do to time is perhaps the most dangerous thing about them—dangerous, that is, from the perspective of a civilization organized on the lines of Christianity and, more recently, capitalism.

Christianity and capitalism are both probably right to detest a plant like cannabis. Both faiths bid us to set our sights on the future; both reject the pleasures of the moment and the senses in favor of the expectation of a fulfillment yet to come—whether by earning salvation or by getting and spending. More even than most plant drugs, cannabis, by immersing us in the present and offering something like fulfillment here and now, short-circuits the metaphysics of desire on which Christianity and capitalism (and so much else in our civilization) depend.***

~

**Most recently, as the medical value of marijuana has been rediscovered, medicine has been searching for ways to "pharmaceuticalize" the plant—find a way to harness its easily accessible benefits in a patch or inhaler that doctors can prescribe, corporations patent, and governments regulate. Whenever possible, Paracelsus's lab-coated descendants have synthesized the active ingredients in plant drugs, allowing medicine to dispense with the plant itself—and any reminders of its pagan past.

***David Lenson draws a useful distinction between drugs of desire (cocaine, for example) and drugs of pleasure, such as cannabis. "Cocaine promises the greatest pleasure ever known in just a minute more . . . But that future never comes." In this respect the cocaine experience is "a savage mimicry of consumer consciousness." With cannabis or the psychedelics, on the other hand, "pleasure can come from natural beauty, domestic tasks, friends and relatives, conversation, or any number of objects that do not need to be purchased."

What, then, *was* the knowledge that God wanted to keep from Adam and Eve in the Garden? Theologians will debate this question without end, but it seems to me the most important answer is hidden in plain sight. The *content* of the knowledge Adam and Eve could gain by tasting of the fruit does not matter nearly as much as its form— that is, the very fact that there was spiritual knowledge of *any* kind to be had from a tree: from nature. The new faith sought to break the human bond with magic nature, to disenchant the world of plants and animals by directing our attention to a single God in the sky. Yet Jehovah couldn't very well pretend the tree of knowledge didn't exist, not when generations of plant-worshiping pagans knew better. So the pagan tree is allowed to grow even in Eden, though ringed around now with a strong taboo. Yes, there *is* spiritual knowledge in nature, the new God is acknowledging, and its temptations are fierce, but I am fiercer still. Yield to it, and you will be punished.

So unfolds the drug war's first battle.

I've removed most all of the temptations from my own garden, though not without regret or protest. Immersed this spring in research for this chapter, I was sorely tempted to plant one of the hybrid cannabis seeds I'd seen for sale in Amsterdam. I immediately thought better of it, however. So I planted lots of opium poppies instead. I hasten to add that I've no plans to do anything with my poppies except admire them—first their fleeting tissue-paper blooms, then their swelling blue-green seedpods, fat with milky alkaloid. (Unless, of course, simply walking among the poppies is enough to have an effect, as it was for Dorothy in Oz.) Unscored and so at least arguably innocent, these poppies are my stand-ins for the cannabis I cannot plant. Whenever I look at their dreamy petals, I'll be reminded of the powers this garden has abjured in order to stay on the safe side of the law.

So I make do with this bowdlerized garden, this densely planted plot of acceptable pleasures—good things to eat, beautiful things to gaze upon—fenced around by heeded laws. If Dionysius is represented in this garden, and he surely is, it's mainly in the flower border. I would be the last person to make light of the power of a fragrant rose to raise one's spirits, summon memories, even, in some not merely metaphorical sense, to intoxicate.

ISHMAEL REED

AMERICA: THE MULTI-NATIONAL SOCIETY

"AMERICA: THE MULTI-NATIONAL SOCIETY" originally appeared in *San Francisco Focus*, a publication of KQED, the local PBS TV station. Since its publication in 1983, it has been reprinted more than any other essay I've written. The reason for this, I believe, is because it challenges the notion that there exists in this country an Anglo-Saxon mainstream that all minorities yearn to enter and that African Americans are the only dissenters to this vision, an argument promoted by *The New York Review of Books* as recently as August 14, 2003, in an article by Andrew Hacker.

Since the essay was published, I have traveled to Asia, Africa, the Middle East, and Europe and discovered that it's not our "Anglo-Saxon mainstream" that interests intellectuals abroad, but our literature, music, art, and film, which are created by men and women of diverse backgrounds. These contributions to world culture might not overcome the outrage that citizens of the globe feel about our politicians lobbing depleted uranium and cluster bombs into civilian neighborhoods indiscriminately, but it exhibits that there is another aspect of American civilization that deserves to be admired.

President Bill Clinton had it right when he said that he didn't care where people came from as long as they subscribed to the Constitution and the Bill of Rights.

—Ishmael Reed

At the annual Lower East Side Jewish Festival yesterday, a Chinese woman ate a pizza in front of Ty Thuan Duc's Vietnamese grocery store. Beside her a Spanish-speaking family patronized a cart with two signs: "Italian Ices" and "Kosher by Rabbi Alper." And after the pastrami ran out, everybody ate knishes.

—The New York Times, 23 June 1983

On the day before Memorial Day 1983, a poet called me to describe a city he had just visited. He said that one section included mosques, built by the Islamic people who dwelled there. Attending his reading, he said, were large numbers of Hispanic people, forty thousand of whom lived in the same city. He was not talking about a fabled city located in some mysterious region of the world. The city he'd visited was Detroit.

A few months before, as I was leaving Houston, Texas, I heard it announced on the radio that Texas's largest minority was Mexican American, and though a foundation recently issued a report critical of bilingual education, the taped voice used to guide the passengers on the air trams connecting terminals in Dallas Airport is in both Spanish and English. If the trend continues, a day will come when it will be difficult to travel through some sections of the country without hearing commands in both English and Spanish; after all, for some western states, Spanish was the first written language and the Spanish style lives on in the western way of life.

Shortly after my Texas trip, I sat in an auditorium located on the campus of the University of Wisconsin at Milwaukee as a Yale professor—whose original work on the influence of African cultures upon those of the Americas has led to his ostracism from some monocultural intellectual circles—walked up and down the aisle, like an old-time southern evangelist, dancing and drumming the top of the lectern, illustrating his points before some serious Afro-American intellectuals and artists who cheered and applauded his performance and his mastery of information. The professor was "white." After his lecture, he joined a group of Milwaukeeans in a conversation. All of the participants spoke Yoruban, though only the professor had ever traveled to Africa.

One of the artists told me that his paintings, which included African and Afro-American mythological symbols and imagery, were hanging in the local McDonald's restaurant. The next day I went to

McDonald's and snapped pictures of smiling youngsters eating hamburgers below paintings that could grace the walls of any of the country's leading museums. The manager of the local McDonald's said, "I don't know what you boys are doing, but I like it," as he commissioned the local painters to exhibit in his restaurant.

Such blurring of cultural styles occurs in everyday life in the United States to a greater extent than anyone can imagine and is probably more prevalent than the sensational conflict between people of different backgrounds that is played up and often encouraged by the media. The result is what the Yale professor, Robert Thompson, referred to as a cultural bouillabaisse, yet members of the nation's present educational and cultural Elect still cling to the notion that the United States belongs to some vaguely defined entity they refer to as "Western civilization," by which they mean, presumably, a civilization created by the people of Europe, as if Europe can be viewed in monolithic terms. Is Beethoven's Ninth Symphony, which includes Turkish marches, a part of Western civilization, or the late nineteenth- and twentieth-century French paintings, whose creators were influenced by Japanese art? And what of the cubists, through whom the influence of African art changed modern painting, or the surrealists, who were so impressed with the art of the Pacific Northwest Indians that, in their map of North America, Alaska dwarfs the lower forty-eight in size?

Are the Russians, who are often criticized for their adoption of "Western" ways by Tsarist dissidents in exile, members of Western civilization? And what of the millions of Europeans who have black African and Asian ancestry, black Africans having occupied several countries for hundreds of years? Are these "European" members of Western civilization, or the Hungarians, who originated across the Urals in a place called Greater Hungary, or the Irish, who came from the Iberian Peninsula?

Even the notion that North America is part of Western civilization because our "system of government" is derived from Europe is being challenged by Native American historians who say that the founding fathers, Benjamin Franklin especially, were actually influenced by the system of government that had been adopted by the Iroquois hundreds of years prior to the arrival of large numbers of Europeans.

Western civilization, then, becomes another confusing category like Third World, or Judeo-Christian culture, as man attempts to impose his small-screen view of political and cultural reality upon a complex world. Our most publicized novelist recently said that Western civilization was the greatest achievement of mankind, an attitude that flourishes on the street level as scribbles in public restrooms: "White Power," "Niggers and Spics Suck," or "Hitler Was a Prophet," the latter being the most telling, for wasn't Adolf Hitler the archetypal monoculturalist who, in his pigheaded arrogance, believed that one way and one blood was so pure that it had to be protected from alien strains at all costs? Where did such an attitude, which has caused so much misery and depression in our national life, which has tainted even our noblest achievements, begin? An attitude that caused the incarceration of Japanese-American citizens during World War II, the persecution of Chicanos and Chinese Americans, the near-extermination of the Indians, and the murder and lynchings of thousands of Afro-Americans.

Virtuous, hardworking, pious, even though they occasionally would wander off after some fancy clothes, or rendezvous in the woods with the town prostitute, the Puritans are idealized in our schoolbooks as "a hardy band" of no-nonsense patriarchs whose discipline razed the forest and brought order to the New World (a term that annoys Native American historians). Industrious, responsible, it was their "Yankee ingenuity" and practicality that created the work ethic. They were simple folk who produced a number of good poets, and they set the tone for the American writing style, of lean and spare lines, long before Hemingway. They worshiped in churches whose colors blended in with the New England snow, churches with simple structures and ornate lecterns.

The Puritans were a daring lot, but they had a mean streak. They hated the theater and banned Christmas. They punished people in a cruel and inhuman manner. They killed children who disobeyed their parents. When they came in contact with those whom they considered heathens or aliens, they behaved in such a bizarre and irrational manner that this chapter in the American history comes down to us as a late-movie horror film. They exterminated the Indians, who taught them how to survive in a world unknown to them, and their encounter with the calypso culture of Barbados resulted in what the tourist guide in Salem's Witches' House refers to as the Witchcraft Hysteria.

The Puritan legacy of hard work and meticulous accounting led to the establishment of a great industrial society; it is no wonder that the American industrial revolution began in Lowell, Massachusetts, but there was the other side, the strange and paranoid attitudes toward those different from the Elect.

The cultural attitudes of that early Elect continue to be voiced in everyday life in the United States: the president of a distinguished university, writing a letter to the *Times*, belittling the study of African civilizations; the television network that promoted its show on the Vatican art with the boast that this art represented "the finest achievements of the human spirit." A modern up-tempo state of complex rhythms that depends upon contacts with an international community can no longer behave as if it dwelled in a "Zion Wilderness" surrounded by beasts and pagans.

When I heard a schoolteacher warn the other night about the invasion of the American educational system by foreign curriculums, I wanted to yell at the television set, "Lady, they're already here." It has already begun because the world is here. The world has been arriving at these shores for at least ten thousand years from Europe, Africa, and Asia. In the late nineteenth and early twentieth centuries, large numbers of Europeans arrived, adding their cultures to those of the European, African, and Asian settlers who were already here, and recently millions have been entering the country from South America and the Caribbean, making Yale professor Bob Thompson's bouillabaisse richer and thicker.

One of our most visionary politicians said that he envisioned a time when the United States could become the brain of the world, by which he meant the repository of all of the latest advanced information systems. I thought of that remark when an enterprising poet friend of mine called to say that he had just sold a poem to a computer magazine and that the editors were delighted to get it because they didn't carry fiction or poetry. Is that the kind of world we desire? A humdrum homogenous world of all brains but no heart, no fiction, no poetry; a world of robots with human attendants bereft of imagination, of culture? Or does North America deserve a more exciting destiny? To become a place where the cultures of this world crisscross. This is possible because the United States is unique in the world. The world is here.

RUTH REICHL

THE QUEEN of MOLD

THE FIRST TIME I read this chapter to an audience someone came up to me afterward and asked, "When did you know that you were funny?"

"I'm not funny," I said.

The man just stared at me as if I was crazy. And that's what I like so much about this particular piece: It made me understand that most of us use humor to hide pain, and that I had been unknowingly doing it all my life.

When I turned in the first draft of *Tender at the Bone* my editor said, "There's a secret buried in this book."

Of course. Every book has its secret, just sitting there, waiting for the reader to dig it up in his own way and in his own time. But I wrote this chapter as I was starting out, still undecided about how much of the secret I was willing to reveal. My mother was a complicated character, a writer's dream, poignant, impossible, filled with life, and I wrestled with her portrait, trying to make her both lovable and funny.

But the truth is that there was more to her, and later I decided to divulge the mental illness that is merely hinted at here. Just writing the words "manic depressive" felt loyal—I knew my mother would be embarrassed by the revelation—but it also felt important to tell the truth. At the time I wasn't quite sure why I had to do it, but after the book was published I finally understood.

I thought the secret was my mother's illness. I was wrong. The secret was that her sickness made me strong, and it took my readers to make me see that. In the years since the book was published I have received dozens of letters from young people with equally impossible parents, all saying how helpful it is to know that they too will be able to survive their childhood.

Humor, of course, helps. These days reading this chapter makes me laugh. I like to think that if Mom were still around she'd be laughing too.

—Ruth Reichl

This is a true story.

Imagine a New York City apartment at six in the morning. It is a modest apartment in Greenwich Village. Coffee is bubbling in an electric percolator. On the table is a basket of rye bread, an entire coffee cake, a few cheeses, a platter of cold cuts. My mother has been making breakfast—a major meal in our house, one where we sit down to fresh orange juice every morning, clink our glasses as if they held wine, and toast each other with "Cheerio. Have a nice day."

Right now she is the only one awake, but she is getting impatient for the day to begin and she cranks WQXR up a little louder on the radio, hoping that the noise will rouse everyone else. But Dad and I are good sleepers, and when the sounds of martial music have no effect she barges into the bedroom and shakes my father awake.

"Darling," she says, "I need you. Get up and come into the kitchen."

My father, a sweet and accommodating person, shuffles sleepily down the hall. He is wearing loose pajamas, and the strand of hair he combs over his bald spot stands straight up. He leans against the sink, holding on to it a little, and obediently opens his mouth when my mother says, "Try this."

Later, when he told the story, he attempted to convey the awfulness of what she had given him. The first time he said that it tasted like cat toes and rotted barley, but over the years the description got better. Two years later it had turned into pigs' snouts and mud and five years later he had refined the flavor into a mixture of antique anchovies and moldy chocolate.

Whatever it tasted like, he said it was the worst thing he had ever had in his mouth, so terrible that it was impossible to swallow, so terrible that he leaned over and spit it into the sink and then grabbed the coffeepot, put the spout into his mouth, and tried to eradicate the flavor.

My mother stood there watching all this. When my father finally put the coffeepot down she smiled and said, "Just as I thought. Spoiled."

And then she threw the mess into the garbage can and sat down to drink her orange juice.

For the longest time I thought I had made this story up. But my brother insists that my father told it often, and with a certain amount of pride.

As far as I know, my mother was never embarrassed by the telling, never even knew that she should have been. It was just the way she was.

Which was taste-blind and unafraid of rot. "Oh, it's just a little mold," I can remember her saying on the many occasions she scraped the fuzzy blue stuff off some concoction before serving what was left for dinner. She had an iron stomach and was incapable of understanding that other people did not.

This taught me many things. The first was that food could be dangerous, especially to those who loved it. I took this very seriously. My parents entertained a great deal, and before I was ten I had appointed myself guardian of the guests. My mission was to keep Mom from killing anybody who came to dinner.

Her friends seemed surprisingly unaware that they took their lives in their hands each time they ate with us. They chalked their ailments up to the weather, the flu, or one of my mother's more unusual dishes. "No more sea urchins for me," I imagined Burt Langner saying to his wife, Ruth, after a dinner at our house, "they just don't agree with me." Little did he know that it was not the sea urchins that had made him ill, but that bargain beef my mother had found so irresistible.

"I can make a meal out of anything," Mom told her friends proudly. She liked to brag about "Everything Stew," a dish invented while she was concocting a casserole out of a two-week-old turkey carcass. (The very fact that my mother confessed to cooking with two-week-old turkey says a lot about her.) She put the turkey and a half can of mushroom soup into the pot. Then she began rummaging around in the refrigerator. She found some leftover broccoli and added that. A few carrots went in, and then a half carton of sour cream. In a hurry, as usual, she added green beans and cranberry sauce. And then, somehow, half an apple pie slipped into the dish. Mom looked momentarily horrified. Then she shrugged and said, "Who knows? Maybe it will be good." And she began throwing everything in the refrigerator in along with it—leftover pâté, some cheese ends, a few squishy tomatoes.

That night I set up camp in the dining room. I was particularly worried about the big eaters, and I stared at my favorite people as they approached the buffet, willing them away from the casserole. I actually stood directly in front of Burt Langner so he couldn't reach the turkey disaster. I loved him, and I knew that he loved food.

Unknowingly I had started sorting people by their tastes. Like a hearing child born to deaf parents, I was shaped by my mother's handicap, discovering that food could be a way of making sense of the world.

At first I paid attention only to taste, storing away the knowledge that my father preferred salt to sugar and my mother had a sweet tooth. Later I also began to note how people ate, and where. My brother liked fancy food in fine surroundings, my father only cared about the company, and Mom would eat anything so long as the location was exotic. I was slowly discovering that if you watched people as they ate, you could find out who they were.

Then I began listening to the way people talked about food, looking for clues to their personalities. "What is she really saying?" I asked myself when Mom bragged about the invention of her famous corned beef ham.

"I was giving a party," she'd begin, "and as usual I left everything for the last minute." Here she'd look at her audience, laughing softly at herself. "I asked Ernst to do the shopping, but you know how absentminded he is! Instead of picking up a ham he brought me corned beef." She'd look pointedly at Dad, who would look properly sheepish.

"What could I do?" Mom asked. "I had people coming in a couple of hours. I had no choice. I simply pretended it was a ham." With that Dad would look admiringly at my mother, pick up his carving knife, and start serving the masterpiece.

Miriam Reichl's Corned Beef Ham

4 pounds whole corned beef	1/4 cup brown sugar
5 bay leaves	Whole cloves
1 onion, chopped	1 can (1 pound 15 ounces)
1 tablespoon prepared mustard	spiced peaches

Cover corned beef with water in a large pot. Add bay leaves and onion. Cook over medium heat about 3 hours, until meat is very tender.

While meat is cooking, mix mustard and brown sugar.

Preheat oven to 325°.

Take meat from water and remove all visible fat. Insert cloves into meat as if it were ham. Cover the meat with the mustard mixture and bake 1 hour, basting frequently with the peach syrup.

Surround meat with spiced peaches and serve.

Serves 6.

Most mornings I got out of bed and went to the refrigerator to see how my mother was feeling. You could tell instantly just by opening the door. One day in 1960 I found a whole suckling pig staring at me. I jumped back and slammed the door, hard. Then I opened it again. I'd never seen a whole animal in our refrigerator before; even the chickens came in parts. He was surrounded by tiny crab apples (*"lady apples"* my mother corrected me later), and a whole wreath of weird vegetables.

This was not a bad sign: the more odd and interesting things there were in the refrigerator, the happier my mother was likely to be. Still, I was puzzled; the refrigerator in our small kitchen had been almost empty when I went to bed.

"Where did you get all this stuff?" I asked. "The stores aren't open yet."

"Oh," said Mom blithely, patting at her crisp gray hair, "I woke up early and decided to go for a walk. You'd be surprised at what goes on in Manhattan at four A.M. I've been down to the Fulton Fish Market. And I found the most interesting produce store on Bleecker Street."

"It was open?" I asked.

"Well," she admitted, "not really." She walked across the worn linoleum and set a basket of bread on the Formica table. "But I saw someone moving around so I knocked. I've been trying to get ideas for the party."

"Party?" I asked warily. "What party?"

"Your brother has decided to get married," she said casually, as if I should have somehow intuited this in my sleep. "And of course we're going to have a party to celebrate the engagement and meet Shelly's family!"

My brother, I knew, would not welcome this news. He was thirteen years older than I and considered it a minor miracle to have reached the age of twenty-five. "I don't know how I survived her cooking," he said as he was telling me about the years when he and Mom were living alone, after she had divorced his father and was waiting to meet mine. "She's a menace to society."

Bob went to live with his father in Pittsburgh right after I was born, but he always came home for holidays. When he was there he always helped me protect the guests, using tact to keep them from eating the more dangerous items.

I took a more direct approach. "Don't eat that," I ordered my best friend Jeanie as her spoon dipped into one of Mom's more creative lunch dishes. My mother believed in celebrating every holiday: in honor of St. Patrick she was serving bananas with green sour cream.

"I don't mind the color," said Jeanie, a trusting soul whose own mother wouldn't dream of offering you an all-orange Halloween extravaganza complete with milk dyed the color of orange juice. Ida served the sort of perfect lunches that I longed for: neat squares of cream cheese and jelly on white bread, bologna sandwiches, Chef Boyardee straight from the can.

"It's not just food coloring," I said. "The sour cream was green to begin with; the carton's been in the refrigerator for months."

Jeanie quickly put her spoon down and when Mom went into the other room to answer the phone we ducked into the bathroom and flushed our lunches down the toilet.

"That was great, Mim," said Jeanie when Mom returned.

"May we be excused?" is all I said. I wanted to get away from the table before anything else appeared.

"Don't you want dessert?" Mom asked.

"Sure," said Jeanie.

"No!" I said. But Mom had already gone to get the cookies. She returned with some strange black lumps on a plate. Jeanie looked at them dubiously, then politely picked one up.

"Oh, go ahead, eat it," I said, reaching for one myself. "They're just Girl Scout mint cookies. She left them on the radiator so all the chocolate melted off, but they won't kill you."

As we munched our cookies, Mom asked idly, "What do you girls think I should serve for Bob's engagement party?"

"You're not going to have the party here, are you?" I asked, holding my breath as I looked around at our living room, trying to see it with a stranger's eye.

Mom had moments of decorating inspiration that usually died before the project was finished. The last one, a romance with Danish modern, had brought a teak dining table, a wicker chair that looked like an egg and hung from a chain, and a Rya rug into our lives. The huge turquoise abstract painting along one wall dated from that period too. But Mom had, as usual, gotten bored, so they were all mixed together with my grandmother's drum table, an ornate breakfront, and some Japanese prints from an earlier, more conservative period.

Then there was the bathroom, my mother's greatest decorating feat. One day she had decided, on the spur of the moment, to install gold towels, a gold shower curtain, and a gold rug. They were no problem. But painting all the porcelain gold was a disaster; it almost immediately began peeling off the sink and it was years before any of us could take a bath without emerging slightly gilded.

My father found all of this slightly amusing. An intellectual who had escaped his wealthy German-Jewish family by coming to America in the twenties, he had absolutely no interest in *things*. He was a book designer who lived in a black-and-white world of paper and type; books were his only passion. He was kindly and detached and if he had known that people described him as elegant, he would have been shocked; clothes bored him enormously, when he noticed them at all.

"No," said Mom. I exhaled. "In the country. We have more room in Wilton. And we need to welcome Shelly into the family properly."

I pictured our small, shabby summer house in the woods. Wilton is only an hour from New York, but in 1960 it was still very rural. My parents had bought the land cheaply and designed the house themselves. Since they couldn't afford an architect, they had miscalculated a bit, and the downstairs bedrooms were very strangely shaped. Dad hardly knew how to hold a hammer, but to save money he had built the house himself with the aid of a carpenter. He was very proud of his handiwork, despite the drooping roof and awkward layout. He was even prouder of our long, rutted, meandering driveway. "I didn't want to cut down a single tree!" he said proudly when people asked why it was so crooked.

I loved the house, but I was slightly embarrassed by its unpainted wooden walls and unconventional character. "Why can't we have the party in a hotel?" I asked. In my mind's eye I saw Shelly's impeccable mother, who seemed to go to the beauty parlor every day and wore nothing but custom-made clothes. Next to her, Mom, a handsome woman who refused to dye her hair, rarely wore makeup, and had very colorful taste in clothes, looked almost bohemian. Shelly's mother wore an enormous diamond ring on her beautifully manicured finger; my mother didn't even wear a wedding band and her fingernails were short and haphazardly polished.

"Nonsense," said Mom. "It will be *much* nicer to have it at home. So much more intimate. I'd like them to see how we live, find out who we are."

"Great," I said under my breath to Jeanie. "That'll be the end of

Bob's engagement. And a couple of the relatives might die, but who worries about little things like that?"

"Just make sure she doesn't serve steak tartare," said Jeanie, giggling.

Steak tartare was the bane of my existence: Dad *always* made it for parties. It was a performance. First he'd break an egg yolk into the mound of raw chopped steak, and then he'd begin folding minced onions and capers and Worcestershire sauce into the meat. He looked tall and suave as he mixed thoughtfully and then asked, his German accent very pronounced, for an assistant taster. Together they added a little more of this or that and then Dad carefully mounded the meat into a round, draped some anchovies across the top, and asked me to serve it.

My job was to spread the stuff onto slices of party pumpernickel and pass the tray. Unless I had bought the meat myself I tried not to let the people I liked best taste Dad's chef d'oeuvre. I knew that my mother bought prepackaged hamburger meat at the supermarket and that if there happened to be some half-price, day-old stuff she simply couldn't resist it. With our well-trained stomachs my father and I could take whatever Mom was dishing out, but for most people it was pure poison.

Just thinking about it made me nervous. "I've got to stop this party," I said.

"How?" asked Jeanie.

I didn't know. I had four months to figure it out.

My best hope was that my mother's mood would change before the party took place. That was not unrealistic; my mother's moods were erratic. But March turned into April and April into May and Mom was still buzzing around. The phone rang constantly and she was feeling great. She cut her gray hair very short and actually started wearing nail polish. She lost weight and bought a whole new wardrobe. Then she and Dad took a quick cruise to the Caribbean.

"We booked passage on a United Fruit freighter," she said to her friends, "so much more interesting than a conventional cruise." When asked about the revolutions that were then rocking the islands she had a standard response: "The bomb in the hotel lobby in Haiti made the trip *much* more interesting."

When they returned she threw herself into planning the party. I got up every morning and looked hopefully into the refrigerator. Things kept getting worse. Half a baby goat appeared. Next there was cactus fruit. But the morning I found the box of chocolate-covered grasshoppers I decided it was time to talk to Dad.

"The plans are getting more elaborate," I said ominously.

"Yes?" said Dad politely. Parties didn't much interest him.

"It's going to be a disaster," I announced.

"Your mother gives wonderful parties," my father said loyally. He was remarkably blind to my mother's failings, regularly announcing to the world that she was a great cook. I think he actually believed it. He beamed when someone mentioned my mother's "interesting dishes" and considered it a compliment when they said, "I've never tasted anything quite like that before." And, of course, *he* never got sick.

"Did you know that she's planning it as a benefit for Unicef?" I asked.

"Really?" he said. "Isn't that nice." He had turned back to the editorials.

"Dad!" I said, trying to get him to see how embarrassing this could be. "She's sending notices to the newspapers. She's inviting an awful lot of people. This thing is getting out of control. It's only a month away and she has nothing planned."

"It'll all work out," Dad said vaguely, folding the newspaper into his briefcase. "Your mother is a very smart woman. She has a PhD." And then, as if there was no more to be said, he added, "I'm sure you'll be a big help."

It was hard to get mad at my father, who was as baffled by my mother's moods as I was, and just as helpless before them. They were like the weather: unpredictable, unavoidable, and often unpleasant. Dad, I think, enjoyed her energy, but then, he could always go to the office when he needed to escape. Which is what he did now. Disgusted, I called my brother.

Bob lived uptown in a fancy apartment and had as little to do with my parents as he could decently get away with.

"She's planning to make my engagement party a benefit?" he asked. "You mean she expects Shelly's family to pay to attend?" I hadn't quite considered that aspect, but I could see his point.

"I guess so," I said. "But that's not the part that worries me. Can you imagine Mom cooking for over a hundred people in the middle of summer? What if it's a really hot day?"

Bob groaned.

"Can't you get called away on business?" I asked. "What if you had a conference you had to go to? Wouldn't she have to call the whole thing off?"

Unfortunately my mother was not the least bit fazed when informed that my brother might not be in town. "The party's not for you," she said to Bob, "it's for Shelly's family. They'll come even if you're too rude not to make an appearance."

"But Mom," said Bob, "you can't ask them to buy tickets to the party."

"Why not?" asked Mom. "I think it's just disgusting the way people who have so much forget about those who are less fortunate. How could you possibly object to raising money for underprivileged children in honor of your marriage? I can't believe I have such a selfish, thoughtless son!" And Mom slammed down the phone.

She always managed to do that, always turned your arguments against you. And so there we were, 150 people invited to lunch on the lawn, a representative from Unicef and photographers promised from all the newspapers. In one of her more grandiose moments Mom wrote her old friend Bertrand Russell in Wales and asked him to come speak; fortunately he was nearing his ninetieth birthday and declined. But he did send a hundred copies of his most recent antiwar booklet, a sort of fairy tale printed on gold paper. It was called *History of the World in Epitome* (for use in Martian infant schools) and it was very short. The last page was a picture of a mushroom cloud.

"These will make wonderful favors!" said Mom smugly, pointing out that they were autographed. She was so pleased she sent out a few more invitations.

"What are you going to serve?" I asked.

"Do you have any ideas?" she replied.

"Yes," I said, "hire a caterer."

Mom laughed as if I had made a joke. But she *was* moved to call and rent some tables and folding chairs, so at least the guests wouldn't be sitting on the ground. I suggested that she hire someone to help cook and serve, but she didn't seem to think that was necessary. "We can do that ourselves," she said blithely. "Can't you get your friends to help?"

"No," I said, "I can't." But I did call Jeanie in the city and ask her to ask her parents if she could come out for the week; she thought my mother was "exciting" and I needed moral support.

As the party approached, things got worse and worse. Mom went on cleaning binges that left the house messier when she was done than when she started, and Jeanie and I went around behind her desperately stuffing things back into closets to create some semblance of order. Mom mowed half the lawn; we mowed the other half. Meanwhile my father, looking apologetic and unhappy, conveniently came up with a big project that kept him in the city.

One morning Mom went to a wholesale food company and came back honking her horn loudly, her car filled to the brim. Jeanie and I rushed out to unload fifty pounds of frozen chicken legs, ten pounds of frozen lump crabmeat, industrial-size cans of tomato and split-pea soup, twenty-five pound sacks of rice, and two cases of canned, spiced peaches.

"This must be the menu," I said to Jeanie.

"What?" she asked.

"I bet she's going to make that awful quick soup she thinks is so great. You know, it's in all the magazines. You mix a can of tomato soup with a can of split pea soup, add a little sherry, and top it with crabmeat."

"Yuck," said Jeanie.

"Then I guess she's going to cook those millions of chicken legs on top of rice, although how she thinks she's going to cook them all in our little oven I don't know. And the canned spiced peaches can be the vegetable; they're easy because all you have to do is open the can and put them on the plates."

I was surprised (and relieved) when she ordered a giant cake from the local bakery. That left only the hors d'oeuvres; I wondered what she had up her sleeve.

The next day I found out. Jeanie and I were playing croquet, but we put down our mallets when Mom's horn started, and watched the car speed through the trees, leaving billows of dust in its wake. We ran out to see what she had dragged home.

"Horn & Hardart was having a sale!" Mom announced triumphantly, pointing to the boxes around her. They were filled with hundreds of small cartons. It looked promising. "It's almost like getting it catered," I said happily to Jeanie as we toted the boxes inside.

My happiness was short-lived; when I began opening the cartons I found that each contained something different.

"The Automat sells leftovers for almost nothing at the end of the day," said Mom, "so I just took everything they had." She was very pleased with herself.

"What are you going to do with it?" I asked.

"Why, serve it," she said.

"In what?" I asked.

"Big bowls," she said.

"But you don't have anything to put in big bowls," I pointed out. "All you have is hundreds of things to put in little bowls. Look," I began ripping the tops off the carton, "this one is potato salad. This one is coleslaw. This one is cold macaroni and cheese. Here's a beet salad. Here's some sliced ham. Nothing matches!"

"Don't worry," said Mom, "I'm sure we can make something out of all of this. After all, everything in it is good."

"Yes," I muttered to Jeanie, "and by the time it gets served everything in it will be four days old. It will be a miracle if it's not moldy."

"I think it would be better if it was," said practical Jeanie. "If people see mold they won't eat it."

"Pray for rain," I said.

Unfortunately, when I woke up on the day of the party there was not a cloud in the sky. I pulled the covers over my head and went back to sleep. But not for long. "Nobody sleeps today," Mom announced, inexorably pulling back the covers. "It's party day!"

Some of the food had acquired a thin veneer of mold, but Mom blithely scraped it off and began mixing her terrible Horn & Hardart mush. "It's delicious!" she cried, holding out a spoonful. It wasn't. Fortunately it looked even worse than it tasted.

I thought the chicken legs were a little dubious too; in order to get them all cooked we had started two days earlier, and the refrigerator couldn't hold them all. But they glistened invitingly, and the oven-baked rice looked fine. We spooned the peaches into Mom's big glass bowls, and they looked beautiful.

I wasn't very happy about the soup. Mom had left the crabmeat out of the freezer to defrost for two days, and even she didn't like the way it was smelling. "I think I'll just add a little more sherry," she kept saying as she poured in bottles of the stuff.

"People will get drunk on the soup," I said.

"Fine," she said gaily, "then maybe they'll donate more to Unicef."

My brother arrived, took one look at the rickety chairs on our uneven lawn, and headed straight for the bar. Mom had hired some local high school boys to be bartenders, and they were pouring whiskey as if it were Coke.

"You've got to stay sober," I said to him. "You've got to make sure that nobody in Shelly's family eats the soup. And they should probably watch out for the chicken too."

Bob had another drink.

My memories of the party are mercifully blurred, but a yellowed clipping from the *Norwalk Hour* tells part of the story. My mother looks radiantly into the camera beneath a headline reading WILTON FAMILY HOSTS BENEFIT FOR UNICEF.

A family photograph of me handing a check to a grinning official in front of a sign that says SECURITY COUNCIL in both French and English tells another part of the tale.

But my brother owns the end of the story. Thirty-five years later his children can still make him turn green by asking, "Remember the time Nana Mimi poisoned everyone?"

"Ooh," he moans, "don't remind me. It was awful. First she extorted money from them. Then she gave out those antibomb favors; it was the early sixties, for Christ sake, and these were conservative businessmen and housewives. But the worse thing was the phone calls. They kept coming all night long. Nobody felt good. Twenty-six of them actually ended up in the hospital having their stomachs pumped. What a way to meet the family!"

I missed all that, but I do remember the phone ringing while we were still cleaning up. Mom was still exulting in the photographer's flashbulbs, and saying for what seemed like the forty-seventh time, "Look how much money we raised!" She picked up the receiver.

"Yes?" said Mom brightly. I think she expected it to be another reporter. Then her voice drooped with disappointment.

"Who doesn't feel well?"

There was a long silence. Mom ran her hand through her chic, short coiffure. "Really?" she said, sounding shocked. "All of them?" She slumped a little as her bright red fingernails went from her hair to her mouth. Then her back straightened and her head shot up.

"Nonsense," I heard her say into the phone. "We all feel fine. And we ate *everything*."

DAN RHODES

From ANTHROPOLOGY

THE STORIES I'VE INCLUDED here were all written in March 1998, when I was working with a degree of energy that I don't think I'll ever recapture. I suspect it will always stand as the most productive month of my writing life. Not having enough money to rent my own place, I had moved into a room above my long-suffering parents' pub in the Kent countryside and found work on a small local fruit and veg farm. As a three-year-old I had dreamed of becoming a Tractor Man, and having just turned twenty-six I found myself reluctantly fulfilling that ambition. My days were spent shivering and squelching from crop to crop, and often an idea for a story would appear while I was repairing holes in the farm track, or having my eyeballs whipped by raspberry canes, and I would turn it over in my head until I got home.

Most evenings I would open the pub at six and wait until the bar staff arrived at seven. I would sullenly serve the occasional customer before going straight back to my envelope or brewery notepad to continue work on my latest story. If anybody tried to engage me in conversation I would brush them off as quickly as possible—whatever they had to say could never begin to compete with my writing. Yes, I was an atrocious barman. Come seven I would escape upstairs with a load of beer (I was spending over half my meagre wages on drink) and start work properly, pounding away at my new idea and obsessively redrafting old stories.

Things weren't looking too bright. The job I had lined up for later in the year, teaching at an international school in Ho Chi Minh City, had vanished in the East Asian slump, nobody I sent my writing to was even slightly impressed by it, I was earning a spectacularly unspectacular wage, and suffering the humiliation of living back at home at the age of twenty-six with no immediate prospect of escape. The stories that would become *Anthropology* were an oasis of order in an otherwise shambolic life. I found myself turning my bottomless well of self-pity (which is surely the most maligned emotion—without self-pity there would be no art) into something positive. It was a physical experience too—when a story finally came together I would feel fire in my bones. It was psychedelic.

It was March 1998 when I really felt the book starting to fly, and I stopped caring about anything else in the world. I felt sure that what I was writing was the closest literature had ever come to pop music, and I still think that. Thirteen stories I wrote that month made the final cut of *Anthropology*, and several of them are firm favourites that I still enjoy reading to audiences. *Anthropology* never quite had the earth-shattering sales I felt it was destined for, and nor did it tear the stuffy book world to shreds as I had hoped it would, but it's still out there somewhere, quietly doing its thing, and I love it every bit as much as I did back then.

—Dan Rhodes

NORMAL

After a blazing row, Harmony joined the nuns. "That's it," she said. "I'm joining the nuns." I was lonely and could hardly sleep, but three days later she escaped and came home. "It was awful," she said. "We had to get up really early, and they made us wear horrible long black dress things and no make-up, and sing all these boring songs." Thankfully things quickly returned to normal, and now she's back to spending her free time joining in with the adverts on TV, and making me get up from the sofa so she can look for her lighter.

PIECES

They kidnapped my girlfriend, and asked for an awful lot of money before they would even think about giving her back. I was grateful for the peace and quiet, so I wasn't in too much of a hurry to settle up. After a while they started posting me little pieces of her, starting with an ear in a soap dish. For some reason they aren't lowering the ransom. It doesn't make sense. They seem to think I'd pay as much for a girl-friend with no thumbs, ears, nose or nipples as I would for one with all her bits still there.

MADRID

I was delighted to find a Spanish girlfriend, and celebrated our first anniversary with a surprise trip to her home city. I landed our helicopter in front of the Palacio Real, and took off her blindfold. "Where is this?" she asked, in her lilting Iberian accent. I was surprised that she didn't recognise such a famous landmark, and suggested she ask a passer-by. She started crying. In a voice I didn't recognise, she told me she was sorry, that there had been a special offer on sunbeds, and it had seemed like the right thing to say at the time.

TRICK

My girlfriend told me she had been the victim of nature's cruellest trick, that although born male she had always felt female. She said she had started dressing in women's clothes at the age of seventeen, and three years later had undergone the necessary surgery. I was stunned, but told her that I loved her first and foremost as a person, and that I would give her all the emotional support she needed. She looked horrified. She had only been joking. She left me. She said she was going to find a real man, not some queer little gayboy like me.

DUST

Xanthe left me. I found out her new address, and returned the kettle she had left behind. The next day I took her a book she had lent me. I found a box of hairgrips, and delivered one each day. If she wasn't home I would post it with a long letter explaining how I had found it on the floor. When I had returned them all, I took her, on the tip of my finger, a tiny ball of dust. "I remember seeing it fall from your dress one afternoon," I said. "The pretty one, with the flowers on it."

BEAUTY

My girlfriend is so beautiful that she has never had cause to develop any kind of personality. People are always wildly glad to see her, even though she does little more than sit around and smoke. She's getting prettier, too. Last time she left the house she caused six car crashes, two coronaries, about thirty domestic disputes and an estimated six hundred unwanted and embarrassing erections. She seems to be quite indifferent to the havoc she causes. "I'm going to the shop for cigarettes," she'll say, yawning with that succulent, glossy mouth. "I suppose you'd better call some ambulances or something."

LESBIAN

My girlfriend and I couldn't decide on a name for our little baby girl. Eventually she took her to the registrar, and said she would think of something on the way. When she returned, I was frantic with anticipation. "So what's she called?"

"I called her Lesbian," she said, smiling at the bundle in her arms. "It's such a pretty name."

I asked her what on earth had possessed her. "Don't you know what it means?" She didn't, so I explained. The poor thing burst into tears.

"I didn't know there were ladies who did that to each other," she sobbed.

TOM ROBBINS

From FIERCE INVALIDS HOME from HOT CLIMATES

∾

AFTER RUMMAGING—METAPHORICALLY—THROUGH attic, cellar, garage, library, underwear drawer, voodoo cabinet, and ammunition depot in search of what I might palm off as a legitimate example of my best work, I eventually settled upon an excerpt from my seventh novel, *Fierce Invalids Home from Hot Climates*. Why? Because in these few pages can be found philosophy, social commentary, humor, poetry, mystery, narrative momentum, and a faint whiff of eroticism; in short, all of the elements that I value most highly in literature.

—Tom Robbins

The distance between Switters and the oasis at last began to shrink. Quite suddenly, in fact, the compound seemed to enlarge, as if, cued by a director and strictly timed, it had burst out (ta da!) on stage. It was no mirage. But what was it? It had better be good because all around it, in every direction, as far as his eyes could see, the world was as empty and dry as a mummy's condom.

He was wondering if he shouldn't have remained with the Bedouins. They were a marvelous people to whom travel was a gift and hospitality a law. The Kurds had been gracious enough, but he preferred the Bedouins, for they were less religious and thus more lively and free. Kurds were essentially settlers who roamed only when forced from their villages by strife. Bedouins were nomadic to the bone. Whereas Kurds were in a constant state of bitter agitation over their lack of an autonomous homeland, Bedouins had no use for such paralyzing concepts. Their homeland was the circle of light around their campfire, their autonomy was in the raw sparkle of the stars.

In almost every nation in the Middle East, Near East, and Africa, nomads were under strong governmental pressure to plant themselves in established settlements. Whatever the socio-political, economic reasons given, underlying it all was that great pathetic lunatic insecurity that drove men to cling to various illusions of certainty and permanence. The supreme irony, of course, was that they clung to those ideals because they were scared witless by the certainty and permanence of death. To the domesticated, nomads were an unwelcome reminder of instinct suppressed, liberty compromised, and control unimplemented.

The fires of this particular band of wandering herdsmen had been noticed by Switters only a few kilometers inside Syria, along the isolated, seasonally fertile wadi down which he'd been driven, headlamps off, to avoid both Iraqi and Syrian border patrols. Knowing that they would be honor bound to receive him hospitably, he ordered the commandeered Jeep stopped about three hundred yards from their encampment, gave the driver a fistful of deutsche marks, and sent him back to his Kurds and fray. "Thanks for the lift, pal. Good luck to you and your homeboys. And if you don't mind me saying so, you ought to switch brands of toothpaste. Give Atomic Flash or Great White Shark a try."

Initially, he'd planned to make his way back into Turkey, where an American with a properly stamped passport and no gunnysacks of gas masks in his possession would have aroused not the slightest suspicion. He might expect to reach the Istanbul airport within the week. But he was full of himself after his little caper, and soon he was full of the Bedouins, as well.

Despite the fleas that prickled him nightly the way stars prickled the desert sky, he loved sleeping on their musky carpets inside their big black tents. (*The universe is organized anarchy*, he thought, *and I'm lying in the folds of its flag.*) He loved their syrupy coffee, earthenware jars, silver ornaments, tilted eyebrows, and the way they danced the *dobqi*, their bare feet as expressive as a ham actor's face. Yes, and he loved it that they were as wild as jackals and yet impeccably neat and polite. Their good manners would put a Newport socialite to shame. Every country had a soul if one knew where to look for it, but for the stateless Bedouins, their soul *was* their country. It was vast, and they occupied it fully. It was also portable, and he felt compelled to follow it awhile.

Should he not have stayed with them indefinitely, devoting his skills and energies to preserving their way of life? The khan, after all, had offered him one of his daughters. "Take your pick among the five," the khan had said, ever the perfect host, and Switters could sense them blushing behind their thin white veils, while the gold coins they wore strung around their heads jingled slightly, as if vibrated by hidden shudders of nuptial anticipation. Their chins were tattooed up to the base of their noses, and at mealtime each would squirt milk from a ewe's teat directly into her teacup. He tried to imagine marriage to such a girl. His hypothetical adulthood-prevention serum would be superfluous, for they had already been inoculated with an ancient genetic Euro-Asian plasma that kept them soft and fiery and curious and frisky to the grave. Imagine romping with a two-legged patchouli-oiled bear cub every moonlit evening on the carpets she would have woven for his own black tent! How primal, how lurid, how timeless and funky and mysterious and frank!

Yet . . .

She would never serve anything but yogurt for breakfast, beer with biscuits and red-eye gravy stricken from his morning repast forever.

She would never discuss *Finnegans Wake* with him, not even on Bloomsday eve.

And neither she nor her kin would get his jokes: for the rest of his life, every bon mot, every wisecrack, destined to fall on uncomprehending ears.

They wouldn't get his jokes even if he told them in Arabic. The Bedouins weren't stiff and somber by any means. They smiled when pleased, which was fairly often, and they laughed as well, but it was a kind of harmlessly mocking laughter, almost invariably directed at an act or an object—his undershorts with the cartoon bunnies, for example—that they considered ridiculous. Unintentional slapstick might delight them, but a deliberate witticism was as alien to their sensibility as a fixed-rate mortgage. Comedy, as such, was not an aspect of Bedouin consciousness, nor of the consciousness of many other archaically traditioned, non-Western peoples.

Begrudgingly, Switters was starting to think that Today Is Tomorrow might be on to something. That goddamned pyramid-headed, grub-eating, drug-drinking, curse-leveling savage from the Amazon bush could have been right on the money when he concluded that it was Western man's comedic sense—his penchant to jibe and quip and pun and satirize and play humorous games with words and images in order to provoke laughter—that was his greatest strength, his defining talent, his unique contribution to the composite soul of the planet.

Conversely, civilized man's great weakness, his flaw, his undoing, perhaps, was his technologically and/or religiously sponsored disconnection to nature and to that disputed dimension of reality sometimes referred to as the "spirit world," both of which were areas to which the Bedouin, the Kandakandero, and their ilk related with ease and understanding, a kind of innate genius, and harmonious grace. Today Is Tomorrow had suggested that if civilized man's humor (and the imagination and individualism that spawned it) could somehow be wed to primitive man's organic wisdom and extradimensional pipeline, the union would result in something truly wondrous and supremely real, the finally consummated marriage of darkness and light.

An interesting idea, the shaman's proposal, but probably even less likely to be achieved than the happy marriage of a Berkeley-educated former CIA agent to a tattooed, teat-squeezing daughter of the khan.

Those were the things Switters was thinking as the nomad band moved deeper and deeper into the distant, slowly rising hills, and he, in the opposite direction, moved closer and closer to the mud walls of the small oasis.

Three of the khan's daughters—yes, he was still thinking of them—had blue eyes, betraying their ancestral origins on Asia's northern steppes. Theirs was not the Sol Glissant swimming-pool blue of Suzy's eyes, however, but a sapphire blue, almost an anthracite blue, as if hardened into being by millions of pounds of chthonian thrust. Their hair was so black that it, too, was nearly blue, and in a dozen other ways they were antithetical to Suzy. Yet, the oldest of them was no more than seventeen, so . . . so what? Seriously. So what? He had certainly not hooked up with the nomads because of young girls, and if they played any part in his impulse to leave, it was due neither to fear nor guilt (emotions quite irrelevant in that milieu) but rather because he had detected something in the girlish laughter wafting from the oasis during the downpour that had seemed glutinous, pulpy, and quilted, as if textured with layers the fleecy Bedouin titters lacked.

However, to what extent those stratified peals had influenced his sudden urge to explore the place, he couldn't honestly say. As mentioned, he was quietly crackling with an emboldened abandon in the aftermath of the Iraqi caper, there was wahoo in his tank, and that was quite likely a more accurate explanation for his whim than the curiosity aroused by distant laughter. In any case, the oasis was decidedly silent now.

It sat there, almost loomed there, like a mud ship becalmed in a rusty bay. Its contours, its lines, were simple but sensuous, organic but intrusive, utilitarian to a fundamental degree yet somehow oddly fanciful, like a collaboration between Antoni Gaudi and a termite colony. The walls, which enclosed an area of about seven or eight acres, were rounded on top, and the single tower that rose above the flat roofs of the two principal buildings inside was also round and bulbous, creating the effect that the whole compound, architecturally at least, had been formed in a gelatin mold. All that was lacking was a dollop of gritty whipped cream. The air around it was so awiggle with heat that one could almost hear a soft shimmering, but not the smallest sound escaped the compound itself. It seemed, in fact, deserted.

The gate—and there was only one—was arched, wooden, and solid. High on the gate was an area of latticed grillwork, but even when standing on his wheelchair, Switters was unable to quite peer through it. From the outside, the compound was as blank as it was hushed. Hanging from a wooden post beside the gate was an iron bell about the size of a football, and beside the bellrope a sign hand-lettered in Arabic and French. It read: TRADESMEN, RING THREE TIMES/THOSE IN NEED, RING TWICE/THE GODLESS SHOULD NOT RING AT ALL.

Switters considered those options for quite a long while before giving the bell exactly one resounding gong.

⌒

After several minutes, having received no response, he next gave the bellrope *four* strong yanks. He waited. The sun was barbecuing the back of his neck, and his canteen was running on empty. What if he was not admitted? Left out in the heat and desolation? Those responsible for the laughter couldn't have vanished in so short a time. Were they deliberately ignoring him? Hiding from him? Trained, perhaps, to respond only to three rings or two, might his unauthorized signals have bewildered them or blown some pre-electrical circuit inside? Switters was always nettled when expected to choose between two modes of behavior, two political, social, or theological systems, two objects or two (allegedly) mutually exclusive delights; between hot and cold, tart and sweet, funny and serious, sacred and profane, Apollonian and Dionysian, apples and oranges, paper and plastic, smoking and nonsmoking, right and wrong. Why only a pair of choices? And why not choose both? Who was the legislator of these dichotomies? Yahweh, who insisted the angels choose between him and his partner, Lucifer? And are tradesmen, as implied here, never in need? Did the bell instructions imply that any visitor who believed in God would, per se, either be needy or have something to sell?

His skull-pot, fairly boiling inside his crumpled Panama hat, was not cooled by this cogitating. He was on the verge of swinging from the bellrope like a spastic Tarzan when he heard a scraping noise, like dog shit being scuffed from a jogging shoe, and looked up to see that the grill had slid open and was framing a human face.

As near as he could tell, the face was female. It was also European, homely, and either middle-aged or elderly, as it was lightly wrinkled and sprigs of graying hair intruded upon its margins. The owner of the face was either standing on a box, or Switters had stumbled upon a nest of Amazons about which University of California basketball recruiters ought to be apprised, for she was staring down at him from a height of more than seven feet.

"*Bonjour, monsieur. Qu'est-ce que vous cherchez?*"

"What am I looking for? The International House of Pancakes. I must have taken the wrong exit."

"*Pardon?*"

"Ran out of gas out past the old Johnson place, and I'm gonna be late for my Tupperware party. Can I use your phone to call Ross Perot?"

"*Mais, monsieur . . .*"

"I'm looking for this very establishment," he said, switching to his best French, which had grown as moldy as Roquefort from lack of use. "What else would I be looking for in this . . ." He paused to search for the French equivalent of *neck of the woods*, though even in English the expression was irrelevant here, there being no woods within hundreds of miles, indeed, not a single tree in any direction except those embosomed by the compound walls. "I was in the neighborhood and thought I'd drop by. May I please come in?"

The hospitality so prodigious in that arid corner of the world was not immediately forthcoming. After a time, the woman said, "I must consult with . . ." At first she said something that seemed to translate as "Masked Beauty," but she quickly corrected herself and uttered, "the abbess." Then she withdrew, leaving him wondering if this desert outpost to which he had been drawn was not some kind of convent.

His suspicion would prove to be well founded, although the kind of convent it was, exactly, was not something he ever could have guessed.

⌒

A quarter hour passed before the slot in the gate reopened. The face in the grill reported (in French) that the abbess wished to know more specifically the nature of his business. "I don't have any business," Switters replied. It was dawning on him that he might have made a dumb mistake in coming here. "I'm a simple wayfarer seeking temporary refuge from a stern climate."

"I see." The woman removed her face from the grill and relayed his words to party or parties unseen. Behind the gate there was a low murmur of voices in what seemed both French and English. Then the face returned to inquire if he was not an American. He confessed. "I see," said the woman, and again withdrew.

A different face, noticeably younger, rosy as a ham hock, and congenial of smile appeared in the aperture. "Good day, sir," this one said in lilting English. "I don't know what you're doing here, but I'm dreadfully afraid we can't let you enter at the moment." Her accent seemed to be Irish. "I'm the only one here now who speaks English, and I haven't got any bleeding authority, if you'll please excuse my coarse speech, so Masked Beauty or rather the mother superior's sent word that your request can't be properly considered until Sister Domino comes back. I'm sorry, sir. You're not from the Church, are you, sir? That would be a different matter, naturally, but you're not from the Church, now are you?"

Switters hesitated a moment before responding, in imitation of R. Potney Smithe, "Bloody well not my end of the field." He was encouraged when the new face seemed to suppress a giggle. "I'm Switters, freelance errand boy and all-around acquired taste, prepared to exchange hard currency for a night's lodging. And what's your name, little darling?"

The new face blushed. Its owner turned away, engaged in brief discussion with the unseen voices, then reappeared. "Sorry, sir, you'll have to wait for herself."

"Wait for how long?"

"Oh, not more than a day or two, sir. She'll be coming back from Damascus."

A day or two! "Wait where?"

"Why, there's a wee shade over there, sir." She rolled her eyes toward a spot along the wall where an overhang of thickly leaved boughs cast a purplish shadow on the sand. "Bloody unaccommodating, ain't it? I can talk like this because only you and God can understand me, and I don't believe either you or God gives a pip. I'd like to hear how you got here in that bloody chair, but they're pulling at my skirts. Good-bye, sir, and God bless."

"Water!" Switters called, as the grill shut down. *"L'eau, s'il vous plaît."*

"Un moment," a voice called back, and in about ten minutes the gate creaked open a few inches. In the crack there stood not the Irishwoman but the Frenchwoman to whom he'd spoken first. She shoved a pitcher of water and a plate of dried figs at him and quickly shut the gate.

"Oh, well," he sighed. He trundled the twenty feet or so to the shaded place, where he spread the blanket and lay down, his heels propped on the chair's footrest, two inches above the ground. The water in the pitcher was cool. The figs had a faint taste of Suzy. Of girl. He fell asleep and dreamed of woolly things.

⌒

When he awoke it was night. Above him, all around him, the sky was a bolt of black velvet awaiting the portrait of Jesus or Elvis. Stars, like grains of opium, dusted it from edge to edge. In one far corner, the moon was rising. It looked like the head of an idol, a golden calf fattened on foxfire.

Why was the air so torrid? It was his experience that the desert cooled quickly after dark. And summer was yet a month away. Not that it mattered, any more than it mattered that his muscles seemed loosened from his bones or that his bones were swimming in gasoline. He felt like the Sleepy Gypsy in Rousseau's great painting, asleep with his eyes half open in a night alive with mystery and fever.

Fever! It gradually occurred to him that it was he who was hot, not the air. The sweat drops on his brow were like tadpoles. They migrated down his neck as if in search of a pond. Still, he didn't care. A night such as this was worth anything! His aching only gave pitch to its beauty.

The stars hopped about like chigger bugs. The moon edged toward him. Once, he had the sensation that it was licking him with a great wounded tongue. He smelled orange blossoms. He was nauseated. He heard himself moan.

His brain, lit as it now was by an unearthly radiance, accepted the fact that the fever that sickened him also protected him. It spun a cocoon around him. *I am the larva of the New Man*, he thought. But then he added, *Much as the paperclip is the larva of the coat hanger.* He cackled wildly and wished that Bobby Case were there.

Moonlight enveloped him like a clown suit—voluminous, chalky, theatrical—into which he was buttoned with fuzzy red pompons of fever. Inside it, his blood sang torch songs, sang them throughout the night, as he drifted in and out of dreams and delirium, unable to distinguish the one from the other. When he vomited, it was a fizzy mixture of bile and girl.

At some point, he realized that the sun was beating him between the eyes like a stick. He covered his face with his hat and grieved for the enchantments of evening. Another time, he was sure he heard female voices, cautious but caring, and sensed that figures were gathered around him like the ghosts of dead Girl Scouts around a spectral weenie roast. *I'm hot enough to toast marshmallows.* He chuckled, pleased with himself for no good reason. The voices faded, but he became aware of a fresh pitcher of water beside him and a silk pillow under his head.

Then, it was night again. He uncovered his face in time to see the moon spin into view like a salt-encrusted pinwheel. Although he couldn't explain why, the night sky made him want to meow. He tried meowing once or twice, but it hurt his gums, which were swollen, and his throat, which felt like a scabbard two sizes too small for its sword. Oddly enough, it never occurred to him that he might be dying. For his composure he could probably thank fever, which nature had programmed to weave illusions of invincibility, and that Amazon shaman, whose ayahuasca had for him forever dissolved boundaries between life and its extreme alternative (lesser alternatives being conformity, boredom, sobriety, consumerism, dogmatism, puritanism, legalism, and things of that sorry ilk). He realized, nonetheless, that he was in a kind of trouble for which he had not bargained.

It was on the second afternoon—or, perhaps, the third—that he emerged from deep torpor to find his forehead being sponged by a vivacious, round-cheeked nun. He studied her face only seconds before blurting out, weakly but passionately, "I love you."

"Oh yeah?" she replied in American English with a faint French accent. "You're out of your cotton-picking mind."

That's true, he thought, and shut his eyes, though he took her smile with him into stupor. The next time he awoke, he was inside the oasis.

RICHARD RODRIGUEZ

SAND

ᕫ

ALL DAY I HAVE been turning pages. Whenever my hand hesitates, paragraphs begin to speak, to recommend themselves: *Look at me!* Or: *See, how I realized your will.* Or: *I have been anthologized more than others.*

Asking a writer to choose his best work!

Some essays I remember quite clearly having written. I remember their difficulties, their solutions. The paths through several are as clear and indelible to me as the lines of my palm, the streets of some cities.

But there are one or two other essays, much more mysterious; so little do I remember having written them, they seem to have been composed by another hand; foreign.

"Sand" is one of those. I had forgotten it altogether. What comes next? (I wondered, this morning, turning a page).

This essay has lain unobserved in a collection of more turbulent and demanding pieces, in a book called *Days of Obligation.* It is not my best—whatever that might mean—but it charms mightily because it is about those years in Los Angeles when, in my vanity, I began to call myself a writer, without knowing what that might mean. Never guessing that I would someday write sentences, paragraphs, entire essays that would come to exist outside of me, and to render me a reader, not their author, upon rereading.

—Richard Rodriguez

The prize for selling 146 subscriptions to the *Catholic Herald* was a red bicycle and a trip to Disneyland.

I wasn't all that thrilled about Disneyland. Yet I remember walking back from the six o'clock mass with my father that morning; the summer's morning silence; the sense of moment. I had never been more than a hundred miles from Sacramento; I had never stayed in a motel.

I rode shotgun alongside Mr. Kelley, the *Herald*'s circulation manager. The second-place winner from Holy Spirit (one hundred subscriptions) sat in the back seat.

All the way down Highway 99, past the truck stops, the Dairy

Queens, the Giant Oranges, past Modesto and Fresno and the turnoffs to hundreds of country roads, in between the yes-pleases and no-thank-yous, we listened to "Monitor"—the weekend service of NBC Radio. Each hour passed with the announcer's intoning from Rockefeller Center: "This is 'Monitor,' going places, doing things."

There had been a typhoon in Asia. Each time the static receded, more green bodies had washed up among the baseball scores. I stared out the car window, dreaming of Rockefeller Center.

Great cities were tall cities. New York promised most glamour for being the tallest, the coolest, the farthest from these even rows of green; this hot, flat Valley floor.

In the late 1950s, it was still possible to imagine Times Square outside the studio—rain-slickened Broadway awash with neon—and the taxicab that brought Miss Arlene Francis to the theater.

Billy Reckers sent me a postcard from L.A. once—white, horizontal, vast—a vast Sacramento. The house where Gracie Allen lived on TV looked like the houses on 45th Street. The streets on *Dragnet* looked like the streets downtown.

But on two festival days, Los Angeles seemed more glamorous than anywhere else in the world.

New Year's Day was blind and cold in Sacramento. We had the tule fog. We chastened our rooms and our memories, replaced the Christmas ornaments in their cardboard boxes, labeled the boxes, packed them away. On our black-and-white television screen, it was always bright for the Rose Parade from sunny Pasadena, the sunlight dancing on chrome, sunlight flashing from the rhinestones of the Rose Queen and her court.

On the night of the Academy Awards, movie stars pretended real lives, getting out of limousines, walking the gauntlet of flash bulbs. Cleopatra, Tarzan, Mrs. Miniver were all neighbors, all lived in ranch-style houses in L.A.

Mr. Kelley got us to Los Angeles by six o'clock, as he had promised. (We'll stop for dinner, stay overnight in a motel in Hollywood; then drive to Disneyland in the morning.)

Was this it? Even Sacramento had its ceremonial entrance, over the Tower Bridge. After the long, straight line of Highway 99 and the drama of the Tehachapi Mountains—ten hours—we had undergone no change. We drove along Sepulveda Boulevard, looking for a place to eat.

We parked under the aerodynamic roof of a restaurant that

looked like a butterfly. I ordered "chicken in the basket."

We found a motel near the famous Hollywood Bowl. We got one room with twin beds. Mr. Kelley took one of the beds. I shared mine with the runner-up from Holy Spirit. We watched *Lawrence Welk*, because Mr. Kelley's uncle was famous. Mr. Kelley's uncle played the champagne organ. Mr. Kelley wandered around the room in his boxer shorts, scratching. I studied the hair on Mr. Kelley's back as he talked to his wife on the telephone.

A few years later, Johnny Carson moved *The Tonight Show* from New York to Los Angeles. Carson told jokes that began with freeways as the metaphor for American innocence, for minding one's own business, for being abroad in the great world ("I was driving along the Ventura Freeway the other day . . .").

By that time, Los Angeles had become the capital of America. By that time, most of America looked like L.A.

⌒

I moved to Los Angeles when I was twenty-eight. The part of the city I knew was the west side, the famous side, from West Hollywood to Santa Monica, north along the coast to Malibu and south to the Palisades. The west side did not define Los Angeles any more than Pasadena did. Pasadena was also Los Angeles and Burbank was also Los Angeles and Torrance and Watts, Glendale, Tarzana, Boyle Heights.

Los Angeles had not yet undergone its metamorphosis—not yet the Pacific Rim capital, crowded with immigrants, choking on tragedy. Los Angeles was a Protestant dream of a city, a low city: separate houses, separate lawns, separate cars. Los Angeles was famous among American cities for being the creation of native-born Americans—"internal immigrants" from Iowa or from Brooklyn. Its tone was comic. Its scale was childish—giant donuts and eight-lane freeways. Los Angeles was not the creation of foreign parents escaping tragedy; Los Angeles was the creation of American children.

People I knew on the west side rarely went to the Mexican side. People in the San Fernando Valley expressed fatuous pride at not having been downtown for years. Orange County was the region's largest attempt to secede from itself. But Los Angeles named everything and everyone, claimed every horizon. The city without a center was everywhere the city. L.A. bestowed metropolitan stature on the suburban. America made fun of L.A.

Europeans admired, especially Brits admired Los Angeles.

In London, I met a specimen of one of England's most congealed bloods who was disappointed to learn that I was from San Francisco, oh dear—he much preferred *Los Annjilleeze.*

In 1971, Reynor Banham, a British architectural critic, published his pop celebration of the city, *Los Angeles: The Architecture of Four Ecologies.* Banham wrote disparagingly of the California alternative— San Francisco—with its "prefabricated Yankee houses and prefabricated New England or European attitudes."

Then David Hockney arrived in L.A. from coal-blackened northern England; dyed his hair, changed into shorts; eased into a primary palette. Hockney sold his canvas to the world: suburban tract villas, blond statue boys, an Aqua Velva Mediterranean.

Europe sought freedom from centuries. Europe craved vulgarity. Europe found innocence.

For all its innocence, L.A. was flattered by Europe's attentions in those years. It was the stuff of sonnets—old men taking young men to the opera at the Dorothy Chandler Pavilion. In a way, Europe was turning a trick on L.A., teaching the capital of childish narcissism the confidence of outward regard. L.A. soon came to believe that it was indeed an important city, a world city. "London, Paris, Beverly Hills," read the perfume bottles. British actors and German divas were flown into town like so many truffles. In return, Los Angeles opened the last great European museum in the world, an authentic Greek temple at the edge of the sea.

I imagined I knew some secret about Los Angeles that other people did not know. The architect who Bauhaused his bungalow was living in a house identical to the house I had grown up in. The Sacramento boy still refused to believe that a horizontal city could be a great city. But there were times when Los Angeles amused me for taking all I dismissed as Sacramento and selling it to the world as glamour. What a joke!

I now realize that Los Angeles was doing the same with me. I was a Mexican from the Central Valley—even then L.A. was the second-largest Mexican city in the world—a Mexican kid from the Central Valley with a big nose and glasses. I had spent my life indoors, reading about London.

But in L.A. I passed for a glamour-boy.

"Because you can talk," one angel explained. "All they want is to be amused."

I had always been intellectually arrogant. In L.A., I yearned to become glamorous enough to be humble, in the manner of the angels.

There was nothing reticent about L.A. Glamour was instant. The city took its generosity from the movies. You're beautiful if L.A. says you're beautiful, goddammit.

It was the sons of Jewish immigrants, the haberdasher's son and the tobacconist's son, who established the epic scale of the movies. Movies taught one big lesson: individual lives have scope and grandeur.

Of course L.A. is shallow. Lips that are ten feet long and faces that are forty feet high! But such faces magnify our lives, reassure us that single lives matter. The attention L.A. lavishes on a single face is as generous a metaphor as I can find for the love of God.

My favorite time in the city was twilight, when theater lights dim, when the curtain opens. Then the basin of L.A. released its cocktail scent, lacrimatory, grenadine, rose. I flew through the brimstone canyons in a borrowed convertible, heedless, drum-driven.

To my first L.A. party. Some gallery opening on Melrose. A Scandinavian diplomat stands all alone with a drink melting in his hand. The gallery is too crowded, too noisy. I have to shout my name in the diplomat's ear. A golden ear, like a scroll.

Who was that? the Scandinavian diplomat later asked the gallery owner, who still later told me this story.

"You mean the professional tennis player?" The owner shrugged, confusing me with one of the Bombay brothers then on the international circuit.

(My first role.)

I became a writer in L.A. I jogged, I house-sat, I watched dragonflies patrol swimming pools. I turned the pages of fashion magazines.

I went apartment-hunting in Santa Monica. The real-estate agent drove me in her borrowed convertible to an apartment not far from the beach. The carpet was rust-colored shag. An aluminum sliding glass door led to a redwood deck overlooking the garage. Dark-green plants were suspended in papooses of hemp. The previous tenant had left the kitchen cupboard filled with neatened piles of *Playboy*.

"It only needs . . . ?" the real-estate agent prompted.

There is a picture of me, taken one afternoon at the UCLA track field. I am stretching, standing on one leg like a tropical bird. The spread, when it was published, was titled BOYS OF SUMMER. I was far from being a boy that day, far from the gravity of the twelve-year-old who won Disneyland. And the day was far from a summer's day. It was December 31.

The most depressing time in L.A. is the moment when the screen dies, the theater lights come up. I came out of the theater on Wilshire, my eyes unaccustomed to the light.

Within a month, I am shivering in a thin sports jacket on a pedestrian island in the middle of Market Street in San Francisco. My pants legs are blowing in the wind. Shadows are stumbling around me in the dark, burping into aluminum cans or raging with sacrilege.

I am carrying a suitcase. If the trolley ever comes, I face several months in the basement apartment of my parents' home, completing a book.

The angelic friends told me I was making a mistake.

I told them I could not find a bright enough apartment in L.A. for the price I was willing to pay.

The truth was, I had doubted. The truth was, I didn't have even enough childish imagination to Bauhaus a Santa Monica apartment.

My last L.A. party: a party in Westwood, where I met the idol of my reading life, an extraordinary critic, a superstar among critics, a word-Adonis. Over there, on the sofa by the lamp, someone whispered, What, but here was a little gray man. He crossed his legs like a woman; his trousers were too high; his socks were too low. I noticed the pale hairless shin as he dandled his foot to and fro.

A writer should be at least as glamorous as his calling. What good are all the gauds and greensleeves of Renaissance poetry, what good are all the leggings and ribbons, the codpieces, quivers, circlets of hair, if they make the banquet of a dry little man?

I will stay in Los Angeles forever.

But what good are leggings and ribbons and weight-lifting salons if your soul is the bathroom mirror?

I've got to get out of this town.

For a time in San Francisco, I continued to wear my shirts unbuttoned far down—Aren't you cold? people asked. I astonished a luncheon companion by dipping my fingers into her San Pellegrino water to anoint my hair. But then I left off. I was starting to go bald anyway.

⌒

Entering the city that day, when I was twenty-eight, I drove down Highway One. If there is a best way to enter Los Angeles, it is this way—from the north and along the Pacific Coast Highway. I drove past Pepperdine, past Malibu, past the gas stations and public beaches. A Saturday afternoon in summer, the great city at play, and the only premonition of tragedy a dab of sun block.

I turned left at Wilshire, passed the statue of Santa Monica pining for her son's conversion.

A few weeks before, I had left graduate school, a sad case in my cotton washpants, my short-sleeved white shirt, my head a well of poetry, a staircase of poetry, and the aforementioned glasses. I was spending the weekend with a college friend, now a professor at UCLA.

I found myself in Beverly Hills. Most of the streets were empty of pedestrians. I got out for a walk.

I paused at the window of a store on Camden. I went inside. No one paid much attention to me. I browsed and I watched. I had never seen people so formally dressed for the sun.

A man behind the counter asked if I wanted anything to drink. I recognized him. A bit actor on television. I . . . cast down my eyes, I asked him about an orange shirt, raising the shirt from the counter with one finger.

"Are you really interested . . . ? All those pins . . ."

I told him I was serious.

And so he unbuttoned the shirt and I put it on.

A second clerk came over and draped a sweater over my shoulders. The two men studied the effect as if I weren't there.

Toooo blue.

The bit actor crossed to a mannequin.

"Don't say no till you've tried it on."

He held the coat with its lining outward to receive my arms. I glanced down at the lapels. Gaudy, black-and-white checks. I didn't dare.

Then I looked into the mirror.

Another man came from behind the counter and placed a straw hat on my head.

"There."

At that moment, the door opened and Cesar Romero walked into the mirror.

"Great-looking coat," he said, tapping my shoulder lightly as he passed.

WITOLD RYBCZYNSKI

GETTING AWAY from IT ALL

I THINK I KNOW which will be my most lasting book, or the one to which readers are most attached, or the one that had had the widest influence. I certainly know my own favorite. But my best?

Best, for me, has something to do with workmanship. I chose a magazine essay. I write a great many essays, and since collections are not a favorite of publishers, they don't always get preserved. This one deserves to be. It starts with a small incident, and slowly spreads to encompass a consequential idea: what we do with our spare time. Leisure defines us more than work, and how we build when we build for fun has always represented the acme of a certain sort of architecture: Villa Rotonda, Biltmore House, Fallingwater.

Architecture was my first love, but this is not really an essay about buildings, or at least not only about buildings. It flits from Karen Blixen, to Mozart, to Saranac Lake. The restlessness, for what it's worth, is probably what I like the most about it.

Incidentally, I sent Danièle and Luc my sketch. They did build their house but they ignored my suggestions. *Tant pis.*

—Witold Rybczynski

Last summer, I was in Montreal on a brief visit from Philadelphia, where I now live. I had some small business to conduct there, but the visit was mainly an opportunity to look up old friends. I called Danièle, whom I hadn't seen in a couple of years, and we arranged to have dinner together that evening. She promised to take me to a new bistro, and I looked forward to it: Montreal is no longer the premier city of Canada—that role now belongs to Toronto—and it seemed a bit shabbier than I remembered, but it still has more than its share of exceptional restaurants.

"Shall we meet there?" I asked.

"No," she said, "you must come by the apartment first." She told me excitedly that she wanted to show me the plans of a weekend house that she and Luc were going to build. Danièle is not an architectural neo-phyte: she had been married to an architect for twenty years. True, the marriage had ended in divorce—Luc, her current beau, is in public rela-tions—and I didn't remember her having expressed strong ideas about architecture in the past. But I knew her ex well; he had been a student of mine. You can't live with someone for twenty years and not be influ-enced by what that person does. At least, that's what my wife tells me. So I was curious to see what sort of house Danièle had come up with.

She and Luc and I sat around the kitchen table, and they showed me snapshots of the site, which was in the Laurentian Mountains, a popular recreation area north of Montreal. The Laurentians are an old volcanic range, and the worn, rounded mountains recall the Berkshires or the Catskills, but they're wilder, with fewer signs of human habita-tion. Though I prefer pastoral scenery—rolling fields and gentle hills—to mountains, I had to admit that Danièle and Luc's land was beautiful: a wooded hilltop with long views in several directions.

I sensed that Danièle was a bit nervous about showing me the drawings of the house. That was understandable. She knew that I taught architecture and wrote about domestic design. She and her hus-band had helped my wife and me when we built our own house in the country. Now it was her turn. Building a house for yourself is exciting, because of the feeling of possibility that a new house carries, and because creating shelter is a basic human urge, whether or not you are an architect. It is the same urge that makes children erect playhouses out of blankets and cardboard boxes, and build sandcastles at the beach. But building a house—a real house—is also scary, and not just because of the money involved or the fear of making mistakes. A new house is revealing. It tells you—and everyone else—"This is how I live. This is what's important to me. This is what I dream about." I think that's why home magazines—from *Ladies' Home Journal* to *Architectural Digest*—have always been popular. It's not just a matter of looking for decorating hints. Rather, houses intrigue us because they tell us so much about their owners.

Danièle spread out the sketches, which had been prepared by a local architect. Siting is always a crucial decision for a country house. I could see that the house would stand almost at the top of the hill, and so would be approached from below, as, ideally, it should be; walking down to a house is always unpleasant. The hilltop had obviously been chosen for the views it offered, but it also meant that the house would be some distance from the road, and would require a short walk through the trees to arrive at the front door.

The floor layout of the house was simple enough. Because of the sloping ground, the lower level, containing two bedrooms and a bathroom, would be dug partly into the ground. The floor above, which could be entered directly from the upper part of the slope, would hold the living areas, and there would be a sleeping loft in a sort of tower. Danièle explained that they wanted to be able to rent a room to skiers during the winter season, which was why the lower level would have its own front door and could be separated from the rest of the house. The exterior would be mainly wood, with several sloping roofs. It was hard to put your finger on the architectural style of the house. It wasn't going to have the curved eaves and dormer windows of the traditional Breton style, which is still popular with many Québécois. Although the functional-looking window frames and rather spare exterior couldn't be called old-fashioned, neither did they seem aggressively modern. I suppose most people would use the term "contemporary."

The three of us got into a long discussion about how best to rearrange one of the bathrooms. I pointed out that if they moved the door to the other side and changed the site of the toilet, they could gain space and improve the circulation in the kitchen area as well. Not very inspirational stuff. I could see that Luc and Danièle expected something more. I had unconsciously fallen into a bad habit of architecture teachers: if you really don't know what to say about a project, focus on some practical improvement, no matter how small. How often had I sat on design juries at the university, taking part in interminable discussions about fire exits or corridor widths, when the real problem was something else entirely.

It wasn't that Danièle and Luc's house looked boring—quite the opposite. "The architect told us that she worked hard to make each side of the house different," Danièle explained. Differences there certainly were, and, I thought, that was part of the problem. The little house was trying too hard to be unusual and interesting. The perimeter was animated by indentations and protrusions—architectural bumps and grinds. Instead of a single sheltering gable, the roof was broken up into several slopes. This is a favorite device of commercial homebuilders and is obviously a crowd pleaser, though the roof has always seemed to me an odd thing to spend your money on. The complexity of the roof was mirrored by the intricacy of the fenestration:

there were half a dozen different window shapes and sizes. The modest house was hardly in a league with Frank Gehry and Peter Eisenman, but it *was* busy.

I realized that I had to say something more substantive about the house, but I wasn't sure where to start. I think that small, inexpensive houses like Danièle and Luc's should be as simple as possible. This is partly a question of economics; complexity costs money, after all, and I would rather see a restricted budget devoted to better-quality materials than to architectural bravura. But it is also an aesthetic issue. I like plain farmhouses and straightforward country buildings. They usually look good in the landscape, and they have a kind of directness and honesty that appeals to me. True, they are often really just boxes, but boxes can be given charm through relatively inexpensive details of construction, such as bay windows, trellises, and even shutters.

A simple way to dress up a house is to add a porch. Porches, with their columns, balustrades, and ornamental fretwork, are pleasant to look at, and they are also pleasant places to sit. They are like rooms, but without walls, and they encourage the sort of lazy inactivity that has always seemed to me to be the essence of leisure. I noticed that Danièle's house didn't have any covered outdoor area, and I suggested that they might consider adding a screened porch. This would also be a useful feature, since the Laurentian summers are notorious for their mosquitoes and blackflies.

"No," Luc said. "A porch won't do at all. Porches and balconies are something for a city house. We want our house to look rustic."

That was interesting. I had always associated porches and verandas with country houses. Evidently, for Danièle and Luc they were an urban feature. (Indeed, Montreal row houses traditionally do have verandas.) A little later, they asked me what sort of material I thought should be used to finish the inside walls. I said that I liked plaster wallboard—that it was inexpensive, you could paint it whatever color you wanted, and, furthermore, it was fire-resistant—an important consideration when you're building miles from a fire station. They looked skeptical and said that they had been thinking, rather, of wood. "We want this to be a different sort of place, where we can get away from our city life," Luc said.

A lot of architecture has to do with images—and imaginings. For one person, getting away means a broad porch with a rocking chair and a slowly turning ceiling fan. The image may be the result of a remembered family photograph, or a painting, or even the experience of a real porch somewhere. That particular porch image has haunted me for years—I think I saw it first in a magazine ad for whiskey. And one of the side benefits of watching the film *Out of Africa* is the beautiful porch of Karen Blixen's plantation house in Kenya, with Mozart's Clarinet Concerto playing on a windup gramophone. Alas, for Luc a porch was just a utilitarian appendage. Moreover, the image it conjured up for him was not rural but urban. I also had the impression that he considered porches to be old-fashioned—or maybe just places for old people.

I have always liked farmhouse kitchens—large, comfortable rooms where you can cook and eat and socialize around the kitchen table. (That's probably a remembered image, too.) The plans of Danièle and Luc's house, on the other hand, showed a small efficiency kitchen, with a separate dining area. It was an arrangement that reminded me—but, obviously, not them—of a city apartment. I realized that their idea of getting away from it all was more dynamic than mine: not a cabin in the woods but a striking ski chalet on a hilltop, with different views from each room, beamed ceilings, knotty-pine walls, and a dramatic fireplace. I was starting to understand why the house looked the way it did. It was not a question of money—theirs was hardly an extravagant house. It reflected a different idea of rusticity.

Getting away from it all has a long history; almost as soon as people started living in towns, they felt the need to build country retreats. In ancient times, it was the common practice of wealthy Romans to decamp periodically to country estates. "You should take the first opportunity yourself to leave the din, the futile bustle, and the useless occupations of the city," Pliny the Younger wrote in a letter to a friend. Pliny owned two country retreats, one a large agricultural estate in present-day Umbria, the other his famous seaside villa in Latium, of which he wrote, "There I do most of my writing, and, instead of the land I lack, I work to cultivate myself." The sentiment—re-creation— is recognizably modern. Modern-sounding, too, is the Renaissance architect Leon Battista Alberti's advice that "if the villa is not distant, but close by a gate of the city, it will make it easier and more convenient to flit, with wife and children, between town and villa, whenever desirable."

In nineteenth-century America, such flitting usually meant taking a steamboat or a train. Summer houses sprang up along the Hudson River, in New York, and the Schuylkill, in Philadelphia, or in places like Newport, Rhode Island. In Newport you'll find many early examples of the Shingle Style, one of the high accomplishments of American architecture. The Watts Sherman house, designed by the great architect H. H. Richardson in 1874, is irregular in composition, and the granite, the half-timbering, and the wooden shingles on the exterior give it the picturesque appearance that is a trademark of the Shingle Style. Still, it is provided with a drawing room, a dining room, and a library, and so is not really a radical departure from a typical middle-class suburban or urban house of the period.

Although rich New Yorkers commuted to their villas in Newport, these were summer houses, not weekend houses. Indeed, the full weekend—a two-day holiday at the end of the workweek—didn't appear until the twentieth century. It arrived first in Britain, as a one-and-a-half-day holiday, and by the early nineteen-hundreds more and more Americans were also working "short Saturdays." Eventually the five-day workweek became commonplace, and the combination of the two-day holiday and the automobile produced the vast proliferation of weekend retreats that we know today.

The weekend cottage continues the time-tested tradition of the summer getaway house, but with a crucial difference. Instead of being used for an entire season, it is chiefly a two-day retreat. Hence it is less a place of long and lazy summers than of sometimes frantic spurts of recreation. Perhaps that's why the architecture is often intentionally unusual, with dramatic fireplaces, tall spaces, and cantilevered decks. That was what Luc meant when he said he wanted "a different sort of place." It was probably the late architect Charles Moore who started the trend toward spatial excitement. In the mid-nineteen-sixties he designed a series of weekend houses, chiefly in Northern California, with deceptively simple exteriors and with interiors that were a cross between barns and jungle gyms. Although designed with considerable sophistication, these houses could also be described as the architectural equivalent of the then popular leisure suit. That is, they were intended to put people instantaneously in a different mood and also to tell the world that here the owner was off duty. Moore's approach was influential, and versions of his houses sprang up in vacation spots from Colorado to Vermont.

Like many people, I spend my weekends in a worn pair of shorts

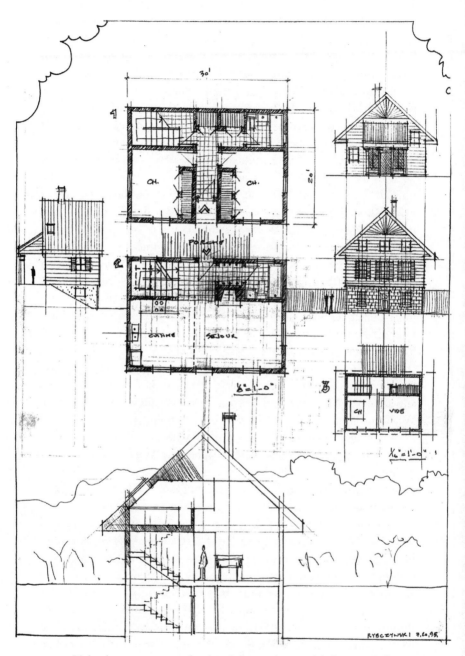

It's hard to comment on—let alone judge—other people's fantasies. Still,
I couldn't resist making my own sketches for Danièle and Luc's house.

and an old polo shirt. Perhaps that's why my ideal of a weekend house is more like a farmhouse—commodious rather than exciting, a place to kick your shoes off and relax, a place that can get scuffed up and still feel comfortable. Sculptural staircases and eye-popping fireplaces are not a priority. Now, I don't want to give the impression that I think weekend houses should be Thoreau-style shacks, without conveniences, or even without luxuries. I would have no objection to a Miele range and a Sub-Zero refrigerator in my country kitchen. After all, that has always been the paradoxical thing about second homes: we want to feel that we're roughing it, but we want our comforts, too. Pliny schlepped around his villa in an old tunic, but he had a proper warmed swimming bath as well as a banqueting hall. When Richardson designed the Watts Sherman house in Newport, he made it look rustic, but he also incorporated a novel amenity: central heating. Even Thoreau, whose cabin at Walden Pond didn't have a kitchen (in warm weather, he cooked outside over an open fire), regularly walked to nearby Concord to have dinner at friends' houses.

I remember once visiting an Adirondack camp on Lower Saranac Lake. It was one of many in the area that had been built by rich New Yorkers during the Gilded Age. The house itself was typical—a charming, rough-hewn log building with a massive granite fireplace, columns made of peeled and polished tree trunks, and spartan Arts-and-Crafts-style furniture. Here was rusticity laid on with a trowel. When this particular camp, Knollwood, was built, in 1899, it consisted of six cottages, a so-called casino (a social gathering place, not a gambling hall), and a boathouse, all designed by William Coulter, the architect of some of the buildings at Sagamore, the Vanderbilts' famous camp. Although the ample cottages contained several bedrooms, there were originally only small service kitchens. That was because the six families and their guests had their meals prepared and served to them in the casino, which did have a large kitchen. You went boating on the lake and hiking in the forest, but that was no reason you couldn't have a proper dinner, prepared by your New York cook. The Knollwood boathouse contains canoes and handmade Adirondack guide boats but also, on the upper floor, a huge billiard table. I don't think I would require a billiard table in my ideal weekend house, but, on the other hand, I wouldn't do without a compact-disk player. Getting away from it all has always involved compromise as well as a certain degree of make-believe.

It's hard to comment on—let alone judge—other people's fantasies. If Danièle and Luc wanted a house in the country, well, they would have to make their own compromises. I don't think I was really much help to my friends; our ideas of weekend houses were probably just too different. Anyway, we all went out to dinner, the atmosphere in the bistro was convivial, the food was excellent, and everyone had a good time. A week later, when I got home to Philadelphia, I just couldn't resist making some sketches of my own, trying to accommodate all their requirements. I drew a little cottage, twenty feet by thirty feet, clapboard above and with a stone base—for the two bedrooms—below. The house was sheltered by a broad gable roof (to accommodate the sleeping loft). The loft looked down on the main living space, a large family room with a kitchen at one end and a sitting area at the other. In the center of the room, a Franklin stove served for warming cold toes and cold plates. A pair of glazed doors opened onto a large screened porch. It was only a sketch, just to keep my hand in, I told myself. But if I shut my eyes I could almost hear the strains of the Clarinet Concerto in the woods.

DAVID SEDARIS

REPEAT AFTER ME

WHILE I'M SURE THE Quality Paperback Book Club means well, I'd feel much more comfortable contributing to an anthology titled "This One's Not So Bad," or "Here Is My Least Worst." The word *Best* is causing me problems, so instead I've chosen what I think of as my favorite story, "Repeat After Me." I wrote it in the summer of 2001, and rewrote it the following fall, while on a lecture tour of the United States. It was right after September 11th, an odd time to travel the country, and reading the story today I am reminded of long security lines, and groups of tired passengers standing around airport televisions. Mostly though, "Repeat After Me" causes me to think about my family, and of the various ways I have exploited them over the years. It's not a pretty picture, but I like the way that the story moves, pausing to light on parrots and maimed Chinese box turtles. If nothing else, I think it accurately conveys the laziness and ease of spending time with someone you love.

—David Sedaris

Although we'd discussed my upcoming visit to Winston-Salem, my sister and I didn't make exact arrangements until the eve of my arrival, when I phoned from a hotel in Salt Lake City.

"I'll be at work when you arrive," she said, "so I'm thinking I'll just leave the key under the hour ott near the ack toor."

"The what?"

"Hour ott."

I thought she had something in her mouth until I realized she was speaking in code.

"What are you, on a speakerphone at a methadone clinic? Why can't you just tell me where you put the goddam house key?"

Her voice dropped to a whisper. "I just don't know that I trust these things."

"Are you on a cell phone?"

448

"Of course not" she said. "This is just a regular cordless, but still, you have to be careful."

When I suggested that actually she *didn't* have to be careful, Lisa resumed her normal tone of voice, saying, "Really? But I heard . . ."

My sister's the type who religiously watches the fear segments of her local Eyewitness News broadcasts, retaining nothing but the headline. She remembers that applesauce can kill you but forgets that in order to die, you have to inject it directly into your bloodstream. Pronouncements that cell-phone conversations may be picked up by strangers mix with the reported rise of both home burglaries and brain tumors, meaning that as far as she's concerned, all telecommunication is potentially life-threatening. If she didn't watch it on the news, she read it in *Consumer Reports* or heard it thirdhand from a friend of a friend of a friend whose ear caught fire while dialing her answering machine. Everything is dangerous all of the time, and if it's not yet been pulled off the shelves, then it's certainly under investigation—so there.

"Okay," I said, "but can you tell me *which* hour ott? The last time I was there you had quite a few of them."

"It's ed," she told me. "Well . . . edd*ish*."

I arrived at Lisa's house late the following afternoon, found the key beneath the flowerpot, and let myself in through the back door. A lengthy note on the coffee table explained how I might go about operating everything from the television to the waffle iron, each carefully detailed procedure ending with the line *"Remember to turn off and unplug after use."* At the bottom of page three, a postscript informed me that if the appliance in question had no plug—the dishwasher, for instance—I should make sure it had completed its cycle and was cool to the touch before leaving the room. The note reflected a growing hysteria, its subtext shrieking, *Oh-my-God-he's-going-to-be-alone-in-my-house-for-close-to-an-hour.* She left her work number, her husband's work number, and the number of the next-door neighbor, adding that she didn't know the woman very well, so I probably shouldn't bother her unless it was an emergency. "P.P.S. She's a Baptist, so don't tell her you're gay."

The last time I was alone at my sister's place she was living in a white-brick apartment complex occupied by widows and single, middle-aged working women. This was in the late seventies, when we were supposed to be living in dorms. College hadn't quite worked out the way she'd expected, and after two years in Virginia she'd returned to Raleigh and taken a job at a wineshop. It was a normal-enough life for a twenty-one-year-old, but being a dropout was not what she had planned for herself. Worse than that, it had not been planned *for* her. As children we'd been assigned certain roles—leader, bum, troublemaker, slut—titles that effectively told us who we were. As the oldest, smartest, and bossiest, it was naturally assumed that Lisa would shoot to the top of her field, earning a master's degree in manipulation and eventually taking over a medium-size country. We'd always known her as an authority figure, and while we took a certain joy in watching her fall, it was disorienting to see her with so little confidence. Suddenly she was relying on other people's opinions, following their advice and withering at the slightest criticism.

Do you really think so? Really? She was putty.

My sister needed patience and understanding, but more often than not, I found myself wanting to shake her. If the oldest wasn't who she was supposed to be, then what did it mean for the rest of us?

Lisa had been marked Most Likely to Succeed, and so it confused her to be ringing up gallon jugs of hearty burgundy. I had been branded as lazy and irresponsible, so it felt right when I, too, dropped out of college and wound up living back in Raleigh. After being thrown out of my parents' house, I went to live with Lisa in her white-brick complex. It was a small studio apartment—the adult version of her childhood bedroom—and when I eventually left her with a broken stereo and an unpaid eighty-dollar phone bill, the general consensus was, "Well, what did you expect?"

I might reinvent myself to strangers, but to this day, as far as my family is concerned, I'm still the one most likely to set your house on fire. While I accepted my lowered expectations, Lisa fought hard to regain her former title. The wineshop was just a temporary setback, and she left shortly after becoming the manager. Photography interested her, so she taught herself to use a camera, ultimately landing a job in the photo department of a large international drug company, where she took pictures of germs, viruses, and people reacting to germs and viruses. On weekends, for extra money, she photographed weddings, which really wasn't that much of a stretch. Then she got married herself and quit the drug company in order to earn an

English degree. When told there was very little call for thirty-page essays on Jane Austen, she got a real estate license. When told the housing market was down, she returned to school to study plants. Her husband, Bob, got a job in Winston-Salem, and so they moved, buying a new three-story house in a quiet suburban neighborhood. It was strange to think of my sister living in such a grown-up place, and I was relieved to find that neither she nor Bob particularly cared for it. The town was nice enough, but the house itself had a way of aging things. Stand outside and you looked, if not young, then at least relatively carefree. Step indoors and you automatically put on twenty years and a 401(k) plan.

My sister's home didn't really lend itself to snooping, and so I spent my hour in the kitchen, making small talk with Henry. It was the same conversation we'd had the last time I saw him, yet still I found it fascinating. He asked how I was doing, I said I was all right, and then, as if something might have drastically changed within the last few seconds, he asked again.

Of all the elements of my sister's adult life—the house, the husband, the sudden interest in plants—the most unsettling is Henry. Technically he's a blue-fronted Amazon, but to the average layman, he's just a big parrot—the type you might see on the shoulder of a pirate.

"How you doing?" The third time he asked, it sounded as if he really cared. I approached his cage with a detailed answer, and when he lunged for the bars, I screamed like a girl and ran out of the room.

"Henry likes you," my sister said a short while later. She'd just returned from her job at the plant nursery and was sitting at the table, unlacing her sneakers. "See the way he's fanning his tail? He'd never do that for Bob. Would you, Henry?"

Bob had returned from work a few minutes earlier and immediately headed upstairs to spend time with his own bird, a balding green-cheeked conure named José. I'd thought the two pets might enjoy an occasional conversation, but it turns out they can't stand each other.

"Don't even *mention* José in front of Henry," Lisa whispered. Bob's bird squawked from the upstairs study, and the parrot responded with a series of high, piercing barks. It was a trick he'd picked up from Lisa's border collie, Chessie, and what was disturbing was that he sounded *exactly* like a dog. Just as, when speaking English, he sounded exactly like Lisa. It was creepy to hear my sister's voice coming from a beak, but I couldn't say it didn't please me.

"Who's hungry?" she asked.

"Who's hungry?" the voice repeated.

I raised my hand, and she offered Henry a peanut. Watching him take it in his claw, his belly sagging almost to the perch, I could understand what someone might see in a parrot. Here was this strange little fatso living in my sister's kitchen, a sympathetic listener turning again and again to ask, "So, really, how are you?"

I'd asked her the same question and she'd said, "Oh, fine. You know." She's afraid to tell me anything important, knowing I'll only turn around and write about it. In my mind, I'm like a friendly junkman, building things from the little pieces of scrap I find here and there, but my family's started to see things differently. Their personal lives are the so-called pieces of scrap I so casually pick up, and they're sick of it. More and more often their stories begin with the line "You have to swear you will never repeat this." I always promise, but it's generally understood that my word means nothing.

I'd come to Winston-Salem to address the students at a local college, and then again to break some news. Sometimes when you're stoned it's fun to sit around and think of who might play you in the movie version of your life. What makes it fun is that no one is actually going to make a movie of your life. Lisa and I no longer got stoned, so it was all the harder to announce that my book had been optioned, meaning that, in fact, someone was going to make a movie of our lives—not a student, but a real director people had actually heard of.

"*A what?*"

I explained that he was Chinese, and she asked if the movie would be in Chinese.

"No," I said, "he lives in America. In California. He's been here since he was a baby."

"Then what does it matter if he's Chinese?"

"Well," I said, "he's got . . . you know, a sensibility."

"Oh brother," she said.

I looked to Henry for support, and he growled at me.

"So now we have to be in a movie?" She picked her sneakers off the floor and tossed them into the laundry room. "Well," she said, "I can tell you right now that you are not dragging my bird into this." The movie was to be based on our pre-parrot years, but the moment she put her foot down I started wondering who we might get to play the role of Henry. "I know what you're thinking," she said. "And the answer is no."

Once, at a dinner party, I met a woman whose parrot had learned to imitate the automatic icemaker on her new refrigerator. "That's what happens when they're left alone," she'd said. It was the most depressing bit of information I'd heard in quite a while, and it stuck with me for weeks. Here was this creature, born to mock its jungle neighbors, and it wound up doing impressions of man-made kitchen appliances. I repeated the story to Lisa, who told me that neglect had nothing to do with it. She then prepared a cappuccino, setting the stage for Henry's pitch-perfect imitation of the milk steamer. "He can do the blender, too," she said.

She opened the cage door, and as we sat down to our coffees, Henry glided down onto the table. "Who wants a kiss?" She stuck out her tongue, and he accepted the tip gingerly between his upper and lower beak. I'd never dream of doing such a thing, not because it's across-the-board disgusting but because he would have bitten the shit out of me. Though Henry might occasionally fan his tail in my direction, it is understood that he is loyal to only one person, which, I think, is another reason my sister is so fond of him.

"Was that a good kiss?" she asked. "Did you like that?"

I expected a yes-or-no answer and was disappointed when he responded with the exact same question: "Did you like that?" Yes, parrots can talk, but unfortunately they have no idea what they're actually saying. When she first got him, Henry spoke the Spanish he'd learned from his captors. Asked if he'd had a good night's sleep, he'd say simply, "*Hola*," or "*Bueno*." He goes through phases, favoring an often repeated noise or sentence, and then moving on to something else. When our mother died, Henry learned how to cry. He and Lisa would set each other off, and the two of them would go on for hours. A few years later, in the midst of a brief academic setback, she trained him to act as her emotional cheerleader. I'd call and hear him in the background, screaming, "We love you, Lisa!" and "You can do it!" This was replaced, in time, with the far more practical "Where are my keys?"

After finishing our coffees, Lisa and I drove to Greensboro, where I delivered my scheduled lecture. That is to say, I read stories about my family. After the reading, I answered questions about them, thinking all the while how odd it was that these strangers seemed to know so much about my brother and sisters. In order to sleep at night, I have to remove myself from the equation, pretending that the people I love expressly choose to expose themselves. Amy breaks up with a boyfriend and sends out a press release. Paul regularly discusses his bowel movements on daytime talk shows. I'm not the conduit, but just a poor typist stuck in the middle. It's a delusion much harder to maintain when a family member is actually *in* the audience.

The day after the reading, Lisa called in sick and we spent the afternoon running errands. Winston-Salem is a city of plazas—midsize shopping centers, each built around an enormous grocery store. I was looking for cheap cartons of cigarettes, so we drove from plaza to plaza, comparing prices and talking about our sister Gretchen. A year earlier she'd bought a pair of flesh-eating Chinese box turtles with pointed noses and spooky translucent skin. The two of them lived in an outdoor pen and were relatively happy until raccoons dug beneath the wire, chewing the front legs off the female and the rear legs off her husband.

"I may have the order wrong," Lisa said. "But you get the picture."

The couple survived the attack and continued to track the live mice that constituted their diet, propelling themselves forward like a pair of half-stripped Volkswagens.

"The sad part is that it took her two weeks to notice it," Lisa said. "Two weeks!" She shook her head and drove past our exit. "I'm sorry, but I don't know how a responsible pet owner could go that long without noticing a thing like that. It's just not right."

According to Gretchen, the turtles had no memories of their former limbs, but Lisa wasn't buying it. "Oh, come on," she said. "They must at least have phantom pains. I mean, how can a living creature not mind losing its legs? If anything like that happened to Chessie, I honestly don't know how I could live with myself." Her eyes misted and she wiped them with the back of her hand. "My little collie gets a tick and I go crazy."

Lisa's a person who once witnessed a car accident, saying, "I just hope there isn't a dog in the backseat." Human suffering doesn't faze her much, but she'll cry for days over a sick-pet story.

"Did you see that movie about the Cuban guy?" she asked. "It played here for a while but I wouldn't go. Someone told me a dog gets killed in the first fifteen minutes, so I said forget it."

I reminded her that the main character died as well, horribly, of AIDS, and she pulled into the parking lot, saying, "Well, I just hope it wasn't a *real* dog."

I wound up buying cigarettes at Tobacco USA, a discount store with the name of a theme park. Lisa had officially quit smoking ten years earlier and might have taken it up again were it not for Chessie, who, according to the vet, was predisposed to lung ailments. "I don't want to give her secondhand emphysema, but I sure wouldn't mind taking some of this weight off. Tell me the truth, do I look fat to you?"

"Not at all."

She turned sideways and examined herself in the front window of Tobacco USA. "You're lying."

"Well, isn't that what you want me to say?"

"Yes," she said. "But I want you to really mean it."

But I *had* meant it. It wasn't the weight I noticed so much as the clothing she wore to cover it up. The loose, baggy pants and oversize shirts falling halfway to her knees: This was the look she'd adopted a few months earlier, after she and her husband had gone to the mountains to visit Bob's parents. Lisa had been sitting beside the fire, and when she scooted her chair toward the center of the room, her father-in-law said, "What's the matter, Lisa? Getting too fat—I mean hot. Getting too hot?"

He tried to cover his mistake, but it was too late. The word had already been seared into my sister's brain.

"Will I have to be fat in the movie?" she asked.

"Of course not," I said. "You'll be just . . . like you are."

"Like I am according to who," she asked. "The Chinese?"

"Well, not *all* of them," I said. "Just one."

Normally, if at home during a weekday, Lisa likes to read nineteenth-century novels, breaking at one to eat lunch and watch a television program called *Matlock*. By the time we finished with my errands, the day's broadcast had already ended, and so we decided to go to the movies—whatever she wanted. She chose the story of a young Englishwoman struggling to remain happy while trying to lose a few extra pounds, but in the end she got her plazas confused, and we arrived at the wrong theater just in time to watch *You Can Count on Me*, the Kenneth Lonergan movie in which an errant brother visits his older sister. Normally, Lisa's the type who talks from one end of the picture to the other. A character will spread mayonnaise onto a chicken sandwich and she'll lean over, whispering, "One time, I was doing that? And the knife fell into the toilet." Then she'll settle back in her seat and I'll spend the next ten minutes wondering why on earth someone would make a chicken sandwich in the bathroom. This movie reflected our lives so eerily that for the first time in recent memory, she was stunned into silence. There was no physical resemblance between us and the main characters—the brother and sister were younger and orphaned—but like us, they'd stumbled to adulthood playing the worn, confining roles assigned to them as children. Every now and then one of them would break free, but for the most part they behaved not as they wanted to but as they were expected to. In brief, a guy shows up at his sister's house and stays for a few weeks until she kicks him out. She's not evil about it, but having him around forces her to think about things she'd rather not, which is essentially what family members do, at least the family members my sister and I know.

On leaving the theater, we shared a long, uncomfortable silence. Between the movie we'd just seen and the movie about to be made, we both felt awkward and self-conscious, as if we were auditioning for the roles of ourselves. I started in with some benign bit of gossip I'd heard concerning the man who'd played the part of the brother but stopped after the first few sentences, saying that, on second thought, it wasn't very interesting. She couldn't think of anything, either, and so we said nothing, each of us imagining a bored audience shifting in their seats.

We stopped for gas on the way home and were parking in front of her house when she turned to relate what I've come to think of as the quintessential Lisa story. "One time," she said, "one time I was out driving?" The incident began with a quick trip to the grocery store and ended, unexpectedly, with a wounded animal stuffed into a pillowcase and held to the tailpipe of her car. Like most of my sister's stories, it provoked a startling mental picture, capturing a moment in time when one's actions seem both unimaginably cruel and completely natural. Details were carefully chosen and the pace built gradually, punctuated by a series of well-timed pauses. "And then . . . and then . . ." She reached the inevitable conclusion and just as I started to laugh, she put her head against the steering wheel and fell apart. It wasn't the gentle flow of tears you might release when recalling an isolated action or event, but the violent explosion that comes when you realize that all such events are connected, forming an endless chain of guilt and suffering.

I instinctively reached for the notebook I keep in my pocket and she grabbed my hand to stop me. "If you ever," she said, "*ever* repeat that story, I will never talk to you again."

In the movie version of our lives, I would have turned to offer her comfort, reminding her, convincing her that the action she'd described had been kind and just. Because it was. She's incapable of acting otherwise.

In the *real* version of our lives, my immediate goal was simply to change her mind. "Oh come on," I said. "The story's really funny, and, I mean, it's not like *you're* going to do anything with it."

Your life, your privacy, your occasional sorrow—it's not like you're going to do anything with it. Is this the brother I always was, or the brother I have become?

I'd worried that, in making the movie, the director might get me and my family wrong, but now a worse thought occurred to me: What if he got us right?

Dusk. The camera pans an unremarkable suburban street, moving in on a parked four-door automobile, where a small, evil man turns to his sobbing sister, saying, "What if I use the story but say that it happened to a friend?"

But maybe that's not the end. Maybe before the credits roll, we see this same man getting out of bed in the middle of the night, walking past his sister's room, and continuing downstairs into the kitchen. A switch is thrown, and we notice, in the far corner of the room, a large standing birdcage covered with a tablecloth. He approaches it carefully and removes the cloth, waking a blue-fronted Amazon parrot, its eyes glowing red in the sudden light. Through everything that's gone before this moment, we understand that the man has something important to say. From his own mouth the words are meaningless, and so he pulls up a chair. The clock reads three A.M., then four, then five, as he sits before the brilliant bird, repeating slowly and clearly the words "Forgive me. Forgive me. Forgive me."

HUSTON SMITH

FLAKES of FIRE,
HANDFULS of LIGHT

AMONG THE VOCATIONAL SLOTS available during my lifetime, none could have fitted me better than that of university professor. I have been happy in its no longer ivy-covered towers, for it has allowed me to do exactly what I want to do in my career. At the same time I have had a lover's quarrel with the university from the start, for it falls far short of what it might be if it were not hampered by unwitting assumptions that impede its search for truth.

When, in the academic year 1976-77, the humanities division of Syracuse University, where I was then teaching, moved into a new building and a lecture series was mounted to celebrate the occasion, I was delegated to speak for the religion department in the series. I think this transcription of my lecture comes as close as any brief statement has to summarizing what I have tried to say in my career. I like it.

—Huston Smith

THE HUMANITIES AS UNCONTROLLED EXPERIMENT

Those of us who saw *Einstein's Universe*, that remarkable television program the British Broadcasting Company created for the centennial of Einstein's birth last March, remember the words that laced it like a theme: "Einstein would have wanted us to say it in the simplest possible way. Space tells matter how to move; matter tells space how to warp." How, in the simplest possible way, can we describe the burden and promise of the humanities today?

I. THE HUMANITIES

First, by identifying their central concern. They have many facets, of course, but we will not be far from the mark if we think of them as custodians of the human image;[1] one way or another, in cycles and epicycles, they circle the question of who we take ourselves to be—what it means to be a human being, to live a human life. We know that self-images are important, for endowed as we are with self-consciousness, we draw portraits of ourselves and then fashion our lives to their likenesses, coming to resemble the portraits we draw. Psychologists who are professionally concerned with behavior modification tell us that a revised self-image is the most important single factor in human change. It is when a person sees himself differently that new ways of behaving come to seem feasible and appropriate.

If then (in company with religion and the arts in our culture at large) the humanities are custodians of the human self-image, what is their burden and promise today?

II. BURDENS: SOCIAL AND CONCEPTUAL

Turning first to their burdens, they are of two kinds, social and conceptual. As the first of these stems from our culture's institutional forms I shall let a social scientist, a colleague, Manfred Stanley, tell the story. "It is by now a Sunday-supplement commonplace," he writes, "that the social, economic and technological modernization of the world is accompanied by a spiritual malaise that has come to be called alienation."[2] The social changes contributing to this alienation reduce most importantly, I suspect—I am not attributing this further point to Professor Stanley—to disruption of the primary communities in which life used to be lived. No longer rooted in such communities, our lives are seen less in their entirety, as wholes, by others; and in consequence (so fully are our perceptions of ourselves governed by others' perceptions of us) we have difficulty seeing *ourselves* as wholes. High mobility decrees that our associates know only limited time segments of our lives—childhood, college, mid-life career, retirement—while the compartmentalization of industrial life insures that at any given life stage our associates will know us in only one of our roles: worker, member of the family, civic associate, or friend. Once again, none know us whole, and as our fellows do not so know us, we have trouble seeing ourselves as wholes as well.

This scattering of our lives in time and their splintering in space tends to fragment self-image and in extreme cases to pulverize it.

Engendering Robert Lifton's "protean man" and abetting the existentialist's conclusion that we *have* no essence, the disruption of the primary community is, as I say, the heaviest burden I see institutional changes laying on our efforts to see ourselves as complete persons. But the conceptual problem our age has wrought is, if anything, even weightier. By this conceptual problem I mean the world view the modern West has settled into: its notion of "the scheme of things entire" as it finally is. The statement by Professor Stanley that I began quoting speaks to this conceptual side of our predicament too—so precisely, in fact, that I shall continue to let him speak for me. He was noting, you will recall, the alienation that modernization has occasioned, and having alluded to some of its social causes drives straight to the heart of the matter as follows:

> At its most fundamental level, the diagnosis of alienation is based on the view that modernization forces upon us a world that, although baptized as real by science, is denuded of all humanly recognizable qualities; beauty and ugliness, love and hate, passion and fulfillment, salvation and damnation. It is not, of course, being claimed that such matters are not part of the existential realities of human life. It is rather that the scientific world view makes it illegitimate to speak of them as being "objectively" part of the world, forcing us instead to define such evaluation and such emotional experiences as "merely subjective" projections of people's inner lives.
>
> The world, once an "enchanted garden," to use Max Weber's memorable phrase, has now become disenchanted, deprived of purpose and direction, bereft—in these senses—of life itself. All that which is allegedly basic to the specifically human status in nature comes to be forced back upon the precincts of the "subjective" which, in turn, is pushed by the modern scientific view ever more into the province of dreams and illusions.[3]

To say that it is difficult—burdensome—to maintain a respectable image of man in a world like this is an understatement. The truth is, it is impossible.[4] If modern man feels alienated from this world he sees enveloping him, it shows that his wits are still intact. He *should* feel alienated. For no permanent standoff between self and world is possible; eventually there will be a showdown. And when it comes, there is no doubt about the outcome: the world will win—for a starter, it is bigger than we are. So a meaningful life is not finally possible in a meaningless world. It is provisionally possible—there can be a temporary standoff between self and world—but finally it is not possible.[5] Either the garden is indeed disenchanted, in which case the humanities deserve to be on the defensive, no noble image being possible in an a-noble—I do not say ignoble—world; or the garden remains enchanted and the humanities should help make this fact known.

To set out to reverse the metaphysical momentum of the last four hundred years might seem a task so difficult as to be daunting, but there is another way to look at the matter. Here, surely, is something worth doing, a project to elicit the best that is within us including resources we might not know we possess; so even if we fail in the attempt we shall do so knowing the joy that comes from noble doings. To get the project underway we must advance into enemy territory— we shall find it to be a contemporary form of what Plato called "upside down existence"—and to do this we must cross a no-man's-land of methodology, "no-man's" being precise here because if either side were to capture it the battle would be theirs. So, a short interlude on method to establish the ground rules for the "war of the worlds" (read "war of the world views") we are about to begin.

III. METHODOLOGICAL INTERLUDE

In a university setting, any move to reinstate the enchanted garden will naturally be met by the question: "How do you *know* it is enchanted?" If we answer that we experience it so, that we find ourselves ravished by its mystery and washed by its beauty and presences—not always, of course, but enough to sustain conviction[6]—we shall be told that this is not to know, it is merely to feel. This crude response requires of us a choice. Either we blow the whistle at once on this cramped and positivistic definition of knowledge (as we shall soon see, its willingness to dignify as knowledge only such kinds as hold the promise of augmenting our power to control rules out the very possibility of knowing things that might be superior to us, it being possible to control only subordinates or at most equals; in a word, it rules out the possibility of knowing transcendence) or we can let this restriction of knowledge to what-can-be-proved stand, in which case knowledge becomes a foundation (one among several) for a higher epistemic yield—call it insight, wisdom, understanding, or even intelligence if we use that word to include, as it did for the Scholastics, Plato's "eye of the soul" that can discern spiritual objects. What we must never, never do is make proof our master. Fear that if we do not subject ourselves to it we may wander into error will always tempt us to this slavery,[7] but to yield to the temptation spells disaster for our discipline. Even physicists, if they be great ones, see (as Richard Feynman pointed out in his Nobel Lecture) that "a very great deal more truth can become known than can be proven." "Not to prove, but to discover"[8] must be the humanities' watchword.

To rise above the tyranny of proof and with pounding heart bid farewell to the world of the inadequate—the rope is cut, the bird is free—is in no wise to abandon thoughts for feelings, as if bogs could accommodate the human spirit better than cages. To relegate the health of our souls to the whims of our emotions would be absurd. To say that in outdistancing proof we take our minds with us is too weak; they empower our flight. At this higher altitude the mind is, if anything, *more* alive than before;[9] in supreme instances the muses take over and our minds go on "automatic pilot," that inspired, ecstatic state Plato called "the higher madness." We cannot here track them to those heights where myth and poetry conspire with revelation and remembrance, science joining them at those times when hunches strike terror in the heart, so fine is the line between inspired madness and the kind that disintegrates. Such ozone atmosphere is not for this essay. Ours is the *to metaxy*, the intermediate realm between proofs that cannot tell us whether the garden is enchanted or not and inspiration that shows us, face to face, that it is. Proofs being unavailable in this "middle kingdom," there remains the possibility that reasons may have something to say—proofs, no; reasons, yes. Even here we should not expect too much, for the more we try to make our reasons *resemble* proofs—in justifications or arguments that compel provided only that the hearer has rational faculties—the more they must take on proof's earthbound character; in grounding them in demonstrations that compel, we will "ground" them in the correlative sense of preventing them from getting off the ground.

This last point is worth dwelling on for a paragraph, for it points to a dilemma the university is caught in but does not clearly see. On the one hand we take it for granted that an important part of our job is to train people to think critically; concurrently we assume that the university is an important custodian of civilization: We have the celebrated retort of the Oxford don who, asked what *he* was doing for the Battle of Britain, replied that he was what the fighting was *for*. What the university does not see is that the criteria for critical thinking it has adopted work against the high image of man that keeps civilizations vital: The Aryans who fanned out in the second millennium B.C.E. to spread the Indo-European language base from India to Ireland—*Aryur*vedic medicine still flourishes in India, and Eyre is simply Aryur spelled differently—called themselves Aryan (noble), while the Muslims who entered history in the greatest political explosion the world has known were powered for that explosion by the Qur'anic assurance, "Surely We created man in the best stature" (XCV, 4). To cite but a single evidence of the contradiction the university is caught in here, "There is no doubt that in developed societies education has contributed to the decline of religious belief";[10] yet students of evolution tell us that "religious behaviors are . . . probably adaptive; [their] dialog with 'nature' . . . is an important integrator of [man's] whole self-view in relation to the world and to activity."[11] I suspect that the conjunction of these two facts—religion is adaptive and the canons of modernity erode it—contributed to Max Weber's pessimism about the future, a pessimism shared by the foremost contemporary British sociologist of religion, Bryan Wilson. Seeing current society as less legitimated than any previous social order, Wilson fears a breakdown of civilizing values in the face of an increasingly anonymous and rationalized culture.[12] I think we should ask ourselves very seriously whether the canons of critical thinking the university has drifted into actually further such a possible breakdown. It has been America's hope that these canons make for a better, more "rational" world. It seems to be her experience that they do not necessarily do so.

But to proceed. If our first methodological point noted that attempts to force the question of the world's worth into the arena of proof preclude a heartening answer by that move alone, the second point concerns an innuendo that must be anticipated and dismissed so discussion can proceed on a decent level. I refer to the charge, more frequently insinuated than openly expressed, that affirmative world views are products of wishful thinking. What are put forward as *good* reasons to support them are not the real reasons. The real reasons are psychological.

At risk of protesting too much, I propose to raise a small electrical storm here to clear the atmosphere. As barometer to show that the storm is needed, I shall refer to the British philosopher and sociologist

Ernest Gellner. In his *Legitimation of Belief* he proposes that only such knowledge as lends itself to "public formulation and repeatability" be considered "real knowledge." He admits that the "moral, 'dehuman- izing' price" of this move is high, for it leads to the conclusion that "our identities, freedom, norms, are no longer underwritten by our vision and comprehension of things, [so] we are doomed to suffer from a ten- sion between cognition and identity"—note the enchantment depart- ing the garden like helium from a punctured balloon. But we should pay this price manfully, Gellner contends, for its alternative is "styles of thought [that are] cheap, . . . cosy [and] meretricious." It is rhetoric like this that demands a storm to dispatch it. Gellner does not argue that the kind of knowledge he baptizes as "real" in fact is so; only that "we have become habituated to and dependent on" such knowledge and so "are constrained" to define knowledge this way. "It was Kant's merit," he acknowledges, "to see that this compulsion is in us, not in things. It was Weber's to see that it is historically a specific kind of mind, not mind as such, which is subject to this compulsion."[13] But if anyone questions the worth of this compulsion to which "we have become . . . bound" and proposes to try to loosen its hold on us, he must face, atop this already demanding task, Gellner's insults. For to take exception to his delimitation of "real knowledge" is, to repeat his charge, to engage in "styles of thought [that are] cheap and meretri- cious." That last word drove me to my dictionary; I wanted to discov- er with precision how my mind works. According to the Oxford English Dictionary it is "showily attractive . . . befitting a harlot."

I deplore this whole descent into name-calling. Unworthy of dis- cussions in a university setting, it leaves a bad taste in my mouth; part of me feels petty for allowing myself to have been dragged into it. But the phenomenon is real, so it must be dealt with. Volumes could be assembled of so-called arguments of this kind where a psychologically angled vocabulary is used without apparently taking into account the effect this is likely to have on uncritical minds. Though this kind of lan- guage is doubtless not intended to degrade the humanities, it does nev- ertheless betray an artless style of thinking of its authors. For if "real knowledge" is restricted to what is public and repeatable, what is left for the humanities is mostly unreal knowledge or no knowledge at all.

I hope we are agreed that *ad hominem* arguments get us nowhere. Naturally, I wonder from time to time if my high regard for life and the world is fathered by desire and mothered by need, but this is a shoe that fits either foot. Psychologists tell us that on average people give themselves more grief through too poor estimates of themselves than through inflated estimates; it is self-contempt, not pride, that we have basically to deal with. So if we insist on playing this psychologizing game perhaps we should invite our prophets of the human nadir to join us on the psychiatrist's couch—Beckett, who admits he was born depressed; Camus, Sartre, whoever your list includes—to see if Diane Keaton in *Manhattan* was right in seeing their gloomy worlds as personal neuroses inflated to cosmic proportions.[14] Wittgenstein once remarked that the world of a happy man is a happy world.

The storm is on its way out, but a last, receding clap of thunder as it makes its departure. When the question of whether we are saved by grace or self-effort became an issue in Japanese Buddhist thought, a militant advocate of self-power (Nichiren) made a statement that was counter-dependent to a degree worthy of Fritz Perls. Personal responsibility being everything, he argued, a single supplication for help from the Buddhas was enough to send a man to hell. To which a member of the other-power school replied that as he was undoubtedly destined for hell anyway, being totally incapable of saving himself, he might as well take his supplications along with him as comforts. I confess that, taste for taste, I find this latter posture more appealing than that of existentialists who strut life's stage histrionically hurling their byronic defiance—"there's no meaning but my meaning; that which each of us personally creates"—at an unhearing universe Ernest Becker is the latest culture hero in this existentialist camp. And I can say *why* I find this latter group less appealing; this switch from the psychologizing and subjectivism I have allowed myself to be dragged into in this discussion to a *reason* is sign that the storm is over. The existentialists are more self-centered—so, at least, their writings come through to me. In countering the mechanistic image of man that science produced, existentialism arose precisely to recall us to ourselves, to remind us of our individuality and freedom—properties that science cannot deal with. In making this correlation it served an important function; we humanists stand greatly in its debt. But there was something it did not see—probably could not see at mid-century. In countering science's push for uniformities and determining forces it uncritically accepted a third scientific premise, the man/world divide that Descartes and Newton first moved into place. This third premise no more describes the actual nature of things than do the first two; all three are science's working principles, no more, no less. This uncritical acceptance of the third working principle of science drove the existentialists into an alienated, embattled, egocentric depiction of the human condition. In mistaking the separate, self-contained part of us for our true part, existentialism made a fatal mistake that has confused and lowered our self-estimate. I use the past tense in speaking of it because increasingly it has a passé flavor. It lingers on because theology and humanistic psychology have not gathered the academic strength to replace it with a convincing alternative, and philosophy has not given them enough help in their efforts.

So we come to our central question, asking not if an image of man loftier than either science or the existentialists have given us is possible in our times—that would again divert us to a psychological question, this time the question of whether Western civilization still has the *vitality* to believe great things. Instead, we ask whether this loftier image is true. Even here, though, we have not reached the bottom line, for as we noted earlier the final question is not whether *man* is noble but whether *reality* is noble, it being impossible to answer the first question affirmatively unless the second is so unanswered.[15] If it be asked why I do not produce a moral culprit for our reduced self-image (evil men who have ground that image into the dirt by exploiting us) or even a social culprit (what hope for man in an age of mechanization and technique?), the answer is that important as these tyrannies are, they are not our final problem. Our final adversary is the notion of a lifeless universe as the context in which life and thought are set, one which without our presence in it would have been judged inferior to ourselves. Could we but shake off our anodynes for a moment we would see that nothing could be more terrible than the condition of spirits in a supposedly lifeless and indifferent universe—Newton's great mechanism of time, space, and inanimate forces operating automatically or by chance. Spirits in such a context are like saplings without water; their organs shrivel. Not that there has been ill intent in turning holyland into wasteland, garden into desert; just disastrous consequences unforeseen. So we must pick up anew Blake's Bow of Burning Gold to support "the rise of soul against intellect" (Yeats) as intellect has come to be narrowly perceived. To continue with Yeats, this time paraphrasing him, we must hammer loud upon the wall till truth at last obeys our call. We must produce some reasons.

IV. LEAVING THE WASTELAND

Aimed not at individuals (scientists, say) or disciplines (science or the
social sciences) but at habits of thought that encroach on us all in the
modern West—"there never was a war that was not inward"
(Marianne Moore)—the reasons are of two sorts, positive and negative.
As the negative reasons mesh better with current styles of thought—
what we currently take to be reasonable—I shall begin with them.
They are negative because they say nothing about what reality is like;
they merely show that the claim that it is a lifeless mechanism has not
a rational leg to stand on. My latest book (*Forgotten Truth*)[16] and essay
("Excluded Knowledge")[17] work out this exposé in some detail; here I
can only summarize their combined argument.

1. We begin with *motivations*. Nothing is more uncompromising
about ourselves than that we are creatures that want.

2. These wants give rise to *epistemologies*. From the welter of
impressions and surmises that course through our streams of consciousness we register, firm up, and take to be true those that stay in
place and support us like stepping stones in getting us where we want
to go. In the seventeenth century Western man stumbled on a special-
ized way of knowing that we call the scientific method, a packet of
directives counseling, first, what we should attend to, and then what we
should do with the objects that come into focus through this attention.
This new epistemological probe dramatically increased our understanding of how nature works and our control over it.[18] As we wel-
comed this increase, we "went with" this way of knowing, enshrining
it as the supreme way of getting at truth, and what it discloses as truth.

3. Epistemologies in turn produce *ontologies*—they create world
views. In the case in question, the epistemology we fashioned to
enlarge our cognitive bite into the natural world produced an ontology
that made nature central. It may not be accurate to call this new ontology materialism, but clearly it is naturalistic. Everything that exists
must have a foothold in nature (space, time, and matter), and in the
end it must be subject to that footing.

4. Finally, ontologies generate *anthropologies*. Man being by definition a part of reality, his nature must obviously conform to what reality
is. So a naturalistic world view produces, perforce, a humanistic view of
man, "humanistic" being used here as adjective not for the humanities

but for a specific doctrine that makes embodied man, man's measure.

So far have we ventured down the road of this promethean epistemology, naturalistic ontology, and humanistic anthropology that it is virtually impossible for us to see how arbitrary the entire outlook is—how like a barren moonscape it would have appeared to our ancestors and continues to appear to everyone but ourselves. My own birth and early experience in China may make it easier for me to see Weber's point, earlier referred to, that the way our Western minds work is not the way human minds must work; but nothing turns on this. I think we can say that the negative way of making our case for the humanities—our point that rationality in no way requires us to think that the garden is not enchanted—has objective standing. We can *argue* with those who question it.

V. ENTERING THE HOLY LAND

Not so with reasons we may adduce for thinking that the garden *is* enchanted. These positive reasons are not *il*logical, but whether we admit the fact grudgingly or glory in it, the fact itself remains: These positive reasons require, as their premises so to speak, sensibilities that are unevenly distributed and cultivated. So purely rational clout cannot be expected of them.[19] But as the Buddha said to Mara the Tempter when the latter tried to persuade him not to bother to teach because there was no hope that others could fathom his culminating insight: "There will be some who will understand." So I shall continue. Over the entrance to the magic lantern show in Hermann Hesse's *Steppenwolf* was inscribed, "Not for Everybody." The following four arguments will seem like such only to those who at some level of their being have not been permitted to forget the immensity of what it means to be truly human.

1. *The argument from the human majority.* No culture save our own has disjoined man from his world, life from what is presumed to be non-life, in the alienating way we have. As Gilbert Durand has pointed out,

> the traditional image of man does not distinguish, nor even *want* to distinguish, the I from the Not-I, the world from man; whereas the entire teaching of modern Western civilization . . . strives to cut the world off from man, to separate the "I think" from what

is thought. Dualism is the great "schizomorphic" structure of Western intelligence.[20]

Laurens van der Post tells of the South African bushmen that wherever they go, they feel themselves known, hence at home. There is no threat, no horror of emptiness or strangeness, only familiarity in a friendly, living environment, hence also the absence of any feeling of loneliness.[21] One of my favorite possessions is a *kakimono* that was given to me by a Japanese friend. In four Chinese characters that are bold and beautiful it proclaims that heaven and earth are pervaded with sentience, infused with feeling. This "majority rule" argument that I am beginning with must naturally face the suspicion that attends all reasonings to the effect that "fifty million Frenchmen can't be wrong." But unless the minority (in this case ourselves) can show *reasons* for thinking the majority is mistaken (and in this case such reasons do not exist: that was the gist of my negative formulation of the case for the humanities) it seems wise to side with the majority. From within Western parochialism the view that man is of a piece with his habitat may look like it belongs to "the childhood of the human race." Freed from that parochialism it looks like man's central surmise when the full range of human experience is legitimated and pondered profoundly: the view that is normal to the human condition because consonant with the complete complement of human sensibilities.

2. *The argument from science.* We must be careful here, for science cannot take a single step toward *proving* transcendence. But because it does prove things in its own domain and that domain has turned out to be impressive in its own right, science has become the most powerful symbol for transcendence our age affords. I shall list three teachings of contemporary science that carry powerful overtones for those with ears to hear.

a. Fred Hoyle tells us that "no literary imagination could have invented a story one-hundredth part as fantastic as the sober facts that [science has] unearthed.[22] That reality has turned out to be quantitatively more extravagant than we had supposed suggests that its qualitative features may be equally beyond our usual suppositions. If the universe is spatially unbounded, perhaps it is limitless in worth as well.

b. Wholeness, integration, at-one-ment—the concept of unity is vital to the humanities; it is not going too far to cite radical *dis*unity (the man/world split as a final disjunction) as the fiction that has reduced the humanities to their present low condition. Yet science has found *nature* to be unified to a degree that, again, we would not have surmised without its proofs. Matter and energy are one. Time and space are one, time being space's fourth dimension. Space and gravity are one: The latter is simply space's curvature. And in the end matter and its space-time field are one; what appears to us as a material body is nothing but a center of space-time's deformation. Once again: If we could be taken backstage into the spiritual recesses of reality in the way physics has taken us into its physical recesses, might we not find harmony hidden there as well—earth joined to heaven, man walking with God?

c. The Cartesian/Newtonian paradigm will not work for quantum physics. It is going to be very difficult to fashion an alternative, for the new physics is so strange that we will never be able to visualize it or describe it consistently in ordinary language. But this is itself exciting. We do not know where we are headed, but at least the door of the prison that alienated us and produced the Age of Anxiety is now sprung. It is true that we do not know where we are going, but scientists themselves are beginning to suggest that our haven may be nowhere in the space-time manifold since that manifold is itself derivative and relative. Our final move may be into a different dimension of reality entirely. David Bohm calls this dimension "the implicate order," an order to which Bell's theorem, Chew's S-matrix bootstrap model as Fritjof Capra interprets it, and Karl Pribram's holographic model of mind all seem (in their various ways) to point.

3. *The argument from human health.* "Pascal's Wager" and James's "Will to Believe" have made their place in philosophy by virtue of their sensible suggestions as to how to proceed in the face of uncertainty. I propose that we add to them what might be called "The Argument from Human Health." I shall use something John Findlay has written about Hegel to make my point here, replacing his references to Hegel with phrases that describe life's final matrix—in this essay what I have been calling, with Weber, life's garden.

> In my not infrequent moods of exaltation I certainly sense my garden to be enchanted. When I do hard theoretical work and succeed in communicating its results to others, I feel that the whole sense of the world lies in endeavours such as mine, that this is the whole justification of its countless atrocious irritants. I feel clear that the world

has sense, and that no philosophy that sees it as disenchanted can express this sense satisfactorily. But in my more frequent mood of mild depression I do not see the world thus. I see it as bereft of sense, and I submit masochistically to its senselessness, even taking more comfort in its cold credibility than in the rational desirability of an enchanted existence. I am not even convinced that there is one best or right perspective in which the world should be viewed: it seems a provocative staircase figure always idly altering its perspective.[23]

The point is this: "Depression" and "masochism" are pathological terms. To cast our lot with them, assuming that we see most clearly when we are unwell rather than well, is itself a pathological move. The healthy move, it would seem, is to ground our outlooks in our noblest intuitions. This leads to my fourth and final consideration.

4. *The argument from special insights.* End meets beginning: I come at my close to my title. The title of William Golding's novel *Free Fall* has obvious affinities with my subtitle, "The Humanities as Uncontrolled Experiment," but it is an account its hero gives of something that happens to him in the course of that story that gives me my title proper. Samuel Mountjoy—his name itself elicits a small gasp in the context of the burden and promise of the humanities—is in a Nazi concentration camp awaiting questioning about plans for a prison break. Frenetically he rehearses the tortures that are sure to be inflicted on him to extract the scrap of information he possesses when suddenly, in his own words, "I was visited by a flake of fire, miraculous and pentecostal; and fire transmuted me, once and forever."[24]

Intimations like these come, and when they do we do not know whether the happiness they bring is the rarest or the commonest thing on earth, for in all earthly things we find it, give it, and receive it, but cannot hold onto it. When it comes, it seems in no way strange to be so happy, but in retrospect we wonder how such gold of Eden could have been ours. The human opportunity, always beckoning but never in this life reached, is to stabilize that gold; to let such flakes of fire turn us into "handfuls of light." This second image comes from a Tradition in Islam that reads, "God took a handful of His light, and said to it 'Be Muhammad.'" In its esoteric, Sufic reading, the Muhammad here referred to is the Logos, the Universal Man, the Image of God that is in us all; our essence that awaits release.

NOTES

¹I have decided not to assume a double gender vocabulary, adding "woman" every time I write "man." I shall rely on the reader to understand that I consciously use "man" in the generic sense in which it appears in "human" or "the humanities." While speaking of genders, I should mention my indebtedness to Kendra Smith. It was in company and conversation with her that many of the ideas in this essay emerged or took final shape.

²Manfred Stanley, "Beyond Progress: Three Post-Political Futures," in *Images of the Future*, ed. Robert Bundy (Buffalo: Prometheus Books, 1976), p. 115.

³Ibid., pp. 115-16.

⁴Christopher Lasch gives us one indication of this in his *The Culture of Narcissism* (New York: W. W. Norton, 1978), which has as its subtitle, *American Life in an Age of Diminishing Expectations*. "We do not think well of ourselves," Saul Bellow noted in his 1976 Nobel Prize address: "we do not think amply about what we are. . . . It is the jet plane in which we commonplace human beings have crossed the Atlantic in four hours that embodies such values as we claim." Lest it be thought that artists and humanists are the only ones who have noticed this decline in our self-regard, I shall add the verdict of a Nobel-laureate neuro-physiologist, John Eccles: Man is not just "a hastily made-over ape. . . . Science has gone too far in breaking down our belief in our spiritual greatness" (*Brain/Mind Bulletin*, February 20, 1978, p. 4).

⁵A certain metaphysical sensitivity is needed to see this—a talent for the long view— but the point must rest here with an anology. From their beginning stars struggle against the force of their own gravity, which they can oppose only by generating tremendous amounts of energy to maintain high internal pressures. But the star can never win the battle, for when its fuel is exhausted, gravity wins and the star must die.

⁶In Alvin Plantinga, *God and Other Minds* (Ithaca, N.Y.: Cornell University Press, 1967), Plantinga says he does not know how to argue the existence of God, whose existence seems as obvious to him as anything he might try to argue it *from*.

⁷"I am so afraid of error that I keep hurling myself into the arms of doubt rather than into the arms of truth" (Petrarch).

⁸Epigraph of Carolly Erickson's *The Medieval Vision* (New York: Oxford University Press, 1976).

⁹"Insight is an *act*, permeated by intense passion, that makes possible great clarity in the sense that it perceives and dissolves subtle but strong emotional, social, linguistic, and intellectual pressures tending to hold the mind in rigid grooves and fixed compartments, in which fundamental challenges are avoided. From this germ can unfold a further perception that is not contained in the entire previously existent field of the known. . . . This perception includes new orders and forms of *reason* that are expressed in the medium of thought and language" (David Bohm, "On Insight and Its Significance for Science, Education, and Values," *Teachers College Record* 80, no. 3 [1979]: 409).

¹⁰Edward Norman, *Christianity and the World Order* (New York: Oxford University Press, 1979), p. 6.

[11]Alex Comfort, *I and That* (New York: Crown Publishers, 1979), pp. 69-70. It is not likely that this estimate of religion's importance, coming as it does from the author of *The Joy of Sex*, is skewed by excess piety.

[12]Bryan Wilson, *Contemporary Transformations of Religion* (Oxford: Clarendon Press, 1976), p. 100.

[13]Ernest Gellner, *Legitimation of Belief* (Cambridge: Cambridge University Press, 1975), pp. 206-07.

[14]"Despair is, theologically considered, not only a sin but the greatest of sins: and yet at the same time there is a sort of pride in it, a pleasure even, as in the only great thing left to us. It is also a kind of revenge on those whom we imagine have driven us to it" (Kathleen Raine).

[15]"Plato understood that all attempts to form a nobler type of man—i.e., all paideia and all culture—merge into the problem of the nature of the divine" (Werner Jaeger).

[16]Huston Smith, *Forgotten Truth* (New York: Harper & Row, 1976).

[17]Huston Smith, "Excluded Knowledge: A Critique of the Modern Western Mind Set," *Teachers College Record* 80, no. 3 (February 1979): 419-45.

[18]It was the corridors of power that yawned before Bacon and his cohorts in the seventeenth century that made science so heady. Forming their Invisible College, they divided power into three kinds. Power over themselves science did not seem to offer. Power over others it did dangle—in the imperialism and colonialism it foreshadowed—but there seemed to be moral ambiguities here so they scratched this topic from their agenda. It was power over nature that excited them as the unqualified good science was deeding to man.

[19]A scientist has written that whatever we consider ultimate reality to be, one of the reasons we find it to be mysterious and awe-inspiring is precisely "its failure to present itself as the perfect and articulate consequence of rational thought" (Henry Marganau in Paul Schilpp, *Albert Einstein: Philosopher-Scientist* [New York: Harper Torchbooks, 1959], p. 250).

[20]Gilbert Durand, "On the Disfiguration of the Image of Man in the West," Monograph published by Golgonooza Press, Ipswich, 1977.

[21]Laurens van der Post, *The Heart of the Hunter* (Baltimore: Penguin, 1965), p. 188.

[22]Fred Hoyle, *The Nature of the Universe* (New York: New American Library, 1950), p. 120.

[23]John Findlay in Alasdair MacIntyre, ed., *Hegel* (South Bend: University of Notre Dame Press, 1976), pp. 19-20.

[24]William Golding, *Free Fall* (New York: Harcourt, Brace, 1960), p. 188.

MARK ALAN STAMATY

From *WHO NEEDS DONUTS?*

TO CHOOSE "MY BEST" work, I should offer a bunch of blank pages. Hopefully hundreds, thousands. That would be in keeping with the words of the colorfully incomparable first-year drawing teacher I had at Cooper Union, Robert Gwathmey, who used to tell us: "Your best painting is always your NEXT painting." So I hope I have yet to do my best work, but I chose these pages from my book *Who Needs Donuts?* because I put my heart and soul into them and because they were a crystallization of endless hours of walking around the city I love, New York, which continues to be a kaleidoscopic source of imagery for my art.

—Mark Alan Stamaty

to look for donuts.

GAY TALESE

FRANK SINATRA HAS a COLD

I GREW UP READING fiction and I read very little nonfiction. My aspiration as a young man—I wrote this when I was in my thirties—was to bring to magazine writing the many aspects of the short story writers I admired, such as John Cheever, John O'Hara, and Irwin Shaw, who were my three favorite short story writers in the '60s. The piece speaks for itself. It's one of my best. It's like being asked, "Of all of your children, who is your favorite child?" You give your best to every piece; you know you've done your best and that's the end of it.

—Gay Talese

Frank Sinatra, holding a glass of bourbon in one hand and a cigarette in the other, stood in a dark corner of the bar between two attractive but fading blondes who sat waiting for him to say something. But he said nothing; he had been silent during much of the evening, except now in this private club in Beverly Hills he seemed even more distant, staring out through the smoke and semidarkness into a large room beyond the bar where dozens of young couples sat huddled around small tables or twisted in the center of the floor to the clamorous clang of folk-rock music blaring from the stereo. The two blondes knew, as did Sinatra's four male friends who stood nearby, that it was a bad idea to force conversation upon him when he was in this mood of sullen silence, a mood that had hardly been uncommon during this first week of November, a month before his fiftieth birthday.

Sinatra had been working in a film that he now disliked, could not wait to finish; he was tired of all the publicity attached to his dating the twenty-year-old Mia Farrow, who was not in sight tonight; he was angry that a CBS television documentary of his life, to be shown in two weeks, was reportedly prying into his privacy, even speculating on his possible friendship with Mafia leaders; he was worried about his starring role in an hour-long NBC show entitled *Sinatra—A Man and His Music*, which would require that he sing eighteen songs with a voice that at this particular moment, just a few nights before the taping was to begin, was weak and sore and uncertain. Sinatra was ill. He was the victim of an ailment so common that most people would consider it trivial. But when it gets to Sinatra it can plunge him into a state of anguish, deep depression, panic, even rage. Frank Sinatra had a cold.

Sinatra with a cold is Picasso without paint, Ferrari without fuel— only worse. For the common cold robs Sinatra of that uninsurable jewel, his voice, cutting into the core of his confidence, and it affects not only his own psyche but also seems to cause a kind of psychosomatic nasal drip within dozens of people who work for him, drink with him, love him, depend on him for their own welfare and stability. A Sinatra with a cold can, in a small way, send vibrations through the entertainment industry and beyond as surely as a President of the United States, suddenly sick, can shake the national economy.

For Frank Sinatra was now involved with many things involving many people—his own film company, his record company, his private airline, his missile-parts firm, his real-estate holdings across the nation, his personal staff of seventy-five—which are only a portion of the power he is and has come to represent. He seemed now to be also the embodiment of the fully emancipated male, perhaps the only one in America, the man who can do anything he wants, *anything*, can do it because he has money, the energy, and no apparent guilt. In an age when the very young seem to be taking over, protesting and picketing and demanding change, Frank Sinatra survives as a national phenomenon, one of the few prewar products to withstand the test of time. He is the champ who made the big comeback, the man who had everything, lost it, then got it back, letting nothing stand in his way, doing what few men can do: he uprooted his life, left his family, broke with everything that was familiar, learning in the process that one way to hold a woman is not to hold her. Now he has the affection of Nancy and Ava and Mia, the fine female produce of three generations, and still has the adoration of his children, the freedom of a bachelor, he does not feel old, he makes old men feel young, makes them think that if Frank Sinatra can do it, it can be done; not that *they* could do it, but it is still nice for other men to know, at fifty, that it can be done.

But now, standing at this bar in Beverly Hills, Sinatra had a cold, and he continued to drink quietly and he seemed miles away in his private world, not even reacting when suddenly the stereo in the other room switched to a Sinatra song, "In the Wee Small Hours of the Morning."

It is a lovely ballad that he first recorded ten years ago, and it now inspired many young couples who had been sitting, tired of twisting, to get up and move slowly around the dance floor, holding one another very close. Sinatra's intonation, precisely clipped, yet full and flowing, gave a deeper meaning to the simple lyrics—"In the wee small hours of the morning / while the whole wide world is fast asleep / you lie awake, and think about the girl. . . ."—it was like so many of his classics, a song that evoked loneliness and sensuality, and when blended with the dim light and the alcohol and nicotine and late-night needs, it became a kind of airy aphrodisiac. Undoubtedly the words from this song, and others like it, had put millions in the mood, it was music to make love by, and doubtless much love had been made by it all over America at night in cars, while the batteries burned down, in cottages by the lake, on beaches during balmy summer evenings, in secluded parks and exclusive penthouses and furnished rooms, in cabin cruisers and cabs and cabanas—in all places where Sinatra's songs could be heard were these words that warmed women, wooed and won them, snipped the final thread of inhibition and gratified the male egos of ungrateful lovers; two generations of men had been the beneficiaries of such ballads, for which they were eternally in his debt, for which they may eternally hate him. Nevertheless here he was, the man himself, in the early hours of the morning in Beverly Hills, out of range.

The two blondes, who seemed to be in their middle thirties, were preened and polished, their matured bodies softly molded within tight dark suits. They sat, legs crossed, perched on the high bar stools. They listened to the music. Then one of them pulled out a Kent and Sinatra quickly placed his gold lighter under it and she held his hand, looked at his fingers: they were nubby and raw, and the pinkies protruded, being so stiff from arthritis that he could barely bend them. He was, as usual, immaculately dressed. He wore an oxford-grey suit with a vest, a suit conservatively cut on the outside but trimmed with flamboyant silk within; his shoes, British, seemed to be shined even on the bottom of the soles. He also wore, as everybody seemed to know, a remarkably convincing black hairpiece, one of sixty that he owns, most of them under the care of an inconspicuous little grey-haired lady who, holding his hair in a tiny satchel, follows him around whenever he performs. She earns $400 a week. The most distinguishing thing about Sinatra's face are his eyes, clear blue and alert, eyes that within seconds can go cold with anger, or glow with affection, or, as now, reflect a vague detachment that keeps his friends silent and distant.

Leo Durocher, one of Sinatra's closest friends, was now shooting pool in the small room behind the bar. Standing near the door was Jim Mahoney, Sinatra's press agent, a somewhat chunky young man with a square jaw and narrow eyes who would resemble a tough Irish plain-clothesman if it were not for the expensive continental suits he wears and his exquisite shoes often adorned with polished buckles. Also nearby was a big, broad-shouldered two-hundred-pound actor named Brad Dexter who seemed always to be thrusting out his chest so that his gut would not show.

Brad Dexter has appeared in several films and television shows, displaying fine talent as a character actor, but in Beverly Hills he is equally known for the role he played in Hawaii two years ago when he swam a few hundred yards and risked his life to save Sinatra from drowning in a riptide. Since then Dexter has been one of Sinatra's constant companions and has been made a producer in Sinatra's film company. He occupies a plush office near Sinatra's executive suite. He is endlessly searching for literary properties that might be converted into new starring roles for Sinatra. Whenever he is among strangers with Sinatra he worries because he knows that Sinatra brings out the best and worst in people—some men will become aggressive, some women will become seductive, others will stand around skeptically appraising him, the scene will be somehow intoxicated by his mere presence, and maybe Sinatra himself, if feeling as badly as he was tonight, might become intolerant or tense, and then: headlines. So Brad Dexter tries to anticipate danger and warn Sinatra in advance. He confesses to feeling very protective of Sinatra, admitting in a recent moment of self-revelation: "I'd kill for him."

While this statement may seem outlandishly dramatic, particular-ly when taken out of context, it nonetheless expresses a fierce fidelity that is quite common within Sinatra's special circle. It is a characteris-tic that Sinatra, without admission, seems to prefer: *All the Way*; *All or Nothing at All*. This is the Sicilian in Sinatra; he permits his friends, if they wish to remain that, none of the easy Anglo-Saxon outs. But if they remain loyal, then there is nothing Sinatra will not do in turn—fabulous gifts, personal kindnesses, encouragement when they're down, adulation when they're up. They are wise to remember, how-ever, one thing. He is Sinatra. The boss. *Il Padrone*.

I had seen something of this Sicilian side of Sinatra last summer at

Jilly's saloon in New York, which was the only other time I'd gotten a close view of him prior to this night in this California club. Jilly's, which is on West Fifty-second Street in Manhattan, is where Sinatra drinks whenever he is in New York, and there is a special chair reserved for him in the back room against the wall that nobody else may use. When he is occupying it, seated behind a long table flanked by his closest New York friends—who include the saloon-keeper, Jilly Rizzo, and Jilly's azure-haired wife, Honey, who is known as the "Blue Jew"—a rather strange ritualistic scene develops. That night dozens of people, some of them casual friends of Sinatra's, some mere acquaintances, some neither, appeared outside of Jilly's saloon. They approached it like a shrine. They had come to pay respect. They were from New York, Brooklyn, Atlantic City, Hoboken. They were old actors, young actors, former prizefighters, tired trumpet players, politicians, a boy with a cane. There was a fat lady who said she remembered Sinatra when he used to throw the *Jersey Observer* onto her front porch in 1933. There were middle-aged couples who said they had heard Sinatra sing at the Rustic Cabin in 1938 and "We knew then that he really had it!" Or they had heard him when he was with Harry James's band in 1939, or with Tommy Dorsey in 1941 ("Yeah, that's the song, 'I'll Never Smile Again'—he sang it one night in this dump near Newark and we danced . . ."); or they remembered that time at the Paramount with the swooners, and him with those bow ties, The Voice; and one woman remembered that awful boy she knew then—Alexander Dorogokupetz, an eighteen-year-old heckler who had thrown a tomato at Sinatra and the bobby-soxers in the balcony had tried to flail him to death. Whatever became of Alexander Dorogokupetz? The lady did not know.

And they remembered when Sinatra was a failure and sang trash like "Mairzy Doats," and they remembered his comeback and on this night they were all standing outside Jilly's saloon, dozens of them, but they could not get in. So some of them left. But most of them stayed, hoping that soon they might be able to push or wedge their way into Jilly's between the elbows and backsides of the men drinking three-deep at the bar, and they might be able to peek through and *see* him sitting back there. This is all they really wanted; they wanted to see him. And for a few moments they gazed in silence through the smoke and they stared. Then they turned, fought their way out of the bar, went home.

Some of Sinatra's close friends, all of whom are known to the men guarding Jilly's door, do manage to get an escort into the back room. But once they are there they, too, must fend for themselves. On the particular evening, Frank Gifford, the former football player, got only seven yards in three tries. Others who had somehow been close enough to shake Sinatra's hand did *not* shake it; instead they just touched him on the shoulder or sleeve, or they merely stood close enough for him to see them and, after he'd given them a wink of recognition or a wave or a nod or called out their names (he had a fantastic memory for first names), they would then turn and leave. They had checked in. They had paid their respects. And as I watched this ritualistic scene, I got the impression that Frank Sinatra was dwelling simultaneously in two worlds that were not contemporary.

On the one hand he is the swinger—as he is when talking and joking with Sammy Davis, Jr., Richard Conte, Liza Minnelli, Bernie Massi, or any of the other show-business people who get to sit at *the* table; on the other, as when he is nodding or waving to his *paisanos* who are close to him (Al Silvani, a boxing manager who works with Sinatra's film company; Dominic Di Bona, his wardrobe man; Ed Pucci, a 300-pound former football lineman who is his aide-de-camp), Frank Sinatra is *Il Padrone*. Or better still, he is what in traditional Sicily have long been called *uomini rispettati*—men of respect: men who are both majestic and humble, men who are loved by all and are very generous by nature, men whose hands are kissed as they walk from village to village, men who would *personally* go out of their way to redress a wrong.

Frank Sinatra does things *personally*. At Christmas time, he will personally pick dozens of presents for his close friends and family, remembering the type of jewelry they like, their favorite colors, the sizes of their shirts and dresses. When a musician friend's house was destroyed and his wife was killed in a Los Angeles mud slide a little more than a year ago, Sinatra personally came to his aid, finding the musician a new home, paying whatever hospital bills were left unpaid by the insurance, then personally supervising the furnishing of the new home down to the replacing of the silverware, the linen, the purchase of new clothing.

The same Sinatra who did this can, within the same hour, explode in a towering rage of intolerance should a small thing be incorrectly done for him by one of his *paisanos*. For example, when one of his men brought him a frankfurter with catsup on it, which Sinatra apparently abhors, he angrily threw the bottle at the man, splattering catsup all over him. Most of the men who work around Sinatra are big. But this never seems to intimidate Sinatra nor curb his impetuous behavior with them when he is mad. They will never take a swing back at him. He is *Il Padrone*.

At other times, aiming to please, his men will overreact to his desires: when he casually observed that his big orange desert jeep in Palm Springs seemed in need of a new painting, the word was swiftly passed down through the channels, becoming ever more urgent as it went, until finally it was a *command* that the jeep be painted *now*, immediately, yesterday. To accomplish this would require the hiring of a special crew of painters to work all night, at overtime rates; which, in turn, meant that the order had to be bucked back up the line for further approval. When it finally got back to Sinatra's desk, he did not know what it was all about; after he had figured it out he confessed, with a tired look on his face, that he did not care when the hell they painted the jeep.

Yet it would have been unwise for anyone to anticipate his reaction, for he is a wholly unpredictable man of many moods and great dimension, a man who responds instantaneously to instinct—suddenly, dramatically, wildly he responds, and nobody can predict what will follow. A young lady name Jane Hoag, a reporter at *Life*'s Los Angeles bureau who had attended the same school as Sinatra's daughter, Nancy, had once been invited to a party at Mrs. Sinatra's California home at which Frank Sinatra, who maintains very cordial relations with his former wife, acted as host. Early in the party Miss Hoag, while leaning against a table, accidentally with her elbow knocked over one of a pair of alabaster birds to the floor, smashing it to pieces. Suddenly, Miss Hoag recalled, Sinatra's daughter cried, "Oh, that was one of my mother's favorite . . ."—but before she could complete the sentence, Sinatra glared at her, cutting her off, and while forty other guests in the room all stared in silence, Sinatra walked over, quickly with his finger flicked the *other* alabaster bird off the table, smashing it to pieces, and then put an arm gently around Jane Hoag and said, in a way that put her completely at ease, "That's okay, kid."

Now Sinatra said a few words to the blondes. Then he turned from the bar and began to walk toward the poolroom. One of Sinatra's other men friends moved in to keep the girls company. Brad Dexter, who had been standing in the corner talking to some other people, now followed Sinatra.

The room cracked with the clack of billiard balls. There were about a dozen spectators in the room, most of them young men who were watching Leo Durocher shoot against two other aspiring hustlers who were not very good. This private drinking club has among its membership many actors, directors, writers, models, nearly all of them a good deal younger than Sinatra or Durocher and much more casual in the way they dress for the evening. Many of the young women, their long hair flowing loosely below their shoulders, wore tight, fanny-fitting Jax pants and very expensive sweaters; and a few of the young men wore blue or green velour shirts with high collars and narrow tight pants, and Italian loafers.

It was obvious from the way Sinatra looked at these people in the poolroom that they were not his style, but he leaned back against a high stool that was against the wall, holding his drink in his right hand, and said nothing, just watched Durocher slam the billiard balls back and forth. The younger men in the room, accustomed to seeing Sinatra at this club, treated him without deference, although they said nothing offensive. They were a cool young group, very California-cool and casual, and one of the coolest seemed to be a little guy, very quick of movement, who had a sharp profile, pale blue eyes, blondish hair, and squared eye-glasses. He wore a pair of brown corduroy slacks, a green shaggy-dog Shetland sweater, a tan suede jacket, and Game Warden boots, for which he had recently paid $60.

Frank Sinatra, leaning against the stool, sniffling a bit from his cold, could not take his eyes off the Game Warden boots. Once, after gazing at them for a few moments, he turned away; but now he was focused on them again. The owner of the boots, who was just standing in them watching the pool game, was named Harlan Ellison, a writer who had just completed work on a screenplay, *The Oscar*.

Finally Sinatra could not contain himself.

"Hey," he yelled in his slightly harsh voice that still had a soft, sharp edge. "Those Italian boots?"

"No," Ellison said.

"Spanish?"

"No."

"Are they *English* boots?"

"Look, I donno, man," Ellison shot back, frowning at Sinatra, then turning away again.

Now the poolroom was suddenly silent. Leo Durocher who had been poised behind his cue stick and was bent low just froze in that position for a second. Nobody moved. Then Sinatra moved away from the stool and walked with that slow, arrogant swagger of his toward Ellison, the hard tap of Sinatra's shoes the only sound in the room. Then, looking down at Ellison with a slightly raised eyebrow and a tricky little smile, Sinatra asked: "You expecting a *storm?*"

Harlan Ellison moved a step to the side. "Look, is there any reason why you're talking to me?"

"I don't like the way you're dressed," Sinatra said.

"Hate to shake you up," Ellison said, "but I dress to suit myself."

Now there was some rumbling in the room, and somebody said, "Com'on, Harlan, let's get out of here," and Leo Durocher made his pool shot and said, "Yeah, com'on."

But Ellison stood his ground.

Sinatra said, "What do you do?"

"I'm a plumber," Ellison said.

"No, no, he's not," another young man quickly yelled from across the table. "He wrote *The Oscar.*"

"Oh, yeah," Sinatra said, "well I've seen it, and it's a piece of crap."

"That's strange," Ellison said, "because they haven't even released it yet."

"Well, I've seen it," Sinatra repeated, "and it's a piece of crap."

Now Brad Dexter, very anxious, very big opposite the small figure of Ellison, said, "Com'on, kid, I don't want you in this room."

"*Hey,*" Sinatra interrupted Dexter, "can't you see I'm talking to this guy?"

Dexter was confused. Then his whole attitude changed, and his voice went soft and he said to Ellison, almost with a plea, "*Why do you persist in tormenting me?*"

The whole scene was becoming ridiculous, and it seemed that Sinatra was only half-serious, perhaps just reacting out of sheer boredom or inner despair; at any rate, after a few more exchanges Harlan Ellison left the room. By this time the word had gotten out to those on the dance floor about the Sinatra-Ellison exchange, and somebody went to look for the manager of the club. But somebody else said that the manager had already heard about it—and had quickly gone out the door, hopped in his car and drove home. So the assistant manager went into the poolroom.

"I don't want anybody in here without coats and ties," Sinatra snapped.

The assistant manager nodded, and walked back to his office.

It was the morning after. It was the beginning of another nervous day for Sinatra's press agent, Jim Mahoney. Mahoney had a headache, and he was worried but not over the Sinatra-Ellison incident of the night before. At the time Mahoney had been with his wife at a table in the other room, and possibly he had not even been aware of the little drama. The whole thing had lasted only about three minutes. And three minutes after it was over, Frank Sinatra had probably forgotten about it for the rest of his life—as Ellison will probably remember it for the rest of *his* life: he had had, as hundreds of others before him, at an unexpected moment between darkness and dawn, a scene with Sinatra.

It was just as well that Mahoney had not been in the poolroom; he had enough on his mind today. He was worried about Sinatra's cold and worried about the controversial CBS documentary that, despite Sinatra's protests and withdrawal of permission, would be shown on television in less than two weeks. The newspapers this morning were full of hints that Sinatra might sue the network, and Mahoney's phones were ringing without pause, and now he was plugged into New York talking to the *Daily News*'s Kay Gardella, saying: " . . . that's right, Kay . . . they made a gentleman's agreement to not ask certain questions about Frank's private life, and then Cronkite went right ahead: 'Frank, tell me about those associations.' *That* question, Kay—*out!* That question should never have been asked. . . ."

As he spoke, Mahoney leaned back in his leather chair, his head shaking slowly. He is a powerfully built man of thirty-seven; he has a round, ruddy face, a heavy jaw, and narrow pale eyes, and he might appear pugnacious if he did not speak with such clear, soft sincerity and if he were not so meticulous about his clothes. His suits and shoes are superbly tailored, which was one of the first things Sinatra noticed about him, and in his spacious office opposite the bar is a red-muff electrical shoe polisher and a pair of brown wooden shoulders on a stand over which Mahoney can drape his jackets. Near the bar is an autographed photograph of President Kennedy and a few pictures of Frank Sinatra, but there are none of Sinatra in any other rooms in

Mahoney's public-relations agency; there once was a large photograph of him hanging in the reception room but this apparently bruised the egos of some of Mahoney's other movie-star clients and, since Sinatra never shows up at the agency anyway, the photograph was removed.

Still, Sinatra seems ever present, and if Mahoney did not have legitimate worries about Sinatra, as he did today, he could invent them—and, as worry aids, he surrounds himself with little mementos of moments in the past when he did worry. In his shaving kit there is a two-year-old box of sleeping tablets dispensed by a Reno druggist—the date on the bottle marks the kidnapping of Frank Sinatra, Jr. There is on a table in Mahoney's office a mounted wood reproduction of Frank Sinatra's ransom note written on the aforementioned occasion. One of Mahoney's mannerisms, when he is sitting at his desk worrying, is to tinker with the tiny toy train he keeps in front of him—the train is a souvenir from the Sinatra film, *Von Ryan's Express*; it is to men who are close to Sinatra what the PT-109 tie clasps are to men who were close to Kennedy—and Mahoney then proceeds to roll the little train back and forth on the six inches of track; back and forth, back and forth, click-*clack*-click-*clack*. It is his Queeg-thing.

Now Mahoney quickly put aside the little train. His secretary told him there was a *very* important call on the line. Mahoney picked it up, and his voice was even softer and more sincere than before. "Yes, Frank," he said. "Right . . . right . . . yes, Frank. . . ."

When Mahoney put down the phone, quietly, he announced that Frank Sinatra had left in his private jet to spend the weekend at his home in Palm Springs, which is a sixteen-minute flight from his home in Los Angeles. Mahoney was now worried again. The Lear jet that Sinatra's pilot would be flying was identical, Mahoney said, to the one that had just crashed in another part of California.

On the following Monday, a cloudy and unseasonably cool California day, more than one hundred people gathered inside a white television studio, an enormous room dominated by a white stage, white walls, and with dozens of lights and lamps dangling: it rather resembled a gigantic operating room. In this room, within an hour or so, NBC was scheduled to begin taping a one-hour show that would be televised in color on the night of November 24 and would highlight, as much as it could in the limited time, the twenty-five-year career of Frank Sinatra as a public entertainer. It would not attempt to probe, as the forthcoming CBS *Sinatra* documentary allegedly would, that area of Sinatra's life that he regards as private. The NBC show would be mainly an hour of Sinatra singing some of the hits that carried him from Hoboken to Hollywood, a show that would be interrupted only now and then by a few film clips and commercials for Budweiser beer. Prior to his cold, Sinatra had been very excited about this show; he saw here an opportunity to appeal not only to those nostalgic, but also to communicate his talent to some rock-and-rollers—in a sense, he was battling The Beatles. The press releases being prepared by Mahoney's agency stressed this, reading: "If you happen to be tired of kid singers wearing mops of hair thick enough to hide a crate of melons . . . it should be refreshing, to consider the entertainment value of a video special titled *Sinatra—A Man and His Music. . . .*"

But now in this NBC studio in Los Angeles, there was an atmosphere of anticipation and tension because of the uncertainty of the Sinatra voice. The forty-three musicians in Nelson Riddle's orchestra had already arrived and some were up on the white platform warming up. Dwight Hemion, a youthful sandy-haired director who had won praise for his television special on Barbra Streisand, was seated in the glass-enclosed control booth that overlooked the orchestra and stage. The camera crews, technical teams, security guards, Budweiser ad men were also standing between the floor lamps and cameras, waiting, as were a dozen or so ladies who worked as secretaries in other parts of the building but had sneaked away so they could watch this.

A few minutes before eleven o'clock, word spread quickly through the long corridor into the big studio that Sinatra was spotted walking through the parking lot and was on his way, and was looking fine. There seemed great relief among the group that was gathered; but when the lean, sharply dressed figure of the man got closer, and closer, they saw to their dismay that it was not Frank Sinatra. It was his double. Johnny Delgado.

Delgado walks like Sinatra, has Sinatra's build, and from certain facial angles does resemble Sinatra. But he seems a rather shy individual. Fifteen years ago, early in his acting career, Delgado applied for a role in *From Here to Eternity*. He was hired, finding out later that he was to be Sinatra's double. In Sinatra's latest film, *Assault on a Queen*, a story in which Sinatra and some fellow conspirators attempt to hijack the *Queen Mary*, Johnny Delgado doubles for Sinatra in some water scenes; and now, in this NBC studio, his job was to stand under the hot television lights marking Sinatra's spots on the stage for the camera crews.

Five minutes later, the real Frank Sinatra walked in. His face was pale, his blue eyes seemed a bit watery. He had been unable to rid himself of the cold, but he was going to try to sing anyway because the schedule was tight and thousands of dollars were involved at this moment in the assembling of the orchestra and crews and the rental of the studio. But when Sinatra, on his way to his small rehearsal room to warm up his voice, looked into the studio and saw that the stage and orchestra's platform were not close together, as he had specifically requested, his lips tightened and he was obviously very upset. A few moments later, from his rehearsal room, could be heard the pounding of his fist against the top of the piano and the voice of his accompanist, Bill Miller, saying, softly, "Try not to upset yourself, Frank."

Later Jim Mahoney and another man walked in, and there was talk of Dorothy Kilgallen's death in New York earlier that morning. She had been an ardent foe of Sinatra for years, and he became equally uncomplimentary about her in his nightclub act, and now, though she was dead, he did not compromise his feelings. "Dorothy Kilgallen's dead," he repeated, walking out of the room toward the studio. "Well, guess I got to change my whole act."

When he strolled into the studio the musicians all picked up their instruments and stiffened in their seats. Sinatra cleared his throat a few times and then, after rehearsing a few ballads with the orchestra, he sang "Don't Worry About Me" to his satisfaction and, being uncertain of how long his voice could last, suddenly became impatient.

"Why don't we tape this mother?" he called out, looking up toward the glass booth where the director, Dwight Hemion, and his staff were sitting. Their heads seemed to be down, focusing on the control board.

"Why don't we tape this mother?" Sinatra repeated.

The production stage manager, who stands near the camera wearing a headset, repeated Sinatra's words exactly into his line to the control room: "Why don't we tape this mother?"

Hemion did not answer. Possibly his switch was off. It was hard to know because of the obscuring reflections the lights made against the glass booth.

"Why don't we put on a coat and tie," said Sinatra, then wearing a high-necked yellow pullover, "and tape this. . . ."

Suddenly Hemion's voice came over the sound amplifier, very calmly: "Okay, Frank, would you mind going back over. . . ."

"Yes I *would* mind going back," Sinatra snapped.

The silence from Hemion's end, which lasted a second or two, was then again interrupted by Sinatra saying, "When we stop doing things around here the way we did them in 1950, maybe we . . ." and Sinatra continued to tear into Hemion, condemning as well the lack of modern techniques in putting such shows together; then, possibly not wanting to use his voice unnecessarily, he stopped. And Dwight Hemion, very patient, so patient and calm that one would assume he had not heard anything that Sinatra had just said, outlined the opening part of the show. And Sinatra a few minutes later was reading his opening remarks, words that would follow "Without a Song," off the large idiot-cards being held near the camera. Then, this done, he prepared to do the same thing on camera.

"Frank Sinatra Show, Act I, Page 10, Take 1," called a man with a clapboard, jumping in front of the camera—*clap*—then jumping away again.

"Did you ever stop to think," Sinatra began, "what the world would be like without a song? . . . It would be a pretty dreary place. . . . Gives you something to think about, doesn't it? . . ."

Sinatra stopped.

"Excuse me," he said, adding, "*Boy*, I need a drink."

They tried it again.

"Frank Sinatra Show, Act I, Page 10, Take 2," yelled the jumping guy with the clapboard.

"Did you ever stop to think what the world would be like without a song? . . ." Frank Sinatra read it through this time without stopping. Then he rehearsed a few more songs, once or twice interrupting the orchestra when a certain instrumental sound was not quite what he wanted. It was hard to tell how well his voice was going to hold up, for this was early in the show; up to this point, however, everybody in the room seemed pleased, particularly when he sang an old sentimental favorite written more than twenty years ago by Jimmy Van Heusen and Phil Silvers—"Nancy," inspired by the first of Sinatra's three children when she was just a few years old.

> If I don't see her each day
>   I miss her. . . .
> Gee what a thrill
>   Each time I kiss her. . . .

As Sinatra sang these words, though he has sung them hundreds and hundreds of times in the past, it was suddenly obvious to everybody in the studio that something quite special must be going on inside the man, because something quite special was coming out. He was singing now, cold or no cold, with power and warmth, he was letting himself go, the public arrogance was gone, the private side was in this song about the girl who, it is said, understands him better than anybody else, and is the only person in front of whom he can be unashamedly himself.

Nancy is twenty-five. She lives alone, her marriage to singer Tommy Sands having ended in divorce. Her home is in a Los Angeles suburb and she is now making her third film and is recording for her father's record company. She sees him every day; or, if not, he telephones, no matter if it be from Europe or Asia. When Sinatra's singing first became popular on radio, stimulating the swooners, Nancy would listen at home and cry. When Sinatra's first marriage broke up in 1951 and he left home, Nancy was the only child old enough to remember him as a father. She also saw him with Ava Gardner, Juliet Prowse, Mia Farrow, many others, has gone on double dates with him. . . .

> She takes the winter
>   And makes it summer. . . .
> Summer could take
>   Some lessons from her. . . .

Nancy now also sees him visiting at home with his first wife, the former Nancy Barbato, a plasterer's daughter from Jersey City whom he married in 1939 when he was earning $25 a week singing at the Rustic Cabin near Hoboken.

The first Mrs. Sinatra, a striking woman who has never remarried ("When you've been married to Frank Sinatra . . ." she once explained to a friend), lives in a magnificent home in Los Angeles with her younger daughter, Tina, who is seventeen. There is no bitterness, only

great respect and affection between Sinatra and his first wife, and he
has long been welcome in her home and has even been known to wander in at odd hours, stoke the fire, lie on the sofa and fall asleep. Frank
Sinatra can fall asleep anywhere, something he learned when he used
to ride bumpy roads with band buses; he also learned at that time,
when sitting in a tuxedo, how to pinch the trouser creases in the back
and tuck the jacket under and out, and fall asleep perfectly pressed.
But he does not ride buses anymore, and his daughter Nancy, who in
her younger days felt rejected when he slept on the sofa instead of giving attention to her, later realized that the sofa was one of the few
places left in the world where Frank Sinatra could get any privacy,
where his famous face would neither be stared at nor cause an abnor-
mal reaction in others. She realized, too, that things normal have
always eluded her father: his childhood was one of loneliness and a
drive toward attention, and since attaining it he has never again been
certain of solitude. Upon looking out the window of a home he once
owned in Hasbrouck Heights, New Jersey, he would occasionally see
the faces of teenagers peeking in; and in 1944, after moving to
California and buying a home behind a ten-foot fence on Lake Toluca,
he discovered that the only way to escape the telephone and other
intrusions was to board his paddle boat with a few friends, a card table
and a case of beer, and stay afloat all afternoon. But he has tried, inso-
far as it has been possible, to be like everyone else, Nancy says. He wept
on her wedding day, he is very sentimental and sensitive. . . .

"What the hell are you doing up there, Dwight?"
    Silence from the control booth.
    "Got a party or something going on up there, *Dwight?*"
    Sinatra stood on the stage, arms folded, glaring up across the cam-
eras toward Hemion. Sinatra had sung "Nancy" with probably all he
had in his voice on this day. The next few numbers contained raspy
notes, and twice his voice completely cracked. But now Hemion was
in the control booth out of communication; then he was down in the
studio walking over to where Sinatra stood. A few minutes later they
both left the studio and were on the way up to the control booth. The
tape was replayed for Sinatra. He watched only about five minutes of
it before he started to shake his head. Then he said to Hemion: "Forget
it, just forget it. You're wasting your time. What you got there,"
Sinatra said, nodding to the singing image of himself on the television

screen, "is a man with a cold." Then he left the control booth, ordering that the whole day's performance be scrubbed and future taping postponed until he had recovered.

Soon the word spread like an emotional epidemic down through Sinatra's staff, then fanned out through Hollywood, then was heard across the nation in Jilly's saloon, and also on the other side of the Hudson River in the homes of Frank Sinatra's parents and his other relatives and friends in New Jersey.

When Frank Sinatra spoke with his father on the telephone and said he was feeling awful, the elder Sinatra reported that *he* was also feeling awful: that his left arm and fist were so stiff with a circulatory condition he could barely use them, adding that the ailment might be the result of having thrown too many left hooks during his days as a bantamweight almost fifty years ago.

Martin Sinatra, a ruddy and tattooed little blue-eyed Sicilian born in Catania, boxed under the name of "Marty O'Brien." In those days, in those places, with the Irish running the lower reaches of city life, it was not uncommon for Italians to wind up with such names. Most of the Italians and Sicilians who migrated to America just prior to the 1900s were poor and uneducated, were excluded from the building-trades unions dominated by the Irish, and were somewhat intimidated by the Irish police, Irish priests, Irish politicians.

One notable exception was Frank Sinatra's mother, Dolly, a large and very ambitious woman who was brought to this country at two months of age by her mother and father, a lithographer from Genoa. In later years Dolly Sinatra, possessing a round red face and blue eyes, was often mistaken for being Irish, and surprised many at the speed with which she swung her heavy handbag at anyone uttering "Wop."

By playing skillful politics with North Jersey's Democratic machine, Dolly Sinatra was to become, in her heyday, a kind of Catherine de Medici of Hoboken's third ward. She could always be counted upon to deliver six hundred votes at election time from her Italian neighborhood, and this was her base of power. When she told one of the politicians that she wanted her husband to be appointed to the Hoboken Fire Department, and was told, "But, Dolly, we don't have an opening," she snapped, "*Make* an opening."

They did. Years later she requested that her husband be made a captain, and one day she got a call from one of the political bosses that began, "Dolly, congratulations!"

"For what?"

"*Captain* Sinatra."

"Oh, you finally made him one—thank you very much."

Then she called the Hoboken Fire Department.

"Let me speak to *Captain* Sinatra," she said. The fireman called Martin Sinatra to the phone, saying, "Marty, I think your wife has gone nuts." When he got on the line, Dolly greeted him:

"Congratulations, *Captain* Sinatra!"

Dolly's only child, christened Francis Albert Sinatra, was born and nearly died on December 12, 1915. It was a difficult birth, and during his first moment on earth he received marks he will carry till death— the scars on the left side of his neck being the result of a doctor's clumsy forceps, and Sinatra has chosen not to obscure them with surgery.

After he was six months old, he was reared mainly by his grandmother. His mother had a full-time job as a chocolate dipper with a large firm and was so proficient at it that the firm once offered to send her to the Paris office to train others. While some people in Hoboken remember Frank Sinatra as a lonely child, one who spent many hours on the porch gazing into space, Sinatra was never a slum kid, never in jail, always well-dressed. He had so many pants that some people in Hoboken called him "Slacksey O'Brien."

Dolly Sinatra was not the sort of Italian mother who could be appeased merely by a child's obedience and good appetite. She made many demands on her son, was always very strict. She dreamed of his becoming an aviation engineer. When she discovered Bing Crosby pictures hanging on his bedroom walls one evening, and learned that her son wished to become a singer too, she became infuriated and threw a shoe at him. Later, finding she could not talk him out of it—"he takes after me"—she encouraged his singing.

Many Italo-American boys of his generation were then shooting for the same star—they were strong with song, weak with words, not a big novelist among them: no O'Hara, no Bellow, no Cheever, nor Shaw; yet they could communicate *bel canto*. This was more in their tradition, no need for a diploma; they could, with a song, someday see their names in lights . . . *Perry Como* . . . *Frankie Laine* . . . *Tony Bennett* . . . *Vic Damone* . . . but none could see it better than *Frank Sinatra*.

Though he sang through much of the night at the Rustic Cabin, he was up the next day singing without a fee on New York radio to get more attention. Later he got a job singing with Harry James's band, and it was there in August of 1939 that Sinatra had his first recording hit—"All or Nothing at All." He became very fond of Harry James and the men in the band, but when he received an offer from Tommy Dorsey, who in those days had probably the best band in the country, Sinatra took it; the job paid $125 a week, and Dorsey knew how to feature a vocalist. Yet Sinatra was very depressed at leaving James's band, and the final night with them was so memorable that, twenty years later, Sinatra could recall the details to a friend: ". . . the bus pulled out with the rest of the boys at about half-past midnight. I'd said good-bye to them all, and it was snowing, I remember. There was nobody around and I stood alone with my suitcase in the snow and watched the taillights disappear. Then the tears started and I tried to run after the bus. There was such spirit and enthusiasm in that band, I hated leaving it. . . ."

But he did—as he would leave other warm places, too, in search of something more, never wasting time, trying to do it all in one generation, fighting under his *own* name, defending underdogs, terrorizing top dogs. He threw a punch at a musician who said something anti-Semitic, espoused the Negro cause two decades before it became fashionable. He also threw a tray of glasses at Buddy Rich when he played the drums too loud.

Sinatra gave away $50,000 worth of gold cigarette lighters before he was thirty, was living an immigrant's wildest dream of America. He arrived suddenly on the scene when DiMaggio was silent, when *paisanos* were mournful, were quietly defensive about Hitler in their homeland. Sinatra became, in time, a kind of one-man Anti-Defamation League for Italians in America, the sort of organization that would be unlikely for them because, as the theory goes, they rarely agreed on anything, being extreme individualists: fine as soloists, but not so good in a choir; fine as heroes, but not so good in a parade.

When many Italian names were used in describing gangsters on a television show, *The Untouchables*, Sinatra was loud in his disapproval. Sinatra and many thousands of other Italo-Americans were resentful as well when a small-time hoodlum, Joseph Valachi, was brought by Bobby Kennedy into prominence as a Mafia expert, when indeed, from Valachi's testimony on television, he seemed to know less than most waiters on Mulberry Street. Many Italians in Sinatra's circle also regard Bobby Kennedy as something of an Irish cop, more dignified than those in Dolly's day, but no less intimidating. Together with Peter Lawford, Bobby Kennedy is said to have suddenly gotten "cocky" with Sinatra after John Kennedy's election, forgetting the contribution Sinatra had made in both fundraising and in influencing many anti-Irish Italian votes. Lawford and Bobby Kennedy are both suspected of having influenced the late President's decision to stay as a house guest with Bing Crosby instead of Sinatra, as originally planned, a social setback Sinatra may never forget. Peter Lawford has since been drummed out of Sinatra's "summit" in Las Vegas.

"Yes, my son is like me," Dolly Sinatra says, proudly. "You cross him, he never forgets." And while she concedes his power, she quickly points out, "He can't make his mother do anything she doesn't want to do," adding, "Even today, he wears the same brand of underwear I used to buy him."

Today Dolly Sinatra is seventy-one years old, a year or two younger than Martin, and all day long people are knocking on the back door of her large home asking her advice, seeking her influence. When she is not seeing people and not cooking in the kitchen, she is looking after her husband, a silent but stubborn man, and telling him to keep his sore left arm resting on the sponge she has placed on the armrest of a soft chair. "Oh, he went to some terrific fires, this guy did," Dolly said to a visitor, nodding with admiration toward her husband in the chair.

Though Dolly Sinatra has eighty-seven godchildren in Hoboken, and still goes to that city during political campaigns, she now lives with her husband in a beautiful sixteen-room house in Fort Lee, New Jersey. This home was a gift from their son on their fiftieth wedding anniversary three years ago. The home is tastefully furnished and is filled with a remarkable juxtaposition of the pious and the worldly—photographs of Pope John and Ava Gardner, of Pope Paul and Dean Martin; several statues of saints and holy water, a chair autographed by Sammy Davis, Jr. and bottles of bourbon. In Mrs. Sinatra's jewelry box is a magnificent strand of pearls she had just received from Ava Gardner, whom she liked tremendously as a daughter-in-law and still keeps in touch with and talks about; and hung on the wall is a letter addressed to Dolly and Martin: "The sands of time have turned to gold, yet love continues to unfold like the petals of a rose, in God's garden of life . . . may God love you thru all eternity. I thank Him, I thank you for the being of one. Your loving son, Francis. . . ."

Mrs. Sinatra talks to her son on the telephone about once a week, and recently he suggested that, when visiting Manhattan, she make use of his apartment on East Seventy-second Street on the East River. This is an expensive neighborhood of New York even though there is a small factory on the block, but this latter fact was seized upon by Dolly Sinatra as a means of getting back at her son for some unflattering descriptions of his childhood in Hoboken.

"What—you want me to stay in *your* apartment, in *that* dump?" she asked. "You think I'm going to spend the night in *that* awful neighborhood?"

Frank Sinatra got the point, and said, "Excuse *me*, Mrs. Fort Lee."

After spending the week in Palm Springs, his cold much better, Frank Sinatra returned to Los Angeles, a lovely city of sun and sex, a Spanish discovery of Mexican misery, a star land of little men and little women sliding in and out of convertibles in tense tight pants.

Sinatra returned in time to see the long-awaited CBS documentary with his family. At about nine P.M. he drove to the home of his former wife, Nancy, and had dinner with her and their two daughters. Their son, whom they rarely see these days, was out of town.

Frank, Jr., who is twenty-two, was touring with a band and moving cross country toward a New York engagement at Basin Street East with The Pied Pipers, with whom Frank Sinatra sang when he was with Dorsey's band in the 1940s. Today Frank Sinatra, Jr., whom his father says he named after Franklin D. Roosevelt, lives mostly in hotels, dines each evening in his nightclub dressing room, and sings until two A.M., accepting graciously, because he has no choice, the inevitable comparisons. His voice is smooth and pleasant, and improving with work, and while he is very respectful of his father, he discusses him with objectivity and in an occasional tone of subdued cockiness.

Concurrent with his father's early fame, Frank, Jr. said, was the creation of a "press-release Sinatra" designed to "set him apart from the common man, separate him from the realities: it was suddenly Sinatra, the electric magnate, Sinatra who is supernormal, not super-*human* but super*normal*. And here," Frank, Jr. continued, "is the great fallacy, the great bullshit, for Frank Sinatra *is* normal, *is* the guy whom you'd meet on a street corner. But this other thing, the supernormal guise, has affected Frank Sinatra as much as anybody who watches one of his television shows, or reads a magazine article about him. . . .

"Frank Sinatra's life in the beginning was so normal," he said, "that nobody would have guessed in 1934 that this little Italian kid with the curly hair would become the giant, the monster, the great living legend. . . . He met my mother one summer on the beach. She was Nancy Barbato, daughter of Mike Barbato, a Jersey City plasterer. And she meets the fireman's son, Frank, one summer day on the beach at Long Branch, New Jersey. Both are Italian, both Roman Catholic, both lower-middle-class summer sweethearts—it is like a million bad movies starring Frankie Avalon. . . .

"They have three children. The first child, Nancy, was the most normal of Frank Sinatra's children. Nancy was a cheerleader, went to summer camp, drove a Chevrolet, had the easiest kind of development centered around the home and family. Next is me. My life with the family is very, very normal up until September of 1958 when, in complete contrast to the rearing of both girls, I am put into a college-preparatory school. I am now away from the inner family circle, and my position within has never been remade to this day. . . . The third child, Tina. And to be dead honest, I really couldn't say what her life is like. . . ."

The CBS show, narrated by Walter Cronkite, began at ten P.M. A minute before that, the Sinatra family, having finished dinner, turned their chairs around and faced the camera, united for whatever disaster might follow. Sinatra's men in other parts of town, in other parts of the nation, were doing the same thing. Sinatra's lawyer, Milton A. Rudin, smoking a cigar, was watching with a keen eye, an alert legal mind. Other sets were watched by Brad Dexter, Jim Mahoney, Ed Pucci; Sinatra's makeup man, "Shotgun" Britton; his New York representative, Henri Giné; his haberdasher, Richard Carroll; his insurance broker, John Lillie; his valet, George Jacobs, a handsome Negro who, when entertaining girls in *his* apartment, plays records by Ray Charles.

And like so much of Hollywood's fear, the apprehension about the CBS show all proved to be without foundation. It was a highly flattering hour that did not deeply probe, as rumors suggested it would, into Sinatra's love life, or the Mafia, or other areas of his private province. While the documentary was not authorized, wrote Jack Gould in the next day's *New York Times*, "it could have been."

Immediately after the show, the telephones began to ring throughout the Sinatra system conveying words of joy and relief—and from New York came Jilly's telegram: WE RULE THE WORLD!

The next day, standing in the corridor of the NBC building where he was about to resume taping his show, Sinatra was discussing the CBS show with several of his friends, and he said, "Oh, it was a gas."

"Yeah, Frank, a helluva show."

"But I think Jack Gould was right in the *Times* today," Sinatra said. "There should have been more on the *man*, not so much on the music. . . ."

They nodded, nobody mentioning the past hysteria in the Sinatra world when it seemed CBS was zeroing in on the *man*; they just nodded and two of them laughed about Sinatra's apparently having gotten the word "bird" on the show—this being a favorite Sinatra word. He often inquires of his cronies, "How's your bird?"; and when he nearly drowned in Hawaii, he later explained, "Just got a little water on my bird"; and under a large photograph of him holding a whisky bottle, a photo that hangs in the home of an actor friend named Dick Bakalyan, the inscription reads: "Drink, Dickie! It's good for your bird." In the song, "Come Fly with Me," Sinatra sometimes alters the lyrics—". . . just say the words and we'll take our birds down to Acapulco Bay. . . ."

Ten minutes later Sinatra, following the orchestra, walked into the NBC studio which did not resemble in the slightest the scene here of eight days ago. On this occasion Sinatra was in fine voice, he cracked jokes between numbers, nothing could upset him. Once, while he was singing "How Can I Ignore the Girl Next Door," standing on the stage next to a tree, a television camera mounted on a vehicle came rolling in too close and plowed against the tree.

"Kee-rist!" yelled one of the technical assistants.

But Sinatra seemed hardly to notice it.

"We've had a slight accident," he said, calmly. Then he began the song all over from the beginning.

When the show was over, Sinatra watched the rerun on the monitor in the control room. He was very pleased, shaking hands with Dwight Hemion and his assistants. Then the whisky bottles were opened in Sinatra's dressing room. Pat Lawford was there, and so were Andy Williams and a dozen others. The telegrams and telephone calls continued to be received from all over the country with praise for the CBS show. There was even a call, Mahoney said, from the CBS producer, Don Hewitt, with whom Sinatra had been so angry a few days before. And Sinatra was *still* angry, feeling that CBS had betrayed him, though the show itself was not objectionable.

"Shall I drop a line to Hewitt?" Mahoney asked.

"Can you send a fist through the mail?" Sinatra asked.

He has everything, he cannot sleep, he gives nice gifts, he is not happy, but he would not trade, even for happiness, what he is. . . .

He is a piece of our past—but only we have aged, he hasn't . . . we are dogged by domesticity, he isn't . . . we have compunctions, he doesn't . . . it is our *fault, not his. . . .*

He controls the menus of every Italian restaurant in Los Angeles; if you want North Italian cooking, fly to Milan. . . .

Men follow him, imitate him, fight to be near him . . . there is something of the locker room, the barracks about him . . . bird . . . bird. . . .

He believes you must play it big, wide, expansively—the more open you are, the more you take in, your dimensions deepen, you grow, you become more what you are—bigger, richer. . . .

"He is better than anybody else, or at least they think he is, and he has to live up to it."

—Nancy Sinatra, Jr.

"He is calm on the outside—inwardly a million things are happening to him."

—Dick Bakalyan

"He has an insatiable desire to live every moment to its fullest because, I guess, he feels that right around the corner is extinction."

—Brad Dexter

"All I ever got out of any of my marriages was the two years Artie Shaw financed on an analyst's couch."

—Ava Gardner

"We weren't mother and son—we were buddies."

—Dolly Sinatra

"I'm for anything that gets you through the night, be it prayer, tran-quilizers or a bottle of Jack Daniel."

—Frank Sinatra

Frank Sinatra was tired of all the talk, the gossip, the theory—tired of reading quotes about himself, of hearing what people were saying about him all over town. It had been a tedious three weeks, he said, and now he just wanted to get away, go to Las Vegas, let off some steam. So he hopped in his jet, soared over the California hills across the Nevada flats, then over miles and miles of desert to The Sands and the Clay-Patterson fight.

On the eve of the fight he stayed up all night and slept through most of the afternoon, though his recorded voice could be heard singing in the lobby of The Sands, in the gambling casino, even in the toilets, being interrupted every few bars however by the paging public address: ". . . Telephone call for Mr. Ron Fish, Mr. Ron Fish . . . *with a ribbon of gold in her hair.* . . . Telephone call for Mr. Herbert Rothstein, Mr. Herbert Rothstein . . . *memories of a time so bright, keep me sleepless through dark endless nights.* . . ."

Standing around in the lobby of The Sands and other hotels up and down the strip on this afternoon before the fight were the usual prefight prophets: the gamblers, the old champs, the little cigar butts from Eighth Avenue, the sportswriters who knock the big fights all year but would never miss one, the novelists who seem always to be identifying with one boxer or another, the local prostitutes assisted by some talent in from Los Angeles, and also a young brunette in a wrinkled black cocktail dress who was at the bell captain's desk crying, "But I want to speak to Mr. Sinatra."

"He's not here," the bell captain said.

"Won't you put me through to his room?"

"There are *no* messages going through, Miss," he said, and then she turned, unsteadily, seeming close to tears, and walked through the lobby into the big noisy casino crowded with men interested only in money.

Shortly before seven P.M., Jack Entratter, a big grey-haired man who operates The Sands, walked into the gambling room to tell some men around the blackjack table that Sinatra was getting dressed. He also said that he'd been unable to get front-row seats for everybody, and so some of the men—including Leo Durocher, who had a date, and Joey Bishop, who was accompanied by his wife—would not be able to fit in Frank Sinatra's row but would have to take seats in the third row. When Entratter walked over to tell this to Joey Bishop, Bishop's face fell. He did not seem angry; he merely looked at Entratter with an empty silence, seeming somewhat stunned.

"Joey, I'm *sorry*," Entratter said when the silence persisted, "but we couldn't get more than six together in the front row."

Bishop still said nothing. But when they all appeared at the fight, Joey Bishop was in the front row, his wife in the third.

The fight, called a holy war between Muslims and Christians, was preceded by the introduction of three balding ex-champions, Rocky Marciano, Joe Louis, Sonny Liston—and then there was "The Star-Spangled Banner" sung by another man from out of the past, Eddie Fisher. It had been more than fourteen years ago, but Sinatra could still remember every detail: Eddie Fisher was then the new king of the baritones, with Billy Eckstine and Guy Mitchell right with him, and Sinatra had been long counted out. One day he remembered walking into a broadcasting studio past dozens of Eddie Fisher fans waiting outside the hall, and when they saw Sinatra they began to jeer, "Frankie, Frankie, I'm *swooning*, I'm *swooning*." This was also the time when he was selling only about 30,000 records a year, when he was dreadfully miscast as a funny man on his television show, and when he recorded such disasters as "Mama Will Bark," with Dagmar.

"I growled and barked on the record," Sinatra said, still horrified by the thought. "The only good it did me was with the dogs."

His voice and his artistic judgment were incredibly bad in 1952, but even more responsible for his decline, say his friends, was his pursuit of Ava Gardner. She was the big movie queen then, one of the most beautiful women in the world. Sinatra's daughter Nancy recalls seeing Ava swimming one day in her father's pool, then climbing out of the water with that fabulous body, walking slowly to the fire, leaning over it for a few moments, and then it suddenly seemed that her long dark hair was all dry, miraculously and effortlessly back in place.

With most women Sinatra dates, his friends say, he never knows whether they want him for what he can do for them now—or will do for them later. With Ava Gardner, it was different. He could do nothing for her later. She was on top. If Sinatra learned anything from his experience with her, he possibly learned that when a proud man is down a woman cannot help. Particularly a woman on top.

Nevertheless, despite a tired voice, some deep emotion seeped into his singing during this time. One particular song that is well remembered even now is "I'm a Fool to Want You," and a friend who was in the studio when Sinatra recorded it recalled: "Frank was really worked up that night. He did the song in one take, then turned around and walked out of the studio and that was that. . . ."

Sinatra's manager at that time, a former song plugger named Hank Sanicola, said, "Ava loved Frank, but not the way he loved her. He needs a great deal of love. He wants it twenty-four hours a day, he must have people around—Frank is that kind of guy." Ava Gardner, Sanicola said, "was very insecure. She feared she could not really hold a man . . . twice he went chasing her to Africa, wasting his own career. . . ."

"Ava didn't want Frank's men hanging around all the time," another friend said, "and this got him mad. With Nancy he used to be able to bring the whole band home with him, and Nancy, the good Italian wife, would never complain—she'd just make everybody a plate of spaghetti."

In 1953, after almost two years of marriage, Sinatra and Ava Gardner were divorced. Sinatra's mother reportedly arranged a reconciliation, but if Ava was willing, Frank Sinatra was not. He was seen with other women. The balance had shifted. Somewhere during this period Sinatra seemed to change from the kid singer, the boy actor in the sailor suit, to a man. Even before he had won the Oscar in 1953 for his role in *From Here to Eternity*, some flashes of his old talent were coming through—in his recording of "The Birth of the Blues," in his Riviera-nightclub appearance that jazz critics enthusiastically praised; and there was also a trend now toward L.P.'s and away from the quick three-minute deal, and Sinatra's concert style would have capitalized on this with or without an Oscar.

In 1954, totally committed to his talent once more, Frank Sinatra was selected Metronome's "Singer of the Year," and later he won the U.P.I. disc-jockey poll, unseating Eddie Fisher—who now, in Las Vegas, having sung "The Star-Spangled Banner," climbed out of the ring, and the fight began.

Floyd Patterson chased Clay around the ring in the first round, but was unable to reach him, and from then on he was Clay's toy, the bout ending in a technical knockout in the twelfth round. A half hour later, nearly everybody had forgotten about the fight and was back at the gambling tables or lining up to buy tickets for the Dean Martin-Sinatra-Bishop nightclub routine on the stage of The Sands. This routine, which includes Sammy Davis, Jr. when he is in town, consists of a few songs and much cutting up, all of it very informal, very special, and rather ethnic—Martin, a drink in hand, asking Bishop: "Did you ever see a Jew jitsu?"; and Bishop, playing a Jewish waiter, warning the two Italians to watch out "because I got my own group—the *Matzia*."

Then after the last show at The Sands, the Sinatra crowd, which now numbered about twenty—and included Jilly, who had flown in from New York; Jimmy Cannon, Sinatra's favorite sports columnist; Harold Gibbons, a Teamster official expected to take over if Hoffa goes to jail—all got into a line of cars and headed for another club. It was three o'clock. The night was young.

They stopped at The Sahara, taking a long table near the back, and listened to a baldheaded little comedian named Don Rickles, who is probably more caustic than any comic in the country. His humor is so rude, in *such* bad taste, that it offends no one—it is *too* offensive to be offensive. Spotting Eddie Fisher among the audience, Rickles proceeded to ridicule him as a lover, saying it was no wonder that he could not handle Elizabeth Taylor; and when two businessmen in the audience acknowledged that they were Egyptian, Rickles cut into them for their country's policy toward Israel; and he strongly suggested that the woman seated at one table with her husband was actually a hooker.

When the Sinatra crowd walked in, Don Rickles could not be more delighted. Pointing to Jilly, Rickles yelled: "How's it feel to be Frank's tractor? . . . Yeah, Jilly keeps walking in front of Frank clearing the way." Then, nodding to Durocher, Rickles said, "Stand up Leo, show Frank how you slide." Then he focused on Sinatra, not failing to mention Mia Farrow, nor that he was wearing a toupee, nor to say that Sinatra was washed up as a singer, and when Sinatra laughed, everybody laughed, and Rickles pointed toward Bishop: "Joey Bishop keeps checking with Frank to see what's funny."

Then, after Rickles told some Jewish jokes, Dean Martin stood up and yelled, "Hey, you're always talking about the Jews, never about the Italians," and Rickles cut him off with, "What do we need the Italians for—all they do is keep the flies off our fish."

Sinatra laughed, they all laughed, and Rickles went on this way for nearly an hour until Sinatra, standing up, said, "All right, com'on, get this thing over with. I gotta go."

"Shaddup and sit down!" Rickles snapped. "I've had to listen to you sing. . . ."

"Who do you think you're talking to?" Sinatra yelled back.

"Dick Haymes," Rickles replied, and Sinatra laughed again, and then Dean Martin, pouring a bottle of whisky over his head, entirely drenching his tuxedo, pounded the table.

"Who would ever believe that staggering would make a star?" Rickles said, but Martin called out, "Hey, I wanna make a speech."

"Shaddup."

"No, Don, I wanna tell ya," Dean Martin persisted, "that I think you're a great performer."

"Well, thank you, Dean," Rickles said, seeming pleased.

"But don't go by me," Martin said, plopping down into this seat, "I'm drunk."

"I'll buy that," Rickles said.

By four A.M. Frank Sinatra led the group out of The Sahara, some of them carrying their glasses of whisky with them, sipping it along the sidewalk and in the cars; then, returning to The Sands, they walked into the gambling casino. It was still packed with people, the roulette wheels spinning, the crapshooters screaming in the far corner.

Frank Sinatra, holding a shot glass of bourbon in his left hand, walked through the crowd. He, unlike some of his friends, was perfectly pressed, his tuxedo tie precisely pointed, his shoes unsmudged. He never seems to lose his dignity, never lets his guard completely down no matter how much he has drunk, nor how long he has been up. He never sways when he walks, like Dean Martin, nor does he ever dance in the aisles or jump up on tables, like Sammy Davis.

A part of Sinatra, no matter where he is, is never there. There is always a part of him, though sometimes a small part, that remains *Il Padrone*. Even now, resting his shot glass on the blackjack table, facing the dealer, Sinatra stood a bit back from the table, not leaning against it. He reached under his tuxedo jacket into his trouser pocket and came up with a thick but *clean* wad of bills. Gently he peeled off a one-hundred-dollar bill and placed it on the green-felt table. The dealer dealt him two cards. Sinatra called for a third card, overbid, lost the hundred.

Without a change of expression, Sinatra put down a second hundred-dollar bill. He lost that. Then he put down a third, and lost that. Then he placed two one-hundred-dollar bills on the table and lost those. Finally, putting his sixth hundred-dollar bill on the table, and losing it, Sinatra moved away from the table, nodding to the man, and announcing, "Good dealer."

The crowd that had gathered around him now opened up to let him through. But a woman stepped in front of him, handing him a piece of paper to autograph. He signed it and then *he* said, "Thank you."

In the rear of The Sands' large dining room was a long table reserved for Sinatra. The dining room was fairly empty at this hour, with perhaps two dozen other people in the room, including a table of four unescorted young ladies sitting near Sinatra. On the other side of the room, at another long table, sat seven men shoulder-to-shoulder against the wall, two of them wearing dark glasses, all of them eating quietly, speaking hardly a word, just sitting and eating and missing nothing.

The Sinatra party, after getting settled and having a few more drinks, ordered something to eat. The table was about the same size as the one reserved for Sinatra whenever he is at Jilly's in New York; and the people seated around this table in Las Vegas were many of the same people who are often seen with Sinatra at Jilly's or at a restaurant in California, or in Italy, or in New Jersey, or wherever Sinatra happens to be. When Sinatra sits to dine, his trusted friends are close; and no matter where he is, no matter how elegant the place may be, there is something of the neighborhood showing because Sinatra, no matter how far he has come, is still something of the boy from the neighborhood—only now he can take his neighborhood with him.

In some ways, this quasi-family affair at a reserved table in a public place is the closest thing Sinatra now has to home life. Perhaps, having had a home and left it, this approximation is as close as he cares to come; although this does not seem precisely so because he speaks with such warmth about his family, keeps in close touch with his first wife, and insists that she make no decision without first consulting him. He is always eager to place his furniture or other mementos of himself in her home or his daughter Nancy's, and he also is on amiable terms with Ava Gardner. When he was in Italy making *Von Ryan's Express*, they spent some time together, being pursued wherever they went by the *paparazzi*. It was reported then that the *paparazzi* had made Sinatra a collective offer of $16,000 if he would pose with Ava Gardner; Sinatra was said to have made a counter offer of $32,000 if he could break one *paparazzi* arm and leg.

While Sinatra is often delighted that he can be in his home completely without people, enabling him to read and think without interruption, there are occasions when he finds himself alone at night, and *not* by choice. He may have dialed a half-dozen women, and for one reason or another they are all unavailable. So he will call his valet, George Jacobs.

"I'll be coming home for dinner tonight, George."

"How many will there be?"

"Just myself," Sinatra will say. "I want something light, I'm not very hungry."

George Jacobs is a twice-divorced man of thirty-six who resembles Billy Eckstine. He has traveled all over the world with Sinatra and is devoted to him. Jacobs lives in a comfortable bachelor's apartment off Sunset Boulevard around the corner from Whiskey à Go Go, and he is known around town for the assortment of frisky California girls he has as friends—a few of whom, he concedes, were possibly drawn to him initially because of his closeness to Frank Sinatra.

When Sinatra arrives, Jacobs will serve him dinner in the dining room. Then Sinatra will tell Jacobs that he is free to go home. If Sinatra, on such evenings, should ask Jacobs to stay longer, or to play a few hands of poker, he would be happy to do so. But Sinatra never does.

This was his second night in Las Vegas, and Frank Sinatra sat with friends in The Sands' dining room until nearly eight A.M. He slept through much of the day, then flew back to Los Angeles, and on the following morning he was driving his little golf cart through the Paramount Pictures movie lot. He was scheduled to complete two final scenes with the sultry blonde actress, Virna Lisi, in the film, *Assault on a Queen*. As he maneuvered the little vehicle up the road between the big studio buildings, he spotted Steve Rossi who, with his comedy partner Marty Allen, was making a film in an adjoining studio with Nancy Sinatra.

"Hey, Dag," he yelled to Rossi, "stop kissing Nancy."

"It's part of the film, Frank," Rossi said, turning as he walked.

"In the garage?"

"It's my Dago blood, Frank."

"Well, cool it," Sinatra said, winking, then cutting his golf cart around a corner and parking it outside a big drab building within which the scenes for *Assault* would be filmed.

"Where's the fat director?" Sinatra called out, striding into the studio that was crowded with dozens of technical assistants and actors all gathered around cameras. The director, Jack Donohue, a large man who has worked with Sinatra through twenty-two years on one production or other, had had headaches with this film. The script had been chopped, the actors seemed restless, and Sinatra had become bored. But now there were only two scenes left—a short one to be filmed in the pool, and a longer and passionate one featuring Sinatra and Virna Lisi to be shot on a simulated beach.

The pool scene, which dramatizes a situation where Sinatra and his hijackers fail in their attempt to sack the *Queen Mary*, went quickly and well. After Sinatra had been kept in the water shoulder-high for a few minutes, he said, "Let's move it, fellows—it's cold in this water, and I've just gotten over a cold."

So the camera crews moved in closer, Virna Lisi splashed next to Sinatra in the water, and Jack Donohue yelled to his assistants operating the fans, "Get the waves going," and another man gave the command, *"Agitate!"* and Sinatra broke out in song. "Agitate in rhythm," then quieted down just before the cameras started to roll.

Frank Sinatra was on the beach in the next situation, supposedly gazing up at the stars, and Virna Lisi was to approach him, toss one of her shoes near him to announce her presence, then sit near him and prepare for a passionate session. Just before beginning, Miss Lisi made a practice toss of her shoe toward the prone figure of Sinatra sprawled on the beach. As she tossed her shoe, Sinatra called out, "Hit me in my bird and I'm going home."

Virna Lisa, who understands little English and certainly none of Sinatra's special vocabulary, looked confused, but everybody behind the camera laughed. She threw the shoe toward him. It twirled in the air, landed on his stomach.

"Well, that's about three inches too high," he announced. She again was puzzled by the laughter behind the camera.

Then Jack Donohue had them rehearse their lines, and Sinatra, still very charged from the Las Vegas trip, and anxious to get the cameras rolling, said, "Let's try one." Donohue, not certain that Sinatra and Lisi knew their lines well enough, nevertheless said okay, and an assistant with a clapboard called, "419, Take 1," and Virna Lisi approached with the shoe, tossed it at Frank lying on the beach. It fell short of his thigh, and Sinatra's right eye raised almost imperceptibly, but the crew got the message, smiled.

"What do the stars tell you tonight?" Miss Lisi said, delivering her first line, and sitting next to Sinatra on the beach.

"The stars tell me tonight I'm an idiot," Sinatra said, "a gold-plated idiot to get mixed up in this thing. . . ."

"Cut," Donohue said. There were some microphone shadows on the sand, and Virna Lisi was not sitting in the proper place near Sinatra.

"419, Take 2," the clapboard man called.

Miss Lisi again approached, threw the shoe at him, this time falling short—Sinatra exhaling only slightly—and she said, "What do the stars tell you tonight?"

"The stars tell me I'm an idiot, a gold-plated idiot to get mixed up in this thing. . . ." Then, according to the script, Sinatra was to continue, ". . . do you know what we're getting into? The minute we step on the deck of the *Queen Mary*, we've just tattooed ourselves," but Sinatra, who often improvises on lines, recited them: ". . . do you know what we're getting into? The minute we step on the deck of that mother's-ass ship. . . ."

"*No*, no," Donohue interrupted, shaking his head, "I don't think that's right."

The cameras stopped, some people laughed, and Sinatra looked up from his position in the sand as if he had been unfairly interrupted.

"I don't see why that can't work . . ." he began, but Richard Conte, standing behind the camera, yelled, "It won't play in London."

Donohue pushed his hand through his thinning grey hair and said, but not really in anger, "You know, that scene was pretty good until somebody blew the line. . . ."

"Yeah," agreed the cameraman, Billy Daniels, his head popping out from around the camera, "it was a pretty good piece. . . ."

"Watch your language," Sinatra cut in. Then Sinatra, who has a genius for figuring out ways of not reshooting scenes, suggested a way in which the film could be used and the "mother" line could be recorded later. This met with approval. Then the cameras were rolling again, Virna Lisi was leaning toward Sinatra in the sand, and then he pulled her down close to him. The camera now moved in for a close-up of their faces, ticking away for a few long seconds, but Sinatra and Lisi did not stop kissing, they just lay together in the sand wrapped in one another's arms, and then Virna Lisi's left leg just slightly began to rise a bit, and everybody in the studio now watched in silence, not saying anything until Donohue finally called out:

"If you ever get through, let me know. I'm running out of film."

Then Miss Lisi got up, straightened out her white dress, brushed back her blonde hair and touched her lipstick, which was smeared. Sinatra got up, a little smile on his lips, and headed for his dressing room.

Passing an older man who stood near a camera, Sinatra asked, "How's your Bell & Howell?"

The older man smiled.

"It's fine, Frank."

"Good."

In his dressing room Sinatra was met by an automobile designer who had the plans for Sinatra's new custom-built model to replace the $25,000 Ghia he has been driving for the last few years. He also was awaited by his secretary, Tom Conroy, who had a bag full of fan mail, including a letter from New York's Mayor John Lindsay; and by Bill Miller, Sinatra's pianist, who would rehearse some of the songs that would be recorded later in the evening for Sinatra's newest album, *Moonlight Sinatra*.

While Sinatra does not mind hamming it up a bit on a movie set, he is extremely serious about his recording sessions; as he explained to a British writer, Robin Douglas-Home: "Once you're on that record singing, it's you and you alone. If it's bad and gets you criticized, it's you who's to blame—no one else. If it's good, it's also you. With a film it's never like that; there are producers and scriptwriters, and hundreds of men in offices and the thing is taken right out of your hands. With a record, you're *it*. . . ."

> But now the days are short
>   I'm in the autumn of the year
> And now I think of my life
>   As vintage wine
> From fine old kegs. . . .

It no longer matters what song he is singing, or who wrote the words—they are all *his* words, *his* sentiments, they are chapters from the lyrical novel of his life.

> Life is a beautiful thing
> As long as I hold the string. . . .

When Frank Sinatra drives to the studio, he seems to dance out of the car across the sidewalk into the front door; then, snapping his fingers, he is standing in front of the orchestra in an intimate, airtight room, and soon he is dominating every man, every instrument, every sound wave. Some of the musicians have accompanied him for twenty-five years, have gotten old hearing him sing "You Make Me Feel So Young."

When his voice is on, as it was tonight, Sinatra is in ecstasy, the room becomes electric, there is an excitement that spreads through the orchestra and is felt in the control booth where a dozen men, Sinatra's friends, wave at him from behind the glass. One of the men is the Dodgers' pitcher, Don Drysdale ("Hey, Big D," Sinatra calls out, "*hey*, baby!"); another is the professional golfer Bo Wininger; there are also numbers of pretty women standing in the booth behind the engineers, women who smile at Sinatra and softly move their bodies to the mellow mood of his music:

> Will this be moon love
> Nothing but moon love
> Will you be gone when the dawn
> Comes stealing through. . . .

After he is finished, the record is played back on tape, and Nancy Sinatra, who has just walked in, joins her father near the front of the orchestra to hear the playback. They listen silently, all eyes on them, the king, the princess; and when the music ends there is applause from the control booth, Nancy smiles, and her father snaps his fingers and says, kicking a foot, "*Ooba-deeba-boobe-do!*"

Then Sinatra calls to one of his men. "Hey, Sarge, think I can have a half-a-cup of coffee?"

Sarge Weiss, who had been listening to the music, slowly gets up.

"Didn't mean to wake ya, Sarge," Sinatra says, smiling.

Then Weiss brings the coffee, and Sinatra looks at it, smells it, then announces, "I thought he'd be nice to me, but it's *really* coffee. . . ."

There are more smiles, and then the orchestra prepares for the next number. And one hour later, it is over.

The musicians put their instruments into their cases, grab their coats, and begin to file out, saying good-night to Sinatra. He knows them all by name, knows much about them personally, from their bachelor days, through their divorces, through their ups and downs, as they know him. When a French-horn player, a short Italian named Vincent DeRosa, who has played with Sinatra since The Lucky Strike "Hit Parade" days on radio, strolled by, Sinatra reached out to hold him for a second.

"Vicenzo," Sinatra said, "how's your little girl?"

"She's fine, Frank."

"Oh, she's not a *little* girl anymore," Sinatra corrected himself, "she's a big girl now."

"Yes, she goes to college now. U.S.C."

"That's great."

"She's also got a little talent, I think, Frank, as a singer."

Sinatra was silent for a moment, then said, "Yes, but it's very good for her to get her education first, Vicenzo."

Vincent DeRosa nodded.

"Yes, Frank," he said, and then he said, "Well, good-night, Frank."

"Good-night, Vicenzo."

After the musicians had all gone, Sinatra left the recording room and joined his friends in the corridor. He was going to go out and do some drinking with Drysdale, Wininger, and a few other friends, but first he walked to the other end of the corridor to say good-night to Nancy, who was getting her coat and was planning to drive home in her own car.

After Sinatra had kissed her on the cheek, he hurried to join his friends at the door. But before Nancy could leave the studio, one of Sinatra's men, Al Silvani, a former prizefight manager, joined her.

"Are you ready to leave yet, Nancy?"

"Oh, thanks, Al," she said, "but I'll be all right."

"Pope's orders," Silvani said, holding his hands up, palms out.

Only after Nancy had pointed to two of her friends who would escort her home, and only after Silvani recognized them as friends, would he leave.

The rest of the month was bright and balmy. The record session had gone magnificently, the film was finished, the television shows were out of the way, and now Sinatra was in his Ghia driving out to his office to begin coordinating his latest projects. He had an engagement at The Sands, a new spy film called *The Naked Runner* to be shot in England, and a couple more albums to do in the immediate months ahead. And within a week he would be fifty years old. . . .

> Life is a beautiful thing
> As long as I hold the string
> I'd be a silly so-and-so
> If I should ever let go. . . .

Frank Sinatra stopped his car. The light was red. Pedestrians passed quickly across his windshield but, as usual, one did not. It was a girl in her twenties. She remained at the curb staring at him. Through the corner of his left eye he could see her, and he knew, because it happens almost every day, that she was thinking, *It looks like him, but is it?*

Just before the light turned green, Sinatra turned toward her, looked directly into her eyes waiting for the reaction he knew would come. It came and he smiled. She smiled and he was gone.

GARRY TRUDEAU

DOONESBURY: THE GOLDEN HOUR

THESE THREE STRIPS, WHICH appeared in the spring of 2004, began a story about sacrifice, about the kind of shattering loss that completely transforms lives. As I had so often in the past, I placed B.D. in harm's way, but this time his charmed life took a sudden, dark turn on a road outside Fallujah. In the opening panels, I showed him in shock, hallucinating, with voices cutting in and out. Medics call this time the golden hour, that small window of opportunity when lives are most easily saved. B.D. was medevaced out, and in the third strip, I reversed the point of view, revealing just how grievous his wound really was. We also saw his hair, its presence almost as startling as the absence of his leg.

What I meant to convey here was that B.D.'s life had been irrevocably changed, that another chapter had begun. He was being sent on an arduous journey of recovery and rehabilitation. There is no culture of complaint among the wounded—most feel grateful to be alive and respectful of those who have endured even worse fates. But for many, a kind of black humor is indispensable in fending off bitterness or despair, so this was what animated the strips that followed.

Whatever we may think about the war in Iraq, we can't tune out the individual tragedies. We have to remain mindful of the terrible losses that are being suffered in our name.

—Garry Trudeau

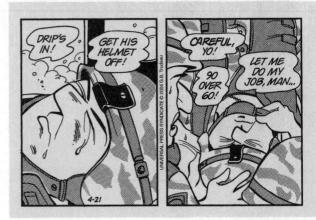

519

SCOTT TUROW

From THE LAWS of OUR FATHERS

FAULKNER REMARKED THAT HE wrote novels only because he had tried and failed, first at writing poems, then at writing short stories. Faulkner could call himself a failure as a short story writer only by comparison with his novels. I, on the other hand, can offer the same comment about myself with no reservations concerning its accuracy.

For a novelist, no excerpt can truly be her or his "best." If the best were there in small pieces, the larger whole would have no reason to exist. But there are snatches of my novels that I reread for inspiration and amusement and what follows is one of them. *The Laws of Our Fathers* is my most personal book, dedicated to my children, and meant as a generational reflection about those of us who came of age in the 1960s. Thematically, the novel is dominated by the passions and mistakes that haunted our youth, especially the conviction that a more just America was within our grasp, and the way that vision has both foundered and changed shape as the years have passed. Naturally, race relations, the original sin of America's conception, play a central part.

Near the end of the novel, Hobie Tuttle, a black lawyer and a lifelong friend of one of the novel's narrators, Seth Weissman, steps forward to speak the eulogy upon the death of Seth's father, Bernhard, a Holocaust survivor.

—Scott Turow

EULOGY FOR BERNHARD WEISSMAN
by Hobart Tariq Tuttle
April 1, 1996

Allah, Yahweh, sweet Jesus—by whatever name we know You, Lord—take the soul of Bernhard Weissman. You caused him in his life to confront terrible wickedness. He now deserves Your eternal peace. Were we all—all of us here—to share our memories of Bernhard

Weissman, You'd hear a lot of different things. There'd be many voices. There are folks here who can tell You he was a genius in his work.
Winners of the Nobel Prize in Economics invited him to their table
and treated him as a peer. His granddaughter, our sweet Sarah, would
tell You he was a great old guy who responded to her kindness. And
You've heard Seth say he was a tough father, and I tell You, I was
around to see that, and it is word.

I can speak only for myself. I *liked* the dude. I'm here as his friend.
Soundin goofy, I know, sayin I was friends with a fella twice my age.
But we *were* friends. When I was a little kid, he scared the livin hell
out of me. I remember him wearing those nasty glasses that looked
like they pinched your nose—pince-nez?—and talking with that
funky Viennese accent? Half the time to start, I couldn't tell if he was
speaking to me or clearing his throat. I wanted no part of this cat.

But by high school, I had gotten into him. I can tell You a lot of
good things about Mr. Weissman. He was funny. Kind of sneaky
funny. He'd catch you. I remember a few years ago, I was visiting, and
we were talking about the things we talked about often, politics, race,
America, and I said I saw how the government had finally relented
and was going to let a group of black and Jewish leaders go together to
visit various capitals in the Middle East, hoping to make peace. "Zere
is no kvestion, Hopie, zat ze government vants zem to go," he told me.
"Zey vould razzer, however, zat zey not come back."

And something else I always appreciated about the man—he liked
me. Part of that, I always knew, was for Seth's sake. Bernhard was
doin the best he could, takin to Seth's main man, even if he couldn't
always do the same for Seth. But he was into me for me, too. I had no
doubt about that. I could make him laugh. And he had no trouble with
a Negro kid being smart. He was not born American and he did not
have a trace of our color-thing, not even of speck of it, on his soul. I
appreciated that, I must say. And I have to allow, on my side, that it
was easier for me to accept him than many other white folks, because
he had paid the price. I couldn't ever say to him, "You don't know
what it's like." He knew. He understood how it felt to be stuck in this
situation, to be labeled and judged, always and constantly under the
weight of something you never really fully chose.

You know, I'm like everybody else on the planet: I am deeply
struck by the suffering of my own. It's a terrible truth that identity is
steeped in the blood of martyrs, a phenomenon you can see clear round

the world, people everywhere grouped under ethnic banners and all of them beefin about the way their kin were treated in times past. The Armenians, the Kurds. The Igbo. The Rom. The list is damn near end-less. Everybody recalls their oppressors. Even the Pilgrims, WASPs, who I grew up thinking had everything, celebrated Thanksgiving to recollect how bad folks back in England had been to them. And the fact is, nobody's makin this stuff up. We cannot bear homage to those who made us without recognizing their suffering. But it's a sad lesson, nonetheless, that we all so often lay claim to our heritage out of fear of those who once hated us and thus may do so again.

But I'm like the rest: I have always known the pain of black folks. All my life. I've felt it in my bones. We had it good in my home, no complaint about that, but it didn't take me very long, even as a little kid, to notice how hard it was for so many others, and to see that a whole lot of those folks had the same skin on them as I did. I'm the first to tell you that I did not have a clue what to do with that. As a young man, I didn't want the burden. And then I discovered I'd never know myself, never accept myself, unless I took it up. And the absolutely amazing part, as I look back, is that the person who taught me more about dealing with that—*the* man in my life—is Bernhard Weissman. I'm sure, if there had been some cagey old ex-slave who lived down the block, I'd have sat at his feet instead. But there wasn't. I guess Bernhard was the closest thing I could find, a firsthand victim of unbearable oppression, someone I could ask what I see now I was always askin him, even though I never once said it out loud, namely, How do you come to terms?

The last time I saw him, I was asking that again. I was truly in a state. Upset. I was trying a lawsuit, a very confusing lawsuit. It was con-fusing to me, because I saw what I see every day in a new light. Usually, I view the life of the ghettoized as a professional. I see it case by case: one crime, one rousting, this thieving client, that dishonest cop. I render what aid I can on that basis, one at a time. But being home, I somehow lost my grip on my professional perspective. I saw the larger picture again, and it was, at moments, heartrending. A terrible thing is happening here. In our midst. And I saw how hatred and desperation may yet engulf us all.

And I talked to Bernhard about this. We walked. We went out there, not far away, and inched along the Midway, that beautiful tree-lined esplanade, with its benches, on the west side of U. Park. It was one of those mysterious late-autumn days in the Midwest, the pewter sky losing the hope of light, the big trees stretching black and stark, the walks slick with moldering yellow leaves. Bernhard listened to me as I confided my anguish, and he confronted me with an odd question.

"Do you know, Hopie," he asked, "vere zis Mid-vay comes from?"

I didn't of course. So he told me the story. During the Civil War, after the Yanks had freed the Mississippi River, they used to freight Confederate prisoners up here, far from the front lines. These rebs— 20,000 of them—ended up imprisoned here on the land that now stands beneath the Midway. The city was pretty much a wreck by then. There were no provisions. Everything was being commandeered for the front. There wasn't food to spare, nor coats nor blankets. And in the dead of winter, these prisoners, Southern boys, some who'd barely seen a frost, just basically stood out here on the Midway and died. Froze to death. More than 12,000 of them. They buried those Confederate soldiers right there. And after Dixie was subdued, the city fathers, embittered by war and eager to forget its horrors, plowed the ground over and planted grass and trees, rather than raise gravestones.

You think about that, though. Those lovely stone mansions, up on Grand Boulevard, they were there by the 1850s. It was a fashionable street. Ladies in their hoop skirts went perambulating up and down every day. They walked their babies. And yonder, behind a mess of wire and fences, stood the rebs, huddling under the trees for cover in the snow, freezing and screaming and carrying on, crying out for mercy, and dying. Every day a couple got shot trying to escape.

It was something for me to think about, of course, because it called up all of an African-American's complicated feelings about the Civil War. I still cleave to a schoolboy's understanding of those events, because I think it is fundamentally correct. In the minds of many of those fighting—probably most—it was the War to Free the Slaves. Oh sure, it had a thousand other motives, too, Genovese and them-all, I've read the books. But for the most part there were Americans, who, no matter how they varnished it over with talk of states' rights or the cotton economy, were willing to die for the right to own a nigger, and other Americans, hundreds of thousands of them, white Americans, prepared to lay down their lives because God wanted all his children, including the black ones, to be free. I often think we'd do well in this country to bear both facts in mind. Surely I had them in mind at that moment. And although a part of me listened to Bernhard's story in shock, to think that I had walked a thousand times across the unmarked graves of young soldiers who died so pitifully in their own country, another part of me—the greater part, I confess—heard this with the parched thirst of a people who have never had a full measure of revenge. For it occurred to me at once that those men, cruelly imprisoned, were slaveholders and their supporters. And I thought to myself, Good, this was good, this was as it had to be. Well, there was a look we shared then, Bernhard and me, he the survivor of a similar captivity and I the great-grandson of slaves. He read the thought passing behind my eyes as surely as if I had spoken it, and I do not believe we exchanged another word as we walked slowly home.

Bernhard made his mistakes. But we cannot lay him to rest without admiring his strength of character. He had the courage to tell me what he meant to out on the Midway, which was that this would never end. He could hardly be faulted for that view, not only because of his own experience, but given what has gone on since, dozens of hideous episodes that seem to show that humankind has not learned a damn thing from all that suffering. Pol Pot's killing fields. Idi Amin. The Chinese slaughters in Tibet. The Ayatollah's annihilation of the Baha'i. The Hutus' dismemberment of the Tutsis. The disappeared in Argentina. The carnage in Bangladesh. In Biafra. In Bosnia. We may only pray it does not happen here.

We cannot blame Bernhard for his pessimism. There are days— many, many days—when I know in my bones he was right. But perhaps there is another way to accept his legacy. Perhaps there is meaning in these millions of seemingly meaningless deaths. Perhaps Darwin—or God—is sending the species signs so large we cannot fail to heed them. Perhaps our survival depends on recognizing that we can be monsters, so that self-awareness reinforces our commitment to what is more noble in us. For in his lifetime, Bernhard also saw freedom in South Africa, the enfranchisement of women in the West, the withering of colonialism, the blooming of democracy in nation after nation, and the growth of a million varieties of the fruit of human cunning which have immeasurably advanced knowledge and well-being across the planet. Perhaps that was what Bernhard meant to tell me, after all: we are both. We are the tyrant *and* the democrat, the captor *and* the survivor, the slaveholder *and* the slave. We are blood heirs to each heritage. On the best days—his and mine—that is what I hope Bernhard would admonish all of us never to forget.

ANNE TYLER

From DINNER at the HOMESICK RESTAURANT

DINNER AT THE HOMESICK RESTAURANT was my ninth novel. I've had sixteen published, all told. In an ideal world, I would be saying that my best book was my sixteenth book. (We all like to believe that we're getting better and better.) And it's true that the work that came later may contain more skillful pieces of writing, and fewer errors of inexperience.

But that fact is that Novel No. 9 is the one I'm proudest to claim. Of all my books, it comes closest to the vision I had in mind when I first began it. Its characters were the most alive to me while I was writing, seizing the plot right out of my hands, startling me with remarks I'd never have dreamed of on my own, breaking my heart a hundred times over—poor beleaguered, angry Pearl and her "good" son Ezra and her "bad" son Cody and her anxious daughter Jenny. Sometimes when I'd finished work for the day I had a sort of scraped feeling deep in my chest, as if I had dug down to the very bottom of my soul to come up with what I'd written.

It didn't win any prizes. It sold all right, I guess, though not as well as the later books. But if you'd told me after I finished it that I would never write anything else, I would still feel that I had done with my life the very best that I could do. I don't think anyone could ask for more than that.

—Anne Tyler

Cody and Ezra and Jenny went shopping for a Christmas present for their mother. Each of them had saved four weeks' allowance, which meant forty cents apiece, and Cody had a dollar extra that he'd taken from Miss Saunders's center desk drawer. That made two dollars and twenty cents—enough for some winter gloves, Cody suggested. Jenny said gloves were boring and she wanted to buy a diamond ring. "That's really stupid," Cody told her. "Even you ought to know you can't buy a diamond ring for two-twenty."

"I don't mean a real one, I mean glass. Or anything, just so it's pretty and not useful."

They were forced to shop in the stores near home, since they didn't want to spend money on carfare. It was mid-December and crowds of other people were shopping too—plowing past with their arms full of packages, breathing white clouds in the frosty air. Further downtown the department store windows would be as rich and bright as the insides of jewel boxes, and there'd be carols and clanging brass bells and festoons of tinsel on the traffic lights, but in this neighborhood the shops were smaller, darker, decorated with a single wreath on the door or a cardboard Santa Claus carrying a carton of Chesterfield cigarettes. Soldiers on leave straggled by in clumps, looking lost. The shoppers had something grim and determined about them—even those with the gaudiest packages. They seemed likely to mow down anyone in their path. Cody took a pinch of Jenny's coat sleeve so as not to lose her.

"I'm serious," she was saying. "I don't want to get her anything warm. Anything necessary. Anything—"

"Serviceable," Ezra said.

They all grimaced.

"If we bought her a ring, though," Ezra said, "she might feel bad about the wastefulness. She might not really enjoy it."

Cody hated the radiant, grave expression that Ezra wore sometimes; it showed that he realized full well how considerate he was being. "What do *you* want for Christmas?" Cody asked him roughly. "World peace?"

"World what? I'd like a recorder," Ezra said.

They crossed an intersection with a swarm of sailors. "Well," said Cody, "you're not getting one."

"I know that."

"You're getting a cap with turn-down earflaps and a pair of corduroy pants."

"Cody!" said Jenny. "You weren't supposed to tell."

"It doesn't matter," Ezra said.

They separated for a woman who had stopped to fit her child's mittens on. "It used to be," Jenny said, "that we got toys for Christmas, and candy. Remember how nice last Christmas was?"

"This one's going to be nice too," Ezra told her.

"Remember down in Virginia, when Daddy bought us a sled, and Mother said it was silly because it hardly ever snowed but December twenty-sixth we woke up and there was snow all over everything?"

"That was fun," Ezra said.

"We had the only sled in town," Jenny said. "Cody started charging for rides. Daddy showed us how to wax the runners and we pulled it to the top of that hill . . . What was the name of that hill? It had such a funny—"

Then she stopped short on the sidewalk. Pedestrians jostled all around her. "Why," she said.

Cody and Ezra looked at her.

"He's really not ever coming home again. Is he," she said.

No one answered. After a minute they resumed walking, three abreast, and Cody took a pinch of Ezra's sleeve, too, so they wouldn't drift apart in the crowd.

Cody sorted the mail, setting aside for his mother a couple of envelopes that looked like Christmas cards. He threw away a department store flyer and a letter from his school. He pocketed an envelope with a Cleveland postmark.

He went upstairs to his room and switched on the goose-necked lamp beside his bed. While the lightbulb warmed, he whistled and stared out the window. Then he tested the bulb with his fingers and, finding it hot enough, wrapped the envelope around it and counted slowly to thirty. After that he pried open the flap with ease and pulled out a single sheet of paper and a check.

. . . says they should be producing to capacity by June of '45 . . . his father wrote. *Sorry the enclosed is a little smaller than expected as I have incurred some . . .* It was his usual letter, nothing different. Cody folded it again and slid it back in the envelope, though it hardly seemed worth the effort. Then he heard the front door slam. "Ezra Tull?" Pearl called. Her cloppy high heels started rapidly up the stairs. Cody tucked the envelope into his bureau and shut the drawer. "Ezra!"

"He's not here," Cody said.

She came to stand in the doorway. "Where is he?" she asked. She was out of breath, untidy-looking. Her hat was on crooked and she still wore her coat.

"He went to get the laundry, like you told him to."

"What do you know about this?"

She bore down on him, holding out a stack of snapshots. The one on top was so blurred and gray that Cody had trouble deciphering it.

He took the whole collection from her hand. Ah, yes: Ezra lay in a stupor, surrounded by liquor bottles. Cody grinned. He'd forgotten that picture completely.

"What could it mean?" his mother asked. "I take a roll of film to the drugstore and I come back with the shock of my life. I just wanted to get the camera ready for Christmas. I was expecting maybe some scenes from last summer, or Jenny's birthday cake . . . and here I find Ezra like a derelict! A common drunk! Could this be what it looks like? Answer me!"

"He's not as perfect as you think he is," Cody told her.

"But he's never given me a moment's worry."

"He's done a lot that might surprise you."

Pearl sat down on his bed. She was shaking her head, looking stunned. "Oh, Cody, it's such a battle, raising children," she said. "I know you must think I'm difficult. I lose my temper, I carry on like a shrew sometimes, but if you could just realize how . . . helpless I feel! How scary it is to know that everyone I love depends on me! I'm afraid I'll do something wrong."

She reached up—for the photos, he thought, and he held them out to her; but no, what she wanted was his hand. She took it and pulled him down beside her. Her skin felt hot and dry. "I've probably been too hard on you," she said. "But I look to you for support now, Cody. You're the only person I can turn to; it may be you and I are more alike than you think. Cody, what am I going to do?"

She leaned closer, and Cody drew back. Even her eyes seemed to give off heat. "Uh, well . . ." he said.

"Who took that picture, anyhow? Was it you?"

"Look," he said. "It was a joke."

"Joke?"

"Ezra didn't drink that stuff. I just set some bottles around him."

Her gaze flicked back and forth across his face.

"He's never touched a drop," Cody told her.

"I see," she said. She freed his hand. She said, "Well, all I can say is, that's some joke, young man." Then she stood up and took several steps away from him. "That's some sense of humor you've got," she said.

Cody shrugged.

"Oh, I suppose it must seem very funny, scaring your mother half out of her wits. Letting her babble on like a fool. Slandering your little brother. It must seem hilarious, to someone like you."

"I'm just naturally mean, I guess," Cody said.

"You've been mean since the day you were born," she told him.

After she had walked out, he went to work resealing his father's letter.

Ezra landed on Park Place and Cody said, "Aha! Park Place with one hotel. Fifteen hundred dollars."

"Poor, poor Ezra," Jenny said.

"How'd you do that?" Ezra asked Cody.

"How'd I do what?"

"How'd you get a hotel on Park Place? A minute ago it was mortgaged."

"Oh, I scrimped and saved," Cody said.

"There's something peculiar going on here."

"Mother!" Jenny called. "Cody's cheating again!"

Their mother was stringing the Christmas tree lights. She looked over and said, "Cody."

"What did I do?" Cody asked.

"What did he do, children?"

"He's the banker," Jenny said. "He made us let him keep the bank and the deeds and the houses. Now he's got a hotel on Park Place and all this extra money. It's not fair!"

Pearl set down the box of lights and came over to where they were sitting. She said, "All right, Cody, put it back. Jenny keeps the deeds from now on; Ezra keeps the bank. Is that clear?"

Jenny reached for the deeds. Ezra began collecting the money.

"And I tell you this," Pearl said. "If I hear one more word, Cody Tull, you're out of the game. Forever! Understood?" She bent to help Ezra. "Always cheating, tormenting, causing trouble . . ." She laid the fives beside the ones, the tens beside the fives. "Cody? You hear what I say?"

He heard, but he didn't bother answering. He sat back and smiled, safe and removed, watching her stack the money.

JOHN UPDIKE

YOUR LOVER JUST CALLED

WHAT COULD BE MORE confining and depleting than this exercise, a popular favorite with questioners in a lecture audience, of asking an author to pick his "best"? If he succumbs, he in an instant relegates all the considerable rest of his work to the status of second-best. If he resists, he implies that he has no best, no standards. I cope with it by trying to pick a different specimen every time I am asked. This time let me name "Your Lover Just Called," a short story about a recurrent fictional couple of mine, Joan and Richard Maple. Over a dozen stories involving them exist, most of them collected in a paperback volume called, in this country, *Too Far to Go* and, in England, *Your Lover Just Called.* This particular story was written in late July 1966 and has a high-summer feel to it; summer loosens up my writerly juices and often squeezes my time at the desk to a few hours before I must rush off to the garden or the golf course. One writes best, possibly, under pressure of a deadline; having all day leads one to dawdle. The story flowed easily: the Maples usually had no trouble talking to each other and generating action of a domestic sort. Here, I of course enjoyed having a telephone as a character, along with the sentimental Mack Dennis, but the image that sticks pleasurably in my mind, as something precious saved from the flux of American middle-class errands and yearning, was the double view Richard enjoys from the dark backyard, of his older daughter in her lemon-colored nightie fiddling with her dolls and scratching an armpit in her well-lit bedroom while below, stereoptically, her mother flirts her head and holds a drink in her hand out safe from being spilled by a kiss. The late John Cheever was amused by this last detail. To me the double sight, and the hero with his cigarettes and scratchy throat halted in amazement on the grass, have something in them of the magic and mournful secrecy of family life, as we each revolve with our separate needs in the transient, loving shelter of the house we all share.

—John Updike

The telephone rang, and Richard Maple, who had stayed home from work this Friday because of a cold, answered it: "Hello?" The person at the other end of the line hung up. Richard went into the bedroom, where Joan was making the bed, and said, "Your lover just called."

"What did he say?"

"Nothing. He hung up. He was amazed to find me home."

"Maybe it was *your* lover."

He knew, through the phlegm beclouding his head, that there was something wrong with this, and found it. "If it was *my* lover," he said, "why would she hang up, since I answered?"

Joan shook the sheet so it made a clapping noise. "Maybe she doesn't love you any more."

"This is a ridiculous conversation."

"You started it."

"Well, what would you think, if you answered the phone on a weekday and the person hung up? He clearly expected you to be home alone."

"Well, if you'll get under these covers I'll call him back and explain the situation."

"*You* think *I'll* think you're kidding but I know that's really what *would* happen."

"Oh, come on, Dick. Who would it be? Freddie Vetter?"

"Or Harry Saxon. Or somebody I don't know at all. Some old college friend who's moved to New England. Or maybe the milkman. I can hear you and him talking while I'm shaving sometimes."

"We're surrounded by hungry children. He's fifty years old and has hair coming out of his ears."

"Like your father. You're not averse to older men. There was that humanities section man when we first met. Anyway, you've been acting awfully happy lately. There's a little smile comes into your face when you're doing the housework. See, there it is!"

"I'm smiling," Joan said, "because you're so absurd. I have no lover. I have nowhere to put him. My days are consumed by devotion to the needs of my husband and his many children."

"Oh, so I'm the one who made you have all the children? While you were hankering after a career in fashion or in the exciting world of business. Aeronautics, perhaps. You could have been the first woman to design a nose cone. Or to crack the wheat-futures cycle.

Joan Maple, girl agronomist. Joan Maple, lady geopolitician. But for that fornicating brute she mistakenly married, this clear-eyed female citizen of our ever-needful republic—"

"Dick, have you taken your temperature? I haven't heard you rave like this for years."

"I haven't been betrayed like this for years. I hated that *click*. That nasty little I-know-your-wife-better-than-you-do *click*."

"It was some child. If we're going to have Mack for dinner tonight, you better convalesce now."

"It *is* Mack, isn't it? That son of a bitch. The divorce isn't even finalized and he's calling my wife on the phone. And then proposes to gorge himself at my groaning board."

"I'll be groaning myself. You're giving me a headache."

"Sure. First I foist off children on you in my mad desire for progeny, then I give you a menstrual headache."

"Get into bed and I'll bring you orange juice and toast cut into strips the way your mother used to make it."

"You're lovely."

As he was settling himself under the blankets, the phone rang again, and Joan answered it in the upstairs hall. "Yes . . . no . . . no . . . good," she said, and hung up.

"Who was it?" he called.

"Somebody wanting to sell us the *World Book Encyclopedia*," she called back.

"A very likely story," he said, with self-pleasing irony, leaning back onto the pillows confident that he was being unjust, that there was no lover.

Mack Dennis was a homely, agreeable, sheepish man their age, whose wife, Eleanor, was in Wyoming suing for divorce. He spoke of her with a cloying tenderness, as if of a favorite daughter away for the first time at camp, or as a departed angel nevertheless keeping in close touch with the abandoned earth. "She says they've had some wonderful thunderstorms. The children go horseback riding every morning, and they play Pounce at night and are in bed by ten. Everybody's health has never been better. Ellie's asthma has cleared up and she thinks now she must have been allergic to *me*."

"You should have cut all your hair off and dressed in cellophane," Richard told him.

Joan asked him, "And how's *your* health? Are you feeding yourself enough? Mack, you look thin."

"The nights I don't stay in Boston," Mack said, tapping himself all over for a pack of cigarettes, "I've taken to eating at the motel on Route 33. It's the best food in town now, and you can watch the kids in the swimming pool." He studied his empty upturned hands as if they had recently held a surprise. He missed his own kids, was perhaps the surprise.

"I'm out of cigarettes too," Joan said.

"I'll go get some," Richard said.

"And a thing of club soda if they have it."

"I'll make a pitcher of martinis," Mack said. "Doesn't it feel great, to have martini weather again?"

It was that season which is late summer in the days and early autumn at night. Evening descended on the downtown, lifting the neon tubing into brilliance, as Richard ran his errand. His sore throat felt folded within him like a secret; there was something reckless and gay in his being up and out at all after spending the afternoon in bed. Home, he parked by his back fence and walked down through a lawn rustling with fallen leaves, though the trees overhead were still massy. The lit windows of his house looked golden and idyllic; the children's rooms were above (the face of Judith, his bigger daughter, drifted preoccupied across a slice of her wallpaper, and her pink square hand reached to adjust a doll on a shelf) and the kitchen below. In the kitchen windows, whose tone was fluorescent, a silent tableau was being enacted. Mack was holding a martini shaker and pouring it into a vessel, eclipsed by an element of window sash, that Joan was offering with a long white arm. Head tilted winningly, she was talking with the slightly pushed-forward mouth that Richard recognized as peculiar to her while looking into mirrors, conversing with her elders, or otherwise seeking to display herself to advantage. Whatever she was saying made Mack laugh, so that his pouring (the silver shaker head glinted, a drop of greenish liquid spilled) was unsteady. He set the shaker down and displayed his hands—the same hands from which a little while ago a surprise had seemed to escape—at his sides, shoulder-high.

Joan moved toward him, still holding her glass, and the back of her head, done up taut and oval in a bun, with downy hairs trailing at the nape of her neck, eclipsed all of Mack's face but his eyes, which closed. They were kissing. Joan's head tilted one way and Mack's another to make their mouths meet tighter. The graceful line of her shoulders was carried outward by the line of the arm holding her glass safe in the air. The other arm was around his neck. Behind them an open cabinet door revealed a paralyzed row of erect paper boxes whose lettering Richard could not read but whose coloring advertised their contents—Cheerios, Wheat Honeys, Onion Thins. Joan backed off and ran her index finger down the length of Mack's necktie (a summer tartan), ending with a jab in the vicinity of his navel that might have expressed a rebuke or a regret. His face, pale and lumpy in the harsh vertical light, looked mildly humorous but intent, and moved forward, toward hers, an inch or two. The scene had the fascinating slow motion of action underwater, mixed with the insane silent suddenness of a television montage glimpsed from the street. Judith came to the window upstairs, not noticing her father standing in the shadow of the tree. Wearing a nightie of lemon gauze, she innocently scratched her armpit while studying a moth beating on her screen; and this too gave Richard a momentous sense, crowding his heart, of having been brought by the mute act of witnessing—like a child sitting alone at the movies—perilously close to the hidden machinations of things. In another kitchen window a neglected teakettle began to plume and to fog the panes with steam. Joan was talking again; her forward-thrust lips seemed to be throwing rapid little bridges across a narrowing gap. Mack paused, shrugged; his face puckered as if he were speaking French. Joan's head snapped back with laughter and triumphantly she threw her free arm wide and was in his embrace again. His hand, spread starlike on the small of her back, went lower to what, out of sight behind the edge of Formica counter, would be her bottom.

Richard scuffled loudly down the cement steps and kicked the kitchen door open, giving them time to break apart before he entered. From the far end of the kitchen, smaller than children, they looked at him with blurred, blank expressions. Joan turned off the steaming kettle and Mack shambled forward to pay for the cigarettes. After the third round of martinis, the constraints loosened and Richard said, taking pleasure in the plaintive huskiness of his voice, "Imagine my discomfort. Sick as I am, I go out into this bitter night to get my wife and my guest some cigarettes, so they can pollute the air and aggravate my already grievous bronchial condition, and, coming down through the back yard, what do I see? The two of them doing the Kama Sutra in my own kitchen. It was like seeing a blue movie and knowing the people in it."

"Where do you see blue movies nowadays?" Joan asked.

"Tush, Dick," Mack said sheepishly, rubbing his thighs with a brisk ironing motion. "A mere fraternal kiss. A brotherly hug. A disinterested tribute to your wife's charm."

"Really, Dick," Joan said. "I think it's shockingly sneaky of you to be standing around spying into your own windows."

"Standing around! I was transfixed with horror. It was a real trauma. My first primal scene." A profound happiness was stretching him from within; the reach of his tongue and wit felt immense, and the other two seemed dolls, homunculi, in his playful grasp.

"We were hardly doing anything," Joan said, lifting her head as if to rise above it all, the lovely line of her jaw defined by tension, her lips stung by a pout.

"Oh, I'm sure, by your standards, you had hardly begun. You'd hardly sampled the possible wealth of coital positions. Did you think I'd never return? Have you poisoned my drink and I'm too vigorous to die, like Rasputin?"

"Dick," Mack said, "Joan loves you. And if I love any man, it's you. Joan and I had this out years ago, and decided to be merely friends."

"Don't go Gaelic on me, Mack Dennis. 'If I love any mon, 'tis thee.' Don't give me a thought, laddie. Just think of poor Eleanor out there, sweating out your divorce, bouncing up and down on those horses day after day, playing Pounce till she's black and blue—"

"Let's eat," Joan said. "You've made me so nervous I've probably overdone the roast beef. Really, Dick, I don't think you can excuse yourself by trying to make it funny."

Next day, the Maples awoke soured and dazed by hangovers; Mack had stayed until two, to make sure there were no hard feelings. Joan usually played ladies' tennis Saturday mornings, while Richard amused the children; now, dressed in white shorts and sneakers, she delayed at home in order to quarrel. "It's desperate of you," she told Richard, "to try to make something of Mack and me. What are you trying to cover up?"

"My dear Mrs. Maple, I *saw*," he said. "I *saw* through my own windows you doing a very credible impersonation of a female spider having her abdomen tickled. Where did you learn to flirt your head like that? It was better than finger puppets."

"Mack always kisses me in the kitchen. It's a habit, it means nothing. You know for yourself how in love with Eleanor he is."

"So much he's divorcing her. His devotion verges on the quixotic."

"The divorce is her idea, obviously. He's a lost soul. I feel sorry for him."

"Yes, I saw that you do. You were like the Red Cross at Verdun."

"What I'd like to know is, why are you so pleased?"

"Pleased? I'm annihilated."

"You're delighted. Look at your smile in the mirror."

"You're so incredibly unapologetic, I guess I think you must be being ironical."

The telephone rang. Joan picked it up and said, "Hello," and Richard heard the click across the room. Joan replaced the receiver and said to him, "So. She thought I'd be playing tennis by now."

"Who's she?"

"You tell me. Your lover. Your loveress."

"It was clearly yours, and something in your voice warned him off."

"Go to her!" Joan suddenly cried, with a burst of the same defiant energy that made her, on other hungover mornings, rush through a mountain of housework. "Go to her like a man and stop trying to maneuver me into something I don't understand! I have no lover! I let Mack kiss me because he's lonely and drunk! Stop trying to make me more interesting than I am! All I am is a beat-up housewife who wants to go play tennis with some other exhausted ladies!"

Mutely Richard fetched from their sports closet her tennis racket, which had recently been restrung with gut. Carrying it in his mouth like a dog retrieving a stick, he got down on all fours and laid it at the toe of her sneaker. Richard Jr., their older son, a wiry nine-year-old presently obsessed by the accumulation of Batman cards, came into the living room, witnessed this pantomime, and laughed to hide his fright. "Dad, can I have my dime for emptying the wastebaskets?"

"Mommy's going to go out to play, Dickie," Richard said, licking from his lips the salty taste of the racket handle. "Let's all go to the five-and-ten and buy a Batmobile."

"Yippee," the small boy said limply, glancing wide-eyed from one of his parents to the other, as if the space between them had gone treacherous.

Richard took the children to the five-and-ten, to the playground, and to a hamburger stand for lunch. These blameless activities transmuted the residue of alcohol and phlegm into a woolly fatigue as pure as the sleep of infants. His sore throat was fading. Obligingly he nodded while his son described an endless plot: ". . . and then, see, Dad, the Penguin had an umbrella smoke came out of, it was neat, and there were these two other guys with funny masks in the bank vault, filling it with water, I don't know why, to make it bust or something, and Robin was climbing up these slippery stacks of like half-dollars to get away from the water, and then, see, Dad . . ."

Back home, the children dispersed into the neighborhood on the same mysterious tide that on other days packed their back yard with unfamiliar urchins. Joan returned from tennis glazed with sweat, her ankles coated with clay-court dust. Her body was swimming in the afterglow of exertion. He suggested they take a nap.

"Just a nap," she warned.

"Of course," he said. "I met my mistress at the playground and we satisfied each other on the jungle gym."

"Maureen and I beat Alice and Judy. It can't be any of those three, they were waiting for me half an hour."

In bed, the shades strangely drawn against the bright afternoon, and a glass of stale water standing bubbled with secret light, he asked her, "You think I want to make you more interesting than you are?"

"Of course. You're bored. You left me and Mack alone deliberately. It was very uncharacteristic of you, to go out with a cold."

"It's sad, to think of you without a lover."

"I'm sorry."

"You're pretty interesting anyway. Here, and here, and here."

"I said really a nap."

"In the upstairs hall, on the other side of the closed bedroom door, the telephone rang. After four peals—icy spears hurled from afar—the ringing stopped, unanswered. There was a puzzled pause. Then a tentative, questioning *pring*, as if someone in passing had bumped the table, followed by a determined series, strides of sound, imperative and plaintive, that did not stop until twelve had been counted; then the lover hung up.

JOHN A. WILLIAMS

SON in the AFTERNOON

MY BEST FICTION IS a short story first published in *Exodus* in 1959 and still appearing in various anthologies, "Son in the Afternoon." The title is an angular takeoff on the Ernest Hemingway novel *The Sun Also Rises*. While I liked much of Hemingway's work, I was uneasy with his treatment of his rare characters of color. "Son" was the work that pushed me to writing novels.

At its first publication I sent a copy to my mother. She was of the generation wary of writings that were not biblical or close to it. "That ole writing," she called it, with something like motherly disdain. She wasn't much interested in reading it—and, in fact, she only began to read son John when the novels came out and I proudly sent them to her. But she *had* read "Son" and I knew she liked the story, knew she'd seen herself in it as the good person, the "subdued" housekeeping lady, the substitute mother, which she certainly had been for many white families while I was a youngster.

As many anthologies as it's been in, "Son" was not snatched up for publication. One editor rejected it, writing, "This story is no go unless we run a picture of the author with it, and that is not possible." Another said, "No way in hell can we run this story." Other editors returned "Son" without comment or never returned it at all, although two did take the trouble to let me know they'd burned it. The publication of "Son in the Afternoon" made me realize, as no other literary experience has, that this writing/publishing business was far deeper than I thought as a young writer, and more fearsome I learned as an older writer.

Living in New York helped me dig in my spikes, fingers splayed along the ground, crouched, butt raised to start the race of getting published. (Note: sprinters raise their butts at the call of "set.") I saw many other writer friends who did not do well or as well. I knew my family was looking on, the way a crowd watches one slide along a tightrope. Now, forty-five years later, I've written and published stories, essays, novels, poems, plays, a libretto, and books of nonfiction; taught writing at several universities; been a journalist (print, radio, television), and I'm not done yet. "Son" was my starting point, and I am still pleased to revisit it now and again to see where it all came together.

—John A. Williams

It was hot. I tend to be a bitch when it's hot. I goosed the little Ford over Sepulveda Boulevard toward Santa Monica until I got stuck in the traffic that pours from L.A. into the surrounding towns. I'd had a very lousy day at the studio.

I was—still am—a writer and this studio had hired me to check scripts and films with Negroes in them to make sure the Negro movie-goer wouldn't be offended. The signs were already clear that one day the whole of American industry would be racing pell-mell to get a Negro, showcase a spade. I was kind of a pioneer. I'm a *Negro* writer, you see. The day had been tough because of a couple of verbs—slink and walk. One of those Hollywood hippies had done a script calling for a Negro waiter to slink away from the table where a dinner party was glaring at him. I said the waiter should walk, not slink, because later on he becomes a hero. The Hollywood hippie, who understood it all because he had some colored friends, said that it was essential to the plot that the waiter slink. I said you don't slink one minute and become a hero the next; there has to be some consistency. The Negro actor I was standing up for said nothing either way. He had played Uncle Tom roles so long that he had become Uncle Tom. But the director agreed with me.

Anyway . . . hear me out now. I was on my way to Santa Monica to pick up my mother, Nora. It was a long haul for such a hot day. I had planned a quiet evening: a nice shower, fresh clothes, and then I would have dinner at the Watkins and talk with some of the musicians on the scene for a quick taste before they cut to their gigs. After, I was going to the Pigalle down on Figueroa and catch Earl Grant at the organ, and still later, if nothing exciting happened, I'd pick up Scottie and make it to the Lighthouse on the Beach or to the Strollers and lis-ten to some of the white boys play. I liked the long drive, especially while listening to Sleepy Stein's show on the radio. Later, much later of course, it would be home, back to Watts.

So you see, this picking up Nora was a little inconvenient. My mother was a maid for the Couchmans. Ronald Couchman was an architect, a good one I understood from Nora who has a fine sense for this sort of thing; you don't work in some hundred-odd houses dur-ing your life without getting some idea of the way a house should be laid out. Couchman's wife, Kay, was a playgirl who drove a white Jaguar from one party to another. My mother didn't like her too much; she didn't seem to care much for her son, Ronald, junior. There's something wrong with a parent who can't really love her own child, Nora thought. The Couchmans lived in a real fine residential section, of course. A number of actors lived nearby, character actors, not really big stars.

Somehow it is very funny. I mean that the maids and butlers knew everything about these people, and these people knew nothing at all about the help. Through Nora and her friends I knew who was laying whose wife; who had money and who *really* had money; I knew about the wild parties hours before the police, and who smoked marijuana, when, and where they got it.

To get to Couchman's driveway I had to go three blocks up one side of a palm-planted center strip and back down the other. The driveway bent gently, then swept back out of sight of the main road. The house, sheltered by slim palms, looked like a transplanted New England Colonial. I parked and walked to the kitchen door, skirting the growling Great Dane who was tied to a tree. That was the route to the kitchen door.

I don't like kitchen doors. Entering people's houses by them, I mean. I'd done this thing most of my life when I called at places where Nora worked to pick up the patched or worn sheets or the half-eaten roasts, the battered, tarnished silver—the fringe benefits of a housemaid. As a teen-ager I'd told Nora I was through with that crap; I was not going through anyone's kitchen door. She only laughed and said I'd learn. One day soon after, I called for her and without knocking walked right through the front door of this house and right on through the living room. I was almost out of the room when I saw feet behind the couch. I leaned over and there was Mr. Jorgensen and his wife making out like crazy. I guess they thought Nora had gone and it must have hit them sort of suddenly and they went at it like the hell-bomb was due to drop any minute. I've been that way too, mostly in the spring. Of course, when Mr. Jorgensen looked over his shoulder and saw me, you know what happened. I was thrown out and Nora right behind me. It was the middle of winter, the old man was sick and the coal bill three months overdue. Nora was right about those kitchen doors: I learned.

My mother saw me before I could ring the bell. She opened the door. "Hello," she said. She was breathing hard, like she'd been running or something. "Come in and sit down. I don't know *where* that

Kay is. Little Ronald is sick and she's probably out gettin' drunk again." She left me then and trotted back through the house, I guess to be with Ronnie. I hated the combination of her white nylon uniform, her dark brown face and the wide streaks of gray in her hair. Nora had married this guy from Texas a few years after the old man had died. He was all right. He made out okay. Nora didn't have to work, but she just couldn't be still; she always had to be doing something. I suggested she quit work, but I had as much luck as her husband. I used to tease her about liking to be around those white folks. It would have been good for her to take an extended trip around the country visiting my brothers and sisters. Once she got to Philadelphia, she could go right out to the cemetery and sit awhile with the old man.

I walked through the Couchman home. I liked the library. I thought if I knew Couchman I'd like him. The room made me feel like that. I left it and went into the big living room. You could tell that Couchman had let his wife do that. Everything in it was fast, dart-like, with no sense of ease. But on the walls were several of Couchman's conceptions of buildings and homes. I guess he was a disciple of Wright. My mother walked rapidly through the room without looking at me and said, "Just be patient, Wendell. She should be here real soon."

"Yeah," I said, "with a snootful." I had turned back to the drawings when Ronnie scampered into the room, his face twisted with rage.

"Nora!" he tried to roar, perhaps the way he'd seen the parents of some of his friends roar at their maids. I'm quite sure Kay didn't shout at Nora, and I don't think Couchman would. But then no one shouts at Nora. "Nora, you come right back here this minute!" the little bastard shouted and stamped and pointed to a spot on the floor where Nora was supposed to come to roost. I have a nasty temper. Sometimes it lies dormant for ages and at other times, like when the weather is hot and nothing seems to be going right, it's bubbling and ready to explode. "Don't talk to *my* mother like that, you little—!" I said sharply, breaking off just before I cursed. I wanted him to be large enough for me to strike. "How'd you like for me to talk to *your* mother like that?"

The nine-year-old looked up at me in surprise and confusion. He hadn't expected me to say anything. I was just another piece of furniture. Tears rose in his eyes and spilled out onto his pale cheeks. He put his hands behind him, twisted them. He moved backwards, away from me. He looked at my mother with a "Nora, come help me" look. And sure enough, there was Nora, speeding back across the room, gathering the kid in her arms, tucking his robe together. I was too angry to feel hatred for myself.

Ronnie was the Couchmans' only kid. Nora loved him. I suppose that was the trouble. Couchman was gone ten, twelve hours a day. Kay didn't stay around the house any longer than she had to. So Ronnie had only my mother. I think kids should have someone to love, and Nora wasn't a bad sort. But somehow when the six of us, her own children, were growing up we never had her. She was gone, out scuffling to get those crumbs to put into our mouths and shoes for our feet and praying for something to happen so that all the space in between would be taken care of. Nora's affection for us took the form of rushing out into the morning's five o'clock blackness to wake some silly bitch and get her coffee; took form in her trudging five miles home every night instead of taking the streetcar to save money to buy tablets for us, to use at school, we said. But the truth was that all of us liked to draw and we went through a writing tablet in a couple of hours every day. Can you imagine? There's not a goddamn artist among us. We never had the physical affection, the pat on the head, the quick, smiling kiss, the "gimmee a hug" routine. All of this Ronnie was getting.

Now he buried his little blond head in Nora's breast and sobbed. "There, there now," Nora said. "Don't you cry, Ronnie. Ol' Wendell is just jealous, and he hasn't much sense either. He didn't mean nuthin'."

I left the room. Nora had hit it of course, hit it and passed on. I looked back. It didn't look so incongruous, the white and black together, I mean. Ronnie was still sobbing. His head bobbed gently on Nora's shoulder. The only time I ever got that close to her was when she trapped me with a bearhug so she could whale the daylights out of me after I put a snowball through Mrs. Grant's window. I walked outside and lit a cigarette. When Ronnie was in the hospital the month before, Nora got me to run her way over to Hollywood every night to see him. I didn't like that worth a damn. All right, I'll admit it: it did upset me. All that affection I didn't get nor my brothers and sisters going to that little white boy who, without a doubt, when away from her called her the names he'd learned from adults. Can you imagine a nine-year-old kid calling Nora a "girl," "our girl"? I spat at the Great Dane. He snarled and then I bounced a rock off his fanny. "Lay down, you bastard," I muttered. It was a good thing he was tied up.

I heard the low cough of the Jaguar slapping against the road. The car was throttled down, and with a muted roar it swung into the driveway. The woman aimed it for me. I was evil enough not to move. I was tired of playing with these people. At the last moment, grinning, she swung the wheel over and braked. She bounded out of the car like a tennis player vaulting over a net.

"Hi," she said, tugging at her shorts.

"Hello."

"You're Nora's boy?"

"I'm Nora's son." Hell, I was as old as she was; besides, I can't stand "boy."

"Nora tells us you're working in Hollywood. Like it?"

"It's all right."

"You must be pretty talented."

We stood looking at each other while the dog whined for her attention. Kay had a nice body and it was well tanned. She was high, boy, was she high. Looking at her, I could feel myself going into my sexy bastard routine; sometimes I can swing it great. Maybe it all had to do with the business inside. Kay took off her sunglasses and took a good look at me. "Do you have a cigarette?"

I gave her one and lit it. "Nice tan," I said. Most white people I know think it's a great big deal if a Negro compliments them on their tans. It's a large laugh. You have all this volleyball about color and come summer you can't hold the white folks back from the beaches, anyplace where they can get some sun. And of course the blacker they get, the more pleased they are. Crazy. If there is ever a Negro revolt, it will come during the summer and Negroes will descend upon the beaches around the nation and paralyze the country. You can't conceal cattle prods and bombs and pistols and police dogs when you're showing your birthday suit to the sun.

"You like it?" she asked. She was pleased. She placed her arm next to mine. "Almost the same color," she said.

"Ronnie isn't feeling well," I said.

"Oh, the poor kid. I'm so glad we have Nora. She's such a charm. I'll run right in and look at him. Do have a drink in the bar. Fix me one too, will you?" Kay skipped inside and I went to the bar and poured out two strong drinks. I made hers stronger than mine. She was back soon. "Nora was trying to put him to sleep and she made me stay out." She giggled. She quickly tossed off her drink. "Another, please?" While I was fixing her drink she was saying how amazing it was for Nora to have such a talented son. What she was really saying was that it was amazing for a servant to have a son who was not also a servant. "Anything can happen in a democracy," I said. "Servants' sons drink with madames and so on."

"Oh, Nora isn't a servant," Kay said. "She's part of the family."

Yeah, I thought. Where and how many times had I heard *that* before?

In the ensuing silence, she started to admire her tan again. "You think it's pretty good, do you? You don't know how hard I worked to get it." I moved close to her and held her arm. I placed my other arm around her. She pretended not to see or feel it, but she wasn't trying to get away either. In fact she was pressing closer and the register in my brain that tells me at the precise moment when I'm in, went off. Kay was very high. I put both arms around her and she put both hers around me. When I kissed her, she responded completely.

"Mom!"

"Ronnie, come back to bed," I heard Nora shout from the other room. We could hear Ronnie running over the rug in the outer room. Kay tried to get away from me, push me to one side, because we could tell that Ronnie knew where to look for his Mom: he was running right for the bar, where we were. "Oh, please," she said, "don't let him see us." I wouldn't let her push me away. "Stop!" she hissed. "He'll *see* us!" We stopped struggling just for an instant, and we listened to the echoes of the word *see*. She gritted her teeth and renewed her efforts to get away.

Me? I had the scene laid right out. The kid breaks into the room, see, and sees his mother in this real wriggly clinch with this colored guy who's just shouted at him, see, and no matter how his mother explains it away, the kid has the image—the colored guy and his mother—for the rest of his life, see?

That's the way it happened. The kid's mother hissed under her breath, "*You're crazy!*" and she looked at me as though she were seeing me or something about me for the very first time. I'd released her as soon as Ronnie, romping into the bar, saw us and came to a full, open-mouthed halt. Kay went to him. He looked first at me, then at his mother. Kay turned to me, but she couldn't speak.

Outside in the living room my mother called, "Wendell, where are you? We can go now."

I started to move past Kay and Ronnie. I felt many things, but I made myself think mostly, *There you little bastard, there.*

My mother thrust her face inside the door and said, "Good-bye, Mrs. Couchman. See you tomorrow. 'Bye, Ronnie."

"Yes," Kay said, sort of stunned. "Tomorrow." She was reaching for Ronnie's hand as we left, but the kid was slapping her hand away. I hurried quickly after Nora, hating the long drive back to Watts.

ABOUT THE AUTHORS

Scott Adams is the creator of Dilbert (www.dilbert.com), which appears in more than two thousand newspapers in sixty-five countries. Adams has twenty-nine books in print with more than eleven million copies sold, including two number one *New York Times* bestsellers.

Ai won the 1999 National Book Award for Poetry for *Vice: New and Selected Poems*. The poet is also the recipient of the Lamont Poetry Award and an American Book Award. She teaches at Oklahoma State University and lives in Stillwater, Oklahoma.

Julia Alvarez is the author of the best-selling novels *How the García Girls Lost Their Accents* (1991) and its sequel, *¡Yo!* (1997). Her father's revolutionary ties inspired *In the Time of Butterflies* (1994). Alvarez's work has won many honors, including the PEN Oakland Award, and has been named as finalists for the National Book Critics Circle Award.

Natalie Angier is a science writer for *The New York Times* and author of *Natural Obsessions*, *The Beauty of the Beastly*, and *Woman: An Intimate Geography*, a bestseller translated into nineteen languages. She edited *The Best American Science and Nature Writing 2002*. In 1991 she won a Pulitzer Prize for her science reporting.

Paul Auster is the author of eleven novels, most recently, *Oracle Night*. He has also published many works of nonfiction and edited *I Thought My Father Was God*, the NPR National Story Project anthology, which was a national bestseller. He lives in Brooklyn, New York.

T. Coraghessan Boyle is the best-selling author of many novels and story collections, including *The Inner Circle*, *Drop City*, *After the Plague*, *Riven Rock*, *The Tortilla Curtain*, *Without a Hero*, *The Road to Wellville*, *East Is East*, *If the River Was Whiskey*, *World's End* (winner of the PEN/Faulkner Award), *Greasy Lake*, *Budding Prospects*, *Water Music*, and *Descent of Man*. His fiction regularly appears in major American magazines, including *The New Yorker*, *GQ*, *The Paris Review*, *Playboy*, and *Esquire*.

Bebe Moore Campbell is a best-selling novelist and journalist. Her fiction includes *Brothers and Sisters, Singing in the Comeback Choir, Your Blues Ain't Like Mine, What You Owe Me,* and *72 Hour Hold.* Campbell's nonfiction has appeared in *The New York Times, The Washington Post, Los Angeles Times, Ms., Essence, Black Enterprise, Ebony, Working Mother,* and *USA Weekend,* among other publications. She is a regular contributor to National Public Radio.

Hayden Carruth has published more than thirty books of poetry, criticism, anthologies—including the classic *The Voice That Is Great Within Us*—and a novel. His work has been awarded many honors, including the National Book Award, the Lenore Marshall Prize, the Whiting Award, the Ruth Lilly Prize, and a Lannan Literary Fellowship.

Sandra Cisneros was born in Chicago in 1954. Internationally acclaimed for her poetry and fiction, she has been the recipient of numerous awards, including the Lannan Literary Award and the American Book Award, and of fellowships from the National Endowment for the Arts and the MacArthur Foundation. Cisneros is the author of the novels *The House on Mango Street* and *Caramelo*; a collection of short stories, *Woman Hollering Creek*, winner of the QPB New Voices Award; a book of poetry, *Loose Woman*; and a children's book, *Hairs/Pelitos*. She lives in San Antonio, Texas.

Chitra Banerjee Divakaruni is the author of the novels *Queen of Dreams, The Vine of Desire, Sister of My Heart,* and *The Mistress of Spices*; the story collections *The Unknown Errors of Our Lives* and *Arranged Marriage,* which received several awards, including the American Book Award; four collections of prize-winning poetry; and children's books. Her work has appeared in *The New Yorker, The Atlantic Monthly, The Best American Short Stories 1999,* and *The New York Times.* Born in Calutta, Divakaruni now lives near Houston, Texas.

Emma Donoghue was born in Dublin, spent many years in England, and now lives in Canada. She is the author of *Life Mask* and *Slammerkin,* as well as two other novels, a collection of short stories, and a collection of fairy tales. Her novels have been translated into eight languages.

Rita Dove, Pulitzer Prize-winning former Poet Laureate, is Commonwealth Professor of English at the University of Virginia. Her collections of poetry include *Thomas and Beulah* and *American Smooth.*

Carolyn Ferrell is author of the short story collection *Don't Erase Me,* awarded the Art Seidenbaum Award from the *Los Angeles Times*, the John C. Zacharis Award given by *Ploughshares,* and the QPB New Voices Award. Her stories have been anthologized in *The Best American Short Stories of the Century*; *Giant Steps: The New Generation of African American Writers*; *Black Silk: A Collection of African American Erotica*; and *Children of the Night: The Best Short Stories by Black Writers, 1967 to the Present.*

Helen Fisher, Ph.D., is one of this country's most prominent anthropologists. Prior to becoming a research professor at Rutgers University, she was a research associate at the American Museum of Natural History in New York City. Dr. Fisher has conducted extensive research on the evolution, expression, and chemistry of love. Her books are *Why We Love, The First Sex, The Anatomy of Love*, and *The Sex Contract.*

Al Franken is the author of four *New York Times* bestsellers, including his latest, *Lies, and the Lying Liars Who Tell Them: A Fair and Balanced Look at the Right*. A master of many mediums, he hosts an eponymous radio show, and is the winner of five Emmy and two Grammy awards.

Martin Gardner is the author of more than sixty-five books and articles including the bestseller *The Annotated Alice*, an analysis of Lewis Carroll's *Alice in Wonderland*, followed by a sequel, *More Annotated Alice*. He has also written two novels, *The Flight of Peter Fromm* and *Visitors from Oz*, and his *Scientific American* columns are collected in fifteen volumes. He now lives in his home state of Oklahoma.

Laurie Garrett is Senior Fellow for Global Health at the Council on Foreign Relations. She is a contributor to such publications as *Vanity Fair*, *Esquire*, the *Los Angeles Times*, and *Foreign Affairs*, and was a health and science writer for *Newsday* for many years. She is the only person to have received all of the top three awards in American journalism: the Pulitzer Prize (for which she has three times been a finalist); the George Foster Peabody Broadcasting Award; and the George C. Polk Award, which she won twice. Her books are *Betrayal of Trust*, *Microbes Versus Mankind*, and *The Coming Plague.*

Marita Golden has written both fiction and nonfiction, including *Don't Play in the Sun, Migrations of the Heart, The Edge of Heaven, A Miracle Every Day,* and *Saving Our Sons*. She is the editor of *Wild Women Don't Wear No Blues: Black Women Writers on Love, Men and Sex*, and coeditor of *Gumbo: An Anthology of African American Writing* and *Skin Deep: Black Women and White Women Write About Race*. She is the founder and CEO of the Hurston/Wright Foundation, which supports African American writers, and lives in Maryland.

A. M. Homes is the author of the novels *The End of Alice, In a Country of Mothers, Music for Torching*, and *Jack*, as well as the short story collections *Things You Should Know* and *The Safety of Objects*. Her fiction has been translated into eight languages, and she is the recipient of numerous awards, including a Guggenheim Fellowship and a National Endowment for the Arts Fellowship. Her fiction and nonfiction appear in magazines such as *The New Yorker* and *Artforum*, among others, and she is a contributing editor at *Vanity Fair, Mirabella, Bomb, Blind Spot*, and *Story*. She teaches in the writing programs at Columbia University and The New School and lives in New York City.

Arianna Huffington is a nationally syndicated columnist, author of ten books, including the national bestseller *Pigs at the Trough*, and co-host of the National Public Radio program *Left, Right, and Center*. She lives in Los Angeles with her two daughters.

P. D. James is the author of eighteen books, most of which have been filmed for television. Before her retirement in 1979, she spent thirty years in various departments of the British Civil Service, including the Police and Criminal Law Departments of Great Britain's Home Office. The recipient of many prizes and honors, she was created Baroness James of Holland Park in 1991.

Gish Jen is the author of the novels *The Love Wife, Typical American*, and *Mona in the Promised Land*, and *Who's Irish?*, a book of stories. Her honors include the Lannan Award for Fiction and the Strauss Living Award from the American Academy of Arts and Letters. She lives with her husband and two children in Cambridge, Massachusetts.

Mary Karr's poems and essays have won Pushcart prizes and have appeared in magazines such as *The New Yorker, The Atlantic*, and *Parnassus*. She was a Bunting Fellow at Radcliffe College, and is now the Jesse Truesdale Peck Professor of English Literature at Syracuse University. Her books are the memoirs *The Liars' Club* and *Cherry*, and the poetry collections *Viper Rum, The Devil's Tour*, and *Abacus*.

Barbara Kingsolver pursued graduate studies in biology and ecology at the University of Arizona in Tucson, where she received a Masters of Science degree. Her articles have appeared in a variety of publications, including *The Nation, The New York Times*, and *Smithsonian*. Her books include *The Bean Trees, Homeland and Other Stories, Animal Dreams, Pigs in Heaven, Prodigal Summer, The Poisonwood Bible*, and the best-selling essay collections *High Tide in Tucson* and *Small Wonders*.

Maxine Hong Kingston is Senior Lecturer for Creative Writing at the University of California, Berkeley. For her memoirs and fiction—*The Fifth Book of Peace, The Woman Warrior, China Men, Tripmaster Monkey,* and *Hawai'i One Summer*—she has earned numerous awards, among them the National Book Award, the National Book Critics Circle Award for Nonfiction, the PEN West Award for Fiction, an American Academy of Arts and Letters Award in Literature, and a National Humanities Medal from the National Endowment for the Humanities, as well as the title of "Living Treasure of Hawai'i."

Neil LaBute's films are *In the Company of Men, Your Friends and Neighbors, Nurse Betty, Possession,* and *The Shape of Things,* based on his stage play. His other plays include *Fat Pig, This Is How It Goes, The Mercy Seat, The Distance from Here,* and *bash: latter-day plays,* which LaBute directed in New York and London in 1999. He is also the author of a collection of short stories, *Seconds of Pleasure.*

Doris Lessing is one of the most celebrated and distinguished writers of the twentieth century. Her best-known novel is the classic *The Golden Notebook,* and her most recent books are the novels *Ben, in the World* and *The Sweetest Dream,* and two volumes of autobiography, *Under My Skin* and *Walking in the Shade.* A Companion of Honor and a Companion of Literature, she was awarded in 2001 the David Cohen Memorial Prize for British Literature and Spain's Prince of Asturias Prize.

Jonathan Lethem is the author of six novels, including the bestsellers *The Fortress of Solitude* and *Motherless Brooklyn,* which won the National Book Critics Circle Award and was named novel of the year by *Esquire.* His stories and essays have appeared in *The New Yorker, Rolling Stone, Esquire, McSweeney's, Tin House, The New York Times, The Paris Review,* and his collections *Men and Cartoons* and *The Disappointment Artist.*

Philip Levine is the author of sixteen collections of poetry and two books of essays. He has received many awards, including the National Book Award in 1980 for *Ashes* and in 1991 for *What Work Is,* and the Pulitzer Prize in 1995 for *The Simple Truth.*

Barry Lopez is the author of six works of nonfiction and eight works of fiction. His writing appears regularly in *Harper's, The Paris Review,* and *The Georgia Review.* He is the recipient of a National Book Award for his *Arctic Dreams,* an Award in Literature from the American Academy of Arts and Letters, a Guggenheim Fellowship, and other honors.

Yann Martel, the son of diplomats, was born in Spain in 1963. He grew up in Costa Rica, France, Mexico, Alaska, and Canada, and as an adult has spent time in Iran, Turkey, and India. After studying philosophy in college, he worked at various odd jobs until he began earning his living as a writer at the age of twenty-seven. Martel is the Man Booker Prize-winning author of *Life of Pi*, and has just published *The Facts Behind the Helsinki Roccamatios*, a collection of short fiction.

Valerie Martin is the author of six novels and two collections of short fiction, including *Property* (for which she won the Orange Prize), *Italian Fever*, *The Great Divorce*, and *Mary Reilly*. She also published a biography of St. Francis, *Salvation*.

Arthur Miller was born in New York City in 1915 and studied at the University of Michigan. His plays include *All My Sons* (1947), *Death of a Salesman* (1949), *The Crucible* (1953), *A View from the Bridge* (1955), and *After the Fall* (1964). Miller was granted the 2001 Medal for Distinguished Contribution to American Letters. He has twice won the New York Drama Critics Circle Award, and in 1949 he was awarded the Pulitzer Prize. His most recent play is *Finishing the Picture*.

Anchee Min was born in Shanghai in 1957. At seventeen, she was sent to a labor collective, where after a number of years a talent scout recruited her for Madame Mao's Shanghai Film Studio. Min came to the United States in 1984 with the help of the actress Joan Chen. Her memoir, *Red Azalea*, won the QPB New Visions Award, was named a New York Times Notable Book of 1994, and was an international bestseller, with rights sold in twenty countries.

Jan Morris, historian, traveler, and travel writer, is the author of over forty books including *Venice*, *Oxford*, and *Pax Britannica*, a three-volume history of the British Empire; and *Conundrum*, an account of the sex-change operation by which she became Jan. She published *Farewell the Trumpets: An Imperial Retreat* (1978), excerpted here, while living as James Morris.

Haruki Murakami was born in Kyoto, Japan, in 1949, grew up in Kobe, and now lives near Tokyo. The most recent of his many honors is the Yomiuri Literary Prize, whose previous recipients include Yukio Mishima, Kenzaburo Oe, and Kobo Abe. Among his novels and story collections are *A Wild Sheep Chase*, *Norwegian Wood*, *The Elephant Vanishes*, *The Wind-Up Bird Chronicle*, and *Hard-Boiled Wonderland and the End of the World*.

Kathleen Norris is the award-winning bestselling author of *Amazing Grace: A Vocabulary of Faith*; *The Cloister Walk*; *Dakota: A Spiritual Geography*; and *The Virgin of Bennington*. Her poems have appeared in *The New Yorker*, in various anthologies, and in her own collections of poetry.

Lynn Nottage is a playwright from Brooklyn. Her plays are *Intimate Apparel*; *Crumbs from the Table of Joy*; *Mud, River, Stone*; *Por'knockers*; and *Fabulation*. Nottage's awards include an AT&T OnStage Award and PEN/Laura Pels Foundation Awards for Drama.

Joyce Carol Oates is a recipient of the National Book Award and the PEN/Malamud Award for Excellence in Short Fiction. She has written some of the most enduring fiction of our time, including the national bestsellers *The Falls*, *We Were the Mulvaneys*, and *Blonde*, which was nominated for the National Book Award. She is the Roger S. Berlind Distinguished Professor of the Humanities at Princeton University and has been a member of the American Academy of Arts and Letters since 1978.

Robert Pinsky founded the Favorite Poem Project during his tenure as Poet Laureate of the United States. He is the author of *The Figured Wheel, The Inferno of Dante*, and many other collections of poetry.

Michael Pollan is a contributing writer for *The New York Times Magazine* as well as a contributing editor at *Harper's*. He is the author of two prize-winning books: *Second Nature: A Gardener's Education*, which won the QPB New Visions Award; *A Place of My Own: The Education of an Amateur Builder*; and *The Botany of Desire: A Plant's Eye View of the World*. Pollan teaches journalism at the University of California, Berkeley.

Ishmael Reed has taught at Harvard, Yale, and Dartmouth and has long been on the faculty at University of California, Berkeley. He is the award-winning author of more than twenty books—novels, essays, plays, and poetry—that have been translated into seven languages. Reed has been a finalist for the Pulitzer Prize and was twice nominated for the National Book Award. He lives in Oakland, California.

Ruth Reichl joined *Gourmet* as Editor in Chief in April 1999. She came to the magazine from *The New York Times*, where she had been the restaurant critic since 1993. Reichl began writing about food in 1972, when she published a book called *Mmmmm: A Feastiary*. Since then, she has authored the critically acclaimed best-selling memoirs *Tender at the Bone, Comfort Me with Apples*, and *Garlic and Sapphires*. She is the editor of The Modern Library Cooking Series and *The Gourmet Cookbook*.

Dan Rhodes is the author of the short story collections *Don't Tell Me the Truth About Love* and *Anthropology*, the internationally acclaimed novel *Timoleon Vieta Come Home: A Sentimental Journey*, and the pseudonymously written *The Little White Car*. After graduating from the University of Glamorgan in 1995 he taught in Saigon and worked at various times at his parents' pub and on a fruit and vegetable farm. Winner of the QPB New Voices Award, Rhodes was chosen as one of Granta's Best Young British Novelists in 2003.

Tom Robbins is the author of eight best-selling novels, *Villa Incognito, Fierce Invalids Home from Hot Climates, Jitterbug Perfume, Still Life with Woodpecker, Skinny Legs and All, Half Asleep in Frog Pajamas, Even Cowgirls Get the Blues,* and *Another Roadside Attraction.*

Richard Rodriguez works as an editor at the Pacific News Service in San Francisco and is a contributing editor for *Harper's* and the Sunday "Opinion" section of the *Los Angeles Times*. He has published numerous articles in *The New York Times, The Wall Street Journal, The American Scholar, Time, Mother Jones,* and *The New Republic*, as well as other publications. He has also written three books: *Brown: The Last Discovery of America*, which won a QPB New Visions award; *Hunger of Memory*; and *Days of Obligation: An Argument with My Mexican Father.*

Witold Rybczynski received Bachelor of Architecture and Master of Architecture degrees from McGill University in Montreal. He is the author of more than fifty articles and papers on the subject of housing, architecture, and technology, including the books *Taming the Tiger, Paper Heroes, The Most Beautiful House in the World, Waiting for the Weekend, Looking Around: A Journey Through Architecture and City Life,* and *The Perfect House.*

David Sedaris is a playwright and a regular contributor to Public Radio International's *This American Life*. He is the author of the best-selling books *Barrel Fever, Naked, Holidays on Ice, Me Talk Pretty One Day,* and *Dress Your Family in Corduroy and Denim*. He travels extensively through Europe and the United States on lecture tours, and now lives in England.

Huston Smith is internationally known as the premier teacher of world religions and for his best-selling books *The World's Religions* and *Why Religion Matters*. He was the focus of a five-part PBS television series with Bill Moyers, and has taught at Washington University, the Massachusetts Institute of Technology, Syracuse University, and the University of California, Berkeley.

Mark Alan Stamaty's political cartoons and comic strips have appeared in *Time, The Village Voice, The Washington Post, The New York Times Book Review,* and *Slate.* His children's books include *Who Needs Donuts?, Alia's Mission, Minnie Maloney and Macaroni,* and *Where's My Hippopotamus?*

Gay Talese is a journalist and international best-selling author whose works include *The Bridge, The Kingdom and the Power, Honor Thy Father, Thy Neighbor's Wife,* and *Unto the Sons.* Currently at work on the follow-up to *Unto the Sons,* he lives in New York City and Ocean City, New Jersey.

Garry Trudeau launched *Doonesbury* in 1970 and five years later became the first comic strip artist to be awarded a Pulitzer Prize for editorial cartooning. Now tracking its seventh presidential administration, Doonesbury appears in more than 1,400 daily and Sunday newspapers around the globe. Trudeau maintains a lively online presence, refreshed daily, at www.doonesbury.com.

Scott Turow is the author of two works of nonfiction, *One L* and *Ultimate Punishment,* and six best-selling novels about the law, from *Presumed Innocent* (1987) to *Reversible Errors* (2002). He is a partner in the Chicago firm of Sonnenschein Nath & Rosenthal, and has been frequently involved with death penalty litigation.

Anne Tyler was born in Minneapolis but grew up in Raleigh, North Carolina. She graduated at nineteen from Duke University and went on to do graduate work in Russian studies at Columbia University. She recently published her sixteenth novel, *The Amateur Marriage*; her eleventh, *Breathing Lessons,* was awarded the Pulitzer Prize in 1988. She is a member of the American Academy and Institute of Arts and Letters.

John Updike was born in Shillington, Pennsylvania. He graduated from Harvard College in 1954 and spent a year in Oxford, England, at the Ruskin School of Drawing and Fine Art. From 1955 to 1957 he was a member of the staff of *The New Yorker* and since 1957 has lived in Massachusetts. He is the author of more than fifty books, including collections of short stories, poems, and criticism. His novels have won the Pulitzer Prize, the National Book Award, the American Book Award, and the National Book Critics Circle Award.

John A. Williams was born in Jackson, Mississippi, in 1925. He has been a foreign correspondent for *Newsweek* as well as Professor of English at Rutgers University. Among his numerous awards are the American Book Award and the National Institute of Arts and Letters Award. An exhibit honoring his work can be found at www.library.rochester.edu/rbk/williams.

ACKNOWLEDGMENTS

Dilbert, October 8, 2001, by Scott Adams. Reprinted by permission of United Feature Syndicate, Inc.

"Jimmy Hoffa's Odyssey," from *Vice: New and Selected Poems* by Ai. Copyright © 1999 by Ai. Used by permission of W. W. Norton & Company, Inc.

"Freedom Cry" from *Before We Were Free* by Julia Alvarez. Copyright © 2002 by Julia Alvarez. Published by Dell Laurel-Leaf and originally in hardcover by Alfred A. Knopf, both imprints of Random House Children's Books. Reprinted by permission of Susan Bergholz Literary Services, NY. All rights reserved. Introduction copyright © 2004 by Julia Alvarez. By permission of Susan Bergholz Literary Services, NY. All rights reserved.

"Confessions of a Lonely Atheist" by Natalie Angier. Copyright © 2001 by Natalie Angier. Reprinted from *The New York Times Magazine*, January 14, 2001. Used by permission.

"Mr. Bones" from *Timbuktu* by Paul Auster, copyright © 1999 by Paul Auster. Reprinted by permission of Henry Holt and Company, LLC.

"Filthy with Things," from *Without a Hero* by T. Coraghessan Boyle, copyright © 1994 by T. Coraghessan Boyle. Used by permission of Viking Penguin, a division of Penguin Group (USA) Inc.

"Chapter 1," from *Sweet Summer* by Bebe Moore Campbell, copyright © 1989 by Bebe Moore Campbell. Used by permission of G. P. Putnam's Sons, a division of Penguin Group (USA) Inc.

"What to Do," from *Scrambled Eggs & Whiskey: Poems 1991-1995* by Hayden Carruth. Copyright © 1995 by Hayden Carruth. Reprinted with the permission of Copper Canyon Press, P.O. Box 271, Port Townsend, WA 98368-0271.

Excerpt from *Caramelo* by Sandra Cisneros. Copyright © 2002 by Sandra Cisneros. Published in paperback by Vintage Books in 2003 and originally in hardcover by Alfred A. Knopf, Inc. Reprinted by permission of Susan Bergholz Literary Services, NY. All rights reserved. Introduction copyright © 2004 by Sandra Cisneros. By permission of Susan Bergholz Literary Services, NY. All rights reserved.

"Mrs. Dutta Writes a Letter" from *The Unknown Errors of Our Lives* by Chitra Banerjee Divakaruni, copyright © 2001 by Chitra Banerjee Divakaruni. Used by permission of Doubleday, a division of Random House, Inc.